MANAGING CULTURAL DIVERSITY IN ASIA

Managing Gender Diversity in Asia: A Research Companion
Edited by **Mustafa F. Özbilgin**, *Professor of Human Resource
Management, University of East Anglia, UK and* **Jawad Syed**, *Lecturer in
Human Resource Management, Kent Business School, University of Kent,
UK*

'Managing Gender Diversity in Asia *is as timely as it is important.
Mustafa F. Özbilgin and Jawad Syed raise the set of issues that all of us,
managers and scholars, need to ponder and address if we are to have a 21st
century defined by equity.'*
                                        – Nancy J. Adler, McGill University, Canada

This timely *Companion* examines the unique codes and processes of
managing gender diversity, equality and inclusion in Asia.

Managing Gender Diversity in Asia covers the whole geography of
Asia through chapters authored by eminent scholars in the field and
thus provides an authoritative tool for a critical and evidence based
understanding of gender diversity management in Asia. The distinctive
nature of Asian institutional structures, approaches and processes
are examined in order to account for variations in representation and
inclusion at work for women and men.

This comprehensive *Companion* will make ideal reading for researchers,
postgraduate students and practitioners who wish to understand the
methodological and thematic idiosyncrasies of researching gender
diversity management in organisational settings.

June 2010   c304pp   ISBN 978 1 84720 644 2

Managing Cultural Diversity in Asia

A Research Companion

Edited by

Jawad Syed

Lecturer in Human Resource Management, Kent Business School, University of Kent, UK

and

Mustafa F. Özbilgin

Professor of Human Resource Management, University of East Anglia, UK

Edward Elgar
Cheltenham, UK • Northampton, MA, USA

© Jawad Syed and Mustafa F. Özbilgin 2010

Published by
Edward Elgar Publishing Limited
The Lypiatts
15 Lansdown Road
Cheltenham
Glos GL50 2JA
UK

Edward Elgar Publishing, Inc.
William Pratt House
9 Dewey Court
Northampton
Massachusetts 01060
USA

A catalogue record for this book
is available from the British Library

Library of Congress Control Number: 2009941280

Mixed Sources
Product group from well-managed
forests and other controlled sources
www.fsc.org Cert no. SA-COC-1565
© 1996 Forest Stewardship Council

ISBN 978 1 84980 094 5

Printed and bound by MPG Books Group, UK

Contents

Contributors

Zulhamri Abdullah, Deputy Director, Centre for Cocurriculum and Senior Lecturer in International Corporate Communication, Department of Communication, University Putra, Malaysia.

F. Pinar Acar, PhD, Department of Business Administration, Middle East Technical University, Ankara, Turkey.

Akram Al Ariss, Assistant Professor of Human Resource Management, Champagne School of Management, Troyes, France.

Kurt April, Professor of Leadership, Diversity and Inclusion, Graduate School of Business, University of Cape Town, South Africa, Research Fellow, Ashridge, UK and Associate Fellow, University of Oxford, UK.

Sharif As-Saber, Senior Lecturer, School of Management, Faculty of Business and Economics, Monash University, Clayton, VIC, Australia.

Nailah Ayub, Mphil, Social and Organizational Psychology, Leiden University, The Netherlands.

Moira Calveley, Senior Research Fellow, Business School, University of Hertfordshire, Hatfield, UK.

David Collings, Lecturer in International Management, Department of Management, National University of Ireland, Galway, Ireland.

Beliz Dereli, Assistant Professor, Career Center Planning Manager, Istanbul Commerce University, Turkey.

Prescott C. Ensign, Associate Professor, Telfer School of Management, University of Ottawa, Canada.

Robert W. Fairlie, Professor, Department of Economics, University of California, Santa Cruz, CA, USA.

Greg Fisher, Associate Professor, Flinders Business School, Flinders University, Australia.

Rana Haq, Assistant Professor, School of Commerce and Administration, Faculty of Management, Laurentian University, Sudbury, Ontario, Canada.

Charmine E.J. Härtel, Professor and Management Cluster Leader (Research), UQ Business School, The University of Queensland, Australia.

Graham Hollinshead, Reader in International HRM, Business School, University of Hertfordshire, Hatfield, UK.

Karen Jehn, Melbourne Business School, University of Melbourne, Australia.

Yang-Im Lee, Director, CSCEO Management Services Limited and Senior Research Fellow, Birkbeck, University of London, UK.

Shannon Lloyd, PhD Candidate, School of Management, Faculty of Business and Economics, Monash University, Clayton, VIC, Australia.

Ruby M.M. Ma, Lecturer, Deakin Business School, Faculty of Business and Law, Deakin University, Burwood, VIC, Australia.

Mustafa F. Özbilgin, Professor of Human Resource Management, Norwich Business School, University of East Anglia, Norwich, UK.

Taran Patel, PhD, Associate Professor, Management and Organizational Behavior, Grenoble Ecole de Management, Grenoble, France.

Ayala Malach Pines, Professor and Chair, Department of Business Administration, Ben-Gurion University of the Negev, Israel.

Edwina Pio, Associate Professor, School of Business and Law, Auckland University of Technology, Auckland, New Zealand.

Jalandhar Pradhan, Assistant Professor of Economics, Department of Humanities and Social Sciences, National Institute of Technology, Rourkela, Orissa, India.

Nicholas P. Robinson, Faculty of Law, McGill University, Montreal and Merchant Law Group LLP, Canada.

Hugh Scullion, Professor and Head of Department, Department of Management, National University of Ireland, Galway, Ireland.

Divya Singhal, Assistant Professor, Department of Management Studies, Goa Institute of Management, India.

Eon Smit, Professor of Business Forecasting and Decision Analysis and Director, University of Stellenbosch Business School, University of Stellenbosch, South Africa.

Ebrahim Soltani, Senior Lecturer in Operations Management, Kent Business School, University of Kent, Canterbury, Kent, UK.

Olca Sürgevil, PhD, Research Assistant, Department of Business Administration, Faculty of Economics and Administrative Sciences, Dokuz Eylul University, Turkey.

Jawad Syed, Lecturer in Human Resource Management, Kent Business School, University of Kent, Canterbury, UK.

David Weir, Professor of Intercultural Management, Liverpool Hope University, Liverpool, UK and Professor Affilié, ESC, Rennes, France.

Daungdauwn Youngsamart, Lecturer, School of Management, Monash University, Australia.

Ahmet Yükleyen, Croft Assistant Professor of Anthropology, Sociology and Anthropology Department, University of Mississippi, Oxford, USA.

Nurit Zaidman, Head of Specialization in Strategy and International Management, Department of Business Administration, Ben-Gurion University, Israel.

1 Introduction: diversity management travels to underexplored territories

Mustafa F. Özbilgin and Jawad Syed

Not a believer inside the mosque, am I
Nor a pagan disciple of false rites
Not the pure among the impure
Neither Moses, nor the Pharaoh
Bulleh! to me, I am not known

Not an Arab, nor Lahori
Neither Hindi, nor Nagauri
Hindu, Turk (Muslim), nor Peshawari
Nor do I live in Nadaun
Bulleh! to me, I am not known

(Bulleh Shah, 1680–1757)

Managing workforce diversity constitutes an important area of global corporate activity (Ferner et al., 2005), although it can be considered a relatively new organisational paradigm (Gilbert et al., 1999). Diversity management continues to fascinate management scholars as diversity promises advancement in knowledge, evolution and innovation (Härtel, 2004). However, the diversity management phenomenon remains underexplored in the Asian context. When we conceived the idea of co-editing this research volume two years ago, we were aware of and also motivated by the fact that the oft-cited studies of diversity, for example, Sanchez and Brock (1996) and Harrison et al. (1998), are limited to the English-speaking geographies. Furthermore, mainstream theorisation in the field has been rather anaemic in terms of contextual detail, namely relating theorisation on diversity to history and geography (see, for example, Harrison and Klein, 2007). Ignoring history and geography in building diversity theory bodes ill for understanding issues pertaining to diversity management in other contexts, that is, places and times that fall outside the mainstream focus in this field of study (Özbilgin, 2009; Syed and Özbilgin, 2009). Even studies of global diversity management remain silent about the Asian context and its unique requirements for the sake of conceptual clarity (Nishii and Özbilgin, 2007).

This volume has been developed with the aim of providing an authoritative overview of cultural diversity management in Asia. Although the

1

Asian context appears at first sight to be irreconcilably divergent in terms of diversity management approaches, in this volume we seek to explore thematic and geographical demarcations of the concepts of diversity and equality at work. The aim is not only to examine diversity management in a particular geography but also to make a marked contribution to the theory of managing diversity and equality by revealing the significance of context, time and space in framing policies and practices of management. Following the call by Bell and Kravitz (2008), we have attempted to bring together studies which theorise the practice of diversity management, in order to help close the gap between practice and theory in this field in Asia. The volume, therefore, offers in the main an evidence-based approach (Özbilgin and Tatli, 2008) in the theorisation of diversity management.

With empirical and conceptual contributions from eminent scholars from across the Asian continent as well as the Asian diaspora, this volume provides a text that allows us to understand practices of equality and diversity management in settings across Asia, and also to understand the key drivers and implications of such practices. The volume examines diversity management from multiple angles; while some chapters examine diversity management in domestic firms in Asian countries, others examine it from a cross-cultural or international perspective.

It is possible and useful to identify overarching patterns and processes of diversity management in this geography with particular attention to cross-national differences. Unprecedented economic growth of countries such as China and India has drawn scholarly attention to management issues in the Asian context. It is, however, well documented that countries in Asia do not enjoy a common approach to management. Similar to the US and the European contexts, evidence of diversity management practices across the Asian countries appears divergent. Nevertheless, while there is a wide spectrum of practices in terms of managing diversity and equality in Asia, there is a finite set of different approaches and there are some common observable patterns of management which stand up well to cross-national scrutiny in this geography. One of the significant patterns of managing diversity in the Asian context is the silence of organisational discourses surrounding this issue. When critical approaches to diversity management are offered to explore inequities of power relations in the European context (for example, Janssens and Zanoni, 2005), Asian scholarship in the field of diversity and equality has remained largely silent. A strong focus on economic development in Asia has almost relegated issues of diversity and equality to the level of secondary importance. We contend in this volume that this attitude towards diversity is misguided and that economic development cannot be studied in isolation from its human consequences, one of which is the inevitability of diverse and intercultural exchanges/interactions. Indeed, what is sorely lacking in the Asian context is a business case for diversity, which is akin to that offered in North America (see, for example, Robinson and Dechant, 1997), but which is based on an emic understanding of dynamics of business in Asia.

The Asian context is characterised as the main source of religious diversity internationally. The world's religions with the largest number of followers, including Buddhism, and Abrahamic religions of Judaism, Christianity and Islam, were all conceived in the Asian continent. With a few exceptions (for example, Özbilgin, 2000; Jain et al., 2003; Ghorbani and Tung, 2007; Syed, 2008), international comparative studies of diversity and equal opportunity mostly neglect this unique character of Asia as the birthplace and stronghold of contemporary religions. The lack of understanding the implication of cultural diversity brought about by religious diversity has been challenged in recent years with management scholarship that focused on the significance of Buddhist and Muslim traditions from the region; for example, White's (1999) theorisation of ethical behaviour in organisations which is the enactment of the principles of elements common to the feminist ethic of care and the Buddhist ethic of compassion, and Saha's (1992) study on Zen and industrial management in Japan.

Previous research suggests that the compatibility of organisational values with the wider societal or cultural values is essential to the long-term success of organisations (Hofstede, 1984; Schuler and Rogovsky, 1998; Harzing and Sorge, 2003). Organisational–societal cultural congruence is important not only to productivity and worker satisfaction (Newman and Nollen, 1996), but also in terms of perceived organisational legitimacy that affects the long-term survival of the business (Kostova and Zaheer, 1999; Giacobbe-Miller et al., 2003). From an institutional perspective, coercive pressure is often brought about by the actions of governmental and other regulatory bodies that have control over an organisation or its critical resources (for example, DiMaggio and Powell, 1983; Oliver, 1991; Kostova and Roth, 2002; James and Wooten, 2006). Cross-national differences in institutional structures are known to result in management practices that vary from country to country (Gooderham et al., 1999). Tatli and Özbilgin (2009) explain that the embedded nature of diversity management requires researchers to account for the meaning of difference and diversity in specific contexts, rather than assuming that diversity theories can be transferred and transposed irrespective of the time and place in which they are conceived.

The divergent trajectories of countries in this volume, in relation to laws, religions, history and economic systems, also make it possible for us to examine the impact of factors such as the interface of tradition, religion and state governance as they inform the way diversity and equal opportunity policies and practices are shaped. In terms of practice, we hope that the volume will inform decision making in private and public sector organisations in Asia. Diversity management and equal opportunity practices are now considered to have strategic importance. Therefore, an understanding of diversity and equality structures, processes and outcomes in this geography is important for formulations of business strategy for public and private sector organisations.

In sum, we hope that the volume will serve to explicate the scope and nature of diversity management policy frameworks in countries in Asia. Contextual (for example, socio-economic, legal and demographic) conditions which drive the development of such policies constitute the focus of some chapters. Besides the contextual perspective, there are chapters which seek to develop, validate and compare various dimensions which frame antecedents, correlates and consequences of diversity management. Outlining and comparing dimensions of diversity and equal opportunity frameworks in national settings, the volume provides a connected understanding of the Asian context. Overall, the volume contributes to the development of theory to explicate the dynamic nature and processes of diversity and equality at work in Asia.

Structure of the volume
Cultural diversity is a consequence of different assumptions which underpin the logic of practice at work. The Asian setting provides a unique site for studying cultural diversity as Asia is the birthplace of many socio-religious discourses which underpin the way in which work and life is organised in contemporary societies. Following this introduction, the first 19 chapters deal with cultural diversity management in Asia. The volume also contains three chapters on the Asian diaspora, exploring the diversity of and among Asian migrants in other continents.

Cultural diversity
At first sight the Asian context appears rich in cultural constructs such as systems of caste, networks of social and economic relations, as well as assumptions of organisation and work. However, this perception of wealth of culture in the region can partly be explained by the perceived dissimilarity of these cultural constructs to the dominant cultural constructs in the English language literatures. In order to demystify cultural constructs which are unique to countries in Asia, the volume houses 19 chapters that study cultural diversity in and among Asian countries.

In his chapter on cultural diversity management in Malaysia, Abdullah (Chapter 2) offers a communication management perspective on cultural diversity in a multicultural environment. The chapter highlights how organisational leaders' perception of diversity management may affect their organisational strategy development. The chapter explores how cultural diversity is practised in multinational corporations in Malaysia. It demonstrates that understanding cultural diversity can be very complicated but unlocking the potential of local cultures may reveal a distinctive identity for today's corporations. The chapter shows that managing cultural diversity requires a holistic approach especially from top management personnel in terms of cultural sensitivity and 'local focus'.

In her chapter on identity salience, occupational commitment and organisational citizenship behaviours, Acar (Chapter 3) offers an exploratory study of multinational teams from the Turkish context. She notes that very few studies, to date, examine national origin as a dimension of diversity. Her chapter aims to remedy this gap in the extant diversity literature by developing a conceptual framework to examine organisational citizenship behaviours in teams composed of members from different nations. Specifically, the chapter investigates the effects of national identity salience on organisational citizenship behaviours. Acar argues that salient subgroup identities will have a negative impact on such behaviours. She also proposes the often understudied occupational commitment as a moderator variable. The framework presented in her chapter suggests that negative influence of salient identities on organisational citizenship behaviours will be weakened by high occupational commitment.

Al Ariss (Chapter 4) focuses on the patterns of religious diversity management in Lebanon. The chapter argues that diversity management challenges faced by the multi-religious Lebanese society reflect the ones that the world is increasingly experiencing with globalisation and migration. The chapter suggests that the 'diversity scheme' in Lebanon refers to power distribution among different religious communities rather than the freedom of practising religions in organisations or in social life. The study is based on 20 qualitative interviews conducted with Lebanese men and women who have spent part of their lives and careers in Lebanon and the other part in France.

April and Smit (Chapter 5) review existing models of motivation and personal expectancy to establish a foundation for a discretionary effort framework, which would be relevant to professional networks. The chapter demonstrates that despite an undifferentiated Western view of Chinese employees, individuals demonstrate behavioural variables that they require to be satisfied before offering their discretionary effort. Additionally, the factors of organisational position and individual educational qualifications are positively correlated towards an individual offering his/her discretionary effort.

Ayub and Jehn (Chapter 6) describe the diversity scenario in Pakistan with the help of survey studies and interviews. The authors discuss the presence of diversity and whether the Pakistani workforce acknowledges and accepts diversity. They examine the prevalent attitudes and grievances regarding diversity at work. The chapter offers some ideas for diversity management in Pakistan in view of the issues expressed by local personnel and corresponding elements from models that have been designed and practised in other countries and cultures.

Calveley and Hollinshead (Chapter 7) investigate workplace discrimination on the grounds of gender and ethnicity in the context of the transformation of the political economy in Russia. The chapter exposes the decline in the status of women in the new liberal economy of Russia and illustrates why a significant number of women are still faced with inequality in the workplace. The chapter also explains how migrant workers are marginalised and discriminated against both in the workplace and in society, despite their significant contribution to the building of the Russian economy.

In her chapter on diversity management in Turkish subsidiaries operating in Asia, Dereli (Chapter 8) explores the importance of cultural diversity management for organisations. The chapter investigates the main problems of the cultural diversity management in Turkish companies which operate in Central Asian countries (Kazakhstan, Uzbekistan, Kyrgyzstan, Turkmenistan and Tajikistan, which gained independence following the collapse of the Soviet Union in 1991) and their human resources management approaches and methods with respect to the problems encountered.

Haq (Chapter 9) offers an analysis of the caste-based quota system in India. The 2001 Census of India recorded that India had crossed the one billion population mark, making it the second most populated country in the world, after China. The people of India are diverse in language, culture and religion since there are 28 states and seven Union Territories, each with a distinct history, culture, cuisine, customs, official language, dialects, religious beliefs and festivals. Haq highlights cross-national differences in the target groups protected by diversity policies and explores the key drivers that underpin the reservations context, practices and outcomes in the realm of India's complex workforce diversity challenges. The focus of this chapter is to provide a discussion on the socio-economic and political influences on the reservations policies, thus contributing to the global discussion on diversity management by examining the antecedents, interventions and outcomes of India's reservations policies. The chapter extends India's reservations issues into the cross-national conversations on managing diversity by informing, educating and raising the awareness of readers, scholars and practitioners unfamiliar with the Indian diversity management context.

In their chapter on intercultural competencies, Härtel, Lloyd and Singhal (Chapter 10) present the findings of preliminary research which explores intercultural business interactions through a comparative survey study undertaken in India and Australia. The authors begin their chapter by reviewing literature addressing the impact of culture on interactions between people from different cultural backgrounds. The chapter then links these findings with the intercultural competencies identified in the literature and investigates whether the same competencies are important across cultures. The chapter examines the full range of core intercultural competencies identified in the taxonomy derived by the first two authors from a comprehensive literature review.

Härtel, Ma and As-Saber (Chapter 11) offer a conceptual analysis of managing Chinese enterprise relationships through *Guanxi*-based diversity management. Increasingly, the forces of globalisation are leading to the necessity for organisations to operate on an international scale in order to remain viable. While these international operations can create a number of benefits for organisations, they also introduce a whole new set of challenges which must be dealt with, not least of which is the challenge of interacting with individuals from diverse backgrounds. In their pursuit of a conceptual analysis of managing Chinese enterprise relationships through *Guanxi*, Härtel et al. develop a model to examine the Sino-Western business relationship-building process, in particular, looking at the factors affecting Chinese business partners' perception of *Guanxi* and how it can influence the relationship. The model extends existing conceptualisations of the cross-cultural communication process by combining theories of emotions and research on *Guanxi* and the second author's own unique understanding and experience of the Chinese perception of *Guanxi* combined with well-accepted theories of contextual, social and cognitive influences on communication and negotiation. The authors explain how culturally founded communication patterns play an important role in the informal and formal phases of business negotiation.

Lee (Chapter 12) undertakes a comparative study of Japanese and South Korean mindsets which provides insights into how management decisions are made in Japan and Korea. The chapter pays attention to both Japanese and Korean organisational culture, which is then followed by empirical research. The exploratory research undertaken relating to both Japanese and Korean culture is outlined and followed by an analysis, and a number of important cultural factors are highlighted. The similarities and differences between the cultures are identified, and a conclusion is provided.

In her conceptual chapter on diversity in India, Patel (Chapter 13) explores some of the discrimination-related issues that plague India today. The chapter addresses the discussion at the national level. It exposes some of the discrimination-related issues faced by different minority groups such as members of the lower castes of the Hindu religion, minority religions – particularly Muslims who constitute about 12 per cent of the Indian population – women, homosexuals and transgenders. The chapter discusses the history of the evolution of affirmative action in India and exposes its current status in India today. It also exposes some of the challenges that Indian society currently faces in implementing affirmative action. The chapter also addresses the diversity debate at the corporate level, providing examples of some diversity-related issues that international managers may have to cope with while working in India.

Pradhan (Chapter 14) deals with the state of the South Asian economy and environment. The chapter also examines a few likely scenarios of long-term economic growth and demographic change and their implications for regional economic relationships. Results suggest that South Asian countries are at a turning point to achieve a 7 to 8 per cent growth rate. The economic reforms on which all these countries are embarking depend on the macroeconomic foundations. Nevertheless, a poor social infrastructure and the low level of human resource development in all the countries with the exception of Sri Lanka impose severe constraints. Absolute poverty is still high in all countries. Demographically, population growth is high, which moderates the process of development in most of the countries. This creates conditions which, if they persist without rapid amelioration, can result in political instability and social unrest within countries, spilling over to the region as a whole.

Few studies have examined how multinational corporations operating in India can manage diversity and create visions that ensure a level of consistency between individual, organisational and societal values. In their chapter on transplanting the meritocracy in India, Robinson and Ensign (Chapter 15) argue that the values embraced by the Indian government (through its constitution, policies and institutions) are a good starting point for organisations that wish to overcome the friction created by prejudice in the subcontinent. The values elaborated in the Indian Constitution can be viewed as an example of the societal aspirations of Indians and must therefore be studied carefully. The chapter suggests that unlike the United States where diversity is largely a question of race, or Europe where diversity has traditionally been largely a question of language and culture, India's diversity is racial, religious, linguistic and even class based, all at once. Further, the breadth and range of diversity is greater than one would find in many other countries, given that people who are polar opposites in one sense or another work side by side. The chapter discusses some of the innovations of the Indian Constitution and reasons for these innovations; some key issues identified by the Constitution and other sources that illustrate practices and social divisions that were perceived as being particularly problematic; and how an MNC might want to go about drafting an enduring vision statement that can assist in achieving corporate goals in India.

The main aim of Soltani, Scullion, Lai and Collings (Chapter 16) is to examine management of diversity and equal opportunity in employment in Iran. While benefits associated with diversity management might be true in the context of developed countries, the authors are critical of their exist-ence in the context of less-developed nations such as Iran. Furthermore, while in most previous research on managing diversity the perspective of managers who had policy-making roles in the organisation dominated the analysis, this chapter tackles this limitation, and advances understanding by providing multiple perspectives on diversity and equal opportunity in employment to encompass both managers' and workers' views. This chapter is based on 76 semi-structured interviews across two industries (construction and manufacturing) with both managers and blue-collar workers. The findings suggest that, in contrast to existing theories, eco-nomic evaluations such as cost-minimisation of the diverse work groups are the major driving force behind adopting equal opportunity practices in employment. Interestingly, the data suggest that such a cost–benefit relationship is also seen as beneficial by the workers.

Sürgevil (Chapter 17) discusses dimensions of diversity management in science and business in Turkey. The chapter draws on data from the Turkish Statistical Institute and examines this data in relation to various categories of diversity. The chapter also brings in data from the Turkish Enterprise and Business Confederation and the Turkish Confederation of Employers' Union, providing a comprehensive assessment of diversity management in Turkey.

In his exploration of diversity management in the context of the Middle East, Weir (Chapter 18) argues that a fundamental theoretical focus on diversity as a determining aspect of post-modern social organisation has come from the continuing philosophical concern with the 'other'. This has ranged from Levinas's call for ethics to be regarded as a first philosophy, prior to ontological and epistemological concerns, to Schutz's elabora-tion of the nature of social understanding. These are not issues that in day-to-day life resonate much with operational managers: nonetheless there is continuing intellectual concern with these topics, exemplified most recently perhaps in the continuing theme in Charles Taylor's work to bridge the Anglo-Saxon and the European approaches to these themes, and these fundamental analyses form an underpinning backdrop to our concerns.

Youngsamart, Fisher and Härtel (Chapter 19) offer a review of the literature on the management of diversity in Thailand and report findings that are relevant to the domain of diversity management drawn from previously unpublished results of four convergent interview-based studies conducted over a 12-year period from 1996 to 2008. While the main focus of each of these studies was not diversity management, each study dealt in some way with culture, race, ethnicity, religion and management issues in Thailand. In this chapter, the authors use incidental results from a number of qualitative studies, to explore and explain the nature of diversity management in the Thai business context. Consistent with literature that examines management in organisations in Thailand, the authors suggest that social class and patron–client relationships are stronger influences on the career outcomes of women, ethnically diverse and religiously diverse employees. Education enables individuals to move through class barriers, and receive career benefits. The fluidity of the patronage system in Thailand creates the opportunity for individuals to develop advantageous relationships, which may be beneficial for those individuals, but overall does not align with the Western concepts of equity in the workplace.

Theoretical discussion on the interaction of globalisation and national diversity management has concentrated on the tension between the particularities of the context and the universal homogenisation of Anglo-American standards. Yükleyen (Chapter 20) examines Islamic civil society and social capital in Turkey and suggests two ways to expand this discussion on diversity management. First, the chapter applies lessons from Western-oriented globalisation on the relationship of diversity and development in the cultural context of Turkey, which is often presented as a 'bridge between East and West'. Turkey's presumed in-between identity indicates that the context of each country regardless of its subjection to occidental or oriental discourse creates particular conditions and approaches to manage diversity. Second, diversity management literature's level of analysis primarily focuses on the company, national or multinational. The goal of increasing market efficiency and respecting human dignity through the recognition of ethnic, racial, gender, religious and other identities within companies could have implications for state–society relations as well. However, the national context in each country significantly shapes the diversity management strategy in each company. On the other hand, lessons of cultural diversity management could fruitfully be applied to state–society interaction. The public (un)recognition of emerging group identities could challenge or facilitate the economic development of a country depending on how cultural diversity is politically managed. This chapter focuses on how the secular Turkish state is (mis) managing the rising Islamic identity within the civil society through the case of a moderate Islamic movement.

Diaspora

Studying the Asian context also requires us to pay attention to the diversity in the Asian diaspora, namely Asians in other continents as migrants and expatriates. In this volume, there are three chapters which examine diversity issues of the Asian diaspora.

Diasporas can be categorised in multiple ways based on characteristics such as: modes of cultural reproduction, sites of engagement, reconstructions of place; nations unbound, long-distance nationalism; a governmental category that represents new geographies; or irreral spaces which are between the real and imagined.

In his chapter on Asian and other migrant entrepreneurs in the US, Fairlie (Chapter 21) examines the contribution of immigrants to business ownership, formation and performance using three large, nationally representative datasets – the Census 5 per cent PUMS Sample, the Current Population Survey (CPS), and the Characteristics of Business Owners (CBO). The Census 5 per cent PUMS Sample is the only nationally representative dataset with large enough sample sizes to examine business ownership among detailed immigrant groups, and the CBO is the only business-level dataset with information on a large sample of immigrants. Using this data, several key questions about immigrant entrepreneurship are explored. The study highlights some key contributions from immigrant entrepreneurs from Asian countries.

Pio's broad objective (Chapter 22) is to stimulate a critical analysis and reflection on the Asian diaspora in New Zealand, through foregrounding ethnicity embedded within the socio-historical context of a particular period and country. By viewing the Asian diaspora through the prism of postcolonialism, Pio's study contributes to the larger debates and scholarship on issues of otherness, governmentality and the significance of positionality in research. The chapter focuses on the Chinese and Indians who form the largest Asian groups in New Zealand and have been recorded as the first Asian settlers in Aotearoa or the Land of the Long White Cloud, which is the Maori name for New Zealand.

A total of 190,000 foreign workers are employed in Israel today; about 50 per cent of them have employment permits while the rest are illegal. Against the backdrop of these labourers, Zaidman and Pines (Chapter 23) address a very different type of foreign worker – educated employees in the highly sophisticated and highly successful Israeli high-tech industry. Today's global economy increasingly requires workers to collaborate in teams that cross cultural and geographic boundaries. The chapter adopts a relational perspective underpinned by a belief in contextually situated phenomena that exist in interconnected relationships, in this case involving the individual workers (their behaviour, coping strategies, stress and burnout) the multicultural team (its cohesion and communication), the organisation (its culture, politics and disturbing aspects), the global sector (high-tech) and culture (Israeli versus Indian).

Overall, we hope that the book will prove a valuable addition to resources on cultural diversity management in Asia and also internationally, equally accessible and useful to research scholars and students as well as managers and policy makers interested in non-orthodox discourses and practices of diversity and equal opportunity. Last but not least we would like to offer our thanks to all contributors for their wonderful and exciting contributions to this volume. In particular, we are grateful to Charmine Härtel and Edwina Pio for their help in reviewing some of the chapters of the current volume. We would also like to thank Ben Booth and Jenny Wilcox of Edward Elgar for closely working with us in designing and completing this book project.

References

Bell, M.P. and Kravitz, D.A. (2008), 'From the editors: what do we know and need to learn about diversity education and training?', *Academy of Management Learning and Education*, **7** (3): 301–8.

DiMaggio, P. and Powell, W. (1983), 'The iron cage revisited: institutional isomorphism and collective rationality in organization fields', *American Sociological Review*, **48**: 147–60.

Ferner, A., Almond, P. and Colling, T. (2005), 'Institutional theory and the cross-national transfer of employment policy: the case of "workforce diversity" in US multinationals', *Journal of International Business Studies*, **36** (3): 304–21.

Ghorbani, M. and Tung, R.L. (2007), 'Behind the veil: an exploratory study of the myths and realities of women in the Iranian workforce', *Human Resource Management Journal*, **17** (4): 376–92.

Giacobbe-Miller, J.K., Miller, D.J., Zhang, W. and Victorov, V.I. (2003), 'Country and organizational-level adaptation to foreign workplace ideologies: a comparative study of distributive justice values in China, Russia and the United States', *Journal of International Business Studies*, **34** (4): 389–406.

Gilbert, J., Stead, B. and Ivancevich, J. (1999), 'Diversity management: a new organisational paradigm', *Journal of Business Ethics*, **21** (1): 31–42.

Gooderham, P.N., Nordhaug, O. and Ringdal, K. (1999), 'Institutional and rational determinants of organizational practices: human resource management in European firms', *Administrative Science Quarterly*, **44**: 507–31.

Harrison, D. and Klein, K. (2007), 'What's the difference? Diversity constructs as separation, variety, or disparity in groups', *Academy of Management Review*, **32**: 1–30.

Harrison, D., Price, K. and Bell, M. (1998), 'Beyond relational demography: time and the effects of surface- and deep-level diversity on work group cohesion', *Academy of Management Journal*, **41**: 96–107.

Härtel, C. (2004), 'Towards a multicultural world: identifying work systems, practices and employee attitudes that embrace diversity', *Australian Journal of Management*, **29** (2): 189–200.

Harzing, A. and Sorge, A. (2003), 'The relative impact of country-of-origin and universal contingencies on internationalization strategies and corporate control in multinational enterprises: world-wide and European perspectives', *Organization Studies*, **24** (2): 187–214.

Hofstede, G. (1984), *Culture's Consequences*, London: Sage.

Jain, H., Sloane, P. and Horwitz, F. (eds) (2003), *Employment Equity and Affirmative Action: An International Comparison*, Armonk, NY: M.E. Sharpe.

James, E.H. and Wooten, L.P. (2006), 'Diversity crises: how firms manage discrimination lawsuits', *Academy of Management Journal*, **49** (6): 1103–18.

Janssens, M. and Zanoni, P. (2005), 'Many diversities for many services: theorizing diversity (management) in service companies', *Human Relations*, **58** (3), 311–40.

Kostova, T. and Roth, K. (2002), 'Adoption of an organizational practice by subsidiaries of multinational corporations: institutional and relational effects', *Academy of Management Journal*, **45** (1): 215–33.

Kostova, T. and Zaheer, S. (1999), 'Organizational legitimacy under conditions of complexity: the case of the multinational enterprise', *Academy of Management Review*, **24**: 64–81.

Newman, K.L. and Nollen, S.D. (1996), 'Culture and congruence: the fit between management practices and national culture', *Journal of International Business Studies*, **27**: 753–79.

Nishii, L.H. and Özbilgin, M.F. (2007), 'Global diversity management: towards a conceptual framework', *International Journal of Human Resource Management*, **18**: 1883–94.

Oliver, C. (1991), 'Strategic responses to institutional processes', *Academy of Management Review*, **16** (1): 145–79.

Özbilgin, M.F. (2000), 'Is the practice of equal opportunities management keeping pace with theory? Management of sex equality in the financial services sector in Britain and Turkey', *Human Resource Development International*, **3** (1): 43–67.

Özbilgin, M.F. (ed.) (2009), *Equality, Diversity and Inclusion at Work: A Research Companion*, Cheltenham, UK and Northampton, MA, USA: Edward Elgar.

Özbilgin, M.F. and Tatli, A. (2008), *Global Diversity Management: An Evidence Based Approach*, Basingstoke and New York: Palgrave.

Robinson, G. and Dechant, K. (1997), 'Building a business case for diversity', *Academy of Management Executive*, **11** (3): 21–31.

Saha, A. (1992), 'Zen and industrial management in Japan', *Journal of Managerial Psychology*, **7** (3): 3–9.

Sanchez, J.I. and Brock, P. (1996), 'Outcomes of perceived discrimination among Hispanic employees: is diversity management a luxury or a necessity?', *Academy of Management Journal*, **39** (3): 704–19.

Schuler, R.S. and Rogovsky, N. (1998), 'Understanding compensation practice variations across firms: the impact of national culture', *Journal of International Business Studies*, **29**: 159–77.

Syed, J. (2008), 'A context-specific perspective of equal employment opportunity in Islamic societies', *Asia Pacific Journal of Management*, **25** (1): 135–51.

Syed, J. and Özbilgin, M.F. (2009), 'A relational framework for international transfer of diversity management practices', *International Journal of Human Resource Management*, **20** (12): 2435–53.

Tatli, A. and Özbilgin, M.F. (2009), 'Understanding diversity managers' role in organizational change: towards a conceptual framework', *Canadian Journal of Administrative Sciences*, **26** (3), 244–58.

White, J. (1999), 'Ethical comportment in organizations: a synthesis of the feminist ethic of care and the Buddhist ethic of compassion', *International Journal of Value-Based Management*, **12** (2): 109–28.

2 Cultural diversity management in Malaysia: a perspective of communication management
Zulhamri Abdullah

Introduction

This chapter addresses the importance of cultural diversity management to today's corporations regardless of what type of business they are involved in. The concept of diversity is a unique one as it is crucial to address how cultural diversity impacts on business strategy in the global context and to what extent the organisation can manage cultural diversity in a multicultural environment. This topic remains a complex facet to understand but unlocking the potential of local cultures may reveal the distinctive identity for today's corporations.

In a turbulent business environment, every corporation must face big challenges in improving its business strategy. It is believed that aligning business strategy with cultural diversity is a great formula for winning businesses' potential in a highly competitive business environment. According to Gardenswartz et al. (2003: 4), managing global diversity is one of the best business approaches to improving organisational goals by optimising total workforce potential with respect to their distinct local cultures in the different countries around the world. Before discussing the development of cultural diversity, we shall examine the background of Malaysia, geographically and historically, to better aid a fundamental understanding of diversity management in that country.

Background

Geographically, Malaysia is the world's oldest rainforest country, covering a total area of 329,758 square kilometres in Southeast Asia, situated between the South China Sea and Indonesia (Anuar, 2000: 183; The World Factbook, 2002). Specifically, Malaysia is divided into two large areas: Peninsular Malaysia, or West Malaysia, and East Malaysia, comprising a federation of 13 states. West Malaysia covers Johor, Kedah, Kelantan, Selangor, Negeri Sembilan, Pahang, Perak, Perlis, Terengganu, Malacca and Penang, while East Malaysia covers Sabah and Sarawak. There are two federal territories: Kuala Lumpur, the capital of the country, and Labuan. It has been said that Malaysia is located at the 'centre of one of the most dynamic regions in the global economy' (Burgess and Muthaly, 2001: 140).

Politically, Malaysia is a constitutional monarchy ruled by a head of state, the *Yang diPertuan Agong*, who acts in accordance with government advice, all within the practice of a parliamentary democracy. The Cabinet rules a federation of 13 states, headed by the prime minister, who is responsible to the parliament (Singh, 2001).

In 2007, the total population was approximately 27.17 million, with a large number of people living in the Peninsula and the rest in East Malaysia. Selangor, the country's centre of political, economic and social development, had the highest population of 4.8 million in 2006 (Department of Statistics Malaysia, 2008). Malaysia is multi-ethnic and multi-religious, with three main ethnic groups: *Bumiputera*, including Malays and other indigenous people (65.1 per cent), Chinese (about 26 per cent) and Indian (7.7 per cent). The four main religions are Islam (60.4 per cent), Buddhism (19.2 per cent), Christianity (9.1 per cent) and Hinduism (6.3 per cent); Confucianism/Taoism/other traditional Chinese religions constitute 2.6 per cent (Department of Statistics Malaysia, 2005). Another important element is that the Malay language, widely used for government affairs, is the first national and official language of the country. However, English is widely used in the private sector, including in private schools and the higher learning institutions, as well as in corporations in their dealings in international affairs and in multi-ethnic communities, particularly in urban areas.

Islam, the official religion of the country, is widely embraced and practised by the *Bumiputera*. Additionally, there are also a small number of Indian-Muslim and Chinese-Muslim communities. Christianity is widely practised by some Chinese and Indians, especially in urban areas, and there are also a small number of Malay-Christians among indigenous groups living in Sabah and Sarawak, North Borneo (Netto, 2002: 179). Importantly, the Federal Constitution specifically allows for freedom of religious belief, and the government has allocated funds to provide for places of religious worship such as mosques, churches, and Chinese and Indian temples (Ministry of Culture, Arts and Tourism, 2005).

Sex equality in employment in Malaysia is not a big issue as many Malaysian women have become successful senior managers in the government sector and multinational corporations (MNCs) (CAPWIP, 2008). For instance, top women leaders of prominent Malaysian universities such as the University of Malaya and the National University of Malaysia have transformed their universities into international research universities with a great focus on internationalisation. However, in many Islamic countries of the Arab Peninsula and the Middle East, gender discrimination in employment has affected organisational performance due to the restriction of religious beliefs. In recent years, with improved liberalisation and internationalisation policies in many Islamic countries, the notions of 'belonging'[1] and 'otherness'[2] may take into account promoting gender diversity in employment by its emphasis on seeking an 'ideal worker' in structuring the suitability of career development (Özbilgin and Woodward, 2004).

Importantly, managing ethnic diversity requires intercultural harmony among three main ethnic groups. In order to promote cultural diversity, in 1990, the government developed the New Development Policy (NDP) to unite all main ethnic groups to transform Malaysia into a developed country by 2020. The policy focuses on a strong and stable government (politics), national economic growth (economy) and the improvement of living standards of ethnic groups (social) (Burgess and Muthaly, 2001: 142). However, there is still a lack of tolerance and intercultural understanding among ethnic groups in building sustainable development (Mustapha, 2008). The success of the NDP strategy has been debated since the New Economic Policy was adopted in 1971. Therefore, in 2004 the government announced a new approach to diversity management by introducing Islam *Hadhari* to Malaysian society.

The uniqueness of Islam *Hadhari*: a descriptive analysis

Islam *Hadhari* or 'Civilised Islam' is viewed as a popular civilisation approach to life, promoting *da'wah* or 'the call to Islam', and is based on 10 principles for building an organic society – particularly in the sense of a modern, multi-ethnic and multi-faith society. Islam *Hadhari* is also considered to be a main political and ideological element of the national development programme, Vision 2020. It is claimed that this approach, emphasising good governance, will benefit both Muslim and non-Muslim society in Malaysia.

The idea of Islam *Hadhari* strongly supports the notion of the Islamic modernist model suggested by Syed (2008: 147)[3] by focusing on an alignment between Islam, modernity and local culture. With an increasing degree of internationalisation in socio-cultural, religious and economic contexts, this approach may improve the image of Islam in the eyes of not only Malaysian society but also society more generally.

The 10 principles of Islam *Hadhari* are: faith and piety in Allah, a just and trustworthy government, a free and independent people, mastery of knowledge, balanced and comprehensive economic development, a good quality of life, protection of the rights of minority groups and women, cultural and moral integrity, safeguarding the environment, and strong defences.

Islam, which is gazetted as an official religion in Malaysia, is generally accepted by non-Muslims, based on the new Islam *Hadhari* concept. However, although the understanding and acceptance of Islam *Hadhari* among non-Muslims is relatively positive, the benefits that they might gain as a result of its implementation are not clear.

Between March and May 2007, a quantitative survey questionnaire was sent to non-Muslims to ascertain their perceptions towards Islam and the Muslim population. Some 260 questionnaires were sent to targeted respondents, using a stratified random sampling. This yielded an effective response rate of 50 per cent, of which 130 are usable responses. The sample included non-Muslim government officers who were selected from the Directory of Malaysian Companies – Year 2006 (*Red Book*) in the Klang Valley.

Islam *Hadhari* has been actively promoted by the government in its aim to establish a civilised and modern society. A recent study (Tamam et al., 2007) on 'the effects of communicating Islam *Hadhari* through public relations campaigns among non-Muslim government officers' showed that almost 40 per cent of the respondents learned about Islam *Hadhari* from the news and stories published in mainstream media such as English (39.3 per cent) and Malay (32.1 per cent) newspapers. Some respondents noted that they learned about Islam *Hadhari* from the news and stories broadcast on television (30.4 per cent) and radio (8.9 per cent), and also from other sources of news such as government brochures/fliers and Malay friends, which accounted for only 25 per cent.

In the survey, non-Muslim employees were asked their general opinion about Islam being gazetted as an official religion in Malaysia. Nearly 80 per cent of the respondents had a favourable opinion of Islam. Almost half of the total number of respondents reported that Islam is a way of life for a particular group only (48.5 per cent) and a universal religion practised in a multi-racial society (41.5 per cent).

The government has keenly promoted Islam *Hadhari* to Malaysian society. Thus, this left the question how much more non-Muslims wanted to learn about Islam *Hadhari*. The survey reported that 40.9 per cent of the respondents expressed an interest in learning more about Islam *Hadhari* and 30.3 per cent were somewhat interested, but 16.7 per cent were not at all interested.

Non-Muslim government officers were asked about Islam *Hadhari*'s contribution to building a civilised society. Some 33.9 per cent of the respondents said that Islam *Hadhari* is an approach that emphasises the importance of progress – from an Islamic perspective – in the economic, social and political fields, and 32.1 per cent noted that it is an approach that fosters an Islamic civilisation built upon the noble values and ideas of Islam. Interestingly, 23.2 per cent of the respondents asserted that Islam

Hadhari focuses on enhancing the quality of life for every citizen, regardless of his or her religion. Regarding the identity of Malaysia, 21.4 per cent commented that Islam *Hadhari* has a distinctive Malaysian identity that differs from the Islam that is portrayed in other Islamic countries.

It is important to know how the results of the implementation of Islam *Hadhari* were seen by non-Muslim government officers. The outcomes can be categorised in three facets of implementation: the image of Islam, the relations between Muslims and non-Muslims, and the protection of minority rights.

The survey showed that almost 40 per cent of the respondents noted that the image of Islam had improved slightly, while 35.6 per cent perceived no such improvement. With regard to the relations between Muslims and non-Muslims, 42.4 per cent of the respondents noted that there was no improvement, while only 30.5 per cent asserted that relations had improved slightly. Finally, regarding the protection of minority rights, more than half of the total number of respondents reported no improvement, while 29.7 per cent noted that protection had improved slightly.

Almost half of the total number of respondents reported 'accept with reservations' when asked about their acceptance of Islam *Hadhari* as an approach towards building a civilised society. The findings left open the question whether the implementation of Islam *Hadhari* is merely government rhetoric or a new approach towards integrating all Malaysian ethnic groups in a better political, economic and social environment, with benefits for all Malaysian citizens.

Since the Malaysian prime minister announced the Islam *Hadhari* policy in 2004, there have been numerous public discussions, which later led to the question of to what extent the Islam *Hadhari* approach had been publicly discussed and promoted. Thus, this study aims to examine how Islam *Hadhari* has been promoted to non-Muslims within a multicultural environment. Although informing Muslims about Islam *Hadhari* has been vigorously publicised, it remains a huge challenge to promote the concept to non-Muslims in terms of understanding, acceptance and conveying a positive image. It is doubtful whether the numerous public relations (PR) campaigns have carried a coherent message to the multicultural society including non-Muslims in terms of it being a universal value. A quantitative survey using a stratified random sampling conducted among non-Muslim government officials at the main central government office, Putrajaya, anticipated that the result would show that a clear message on Islam *Hadhari* was being sent by emphasising universal values that are favourable to non-Muslims, rather than portraying Islam *Hadhari* for a Muslim world *per se*.

In the context of Malaysian business and commerce, the government's role in its structural and operational approach of Islam *Hadhari* substantially affects the way MNCs and government-linked corporations (GLCs) operate their business, such as promoting Islamic banking services and developing *Halal*⁴ foods hubs. In Malaysia, it is generally said that the intervention of government in business and commerce shapes economic growth as a whole. Thus, we shall describe Malaysia's economic background in the following section.

Business and economic background

From 1990 to 1997, Malaysia had strong economic growth, with gross domestic product (GDP) averaging 8.7 per cent annually (Icon Group International, 2000: 127). During the 1990s, the primary investment was in the manufacturing industry. Low inflation rates, steady increments in per capita income and low poverty rates were key factors that contributed to the socio-economic growth. However, as a result of the Asian financial crisis of 1997–98, Malaysia's GDP in 1997 fell to only about 6 per cent (ibid.: 128). There were then sharp increases in unemployment and currency depreciation, and a slow GDP growth during the economic recession. In July 1998, the government launched the National Economic Recovery Policy in an effort to improve and strengthen the economy. This policy was introduced with a stringent regulatory system, intended to control the currency by imposing a fixed exchange rate between the Malaysian Ringgit and the US dollar (RM3.8/US$1) in September 1998 (EIA, 2005; ILO, 2005).

The economic recovery was also driven by a number of significant factors such as an increase in sales and marketing in corporate sectors, a growth in consumer credit and mortgage approvals, and a sharp increase in the Kuala Lumpur Stock Exchange. There was a major restructuring of the financial and banking sectors in 2000 to boost the economy. Furthermore, in 2001, the government encouraged more spending in its budget, causing a reduction in the government budget deficit from 2003 to 2004 (EIA, 2005; ILO, 2005).

With a significant effort, Malaysia ultimately achieved strong economic growth and a sharp increase in GDP of 7.1 per cent in 2004 compared to 5.3 per cent in 2003. Currently, Malaysia is experiencing steady economic growth with a rapid expansion in exports and robust competition in corporate sectors such as consumer products, telecommunications, banking, manufacturing, health and suchlike (EIA, 2005; ILO, 2005). Key statistics in Table 2.1 demonstrate a high growth rate, a high inflation rate and low unemployment rates. However, due to recent dramatic hikes in the price of fuel and food, the GDP growth rate may be decreasing by the beginning of 2008. This could both directly and indirectly affect the development

Table 2.1   Malaysia: GDP growth, inflation and employment

Key economic & labour indicators	2005	2006	2007	1st Quarter 2008
Gross domestic product / gross national income				
GDP: (in 1987 constant prices)	262,175	277,673	294,373	n/a
GNP: (in 1987 constant prices)	246,210	261,930	275,719	n/a
Inflation rate (%)	3.0	3.6	2.6	3.7
Employment				
Total labour force (million)	11,291	11,545	10,889.5	10,923.3
Employed (million)	10,893	11,144	10,538.1	10,525.3
Unemployed rate (%)	3.5	3.5	3.2	3.6

Source: Adapted from Department of Statistics, Malaysia (2008).

of cultural diversity management in Malaysia. Indeed, the country's economic growth has been developed significantly by three main races – Malay, Chinese and Indian. Further discussion on Malaysia's socio-economic background is highlighted in the following sections.

Cultural diversity
Malaysia's socio-economic background is crucial to an understanding of the country's rich multiculturalism, for cultural diversity is an essential element in discussing how Malaysians – who are multilingual, multi-ethnic and multi-religious – live in peace and harmony. Indeed, Malaysia is 'one of the most culturally and economically diverse regions of the world' (Fisher, 1996: 1). The mastering of the dominant languages such as English and Malay as mediums of communication is also central to this diversity and is crucial in today's competitive business environment.

As indicated, Malaysia proclaims itself to be an Islamic country (Netto, 2002), but is unique in terms of certain characteristics when compared to other countries in the world, owing to its vigorous and diverse political, economic and social development (Bhuiyan, 1997; Chen et al., 2004). However, it is not sufficient to identify the importance of cultural diversity without relating it to religion, race and language. According to Census 2000, there is a high correlation between religion and ethnicity (Department of Statistics, Malaysia, 2005).

Cultural diversity management: a perspective of public relations
In an organisational context, it is fruitful to discuss cultural diversity management from a PR perspective as public relations is a profession that

requires a management function to build favourable relationships between the organisation and its public (a multi-racial society such as Malay, Chinese and Indian). Rex F. Harlow, a PR scholar, defines PR as:

> The distinctive management function which helps establish and maintain mutual lines of communication, understanding, acceptance and cooperation between an organization and its publics; involves the management of problems or issues; helps management to keep informed on and responsive to public opinion; defines and emphasizes the responsibility of management to serve the public interest; helps management keep abreast of and effectively utilize change, serving as an early warning system to help anticipate trends; and uses research and sound and ethical communication as its principal tools. (Cited in Cutlip et al., 2000: 4)

Furthermore, considering concepts of multiculturalism, Banks (1995: 21) points out that PR is:

> The management of formal communication between organisations and their relevant publics to create and maintain communities of interest and action that favor the organisation, taking full account of the normal human variation in the systems of meaning by which groups understand and enact their everyday lives.

This comes close to describing best practice in PR, which is concerned with mutual understanding between an organisation and its publics and also stresses the importance of culture and diversity for different communities in different locations. An added definition initiated by Hutton (1999: 211) describes PR as 'managing strategic relationships'. Hutton argued that the key elements of PR include management, leadership and mutual understanding. Banks's and Hutton's definitions and the consideration of diversity management showed the importance of multicultural PR in preparing for major challenges in future PR roles.

In a multicultural country like Malaysia, PR practitioners are clearly aware of the importance of 'diversity', 'cultural values' and 'nationality' repertoires in their daily practice. Generally, in a communications department, there are three main races – Malays, Chinese and Indians – working together to fulfil their multicultural clients' needs (Idid, 2004: 230). Syed Arabi Idid (ibid.: 230) also notes that most of their activities are aligned with their local norms, especially religious traditions such as *Eid al Fitr*, *Eid al Adha*, Chinese New Year, *Chap Gog Mei*, *Diwali*, *Thaipusam* and Christmas.

However, there are significant differences between these three main races in practising PR in the context of their cultural values, for different races have distinct cultures (Moses, 2002). Indeed, employers often provide a prayer room, such as the *surau*, in their workplace where Muslim employees can pray. Also reflecting this accommodation, vegetarian food is often served for those from the Indian community. In Malaysia, business and religion are impossible to separate. For example, activities such as the sale of alcohol, gambling and the sale of non-*Halal* foods are illegal for the Muslim community, but non-Muslims may freely practise these activities since they may have different rules in their own cultures. Generally, though, all main races understand their cultural differences in their workplace (Idid, 2004: 230).

Mastering multiple languages is one of the most important issues in nurturing PR practitioners. English is seen as the language of global commerce in Malaysia, while *Bahasa Malaysia* (Malay language) is the nation's official and national language. Kameda (2005: 168) stresses the importance of English as the agent of globalisation for Japanese corporations facing international business communication. Thus, practising global (international) PR requires PR practitioners to master multiple languages, especially English, in order to widen their knowledge about global issues.

Although *Bahasa Malaysia* is the national language, English proficiency for university graduates is also considered essential. However, an enormous number of local graduates from public universities have failed to perform to employers' expectations, particularly in the private sector. Therefore, since almost all organisations in the private sector use English as their principal language of administration (as discussed above), and to enable more Malaysians to become more proficient in English, the government has imposed new educational policies.

For instance, the government has announced a new policy requiring that two core subjects, mathematics and science, should be taught in English rather than in the Malay language at secondary school level in order to improve students' performance (Mohamed, 2003: 1). Thus it is hoped that students will perform better when they further their studies at higher learning institutions. In addition, the National Cultural Policy has proposed English as the medium of communication at public schools with the aim of integrating civil society and preparing students to face the challenges of globalisation (Khattab, 2004: 176). This policy also reflects the heightened awareness of the government in relation to national aspirations and *Wawasan 2020*[5] or Vision 2020 (see Chen et al., 2004), particularly in the wake of the information technology era. *Wawasan 2020* is the ultimate goal of Malaysia to be a fully developed country. This goal can also be achieved by developing the planning and implementation of national information and communication technology policies. In all these contexts, Malaysians are strongly encouraged to be bilingual or multilingual, rather than monolingual, in order to enhance national development and cultural diversity.

Keeping the importance of the diversity of languages in mind, it seems clear that the Malaysian PR industry has been substantially influenced by Western PR philosophies from the early establishment of PR, and that this influence continues in today's development of the profession, not least in the use of English in much of the sector. Notably, in Malaysia, PR practitioners and business communicators are still likely to be practising traditional, one-way communication functions such as media relations and event management. These major PR functions can be interpreted as a technical role. Grunig and Grunig (2003) argue that the press agency or publicity model is the most ineffective way to develop PR practice. This has also been shown by Malaysian research carried out by Kiranjit Kaur (1997) on 'the impact of privatisation on public relations and the role of public relations and management in the privatisation process'.

It might thus be worthwhile for the Malaysian PR industry to adapt Western philosophies to local PR practice. It should also move towards strategic managerial functions such as counselling and reputation management based on applied research and educational development. It seems that although the professional body, the Institute of Public Relations Malaysia, has eagerly promoted rewards for excellence for Malaysian PR practitioners and students, it is more likely to publicise and conduct social activities such as 'Tea Talks', 'Breakfast Talks', contests, glittering ceremonies and similar activities, rather than developing rigorous management research. More funding has been spent on glamorising the activities by inviting top business leaders and politicians in the interests of attracting media coverage from local mainstream media; however, this can be interpreted as polishing the image of the discipline rather than contributing to its maturation. Importantly, the funding could be used to conduct research development and continuous professional development to improve the discipline.

Furthermore, in terms of the medium of communication, learning a new language should be viewed as an entry to another world where users may unlock new opportunities and learn about different cultures. In order to become a 'global' practitioner, they must master at least two languages that are frequently used in the workplace so as to reach a wider market. A case study by Jon White on managing diversity is a good example here: in South Africa, reflecting concern with cultural diversity, different languages were used by members of the top management of Barloworld to describe their organisational strategy development. The company produced the 1999 Annual Report focusing on the key concept – 'creating shareholder value by building powerful industrial brands and long-term relationship'. It seems that the company has determined 'its unique strengths as an ability to manage diversity' and this must be aligned with the organisation's business strategy (White, 2002: 84).

The importance of multicultural public relations

Malaysia, seen as one of the fastest developing countries (Sriramesh and Vercic, 2003), has a rich multiculturalism and cultural diversity. It is worth stressing that multiculturalism and cultural diversity have a significant impact on PR practice in developed and developing countries (Wakefield, 1996: 17).

In keeping with Marshall McLuhan's notion of a global village, people now live and interact in a multi-complex environment where the diversity of races, religions, cultures and languages is taken into account (Motau, 2004). In a survey by the Public Relations Society of America conducted in October 2004 and January 2005, a lack of promotional efforts to attract additional multicultural employees and a complacency by PR employment agencies regarding vacancies for multicultural candidates were found to be major challenges faced by the PR industry in understanding multiculturalism and cultural diversity (Adam, 2005: 6).

Over the years, models of multiculturalism have been ignored, even though they are now acknowledged as essential to good PR in developed and particularly developing countries. A case study by Cummings and DeSanto (2002) revealed that in the 1960s, the International Public Relations Group of Companies (IPRGoC), which served various prominent Japanese companies (but which used Canadian PR practices), failed to convince their local and national clients in Asia, especially in Japan. Additionally, this organisation had to compete with its close competitor, Shandwick International, which was endeavouring to strengthen its local capacity in Japan. Due to some corporate issues, such as internal politicking, a power struggle among various dominant members and the stiff competition with Shandwick International, the IPRGoC collapsed. As a result, former personnel decided to build a new organisation, Worldcom Public Relations Group. Under new leadership and with strong personal relationships among its members, this organisation has developed international networks based on the concept of partnership. By emphasising 'glocalisation' (adaptation to local orientation), the organisation has become the world's third largest PR organisation.

In a highly global setting, most organisations have focused their strategic PR programmes on a diverse range of stakeholder groups, ranging from an individual stakeholder to local communities (Cornelissen, 2004; see also Argenti, 1998), instead of focusing on a single public. In the dynamic business environment, most organisations have also employed multicultural PR practitioners from different educational backgrounds, cultures and characteristics, as well as from different countries to run their strategic PR programmes. Diversity management, based on a symmetrical approach to PR, requires the holistic approach (Wakefield, 1996: 17).

Understanding cultural diversity and multiculturalism is very important to articulate a sensitive and multi-aspect approach to excellent PR, especially in a rapidly developing country like Malaysia. Thus, understanding cultural sensitivity, including language, religious rituals, taboos and suchlike, may reduce conflict within an organisation and enhance organisational performance (LaBahn and Harich, 1997). For example, in an Islamic country, considerable attention should be paid to appreciating religious rituals in the workplace, as, if it is effectively performed, religious faith may enhance employees' performance and the productivity of the organisation. Learning from the calamitous experiences of the IPRGoC, Cummings and DeSanto (2002: 246) suggest that expatriate PR practitioners working in a particular country such as Japan should be sensitive to local cultures and encouraged to communicate in their clients' language.

In addition to this, although Western PR theories (predominantly from the US) have been well developed and are widely practised by global corporations, it would be useful to apply international (global) PR in their practitioners' activities. Sriramesh (2003: 511) argues that with regard to PR education, many Asian countries have come to favour a 'West is best' mentality, as they have adopted US PR curricula, course materials, and so forth rather than developing international (global) PR. He argues that to be 'multicultural professionals, a comprehensive public relations education should deliver knowledge on the linkages between public relations and key environmental variables that influence the practice internationally' (ibid.).

Using Hofstede's intercultural dimensions, Wilhelm (1998) points out significant cultural differences in management skills between Malaysian and American academics. In this regard, Sriramesh (2003) stresses that PR theories require multicultural sensitivity, particularly in a transitional country, as the existing theories have been profoundly influenced by Western philosophy.

Sriramesh and White (1992: 609) argue that there are strong linkages between culture, communication and PR. They are all affected directly and indirectly by the way organisations operate their businesses. Understanding of international PR requires a holistic view and a global and multilingual approach (Sriramesh, 2003) rather than merely polishing the image of communication services. Indeed, there is an urgent need to develop international PR and bring out the implications of its practice in a rapidly developing or transitional country like Malaysia, which is multilingual, multi-ethnic and multi-religious. Banks (1995: 116) points out that:

Training for cultural sensitivity, international adjustment, intercultural communication, and valuing diversity are essential to creating personal changes in multicultural settings. A diverse and rapidly expanding variety of approaches to these sorts of training are available, and organisations should assess their needs and select a training modality that suits their conditions.

In Malaysia and Singapore, communication campaigns have always been aligned with 'intercultural harmony' (Sriramesh, 2003: 515). Examples are the celebration of *Hari Merdeka* or Independence Day, which is concerned with local cultures for all races in those countries. To cater for such circumstances, 'every public relations professional must become a multicultural communicator' (ibid.: 505), with specialised training and development on multicultural facets such as corporate culture, religion, language and suchlike taken into account. This concept gives special advantages to PR professionals who may work with any ethnic group and any country in the world. Thus, it is hypothesised that in the globalisation era, becoming a multicultural communicator can add value to PR roles.

This exploratory study (Abdullah, 2006) looked at how organisational leaders perceived that managing cultural diversity can improve their organisational strategy development. Because PR is a crucial part of organisational systems, the study identified CEO expectations about how PR can be used to manage stakeholders through the management of cultural diversity. The study also determined whether cultural diversity is seen as a barrier or an opportunity to improving their business strategy.

Qualitative method of the study
Unlike quantitative methods, this qualitative tool requires an interviewer to participate actively in discussing particular topics (Seidman, 1998; also see Daymon and Holloway, 2002). In terms of the size of the sample, Saunders et al. (1997) argued that the positivistic approach (a quantitative method) needs a large sample of respondents; in contrast, the phenomenological approach (qualitative method) requires a small number of informants. Thus, a series of interviews were conducted with CEOs and senior directors of large corporations, especially public listed companies, who have a view on the real value of PR. Specifically, key respondents were selected based on an updated directory of the Institute of Public Relations Malaysia (IPRM). A general profile of key respondents showed that they were major clients of PR services and/or operated a huge PR division in their organisation, respectively. The key respondents (CEOs and senior directors) were involved in various service industries which employed a huge number of employees among Malay, China, Indian and expatriates in a multicultural environment (Table 2.2).

Between mid-November 2005 and February 2006,[6] the researcher

Table 2.2   Interviews: chief executive officers/senior directors

Corporation	Job designation	Size of company & sector	Year listed in KLSE*	Diverse employees	Major clients/ supervisors of senior PR staff
C1	Chief Executive Officer	Large/Oil & refinery	1960	Malay, Chinese, Indian & expatriates	Major client
C2	Chief Executive Officer	Large/Waste management	–	Malay, Chinese, Indian & expatriates	Major client
C3	Chief Executive Officer	Large/ Automobile	1990	Malay, Chinese, Indian & expatriates	Major client
C4	Chief Executive Officer	Large/Property development	2000	Malay, Chinese, Indian & expatriates	Major client
C5	Chairman	Large/Banking	1967	Malay, Chinese, Indian & expatriates	'Supervisor' of senior PR staff / major client
C6	Chairman	Large/Conglomerates: properties, hotel, plantation and manufacturing	1990	Malay, Chinese, Indian & expatriates	'Supervisor' of senior PR staff
C7	Chairman	Large/World class/Shipping	–	Malay, Chinese, Indian & expatriates	'Supervisor' of senior PR staff / major client
C8	Deputy Chairman	Large/ Conglomerate: properties, construction, manufac-turing, education, and healthcare	1984	Malay, Chinese, Indian & expatriates	'Supervisor' of senior PR staff / major client
C9	Adviser to Chief Executive Officer	Large/ Telecommu-nication	2002	Malay, Chinese, Indian & expatriates	'Supervisor' of senior PR staff

Table 2.2   (continued)

Corporation	Job designation	Size of company & sector	Year listed in KLSE	Diverse employees	Major clients/ supervisors of senior PR staff
C10	Senior General Manager of Legal counsel, Corporate affairs & Facilities management	Large/Oil & refinery	1994	Malay, Chinese, Indian & expatriates	'Supervisor' of senior PR staff / major client

Note: *KLSE: Kuala Lumpur Stock Exchange.

conducted a series of interviews with CEOs and senior directors of large corporations and/or major clients of PR services in the Klang Valley who understand the real value of PR and communication management. Sending emails to a number of PR leaders to find business leaders who have contributed to the PR industry, such as those to whom the IPRM has awarded the 'Most PR Savvy CEO' award, was a part of the strategy in framing the sample of the study. Of 26 selected business leaders with large corporations and/or major clients of PR services, only 10 replied and agreed to be interviewed. Five of them replied but declined for some reason, such as, 'too busy' or 'matter of policy'. Eleven did not respond. All potential informants were contacted through email, telephone and fax. The cover letter and the interview schedule were officially sent to their corporate communication managers asking their help to arrange interviews with their bosses/supervisors.[7] Then, appointments were set up to conduct face-to-face interviews at the informants' office. The interviews lasted about one to two hours. During the interview, central questions were asked about the value of PR, specifically on how multicultural issues may affect their organisational strategy development and the role of their PR managers in handling particular situations. Some probing questions were asked to seek more information and clarify their opinions/expectations. A digital voice recorder was used to record conversations between the interviewer and interviewees after permission was obtained. All data were transferred to computer software, and a digital wave player for the process of transcribing. All valuable inputs were then analysed and interpreted as findings of this study.

CEO views on cultural diversity

Generally, most CEOs/chairmen agreed that PR is a profession that involves managing stakeholders, especially in an external business environment. It is worth discussing how PR can contribute substantially to organisations by managing cultural diversity and reducing any complexities that affect business performance.

There was complete agreement among the 10 top business leaders interviewed that managing cultural diversity is quite important in determining business success. Malaysia is a multi-ethnic country where multicultural facets can affect organisational strategy development directly and indirectly. It is important to explore the role that PR practitioners can play in improving PR business strategy and reducing any complexities in understanding multicultural issues among the three major ethnic groups – Malay, Chinese and Indian – as well as other ethnicities, including expatriates.

The 10 top executives disclosed that understanding cultural sensitivity among all ethnic groups is very important in formulating and conducting their business strategy, as all corporations studied are manned by diverse employees, especially in corporate communication departments. The chairman of one of the most dynamic banking institutions remarked:

> Organisations in Malaysia are born and bred out of multiculturalism. So it comes quite naturally with the corporation being born and bred here to uphold excellent multicultural values. Our employees come from multi-ethnic backgrounds. The working culture encourages a strong spirit of teamwork, sharing and caring among all races. We have a deliberate policy of observing all festive occasions and observance of respect and appreciation of each other's cultures in the organisation. Observing sensitivities in cross-culture communication is part of our communication policy. [Our banking institution] is a colourful organisation indeed.

They also emphasised that in global business practice, business and multicultural facets cannot be separated, as understanding different cultures may benefit their organisational strategy development. Therefore, managing their business services using a PR strategy which takes account of multicultural sensitivities is vital for business success. Specifically, the chairman of a big shipping company remarked:

> The approach to PR has to be Malaysian based and one that enhances the harmonious working relationship within and outside the business. For example, our corporation has its musical fusion featuring Indian, Malay and Chinese in a two-minute video clip of a 40-piece band playing various instruments.

One of their organisational strategies in adapting their business interests to fit the country's culture and norms is nurturing local PR employees who fully understand the multicultural issues in the country in which the organisation invests. The CEO adviser of the leading telecommunications company disclosed:

> We think diversity will add value to our company. It makes you more prepared and more rounded and more comprehensive. [For example], we wanted to purchase a telecommunications company in India and we are now waiting for approval from the Indian government. So, we looked for a good PR consultancy in India to help us to manage our relationships with regulatory bodies. We wanted to appoint local employees to build our relationships with the Indian government in the interest of buying the telecom company – so they understand their own market and can organise it.

Nurturing local PR employees here is about encouraging global and local firms to employ diverse local employees in order to understand cultural sensitivities such as taboos, religious values and norms that have been practised over the decades in the particular country. This element is aligned with the slogan 'Think locally, act globally'. The chairman of the main multi-purpose gateway port said 'to be aware of cultural sensitivity – "Think locally, act globally" but in acceptance of the norms and customs of the locality'. The chairman of one of the top banking institutions remarked: '[We need to] promote appreciation of local culture, local brands to the world. [We] have to promote a balance between Western and Eastern values. Contributing to global harmony remains their challenge'. Additionally, 'we must become a cultural exporter to the other part of the world', stressed one informant in the oil and refinery business. It is a great challenge for PR practitioners to be cultural diversity experts who can adapt their PR strategy to the country's cultural values and norms in order to harmonise the relationships between the organisation and its stakeholders. Teambuilding, dialogue sessions and management briefings are several key cultural diversity management tools identified as a result of interviewing one business leader in the services sector.

When asked whether the organisation provides a cultural diversity policy that is practised by their diverse employees, five interviewees confirmed that their cultural diversity policy could add value to the harmonisation among different ethnic groups. The CEO of a top global oil company disclosed:

> We have a written agenda that is called 'diversity and inclusiveness'. We say 'inclusiveness' as we value the inputs that our employees contribute. We really value diversity and the different ethnic groups and gender diversity among our employees. Being a multinational company, we must share values as differentiators.

Business leaders were also asked whether they see any difference in multicultural PR in the country where they operate their business. They see that every country has a unique multiculturalism but they are all the same in terms of understanding cultural sensitivity, as there is a diversity of major races such as Chinese and Indian being employed by global corporations and being located in both Western and Eastern worlds. There is a need for PR practitioners to understand the dominant religions such as Islam, Christianity and Hinduism that are practised all over the world. Importantly, global PR practitioners must play a substantial role in informing and advising top management about cultural issues in the country in which they want to invest. Showing great concern about cultural sensitivity with regard to taboos and superstitions, for example, the Chinese belief that their life is influenced by numbers, the CEO of a service corporation disclosed:

> Being multinational companies, you must understand any culture in this world. You must be sensitive to cultural issues. [For example], Alpha Romeo launched a car 164, but number '4' is very bad for the Chinese [unlucky number]. When this new product, a car, was brought to Malaysia, China and Taiwan, the Chinese wouldn't buy [it]. The sales didn't pick up. After [this], they changed the number to 'Alpha Romeo 166'. Look! how cultural sensitivity may affect your business. I think competent PR practitioners must consult with their CEOs and senior management teams about this matter. Because they are the ones who should know about situational issues within an external environment. That's why PR becomes very important. CEOs don't like surprises. The small mistake may result in a big loss.

Concerning cultural sensitivity in the Muslim world with regard to food/meat production, the chairman of a leading conglomerate company stressed: '*Halal* products are very important for the Muslim world. We can also market it to non-Muslims as *Halal* [can be described as] a guarantee "certificate" of health. It is very hygienic indeed'. In this case, he wanted PR practitioners to have a holistic view, especially knowing the facts about the quality of products and services whose values can be shared among different ethnic groups.

In relation to cultural sensitivity in operating their business with respect to the terms/names they use for their products, the CEO of a top automotive corporation remarked:

> I think that most countries have multicultural issues. Understanding cultural sensitivity is quite important, otherwise, you may offend other parties. For example, when we launch *Proton Iswara* that is a Hindu term, *iswara*' also means butterfly. It has a great value for our Malaysian people. We also used to sell *Proton Saga* (the first edition). For Malaysian people, *saga* is a type of fruit which is red and bright. But when we export our cars to Europe, we cannot use *Proton Saga* because *saga* has a bad connotation for European cultures. Then,

we used *Proton Persona*, because *persona* is about impression or personality. We are always concerned about cultural diversity when doing business in a particular country. I think it is PR responsibility to do research and consult with us about this matter.

Cultural sensitivity is also considered in creating their company brand statement. As a company with a 'human touch', the senior general manager of a petroleum organisation emphasised:

I see a human entity has a universal value. It cuts across all cultural or religious issues. Our brand statement is: 'Energy receive and energy return – aspiring people everywhere'. So, based on our brand statement, when we do business in other countries like Sudan or Europe, we are always bound to this statement. As a national company, we are part of Malaysian society. We touch the hearts of other people. So, it is a part of our responsibilities to protect our own heritage and culture. In Sudan, the main problems are education, health and hygiene. This country is left far behind. In Vietnam, it is about the same things. [Therefore], it is our role to inject education and capacity building.

Six informants interviewed also voiced their concern about the lack of understanding about cultural sensitivity among Western expatriates, including PR expatriates, who operate their business in a multicultural country like Malaysia. Informants expected that a greater understanding about cultural diversity would be a key to relationship management between global corporations and their stakeholders all around the world. The deputy chairman of a leading conglomerate organisation remarked:

Many years ago, I was asked to attend some professional courses. They were held by London Worldwide almost every year. They have 300 senior officers from all over the world. But they wanted to do one managerial course over *Eid al-Fitr* [a major Islamic festival] dates. In Malaysia and the Middle East, we have been celebrating *Eid al-Fitr* for more than a hundred years. I was upset because they didn't consider that *Eid al-Fitr* celebration is very important for Muslim delegates. There were many senior officers from Malaysia, Jordan, Saudi Arabia and Indonesia who attended the courses as well. To me, they weren't really sensitive to others' cultures. Then, they realised that they should not hold courses during religious celebrations. Now it is better and people are more aware of it.

From the point of view of business leaders, the importance of cultural diversity management is a crucial and significant part of global PR practice and it is becoming a critical success factor for their businesses.

Discussion

Cultural diversity is on the rise. The question is whether cultural diversity has a significant effect on practising PR business strategy in a multicultural environment. In the global picture, where PR is practised by various ethnic groups from Eastern and Western worlds, cultural sensitivity is central to good PR practice. Thus, cultural diversity should not be seen as a barrier to business performance but should be recognised as an opportunity for organisations to develop better relationships with their stakeholders. As mentioned earlier, the role and functions of PR have a strategic external function, and mastering knowledge of cultural diversity opens a new window of expertise for PR practitioners. Thus, PR practitioners act as cultural exporters and should be able to adapt their work to different environments, which would certainly add value to their expertise.

One of the most striking findings of this study is that understanding sensitivity about distinct culture in Asian countries is crucial for the value creation of business strategy development. The evidence showed that local culture can be considered as a unique and distinctive value which, if properly designed, can be turned into business opportunities for effective marketing communication strategies. However, failing to understand intercultural sensitivity may be damaging to MNCs as culture is a way of life for many diverse Asian societies.

Specifically, drawing on the evidence in this study (Abdullah, 2006), almost all business leaders noted the importance of Malaysian organisational cultures and local norms in their practice. They all also agreed that mastering English as a global language of commerce is an essential skill for competent PR practitioners, but they did not deny that the Malay language[8] needs to be used to maintain the identity of Malaysia. Indeed, Malaysian PR practitioners and PR expatriates should be more sensitive to the local norms and organisational cultures in order to foster a favourable relationship between an organisation and its environment. In a multicultural country, understanding diversity management and cultural values may increase the productivity of an organisation and also create harmony between an organisation and the local society, especially in Malaysia among the three main races, Malay, Chinese and Indian.

Drawing on the evidence, cultural diversity has been of great concern to business leaders as Malaysian corporations encourage diversity in employment among three multi-ethnic groups at the workplace. This creates a harmonised high-performance team culture to deliver values for structuring its organisational strategy development. Sharing values across distinct cultures is very important among diverse employees as they can create opportunities and avoid complexities in their workplace. To strengthen this notion, a series of management policies have been developed and implemented to highlight the concern over diversity management in employment.

Interestingly, the Malaysian corporations studied have been immune to the cultural diversity in their policy development pertaining to celebrating all festive occasions for all main religions – *Eid al Fitr*, *Eid al Adha*, the Chinese New Year and Christmas. This policy has been treated with great respect by and appreciation of diverse local employees. However, some expatriates who work with Malaysian corporations did not seem to understand intercultural sensitivity. Observing and learning sensitivities across cultures is very important to create harmony among all employees.

Indeed, cultural diversity here is seen as a universal concept, as every country has different religious and tribal groups. PR has been practised according to various ethnic groups with different religions and tribes. Thus, building mutual relationships between organisations and external stakeholders requires an understanding of cultural differences to reduce any complexities that may affect business performance.

Implications

The study gives rise to some implications for future managers and researchers pertaining to the importance of cultural diversity management to today's corporations. In Islamic countries, the issue of intercultural sensitivity is of paramount importance. Significantly, there is ample evidence in Malaysia that many corporations have established a cultural diversity policy for their employees to ensure that intercultural sensitivity is treated fairly.

The findings suggest some implications for organisations, specifically private companies and MNCs. Corporations should be able to provide comprehensive training on cultural diversity management. The content of training should focus on understanding three pillars of cultural competency – distinct tribal ethnic groups, religions, and languages. There should be compulsory training courses for new and existing expatriates who are employed by Malaysian corporations. The human resource management department should be able to design and implement training courses on cultural diversity strategically.

The findings also suggest the importance of effectively communicating cultural diversity to all employees from supporting staff to top management personnel. It is a significant responsibility of the corporate communication department to communicate value on diversity management through downward and upward communication. A communication policy should be formulated and practised to ensure that the notion of cultural diversity is understood by all employees. The corporate communication department is responsible for designing effective communication strategies pertaining to cultural diversity.

In a globalising world, every communication practitioner must become a multicultural communicator. Therefore, it is crucial for communication practitioners to be equipped with profound knowledge and skills in distinct cultures, politics and economic systems that should be taught in their formal education and continuing professional development programmes. There is sufficient evidence to note that cultural diversity in organisations should be managed by PR people as perceived by organisational leaders. Strong support from other divisions such as the human resource department and top management is crucial to strengthen the communication policy on cultural diversity management specifically.

In the future, it will be a great challenge for practitioners and researchers to align distinct culture and business strategy in order to improve the value creation of Malaysian corporations in a highly competitive global business environment. Ultimately, it is hoped that in achieving excellent business practice, great attention will be paid to the theoretical and practical knowledge of diversity management as the world becomes more multicultural.

Conclusion

In respecting cultural diversity, understanding cultural differences is vital for PR practitioners and all employees generally. There is a dire need to develop a cultural diversity policy and to examine case studies describing how multicultural issues may affect PR business strategy and organisational strategy development. In respect of the richness of multiculturalism in a multicultural country such as Malaysia, there is great scope for Western and Asian companies to learn from each other.

Indeed, the chapter gives insights, perceptions, concepts and argumentative notions about cultural diversity management in Malaysia, beginning from a broader scope of political, economic and social aspects and narrowing to a micro scope of the practice of cultural diversity through PR management in MNCs and GLCs. It is argued that this study is among the first to examine the views of Malaysian CEOs and senior directors regarding the standards of cultural diversity, drawing from multiple perspectives – public relations, corporate communication, strategic management and multiculturalism. Thus, a multidisciplinary approach to studying cultural diversity can substantially contribute to the body of diversity management knowledge.

Notes

1. 'Belonging' refers to the feeling or experience of being part of a group (Özbilgin and Woodward, 2004: 677).
2. 'Otherness' refers to the feeling or experience of being an outsider excluded from a group (Özbilgin and Woodward, 2004: 677).
3. There are three Islamic models of equal employment opportunity in Islamic societies – Islamic Orthodox, Islamic Western and Islamic Modernist (Syed, 2008).

4. *Halal* is an Arabic word which means permitted and lawful (Hawkins, 1997). *Halal* means that the food must be free from pork and alcohol. Meat must be slaughtered in the manner prescribed by the *shari'a* (Irfan, 2002).
5. 'Malaysia should not be developed only in the economic sense. It must be a nation that is fully developed along all the dimensions: economically, politically, socially, spiritually, psychologically and culturally. We must be fully developed in terms of national unity and social cohesion, in terms of our economy, in terms of social justice, political stability, system of government, quality of life, social and spiritual values, national pride and confidence' (Speech by former Prime Minister of Malaysia, Dr Mahathir Mohamad, to the Malaysian Business Council) (Mohamad, 2005).
6. Note: between mid-November and December 2005: scheduling appointments; and between January and February 2006: visiting and interviewing informants.
7. Corporate communication managers report directly to CEOs/chairmen.
8. The Malay language is an official language used by the three main races – Malay, Chinese and Indian.

References

Abdullah, Z. (2006), 'Towards the Professionalisation of Public Relations in Malaysia. Perception Management and Strategy Development', unpublished doctoral thesis, Cardiff University, Wales.

Adam, V. (2005), 'Survey on multicultural PR PROs shows major barriers to diversity', *PR News*, **23** (61), June 8, available at: www.prnewsonline.com (accessed 20 November 2007).

Anuar, M. (2000), 'Malaysian media and democracy', *Media Asia*, **27** (4), 183–9.

Argenti, P. (ed.) (1998), *Corporate Communication*, Boston, MA: Irwin/McGraw-Hill.

Banks, S.P. (1995), *Multicultural Public Relations: A Social-Interpretive Approach*, London: Sage.

Bhuiyan, S.I. (1997), 'Malaysia's MSC and Singapore's status as Southeast Asia's technology capital', *Media Asia*, **24** (4), 214–19.

Burgess, J. and Muthaly, S. (2001), 'Malaysia', in M. Patrickson and P. O'Brien (eds), *Managing Diversity in the Asia–Pacific*, Brisbane: Jacaranda Wiley, pp. 139–54.

CAPWIP (2008), 'Malaysia report', *Center for Asia-Pacific Women in Politics*, the Philippines.

Chen, A., Ngu, T. and Taib, A. (2004), 'Vision 2020: multicultural Malaysia's campaign for development', Institute for Public Relations Research and Education, Gainesville available at: www.instituteforpr.com (accessed 20 November 2007).

Cornelissen, J.P. (2004), *Corporate Communication: Theory and Practice*, London: Sage.

Cummings, B. and DeSanto, B. (2002), 'Worldcom Public Relations Group: Global Access, Local Focus', in D. Moss and B. DeSanto (eds) (2002), *Public Relations Cases: International Perspectives*, London: Routledge, Taylor & Francis, pp. 246–58.

Cutlip, S.M., Center, A.H. and Broom, G.M. (2000), *Effective Public Relations*, London: Prentice-Hall.

Daymon, C. and Holloway, I. (2002), *Qualitative Research Methods in Public Relations and Marketing Communications*, London: Routledge.

Department of Statistics, Malaysia (2005 and 2008), 'Key statistics', Statistic Agency, Kuala Lumpur, available at: www.statistics.gov.my (accessed 15 April 2007 and 26 July 2008).

EIA (2005), 'Country analysis briefs', Energy Information Administration, Washington, available at: www.eid.doe.gov (accessed 23 December 2008).

Fisher, H.T. (1996), 'Multiculturalism in Malaysia and Australia', Australian Department of Foreign Affairs and Trade, Canberra, available at: www.dfat.gov.au (accessed 9 September 2007).

Gardenswartz, L., Rowe, A., Digh, P. and Bennett, M. (2003), *The Global Diversity Desk Reference: Managing An International Workforce*, San Francisco, CA: Pfeiffer.

Grunig, L.A. and Grunig, J.E. (2003), 'Public relations in the United States: a generation of maturation', in Sriramesh and Vercic (eds), pp. 323–55.

Hawkins, J.M. (ed.) (1997), *Kamus Dwibahasa Oxford Fajar* (Bilingual Dictionary), Shah Alam: Penerbit Fajar Bakti.

Hutton, J.G. (1999), 'The definition, dimensions, and domain of public relations', *Public Relations Review*, **25** (2), 199–214.

Icon Group International (2000), 'Executive Report on Strategies in Malaysia', available at: www.icongroupedition.com accessed 23 December 2007).

Idid, S.A. (2004), 'Public relations in Malaysia: its colonial past to current practice', in Sriramesh (ed.), pp. 217–30.

International Labour Organization (ILO) (2005), Thirteenth Asian Regional Meeting, Geneva, 28–31 August, available at: www.ilo.org (accessed 23 December 2007).

Irfan, H. (2002), 'The halal meat industry: was your Eid sheep really halal?', Health and Science Section, *Islam Online*, available at: www.islamonline.net (accessed 7 March 2007).

Kameda, N. (2005), 'A research paradigm for international business communication', *Corporate Communication: International Journal*, **10** (2), 168–82.

Kaur, K. (1997), 'The Impact of Privatisation on Public Relations and the Role of Public Relations and Management in the Privatisation Process', unpublished doctoral thesis, University of Maryland, College Park, MD.

Khattab, U. (2004), 'Wawasan 2020: engineering a modern Malaysia', *Media Asia*, **31** (3), 170–77.

LaBahn, D.W. and Harich, K.R. (1997), 'Sensitivity to national business culture: effects on U.S.–Mexican channel relationship performance', *Journal of International Marketing*, **5** (4), 29–51.

Ministry of Culture, Arts and Tourism (2005), *About Tourism Malaysia*, Kuala Lumpur, available at: www.mocat.gov.my (accessed 22 November 2007).

Mohamed, M. (2003), 'Study shows use of English effective', *The Star Online*, available at: www.thestar.com.my (accessed 10 April 2007).

Mohamad, M. (2005), '*Wawasan 2020*' (Vision 2020) Malaysian Business Council, Prime Minister's Office, Kuala Lumpur.

Moses, B. (2002), 'Ethnic reporting in the Malaysian media', *Media Asia*, **29** (2), 102–6.

Motau, S. (2004), 'Multicultural communication and relationships – a perspective from South Africa', *Global Alliance for Public Relations and Communication Management*, available at: www.globalpr.org (accessed 23 November 2007).

Mustapha, R. (2008), 'Unity amid diversity: the Malaysian multicultural experience', *International Journal of Diversity in Organisations, Communities and Nations*, **6** (2), 67–74.

Netto, A. (2002), 'Media in divided societies: Malaysia', *Media Asia*, **29** (3), 179–83.

Özbilgin, M. and Woodward, D. (2004), '"Belonging" and "otherness": sex equality in banking in Turkey and Britain', *Gender, Work, and Organization*, **11** (6), 669–88.

Saunders, M., Lewis, P. and Thornhill, A. (1997), *Research Methods for Business Students*, London: Financial Times Management.

Seidman, I. (1998), *Interviewing as Qualitative Research: A Guide for Researchers in Education and the Social Sciences*, London: Teachers' College Press.

Singh, B. (2001), 'The media environment in Malaysia', *Media Asia*, **28** (2), 88–96.

Sriramesh, K. (2003), 'The missing link: multiculturalism and public relations education', in Sriramesh and Vercic (eds), pp. 505–22.

Sriramesh, K. (ed.) (2004), *Public Relations in Asia*, Australia: Thomson Learning.

Sriramesh, K. and Vercic, D. (eds) (2003), *The Global Public Relations Handbook*, Hillsdale, NJ: Lawrence Erlbaum.

Sriramesh, K. and White, J. (1992), 'Societal culture and public relations', in J. Grunig (ed.), *Excellence in Public Relations and Communications Management: Contributions to Effective Organizations*, Hillsdale, NJ: Lawrence Erlbaum, pp. 597–616.

Syed, J. (2008), 'A context-specific perspective of equal employment opportunity in Islam societies', *Asia Pacific Journal of Management*, **25** (1), 135–51.

Tamam, E., Abdullah, Z., Omar, S.Z. and Bolong, J. (2007), 'The effects of communicating Islam *Hadhari* through public relations campaigns among non-Muslim government officers', paper presented at the World Communication Association Conference, Queensland University of Technology, Brisbane, July.

The World Factbook (2002), *About Malaysia*, available at: www.bartleby.com (accessed 3 September 2007).

Wakefield, R.I. (1996), 'Interdisciplinary theoretical foundations for international public relations', in H.M. Culbertson and N. Chen (eds), *International Public Relations: A Comparative Analysis*, Hillsolale, NJ: Lawrence Erlbaum, pp. 17–30.

White, J. (2002), 'Barloworld: communicating strategic direction to increase shareholder value', in D. Moss and B. DeSanto (eds), *Public Relations Cases: International Perspectives*, London: Routledge, pp. 78–84.

Wilhelm, K.H. (1998), 'Hofstede's intercultural dimensions and the decision-making process: Americans and Malaysians in a cooperative university setting', in K.S. Sitaram and M. Prosser (eds), *Civic Discourse: Multiculturalism, Cultural Diversity, and Global Communication*, Stamford, CT: Ablex, pp. 265–80.

3 Identity salience, occupational commitment and organizational citizenship behaviour in multinational teams: an exploratory study from the Turkish context
F. Pinar Acar

Introduction

Managing a culturally diverse workforce is one of the most critical challenges faced by contemporary managers (Adler and Ghadar, 1990; Adler, 2002; Schneider and Barsoux, 2003; Abdullah, ch. 2, this volume; Sürgevil, ch. 17, this volume). The importance of diversity is reflected in the large volume of research directed at understanding its consequences (for comprehensive reviews of diversity research, see Milliken and Martins, 1996; Williams and O'Reilly, 1998; Ashkanasy et al., 2002; Jackson et al., 2003). Unfortunately, very few studies, to date, examine national origin as a dimension of diversity. Jackson et al. (2003) reviewed 63 empirical studies and found that of the total number of effects reported, only one corresponded to the effect of nationality diversity and two to the effects of cultural value diversity. With the increased use of team-based management techniques, the influence of cultural diversity on the functioning of teams has become an important but neglected area (Millhous, 1999; Zaidman and Pines, ch. 23, this volume). This chapter aims to remedy this gap in the extant diversity literature by developing a conceptual framework to examine an important aspect of teamwork, organizational citizenship behaviours, in teams composed of members from different nations.

Specifically, the chapter investigates the effects of national identity salience on organizational citizenship behaviours. It is proposed that salient subgroup identities will have a negative impact on such behaviours. The current study also proposes the often understudied occupational commitment as a moderator variable. The framework presented suggests that negative influence of salient identities on organizational citizenship behaviours will be weakened by high occupational commitment.

Conceptual framework and propositions

With the rise in global trade, countries and companies alike are becoming increasingly multinational (Glazer and De la Rosa, 2008) and the prevalence of multinational teams in organizations is rising (Watson et al., 1998; Millhous, 1999; Adler, 2002). Effectiveness of multinational teams, like that of any other team, partly depends on members' collaboration with each other by sharing relevant information and helping one another with tasks and problems. Such behaviours are commonly labelled as organizational citizenship behaviours (OCBs).

OCBs represent individual behaviours that are discretionary, not part of an employee's job description and thus not enforceable by supervisors, and not directly or explicitly recognized by the formal reward system (Organ, 1988). Performance of OCBs in the aggregate promotes the efficient and effective functioning of the system (ibid.). Therefore, OCBs are important for team effectiveness (Van Der Vegt et al., 2003). Some examples of OCB include helping team members, assisting newcomers to the team, not abusing the rights of team mates, not taking extra breaks, and enduring minor impositions that occur when working as part of a team (Kidwell et al., 1997).

OCBs encompass several kinds of behaviour and scholars distinguished among different types. Organ (1988), for instance, identified five dimensions: altruism, courtesy, sportsmanship, conscientiousness and civic virtue. Morrison (1994) also identified five dimensions: altruism, conscientiousness, sportsmanship, keeping up with changes and involvement. Moorman and Blakely (1995), building on earlier work, developed a scale that measured four types of OCBs – loyal boosterism, interpersonal helping, individual initiative and personal industry. As a result of a literature review, Podsakoff et al. (2000) suggested a seven-dimension model of OCB: helping behaviour, sportsmanship, organizational loyalty, organizational compliance, individual initiative, civic virtue and self-development. Finally, Coleman and Borman (2000) identified three dimensions of OCB: interpersonal citizenship performance (reflects behaviour that benefits other organizational members), organizational citizenship performance (specifies behaviour that benefits the organization), and job-task citizenship performance (identifies extra effort and persistence on the job, dedication to the job, and the desire to maximize one's own job performance).

The above examined research suggests that various types of OCBs fall into two broad categories such that some of these are directed at the system (for example, the team), whereas others are directed at the peers (Williams and Anderson, 1991). In the context of multinational teams, behaviours which involve helping team members with task-related problems are likely to be most important for team effectiveness, and identity salience is expected to have a greater influence on such behaviours (Chattopadhyay, 1999). Therefore, the focus here is on behaviours that involve voluntary aiding of team mates with task-related problems.

Helping fellow team members is a key element to all models of OCB. Organ (1988) refers to this dimension of OCB as 'altruism'. Altruism refers to providing assistance to other team members with tasks and problems (ibid.). Janssen and Huang (2008) identified cooperative behaviours, such as helping others, as critical determinants of individual effectiveness as a team member. To date little research attention has been devoted to understanding the antecedents of altruism in multinational teams.

However, indirect evidence from literature on team diversity suggests that demographic dissimilarity, such as differences in nationality, may negatively affect how group members interact with each other (for example, O'Reilly et al., 1989; Harrison et al., 1998, 2002; Chatman and Flynn, 2001; Jehn and Mannix, 2001) and that attaining cooperation from members of a multinational group could be problematic. Although extant diversity literature makes a valuable contribution to our understanding of the effects of member differences on group dynamics, it has one major shortcoming. It concentrates on 'objective' diversity; that is, the diversity that is present on a team without taking into consideration whether members are aware of and perceive the differences examined as relevant.

Members of a team may not be aware of each and every difference team mates may have, because some differences may not be salient to them (Randel, 2002; Acar, 2008). Therefore, objective conceptualizations of diversity may not be identical to what is perceived by team members and members' perceptions of diversity may be more relevant in explaining their behaviour (Randel, 2002; Hobman et al., 2003; Acar, 2008; Ayub and Jehn, ch. 6, this volume). When an identity is salient, team members are aware of their differences and that identity is the main trigger of member behaviour. According to Randel (2002), identity salience should predict member behaviour more precisely than objective measures of diversity being present within the team. In a study of work groups diverse with respect to gender, Randel showed that gender identity salience moderated the gender diversity–conflict link and that gender identity salience was more strongly associated with emotional conflict for men.

In sum, the majority of diversity literature conceptualizes group diversity in terms of presence of some demographic characteristics. The present chapter takes a different approach and argues that it is the members' perceptions of salient identities that determine how members interact with each other and their tendency to engage in altruism.

Identity salience and OCBs

Identity is one of the root constructs (Ashforth et al., 2008) and one of the most popular topics in organization studies (Sveningsson and Alvesson, 2003). Identity is viewed as having a widespread influence on many organizational behaviour issues and especially relevant for teamwork (Randel, 2002; Sveningsson and Alvesson, 2003). Ashforth et al. (2008) indicate that every individual needs to have a sense of who she/he is, who others are, and how individuals are associated. As such, identities help individuals make sense of the social landscape and identify the kinds of behaviour that are appropriate (Randel, 2002; Ashforth et al., 2008).

One of the most popular conceptualizations of identity in organizational studies is provided by the social identity theory and its development self-categorization theory (Ashforth et al., 2008). Social identity theory and self-categorization theory distinguish between personal identity and social identity (Hogg et al., 2004; Ashforth et al., 2008). Tajfel (1978: 63) defined social identity as that 'part of an individual's self concept which derives from his knowledge of his membership of a social group together with the value and emotional significance attached to that membership'. Personal identity, on the other hand, is 'a self-construal in terms of idiosyncratic personality attributes that are not shared with other people or close relationships that are tied entirely to the specific other person in the dyadic relationship' (Hogg et al., 2004: 251). Because personal identity has little to do with group processes, the focus of social identity approach is on social identity.

According to the social identity approach, individuals have multiple social identities (Hogg et al., 2004; Ashforth et al., 2008). These identities are related to each other in an antagonistic way (Turner et al., 1994), such that as one identity becomes salient, others fade away (Chatman et al., 1998). For instance, Chatman et al. demonstrated that the salience of demographic identity diminished as the salience of organizational identity increased. Thus, in any given situation, only one identity can be 'psychologically real' (Hogg et al., 2004: 252) and it is the identity that is salient that shapes the self-concept, perception, and behaviour of the individuals (Randel, 2002; Hogg et al., 2004; Ashforth et al., 2008). Randel (2002) defines salience as 'an individual-level measure of how prominently a demographic category is used to describe one's group members' (p. 750). Thus, through salient identities group members describe themselves, interpret the group context and interact with group members (Randel, 2002; Hogg et al., 2004; Ashforth et al., 2008).

According to Tajfel and Turner (1986: 16) social identities are 'relational and comparative'. That is, identity salience depends on the context. Two principles govern identity salience – accessibility and fit (Oakes,

1987). Accessibility refers to the perceiver's readiness to activate a particular category (Turner and Haslam, 2001; Van Knippenberg et al., 2004). Categorizations that are more widely accepted in the social context, frequently employed, as well as those that are self-evident and easily noticed are more readily accessible and therefore more likely to be used (Hogg et al., 2004; Van Knippenberg et al., 2004). Hence, categorizations based on readily detectable characteristics such as nationality are more likely to be used.

Fit refers to the match between the category and reality (Turner and Haslam, 2001). Thus, categories which are subjectively meaningful to perceivers (Van Knippenberg et al., 2004) and for which intergroup differences are larger than intragroup differences (Turner and Haslam, 2001) are more likely to be used. In the context of multinational teams, nationality provides a meaningful category that clearly distinguishes between groups. Thus, the above discussions of accessibility and fit indicate that national origin is likely to be quite salient in multinational teams.

According to Tajfel and Turner (1986), social identities are also comparative. That is, individuals derive social identities by classifying themselves and others into social categories on the basis of demographic characteristics such as gender and race. Individuals use salient characteristics to define themselves and others as members of social categories (Turner, 1987). In the case of a multinational team, as discussed above, members are likely to use nationality for categorization purposes. On a multinational team, individuals may perceive other team members as either members of the same category (that is, nationality) as themselves or as members of a category different from their own. Thus, members of a multinational group may perceive themselves and those with the same national origin with them as forming an ingroup, and may see members from other nations as forming an outgroup.

The underlying motivation for categorization is self-enhancement (Tajfel and Turner, 1986; Turner and Haslam, 2001; Hogg et al., 2004). According to the social identity approach, individuals are driven to achieve a positive identity and to enhance their self-esteem (Tajfel and Turner, 1986). When a social identity is salient, 'the self in self enhancement and self esteem is the collective self, social identity' (Hogg et al., 2004: 256). Thus, individuals' self-enhancement depends on creating a positive social identity for the group. In turn, positive social identity is attained and maintained by positively comparing the ingroup to a comparison outgroup (Tajfel and Turner, 1986). This may involve favouring ingroup members and forming biases and negative attitudes towards outgroup members.

Hence, categorization process results in individuals identifying with a social category and perceiving their faiths intertwined with that group. This perception of oneness with the group motivates individuals to favour their fellow ingroup members and try to act in ways that represent the ingroup positively (Van Dyne et al., 1995; Hogg et al., 2004). Under certain conditions, categorization may also lead to negative feelings, distrust and dislike of outgroup members and may result in discriminatory behaviour towards outgroup members (Tajfel and Turner, 1986). For these effects of social categorization to occur, it must be psychologically real (that is, salient) as the basis for perception and self-conception (Hogg et al., 2004).

When members of a multinational team perceive nationality as the salient identity, ingroups and outgroups will be formed along national origins. Randel and Jaussi (2003) propose that identification with a demographic category can result in self-serving behaviours that are detrimental to individual effectiveness as a team member. Van Der Vegt et al. (2003) investigated effects of informational dissimilarity, team identification, and OCBs for individuals working under different configurations of interdependence, and found that information dissimilarity was negatively related to team identification and helping behaviour under conditions of incongruent goal and task interdependence. According to Chattopadhyay (1999) an individual is likely to behave in a fashion consistent with her or his self-image to avoid cognitive dissonance, and since OCBs are defined as a contribution towards the work group for which there is no concrete and immediate reward, occurrence of altruism is more likely in homogeneous teams.

When team members see themselves and team mates as part of an inclusive grouping such as the multinational team, they will include all the team members in the ingroup (Thatcher and Jehn, 1998). Under these conditions, members will identify with the team and experience a sense of oneness with the team which motivates members to behave in cooperative ways to promote their social identity as team members (Van Dyne et al., 1995; Janssen and Huang, 2008). According to Chattopadhyay (1999), individuals are attracted more to ingroup members and they engage in higher levels of OCB towards ingroup members, because such behaviour is consistent with the higher attraction, and to behave otherwise might create cognitive dissonance. Van Knippenberg (2000) suggested that because of their discretionary nature, OCBs are more likely to be performed when member identification with the team is high. Christ et al. (2003) found that team identification was strongly associated with citizenship behaviours aimed at helping colleagues. In a survey study of middle management teams in Dutch banks, Janssen and Huang (2008) found that when individuals identify more strongly with their team, they engaged in more citizenship behaviours towards other team members. Van Dyne et al. (1995) indicated that similar members identify with their team and will try to maintain their positive social identities by acting prosocially towards other team members. Building on the above discussion, the following proposition is developed:

Proposition 1: The higher the salience of national identity for multinational team members, the lower the level of altruism they will demonstrate.

Occupational commitment as a moderator of identity salience OCB link
While investigating the effects of identity salience on OCBs, this chapter also focuses on occupational commitment as a moderator of the effects of identity salience on altruism. 'Occupational commitment' is the term used to describe the degree of attachment to an occupation (Meyer et al., 1993; Snape and Redman, 2003). Although organizational commitment has long been considered among the most important antecedents of OCBs and widely examined (for example, Mowday et al., 1982; Organ and Ryan, 1995; Podsakoff et al., 2000), occupational commitment is mostly overlooked. However, occupational commitment may be more relevant for today's workforce (Wallace, 1993; Snape and Redman, 2003).

Recent changes in the economy and in the way business is conducted are causing jobs both in the private and public sectors to be less secure and less stable (Cappelli, 1999; Mir et al., 2002). Competition has become fiercer and product life cycles are shorter, forcing companies to outsource all functions not central to their capabilities, resulting in restructuring and rightsizing of organizations (Cappelli, 1999). Such measures not only strain the relationship between organizations and their members (Mir et al., 2002) but also decrease the prospects for advancement within organizations and encourage employees to look to other companies for career opportunities (Cappelli, 1999). In the face of the transient and less secure relationship members have with their organization, occupation which transcends any given organization may become the major basis of identification (Ashforth et al., 2008). Hence, 'employees shift their commitment from increasingly transient work organizations to the relative stability of their occupations' (Snape and Redman, 2003: 152). Further, as a result of internationalization of operations, members of multinational teams are usually working away from their organizations. This far distance, and relatively bounded relationships with their organizations, may also decrease members' commitment to the organization.

The above discussion suggests that members of multinational teams may not have a strong sense of belonging to a specific organization and occupation commitment may be more relevant in explaining member behaviour in such teams. In a qualitative study, Blatt (2008) argues that in the absence of a long-term relationship or strong organizational identification with an organization, occupation commitment may be the trigger of OCBs. She examined accounts of helping behaviours by temporary knowledge workers and found that the most prominent theme in explanations of why such workers engaged in OCBs was their perceived norms of professional behaviour for their occupation.

The growing body of research on occupational commitment indicates that similar to organizational commitment, occupational commitment is multidimensional (Meyer et al., 1993; Snape and Redman, 2003). Studies by Meyer et al. (1993), Irving et al. (1997) and Snape and Redman (2003) validated the three-dimensional conceptualization of commitment (Meyer and Allen, 1993) in the occupation domain. According to this model, occupation commitment has three distinct dimensions: affective, continuance and normative. Affective commitment is value-based attachment to the occupation. Continuance commitment is based on an assessment of costs and benefits and develops as employees recognize that they have accumulated investments or 'side bets' that would be lost if they were to leave the organization, or as they recognize that the availability of comparative alternatives is limited. Finally, normative commitment is obligation based and develops as the result of socialization experiences that emphasize the appropriateness of remaining loyal to one's employer or through the receipt of benefits that create within the employee a sense of obligation to reciprocate.

Meyer et al. (1993) suggest that the different dimensions of occupational commitment may have different implications for behaviour and researchers must clearly identify the form of dimension they are examining. For instance, from a sample of registered nurses, Meyer et al. found that of the three dimensions of occupation commitment, only affective commitment was associated with helping behaviour. Similarly, Snape and Redman (2003) proposed that three dimensions of occupation commitment would have different effects on human resource management specialists' intention to actively participate in professional association. Specifically, they found that affective commitment was strongly related to such extra-role and discretionary behaviour, whereas normative commitment was weakly related and continuance commitment was not related to participating in professional activities. Drawing upon the above discussion, the following proposition is suggested:

Proposition 2: Affective occupational commitment will moderate the relationship between national identity salience and altruism.

An exploratory study from Turkey

Turkish context
Despite the rather large literature concerning diversity, the vast majority of studies have been done in the US and other Western countries. Turkey

is rarely explored in diversity management research. However, Turkey presents a rich context to examine the effects of differences in nationality. Over the last two decades, several developments and changes in the economic and socio-cultural domains in Turkey have created opportunities for multinational interface. As a result of the globalization of the world economy, and the development of transportation, and information and communication technology, large American and Western multinational companies entered the Turkish market. At the same time, Turkish companies also opened up to the world. Thus, the international joint ventures and foreign direct investment in Turkey as well as Turkish companies' attempts to operate in foreign markets have contributed to the creation of a multinational workforce. With the fall of the Berlin Wall and the Soviet bloc, Turkey also faced a flood of immigrants from Eastern Europe and Central Asia, further increasing the national diversity of its workforce. Finally, Turkey's bid to join the European Union is creating a multinational interface at the realm of state organizations. In an attempt to adapt to European Union laws and regulations, several state agencies and ministries are carrying out projects with their European counterparts as part of multinational teams.

Turkey lies between Europe and Asia, bridging the two continents not only geographically but also culturally (Aycan and Eskin, 2005). Hofstede's work (1980) suggested that Turkish culture is a collectivist one with a relatively high power distance, uncertainty avoidance and feminine values. The GLOBE study shows that Turkish culture is high in collectivism but relatively low on performance and future orientation (Bodur and Kabasakal, 2002). Cross-cultural studies indicate that there may be significant differences in cultural values that prevail across nations and such values can influence a diverse set of work-related behaviour, as well as the functioning and culture of organizations. For instance, in a study of multinational companies, privately held Turkish companies and Turkish state agencies, Ölmez et al. (2004) found that Turkish institutions did not put much emphasis on formal rationality in terms of efficiency, calculability, predictability and control as much as their multinational counterparts. Metcalf et al. (2006) found significant differences between Finland, India, Mexico, Turkey and the USA in terms of negotiation behaviour. Aycan et al. (2000) suggested that societal values influenced internal work culture and human resource management practices of organizations. Managers from 10 countries including Turkey participated in the study and the results indicate that each country had a somewhat different profile. For instance, Turkey was found to be highly paternalistic, moderately collectivistic and hierarchical, and non-fatalistic. Thus, Turkey occupies a distinct culture that has a strong influence on work behaviour, practices and organization structure which it provides in a unique cultural context which, to date, has not been the setting for a research on diversity.

Sample and procedures

The objective of the current chapter is to develop a conceptual framework that explains the occurrence of altruism in multinational teams whose members may be more committed to their occupations than to their employing organizations. The propositions suggested above were assessed by an exploratory study from two multinational teams from Turkey. One of the teams was the multinational faculty of a bilingual school that provides pre-kindergarten to grade twelve education to a body of multinational students. The second team was a symphony orchestra that consisted of multinational musicians. The composition of both teams was similar: 50 per cent Turkish and 50 per cent foreign nationals. The foreign nationalities represented in the private school included English-speaking countries such as the UK, Canada and the USA, as well as former Soviet bloc countries such as Kazakhstan and Azerbaijan. In the case of the symphony orchestra, the foreign nationalities are all from former Soviet bloc (for example, Russia and Ukraine) and Eastern European (for example, Bulgaria and Romania) countries.

A questionnaire was designed that measured constructs of interest in this chapter as well as additional variables as part of a broader study on diversity, identity and team effectiveness. Questionnaires were distributed in both teams by contact persons. Completed surveys were returned to the contact persons who delivered them to the researcher. A total of 40 questionnaires were distributed in the private school. Thirty-six of these were completed, with a response rate of 90 per cent. Eighty-three questionnaires were distributed to the members of the symphony orchestra. Twenty-five of them were filled in, with a response rate of 30 per cent. The resulting sample consisted of 61 individuals of whom 38 were Turks, three were Canadians, two were Americans, and 18 were from former Soviet bloc and Eastern European countries.

Among the constructs assessed in the questionnaire, national identity salience, affective occupational commitment and altruism were used for the purposes of the current chapter. To operationalize national identity salience, the national identity salience scale developed by Randel (2002) was used. A sample item for this scale was: 'When people ask me about who is in the group, I initially think of describing group members in terms of national composition (e.g., 2 Turks, 3 Americans, and 2 Portuguese)'. To operationalize affective occupational commitment, Meyer et al.'s (1993) six-item scale was used. A sample item for affective commitment was: 'My profession is important to my self-image'. Finally, altruism was operationalized using Podsakoff et al.'s (1990) altruism scale. A sample item for altruism was: 'In this project group, I am always ready to lend a helping hand to those around me'. The questionnaire used a five-point rating scale anchored by 1 = 'Strongly Disagree' to 5 = 'Strongly Agree'.

For native Turkish speakers these scales were back translated to Turkish. Two bilingual graduate students from the Department of Psychology at Middle East Technical University, who were blind to the propositions of this study, translated the English version of the scales into Turkish. Then, another bilingual graduate student from the same department, who was again blind to the hypotheses of the study, translated the scales back to English. Later, the back-translated version was compared to the original. Some minor corrections were made on the Turkish version.

Similarly, for Russian native speakers, the questionnaire was back translated to Russian. First, a professional translator, who was blind to the propositions of the study, translated the English questionnaire to Russian. Then, another translator, who was also blind to study propositions, translated the Russian version back to English. The back-translated version was compared to the original and minor changes were made on the Russian version.

Results
Table 3.1 depicts means and standard deviations for each variable and correlations between the variables in the model. Data were analysed using hierarchical regression. Table 3.2 provides the results of the regression analysis.

Looking at the intercorrelations, it can be seen that, as predicted in this chapter, national identity salience is negatively and significantly correlated with altruism. Contrary to the expectations, however, affective occupational commitment is not significantly correlated with altruism. Although insignificant, the correlation between affective occupational commitment and altruism is in the predicted direction. The correlational analysis

Table 3.1   Means, standard deviations and intercorrelations

Variables	1	2	3
1. Affective commitment		−0.16	0.16
2. Identity salience			−0.17*
3. Altruism			
Mean	4.27	2.45	4.18
Std dev.	0.66	1.00	0.56

Note: *significant at $p < 0.1$; $N = 61$.

Table 3.2   Results of hierarchical regression analysis: altruism as the dependent variable

Independent variables	Model 1	Model 2	Model 3
Controls			
Affective commitment (*AC*)	0.13	0.11	0.15
Predictors			
Identity salience (*IS*)		−0.08	−0.03
Interactions			
IS*AC			−0.01
R square	0.02	0.05	0.05

Note: *N* = 61.

reveals no significant correlation between national identity salience and affective occupational commitment.

When the results of the regression analysis are examined, it can be seen that neither of the propositions of this study was supported. Proposition 1 states that as the salience of national identity for multinational team members increases, the level of altruism they will demonstrate will decrease. The results of hierarchical regression analysis indicate that although the beta coefficient of national identity salience is in the right direction, it is not significant.

Proposition 2 states that affective occupational commitment will moderate the relationship between national identity salience and altruism. The beta coefficient for the interaction term, as shown in Table 3.2, is also insignificant.

Discussion

Multinational teams are increasingly being used by organizations around the world as well as in Asia. The present study was as a first step to examine the link between identity salience, occupational commitment, and altruism in this increasingly popular organizational form. Although the propositions of the current chapter were not supported as a result of hierarchical regression, analysis of the intercorrelations indicates that national identity salience tends to be negatively associated with altruism. Hence, when individuals are aware of their differences in nationality, they may be less inclined to engage in helping behaviours towards each other.

Previous research on diversity invokes social identity theory and self-categorization theory to explain consequences of diversity. An important assertion in the social identity approach is that social categorization processes occur as a result of salient identities. However, diversity literature generally focuses on objective measures of diversity without taking into account whether difference in question are being perceived and, therefore, influencing cognition and behaviour. For instance, previous research that attempted to link diversity and OCB investigated the impact of age, race and gender dissimilarity (Chattopadhyay, 1999) and informational dissimilarity (Van Der Vegt et al., 2003) on OCB. One potential reason for inconclusive results prevalent in the extant diversity literature (for example, Jackson et al., 2003) may be the exclusive focus on objective diversity.

The approach taken in the present chapter indicates that it is more important to focus on the salience of identities because the categorization processes are triggered only when an identity is salient (Tajfel and Turner, 1986). According to the conceptual framework presented, at a given time, it is the identity that is salient to group members that will influence members' self-conception and their likelihood of displaying altruistic behaviour. Thus, one implication of this framework for practising managers is that one way to avoid potential negative outcomes of diversity such as lower levels of altruism, managers and/or team leaders may be to try to decrease the salience of subgroup identities. At the same time, managers and/or team leaders may attempt to highlight the multinational team itself as a desirable social group with which members can identify (Thatcher and Jehn, 1998). Such an inclusive categorization will encourage multinational team members to categorize their team mates as ingroup members and behave in an altruistic way towards all members.

The current chapter also proposes occupational commitment as a possible moderator of the identity salience–OCB relationship. Growing research in the area of occupational commitment suggests that occupational commitment may be more relevant for members of multinational teams than organizational commitment. It was suggested here that affective occupational commitment would moderate the relationship between national identity salience and altruism such that multinational team members would be more likely to be altruistic when members had high affective occupational commitment than when they had low occupational commitment. Blatt (2008) suggests that managers/team leaders of multinational teams can encourage higher levels of occupational commitment by enabling members to interact with peers from their own occupational communities and by providing opportunities for professional development. Unfortunately, the results of the exploratory study presented here did not find support for the moderating role of occupation commitment. One reason for this finding may be that the present study examined only the affective dimension of occupational commitment. Normative and continuance dimensions of occupation commitment were not included in this study. However, Snape and Redman (2003) suggest that the effects of different dimensions of occupation commitment may depend on the levels of the other dimensions. Future research should take into account all three dimensions of occupation commitment as well as their interactions with each other.

Limitations and directions for future research

Altruism is an important dimension of all OCB models. It is noted to be particularly relevant for teamwork (Chattopadhyay, 1999; Van Der Vegt et al., 2003; Janssen and Huang, 2008). However, antecedents of altruism in a multinational team context have not been addressed prior to the present study. The current study suggests that national identities and occupational commitment may be important determinants of altruism in such teams. However, results of the exploratory study reported in this chapter were mostly insignificant. These insignificant results may be due to the small sample size. Future research should examine the effects of national identity salience on OCB using larger sample sizes. Further, the sample of the current study consisted of a private school and a symphony orchestra, both not-for-profit organizations. The proposed framework should also be examined in other contexts such as business organizations.

It should also be noted that although OCB encompasses several dimensions of behaviour directed at the system and peers, the current study examined only one dimension, altruism. Future research should investigate other dimensions of OCB as well. Similarly, members of a team may belong to several social categories, such as gender, age and functional background. Recent research on team identity suggests that more than one identity may be salient simultaneously (for example, Janssen and Huang, 2008) and that identities may interact with each other (Ashforth et al., 2008). Thus one reason for insignificant findings may be the ignored identities that might have been simultaneously salient. Future research should take into account salience of multiple identities.

References

Acar, F.P. (2008), 'Analyzing the effects of diversity perceptions and shared leadership on emotional conflict: a dynamic approach', Working Paper, *Department Business of Administration*, Middle East Technical University, Ankara.

Adler, N.J. (2002), *International Dimensions of Organizational Behavior*, Cincinnati, OH: Southwestern.

Adler, N.J. and Ghadar, F. (1990), 'International strategy from the perspective of people and culture: the North American context', in A.M. Rugman (ed.), *Research in Global Strategic Management: International Business Research for the Twenty-first Century*, Greenwich, CT: JAI, pp. 179–205.

Ashforth, B.E., Harisson, S.H. and Corley, K.G. (2008), 'Identification in organizations: an examination of four fundamental questions', *Journal of Management*, **34**, 325–74.

Ashkanasy, N., Härtel, C. and Dass, C. (2002), 'Diversity and emotion: the new frontiers in organizational behavior research', *Journal of Management*, **28** (3), 307–38.

Aycan, Z. and Eskin, M. (2005), 'Relative contributions of childcare, spousal support, and organizational support in reducing work–family conflict for men and women: the case of Turkey', *Sex Roles*, **53**, 453–71.

Aycan, Z., Kanungo, R.N., Mendonca, M., Yu, K., Deller, J., Stahl, G. and Kurshid, A. (2000), 'Impact of culture on human resource management practices: a 10-country comparison', *Applied Psychology: An International Review*, **49** (1), 192–221.

Blatt, R. (2008), 'OCB of temporary knowledge workers', *Organization Studies*, **29**, 849–66.

Bodur, M. and Kabasakal, H. (2002), 'Türkiye-Arap kümesinde kurumsal kültür: GLOBE araştırması' (Institutional culture in Turkey–Arab cluster: the GLOBE research), *Yönetim Araştırmaları Dergisi* (Journal of Management Research), **2** (1), 5–22.

Cappelli, P. (1999), 'Career jobs are dead', *California Management Review*, **42**, 146–67.

Chatman, J.A. and Flynn, F.J. (2001), 'The influence of demographic heterogeneity on the emergence and consequences of cooperative norms in work teams', *Academy of Management Journal*, **44**, 956–74.

Chatman, J.A., Polzer, J.T., Barsade, S.G. and Neale, M.A. (1998), 'Being different yet feeling similar: demographic contribution and organizational culture on work processes and outcomes', *Administrative Science Quarterly*, **43**, 749–80.

Chattopadhyay, P. (1999), 'Beyond direct and symmetrical effects: the influence of demographic dissimilarity on organizational citizenship behavior', *Academy of Management Journal*, **42** (3), 273–87.

Christ, O., Van Dick, R., Wagner, U. and Stellmacher, J. (2003), 'When teachers go the extra mile: foci of organizational identification as determinants of different forms of organizational citizenship behavior among school teachers', *British Journal of Educational Psychology*, **23**, 239–90.

Coleman, V. and Borman, W. (2000), 'Investigating the underlying structure of the citizenship performance domain', *Human Resource Management Review*, **10**, 25–44.

Glazer, S. and De la Rosa, G. (2008), 'Immigrant status as potential correlate of organizational commitment', *International Journal of Cross Cultural Management*, **8**, 5–22.

Harrison, D.A., Price, K.H. and Bell, M.P. (1998), 'Beyond relational demography: time and the effects of surface- and deep-level diversity on work group cohesion', *Academy of Management Journal*, **41**, 96–107.

Harrison, D.A., Price, K.H., Gavin, J.H. and Florey, A.T. (2002), 'Time, groups, and task performance: changing effects of surface- and deep-level diversity on group functioning', *Academy of Management Journal*, **45**, 1029–45.

Hobman, E.V., Bordia, P. and Gallois, C. (2003), 'Consequences of feeling dissimilar from others in a work team', *Journal of Business and Psychology*, **17** (3), 301–25.

Hofstede, G. (1980), *Culture's Consequences: International Differences in Work-related Values*, Beverly Hills, CA: Sage.

Hogg, M.A., Abrams, D., Otten, S. and Hinkle, S. (2004), 'The social identity perspective: intergroup relations, self-conception, and small groups', *Small Group Research*, **3**, 246–76.

Irving, P., Coleman, D. and Cooper, C. (1997), 'Further assessments of a three-component model of occupational commitment: generalizability and differences across occupations', *Journal of Applied Psychology*, **82**, 444–52.

Jackson, S.E., Joshi, A. and Erhardt, N.L. (2003), 'Recent research on team and organizational diversity: SWOT analysis and implications', *Journal of Management*, **29**, 801–30.

Janssen, O. and Huang, X. (2008), 'Us and me: team identification and individual differentiation as complementary drivers of team members' citizenship and creative behaviors', *Journal of Management*, **34** (1), 69–88.

Jehn, K.A. and Mannix, E.A. (2001), 'The dynamic nature of conflict: a longitudinal study of intragroup conflict and group performance', *Academy of Management Journal*, **44** (2), 238–51.

Kidwell, R., Mossholder, K. and Bennet, N. (1997), 'Cohesiveness and organizational citizenship behavior: a multilevel analysis using work groups and individuals', *Journal of Management*, **23**, 777–93.

Metcalf, L., Bird, A., Shankarmahesh, M., Aycan, Z., Larimo, J. and Valdelamar, D. (2006), 'Cultural tendencies in negotiation: a comparison of Finland, India, Mexico, Turkey, and the United States', *Journal of World Business*, **41**, 382–94.

Meyer, J.P. and Allen, N.J. (1993), 'A three-component conceptualization of organizational commitment', *Human Resource Management Review*, **1**, 61–89.

Meyer, J.P., Allen, N.J. and Smith, C.A. (1993), 'Commitment to organizations and occupations: extension and test of a three-component conceptualization', *Journal of Applied Psychology*, **4**, 538–51.

Millhous, L.M. (1999), 'The experience of culture in multicultural groups: case studies of Russian–American collaboration in business', *Small Group Research*, **30** (3), 280–308.

Milliken, F.J. and Martins, L.L. (1996), 'Searching for common threads: understanding the multiple effects of diversity in organizational groups', *Academy of Management Review*, **21**, 402–33.

Mir, A., Mir, R. and Mosca, J.B. (2002), 'The new age employee: an exploration of changing employee–organization relations', *Public Personnel Management*, **31** (2), 187–201.

Moorman, R. and Blakely, G. (1995), 'Individualism–collectivism as an individual difference predictor of organizational citizenship behavior', *Journal of Organizational Behavior*, **16**, 127–42.

Morrison, E. (1994), 'Role definitions and organizational behavior: the importance of the employee's perspective', *Academy of Management Journal*, **37**, 1543–67.

Mowday, R., Steers, R. and Porter, L. (1982), 'The measurement of organizational commitment', *Journal of Vocational Behavior*, **14**, 224–47.

O'Reilly, C.A. III, Caldwell, D.F. and Barnett, W.P. (1989), 'Work group demography, social integration, and turnover', *Administrative Science Quarterly*, **34**, 21–37.

Oakes, P. (1987), 'The salience of social categories', in J. Turner, M. Hogg, P. Oakes, S. Reicher and M. Wetherell (eds), *Rediscovering the Social Group: A Self-Categorization Theory*, Oxford: Blackwell, pp. 117–41.

Ölmez, A.E., Sümer, H.C. and Soysal, M. (2004), 'Organizational rationality in public, private and multinational firms in Turkey', *Information Knowledge Systems Management*, **4**, 107–18.

Organ, D. (1988), *Organizational Citizenship Behavior: The Good Soldier Syndrome*, Lexington, MA: Lexington Books.

Organ, D.W. and Ryan, K. (1995), 'A meta-analytic review of attitudinal and dispositional predictors of organizational citizenship behavior', *Personnel Psychology*, **8**, 775–802.

Podsakoff, P., MacKenzie, S., Moorman, R. and Fetter, R. (1990), 'Transformational leader behaviors and their effects on followers' trust in leader, satisfaction, and organizational citizenship behaviors', *Leadership Quarterly*, **1**, 107–42.

Podsakoff, P., MacKenzie, S., Paine, J. and Bachrach, D. (2000), 'Organizational citizenship behaviors: a critical review of the theoretical and empirical literature and suggestions for future research', *Journal of Management*, **26** (3), 513–63.

Randel, A.E. (2002), 'Identity salience: a moderator of the relationship between group gender composition and work group conflict', *Journal of Organizational Behavior*, **23**, 749–66.

Randel, A. and Jaussi, K. (2003), 'Functional background identity, diversity, and individual performance in cross-functional teams', *Academy of Management Journal*, **46**, 763–74.

Schneider, S.C. and Barsoux, J.L. (2003), *Managing across Cultures*, Harlow: Financial Times Prentice-Hall.

Snape, E. and Redman, T. (2003), 'An evaluation of a three-component model of occupational commitment: dimensionality and consequences among United Kingdom human resource management specialists', *Journal of Applied Psychology*, **88**, 152–9.

Sveningsson, S. and Alvesson, M. (2003), 'Managing managerial identities: organizational fragmentation, discourse and identity struggle', *Human Relations*, **56** (10), 1163–93.

Tajfel, H. (1978), *Differentiation between Social Groups*, London: Academic Press.

Tajfel, H. and Turner, J. (1986), 'The social identity theory of intergroup behavior', in S. Worchel and W. Austin (eds), *Psychology of Intergroup Relations*, Chicago, IL: Nelson Hall, pp. 7–24.

Thatcher, S.M.B. and Jehn, K.A. (1998), 'A model of group diversity profiles and categorization processes in bicultural organizational groups', in D. Ancona (ed.), *Research on Managing Groups and Groups*, vol. 1, Greenwich, CT: JAI, pp. 1–20.

Turner, J.C. (1987), *Rediscovering the Social Group: A Self-categorization Theory*, New York: Basil Blackwell.

Turner, J. and Haslam, S. (2001), 'Social identity, organizations, and leadership', in M. Turner (ed), *Groups at Work: Theory and Research*, Hillsdale NJ: Lawrence Erlbaum, pp. 25–65.

Turner, J., Oakes, P., Haslam, S. and McGarty, C. (1994), 'Self and collective: cognition and social context', *Personality and Social Psychology Bulletin*, **20**, 454–63.

Van Der Vegt, G.S., Van De Vliert, E. and Oosterhof, A. (2003), 'Informational dissimilarity and OCB: The role of intrateam interdependence and team identification', *Academy of Management Journal*, **46** (6), 715–27.

Van Dyne, L., Cummings, L. and Parks, J. (1995), 'Extra-role behaviors: in pursuit of construct and definitional clarity (a bridge over muddied waters)', in L. Cummings and B. Staw (eds), *Research in Organizational Behavior*, vol. 17, Greenwich, CT: JAI, pp. 215–85.

Van Knippenberg, D. (2000), 'Work motivation and performance: a social identity perspective', *Applied Psychology: An International Review*, **49**, pp. 357–71.

Van Knippenberg, D., De Dreu, C.K.W. and Homan, A.C. (2004), 'Work group diversity and group performance: an integrative model and research agenda', *Journal of Applied Psychology*, **89**, 1008–22.

Wallace, J. (1993), 'Professional and organizational commitment: compatible or incompatible', *Journal of Vocational Behavior*, **42**, 333–49.

Watson, W., Johnson, L. and Merritt, D. (1998), 'Team orientation, self-orientation, and diversity in task groups: their connection to team performance over time', *Group and Organization Management*, **23** (2), 161–88.

Williams, K.Y. and O'Reilly, C.A. (1998), 'Demography and diversity in organizations: a review of 40 years of research', in B. Staw and L. Cummings (eds), *Research in Organizational Behavior*, Greenwich, CT: JAI, pp. 77–140.

Williams, L.J. and Anderson, S.E. (1991), 'Job satisfaction and organizational commitment as predictors of organizational citizenship and in-role behaviors', *Journal of Management*, **17** (3), 601–17.

4 Religious diversity in Lebanon: lessons from a small country to the global world
Akram Al Ariss

Introduction

The term 'diversity' is largely used in the American and British management literatures in the context of a workplace where different people interact. For example, people could differ in non-visible attributes such as education and professional experience and in visible attributes like gender and ethnicity (Pelled, 1996). The meaning of diversity varies across societies (Jones et al., 2000; Hofstede, 2007). For instance, while in the United States, diversity is used in regard to ethnic groupings such Asians or Latinos (Casey and Corday, 2006), in France it is largely understood in terms of gender (for example, Ariss, 2006; Battle, 2007) and cultural differences (Point and Singh, 2003). In Lebanon, a 10,452km² Arab country located in Western Asia, there are 17 religious communities officially acknowledged by the government (Maktabi, 1999). Accordingly, diversity is officially implemented and commonly understood in Lebanese society in terms of religious belonging (Kabbara, 1991; Picard, 1997; Hudson, 1999).

Religious communities in Lebanon are commonly denoted by the term 'confessions' (Haddad, 2002), most of them belong to Christian (such as Maronites and Protestants) and Muslim (such as Sunnis and Shiites) religions (ibid.). Confessionalism in Lebanon is an official religious diversity scheme that distributes institutional power proportionally among various religious communities. The aim of this scheme is to secure balanced power sharing. Hence, positions in government and parliament are allocated between religious communities according to their demographic proportion in the country. In this way, the Lebanese government formally acknowledges rights of religious groups (majority and minorities) by securing a supposed equitable sharing of institutional, political, economic and social power among them. Hence, confessional diversity is restricted to power distribution among different religious groups.

The field study of this chapter generated 20 interviews with Lebanese people. The chapter breaks the silence in the management literature, which remains very underdeveloped on religious diversity matters. By explaining how participants experienced career difficulties linked to a confessional diversity scheme in Lebanon, the chapter makes an original contribution by challenging existing diversity rhetoric, which calls for better representation of people at the workplace according to group membership. In the case of Lebanon, it is shown how diversity discourse, focusing on representation of people at the workplace and in institutions and ignoring merit-based and moral matters, obstructed individuals' career choices and opportunities. The chapter proposes that recognising and valuing differences among employees can only be efficient when coupled with merit-based treatment.

The chapter is divided as follows. It starts by reviewing diversity management literature and particularly the one related to religious diversity. Next, diversity trends in Arab countries and patterns of diversity management in Lebanon are explained. After that, the methods used to collect data are discussed. Finally, analysis of interviews and discussion of the results are presented.

Reviewing the diversity management literature

Diversity has been increasingly propounded with the globalisation of organisations (Yaprak, 2002) leading to an increased interest in women as well as minorities in the workforce (Friedman and DiTomaso, 1996; Jehn and Bezrukova, 2004). Between 1960 to 1990, equal opportunity legislation in the United Kingdom instituted treating individuals equally at work based upon their merit rather than on their membership to any group (Wilson, 1997). This approach has been criticised for ignoring differences among individuals (for example, Montes and Shaw, 2004) and for neglecting organisational expectations in terms of best utilising a diverse workforce.

Beyond the equality discourse discussed above, since the year 1990, equitability has been brought forward in the literature as beneficial to organisational performance (Morrison, 1992) under the term 'business case' (Özbilgin, 2000). Business case proponents, often concerned with talented people, suggest that recognising and valuing differences among employees enhance creativity in terms of problem solving and decision making in organisations (Bantel and Jackson, 1989; Cox et al., 1991; Pelled et al., 1999). Moreover, including a diverse workforce is presented as being useful in increasing market reach, that is, new customers coming from diverse social segments may tend to buy from organisations supporting diversity (Wilson and Iles, 1996; Hicks-Clarke and Iles, 2004). Such organisations are assumed to better attract international investors (Point and Singh, 2003). With some exceptions (Jackson et al., 1991; Schippers et al., 2003), this literature concludes that diversity enhances organisational performance (Richard et al., 2007).

While the business case supporters focus on managing diverse work-force equitably by valuing their differences (Bantel and Jackson, 1989; Cox et al., 1991; Pelled et al., 1999), equality promoters propose treating individuals according to merit rather than group membership (Wilson, 1997). Equality and equity models of diversity are often presented in the management literature as alternatives rather than complementary (Richard et al., 2007).

It might seem that no connection exists between the diversity models discussed above and the religious diversity scheme in Lebanon. Moreover, research on this issue is very scarce. This could be due to three reasons. First, very few scholars work on religious diversity matters in Lebanon: questioning the validity of the religious diversity scheme remains taboo and could lead to conflicts in society, especially with the current political instability in the country. Second, research in general is very scarce in Lebanese universities. Finally, as French remains the dominant language in Lebanon, few Lebanese scholars publish in English and in Anglo-Saxon journals.

Three strong links can be identified between the Western diversity context discussed above and the one in Lebanon: (a) like in Western societies, there are religious minority groups in Lebanon; (b) similarly to diversity models in Europe and the United States, diversity in Lebanon, especially after the Lebanese civil war, is assumed to empower minorities; and (c) like the debate between equality and equity models of diversity in Western countries, there is a growing, although silenced, demand from many Lebanese intellectuals to include more merit-based rather than representation criteria. By examining the case of religious diversity in Lebanon and linking it to diversity rhetoric in the management literature, this chapter demonstrates that recognising differences among employees should be further connected with merit-based treatment.

Religious diversity in the management literature: breaking the silence
With the global world characterised by religiously diverse societies (Turner, 2007), democratic states, even when secular, are increasingly expected to consider the public dimension of religion in social life and at the workplace (Koenig, 2000). Surprisingly, using Google Scholar, a literature review of the management literature yields few results on religious diversity. Religious diversity matters are addressed in this literature at the institutional and organisational levels but are underdeveloped at the individual level (Hicks, 2002; Jackson et al., 2003). For instance, at the institutional level, European policy-making research suggests that recognising religious diversity would encourage people from different religions to participate in public life (Vertovec and Wessendorf, 2004). Accordingly, in Norway

there are calls for reformulating equal opportunity policies to take into account immigrants' religious diversity (Furseth, 2000). On the organisational level, this literature promotes religious diversity at the workplace as this would improve teamwork (Hicks, 2002) among a diverse workforce (Rosenzweig, 1998). Religious diversity is promoted in terms of better representing individuals belonging to religious minorities in institutions and organisations (Turner, 2007). Freedom of practising in organisations and social life is also discussed in this literature (Koenig, 2000).

Such diversity models are comparable to religious diversity in Lebanon, understood and practised in public institutions, in terms of representation of the different religious groups in the country. Empirical grounding concerning the way individuals experience religious diversity throughout their career is absent in this same literature. In an attempt to fill this knowledge gap, this chapter considers the way Lebanese professionals experienced confessional diversity in Lebanon. Findings challenge religious diversity discourse, and more generally diversity theories, which call for better representation of people (that is, in organisations and institutions) according to religious belonging and which neglect considering moral issues and merit-based criteria.

Patterns of diversity management in Arab-Asian countries: understanding the case of Lebanon

Arab nations rely on the Anglo-American management research (Ali and Camp, 1995). Hence, diversity research outside the United States (Bell and Kravitz, 2008) and particularly in the Arab-Asian countries is lacking (Neal et al., 2005). For instance, a simple search on Google Scholar using 'diversity management Arab countries' would give few relevant results (for example, Ali and Camp, 1995; Atiyyah, 1996; Neal et al., 2005). These studies present Arab countries as a uniform entity (Hofstede, 1980) and suggest that diversity management implementations are missing. For example, it is reported that in Qatar and Saudi Arabia (Atiyyah, 1996) Asian workers are discriminated against by being paid less in comparison to European and American nationals when performing the same tasks (Konovsky, 1986). Additionally, while Arab women are progressively becoming more accepted at work (for example, Al-Ghazali, 1990) and in power positions (ILO, 1998; Salloum, 2003), their role is mainly limited to family matters and motherhood (Neal et al., 2005; Sidani, 2005). Syed (2010) notes that in Saudi Arabia women have limited employment opportunities and are still prohibited from driving without a male guardian.

In an attempt to overcome uniform representations of diversity management in Arab countries (Hofstede, 1980), this section presents patterns of Lebanese confessional diversity. Even though gender and ethnic diversity are not within the scope of this chapter, these are briefly discussed to familiarise readers with diversity in Lebanon.

Confessional diversity

Understanding the history of Lebanon allows a better comprehension of its confessional diversity scheme. In contrast to diversity programmes in Western countries that attempt to eliminate discrimination, religious diversity in Lebanon was established as a power control tool by French colonisation. After the First World War, Lebanon, which had been a part of the Ottoman Empire, was occupied by the French as a mandated territory. The country achieved its independence in 1943 (El-Solh, 2004). The French secured power distribution in the country on a confessional basis whereby the Lebanese president would be a Maronite (Christian), the prime minister a Sunni (Muslim) and the speaker of the chamber of deputies a Shiite (Muslim) (Maktabi, 1999). Furthermore, positions in the parliament and in public institutions were distributed among confessional groups (Seaver, 2000). Through this scheme, the French controlled the Lebanese state by giving key governmental positions to Christians rather than to Muslims. Moreover, the French divided the institutional power in the country among the different religious groups rather than constructing a powerful secular nation. In 1975, the lack of policies promoting equality among all Lebanese, stimulated isolation and disparities between different confessions, leading to a civil war that lasted 15 years. In 1989, the Lebanese government reached an agreement (Haddad, 2002) to balance Muslim and Christian representation in power positions (Kiwan, 2005b), thus putting an end to the civil war but confirming confessional divisions (Kabbara, 1991; Picard, 1997; Hudson, 1999). Therefore, confessional diversity in Lebanon refers mainly to power sharing in political, economic and social life between religious groups. The word 'confessional' simply denotes power-sharing schemes.

Nowadays recruitment in public institutions (Kiwan, 2005b) is regulated with compulsory confessional diversity (Kabbara, 1991; Picard, 1997; Hudson, 1999; Aoun, 2007). In the private sector, most of the Lebanese organisations are small family businesses (Mikdashi, 1999) managed by people belonging to one confession. Additionally, private schools and universities, student unions, professional associations, sports clubs and the media have confessional characters (Kiwan, 2005a). While Lebanon is a small country, the diversity management challenges faced by its multi-religious society reflect the ones that the world is increasingly experiencing (Koenig, 2000) as a consequence of globalisation (Turner, 2007) and increased migration (UN, 2000).

Gender diversity
Although Lebanese women are increasingly accessing education and integrating in the job market (UNDP, 2003), gender diversity policies and practices remain very limited (for example, Jamali et al., 2006). For instance, the national level of illiteracy among females (17.8 per cent) is twice that for males (MSA, 1996). Moreover, in 1996 women occupied only 8.5 per cent of the high managerial positions (IWSAW, 1998). For example, in the banking sector women rarely had access to managerial positions (for example, Jamali et al., 2006). Hence, diversity management rhetoric has not translated into improving women's career advancement (Jamali and Abdallah, 2010). This feature of gender-related discrimination is also present in developed countries where women encounter career obstacles (for example, Lyness and Thompson, 2000; Wellington et al., 2003; Baruch, 2006). Furthermore, Lebanese females are remunerated on an average less than men when performing the same job (UNDP, 1998). It is important to note, in this context, that Lebanese laws prevent women married to foreigners from giving citizenship to their husband and children (Abou-Habib, 2003; Diab, 2005).

Ethnic diversity
Lebanon is a destination country for Arab political refugees (Jureidini and Moukarbel, 2000) and for thousands of low-skilled Asian workers who work in domestic services (UN, 2006) and construction. In stark contrast with principles of equal opportunities of the International Labour Organization, immigrants in Lebanon (Jureidini and Moukarbel, 2000) are subject to institutional discrimination in terms of job opportunities and career advancement. For example, the thousands of Palestinians who fled to Lebanon as refugees in 1948 after the declaration of an Israeli state in Palestine (Halabi, 2004) and following the Arab–Israeli war of 1967 were subject to Lebanese legislation that prevents them from working (ibid.). Moreover, migrant workers do not benefit from basic employment rights as Lebanese nationals do (Baaklini, 2000). For example, unskilled workers (for example, domestic workers) are denied rights to a minimal wage, or to work a limited number of hours per month, or even to have vacations and to join labour unions (Young, 2000). The scope of this chapter does not cover ethnic diversity in Lebanon. However, other chapters in this book (for example, Pio, ch. 22) do cover aspects of ethnic diversity of Asian migrants.

Methodology
Twenty qualitative interviews were conducted by this chapter's author in 2007 with a diverse group (that is, in terms of religious belonging, gender,

age and work experience) of Lebanese migrants who lived in Lebanon prior to moving to France (see Appendix Table 4 A.1 for the demographic profiles of participants). Participants discussed experiences of facing diversity practices such as through education, training and work.

Purposeful sampling (Patton, 1990; Sackmann, 1992; McNeill, 1994; Maxwell, 1996; Seidman, 1998) was used to select information-rich cases for in-depth study (Fridah, 2002). The author of this chapter, being Lebanese, had a relatively easy access to informants. The semi-structured qualitative interviews that were conducted addressed the interviewees' social backgrounds, education, training and work experiences (Arksey and Knight, 1999). This method allowed detailed responses to be generated (Rapley, 2004: 15). Interviews were tape-recorded in order to capture tone, comments and oral expressions of participants, allowing the context of discussions to be re-situated. In addition, notes were taken concerning observational issues such as participants' work environments and outside interactions.

Analysis
Confessional diversity emerged as salient to participants' work and life experiences. The confessional scheme obstructed the way informants integrated the job market and an advanced career. Thus, the lack of merit-based work opportunities increased their propensity to emigrate. For 18 participants, the confessional scheme was perceived as being unfair and unhelpful for professional advancement. For instance, those who left Lebanon 30 years ago and others who left two years ago suffered equally from the lack of merit-based career opportunities.

Access to education
All participants except for four (François, Kamal, Salim and Stéphane) attended Lebanese schools managed by confessional groups. Only Karima and Charles experienced a confessional burden during their access to education. Karima studied in public academic institutions in Lebanon. She reported dissatisfaction with state policies, which select students on a confessional basis upon entry to public Lebanese universities. Karima later travelled to France, where she has been living for more than 25 years.

> Karima: [when talking about how the confessional scheme influenced her educational and career path in Lebanon] I come from a Shiite family, and when I had my exam in the university in Lebanon, they classified people according to their religious belonging. They [the state] needed to choose 10 Maronites, 10 I don't know what . . . so it wasn't like those who have the best grades are chosen but rather those who are the best 10 among a confessional community! This was the first shock. Many people suffered from this scheme . . . I found this crazy!

. . . [T]here is also a form of nepotism which has a big influence; if you know somebody, you might be able to take the place of others.

Another example is Charles, a secular Christian in his late twenties. Charles described the school he attended in Lebanon as relatively restricted to Christians:

Charles: [I]t is a private school, managed by Christians priests . . . I have done all my studies in this school, which is a very good one but has some defects that I noticed later; it is not very open to . . . eh . . . to all religions in Lebanon . . . It was a Catholic school . . . however, Catholic teaching was not imposed in a very strict manner.

While the confessional representation scheme guarantees the rights of religious minorities to access educational establishments, people with strong merit may be treated unfairly as reported by Charles and Karima. Neverthless, most participants did not report problems linked to confessional belonging during their education. For instance, Muslims and Christians attended secular and non-secular schools and universities without major problems.

Access to the job market
Seven participants out of 14 who worked in Lebanon faced downward career mobility upon entering the labour market due to a lack of merit-based recruitment criteria. Instead, subjective experiences of participants indicated that confessional belonging constituted a principal selection standard when accessing jobs in public and private sectors. For instance, Kamal, a secular Shiite Muslim in his early sixties was born in Senegal and lived there until the age of 18. After earning a medical degree in cardiology from France, he went to Lebanon in search of work opportunities. During his sojourn in Lebanon, Kamal lived next to a private hospital managed by a Sunni Muslim family but could not get a job there because he was Shiite. Thus he had to work in a hospital relatively far away where Shiite doctors could practise:

Kamal: In Lebanon I had a cardiology clinic in Beirut and I used to work in the public hospital [name of the hospital] in the south [of Lebanon]. It was the war . . . it was difficult. The hospital was closed after it was destroyed by the Israeli army in 1982. I continued to work in my clinic . . . I used to live about 300 meters from the [name of a private hospital] . . . but I wasn't able to work there . . . I think because I am not Sunni . . . It is the confessional scheme . . . the drama of Lebanon!

Although Lebanon suffers from a brain drain (Fargues, 2005), the lack of merit-based career opportunities in the country did not encourage expatriates to return (for example, Helou, 1995; Safieddine et al., 2004a, 2004b, 2004c). In line with this, when Kamal decided to return to Lebanon he came up against confessional favouritism which influenced his decision to leave permanently for France. He has been living there for more than 20 years, and now owns a cardiology clinic in Paris.

Similarly, when discussing his reasons for leaving Lebanon, François pointed to confessional inequalities:

> François: . . . It was a desire to leave, to discover the world . . . discover other horizons because in Lebanon, despite everything, we are a closed-minded people . . . As for me I am secular, when I establish a relation with somebody, I establish a relation with the person as a Lebanese . . . And in Lebanon if you don't belong to a family [meaning an influential Lebanese family] or to a religion, you don't have your place there. I did not like this.

François has been living permanently in France for more than 20 years. He now owns a small engineering company. In 2000, he attempted to establish a business in Lebanon but never succeeded in doing so. François expressed his refusal to draw on confessional relationships in order to advance his career:

> François: Lebanon needs a secular scheme rather than a confessional one! And today it is similar to when I left 28 years ago, nothing has changed, there is no progress in this domain. . . . I have tried several times, not to live and work in Lebanon 100 per cent but to find a mix . . . as I am a consultant . . . I can work everywhere . . . but in Lebanon what is difficult is that I don't have a relational network. In Lebanon if you don't belong to a family, religion or maybe class, you cannot enter . . . I have tried several times but it did not work . . . what blocks me most is the relational network, I don't have a relational network! I don't have a network and I am not able to do as the Lebanese of Lebanon do . . . meaning to pay someone, I am not able to do like the Lebanese of Lebanon . . . and I cannot understand how the Lebanese do that! There is also the problem of religions, you come with good ideas but because you belong to such or such religion [meaning a confessional group] you cannot access the right person . . . you have to deal with a particular person because you have the same religion [confessional groups], even if you trust this person . . . this is penalising! . . . if someone tells me you are Shiite [referring to himself as he is from a Shiite family] you should deal with such a person [a person from your confessional group] . . . I say no!

Both Kamal and François decided to return and invest in Lebanon, but, confessional-based discrimination obstructed their efforts. For both Kamal and François, leaving Lebanon seemed to be a way of building merit-based career experiences.

Another case was Wafa, a Muslim lady in her late forties, who undertook technical studies in Lebanon before emigrating to France. Prior to leaving, she worked in quality assurance activities in a Lebanese chemical industry for several years. During her sojourn in Lebanon, Wafa noticed that recruitment and career advancement of individuals is ruled by their confessional belonging rather than their merit:

> Wafa: In Lebanon there are a lot of things to be done. Unfortunately, the confessional scheme . . . speaking of discrimination and confessions . . . all of that, I hope, still, one day we shall reach a stage where the merit, the competency of people, will be the criteria for professional advancement. Thus, I hope . . . There are a lot of things to be done.

Wafa is now married to a Tunisian man and has four children. She has been living in France for the past 20 years.

In the same way, Elie, a Christian computer engineer in his late twenties, worked for six months in a Lebanese bank before leaving for France. Elie considered that his job in Lebanon did not match his qualifications and that talent does not feature among the most significant recruitment criteria in the private and public organisations in Lebanon:

> Elie: [N]epotism is a big problem in Lebanon. . . . we try to favour . . . incompetent people that we know. It has an impact on the management of private and public organisations; it is something that affects negatively the development of the economy and of the organisations. It is very badly managed . . . nepotism could be at the level of family relations, confessional belongings, political affiliations . . . it is something that has a considerable effect on the economy in general!

Mustafa, a Muslim engineer in his mid-twenties, did two internships in Lebanon prior to emigrating to France. During his stay in Lebanon, he felt that access to work opportunities was dependent on one's confessional belonging rather than on one's talents:

> Mustafa: Discrimination in Lebanon, yes you feel it, you feel it! For instance, there is a confessional repartition in Lebanon so you cannot access one position or another if you don't belong to a certain confession. So it is . . . eh . . . our country is based upon confessional distribution and discrimination! We cannot hide this. Yes . . . I feel the discrimination in Lebanon very strongly!

Mustafa undertook graduate management studies in France. He has been working and living there for the past three years.

Patrick, Tatiana, Yolla and Wael were all aware that the confessional diversity scheme was lacking merit-based dimensions. However, they did not personally face difficulties linked to this. This could be explained by the fact that they all worked and lived within their own confessional groups and thus were not penalised due to their religious belongings. For instance, Patrick is a secular Christian engineer in his mid-forties. In

Lebanon, he worked for six years in companies managed by people from his own confessional group:

> Patrick: I could not face discrimination because at that period I was Christian . . . I lived in the Christian part [in a majority Christian Lebanese city]. . . . I worked in companies, let us say, managed by Maronites. When you are part of the main branch of things, you cannot be . . . you are not different. I am not black, I was not Shiite in Ashrafieh [a majority Christian Lebanese city] or a Druze in Ashrafieh so this was not problematic.

In summary, in contrast to diversity rhetoric in Lebanon, the confessional system failed to offer real, fair career opportunities to individuals. Instead, the diversity scheme was discriminatory against most participants, regardless of their religious belonging. For instance, education, training and professional experiences gained by individuals (for example, Becker, 1993; Haque and Kim, 1995; Rodríguez-Pose and Vilalta-Bufí, 2004; Gabriel et al., 2005) were not sufficient to overcome discrimination barriers. Thus, informants reported experiences of inequalities leading to talent waste (for example, underemployment or unemployment). By leaving Lebanon, they attempted to build a career that better suited their expectations in terms of professional advancement and fair treatment.

Discussion and conclusion
By explaining how Lebanese professionals experienced career difficulties linked to the confessional diversity scheme in Lebanon, this chapter makes an original contribution by challenging existing diversity theories that suggest that equality and equity models are alternatives rather than complementary (Richard et al., 2007). For instance, while business case supporters focus on managing the diverse workforce equitably by valuing their differences (Bantel and Jackson, 1989; Cox et al., 1991; Pelled et al., 1999), equality promoters propose treating individuals according to their merit rather than their membership to any group (Wilson, 1997).

The chapter fills a gap in the management literature that has hitherto been lacking in terms of religious diversity research. It suggests that religious diversity based on power distribution among religious groups in Lebanon fails to offer merit-based job opportunities and obstructs career advancement. This is problematic as individuals' qualifications (for example, education and professional experience) are overlooked in recruitment and job progression. For instance, participants reported that private organisations held by one confessional group only recruited people belonging to their own group. Diversity was thus seen as discriminatory and deepened inequalities instead of securing equal and equitable opportunities.

Findings indicate that talents may be wasted when diversity policies and practices are focused on representation issues while neglecting merit-based criteria for recruitment and career advancement. For instance, education, training and professional experiences (for example, Becker, 1993; Haque and Kim, 1995; Rodríguez-Pose and Vilalta-Bufí, 2004; Gabriel et al., 2005) of participants were not sufficient to surmount discrimination. Thus, institutions and organisations attempting to increase representation of minorities in order to enhance organisational performance (Bantel and Jackson, 1989; Cox et al., 1991; Pelled et al., 1999) should consider having both equity (Richard et al., 2007) and equality (for example, Montes and Shaw, 2004) strategies. In this way, recognising and valuing the differences and similarities of individuals should always be coupled with human resource management that attempts to best use people's talents (Bantel and Jackson, 1989; Cox et al., 1991; Pelled et al., 1999).

Attention to diversity matters has been increasing in Western countries in an attempt to cope with national and international policies aimed at eliminating discrimination (Nishii and Özbilgin, 2007). This is not the case in Lebanon. Accordingly, understanding the Lebanese religious diversity scheme requires a deeper questioning of the historical legacy of French colonisation that produced it in the first place in order to control power and create divisions in the country. This religious diversity proved to be counterproductive for organisations and institutions in Lebanon which failed to make full use of Lebanese human resources.

Decision makers in Lebanon and in other parts of the world should be aware that successful diversity policy making should always be coupled with merit-based dimensions. This would provide individuals, regardless of their group membership, merit-based career opportunities and would consequently benefit organisations and institutions that will fully use their skills.

I would like to conclude on a positive note. With globalisation (Turner, 2007) and migration (UN, 2000), religious diversity challenges in Lebanon are of major significance to developed countries fraught with religious-diverse societies (Vertovec and Wessendorf, 2004). If lessons are to be taken from the Lebanese case, religious diversity policies at both organisational and institutional levels should focus on enhancing moral issues such as tolerance in society and freedom of religious practice (Koenig, 2000) rather than on improving representation of people from diverse religions (Turner, 2007). For example, this could be done through tolerance training programmes run within organisations and institutions. Such programmes could even be integrated at an early stage into the educational school and university modules. In this way, diversity becomes concretely implemented beyond representation and rhetoric.

This chapter has several limitations. It did not empirically examine dimensions of diversity linked to the employment of foreign workers in Lebanon. This could be a research agenda as it remains an omission in the diversity management literature. Moreover, the chapter did not include gender diversity aspects. Readers who wish to learn more about gender diversity in Arab countries can refer to Al-Dajani (2010), who suggests that gender diversity should be recognised further in academic research in Arab countries and accordingly appropriate policies should also be implemented. Future research in Lebanon and in other Arab countries should examine diversity-related matters for people with disabilities, as little has been written on this subject (for example, Wehbi and El-Lahib, 2007).

References

Abou-Habib, L. (2003), 'Gender, citizenship and nationality in the Arab region', *Gender and Development*, **11** (3), 66–75.

Al-Dajani, H. (2010), 'Diversity and inequality among women in employment in the Arab Middle East region: a new research agenda', ch.2 in M. Özbilgin and J. Syed (eds), *Managing Gender Diversity in Asia: A Research Companion*, Cheltenham, UK and Northampton, MA, USA: Edward Elgar, pp. 8–31.

Al-Ghazali, M. (1990), *Kadaya Al-Mar'ah – Women's Issues*, Cairo: Shurook.

Ali, A.J. and Camp, R.C. (1995), 'Teaching management in the Arab world: confronting illusions', *International Journal of Educational Management*, **9** (2), 10–17.

Aoun, G. (2007), 'Report of an international forum on managing diversity', *Equal Opportunities International*, **26** (1), 67–70.

Ariss, A.A. (2006), 'Report on the "History/Gender/Migration" conference in Paris', *Equal Opportunities International*, **25** (2), 146–9.

Arksey, H. and Knight, P. (1999), *Interviewing for Social Scientists*, London: Sage.

Atiyyah, H.S. (1996), 'Expatriate acculturation in Arab Gulf countries', *Journal of Management Development*, **15** (5), 37–47.

Baaklini, S. (2000), 'Les employées de maison, une catégorie lésée qui ignore souvent leurs droits', (Domestic servants, a category that often neglects its rights) *L'Orient – Le Jour*, 3 October.

Bantel, K.A. and Jackson, S.E. (1989), 'Top management and innovations in banking: does the composition of the top team make a difference?', *Strategic Management Journal*, **10** (S1), 107–24.

Baruch, Y. (2006), 'Career development in organisations and beyond: balancing traditional and contemporary viewpoints', *Human Resource Management Review*, **16** (2), 125–38.

Battle, A. (2007), *Construire l'avenir avec les femmes: les femmes agents de transformation, moteurs d'innovation* (Building the future with women: women transformation agents, power of innovation), Paris: Futuribles.

Becker, G.S. (1993), *Human Capital: A Theoretical and Empirical Analysis, with Special Reference to Education*, Chicago, IL: University of Chicago Press.

Bell, M.P. and Kravitz, D.A. (2008), 'From the Guest Co-Editors: What do we know and need to learn about diversity education and training?', *Academy of Management Learning and Education*, **7** (3), 301–8.

Casey, J. and Corday, K. (2006), 'Managing diversity: toward a globally inclusive workplace', Interview with Michàlle Mor Barak, *Network News*, 8.

Cox, T.H., Lobel, S.A. and McLeod, P.L. (1991), 'Effects of ethnic group cultural differences on cooperative and competitive behavior on a group task', *Academy of Management Journal*, **34** (4), 827–47.

Diab, N.A. (2005), *Liban: le cadre juridique de la migration* (Lebanon: the legal migration framework), Florence: European University Institute.

El-Solh, R. (2004), *Lebanon and Arabism: National Identity and State Formation*, London: I.B. Tauris.

Fargues, P. (2005), *Migrations méditerranéennes: rapport 2005* (Mediterranean migration: report 2005), Florence: Robert Schuman Centre for Advanced Studies, European University Institute.

Fridah,W.M. (2002), 'Sampling in research', available at: www.socialresearchmethods.net (accessed 15 October 2006).

Friedman, N. and DiTomaso, J. (1996), 'Myths about diversity: what managers need to know about changes in the US labor force', *California Management Review*, **38** (4), 54–7.

Furseth, I. (2000), 'Religious diversity in prisons and in the military – the rights of Muslim immigrants in Norwegian state institutions', *International Journal on Multicultural Societies*, **2** (1), 40–52.

Gabriel, J., Navarro, C. and Moya, B.R. (2005), 'Business performance management and unlearning process', *Knowledge and Process Management*, **12** (3), 161–70.

Haddad, S. (2002), 'Cultural diversity and sectarian attitudes in postwar Lebanon', *Journal of Ethnic and Migration Studies*, **28** (2), 291–306.

Halabi, Z. (2004), 'Exclusion and identity in Lebanon's Palestinian refugee camps: a story of sustained conflict', *Environment and Urbanization*, **16** (2), 39–48.

Haque, N. and Kim, S. (1995), 'Human capital flight: impact of migration on income and growth', *IMF Staff Papers*, **42**, 577–607.

Helou, M. (1995), 'Contingency planning for systems evolution after crisis: reconstructive brain drain policy-oriented implications – the case of Lebanon, 1975–1994', *Journal of Contingencies and Crisis Management*, **3** (3), 149–64.

Hicks, D.A. (2002), 'Spiritual and religious diversity in the workplace. Implications for leadership', *The Leadership Quarterly*, **13** (4), 379–96.

Hicks-Clarke, D. and Iles, P. (2004), 'Gender diversity and organizational performance', in M.J. Davidson and D.S.L. Fielden (eds), *Individual Diversity and Psychology in Organizations*, Chichester: Wiley-Blackwell, pp. 171–92.

Hofstede, G. (1980), *Culture's Consequences: International Differences in Work-related Values*, London: Sage.

Hofstede, G. (2007), 'Asian management in the 21st century', *Asia Pacific Journal of Management*, **24** (4), 411–420.

Hudson, M. (1999), 'Lebanon after Ta'if: another reform opportunity lost', *Arab Studies Quarterly*, **21** (1), 27–35.

ILO (1998), *World Employment Report 1998–1999: Employability in the Global Economy: How Training Matters*, Geneva: International Labour Organization.

IWSAW (1998), *The Female Labor Force in Lebanon*, Beirut: Institute for Women Studies in the Arab World.

Jackson, S.E., Brett, J.F., Sessa, D.M., Cooper, D.M., Julin, J.A. and Peyronnin, K. (1991), 'Some differences make a difference: individual dissimilarity and group heterogeneity as correlates of recruitment, promotions, and turnover', *Journal of Applied Psychology*, **76** (5), 675–89.

Jackson, S.E., Joshi, A. and Erhardt, N.L. (2003), 'Recent research on team and organizational diversity: SWOT analysis and implications', *Journal of Management*, **29** (6), 801–30.

Jamali, D. and Abdallah, H. (2010), 'Diversity management rhetoric versus reality: insights from the Lebanese context', ch.8 in M. Özbilgin and J. Syed (eds), *Managing Gender Diversity in Asia: A Research Companion*, Cheltenham, UK and Northampton, MA, USA: Edward Elgar, pp. 119–39.

Jamali, D., Safieddine, A. and Daouk, M. (2006), 'The glass ceiling: some positive trends from the Lebanese banking sector', *Women in Management Review*, **21** (8), 625–42.

Jehn, K.A. and Bezrukova, K. (2004), 'A field study of group diversity, work group context, and performance', *Journal of Organizational Behavior*, **25** (6), 703–29.

Jones, D., Pringle, J. and Shepherd, D. (2000), 'Managing diversity meets Aotearoa', *New Zealand Personnel Review*, **29** (3), 364–80.

Jureidini, R. and Moukarbel, N. (2000), 'Brief on foreign female domestic maids in Lebanon', Lebanese NGO Forum, Beirut: American University of Beirut, Department of Social and Behavioral Sciences.

Kabbara, N. (1991), *Critique of the Lebanese Theory of Consociationalism*, Lyon: Maison de l'Orient.

Kiwan, F. (2005a), 'Consolidation ou recomposition de la société civile d'après guerre?' (Consolidation or re-composition of the after war civil soceity), Confluences Méditerranée, **47**.

Kiwan, F. (2005b), *La dimension politique et sociale des migrations au Liban* (The political and social dimension of migration in Lebanon), in P. Fargues (ed.).

Koenig, M. (2000), 'Managing religious diversity in a global context', *International Journal on Multicultural Societies*, **2** (1), 1–4.

Konovsky, E. (1986), 'Migration from the poor to the rich Arab countries', *Middle East Review*, **18** (3), 28–35.

Lyness, K.S. and Thompson, D.E. (2000), 'Climbing the corporate ladder: do female and male executives follow the same route?', *Journal of Applied Psychology*, **85** (1), 86–101.

Maktabi, R. (1999), 'The Lebanese Census of 1932 revisited. Who are the Lebanese?', *British Journal of Middle Eastern Studies*, **26** (2), 219–41.

Maxwell, J.A. (1996), *Qualitative Research Design*, Vol. 41, Newbury Park, CA: Sage.

McNeill, P. (1994), *Research Methods*, London: Routledge.

Mikdashi, T. (1999), 'Constitutive meaning and aspects of work environment affecting creativity in Lebanon', *Participation and Empowerment: An International Journal*, **7** (3), 47–55.

Montes, T. and Shaw, G. (2004), 'The future of workplace diversity in the new millennium', in M.J. Davidson and D.S.L. Fielden (eds), Chichester: Wiley-Blackwell, *Individual Diversity and Psychology in Organizations*, pp. 385–402.

Morrison, A.M. (1992), *The New Leaders: Guidelines on Leadership Diversity in America*, San Francisco, CA: Jossey-Bass.

MSA (1996), 'Population and Housing Survey', Beirut: Ministry of Social Affairs and United Nations Population Fund.

Neal, M., Finlay, J. and Tansey, R. (2005), '"My father knows the minister": a comparative study of Arab women's attitudes towards leadership authority', *Women in Management Review*, **20** (7), 478–97.

Nishii, L.H. and Özbilgin, M.F. (2007), 'Global diversity management: towards a conceptual framework', *International Journal of Human Resource Management*, **18** (11), 1883–94.

Özbilgin, M.F. (2000), 'Is the practice of equal opportunities management keeping pace with theory? Management of sex equality in the financial services sector in Britain and Turkey', *Human Resource Development International*, **3** (1), 43–67.

Patton, M.Q. (1990), *Qualitative Evaluation and Research Methods*, Newbury Park, CA: Sage.

Pelled, L.H. (1996), 'Demographic diversity, conflict, and work group outcomes: an intervening process theory', *Organization Science*, **7** (6), 615–31.

Pelled, L.H., Eisenhardt, K.M. and Xin, K. R. (1999), 'Exploring the black box: an analysis of work group diversity, conflict, and performance', *Administrative Science Quarterly*, **44** (1), 1–28.

Picard, E. (1997), 'Le communautarisme politique et la question de la démocratie au Liban' (The political clannishness and the democracy question in Lebanon), *Revue Internationale de Politique Comparée*, **4** (3), 639–56.

Point, S. and Singh, V. (2003), 'Defining and dimensionalising diversity: evidence from corporate websites across Europe', *European Management Journal*, **21** (6), 750–61.

Rapley, T. (2004), 'Interviews', in C. Seale, G. Gobo, J.F. Gubrium and D. Silverman (eds), *Qualitative Research Practice*, London: Sage, pp. 15–33.

Richard, O.C., Murthi, B.P.S. and Ismail, K. (2007), 'The impact of racial diversity on intermediate and long-term performance: the moderating role of environmental context', *Strategic Management Journal*, **28** (12), 1213–33.

Rodríguez-Pose, A. and Vilalta-Bufí, M. (2004), *Education, Migration, and Job Satisfaction: The Regional Returns of Human Capital in the EU*, Brussels: College of Europe.

Rosenzweig, P. (1998), 'Managing the new global workforce: fostering diversity, forging consistency', *European Management Journal*, **16** (6), 644–52.

Sackmann, S.A. (1992), 'Culture and subcultures: an analysis of organizational knowledge', *Administrative Science Quarterly*, **37** (1), 140–61.

Safieddine, A., Jamali, D. and Daouk, M. (2004a), 'Brain-drain paradox: sometimes leaving is better for everyone', Lebanonwire.

Safieddine, A., Jamali, D. and Daouk, M. (2004b), 'Brain drain or brain gain? A Lebanese perspective', Lebanonwire.

Safieddine, A., Jamali, D. and Daouk, M. (2004c), 'Exploiting expatriate human capital by turning brain drain into a brain gain', Lebanonwire.

Salloum, H. (2003), 'Women in the United Arab Emirates', *Contemporary Review*, **283** (August), 101–5.

Schippers, M.C., Hartog, D.N.D., Koopman, P.L., and Wienk, J.A. (2003), 'Diversity and team outcomes: the moderating effects of outcome interdependence and group longevity and the mediating effect of reflexivity', *Journal of Organizational Behavior*, **24** (6), 779–802.

Seaver, B.M. (2000), 'The regional sources of power-sharing failure: the case of Lebanon', *Political Science Quarterly*, **115** (2), 247–71.

Seidman, I. (1998), *Interviewing as Qualitative Research*, New York: Teachers' College Press.

Sidani, Y. (2005), 'Women, work, and Islam in Arab societies', *Women in Management Review*, **20** (7), 498–512.

Syed, J. (2010), 'From gender empowerment to gender diversity: measuring the gender gap in Muslim majority countries', ch.12 in M. Özbilgin and J. Syed (eds), *Managing Gender Diversity Management in Asia: A Research Companion*, Cheltenham, UK and Northampton, MA, USA: Edward Elgar, pp. 210–26.

Turner, B.S. (2007), 'Managing religions: state responses to religious diversity', *Contemporary Islam*, **1** (2), 123–37.

UN (2000), 'Replacement Migration: Is It a Solution to Declining and Ageing Populations?', New York: United Nations, Department of Economic and Social Affairs, Population Division.

UN (2006), 'International migration in the Arab region, United Nations expert group meeting on international migration and development in the Arab region: challenges and opportunities', Beirut, Lebanon: United Nations, Economic and Social Commission for Western Asia, Population Division, Department of Economic and Social Affairs.

UNDP (1998), *National Human Development Report: Youth and Development*, Beirut: United Nations Development Programme.

UNDP (2003), Millennium Development Goals, Beirut: United Nations Development Programme Lebanon.

Vertovec, S. and Wessendorf, S. (2004), *Migration and Cultural, Religious and Linguistic Diversity in Europe: An Overview of Issues and Trends*, Oxford: Centre on Migration, Policy and Society University of Oxford.

Wehbi, S. and El-Lahib, Y. (2007), 'Organising for voting rights of people with disabilities in Lebanon: reflections for activists', *Equal Opportunities International*, **26** (5), 449–64.

Wellington, S., Kropf, M.B. and Gerkovich, P.R. (2003), 'What's holding women back', *Harvard Business Review*, **81** (6), 18–19.

Wilson, E. and Iles, P. (1996), 'In managing diversity: evaluation of an emerging paradigm', paper presented at the Proceedings of the British Academy of Management Annual Conference, Aston.

Wilson, T. (1997), *Diversity at Work: The Business Case for Equity*, New York: John Wiley.

Yaprak, A. (2002), 'Globalization: strategies to build a great global firm in the new economy', *Thunderbird International Business Review*, **44** (2), 297–302.

Young, M. (2000), 'Migrant workers in Lebanon', available at: http://www.lnf.org.lb/migrationnetwork/mig1.html (accessed 12 December 2007).

Appendix

Table 4A.1   Demographic profiles

Pseudonym	Marital status	Age	Sex	Religious background	Observe a religion	Education partly or fully Lebanon	Worked/ training in Lebanon
Antoine	Married	49	Male	Christian	No	Yes	Yes
Charles	Married	27	Male	Christian	No	Yes	No
Elie	Single/ with friend	29	Male	Christian	Occasional	Yes	Yes
François	Married	49	Male	Muslim	No	Yes	Yes
Ihab	Single/no friend	26	Male	Christian	No	Yes	Yes
Imane	Divorced	54	Female	Muslim	No	Yes	Yes
Jean-Jacques	Divorced	42	Male	Muslim	Occasional	Yes	No
Kamal	Married	61	Male	Muslim	No	No	Yes
Karima	Divorced	49	Female	Muslim	No	Yes	No
Mustafa	Single/no friend	25	Male	Muslim	Yes	Yes	Yes
Patrick	Married	45	Male	Christian	No	Yes	Yes
Salim	Married	55	Male	Unknown	Yes	Yes	No
Samah	Divorced	57	Female	Muslim	No	Yes	No
Samir	Married	55	Male	Muslim	Occasional	Yes	Yes
Stéphane	Married	47	Male	Christian	Occasional	Yes	No
Tatiana	Single/ with friend	47	Female	Christian	No	Yes	Yes
Wael	Single/no friend	30	Male	Muslim	Occasional	Yes	Yes
Wafa	Married	46	Female	Muslim	Occasional	Yes	Yes
Walid	Single/ with friend	31	Male	Christian	Occasional	Yes	Yes
Yolla	Single/no friend	27	Female	Christian	Unknown	Yes	Yes

5 Diverse discretionary effort in workplace networks: serving self over community in China

Kurt April and Eon Smit

Introduction

Historically, the flow of management and diversity theory, relating to multinational companies, has been from mainly Western (Anglo, Franco, American) roots to developing/emerging economies. As a result, workplace relations, employee engagement and, in fact, the very notion of human nature has been addressed in terms of an implicit standard that is primarily White, primarily male, and primarily Western. The possibility for employees who are not White, male or Western to be heard in their own way and on their own terms, reflecting their own interests and ways of knowing, learning and engaging, have traditionally been institutionally denied. These conditions do not reflect mere chance, but rather the ability of those in power to create the terms according to which social reality will be encountered (Wlodkowski and Ginsberg, 1995), and the manner and forms of engagement which are credible (Rowley et al., 2010). To deny these political aspects of multinational workplaces in Asia is dangerous, in that it denies the Asian employee the possibility to make meaning of his/her world and the ability to deliver his/her best within a team when, for instance, engagement is irrelevant and cannot be self-determined. The latter (lack of choice and voice), we know, is experienced as strange, with fear, with annoyance, and Asian employees implicitly know that they are engaging through, and because of, someone else's domination or discursive control (that is, being continually thought of, and treated through, an Asian group lens). Contextual sensitivity is important for moral considerations (Miller, 1994), which ultimately affects determinism attitudes and can also lead to fatalism orientation, with the locus of control perceived as either inside (Rotter, 1966) or outside (Frazee, 1998) the individual.

Personal relevance is the degree to which employees can identify their perspectives and values in their workplace relations, discussions and ways of working. In other words, the ways in which they work and engage others are connected to who they are, their extended families and communities, what they care about, how they perceive and know, what has valency for them, and how they are able to contribute and move forward.

Their natural curiosity for challenges emerges, they want to make sense of things and seek out challenges that are outside of their range of current capabilities and values – this results in employees willingly offering their discretionary effort to an organisation, that is, unsolicited goodwill which leads to effort over and above expected role requirements (for which they usually do not get paid, and the lack-of for which they cannot be fired) and as opposed to traditional effort (for which they usually get paid, and the lack-of for which they can be fired). If employees can be spontaneous and authentic, acting from their deepest and most vital selves, they naturally strive for coherence among the aspects of themselves and their world that are in their awareness (Deci and Ryan, 1991). Self-determination is the need to be the origin of one's behaviour (Wlodkowski and Ginsberg, 1995), to personally endorse one's engagement with others, and being free to choose what one is doing (de Charms, 1968; Deci and Ryan, 1991) and the level of commitment one brings to the behaviour that leads from the choice.

The context of our study is within a multinational firm, that is, specifically a leading global FMCG (fast moving consumer goods) firm operating around the globe – however, our concern was its operations in China. In order to satisfy Bronfenbrenner's (1979) requirement for consistent values socialisation among, and across settings, and its link to group development, the FMCG firm specifically hired certain types of employees (in all of its operations around the globe), that is, those who were personally highly motivated, self-determined, excelled in a high-performance workplace, and required minimum hands-on management. When such consistency exists, socialisation, for this firm, has tended to be efficient and effective. The firm believed that when it is unable to achieve such consistency, socialisation would become fractured and employees would adhere to, and behave according to, 'group type', for example, the Chinese group identity would supersede the individual's choices, thereby negatively affecting the socialisation consistency. However, of concern to the firm was Bronfenbrenner's second condition, in which his colligation of socialisation processes also indicates that events inside the workplace are substantially influenced by the cultural background of the employees – given the Chinese context, the FMCG firm understood that, while it hired a certain type of employee, it still needed a deeper understanding of the interface between the high-performance institutional culture of the firm and the (increasingly) diverse cultural heritage of the constituents.

The study serves to form a theoretical and practical framework for analysing the concept of diverse discretionary effort. It is based on an individual's experience in his/her professional network at the workplace, that is, the people an individual seeks advice from, works with and depends on, to complete his/her work successfully. Expectancy refers to an individual's strength of belief and conviction about whether or not what he/she sets out to do on a personal level is achievable and desirable on a workplace level, in terms of effort and productivity (Vroom, 1964). Underpinning this expectancy is the fact that different and diverse people have different expectations and levels of confidence about their capabilities. Desire and expectation are interwoven, and only mitigated by workplace issues and openness to their expectations, as well as by personal self-esteem and self-confidence issues within a context, that is, in this case, an Asian context.

Rowley et al. (2010) warn that we should be cautious of the rhetoric regarding the assumptions linking traditional diversity and workplace productivity and creativity. It is for this reason that our locus of diversity is situated in individual expectancy. We believe that individuals enter networks often willingly or sometimes unwillingly, with certain expectations – inclusive of Rowley et al.'s gender expectations. Individual productivity, and therefore workplace performance, is linked to the (diverse) associations the people make towards expected outcomes and their contributions to those outcomes. It is our hypothesis that initially the outcome becomes bigger than the self and, subsequently, thus indirectly, the self gains affirmation as the person's expectations are met. The self is therefore ultimately served, thus causing individuals to freely offer their discretionary effort.

Engagement and discretionary effort
It is common cause that people are the most important resource of any organisation (Posner et al., 1986) and that an organisation's success is dependent on the success and happiness of its employees. Vora (2004) argues that the driving factor in winning customer satisfaction is to achieve employee satisfaction. Organisations are beginning to realise that their human capital is one of the last resources of strategic and competitive advantage (Fink, 2006). Gorelick et al. (2004) argue that there are direct links between employee motivation and behaviour, the creation of value for customers and the maximisation of shareholder value. For an organisation's performance to be optimal, a combination of situational and personal factors are required to be in place (Lawler, 1994). Pinder (1984) lists these factors as the individual effort of the employee, the ability of the employee, the amount of support received from the supervisor and team members and the availability of tools and materials. However, Govindarajulu and Daily (2004) suggest that management commitment, employee commitment, rewards and feedback and reviews, are key to encouraging employees in improving personal and team performances. The Accel Team (2006) broadens these factors by listing praise and recognition, trust and respect, job enrichment, communication, incentives,

removal of barriers, provision of optimal learning and the provision of the necessary tools. Peppas et al. (1999) showed that the highest priority attributes, for Chinese respondents in their study, were motivation, initiative, company knowledge, leadership and loyalty (given the importance of group spirit in the Chinese culture, as specified again by Härtel et al. (ch. 11, this volume), these researchers had not expected 'initiative' to be rated second in importance by the Chinese) – they claim that the Chinese place more importance on job attributes that could directly benefit the organisation, as opposed to the interpersonal focus of traditionally Western motivations.

Lawler (1994: 1), however, argues that: 'motivation seems to be the single most important determinant of performance'. Employee motivational principles have been studied in order to achieve higher productivity in the workplace. The Accel Team (2006) argues that the goal of motivational theory is to bring together a collection of resources that describe and comment on key variables within the organisational environment, and that relate to both employee motivation and productivity. The appropriate mix of theories is applied in a way that engages the needs and aspirations of the people who are sought to be motivated.

Work motivation is defined as 'a set of energetic forces that originate both within as well as beyond an individual's being, to initiate work-related behaviour, and to determine its form, direction, intensity, and duration' (Pinder, 1984: 8). 'The study of motivation has to do with the analysis of the various factors which incite and direct an individual's actions' (Atkinson, 1964: 1 in Lawler, 1994: 3). Bindra (1959) argues that at the core of the challenge of motivation, lies the goal-directed aspect of an employee's behaviour. The main premise of any motivational theory is to attempt to explain why people make voluntary choices from the range of behavioural options available. Traditional motivational theories have allowed for the wide variety of individual needs, expectations, values and attitudes to be investigated. It has been stated that motivation, which is supposedly observed to be under the employee's control, is driven by the two factors of arousal and the choice of the employee's behaviour (Mitchell, 1982).

With arousal theory, the work of researchers such as Abraham Maslow, Douglas McGregor and Frederick Hertzberg suggest that, generally, work organisations dedicate their efforts to determining how to satisfy employees' lower-level needs (Mitchell, 1982). These theorists described lower-level needs as a work environment with an emphasis on pay systems and the employees' hours of work. One of the major theories of choice is linked to an individual's expectancy. Expectancy theories are closely linked to the rewarding of performance-enhancing behaviour and argue that people are affected by previous and present outcomes. Vroom's (1964) expectancy theory suggests that an individual's behaviour, the primary purpose of which is to maximise pleasure and minimise pain, results from conscious choices from a range of alternatives. Vroom posited that an employee's performance is based on individual factors such as personality, skills, knowledge, experience and abilities. He further states that an employee's beliefs about expectancy, instrumentality and valence interact psychologically to create a motivational force such that the employee acts in ways that bring pleasure and avoid pain. It is on this basis of expectancy theory that this study aims to extend motivational theory to build a foundation for the concept of diverse discretionary effort within multinationals operating in Asia. Discretionary effort (DE) is formally defined as: 'energy over which an individual has control, beyond that which is minimally required by the organisation, expended pro-organisationally (to benefit the organisation), consistent with organisational goals and requiring both a behavioural as well as cognitive expenditure by the individual' (Entwistle, 2001: 7). DE focuses on the willing effort that is under the control of the employee rather than the organisation. Effort is treated as a consequence and primary indicator of motivation.

The level of DE in the workplace is declining (Kowalski, 2003), with the current work environment being described as 'one of disillusioned employees, unhealthy or non-existent relationships between employees and their employers, high stress levels, a lack of security and little or no trust' (Entwistle, 2001: 17). Yankelovich and Immerwahr (1983) demonstrate that by the early 1980s, 23 per cent of the workforce surveyed offered a high level of DE to their jobs, and 44 per cent perceived their job as low discretion, admitting to only doing what was necessary to keep their job, while 75 per cent of the respondents agreed that they could be more effective in their workplace than they currently were. A 2005 research survey of 990 respondents reports that 70 per cent of employees reviewed indicated that they planned to stay with their current organisation for the near future, but only 21 per cent of those indicated that they offered their full DE to their current job (BlessingWhite, 2005). Kowalski (2003) points out that younger workers surveyed indicated that they would rather work for themselves than for an organisation. These trends clearly indicate that organisations are losing their DE and intellectual capital that was once willingly offered by employees. In China, however, before the Chinese economic reform (starting around 1978), all enterprises were owned by the government in a planned economy framework – this, in many ways, forced people who were not employed by the government, to be entrepreneurial (but unlike the generally accepted Western sense that entrepreneurs are people with a high need for achievement, much of the Chinese entrepreneurialism was of the survivalist nature) – these entrepreneurs can now seek employment in private, stock, partial state-owned, foreign-fund, and joint-venture companies. The traditional government employee is now also a new emerging (intrapreneurial) class within corporate China, as well as in multinationals. According to Zheng (2010), the state and private sphere in Chinese society have never been clearly separated. Additionally, in recent years, a Chinese elite that had studied in Europe and the USA, including at places like the IESE Business School (University of Navarra, Spain) and Harvard, has started to emerge. All of this creates some interesting workplace dynamics and changing forms of engagement within all organisations inside China, including multinationals.

This research study proposes that the more employees perceive their personal expectancies to be fulfilled through their work, the more the employee's self will become affirmed, thus leading the employee to willingly offer his/her DE. Employees eventually seek to affirm their self-worth within their origination. Self-affirmation theory can be described as the theory that asserts that people seek ways to see themselves as: 'competent, good, coherent, unitary, stable, capable of free choice, capable of controlling important outcomes' (Steele, 1988: 262). This theory strives to explain that people will reduce the impact of a threat to their self-concepts by focusing on, and affirming, their competence in some other area. 'Selective self-affirmation can lead people to modify their self-concepts by identifying with self-aspects that justify dissonant behaviour and by disidentifying with the standards that such behaviour violates' (Aronson et al., 1995: 986). If the workplace begins to 'violate' an employee's concepts of self-worth by not engaging the employee in an effective way, then the employee will disengage some part of him/herself from the organisation. This disengagement is crucial to the investigation of self-affirmation and thus DE.

Little has been done to systematically develop a DE framework necessary for testing the theory about its origins and constructs. It is the aim of this research study to lay the necessary conceptual and empirical framework that might advance the knowledge about DE, within a multinational in China, utilising the developed April–Smit DE model to investigate the link between DE and the concept of self-affirmation within professional networks.

Literature review

The April–Smit discretionary effort model, which we developed for the purposes of this research, is founded upon motivational theory. Traditionally, however, organisations have focused exclusively on the jobs performed by employees and on how those jobs could be made more efficient. Any failures to achieve expected results were explained by faults in the training of the individual (Barr et al., 1992), in the methods that the individual used to achieve the task (Accel Team, 2006), or incongruency between institutional and employee cultures (Scheeres and Rhodes, 2006).

Motivational theories
From earliest recorded time, people have organised themselves into teams in order to achieve goals; efforts have been coordinated and controlled to achieve planned outcomes. As early as 1933 the traditional management concepts of motivation were used in work organisations. Mayo (1933) concentrated on fatigue and monotony with specific reference to how the factors of work – breaks, hours, temperature and humidity – affected organisational productivity. He demonstrated the importance of the social contracts that a worker has at the workplace (the Hawthorne effect), that boredom and repetitiveness of tasks lead to reduced motivation. Mayo believed that workers could be motivated by acknowledgement of their social needs and by making them feel important. As a result, employees were given the freedom to make decisions on the job, and greater attention was paid to informal work groups. His model overemphasised the importance of situations for motivating employees.

Maslow (1943) suggested that the behaviour of an individual is determined by his/her strongest need. This would imply that managers would need to have a good understanding of the common needs of individuals in order to encourage them to be more productive. Maslow's hierarchy of needs is often depicted as a pyramid consisting of five levels: the four lower levels are grouped together as 'deficiency needs' associated with 'physiological needs', while the top level is expressed as 'growth needs' associated with 'psychological needs'. While deficiency needs must be met, growth needs are continually shaping behaviour. The basic concept is that the higher needs in this hierarchy only come into focus once all the needs lower down on the pyramid are mainly, or entirely, satisfied. Physiological requirements and safety must be satisfied before higher-level needs such as self-fulfilment are sought. Growth forces create upward movement in the hierarchy, whereas regressive forces push preponent needs further down the hierarchy. While Maslow's theory was regarded as an improvement over previous theories of personality and motivation, it has its detractors. In their extensive review of research dependent on Maslow's theory, Wahba and Bridwell (1976) found little evidence for the ranking of needs that Maslow described or even for the existence of a definite hierarchy at all. For example, less individualistic forms of society than those described by Maslow in this theory, such as the Chinese, might value their social relationships (for example, family, clan or group) higher than their own physiological needs. Maslow's framework, however, is not intended to be the definition of motivational behaviour; rather, it is intended to be used in predicting behaviour on a high- or low-probability basis.

McGregor (1960) investigated the organisational behaviour of individuals at work. From his research he developed two models, which he named Theory X and Theory Y. McGregor's work was based on Maslow's hierarchy of needs; he grouped Maslow's hierarchy into 'lower order' needs (Theory X) and 'higher order' needs (Theory Y). He suggested that management could use either set of needs to motivate employees. According to Theory X, management assumes that its employees are inherently lazy and will avoid work whenever possible. Workers need to be closely supervised and comprehensive systems of controls need to be developed. A hierarchical structure is needed with a control mechanism at each level. According to this theory, employees will show little ambition without an enticing incentive programme and will avoid responsibility whenever they can. A 'Theory X' manager believes that his or her employees do not really want to work, that they would rather avoid responsibility and that it is the manager's job to structure the work and energise the employee. In contrast under Theory Y, management assumes that its employees are ambitious, self-motivated, and anxious to accept greater responsibility and exercise self-control and self-direction. Employees enjoy their mental and physical work activities and have the desire to be imaginative and creative in their jobs. If these employees are afforded the opportunity, the results will be greater productivity. A 'Theory Y' manager believes that, given the right conditions, most people will want to do well at work. They believe that the satisfaction of doing a good job is a strong motivator within the organisation (McGregor, 1960). 'Theory Y bore such fruits as self-directed work teams, self-management, job enrichment, and empowerment' (Carson, 2005: 450).

The DE model underlying this research is closely associated with McGregor's Theory Y, given the 'employee-type' targeted by the FMCG firm. Extending McGregor's theory, the research asserts that an employee's desires, within an organisation, are closely linked to his/her personal and team expectancies. An employee will only offer his/her DE, by having personal expectancies met and becoming self-affirmed.

Herzberg formulated two theories of motivation, stating that job satisfaction and job dissatisfaction act independently of each other. Herzberg's two-factor theory states that there are certain factors in the workplace that cause job satisfaction, while a separate set of factors cause dissatisfaction (Herzberg et al., 1959). Both these models (hygiene and motivation) must be applied simultaneously. Employees had to be treated as fairly as possible, so as to minimise their dissatisfaction. Herzberg found that when these motivators, such as sense of achievement, recognition, the work itself, responsibility, advancement and growth are added to employees' jobs, they are more satisfied with their job and become more productive. Herzberg classified human actions, and the premise behind why these actions were being formed; if an individual performed a work-related action because he/she 'had to', then this was classed as movement, but if the individual performed a work-related action because he/she 'wanted to', then this was classed as motivation (ibid.). Subsequent research has not been very supportive of Herzberg's theory. Phillipchuk and Whittaker (1996: 15) replicated Herzberg's original study and found that, in the current work environment, the results 'showed a decrease in recognition, advancement, and responsibility satisfiers and the disappearance of salary and work conditions as motivators or de-motivators'.

McClelland (1961) proposed a content theory of motivation based on Murray's (1938) theory of personality. This theory describes a comprehensive model of human needs and motivational processes. McClelland's theory is also related to Herzberg's motivation-hygiene theory, in the sense that people with high-achievement motivation tend to be interested in the motivator, which is the job itself (Accel Team, 2006). McClelland asserted that human motivation comprises three dominant needs: the need for achievement (N-Ach), the need for power (N-Pow) and the need for affiliation (N-Affil). The importance of each need varies from individual to individual, and also depends on an individual's cultural background. McClelland's theory supports the expectancy dimension of the DE model; the chapter authors' assert that individuals have expectancies (needs) that differ, and it is the satisfaction of these expectancies that will lead to self-affirmation and thus DE.

Argyris and Schön (1974) argued that people have mental maps with regard to how to act in certain situations. Their results concluded that it is these maps, including the way people plan, implement and review their actions that guide people's actions. Argyris (1980) found that few people are aware of the maps or theories they use. His research was an extension of McGregor's X and Y theory in that the research compared bureaucratic/pyramid values (the organisational counterpart to Theory X assumptions about people) that still dominate most organisations with a more humanistic/democratic value system (the organisational counterpart to Theory Y assumptions about people). For the purpose of this study, we link Argyris's theory, and culturally based mental maps, to an individual's strength of belief and conviction about whether or not what the individual set out to do on an individual level is achievable and desirable on a workplace level in terms of effort and productivity.

Vroom's (1964) 'expectancy theory' is a widely known example of a process theory. Process theories stress the differences in people's needs and focus on the human cognitive processes that create differences between individuals. Content theories, on the other hand, assume that all individuals possess the same set of needs. Vroom suggests that a manager's leadership style should be tailored to the particular situation and group, and this theory also helps to explain how an individual's goals influence individual performance. Vroom provided an in-depth explanation of his process theory, developed around the concepts of expectancy, valence and instrumentality. Vroom's theory (pp. 14–15) assumes that, 'the choices made by a person among alternative courses of action are lawfully related to psychological events occurring contemporaneously with the behaviour'. In other words, a person's work behaviour results from conscious choices from a range of alternatives and these choices (behaviours) are related to their psychological processes, particularly perception and the formation of beliefs and attitudes. Vroom's motivational theory can be summarised in the following equation (Figure 5.1):

$$\text{Motivation} = \text{Expectancy (E)} \times \text{Instrumentality (I)} \times \text{Valence (V)}$$

With Expectancy, employees have different expectations and levels of confidence about what they are capable of doing (Vroom, 1964). Vroom considers Instrumentality as the perception of employees that there will actually be an outcome associated with completing the assigned task (Pinder, 1984). Valence refers to the emotional orientations people hold with respect to outcomes (rewards) (Vroom, 1964).

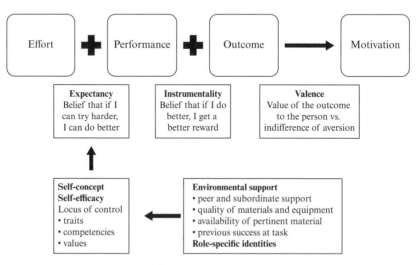

Figure 5.1   Vroom's expectancy theory model

There are two critical components of valence, as identified by Isaac et al. (2001), that concern the chapter authors' and the DE model. First, the attractiveness of an expected outcome differs among different individuals (Snead and Harrell, 1994), and second, 'leaders must expend a significant amount of effort to ensure alignment between the personal goals of their followers and those of the organisation' (Isaac et al., 2001: 219). It is these personal goals that are core to the expectancy model as they form the foundation for the April–Smit DE model.

According to Pinder (1984: 154), the shortcoming in Vroom's expectancy theory and the VIE constructs, is the assumption 'that these constructs are responsible for arousing and directing work effort through the development of intentions'. Pinder (ibid.) further states that 'VIE beliefs cannot be expected to automatically result in specific work behaviours' and that the VIE theory is not 'totally capable of predicting levels of work effort or decisions either to participate in, or to withdraw from, organisational settings'.

Professional networks
In the current business environment of constant change, formal, professional and social networks are becoming increasingly important to organisations. 'Effective investments in your networks can make you smarter, more knowledgeable, and better grounded, as well as a more agile learner and collaborator. These capabilities are critical to solving problems and taking advantage of opportunities at the pace necessary for success today' (Dulworth, 2006: 37). Professional (work-based) networks span regional–organisational boundaries, thereby enhancing the concept of working virtually. Working virtually can benefit the organisation strategically, but it is more challenging to manage than traditional working environments with regard to trust, communication and learning (Eden, 2006). Virtual employees and teams often do not interact face to face with all members of the organisation. These employees thus lack the social interaction of traditional organisations (Dewar, 2006). In traditional work environments, various exercises such as team-building help to instil organisational expectations for obtaining goals (Mitchell, 1982). Whether the employees work virtually or are co-located, this research study proposes that employees enter into professional networks with personal expectations (which we categorise and define below) that are crucial for the DE framework.

Self-affirmation
Steele (1988) first introduced self-affirmation theory, which states that the overall goal of an individual's self-system is to protect an image of his/her self-worth and relates to his/her ability to adapt competently to change.

Sherman and Cohen (2006: 189) argue that self-affirmation not only affects an individual's reaction to threatening situations or events 'but also [his/her] physiological adaptations and actual behaviour'. Such insights have important implications for Chinese employees, in particular – both because of the dominance of Western approaches to management and business, as well as the lingering influences of gender stereotyping reinforced by Confucianism (Rowley et al., 2010). These self-threat concepts have also been related to other areas of self-reinforcement; these include Dunning et al.'s (1995) theories of self-serving, and Brown and Smart's (1991) exaggerated self-ratings of social qualities. In each of these theories, the responses to threats of self-worth were countered by displaying the various forms of self-enhancement at greater levels than those of subjects who were not threatened. It would seem therefore that a threat to an individual's self-worth increases one's need to self-enhance (Meirick, 2005). This process helps individuals to 'accept experiences and information that, although threatening, hold important lessons for self-change' (Sherman and Cohen, 2006: 190).

Underlying self-affirmation theory is the paradigm of cognitive dissonance. Cognitive dissonance is the perception of incompatibility between two cognitions, which can be defined as any element of knowledge, including attitude, emotion, belief or behaviour (Festinger, 1957). The theory of cognitive dissonance states that contradicting mental models serve as a motivator to compel the mind to develop new, or to modify existing, beliefs, so as to diminish the measure of inconsistency between cognitions. Disconfirmed expectancies of both failure and of success lead people's attempts to change responses to those expectancies. It is on this premise that the April–Smit DE model was developed. It is proposed that, once an individual's expectations in the workplace/professional network are met, the individual's dissonance between personal expectation and self-affirmation will be reduced, and the individual will become self-affirmed.

Interpersonal-performance expectancy
'Leaders, through a process of social influence, guide and inspire followers toward desired outcomes' (Spreitzer, 2006: 305). This can occur through formal or informal learning structures. Research on the mentoring process and professional networks has indicated support for personal learning and the development of individual careers (Chandler and Kram, 2005). Lave (1991) and Lave and Wenger (1991) were the first to propose that the key component of learning within professional networks (communities of practice), was to gradually develop the knowledge for new employees with the guidance of a mentor. Eventually the new employee becomes the centre

of 'the community', gaining the necessary knowledge required to perform his/her work function. These 'skilled' employees then continue the cycle and take on new employees as protégés. Rowley et al. (2010) remind us, though, that in male-gendered workplace environments, women often are denied access to the requisite informal networks – thereby engendering interpersonal, as well as career, barriers. Protégés are not the only individuals who benefit from access to mentoring programmes; according to Reisz (2004: 42), for mentors, the mentoring process 'validates their career learning and accomplishments, allows them to pass along their intellectual capital, and provides them the fulfilment that comes from giving something back to their organisation and their profession'. Reisz (p. 42) further states that 'an information mentor provides coaching, listening, advice, sounding board reactions, or other help in an unstructured, casual manner'. Pullins and Fine (2002) argue that taking part in a mentoring programme or helping a fellow employee helps the mentor in his/her own performance appraisal. This 'may provide recognition that serves as a higher-order reward to the mentor, in addition to lower-order rewards such as pay'. The recognition remotivates the mentor, and thus causes him/her to give further attention to the performance area in his/her work (ibid.: 266).

Effort-learning expectancy
Expectancy theory states that individuals engage in behaviours to the extent that they expect those behaviours to result in positive outcomes (Vroom, 1964). The respondents, in this research, have indicated that to achieve their workplace goals, they believe that emphasis placed on personal learning will have value-added learning organisational benefits. Senge (1990) argues that for an organisation to be successful, it will be necessary for people to learn new skills and develop new orientations. In order for a company and individual to advance in business, the individual must change in some way; this can be done by increasing one's knowledge and/or skills. Rampersad (2006) argues that for any significant organisational change to take place, the employees within the organisation must first change. This begins with 'self-learning, and self-learning starts with self-knowledge' (ibid.: 437). Congruent with the present research into DE, Rampersad (ibid.: 437) states that 'if there is an effective balance between the interests of individual employees and those of the organisation, employees will work with greater commitment toward the development of their organisation'. In this sense, Hutton's (1999, quoted in Abdullah, ch. 2, this volume) condition of mutual understanding for public relations is satisfied – individual behaviours that ultimately serve and are constrained by the 'public good'.

Leading-visibility expectancy
'[A] company that supports and encourages career self-management may ultimately have more highly-skilled and flexible employees, because employees understand the need to continuously refresh and update their skills' (Meister, 1998: 25). As an organisation grows and increases its knowledge base, the company builds its intellectual capital and knowledge becomes a competitive asset (Bogdanowicz and Bailey, 2002). The education and development of employees are a valuable commodity, and organisations that support education will hold a distinct competitive advantage over organisations that do not (Leach, 2001). This is most evident in focused Malaysian organisational life, driven by respect and acceptance for multiculturalism, visible and explicit appreciation of local individual and group norms (Abdullah, ch. 2, this volume). The rate of generation of new knowledge around the globe is increasing (Bourner, 1998). '[E]ducation and training should focus less on delivering knowledge and more on helping people to learn how to find out for themselves' (ibid.: 14). Bourner demonstrates that employees understand that acquiring new information, and being seen to do so, is critical to meeting personal expectancies. Employees understand that once their existing knowledge becomes part of the organisation's intellectual capital, they need to keep engaging in acquiring new knowledge, to prevent themselves from becoming redundant (Garrick and Clegg, 2000). '[For a] learning organisation it is not enough to survive ... "adaptive learning" is important – indeed it is necessary. For a learning organisation, "adaptive learning" must be joined by "generative learning", learning that enhances our capacity to create' (Senge, 1990: 14).

Team-sustainability expectancy
Professional network teams or communities of practice provide an ideal platform for developing, sharing and entrusting of information within an organisation (Chua, 2006). To compete in the global arena, old organisational cultures become barriers to being innovative and productive (Gadman and Cooper, 2005). Professional teams are effective in overcoming these barriers. 'Communities of practice are a natural part of organisational life. They exist and develop on their own whether or not the organisation recognises them or encourages their creation' (Chua, 2006: 121). Work teams often fail during infancy due to unrealistic expectations regarding the effort during start-up (Lathin, 1995). 'The key to team sustainability may lie in the effective use of positive cognitive strategies at the team level' (Houghton et al., 2003: 39). Respondents value their own ability to sustain the current and future status of the team. Individuals in a work team are of more value than the sum of the individuals together.

Organisations that successfully use professional networks to foster knowledge must implement processes to sustain and protect the team synergy, as team-wellness sustainability requires ongoing attention to both internally driven team processes and externally supported organisational processes.

Individual-network learning expectancy

According to Senge (1990: 3) learning organisations are 'organisations where people continually expand their capacity to create the results they truly desire, where new and expansive patterns of thinking are nurtured, where collective aspiration is set free, and where people are continually learning to see the whole together'. The capacity for an organisation to be a learning organisation starts with an individual (Barker and Neailey, 1999). Geiger and Turley (2005) argue that for an organisation to be effective, individuals must share their personal knowledge with others; which, in a Chinese context, Härtel et al. (ch. 11, this volume) claim is premised on very personal interactions – the basis for *guanxi*. Wong (1998) argues for the requisite social interactions necessary for such sharing to take place, which Davies et al. (1995) later claimed was the basis for *guanxi* networks. Garrick and Clegg (2000: 281) state that a 'knowledge worker now becomes a calling equivalent to a vocation: knowledge workers help organisations and industries meet contemporary market challenges'. Respondents to this research seem to understand this concept and place critical value on the personal learning.

> [W]hen you ask people about what is it like being part of a great team, what is most striking is the meaningfulness of the experience. People talk about being part of something larger than their experiences as part of truly great teams stand out as singular periods of life lived to the fullest. Some spend the rest of their lives looking for ways to recapture that spirit. (Senge, 1990: 13)

Through learning individuals are able to re-create themselves.

Research methodology

The model

The research study was based upon the maintained hypothesis of the April–Smit discretionary effort model (Box 5.1).

Although there is a significant amount of research that has been conducted into the concept of motivation in the organisational workplace, that concept of DE has hardly any empirical research accredited to it. This is a strong disadvantage to the modern organisation, as DE is a crucial element that can allow managers and leaders to understand how

---

BOX 5.1   THE APRIL–SMIT DISCRETIONARY EFFORT MODEL

Discretionary Effort (DE) = $(0.1*I) \times (0.2*O) \times V \times (0.1*A)$

where:

I = Importance of the Expectancy Construct to the Individual
O = Measure of Desired Outcome Materialising in Workplace
  = Effort Expectancy Construct (EE) + Performance Expectancy Construct (PE)
V = Valence
  = Workplace Orientation for Desired Outcome / Emotional Orientation for Desired Outcome at Workplace
  = (Importance Value of the Expectancy Construct to the Workplace (W) + Achievement of Workplace Goals (WG)) / Emotional Orientation for Desired Outcome at the Workplace (EO)
A = Affirmation of Self through Expectancy (Self-Esteem)
  = Positive Comparison of Expectancy with Peers Meaningfully Evaluated by Workplace (PC) + Self is Perceived to have Capacity for Efficacious Action as evaluated by Workplace (EA)

---

and why individuals differentially offer more than they have to, in terms of their time and effort, with regard to their designated position within an organisation. To this end, the current research has drawn upon existing models of motivation as a framework for the foundation of a DE model. Even though theory has a critical part to play in this type of research, 'it is the application of theory that is important in this case' (Easterby-Smith et al., 2002: 9). The rationale of this research is to add insight to the existing concept of DE, by proposing a model that can be utilised by leaders in organisations, including multinationals in Asia, to put to practical use when addressing the issue of diverse personal productivity and diverse personal expectancy of employees, with regard to motivation.

Variables and questionnaire

The measurement variables that were used in the research are listed below.

The dependent variables measured are:

- industry;
- age;
- gender;
- nationality;
- ethnicity;
- highest organisational position;
- years work experience;
- highest qualification; and
- virtual or co-located work.

The independent variables measured are:

- effort-performance expectancy (EP);
- interpersonal-performance expectancy (IP);
- effort-learning expectancy (EL);
- leading-visibility expectancy (LV);
- network-performance expectancy (NP);
- internal-recognition expectancy (IR);
- mutual-reciprocity expectancy (MR);
- individual-network learning expectancy (NL);
- performance-outcome expectancy (PO);
- team-sustainability expectancy (TS);
- effort expectancy constructs (EE);
- performance expectancy constructs (PE);
- achievement of workplace goals (WG);
- emotional orientation for desired outcome (EO);
- positive comparison of expectancy with peers (PC); and
- self is seen to have capacity for efficacious action (EA).

A questionnaire was developed for data collection. The questionnaire (Appendix 5A) is designed to assist interviewees, in a self-assessment, in thinking through the critical behaviours in 10 key areas for effectively engaging in, utilising and creating and conducting, value-adding, professional network relationships. The DE questionnaire was designed, using standard guidelines, to assist our understanding of the mediating effects of expectancies in professional network performance and learning that will eventually lead to self-affirmation, and thus influencing individuals to freely offer their DE. The questionnaire was tested and was found to satisfy the standard requirements.

The questionnaires were sent out via email, fax and as setup electronically using website survey software. These responses were collected during leadership courses at the Graduate School of Business, University of Cape Town and at Rotterdam School for Management. The permission for the use of these questionnaires had been obtained from the respondents. The sample includes managers from 21 different nationalities, 17 different economic sectors, five different managerial levels, diverse qualifications and a spectrum of work experience and age. They have in common the fact that they have been enrolled on a management development programme, but no claim is made to representativeness. They rather reflect the richness and diversity of international managers.

For the purpose of this research, the data were classified into both categorical and quantitative variables. The design of the questionnaire imparts itself to categorical questions such as gender, ethnicity and virtual or co-located work. The questionnaire also has quantifiable components; the questions on effort-performance expectancy, interpersonal-performance expectancy, and effort-learning expectancy were classified as quantitative as they are all measured on a five-point Likert scale.

Results

Descriptive measures

In the overall sample, there were 1,548 observations, however, not all cases contained complete information and in the data summary and analysis that follows, missing observations were case-wise deleted.

Table 5.1 reports on gender and Table 5.2 presents the age distribution. The data reflects a relative young group of managers, predominantly male, with more than 60 per cent of the respondents younger than 35 years.

The frequency distribution for position in the organisation and highest qualification, respectively, are shown in Tables 5.3 and 5.4, reflecting a relatively well-educated group of people operating mainly at middle-management level. A sectoral distribution of the data indicates a more-or-less random distribution between economic sectors with two exceptions – a preponderance of observations in the financial and engineering sectors.

Table 5.5 reports some descriptive statistics for the personal expectancies and the workplace expectancies (see Appendix 5A for definition of variables). The subscript P refers to a personal expectancy while the subscript W refers to a workplace expectancy.

Statistical differences between biographical categories

The expectancy scores were investigated for statistical differences between the different categories of the biographical data. Four variables indicated significant differences between males and females (see Table 5.6).

Table 5.1   Frequency distribution for gender

Gender	Frequency	%
Male	1,005	64.9
Female	543	35.1
Total	1,548	100.0

Table 5.2   Frequency distribution for age

Age category	Frequency	%
≤ 30	513	33.3
31–35	413	26.8
36–40	235	15.2
41–45	146	9.4
46–50	78	5.1
> 50	157	10.2
Total	1,542	100.0

Table 5.3   Frequency distribution for position in organisation

Position	Frequency	%
Manager	777	50.8
Director	230	15.0
Specialist	353	23.1
CEO	84	5.5
Section head	87	5.1
Other	7	0.5
Total	1,538	100.0

Table 5.4   Frequency distribution of highest qualification

Highest qualification	Frequency	%
Doctorate	50	3.3
Master's degree	286	18.7
Bachelor's degree	733	47.9
Diploma	244	15.9
Matric	146	9.5
Not reported	71	4.6
Total	1,530	100.0 (rounded)

*Table 5.5   Means and standard deviations of expectancies (*n=1540*)*

Variable	Mean	Std dev.
EP_p	4.498	0.620
EP_w	4.263	0.797
IP_p	4.206	0.730
IP_w	3.937	0.866
EL_p	4.202	0.772
EL_w	3.838	0.883
LV_p	3.871	0.850
LV_w	3.792	0.952
NP_p	3.828	0.850
NP_w	3.915	0.923
IR_p	3.792	0.962
IR_w	3.560	0.974
MR_p	3.790	0.857
MR_w	3.522	0.946
NL_p	4.284	0.729
NL_w	3.823	0.916
PO_p	4.317	0.750
PO_w	4.072	0.854
TS_p	4.110	0.868
TS_w	4.062	0.921

Table 5.6   T-test for significant differences between gender categories

Variable	Male mean	Female mean	p-value
LV_p	3.906	3.806	0.027
NP_w	3.871	3.996	0.011
IR_p	3.754	3.861	0.036
TS_w	4.013	4.152	0.005

As far as age categories are concerned, six different categories were distinguished and analysed by means of one-way ANOVA (analysis of variance). The variables where significant differences were observed between at least two categories are listed in Table 5.7. The six categories relate to ages less than 30, 31–35, 35–40, 41–45, 46–50 and older than 50. The analysis of class means shows great consistency in so far as the measurements increase with increasing age.

A one-way ANOVA was executed on the five different qualification categories namely matric, diploma, bachelor's degree, master's degree and doctorate. Three of the expectancy variables indicated significant

Table 5.7   F-tests for significant differences between age categories

Variable	p-value
EP_p	0.007
IP_p	0.005
MP_p	0.012
MR_p	0.014
MR_w	0.017
NL_p	0.023
PO_p	0.006
TS_p	0.000
TS_w	0.013

Table 5.8   F-tests for significant differences between qualification categories

Variables	p-value
IP_p	0.000
LV_p	0.001
IW_w	0.006

differences between the qualification categories (see Table 5.8). The analysis of the class means for the significant variables indicates a strong trend for the class means to increase with higher levels of education. In all cases, the mean of the doctoral class is significantly greater than the other class means.

The five different means for the variable that pertains to the position in the company, namely specialist, section head, manager, director and CEO were also compared in a one-way ANOVA (see Table 5.9). For four variables, significantly different class means could be demonstrated. As in the previous two analyses, there is a notable tendency for the class means to increase with the seniority of the position in the organisation.

The personal and work expectancies were also investigated for significant differences between the means of co-located workers and virtual workers. In two cases, significant differences were observed (Table 5.10). The Pearson product-moment correlation coefficients were calculated for each variable pair in Table 5.10. All the correlation coefficients were greater than 0.90 and all were statistically significant at the 1 per cent level of significance.

Principal component analysis was applied both to the five personal behaviour and the five workplace variables and in both cases a single

Table 5.9   F-tests for significant differences between positional categories

Variable	p-value
LV_w	0.019
NP_p	0.001
NL_w	0.046
TS_p	0.000

Table 5.10   T-tests for the means of personal and work expectancies between co-located workers and virtual workers

Variables	p-value
IP_p	0.025
TS_w	0.000

factor, with all factor loadings in excess of 0.95, explained more than 95 per cent of variability in the variables.

Item analysis
The next stage in the analysis involved an item analysis for the questions pertaining to personal behaviour and the meaningfulness to the workplace (see Appendix 5A).

The following variables were analysed:

- effort expectancy (*EE*);
- performance expectancy (*PE*);
- achievement of workplace goals (*WG*);
- emotional orientation of desired outcome (*EO*);
- positive outcome comparison with peers (*PC*); and
- capacity for efficacious action (*EA*).

Each variable was measured using five items and the Cronbach alpha coefficients were calculated for each item. Where the reliability of the sum scales could be improved by deleting items, this was done. Table 5.11 summarises the overall scale reliabilities and the items retained for further analysis.

Canonical correlation
The variables in the April–Smit Discretionary Effort Model are now defined and estimated as follows:

Table 5.11   Cronbach alphas for items retained

Variable	Cronbach alpha	Items retained
EE_p	0.664	1–5
EE_w	0.817	1–5
PE_p	0.625	1–5
PE_w	0.827	1–5
WG_p	0.979	1–5
WG_w	0.981	1–5
EO_p	0.910	1–4
EO_w	0.420	1–3.5
PC_p	0.405	1–4
PC_w	0.514	1–4
EA_p	0.418	1–4
EA_w	0.798	1–5

$\overline{P}$ denotes the mean of the 10 personal expectancies and $\overline{W}$ the mean of the 10 work expectancies.

I = Importance of the expectancy construct to the individual = $\overline{P}$;

O = Measure of desired outcome materialising in workplace = Effort expectancy construct + Performance expectancy construct = EE_w + PE_w;

V = Valence = Workplace orientation to desired outcome / Emotional orientation to desired outcome at workplace

= $(\overline{W} + WG_w) / EO_w$;

A = Affirmation of Self through expectancy (self-esteem)

= Positive comparison of expectancy with peers meaningfully evaluated by workplace + Self is perceived to have capacity of efficacious action as evaluated by workplace

= $PC_w + EA_w$.

Discretionary effort in general (EP)
= $(0.1I)(0.2O)(0.1A)$ with the 0.1 and 0.2 arbitrary scaling constants.

For each expectancy, the discretionary effort can therefore be calculated as:

$$DE\ (EP) = \{[0.1\ EP_p]\ [0.2\ (EE_w + PE_w)]\ [(\overline{W} + WG_w) / EO_w]$$
$$+ [0.1]\ (PC_w + EA_w)]\}\ \text{etc.}$$

To investigate the relationship between the dimension of expectancy and personal behaviours, canonical correlation analysis was used between

*Table 5.12   Chi-square test with successive roots removed (R = 0.615,
p = 0.000)*

Root removed	Canonical R	p
0	0.615	0.000
1	0.237	0.000
2	0.191	0.000
3	0.091	0.471
4	0.069	0.777
5	0.023	0.977

Table 5.13   Factor structure: personal expectations

Variable	Root 1	Root 2	Root 3	Root 4	Root 5	Root 6
EP_p	0.577	−0.194	−0.280	0.229	0.363	−0.459
IP_p	0.616	−0.280	−0.099	−0.375	−0.386	−0.264
EL_p	0.671	0.133	0.176	−0.242	0.164	0.175
LV_p	0.591	0.642	0.071	0.175	−0.094	−0.118
NP_p	0.482	−0.387	0.648	0.429	−0.057	−0.010
IR_p	0.468	0.038	0.149	−0.053	−0.093	0.369
MR_p	0.154	−0.200	0.077	−0.205	0.640	0.373
NL_p	0.719	−0.047	−0.025	−0.201	0.048	−0.052
PO_p	0.635	−0.024	−0.353	0.411	0.028	0.028
TS_p	0.218	−0.347	−0.296	0.105	−0.294	0.364

the 10 personal expectational variables EP_p to TS_p and the six averaged personal behavioural variables EE_p to EA_p.

The overall canonical R is fairly substantial and highly significant. Table 5.12 indicates that the first two canonical roots are significant and need further examination.

Using 0.6 as cut-off, IP_p, EL_p, NL_p and PO_p show substantial loadings on the first canonical factor, that is, they correlate highly with that factor. The variable LV_p is substantially correlated with the second canonical factor. The first two roots extract an average of about 38 per cent of the variance of the personal expectations (Table 5.13).

This first canonical root of the personal behaviour variables is marked by high loadings on EE_p, PE_p, WG_p and PC_p while EA_p loads highly on the second canonical root. The first two roots account for about 53 per cent of the variance in the personal behaviour variables (Table 5.14).

Overall it is concluded that IP_p, EL_p, NL_p and PO_p affect EE_p, PE_p, WG_p and PC_p while LV_p has a strong influence on EA_p.

Table 5.14   Factor structure: personal behaviours

Variable	Root 1	Root 2	Root 3	Root 4	Root 5	Root 6
EE_p	0.915	−0.040	0.000	0.171	0.213	−0.293
PE_p	0.842	−0.207	−0.295	−0.066	−0.258	0.296
WG_p	0.725	0.110	0.306	−0.122	0.341	0.486
EO_p	0.554	−0.335	0.101	−0.734	0.146	−0.089
PC_p	0.665	−0.140	0.632	−0.058	−0.363	0.042
EA_p	0.570	0.690	0.063	−0.400	−0.180	−0.017

Finally, DE was analysed using ANOVA to test for the significance of the demographic grouping variables. No significant differences (at the 5 per cent level) could be observed between males and females, between the different age groupings or between the different positions in the organisations.

Significant differences, however, could be observed between different qualification levels with diplomas leading to significantly higher DE values that high school, first degree or master degree qualifications induce.

Conclusion

> there exist innumerable forces which interlace, an infinite number of parallelograms of forces giving a resultant, the historical happening. This in its turn can be regarded as the outcome of a force acting as a whole, without consciousness or will. For that which each individual wishes separately, is hindered by all the others, and the general upshot is something which no one in particular has willed.
>
> (Engels, 1941: 55)

In the management of humans there is a trend to emphasise certain visual and group traits, modes of connection and relationship development, and ways of communicating which have proved, in part, to favour the maintenance of norming and stability. In the course of time these manners of regulating affairs restrict the desires of individuals to function diversely or outside of the dominant norm. These desires are generally resisted by both the gatekeepers of the norm (typically organisational management within the workplace) and those whose organisation-based self-esteem is quite low.

The process, emergent self-organisation around a replicating discourse, can be argued as a relatively simple case of a more general phenomenon. In 1976, Dawkins suggested a cultural replicator: the meme – essentially a belief, fashion or idea which replicates, in the broad sense, through imitation. The case for memes has been argued elsewhere; as underpinning a theory of socially contagious behaviour in individuals (Marsden, 1998; Blackmore, 1999) or as the foundation of a more general theory of individual consciousness (Dennet, 1991; Gabora, 1997). A wider view would see memes, or complexes of coexisting memes, as encoding a schemata for cultural organisation (Hull, 1990; Williams, 2000; Weeks and Galunic, 2003). With differences of emphasis, these authors all argue that organisational 'rules' are products of self-replicating systems of ideas and dialogue; in essence, Foucauldian discourses.

The field of diversity management, and diversity scholarship, can be considered as an emergent property of organisations enabled by, and dedicated to the maintaining of, particular paradigms. More generally, understanding of diversity depends on the mainly unwritten organisational 'rules and procedures' (Hannan and Freeman, 1977; Scott-Morgan, 1994), 'institutions' (Powell and DiMaggio, 1991) or 'cultural hegemony' (Gaudelli, 2001) and may be called into existence through organisational discourse; discourse frequently shaped by the metaphors which give it meaning (Morgan, 1996), such as seeing and treating all Chinese employees in the same way (through the generalised lens of culture), treating culture in an undifferentiated manner at both individual and group level (through the lens of national culture) (Härtel et al., ch. 11, this volume), or seeing and treating all multinational employees in the same way (through the lens of self-serving behaviour, towards their own career and financial ends). We find that such generalisations of Chinese, or Asian employees in general, draw diverse individuals into an otherwise undifferentiated mass, based on a particular commonality. This practice tends to victimise people, and leave them in a state of dependency or disempowerment of being, as their classification is imposed upon them by (powerful) others. The extent to which these generalised constructions impose a hierarchy of power is particularly disturbing to us. Within Asia, China can be seen as a cluster of cultures from different regions. This is similar to how it is in Europe, that instead of it being a single country it is a union of countries. China has many different regions and almost 40 nationalities, plus many different languages. In some cases, Chinese cannot understand other Chinese who live just across the river. Such understanding of the diversity of Chinese culture renders the generalised cultural discourse irrelevant.

Complexity arises from viewpoints, beliefs and actions of agents/people in the system, and is enabled by emergence of a replicative meme (discretionary effort), as opposed to an imposed meme (culture). Our research, which looked at individuals with high organisation-based self-esteem, has raised the fact that individuals do in fact act outside of, or contrary to, particular paradigms, that is, in our FMCG firm, Chinese employees were displaying highly individual behaviour (which challenges the accepted collectivist/groupthink cultural paradigm traditionally used to describe Chinese employees); however, these diverse discretionary efforts were not ultimately self-serving but for the collective organisation to do well. We felt that focusing research on diverse discretionary effort will go some way in decoupling the commonality/cultural discourse from individual choice and action – and, hence, sought to develop a model to both account for, but also measure, diverse levels of discretionary effort. Our research, conducted on a sample similar in locus of control, showed that known demographic variables do not account for significant differences in discretionary effort, but that further study needed to be conducted on the role of qualifications in discretionary effort mitigation.

Each society produces contradictions within a given time–space continuum, and each individual develops according to his/her needs, and these needs eventually conflict with the dominant paradigm. Because each person is an individual and hence unique, it would be impossible for there not to be acute contradictions, at some time, between the emotional investments and subsequent efforts of the modern Asian individual to solve his/her unique problem and the effort of society to reward previously tried and tested methods of so doing. It is this contradiction which served as our stimulus to conduct this research study, and we hope which will provide the impetus for thinking more critically about diversity in Asia.

References

Accel Team (2006), 'Employee motivation, the organizational environment and productivity', available at: http://www.accel-team.com/motivation/intro.html (accessed 11 March 2008).

Argyris, C. (1980), *Inner Contradictions of Rigorous Research,* New York: Academic Press.

Argyris, M. and Schön, D. (1974), *Theory in Practice: Increasing Professional Effectiveness,* San Francisco, CA: Jossey-Bass.

Aronson, J., Blanton, H. and Cooper, J. (1995), 'From dissonance to disidentification: selectivity in the self-affirmation process', *Journal of Personality and Social Psychology,* **68** (6), 986–96.

Barker, M. and Neailey, K. (1999), 'From individual learning to project team learning and innovation: a structured approach,' *Journal of Workplace Learning,* **11** (2), 60–67.

Barr, P.S., Stimpert, J.L. and Huff, A.S. (1992), 'Cognitive change, strategic action and organisational renewal', *Strategic Management Journal,* **13**, 15–36.

Bindra, D. (1959), *Motivation: A Systematic Reinterpretation,* New York: Ronald Press.

Blackmore, C. (1999), *The Meme Machine,* Oxford: Oxford University Press.

BlessingWhite (2005), 'Employee Engagement Report 2005', available at: http://www.bless ingwhite.com, accessed 9 April 2008.

Bogdanowicz, M.S. and Bailey, E.K. (2002), 'The value of knowledge and the values of the new knowledge worker: generation X in the new economy', *Journal of European Industrial Training,* **26** (2), 125–9.

Bourner, T. (1998), 'More knowledge, new knowledge: the impact on education and training', *Education + Training,* **40** (1), 11–14.

Bronfenbrenner, U. (1979), *The Ecology of Human Development: Experiments by Nature and Design*, Cambridge, MA: Harvard University Press.

Brown, J.D. and Smart, S.A. (1991), 'The self and social conduct: linking self-representations to prosocial behavior', *Journal of Personality and Social* Psychology, **60**, 368–75.

Carson, C.M. (2005), 'A historical view of Douglas McGregor's Theory Y', *Management Decision*, **43** (3), 450–61.

Chandler, D.E. and Kram, K.E. (2005), 'Applying an adult development perspective to developmental networks', *Career Development International*, **10** (6/7), 548–68.

Chua, A.Y.K. (2006), 'The rise and fall of a community of practice: a descriptive case study', *Knowledge and Process Management*, **13** (2), 120–28.

Davies, H., Leung, K.P.T., Luk, S.T.K. and Wong, Y.H. (1995), 'The benefits of "Guanxi": the value of relationships in developing the Chinese market', *Industrial Marketing Management*, **24**, 207–14.

Dawkins, R. (1976), *The Selfish Gene*, 2nd edn 1989, Oxford: Oxford University Press.

de Charms, R. (1968), *Personal Causation: The Internal Affective Determinants of Behaviour*, San Diego, CA: Academic Press.

Deci, E.L. and Ryan, R.M. (1991), *Intrinsic Motivation and Self-Determination in Human Behavior*, New York: Plenum.

Dennett, D.C. (1991), *Consciousness Explained*, Boston, MA: Little Brown.

Dewar, T. (2006), 'Virtual teams, virtually impossible', *Performance Improvement*, **45** (5), 22–7.

Dulworth, M. (2006), 'Enhancing personal and professional development: the role of peer networks', *Employee Relations Today*, **33** (3), 37–41.

Dunning, D., Leuenberger, A. and Sherman, D.A. (1995), 'A new look at motivated inference: are self-serving theories of success a product of motivational forces?', *Journal of Personality and Social Psychology*, **69**, 58–68.

Easterby-Smith, M., Thorpe, R. and Lowe, A. (2002), *Management Research: An Introduction*, 2nd edn, London: Sage.

Eden, K. (2006), 'Building people-centric communities at Oracle', *Knowledge Management Review*, **9** (3), 12–18.

Engels, F. (1941), in G.V. Plekhanoc (ed.), *Fundamental Problems of Marxism*, London: Lawrence & Wishart.

Entwistle, G.H. (2001), *Measuring Effort Expended in the Workplace: Discretionary Effort and Its Relationship to Established Organizational Commitment and Attachment Dimensions*, Boston, MA: Boston University.

Festinger, L. (1957), *A Theory of Cognitive Dissonance*, Palo Alto, CA: Stanford University Press.

Fink, L.S. (2006), 'The Workforce Scorecard: managing human capital to execute strategy', *Mid-American Journal of Business*, **21** (2), 72–3.

Frazee, V. (1998), 'Working with Indians (cross cultural communication)', *Workforce*, **7**, S10–S12.

Gabora, L. (1997), 'The origin and evolution of culture and creativity', *Journal of Memetics – Evolutionary Models of Information Transmission*, **1**, available at: http://www.cpm.mmu. ac.uk/jom-emit/vol1/gabora_1.html (accessed 12 July 2007).

Gadman, S. and Cooper, C. (2005), 'Strategies for collaborating in an interdependent impermanent world', *Leadership and Organization Development Journal*, **26** (1), 23–35.

Garrick, J. and Clegg, S. (2000), 'Knowledge work and the new demands of learning', *Journal of Knowledge Management*, **4** (4), 279–86.

Gaudelli, W. (2001), 'Identity discourse: problems, presuppositions, and educational practice', *International Journal of Sociology and Social Policy*, **21** (3), 60–81.

Geiger, S. and Turley, D. (2005), 'Personal selling as a knowledge-based activity: communities of practice in the sales force', *Irish Journal of Management*, **26** (1), 61–71.

Gorelick, C., April, K. and Milton, N. (2004), *Performance Through Learning: Knowledge Management in Practice*, Burlington, MA: Elsevier Butterworth-Heinemann.

Govindarajulu, N. and Daily, B.F. (2004), 'Motivating employees for environmental improvement', *Industrial Management + Data Systems*, **104** (3/4), 364–72.

Hannan, M.T. and Freeman, J. (1977), 'The population ecology of organizations', *American Journal of Sociology*, **82** (5), 929–64.

Herzberg, F., Mausner, B. and Snyderman, B.B. (1959), *The Motivation to Work*, New York: John Wiley.

Houghton, J.D., Neck, C.P. and Manz, C.C. (2003), 'We think we can, we think we can, we think we can: the impact of thinking patterns and self-efficacy on work team sustainability', *Team Performance Management*, **9** (1), 31–41.

Hull, D. (1990), *Science as a Process: An Evolutionary Account of the Social and Conceptual Development of Science*, Chicago, IL: University of Chicago Press.

Hutton, J.G. (1999), 'The definition, dimensions, and domain of public relations', *Public Relations Review*, **25** (2), 199–214.

Isaac, R.G., Zerbe, W.J. and Pitt, D.C. (2001), 'Leadership and motivation: the effective application of expectancy theory', *Journal of Management Issues*, **13** (2), 212–26.

Kowalski, B. (2003), 'The engagement gap', *Training*, **40** (4), 62.

Lathin, D. (1995), 'In the midst of the re-engineering forest', *Journal for Quality and Participation*, **18**, 56–70.

Lave, J. (1991), *Situating Learning in Communities of Practice: Perspectives of Socially Shared Cognition*, Washington, DC: American Psychological Association.

Lave, J. and Wenger, E. (1991), *Situated Learning: Legitimate Peripheral Participation*, Cambridge: Cambridge University Press.

Lawler, E.E. (1994), *Motivation in Work Organizations*, New York: Jossey-Bass.

Leach, M.A.L. (2001), 'Knowledge building: developing employees through education', *International Journal of Value-Based Management*, **14** (2), 147–56.

Marsden, P. (1998), 'Memetics and social contagion: two side of the same coin?', *Journal of Memetics – Evolutionary Models of Information Transmission*, **2**, available at: http://cfpm.org/jom-emit/1998/vol2/marsden_p.html (accessed 30 July 2009).

Maslow, A.H. (1943), 'A theory of human motivation', *Psychological Review*, **50**, 370–96.

Mayo, E. (1933), *The Human Problems of an Industrial Civilisation*, New York: Macmillan.

McClelland, D.C. (1961), *The Achieving Society*, Princeton, NJ: Van Nostrand.

McGregor, D. (1960), *The Human Side of Enterprise*, New York: McGraw-Hill.

Meirick, P.C. (2005), 'Self-enhancement motivation as a third variable in the relationship between first- and third-person effects', *International Journal of Public Opinion Research*, **17** (4), 473–83.

Meister, J.C. (1998), 'The quest for lifetime employability', *Journal of Business Strategy*, **19** (3), 25–9.

Miller, J.G. (1994), 'Cultural diversity in the morality of caring: individually-oriented versus duty-based interpersonal moral codes', *Cross-Cultural Research. The Journal of Comparative Social Science*, **28** (1), 3–39.

Mitchell, T.R. (1982), 'Motivation: new directions for theory, research and practice', *Academy of Management Review*, **7** (1), 80–89.

Morgan, G. (1996), 'An afterword: is there anything more to be said about metaphor', in D. Grant and C. Oswick (eds), *Metaphor and Organizations*, London: Sage, 227–40.

Murray, H.A. (1938), *Explorations in Personality*, New York: Oxford University Press.

Peppas, S.C., Peppas, S.R. and Jin, K. (1999), 'Choosing the right employee: Chinese vs. US preferences', *Management Decision*, **37** (1), 7–13.

Phillipchuk, J. and Whittaker, J. (1996), 'An Inquiry into the continuing relevance of Herzberg's motivation theory', *Engineering Management Journal*, **8**, 15–20.

Pinder, C.C. (1984), *Work Motivation: Theories, Issues, and Applications*, Chicago, IL: Scott, Foresman.

Posner, B.Z., Hall, J.L. and Harder, J.W. (1986), 'People are our most important resource: encouraging employee development', *Business Horizons*, **29** (5), 52–4.

Powell, W.W. and DiMaggio, P.J. (eds) (1991), *The New Institutionalism in Organizational Analysis*, Chicago, IL and London: Chicago University Press.

Pullins, E.B. and Fine, L.M. (2002), 'How the performance of mentoring activities affects the mentor's job outcomes', *Journal of Personal Selling and Sales Management*, **22** (4), 259–72.

Rampersad, H. (2006), 'Change your organization, start with yourself', *Training and Management Development Methods*, **20** (4), 437–49.

Reisz, S. (2004), 'Mentoring: a cost-effective retention tool', *Catalyst*, Dublin: May/June, 42–7.

Rotter, J.B. (1966), 'Generalized expectancies for internal versus external control of reinforcement', *Psychological Monographs: General and Applied*, 80, p. 609.

Rowley, C., Yukongdi, V. and Qi Wei, J. (2010), 'Managing diversity: women managers in Asia', ch. 11 in M. Özbilgen and J. Syed (eds), *Managing Gender Diversity in Asia: A Research Companion*, Cheltenham, UK and Northampton, MA, USA: Edward Elgar, pp. 183–209.

Scheeres, H. and Rhodes, C. (2006), 'Between cultures: values, training and identity in a manufacturing firm', *Journal of Organizational Change Management*, **19** (2), 223–36.

Scott-Morgan, P. (1994), *The Unwritten Rules of the Game*, New York: McGraw-Hill.

Senge, P.M. (1990), *The Fifth Discipline: The Art and Practice of the Learning Organization*, London: Random House.

Sherman, D.K. and Cohen, G.L. (2006), 'The psychology of self-defense: self-affirmation theory', *Advances in Experimental Social Psychology*, **38**, 183–242.

Snead, K.C. and Harrell, A.M. (1994), 'An application of expectancy theory to explain a manager's intention to use a decision-support system', *Decision Sciences*, **25** (4), 499–513.

Spreitzer, G.M. (2006), 'Leadership development lessons from positive organizational studies', *Organizational Dynamics*, **35** (4), 305–15.

Steele, C.M. (1988), 'The psychology of self-affirmation: sustaining the integrity of the self', *Advances in Experimental Social Psychology*, **21**, 261–302.

Vora, M.K. (2004), 'Creating employee value in a global economy through participation, motivation and development', *Total Quality Management and Business Excellence*, **15** (5), 793–806.

Vroom, V.H. (1964), *Work and Motivation*, New York: Wiley.

Wahba, M.A. and Bridwell, L.G. (1976), 'Maslow reconsidered: a review of research on the need hierarchy theory', *Organizational Behavior and Human Performance*, **15**, 212–40.

Weeks, J. and Galunic, C. (2003), 'A theory of the cultural evolution of the firm: an intra-organizational ecology of memes', *Organization Studies*, **24** (8), 1309–52.

Williams, R. (2000), 'The business of memes: memetic possibilities for marketing and management', *Management Decision*, **38** (4), 272–9.

Wlodkowski, R.J. and Ginsberg, M.B. (1995), *Diversity and Motivation: Culturally Responsive Teaching*, San Francisco, CA: Jossey-Bass.

Wong, Y.H. (1998), 'The dynamic of Guanxi in China', *Singapore Management Review*, **20** (2), 25–42.

Yankelovich, D. and Immerwahr, J. (1983), *Putting the Work Ethic to Work: A Public Agenda Report on Restoring America's Competitive Vitality*, New York: Public Agenda Foundation.

Zheng, T. (2010), 'State management of the sex industry in China's past and present', ch. 14 in M. Özbilgen and J. Syed (eds), *Managing Gender Diversity in Asia: A Research Companion*, Cheltenham, UK and Northampton, MA, USA: Edward Elgar, pp. 250–70.

Appendix 5A   Research questionnaire

PROFESSIONAL NETWORK EXPECTANCY QUESTIONNAIRE
Self-Assessment Tool for Expectancies within Professional Networks

---

The following self-assessment tool is designed to assist you in thinking through critical behaviours in 10 key areas for effectively engaging in, utilising, and creating conducive, value-adding, professional network relationships. Through self-reflection, the tool highlights areas for personal growth, and raises personal awareness with regard to working through a professional network. It will also assist the researcher in establishing a baseline against which to measure future development and success of employees and managers such as yourselves, and gain understanding of the enhancing and mediating effects of expectancies in professional network performance and learning.

INDUSTRY	CURRENT AGE	GENDER	NATIONALITY	ETHNICITY
HIGHEST ORGANISA-TIONAL POSITION	YEARS WORK EXPERIENCE		CURRENT & PRIOR QUALIFICATIONS	
circle YES / NO	circle YES / NO		circle YES / NO	CL% V%
CO-LOCATED WORK EXCLUSIVELY	VIRTUAL WORK EXCLUSIVELY		MIX OF CO-LOCATED & VIRTUAL WORK	APPROX. % MIX

This questionnaire is designed so as to help you to reflect on your own experiences in your professional network (possibly team) in the workplace, that is, the people you draw on, work with and count on, to complete your work successfully. Expectancy refers to a person's strength of belief and conviction about whether or not what they set out to do on a personal level is achievable, and desirable, on a workplace level, of their effort and productivity. Underpinning this expectancy, is the fact that people have different expectations and levels of confidence about what they are capable of doing. Desire and expectation are interwoven, and only mitigated by workplace issues and openness to their expectations, as well as personal self-esteem and self-confidence issues.

Please initially complete the table provided below, in which you rate the ten expectancies we have defined, on a 1 to 5 scale:

(a) *the value of each expectancy to yourself (what value you personally place on a particular expectancy)* (5=exceptionally high personal value to you; 4=high personal value to you; 3=moderate personal value to you; 2=low personal value to you; 1=very low personal value to you); and,
(b) *the value of each expectancy to your workplace (what value you think your workplace would place on a particular expectancy)* (5=exceptionally high personal value to your workplace; 4=high personal value to your workplace; 3=moderate personal value to your workplace; 2=low personal value to your workplace; 1=very low personal value to your workplace).

RATING OF EXPECTANCY VALUE – TO THE INDIVIDUAL & THE WORKPLACE:

EXPECTANCY DEFINITION	PERSONAL VALUE OF EXPECTANCY (II)	VALUE OF EXPECTANCY TO YOUR WORKPLACE (IW)
EFFORT-PERFORMANCE EXPECTANCY (EP): Network member (you) believes that desired levels of performance are possible, given the resources, competencies and skills s/he possesses		
INTERPERSONAL-PERFORMANCE EXPECTANCY (IP): Network member (you) believes that s/he is seen to be assisting, and developing, others		
EFFORT-LEARNING EXPECTANCY (EL): You believe that expended personal effort will have future, value-adding learning benefits		
LEADING-VISIBILITY EXPECTANCY (LV): You are seen to be in step with new trends and the cutting-edge, and acknowledged as being knowledgeable and practising at the forefront		

NETWORK-PERFORMANCE EXPECTANCY (NP): Network member (you) believes that his/her colleagues are committed to the goals and objectives of the network		
INTERNAL-RECOGNITION EXPECTANCY (IR): Network member (you) believes that s/he will be recognised (with little or no financial rewards), both within the network and the greater organisation, for the contribution s/he has made		
MUTUAL-RECIPROCITY EXPECTANCY (MR): Network members returning directly, or indirectly, aid, resources and/or friendship offered by another network member		
INDIVIDUAL-NETWORK LEARNING EXPECTANCY (NL): Network member believes that his or her own personal learning, knowledge and insights are of value, and can contribute, to the network's learning		
PERFORMANCE-OUTCOME EXPECTANCY (PO): Network member (you) believes that what s/he is doing will lead to certain outcomes		
TEAM-SUSTAINABILITY EXPECTANCY (TS): Network member (you) focused on sustaining the network, and its future		

Please now review each item below and fill in the applicable numbers (in the boxes on the right-hand side of the row) that describes, (a) your most appropriate personal response, and (b) your perception of how meaningful each response is to your workplace (please note: there are no right and wrong answers).

(a) Personal Behaviour Legend – pers – (1–5) (b) **ME** – Meaningful to Workplace & Evaluated Legend – wkpl – (1–5):

5	FREQUENTLY
4	SOMETIMES
3	OCCASIONALLY
2	RARELY
1	NEVER

5	MEASURED & REFLECTED IN PERSONAL PERFORMANCE REVIEW, AND CONSIDERED EXTREMELY IMPORTANT
4	MEASURED AND CONSIDERED EXTREMELY IMPORTANT
3	MEASURED AND CONSIDERED IMPORTANT
2	NOT MEASURED, BUT CONSIDERED IMPORTANT
1	NOT MEASURED AT ALL

	SPECIFIC RESPONSES	pers (1–5)	**ME** wkpl (1–5)
EE	Provide network members with the necessary resources, to play meaning roles in something that is quite significant to the network, and/or organisation		
EE	Insist on, and am known to insist on, the same high standards of cooperation as I personally demonstrate in my dealings with my network members		
EE	Seek to involve myself in activities that exposes me to knowledge and learning, that could eventually aid my future career(s), inside my current organisation, or outside of it		
EE	Put aside specific time slots/periods for sharing, informally and formally, personal knowledge and insights with other network members		
EE	Personally play a pivotal role in consistently ensuring the achievement of desired organisational outcomes (that is, I am needed and valuable to organisational success)		

SPECIFIC RESPONSES		pers (1–5)	ME wkpl (1–5)
PE	Show courage and sense of purpose to stand up for what I believe, in pushing for the desired levels of network performance		
PE	When appropriate, honestly acknowledge to my network when I am unable to contribute significantly or am 'lost' (that is, don't fully know what I am doing nor do I know what to do next)		
PE	Believe that, with some effort, I am capable of learning the required amount, and at the required pace, in order to work competently in all workplace eventualities and situations		
PE	Provide accurate and constructive feedback to my network members regarding their understanding or misunderstanding of important milestones relating to our network's work		
PE	In consultation with stakeholders of my network's contribution (not network members), build a coherent set of both achievable-, and stretch, long-term goals for the professional network		

SPECIFIC RESPONSES		pers (1–5)	ME wkpl (1–5)
WG	Purposefully explore unconventional ideas and different approaches that could eventually (currently, or in the future) be important for my network to know		
WG	Monitor whether individual network members proactively seek project engagements, and periods of projects, that suit (are aligned to) their personal team styles		
WG	Consistently work at, and seek through the eliciting of their viewpoints, the integration and alignment of my work goals with the goals of reciprocal (other contributing) members		
WG	Continuously seek to improve network processes and communication to achieve more effective network cooperation and higher levels of reciprocity among network members		

SPECIFIC RESPONSES		pers (1–5)	ME wkpl (1–5)
WG	Build a broad base of support, for my network, among key stakeholders by identifying and positioning ideas to satisfy their needs, interests and concerns		

SPECIFIC RESPONSES		pers (1–5)	ME wkpl (1–5)
EO	Allow for the expression of emotion as it relates to the performance and under-performance of network members, without allowing it to impact negatively on others or the organisation		
EO	Proactively seek out opportunities to assist network members in challenging projects, or help them to do something extra, beyond the minimal requirements of workplace performance		
EO	Prefer non-financial rewards over financial rewards (extended leave, flexible work hours, attend conferences, sent on courses not related to work issues, explicit peer recognition, and so on)		
EO	My preference is for specific recognition and feedback concerning my contribution (not general platitudes & global statements) from other network members		
EO	Consistently demonstrate high levels of respect for my network members in conversations and dealings with other non-members (in & out of the presence of my network members)		

SPECIFIC RESPONSES		pers (1–5)	ME wkpl (1–5)
PC	Regularly feed back new and different information and knowledge to my network members (information and knowledge that they may not have come across)		
PC	Believe that my network members will match my effort in ensuring our shared success in overcoming challenging tasks/ projects or navigating areas not previously ventured into		

SPECIFIC RESPONSES		pers (1–5)	ME wkpl (1–5)
PC	Deal with would-be dominant network individuals, who no longer appear to share the same underlying intent & values of the network (for example, warning, communicate, formal complaint, and so on)		
PC	Share reputation and successes of network members with other networks (inside and outside of organisation)		
PC	Ensure that my network members' personal goals and needs are aligned with the desired network outcome(s), and therefore their needs are gratified when achieved		

SPECIFIC RESPONSES		pers (1–5)	ME wkpl (1–5)
EA	Expend my personal energy and effort only in those things/processes/projects that currently have personal learning benefit for me, or will have in the future		
EA	Actively seek to ensure the transference of my knowledge and insights across, and outside my, discipline/functional boundaries (both within and outside of the organisation)		
EA	Regularly subject my ideas to scrutiny from non-network members (that is, present at conferences, publish in international peer-reviewed journals, write books, and so on)		
EA	Achieve more of the network milestones/goals compared to other network members, given equal access to resources and aid		
EA	Seek to pull knowledgeable people, and sources of learning and knowledge, into my network (who/that do not yet have informal, or formal, membership of my network)		

6 The diversity scenario in Pakistani organizations
Nailah Ayub and Karen Jehn

Introduction

Diversity is being promoted by laws and regulations, immigration and globalization, and at times by economic pressures. In essence, the workforce has always been diverse with regard to some characteristics when individuals with unique qualities and wisdom work towards a common task. Recent trends have brought women into formal professions and facilitated the disabled, and equal opportunities laws have introduced a culturally diverse workforce. Diversity training and practices are being observed while norms and regulations are being reviewed and revised for improvements. Ambitious organizations have included diversity management not only for improvements in organizational achievements but also for their workers' well-being.

Diversity, generally defined as perceived differences, has been advocated by many diversity researchers to be good for effective and productive work groups and organizations (for example, Watson et al., 1993; McLeod et al., 1996; Jehn et al., 1999). On the other hand, others have negative findings regarding diversity, for reasons such as lack of social integration and high turnover (O'Reilly et al., 1989; Jackson et al., 1991), conflict (Jehn et al., 1999; Mannix and Neale, 2005), and demographic differences (Tsui and O'Reilly, 1989; Alexander et al., 1995). Diversity research reveals a collection of contradictory results concerning the effects of diversity on group outcomes (Guzzo and Dickson, 1996; McLeod et al., 1996; Barsade and Gibson, 1998; Williams and O'Reilly, 1998; Jackson et al., 2003; Mannix and Neale, 2005) leaving us with an inconclusive stance about the effects of diversity or when and what type of diversity is helpful.

In contrast to the rather positive side of the picture, research indicates that diversity is not celebrated in reality as desirable for its potential or as required by law. As Lunardini (1996) and Wirth (2002) noted, women still continue to fight for equal rights in the workplace, such as for equal pay, and the opportunity to develop and advance. Minorities and immigrants still face discrimination with regard to selection, evaluation and promotion (Akrami et al., 2000; Syed, 2008a). While all these workplace issues are a matter of concern in countries around the world, certain problems are more worrying in some countries, depending on their internal context-specific situation. Thus there is a need to consider context (Hofstede, 1993), especially the cultural context, when dealing with an issue, be it diversity in the workplace or in the community, or indeed any issue generally.

Diversity at work

Pakistan emerged as an independent state in South Asia from British rule under the leadership of Muhammad Ali Jinnah in 1947. It is a highly diverse country with regard to religion, ethnicity, language, cultural practices and other attributes (see also Syed, 2008b). Islam is the religion of the majority, with few people of minority religions. The Muslims are further segregated into religious groups and sects based on schools of thoughts and jurisprudence. The major ethnic groups are Punjabis, Pathans, Sindhis, Seraikis, Muhajirs and Balochis. In addition, there are about 2 million registered Afghan refugees as of 2007 (NADRA, 2007), while a smaller number of refugees have come from places like Iran, Burma and Tajikistan. Urdu is the national language and lingua franca, but English is the official language, although it is spoken only by the educated elite. There are 75–80 known local languages. With Punjabi as the largest indigenous language, other significant languages spoken include Pashto, Sindhi, Seraiki and Balochi. These ethnic groups and languages, among other characteristics, contribute to the very diverse cultural scenario.

Pakistan's history has been characterized by periods of economic growth, military rule and political instability. Goldman Sachs identified Pakistan as one of the next 11 countries having the potential of becoming among the world's largest economies along with Brazil, Russia, India and China (*Daily Times*, 2006). Agriculture accounts for approximately 20 percent of the GDP, while the services sector accounts for 53 percent. Among the world's emerging markets, the Karachi Stock Exchange has also increased in value. Major industries include software, automotives, textiles, cement, fertilizer, steel, ship building and aerospace. Foreign investments have been made in several areas including telecommunications, real estate and energy (*Pak Tribune*, 2007). However, considering the high inflation rate, government deficit, external debts, political instability and corruption, Pakistan remains one of the lowest performers. The poverty rate is estimated to be between 23 and 28 percent (World Bank, 2006), with continued inflationary pressures making it difficult to sustain a high growth rate.

Jinnah, the founder of Pakistan, hoped that Pakistan would profit from its diversity. When asking for unity, faith and discipline (Jinnah 1947 [1989], p. 118), Jinnah was well aware of the diverse characteristics that the country had inherited and hoped that Pakistanis would unite despite their diversity – of course, diversity would remain and should be respected:

> You are free; you are free to go to your temples. You are free to go to your mosques or to any other place of worship in this State of Pakistan. You may belong to any religion or caste or creed – that has nothing to do with the business of the State.

Jinnah was optimistic about the positive change and continued: 'We should begin to work in that spirit and in the course of time all these angularities of the majority and minority communities will vanish' (Ibid., pp. 46–7).

In addition to discouraging religious- or ethnicity-based segregation or discrimination, Jinnah recognized the significance of younger people and women. He looked to the youth to educate themselves and contribute towards the prosperity of the country: 'My young friends, I look forward to you as the real makers of Pakistan . . . Set an example of what youth can do' (Jinnah, 1948). Jinnah repeatedly emphasized the role of women as shown by several of his statements. For example,

> I have always maintained that no nation can ever be worthy of its existence that cannot take its women along with the men. No struggle can ever succeed without women participating side by side with men. There are two powers in the world: one is the sword and the other is the pen. There is a great competition and rivalry between the two. There is a third power stronger than both, that of the women. (Jinnah 1940 [1996], p. 1189)

Jinnah's comments, along with several others that he made, unfortunately are ignored as guidelines in the present Pakistan. Unrest, distress and conflict prevail between subgroups formed on the basis of religion and ethnicity in all kinds of groups including in the workplace.

The diversity scenario

A survey of 193 university students was carried out to reflect the diversity characteristics of the potential workforce. The students were aged between 20 and 26 years with a mean and median of 22 and included 55 females (28.5 percent). The students reported at least eight ethnic categories, namely Punjabi (71.0 percent), Pathan (6.7 percent), Saraiki (4.7 percent), Urdu-speaking (3.6 percent), Sindhi (3.1 percent), Kashmiri and non-Pathan inhabitants of the Northwestern Frontier Province (2.6 percent of each), and Baloch (2.1 percent). Since the universities are located in the Punjab province, the majority of the students are Punjabis. At least nine castes were reported by six or more students and 29 other castes, such that there were 38 different castes reported in total. Seven languages were identified as the mother tongue (reported by five or more students) with Punjabi and Urdu as the first and second most reported, respectively. Although all the students reported Islam as their religion, there was a diversity of religious sects. Whereas 28 refused to respond, six asserted that they did not believe in sect and preferred to be identified as Muslims only. The majority of the sample described themselves as Sunni (44.6 percent) and others were even more specific and described themselves as Brelvi and Deobandi (subsects of Sunni), while others identified themselves as belonging to the Jaafri, Ahle-Hadith or Ahle-Sunnat schools of faith. Eight different sects were reported by five or more students.

The students claimed to have a somewhat high belief in diversity (belief in the value of diversity for the group's functioning; van Knippenberg and Haslam, 2003; Homan et al., 2010). Although the students on average showed openness to diversity, direct observations were somewhat different. There was clear gender segregation in the lecture rooms with regard to seating and in discussions. While some participated reluctantly, four students refused to participate at all in the group discussion exercise that was conducted along with the survey questionnaires. After cautious inquiry, we learned that these students would not sit in a group with women. They believed it was religiously and socially objectionable to interact with women. The flexibility of the students could be ascertained through the choices they made during the discussion exercise. They were asked to choose a nationality to work with and then they were put into groups to discuss their individual choices. After the discussion, they were asked to write down the group's choice and then choose again as an individual. Out of the 67 students with individual choices different from that of the group's choice, 34 decided to stay with their individual choice while 18 changed their individual choice after the group discussion in consensus with the group's choice. The diversity beliefs and the decision to change shows that people will change if there are effective change strategies with adequate information available and the opportunity to learn.

In order to investigate those who have already entered the real workplace, we conducted a survey with employees of an IT industry in Islamabad, the capital city of Pakistan. The sample consisted of 137 employees with a mean age of 29.58 years, including 23 females (8.4 percent). The participants reported six languages, 11 ethnicities, 30 castes, and three major religious sects (the students had been more specific in reporting religious sects and subsects. It was unclear whether the working respondents were being more careful in revealing their religious beliefs). Correlation coefficients computed with the help of SPSS software showed that when the members perceived ethnic diversity in their work groups, they also perceived less respect, less cooperation, less trust, and that the group members liked each other less as compared to ethnically homogenous groups. In addition, the employees who perceived high ethnic diversity in their work groups reported less satisfaction, less group performance, and less efficiency. With the lack of perceived respect and cooperation, there was a greater chance of more task-related conflict as well as interpersonal conflict. Such conflicts were likely to influence intragroup feelings and emotions negatively (trust, helping behavior, liking, satisfaction, happiness), and in turn the group performance as shown by significant correlations for the sample data. When religious diversity was perceived, members perceived less respect, less trust and less group performance than groups with religious homogeneity. Perceived gender diversity was associated with less cooperation, less trust and less liking among the group members. Considering the actual diversity in the groups, we observed that the results were significant when diversity was subjectively perceived compared to the actual group composition. This denotes the importance of perception of differences in studying any kind of differences (Greer and Jehn, 2008; Zellmer-Bruhn et al., 2008).

Diversity and diversity issues: views of the managed and the managers

Since we were curious to know what the working people understood by diversity, we conducted semi-structured interviews with people working in different cities of Pakistan. Below, we shall share some comments of the managers and the managed on diversity in the workplace. We learned that differences based on a variety of demographics were recognized in the work groups. Interestingly, one manager (human resource management services) defined diversity as 'difference, variety, and inequality'. Apparently, he believed that differences endorsed inequalities; that is, inequality is to be expected whenever there is diversity.

When asked about diversity characteristics that were present in their work groups, gender, age, ethnicity, religious sects, language, culture, caste, racial divisions, disability, education and personality were listed by almost every interviewed worker and manager. Only two of the men listed gender diversity while everyone referred to ethnicity. To explain the concept of diversity, one manager stated, 'A team of people consisting of Punjabis, Sindhis, and Pathans is a diverse group'. A senior scientist noted that less than 5 percent at his workplace were females and that there was not a single worker from a particular province of Pakistan.

A manager at a government institute also noted that 'diversity is more common in larger cities while the remote areas are still suffering from "ancient" rules and regulations where men and women cannot work together (except for the family). In these villages, outsiders are not usually welcomed either'. Workplace diversity in Pakistan is more a character of cities, reflecting perhaps, upon the economic pressure that drives all kind of city dwellers to work. It is more usual to own agricultural land in the villages where women work for their family within the limits of their property (thus not really violating the rule of staying within designated boundaries). These women are neither paid nor appreciated for their work.

Some more interesting diversity characteristics noted were socio-economic status and political ideology. Workers could be highly segregated depending upon their residential location and type of residence as well as the amount of wealth possessed (that is, socio-economic status) even if they held the same qualifications or had the same job status. Having other things in common, political ideology and identification or affiliation with a particular political party was another strong difference that divides people into different groups and is a source of fierce conflict among Pakistani workers.

An engineer depicted the language diversity situation in the workplace as follows: 'There should be no restriction on any individual for speaking his/her mother tongue but the case is different at our workplaces'. Interestingly enough, he followed up with reasons for his own interaction preferences for those who speak the same language: 'People speaking the same language can interact with each other much more easily as compared to the other people who speak a different language'. Another engineer divulged: 'The people speaking the same language support each other. . . . It has created groups and sometimes people get advantages due to their language only'. While the discontent about subgroup formation is not directly job-related, we know from research that categorizations among work-group members increase conflict, which reduces cohesion, communication and consequently group performance (for example, Tsui et al., 1992; Pelled et al., 1999).

When asked about the diversity issues, it appeared that Pakistani workers do not have a problem with diversity itself; indeed, the overall response is positive. For example, one manager describes his diversity belief as follows: 'People of different backgrounds bring in different opinions and open up the workplace to new ideas'. He then mentioned the negative current situation, 'Unfortunately, people are unable to speak up and present their suggestions to the management in Pakistan, therefore limiting the influx of change'. Pakistanis realize that diversity has become an essential element of the workplace through increased social and economic needs, education and awareness, and global interaction, and thus should be facilitated through rules and a change in attitude. They are actually troubled, as indicated by several of those interviewed, by the many issues introduced by unmanaged diversity. Then they tended to question whether diversity is a good thing, and if a hired woman who has replaced a man was for the general good. The issues that came up during the interviews included, among others, forced obedience. The disadvantaged or the minority must conform and obey in order to survive in a job (for example, a Pathan in a Punjabi dominant work group). More than once, we were told of a series of incidents where the member of an ethnic group in a minority situation was forced to leave the job because of continuing tensions with the majority ethnic group members. For example, a Pathan had to leave a Punjabi-dominated work group in the Islamabad area. On the other hand, a Punjabi found it very difficult to be in a Pathan-dominated work group in Peshawar, particularly because of his/her inability to speak their language; 'if you are living in Peshawar, you have to learn Pashto [language] to live there comfortably'. A senior scientist (Hindko-speaking) described an exchange with a Pathan who was curious about the miserable conditions that Pathans experienced in Punjab. He had heard stories about how Pathans were viciously discriminated against by Punjabis. The scientist, in turn, left the Pathan speechless by asking him if he could justify the same discrimination that a Punjabi might experience in Peshawar. Such discrimination, whether true or alleged, has caused a huge rift between the different ethnicities, and is usually based on a lack of mutual understanding and negative stereotypes that must be addressed in the organizational set-up as well as in communities at large. The lessons of tolerance, adaptability and flexibility also need to be revised.

Several issues related to diversity in the workplace were raised in the following statement of a worker:

> The Pakistani workplace is a male-dominated community and women are not encouraged to work. It is becoming more acceptable for women to work in larger cities, but they are hugely outnumbered and do not enjoy high-paying jobs with increased responsibility. People of religions other than Islam face severe discrimination, and even cultural diversity is not widely accepted. A Punjabi is less likely to accept a Sindhi worker than another Punjabi. . . . The limited diversity has not opened up the Pakistani workplace to new ideas and challenges.

With regard to religious minorities, one engineer commented: 'Pakistan is a declared Islamic state but people of other religions also live here as minorities. The rights of these minorities have the protection of law but enforcement of law in itself is doubtful in Pakistan'. The conflict is not only between Muslims and non-Muslims – one worker noted that there were strong clashes based on religious sects that exist within Muslims. Although completely irrelevant to the tasks and work responsibilities, differences in religious beliefs have a heavy impact on the work groups through subgrouping or coalition formation, and unwillingness to cooperate, assist, or communicate with those of a different religious school of thought or sect. Montalvo and Reynal-Querol (2005) noted that ethnic and religious segregation largely affects economic development and increases the probability of civil conflict. In organizations, ethnic and religious differences are apparently negatively affecting performance and causing interpersonal conflict.

In response to the diversity issues, both workers and managers had similar suggestions. One worker commented:

> Cultural and language barriers need to be overcome for diversity to deliver positive effects. Ineffective communication results in confusion, lack of teamwork, and low morale. Resistance to attitude change can be commonly witnessed in Pakistan. We have heard people saying that 'we've always done it this way'.

Similarly, an engineer remarked that grouping based on language or caste should be discouraged.

The majority of those interviewed agreed that lack of education or awareness is a major hurdle, as described by an IT manager:

> Lack of education is probably the biggest issue. The general public does not understand what diversity is and its benefits to the organization and the society as a whole. Even most managers do not understand or fully grasp the potential of a diverse workforce. In most cases, the manager himself/herself is not educated about the benefits of diversity. Misunderstanding and/or misrepresentation of the Islamic religion is also a hurdle. Women are strictly prohibited in some areas from even thinking about working, let alone diversity.

Another worker from an agricultural research institute added that there are no standard diversity management practices and every manager enjoys his/her own power over the workers: 'Pakistani workplaces are mainly based on one's own experience or will, which may not be correct. Policies do exist but are rarely followed, and there is a strong practice of bossism. . . . There is a general attitude of creating problems instead of helping each other'. Unemployment and socio-economic stresses have had various negative effects, arising from intense competition over acquiring and holding on to a job. Creating problems, favoring the 'ingroup members', leg-pulling of the 'outgroup' members, low cooperation, and fierce conflicts are some of the common grievances.

'Diversity is bad' commented one worker when asked if diversity was improving work performance. A research officer explained that he believed that diversity can be good in principle, but that is not what he sees in practice as a result of a diverse workplace: 'Diversity is there, but there are several issues and generally it has negative rather than positive effects'.

The next question related to how diversity was being managed in

Pakistan. Every respondent, with the exception of three, denied knowledge of any such practices. The problems that arise are handled on an individual basis and only after they have arisen. Even after a problem has been identified, the general management does not revise its practices in favor of future improvements. There is a strong power hierarchy, which is impossible to challenge or bypass. This power hierarchy and the biased practices of those in power discourage diversity and ignore its potential in Pakistani organizations. One manager commented: 'A vast majority of local companies do not really care for diversity and curb any kind of input from anyone'.

Diversity management: views of the managed and the managers

The government has taken some steps to promote diversity and inclusion. Laws and regulations exist, and some effort to promote equal opportunity is somewhat apparent. The most prominent example is the quota system that sets a fixed number of seats for women in parliament; promotes women, the disabled, and provincial/ethnic representations in the workplace; and supports provincial/ethnic admission to educational institutions. The First Women Bank was introduced to encourage women to enter into the banking profession with assured workplace security, especially freedom from harassment. Furthermore, the armed forces and the police have started recruiting women into certain departments.

Women are now participating in almost every industry, depending on accessibility and approach (with regard to the socio-economic and cultural context that encourages/discourages women in different locales). 'Gender diversity is being encouraged in Pakistan, but being a patriarchal and a conservative society in general, the social system is an obstacle for such diversity growth' is a reflection of the women's comments on gender equality and opportunity but was mentioned by only a few of the men. Ironically, women themselves discourage other women from working or seeking an education: 'You are continuing with your higher education because you haven't been able to get married' is a common remark, and was even made by a female professor of psychology who taught one of the authors. It is a common observation that women become accustomed to social limitations and accept the patriarchal practice that is an integral part of their personal experience.

The disabled are discouraged from contributing to the economy, except as a beggar in poor families. A combination of gender and disability is certainly a recipe for disaster. A disabled friend (in a wheelchair), who has a Master of Psychology degree, was unsuccessfully interviewed for several jobs before giving up. She was advised to forget working and stay at home as she would be unable to perform satisfactorily in any job because of her mobility issues. The problems that job seekers and job holders face in a diverse workplace are what makes diversity disagreeable, especially when it is not managed properly and effectively, leaving workers aggrieved, burned out, or even unemployed.

One question asked whether there were diversity management practices, and if so, were they effective? Once again, the responses were not very positive, and most of them can be represented by an IT manager's comments:

> No! Pakistan has a long way to go towards understanding diversity. It is not effectively managed due largely to lack of education. Very few people understand what diversity is (those who do are usually educated overseas) and its benefits. Women are a minority and suppressed, religious bias is everywhere, as well as cultural discrimination.

A few respondents mentioned some diversity management efforts that have been made in private organizations for 'economic reasons'. One manager from an agriculture research institute stated that private organizations are more concerned with their profit and production, while public organizations are still largely indifferent as the government is not directly affected by their progress. A manager associated with a multinational project commented: 'Very little [is being done regarding diversity management]. Only the foreign companies in Pakistan have embraced the idea of a diverse workplace'. Another manager recognized some management measures: 'All those organizations/groups who have accepted the change are making progress, while those following the same path are still faced with problems and inefficiency'. This comment shows that diversity initiatives, if taken, can also be effective in Pakistani organizations.

Diversity management: recommendations from managers
The diversity issues described by the interviewees are precisely the issues that require proper management in Pakistani organizations. The main points include conflicts between ethnic (and linguistic) and religious groups, gender discrimination and harassment, biased behavior and favoritism, and grievances regarding unequal employment opportunities as well as unequal treatment and unjust promotion (due to favoritism and discrimination).

Expressing their views on diversity and related issues, the managers had suggestions for diversity management: 'Pakistani society is multilingual and multicultural, and sectarian in nature. [We need to] create a balance between the people and induce law or power in this regard so that management issues of diversity in Pakistan are settled'. It is obvious from this bank manager's statement and the quotes above, that the major diversity issue is that of differences and conflicts based on ethnicity and religious sects, perhaps even more than gender discrimination and harassment. 'Grouping based on language should not be encouraged' was a suggestion by a worker troubled by discrimination based on language differences. The necessary steps to be taken should include discouraging subgroup formation on the basis of race, ethnicity, language, or religious beliefs.

The majority of the interviewees stressed the need for diversity education and management training. 'Recognizing the issues concerned with diversity is the first requirement and only then can there be a second step' was the comment of a research officer. It is evident that lack of awareness, lack of empowerment, and lack of commitment to change are the major hurdles to addressing diversity issues in Pakistani organizations. Based on our observations through the surveys and the interviews, we shall now discuss some diversity management models and strategies that have been proposed and put into practice elsewhere, and that might be used for effective diversity management within Pakistani organizations using a context-sensitive approach.

Recommendations for diversity management
Diversity in itself is perhaps not such an issue, at least in the cities of Pakistan, as other factors that have been mentioned. Organizations experience the differences (such as those of gender, ethnicity and religion) but not the diversity that can be beneficial to the organization. We shall present a recap of the diversity issues in the words of an interviewee. Presently serving on the board of directors of an organization, the interviewee was clearly frustrated and aggrieved about the present situation but with a strong desire for improvement:

> I can say with confidence that there is no real desire to bring about diversity in the Pakistani workplace. Statutory provisions aside, there have been no concrete efforts in the public sector to promote diversity . . . I am not aware of any specific efforts towards ensuring diversity across the nation. When it comes down to statistics from Baluchistan, interior Sindh, FATA [federally administered tribal areas], FANA [federally administered northern areas] and some parts of Punjab, the very idea of 'workplace' changes altogether. Suppression, repression, subjugation, utter discrimination and abuse are the common norms. No diversity, no rights are the orders . . . Economic crises, a worsening law and order situation, political void, regional hostility, provincial unrest, the absence of ethnic harmony, political animosity, unbearable poverty, nepotism, and many such menaces are our problem. . . . The notion of diversity needs to be understood first. Organizations and businesses need to be convinced of diversity and its benefits. All entities should be educated and encouraged to envisage diversity programs and their implementation. There must be repercussions against discrimination and harassment at the workplace . . . Stereotyping, biases and discrimination must be addressed, and addressed with conviction.

The above quote covers everything that needs to be managed. First, there is a need to gain knowledge about diversity, accept it through improved attitudes toward those who are different, and develop the necessary skills for responsive experiences (Manning, 2000). Pakistani organizations need to transform themselves and not merely change, that is, there is a need to revise the whole structure, system, vision and attitudes (Plantenga, 2004). Dealing with individual problems and incidents or getting rid of the individual problem creators will not help to bring about positive change. Pakistani organizations need structured diversity initiatives to formulate a business strategy, for implementation and for managerial practice (Davidson, 1999) with clear lines of communication to the employees who are involved in the system and recognized as respected members. When designing these policies and strategies, the management must take into account the full context of the employees, including work, educational institution, and social and family situation.

Before discussing recommendations, we shall share our experience of diversity research, which will help future research as well as diversity planning and management initiatives in Pakistani organizations. First, there are no research measures available in the Pakistani context. We need to translate and adapt measures according to situational needs. That is, an English measure need not be translated if it is used at higher organizational levels in the larger cities. The economic situation has greatly de-motivated Pakistanis in general. This general social and economic pessimism makes it difficult for one to be convinced that a research study will bring about any positive change in the set-up. Information sharing will not occur without a solid incentive. Even the management do not believe that research will benefit the organization in any way, and thus any research is considered a waste of time. Rather, the general distrust (regarding confidentiality and anonymity) leads to instant suspicion about the research purposes and consequences, and thus a reluctance to participate or respond honestly. Almost all organizational levels are 'closed' to research, because of skepticism and a lack of appreciation for its potential. The political situation in and outside of Pakistan discourages non-Pakistani researchers from approaching an organization. Even a local researcher cannot conduct research without a strong network with those in power (political or organizational). Personal contacts are essential to obtain permission for conducting a research study. In order to convince the management to cooperate, there must be a strong demonstration of the practical benefits that any study can offer. Once permission is obtained, a detailed research orientation is required to inform the workers and managers about the research and how they can participate, even if it is a simple survey study. The offer of a physical reward can increase the participation rate as well as motivate involvement. Feedback and recommendations must follow data collection so that the organization can benefit from the study and be more receptive to further research. People will participate more if they are shown the benefits of research. While we recognize the need for diversity research, we shall now return to diversity management which requires urgent attention in Pakistani organizations.

Interaction with a willingness to learn will help to bring about improvement in the negative attitudes that currently prevail among Pakistani workers. Social interaction is especially important in the collectivist culture since it is known to enhance performance in diverse groups (Chatman et al., 1998). A careful formal recategorization beginning with an introductory orientation to avoid anxiety and conflict will help to discourage subgroup segregation and encourage mutual cooperation as well as learning. Such orientation is important to explain the purpose of creating job-focused groups and for the active cognizant involvement of the group members. Several researchers have elaborated recategorizations with the help of inclusive group boundaries to reduce the negative effects of intergroup biases (for example, Kramer and Brewer, 1984; Polzer et al., 1999).

Any recategorization should be carefully introduced so that personal identities are not neglected or disregarded. Plantenga (2004) noted that the different identities a person has (for example, gender, ethnicity, class, religion) are all interconnected and are inseparable. All these must be considered together while planning for diversity management. The differences that divide a group are unique to that group and each aspect should be scrutinized to ensure a clear understanding of the situation. The training methodology proposed by Plantenga includes four core principles: focus on people as central to the process of learning and change; acknowledge diversity and the inherent patterns of dominance; empower individuals as well as groups; and recognize and break the dichotomous perceptions in thinking. 'Pakistan-First' was a slogan used in an attempt to unite all Pakistanis incorporating all the differences within their personal identity, but the majority of Pakistanis did not seem to identify with the slogan. The slogan probably served as a rather superordinate identity (Mackie and Goethels, 1987; Ashforth and Mael, 1989) that has been opposed by those researchers who believe that the idea denies the very potential of diversity by de-emphasizing the differences or distinctiveness of identity (Swann et al., 2004). Jackson and Ruderman (1995), however, noticed that the common ingroup identity model (Gaertner et al., 1993) could be used to enhance common group membership over differentiated categories without refuting or discounting primary identities as the basis for loyalties and attachments. Pakistanis identify with their country, but every Pakistani also has multiple identities that are more or less relevant within a context. Pakistan-First, according to some Pakistanis, should have been Muslim-First or Punjabi-First based on the perceived political or geographical context and the religious or cultural identity. Not denying the promise of superordinate identity, any such identity should be introduced with a clear orientation with a personal motive and meaning. For example, a woman or a person from a different ethnic group could be included in a work group as an equally capable and qualified employee, and not as a woman or a member of a particular ethnicity. The group should then be encouraged and facilitated to cooperate in order to accomplish interdependent tasks. Strategies must be undertaken to keep the focus on positive inclusion where every member is perceived as equally important for the group performance. These may include announcements where individual performance is clearly related to group performance; incentives for the best group rather than for individuals; and norms and incentives as well as a formal structure for cooperation and collaboration in place of individual progress.

Trust, respect, cooperation and mutual understanding are absent in Pakistani work groups. Trust is not only important for a group's co-operation and cohesion but is also an important requirement for change. Respect gives reassurance and serves for the self-verification purposes of the members that everyone is accepted and included as a significant member of the group. Without trust and respect, it is difficult to foster a spirit of cooperation, and yet cooperation is crucial for group functioning and progress (Jackson, 1991; Byrne, 1993; Smith et al., 1995). The economic and employment facts of Pakistan show that members will remain in a group whether they like it or not for the sake of retaining their job, but cooperation is likely to be low. Chen et al. (1998) discuss cooperation with regard to the common group identity and superordinate identity (Gaertner and Dovidio, 2000; Gaertner et al., 2000), specifically in collectivist cultures. They believe that within a culture, cooperation may be fostered through establishing positive goal relationships among the members. That is, the focus should be on a task-directed relationship and then we should also expect change to occur at the interpersonal and attitudinal levels as well. While trust may induce cooperation, we believe task-focused cooperation will also improve trust. The path from cooperation to trust seems more viable, than otherwise, at least in Pakistani work groups where the members are mutually distrustful but must work together. Rewards and incentives are two of the most attractive options that a job can offer. Again, the reward and incentive structure can be used as group complementarity mechanisms to improve group cooperation and communication (for reviews of cooperation mechanisms, see Messick and Brewer, 1983; Komorita and Parks, 1999).

In the light of the interviews and survey findings, accountability is strongly needed in Pakistani organizations at present. Affirmative action of monitoring and follow-up corrective measures (Crosby et al., 2006) in personnel selection and promotions should be encouraged. Accountability is necessary to benefit diversity (Welle and Lyness, 2002) and quell the great distrust that currently prevails among the workers. Accountability by itself, however, is not sufficient to bring about the desired change or transformation. Fear of accountability may only serve to make workers and managers more cautious about displaying a prejudicial or discriminatory attitude. Instead, trust, respect, openness, communication, interpersonal contact and learning, and social integration are more likely to bring about positive change and highlight the value of diversity. An effective accountability program requires a carefully designed managerial training and assessment (see Bielby, 2008), with transparent accountability of management and top leadership perhaps more important than subordinate liability. In the prevailing strong power hierarchy, the top levels are expected to institute changes and regulations while subordinates do not consider themselves capable of being, and thus are not expected to be, the agents of change. Even if subordinates are unhappy with the system, they would merely await a change from above since the higher-ups are seen as the agents responsible for change (Zemba et al., 2006). Also, those in a powerful position would be unlikely to tolerate any protest from the lower levels, and indeed tend to suppress any attempt to enforce change for fear of empowerment of the workers and resistance against the management. Therefore, a flatter hierarchy is unlikely to be an effective initial action. Nor does informal mentoring seem to help the present Pakistani situation, which is corrupt with nepotism and social, cultural, ethnic and religious biases (see Pelled and Xin, 1997). Even formal mentoring seems inappropriate, since the organizations are completely new to the idea. To begin with, a flexible work environment with interdependent job-sharing work could be encouraged that portrays the benefits of teamwork and encourages information sharing and cooperative learning (for example, Johnson and Johnson, 1983). Recognition awards should be announced based on a variety of criteria including task-related behaviors as well as behaviors that help promote diversity (such as diversity affirmative actions, cooperation, helping, information sharing, and citizenship behavior). Such action may help to develop a communal feeling that reduces the tendency to categorize and discourages biases.

Recognizing the moral dilemmas and emotional turmoil that women in Pakistani organizations experience, Syed (2008b) offers an emotion regulation model using Grandey's (2000) perspective as a guide. Somewhat similar to 'rooting' (staying with one's identity) and 'shifting' (accommodating with the group), the model explains the emotion regulation process, which is likely to lead to burnout and low job satisfaction at the individual level and may also affect the overall performance of the organization. Clearly, if a worker is uncomfortable with the emotional adjustments or compromises that s/he makes at work, it will take its toll in some form. Note again the necessity of providing a safe environment (social and organizational) over and above the opportunity to work, in order to encourage and sustain diversity in the workplace. Syed (2008b) suggests provision of job autonomy and supervisor and co-worker support as helping factors for women in Pakistani organizations. In the interviews we conducted, the majority of respondents expressed dissatisfaction with the management. This means that trust-building efforts should be made between the management and their subordinates, especially since any desirable change would occur only if it is supported by and clearly identified with the top leadership and integrated into the organizational culture (Rapoport et al., 2002).

Syed (2008c) emphasizes the need for a context-sensitive approach to the employment opportunity concept in a Muslim context while discussing the challenges of 'orientalist' bias and a number of schools of thought within the Islamic religion. In view of the social and cultural practices and the status of women in countries like Pakistan, Syed (ibid.) offers a transition model from Islamic orthodox to Islamic modernist so that the change can be identified as one's own and does not offend local value systems while improving women's economic contribution. Realizing the historical, political and socio-economic specificities of a national context in which the individuals, the organizations, and the national structures are interrelated, Syed and Özbilgin (2009) advocate a multilevel relational approach to the context-specific transfer of management practices that takes into consideration the national structure and institutions. Their propositions start with the acknowledgment that the local context shapes diversity management practices, and emphasize the relational perspective as the link between research and practice. What follows is a discussion of macro, meso and micro levels of organizational context, thus leading to the propositions that management policies and practices should take into account the individual-level relationships and micro-politics of the organization while keeping under consideration the macro-national context as well as the history.

The description and issues of diversity discussed above show that several diversity characteristics are already present in Pakistani organizations with or without formal efforts, but, there are no structured diversity management programs. None of those interviewed denied the potential benefits of diversity, but all lamented the inability to profit from it due to ineffective management practices or lack of awareness. The discussion of possible management strategies shows that it is important to recognize and respect the multiple identities and the social cultures of the employees while considering any change strategy. Pakistani organizations seriously need to adopt an integration-and-learning perspective (Thomas and Ely, 1996; Ely and Thomas, 2001) with an enthusiastic leadership committed to diversity, organizational policies and practices where diversity is connected to work-related values, and an organizational culture that promotes openness and respect allowing for personal development (see also Mannix and Neale, 2005; Sabattini and Crosby, 2008).

Any management or training program must start with an orientation that highlights the positive potential of the change to the benefit of all, in order to achieve an informed change with an understanding of value in diversity and a commitment to diversity, and at the same time to avoid resistance. For a commitment to diversity program, the organizations need reassurance, especially in view of the economic crises in Pakistan, that a change will certainly help and not hurt the economic situation. To reduce the negative intergroup biases, there is a need for training and activities that will familiarize staff with other groups, engagement in positive behavior towards outgroup members, creation of positive emotions through intergroup friendships, gaining insights about the ingroup in the presence of social sanctions (Pettigrew, 1998; Jackson et al., 2003), and fostering appropriate mutual adaptation (Thomas, 1995). Kulik and Roberson (2008) describe an approach involving affirmative action, diversity training, awareness training, skill training and mentoring. All of these approaches can be adapted but perhaps awareness training is more crucial than mentoring, at present. Perhaps mentoring can be considered in organizations where other more important diversity initiatives and prejudice reduction targets have already been achieved. First and foremost, Pakistani organizations need awareness, empowerment and a commitment to change.

References

Akrami, N., Ekehammar, B. and Araya, T. (2000), 'Classical and modern racial prejudice: a study of attitudes towards immigrants in Sweden', *European Journal of Social Psychology*, **30** (4), 521–32.

Alexander, J., Nuchols, B., Bloom, J. and Lee, S. (1995), 'Organizational demography and turnover: an examination of multiform and nonlinear heterogeneity', *Human Relations*, **48** (12), 1455–80.

Ashforth, B.E. and Mael, F. (1989), 'Social identity theory and the organization', *Academy of Management Review*, **14**, 20–39.

Barsade, S.G. and Gibson, D.E. (1998), 'Group emotion: a view from top and bottom', *Research on Managing Groups and Teams*, **1**, 81–102.

Bielby, W.T. (2008), 'Promoting racial diversity at work: challenges and solutions', in A.P. Brief (ed.), *Diversity at Work*, Cambridge: Cambridge University Press, pp. 53–86.

Byrne, J. (1993), 'The horizontal corporation', *Business Week*, December 20, 76–81.

Chatman, J.A., Polzer, J.T., Barsade, S.G. and Neale, M.A. (1998), 'Being different yet feeling similar: the influence of demographic composition and organizational culture on work processes and outcomes', *Administrative Science Quarterly*, **43** (4), 749–80.

Chen, C.C., Chen, X. and Meindl, J. R. (1998), 'How can cooperation be fostered? The cultural effects of individualism–collectivism', *Academy of Management Review*, **23** (2), 285–304.

Crosby, F.J., Iyer, A. and Sincharoen, S. (2006), 'Understanding affirmative action', *Annual Review of Psychology*, **57**, 585–611.

Daily Times (2006), 'Growth potential of emerging economies: Pakistan asked to put in place long term initiatives', December 21, available at http://www.dailytimes.com.pk/default.asp?page=2006%5C12%5C21%5Cstory_21-12-2006_pg5_1 (accessed October 25, 2008).

Davidson, M.N. (1999), 'The value of being included: an examination of diversity change initiatives in organizations', *Performance Improvement Quarterly*, **12**, 164–80.

Ely, R. and Thomas, D. (2001), 'Cultural diversity at work: the effects of diversity perspectives on workgroup processes and outcomes', *Administrative Science Quarterly*, **46**, 229–73.

Gaertner, S.L. and Dovidio, J.F. (2000), *Reducing Intergroup Bias: The Common Ingroup Identity Model*, Philadelphia, PA: Psychology Press.

Gaertner, S.L., Dovido, J.F., Anastasio, P.A., Bachman, B.A. and Rust, M.C. (1993). 'The common ingroup identity model: recategorization and the reduction of intergroup bias', in W. Stroebe and M. Hewstone (eds), *European Review of Social Psychology*, Volume 4, Chichester: Wiley, pp. 1–26.

Gaertner, S.L., Dovidio, J.F., Banker, B.S., Houlette, M., Johnson, K.M. and McGlynn, E.A. (2000), 'Reducing intergroup conflict: from superordinate goals to decategorization, recategorization, and mutual differentiation', *Group Dynamics: Theory, Research, and Practice*, **4** (1), 98–114.

Grandey, A.A. (2000), 'Emotion regulation in the workplace: a new way to conceptualize emotional labor', *Journal of Occupational Health Psychology*, **5** (1), 95–110.

Greer, L.L. and Jehn, K.A. (2008), 'Where perception meets reality: the effects of different types of faultline perceptions, asymmetries, and realities on intersubgroup conflict and group outcomes', *Academy of Management Best Paper Proceedings*, Washington, DC: Academy of Management.

Guzzo, R.A. and Dickson, M.W. (1996), 'Teams in organizations: recent research on performance and effectiveness', *Annual Review of Psychology*, **47**, 307–38.

Hofstede, G. (1993), 'Cultural constraints in management theories', *Academy of Management Executive*, **7** (1), 81–94.

Homan, A.C., Greer, L.L., Jehn, K.A. and Koning, L. (2010), 'Believing shapes seeing: the impact of diversity beliefs on the construal of group composition', *Group Processes & Intergroup Relations*, in press.

Jackson, S. E. (1991), 'Team composition in organizational settings: issues in managing an increasingly diverse workforce', in S. Worchel, W. Wood and J. Simpson (eds), *Group Process and Productivity*, Beverly Hills, CA: Sage, pp. 138–71.

Jackson, S.E. and Ruderman, M.N. (1995), *Diversity in Work Teams*, Washington, DC: American Psychological Association.

Jackson, S.E., Brett, J.F., Sessa, V.I., Cooper, D.M., Julin, J.A. and Peyronnin, K. (1991), 'Some differences make a difference: individual dissimilarity and group heterogeneity as correlates of recruitment, promotions, and turnover', *Journal of Applied Psychology*, **76** (5), 675–89.

Jackson, S.E., Joshi, A. and Erhardt, N.L. (2003), 'Recent research on team and organizational diversity: SWOT analysis and implications', *Journal of Management*, **29** (6), 801–30.

Jehn, K.A., Northcraft, G.B. and Neale, M.A. (1999), 'Why differences make a difference: a field study of diversity, conflict, and performance in workgroups', *Administrative Science Quarterly*, **44** (4), 741–63.

Jinnah, M.A. (1876–1948 [1996]), *Speeches, Statements and Messages of the Quaid-e-Azam*, ed. K.A.K Yusufi, Lahore: Bazm-e-Iqbal, vol. 2, p. 1189.

Jinnah, M.A. (1947 [1989]), *Speeches and Statements As Governor General of Pakistan 1947–48*, new edn, Islamabad: Government of Pakistan Ministry of Information and Broadcasting Directorate of Films and Publications.

Jinnah, M.A. (1948), 'Speeches and quotes: National consolidation', available at: http://www.quaid.gov.pk/speech30.htm (accessed October 28, 2008).

Johnson, D.W. and Johnson, R.T. (1983), 'The socialization and achievement crises: are cooperative learning experiences the solution?', in L. Bickman (ed.), *Applied Social Psychology Annual*, Beverly Hills, CA: Sage, pp. 119–64.

Komorita, S.S. and Parks, C.D. (1999), 'Reciprocity and cooperation in social dilemmas: review and future directions', in D. Budescu and I. Erev (eds), *Games and Human Behavior: Essays in Honor of Amnon Rapoport*, Mahwah, NJ: Erlbaum, pp. 315–30.

Kramer, R.M. and Brewer, M.B. (1984), 'Effects of group identity on resource use in a simulated commons dilemma', *Journal of Personality and Social Psychology*, **46**, 1044–57.

Kulik, C.T. and Roberson, L. (2008), 'Diversity initiative effectiveness: what organizations can (and cannot) expect from diversity recruitment, diversity training, and formal mentoring programs', in A.P. Brief (ed.), *Diversity at Work*, Cambridge: Cambridge University Press, pp. 265–317.

Lunardini, C.A. (1996), *Women's Rights*, Phoenix, AZ: Oryx Press.

Mackie, D.M. and Goethals, G.R. (1987), 'Individual and group goals', in C. Hendrick (ed.), *Review of Personality and Social Psychology*, Newbury Park, CA: Sage, pp. 144–66.

Manning, M.L. (2000), 'Understanding diversity, accepting others: realities and directions', *Educational Horizons* (winter), 125–7.

Mannix, E. and Neale, M.A. (2005), 'What differences make a difference? The promise and reality of diverse teams in organizations', *Psychological Science in the Public Interest*, **6** (2), 31–5.

McLeod, P.L., Lobel, S.A. and Cox, T.H. (1996), 'Ethnic diversity and creativity in small groups', *Small Group Research*, **27**, 248–64.

Messick, D.M. and Brewer, M.B. (1983), 'Solving social dilemmas: a review', in L. Wheeler and P. Shaver (eds), *Review of Personality and Social Psychology*, Beverly Hills, CA: Sage, pp. 11–44.

Montalvo, J.G. and Reynal-Querol, M. (2005), 'Ethnic diversity and economic development', *Journal of Development Economics*, **76** (2), 293–323.

National Database and Registration Authority (NADRA) (2007), 'NADRA has Registered 2.15 Million Afghan Refugees', Government of Pakistan, available at: http://www.nadra.gov.pk/DesktopModules/top/topmore.aspx?tabID=0&ItemID=48&bID=0&Mid=3026 (accessed October 25, 2008).

O'Reilly, C., Caldwell, D. and Barnett, W. (1989), 'Work group demography, social integration, and turnover', *Administrative Science Quarterly*, **34**, 21–37.

Pak Tribune (2007), 'Foreign investment to reach $7 billion during current fiscal: Governor SBP', April 1, available at: http://www.paktribune.com/news/index.shtml?173789 (accessed October 25, 2008).

Pelled, L.H. and Xin, K.R. (1997), 'Work values and their human resource management implications: a theoretical comparison of China, Mexico, and the United States', *Journal of Applied Management Studies*, **6** (2), 185–9.

Pelled, L.H., Eisenhardt, K.M. and Xin, K.R. (1999), 'Exploring the black box: an analysis of work group diversity, conflict, and performance', *Administrative Science Quarterly*, **44**, 1–28.

Pettigrew, T.F. (1998), 'Intergroup contact theory', *Annual Review of Psychology*, **49**, 65–85.

Plantenga, D. (2004), 'Gender, identity, and diversity: learning from insights gained in transformative gender training', *Gender and Development*, **12** (1), 40–46.

Polzer, J.T., Stewart, K.J. and Simmons, J.L. (1999), 'A social categorization explanation for framing effects in nested social dilemmas', *Organizational Behavior and Human Decision Processes*, **79** (2), 154–78.

Rapoport, R., Bailyn, L., Fletcher, J.K. and Pruitt, B.H. (2002), *Beyond Work/Family Balance: Advancing Gender Equity and Workplace Performance*, San Francisco, CA: Jossey-Bass.

Sabattini, L. and Crosby, F. (2008), 'Overcoming resistance', in K. Thomas (ed.), *Diversity Resistance in Organizations*, Hillsdale, NJ: Lawrence Erlbaum, pp. 273–302.

Smith, K.G., Carroll, S.J. and Ashford, S.J. (1995), 'Intra- and interorganizational cooperation: toward a research agenda', *Academy of Management Journal*, **38** (1), 7–23.

Swann, W.B., Polzer, J.T., Seyle, D.C. and Ko, S. (2004), 'Finding value in diversity: verification of personal and social self-views in diverse groups', *Academy of Management Review*, **29** (1), 9–27.

Syed, J. (2008a), 'Employment prospects for skilled migrants: a relational perspective', *Human Resource Management Review*, **18**, 28–45.

Syed, J. (2008b), 'The representation of cultural diversity in Urdu-language newspapers in Pakistan: a study of Jang and Nawaiwaqt', *South Asia: Journal of South Asian Studies*, **31** (2), 317–47.

Syed, J. (2008c), 'A context-specific perspective of equal employment opportunity in Islamic societies', *Asia Pacific Journal of Management*, **25**, 135–51.

Syed, J. and Özbilgin, M. (2009), 'A relational framework for international transfer of diversity management practices', *International Journal of Human Resource Management*, **20** (12), 2435–53.

Thomas, D. and Ely, R. (1996), 'Making differences matter: a new paradigm for managing diversity', *Harvard Business Review*, **74**, 79–90.

Thomas, R.R. (1995), 'A diversity framework', in M.M. Chemers, S. Oskamp and M.A. Costanzo (eds), *Diversity in Organizations*, Beverly Hills, CA: Sage, pp. 245–63.

Tsui, A.S., Egan, T.D. and O'Reilly, C.A. (1992), 'Being different: relational demography and organizational attachment', *Administrative Science Quarterly*, **37** (4), 549–79.

Tsui, A.S. and O'Reilly, C.A. (1989), 'Beyond simple demographic effects: the importance of relational demography in superior-subordinate dyads', *Academy of Management Journal*, **32** (2), 402–23.

van Knippenberg, D. and Haslam, S.A. (2003), 'Realizing the diversity dividend: exploring the subtle interplay between identity, ideology, and reality', in S. A. Haslam, D. van Knippenberg, M. Platow and N. Ellemers (eds), *Social Identity at Work: Developing Theory for Organizational Practice*, New York: Psychology Press, pp. 61–77.

Watson, W.E., Kumar, K. and Michaelsen, L.K. (1993), 'Cultural diversity's impact on interaction process and performance: comparing homogenous and diverse task groups', *Academy of Management Journal*, **36**, 590–602.

Welle, B. and Lyness, K.S. (2002), 'Perceived inclusion and the experience of fair treatment: an examination of gender and justice', paper presented at the Academy of Management National Conference, Denver, 9–14 August.

Williams, K.Y. and O'Reilly, C.A. (1998), 'Demography and diversity in organizations: a review of 40 years of research', *Research in Organizational Behavior*, **20**, 77–140.

Wirth, L. (2002), *Breaking through the Glass Ceiling: Women in Management*, Geneva: International Labour Office.

World Bank (2006), 'UNDP question poverty estimates', *Dawn*, June 20, available at: http://www.dawn.com/2006/06/20/top1.htm (accessed October 25, 2008).

Zellmer-Bruhn, M.E., Maloney, M.M., Bhappu, A.D. and Salvador, R. (2008), 'When and how do differences matter? An exploration of perceived similarity in teams', *Organizational Behavior and Human Decision Processes*, **107** (1), 41–59.

Zemba, Y., Young, M.J. and Morris, M.W. (2006), 'Blaming leaders for organizational accidents: proxy logic in collective versus individual-agency cultures', *Organizational Behavior and Human Decision Processes*, **101** (1), 36–51.

7 Diversity in Russia
Moira Calveley and Graham Hollinshead

Introduction

Consideration of the Russian case potentially offers unique insights into the field of diversity as the country's population, estimated at 141 million (CIA, 2008) combines and juxtaposes strong Asian as well as European influences (Domsch and Lidokhover, 2007b). Yet, throughout the period of communist rule, the protective and authoritarian blanket of state socialism provided little scope for the assertion of individual or ethnic identity. As Antonova (2005, p. 47) argues, in the Soviet era 'ethnic or national peculiarities were presented within the U.S.S.R. through presenting national costumes, ethnic food and pointing out the unity of the "fifteen republics–fifteen sisters" within the Soviet Union'. Thus the Soviet doctrine of 'internationalism' presumed the supremacy of communist ideology and the domination of 'official' Russian culture. Similarly, an idealised notion of women's role permeated Soviet value systems, epitomised by International Women's Day on 8 March, on which Russian men heap flowers, chocolates and perfume on wives and girl-friends (Blagov, 2000). Soviet propaganda was used to highlight the supposed equality of the sexes, the first Soviet female cosmonaut, Valentina Tereshkova, being perceived as a role model, and women with more than five children praised as 'mother heroes' (ibid.). As Gerasimova (2006) states, discrimination is endemic in Russian society and employment on the grounds of gender, age, pregnancy, child-rearing, trade union activity and residence, and against migrant workers. Despite the formal prohibition of discrimination in the constitution and the Labour Code, it persists due to problems of legal enforcement, the possibility of victimisation against those defending their rights and perhaps above all, a widespread lack of concrete understanding concerning its nature and how to fight it.

In this chapter, we place issues of discrimination on the grounds of gender and race in the broader context of radical economic and political transformation in Russia. In examining diversity in the 'new' Russia, a country which is now characterised by a polarisation of economic wealth, we focus first on the downgraded status of women in emerging capitalistic labour market structures. We consider how despite the rhetoric of equality under the previous Soviet regime, the prevailing reality was in fact a patriarchal society which was so embedded within Soviet culture that the 'new' Russia has struggled to overthrow discriminatory attitudes. As a result, a significant number of women are still faced with inequality in the workplace. The chapter then goes on to examine the position of migrant workers who face marginalisation and discrimination both in the workplace and in society while being, at the same time, vital to the building of the Russian economy. The chapter will demonstrate that, albeit for different reasons, women and migrant workers are most likely (although not exclusively) to be at the lower end of the economic stratum, and thus they find themselves in the position of competing for lower-paid work. These two groups provide a contemporary focus in a chapter considering diversity; nonetheless, we are aware that concentration on these groups inevitably presents a selective view of diversity in Russia.

Context

Following the collapse of the Russian empire in 1917, the Union of Soviet Socialist Republics (USSR) came under communist rule, introduced a centrally planned economic order involving rapid industrialisation and effectively closed its doors to the rest of the world. Although the USSR excelled in many fields, not least science and education, this regime ultimately led to a stagnation of the Russian economy and prompted the General Secretary Mikhail Gorbachev in the mid-1980s to introduce a programme of change. Under his direction, the USSR government initiated policies of greater openness (*glasnost*) and renewal (*perestroika*). These policies were welcomed by reformers within the USSR and gradually the Communist party began to lose its tight control over the country. Shortly after Boris Yeltsin became the first democratically elected president in 1991, the Communist party was outlawed and the USSR was officially dissolved, with Russia becoming the largest of 15 independent states.

Russia then entered a period of transformation as moves were made to open the country to the world and create a free-market economy. The initial liberalisation of the Russian economy in the early 1990s occurred in chaotic and disorderly fashion. In January 1992, the Russian government removed most controls on prices, wages, trade and currency exchange, which immediately exposed Russian firms to foreign competition. Simultaneously, planning and mandatory state orders were eliminated, enterprise subsidies were curtailed, restrictions on private ownership of productive assets were removed and small firms privatised (Gerber and Mayorova, 2006). The conditions of 'anarcho-capitalism' (Datamonitor, 2004) served to take the country down an economic spiral, with Russia arguably experiencing 'the greatest economic collapse in peacetime of any country in history' (Sakwa, 2008, p. ix). With prices being freed almost immediately, inflation soared and personal savings were wiped out (Stiglitz, 2002, p. 142). Many Russian citizens were plunged into poverty.

In order to stabilise the economy, the government intervened and introduced a programme of privatisation of state-owned industries. This process was hampered through endemic corrupt practice, and state assets falling into the hands of a rich and powerful cadre of 'oligarchs' (Stiglitz, 2002). Furthermore, Stiglitz argues that the transmutation from communism to capitalism, following prescriptions of the International Monetary Fund (IMF) and the World Bank, occurred in a highly precipitate fashion and was based upon the application of 'shock therapy' economic treatment. Accordingly, the pace of privatisation could not be upheld by underlying institutional and regulatory frameworks. In particular, privatisation of state assets preceded the establishment of legal systems to enforce property rights. Despite possessing rich natural resources, particularly gas and oil, with the exception of a brief respite in 1997 the Russian economy plummeted and poverty levels soared. During this period there was a massive reduction in state spending, including the provision of welfare and pensions, and an increase in unemployment and a growth of the informal economy.

Following the election of President Vladimir Putin in March 2000, the Russian economy has witnessed a period of sustained growth, largely based on its possession and control of natural resources. Possessing reformist instincts (Datamonitor, 2004) Putin has sought to 'legitimise' the Russian business environment (May and Ledgerwood, 2007) and is noted for his determination to control and eradicate the oligarchs (Sakwa, 2008) and to remove 'webs of patronage', although it should be noted that 'crony capitalism' including bribes, 'kickbacks' and unofficial payments remains rife (Datamonitor, 2004). The Putin administration has delivered favourable overtures to Western leaders, particularly in the wake of the September 11, 2000 terrorist attacks; Russia has been designated as a 'market economy' by the USA and the European Union (EU) for the purpose of gaining membership of the World Trade Organization (WTO) (ibid.). However, as Datamonitor reports, Putin's attitude to civil liberties is less certain, given his role in the Russian military's bloody campaign in Chechnya and the government's closure of a leading independent television station in June 2003.

Putin remained in office for two presidential terms, having been precluded by the Russian constitution from standing for a third consecutive term of office. He was replaced in May 2008 with a landslide win by his protégé Dmitry Medvedev. It is expected that Putin will stand for election again in 2012. Medvedev has announced that his own governmental policies would be 'a direct continuation of that path which is being carried out by President Putin' (BBC, 2008). Datamonitor (2004, p. 20) reports that Russia has showed 'renewed vitality' since emerging from the 1998 financial and currency crisis, as reflected in positive trends in growth, exports and investment. Moreover, improvements have been observed in the state of public finances, the curtailment of inflation and the stability of the currency, all underpinned by institutional reform. However, continued economic growth is highly dependent upon the maintenance of the price of oil and gas, fuels constituting the bulk of Russia's exports. Economic progress continues to be hampered by monopolistic tendencies, a weak legal infrastructure and an underdeveloped financial sector (ibid.).

Reform and socio-economic fragmentation
While 'headline' statistics may encourage optimistic interpretation of Russia's current state of economic affairs, a more sanguine analysis of the social effects of reform reveals disadvantage for a major part of the population. As Hollinshead (2007) states, liberalisation of the Russian economy has occurred in a highly fractured fashion, leading to a polarisation of fortunes for 'winners' and 'losers'(Stiglitz, 2002).

As the Moscow-based Levada Center (2006) reveals, approximately 85 per cent of the population live in 'poor' Russia. This group earns 43 per cent of all incomes and possesses 15 per cent of all savings. Approximately 27 per cent of the Russian population live below the subsistence level, which has been calculated at 2,500 roubles a month (70 euros) (ILO, 2004; World Bank, 2004). The position of the new poor in Russia has been worsened since 2004 by governmental measures serving to cut and commoditise welfare provision. Social benefits including free use of public transport, discounts on residential utilities, free local telephones, free medication, free annual treatment at sanatoriums and health resorts, free artificial limbs, wheelchairs for invalids and guaranteed employment for the disabled have been replaced with monetary compensation varying between 300 roubles (8 euros) to 1,550 roubles (42 euros) a month (Volkov and Peters, 2004). Cuts in state subsidiaries have been particularly at the expense of people with dependent children, pensioners, teachers and doctors in rural areas, and students.

On the other hand, around 15 per cent of the population inhabit the 'rich' Russia (Levada Center, 2006), earning 37 per cent of all incomes and possessing 85 per cent of all savings. An article in the *New York Times* (2005) reveals that Russia now has 27 billionaires, exceeded only by 57 in Germany and 341 in the USA. The majority of the Russian 'super rich' control raw materials and associated industries, while others are involved in new business fields including telecommunications, construction, food production and retail. The greatest part of the shareholdings in the largest

Russian enterprises is in the hands of this small social grouping, the 23 largest business groups accounting for approximately 57 per cent of all Russia's industrial production (World Bank, 2003).

The 'new' Russia, therefore, presents a fragmented picture of capitalist development in the early part of the new millennium. The social and economic ruptures which have been experienced since the inception of *glasnost* and *perestroika*, reflect the uneasy and rapid superimposition of capitalist systems on embedded institutional and cultural facets deriving from the Soviet era. It is perhaps not surprising, given the real decline in living standards of a majority of the population, that the security associated with communism is viewed with fond nostalgia by many Russian inhabitants, and particularly the older generation (Camiah and Hollinshead, 2003) who are often living on the edge of poverty (Kendall, 2007). It is within this context of radical economic change combined with cultural and social legacy that our discussion of diversity occurs.

Gender

Under the Soviet constitution, women possessed equal rights in training and remuneration. They were expected to take an equal part in social and political life and were encouraged to combine these activities with the responsibilities of motherhood through paid maternity leave and reduced working hours (White, 2000). White reveals that nearly all women were in employment in the late Soviet era, representing just over half of the workforce. Segregation of employment occurred, with women being concentrated in occupations such as teaching, translating, book-keeping and librarianship. They also, however, represented 60 per cent of engineers, economists and officials in management and administration, and around two-thirds of all doctors (Vestnik statistiki, 1992a). Despite official rhetoric, women's earnings only approximated to two-thirds of male income by the early 1990s (Vestnik statistiki, 1992b). Moreover, manifesting patriarchal traditions in Russian society, female duties were overloaded; demanding fulfilment of maternity and household chores were combined with official employment and social activities (ILO, 2000). Apart from being regarded as an 'economic duty', work also represented a form of social and political integration (Ashwin, 2006a). With technical full employment and little employment mobility, a tight labour market prevailed. As wage differentials were suppressed (Stiglitz, 2002) competition for workers occurred through the state-sponsored provision of welfare (Round et al., 2008) which was devolved to the level of the enterprise. Teplova (2007, p. 289) describes how each enterprise constituted 'a microwelfare state in itself, with its own system of childcare facilities (kindergartens and nurseries), transportation, schools, food provision, pioneer camps, and rest houses'. Following Gerber and Mayorova (2006), the centralised system for determining wages and the existence of a general mandatory pay scale restricted the differential allocation of pay by employers, thus embedding the parameters of the gender pay gap.

Undoubtedly patriarchal attitudes regarding male supremacy persisted throughout the Soviet era, albeit outwardly suppressed by the state (Oglobin, 1999; LaFont, 2001). In post-Soviet times, 'neo-familial' concepts concerning the role of women have emerged, as social and political pressure has been exerted upon women to assume the traditional role of mother and homemaker (Degtiar, 2000). This was articulated by a Russian labour minister in 1993 when he asserted that it was 'better that men work and women take care of the children and do housework' (cited in Ashwin, 2006b, p. 53). Thus, as statutory support for working women has receded, latent patriarchal attitudes and overt discrimination have been given free reign (Gerber and Mayorova, 2006). As Teplova (2007) explains, 'the neofamilialist model draws on a traditional understanding of gender roles (male-breadwinner, female home-maker) and provides support, mainly through the provision of paid parental leave, for those who prefer to care for their children at home' (p. 286).

Following the moves towards economic liberalisation in the early 1990s, there has been a re-ordering of occupational status associated with the downgrading of occupations in education, health, culture, social welfare, personal services and catering (Ahlander, 2001) in which female employment prevails, and bolstering new 'masculine' fields of work in trade, finance and commerce. As stated by Snezhkova (2004), traditional spheres of women's work such as trade, finance, credit and insurance have given way to a concentration of males 'because the opportunity to make good money turned out to be greater in those sectors' (ibid. pp. 86–7). Similarly, Clark and Sacks (2004, p. 542) assert that 'substitution' has taken place, with men moving into former female-dominated areas of employment and women being 'crowded out'. According to Gerber and Mayorovo (2006, p. 2047):

> Women are disadvantaged in the labour market to the extent that, relative to men, they have *higher* rates of layoff and voluntary employment exit, *lower* rates of employment entry and job mobility, *higher* odds that their new jobs are low-quality positions and *lower* odds that they are high quality (italics in original).

Utilising human capital theory, these authors argue that, despite the equalling and surpassing by women of men's educational achievements, the precise skills and endowments possessed by women tend to be less valued and subject to systematic degradation in capitalistic, as opposed to socialistic, milieus (Nee, 1996). Problems of women's integration into liberalised labour markets are exacerbated by their accrual of fewer years' work experience than men due to their role as primary family caretakers (Oglobin, 1999). Based upon a nationally representative household survey, Oglobin (2005) finds that, adjusted for hours worked, women's monthly earnings were 62 per cent of men's between 2000 and 2002. While women's higher human capital endowments reduce the differential, job segregation and discrimination against women were important contributory factors to its widening (ibid.).

In considering why women are disposed to accept poorer-quality jobs, Gerber and Mayorovo (2006) assert that self-reproducing norms from the Soviet era have obliged women to accept lower wage thresholds, particularly in times of economic crisis. Similarly, Ashwin (2002) contends that the 'gender order' in Soviet times, despite encouraging women to work, expected them to put their families first and accept secondary status at work as natural. As a legacy of this tradition, women tend to emphasise income stability rather than level of pay or status (Gerber and Mayorovo, 2006). Women are also disposed to accept part-time work, which has increased during the transition (Teplova, 2007) and are also highly represented in the burgeoning shadow economy, which is completely unregulated and potentially hazardous (ILO, 2000). Such developments have occurred as poverty has become 'feminised' (White, 2000). Thus families with more than two children have found themselves in acute financial difficulty, particularly if headed by a single mother.

Discrimination against women, both covertly during the Soviet era and in a more obvious fashion since, may be explained by women's relative exclusion from both formal and informal networks of influence, which have a vital role to play in social and economic systems. According to Gerber and Mayorova (2006), women were underrepresented in the Communist Party of the Soviet Union (CPSU), membership of which offered opportunities to 'be noticed', particularly regarding one's ambition, motivation and organisational skills (van der Lippe and Fodor, 1998; Gerber, 2000, 2001). According to Blagov (2000) the exclusion of women from the corridors of power has persisted in the 'new' Russia, with cabinet positions being held virtually exclusively by men. A notable exception is former diplomat Valentina Matviyenko, who has been appointed Deputy Prime Minister for Social Programmes. Controversy and lack of resolution still surrounds the assassination of politician Galina Starovoitova in 1998 who was Co-chairperson of the Democratic Russia party and an outspoken pro-democracy campaigner. At the informal level, *blat* has been a prominent feature of life in Russia, this referring to the informal exchange of favours by which resources of the Soviet centralised distribution network have been channelled into informal networks (Ledeneva, 2001). As May and Ledgerwood (2007, p. 32) suggest, in the Soviet era 'personal networking and social connections . . . were paramount to survival'. According to these authors, *blat* remains a feature of the 'new' Russia, although it has been subject to some reconstruction in so far as modern organisations have found personal network channels a vital resource in maximising competitive advantage. We would note that the potency of informal networks is not unique to Russia, and that, in particular, the equivalent phenomenon of *guanxi* continues to condition business relationships in China (Härtel et al., ch. 11, this volume). Of course, at both formal and informal levels, the perpetuation of closed networks for social influence merely reinforces existing power structures, including those based on gender. As Gerber (2000) asserts, powerful individuals who were able to exert leverage in Soviet times frequently continue to hold sway in the new 'Russia', albeit following a degree of personal reinvention.

As *blat* and its associated informal networking influences recruitment processes it will, by definition, give rise to discrimination. As people recommend family and friends for positions in organisations, propagation of similar cultures and backgrounds is witnessed. Further, both horizontal and vertical segregation can become more manifest especially when, as is the case of the 'new' Russia, the more-valued occupations remain, or become, the domain of men. Clearly, if equal opportunities are to be achieved at organisational level, greater transparency is needed in recruitment and promotion practices.

Ethnicity and migrant labour

Although some 84 per cent of the Russian population comprises ethnic Russians, it comprises around 100 other ethnic or national groupings (Amnesty International, 2003). Despite initial tolerance towards cultural minorities immediately following the 1917 revolution, the period of Stalinism witnessed the widespread arrest of political and cultural leaders (ibid.). During the Second World War, the forcible removal of potential 'enemies within' occurred solely on the basis of ethnic or national origins, including Chechens, Ingush, Karachais, Balkars, Meskhetians, Crimean Tatars, Pontic Greeks, Kurds, Koreans, Kalmyks and Germans from the Volga and Ukraine (ibid.). Such groups were subject to severe restrictions of their movement until Stalin's death in 1953, by which time returning to their original homes became impossible (ibid.). During the Soviet era, anti-semitism was frequently an official policy and expression of minority culture and language was forcefully constrained in the drive towards 'Russification' (ibid.). During *perestroika* in the late 1980s, a programme of rehabilitation and re-housing was introduced for displaced ethnic groups, although this was confronted with many practical problems. The end of Soviet rule also saw the emergence of 15 republics, each with its own languages, cultures and religious traditions, as sovereign states, and comprising Russian, Ukrainian, Uzbek, Belarusian, Kazak, Azeri, Armenian, Tajik, Georgian, Moldavian, Lithuanian, Turkmen, Kyrgyz, Latvian and Estonian nationalities (ibid.). The break-up of the Soviet Union has been accompanied by several conflicts, most notably in Chechnya. Many economies of the new sovereign states remain economically weak, although Latvia and Lithuania are now EU members.

In a study of multiculturalism in Russia, Antonova (2005) reflects that the Soviet doctrine of 'internationalism' actually presumed the supremacy of communist ideology, the domination of 'official' Russian culture within the Soviet Union and the underestimation of the value of different cultures. According to Antonova, citizens of certain Asian cultures such as Uzbekistan and Turkmenistan were considered to be less intellectual and educated than Russians. In a study of 32 senior civil servants in Perm and Saratov, Antonova reveals a persistence of colour/ethnicity 'blindness' in the post-Soviet era, participants finding the nationality question 'painful' and, despite their awareness of discrimination on ethnic grounds, preferring to leave this problem secret and concealed. This orientation is well exemplified by the following quotation:

> Discrimination in terms of national origin can be revealed in our region at all levels of bureaucracy without an exception. The main gate for the discrimination is an appointment process. Although officially there is open competition for the majority of posts within the regional civil service – all talk about the fairness and transparency of that competition is just rubbish. This is just for show. The real candidate either had been already working for this post for a while, needing to be officially confirmed through the competition procedure, or he/she has already been approved for the vacancy. Thus all this 'performance' with the competition is nothing less than window dressing, the necessity to show that everything is legal. (Ibid., p. 49)

In probing the nature of the Russian identity, Solovei (2008) reveals profound changes occurring in the post-Soviet era. Solovei asserts that, following a period of self-disparagement in the preliminary chaotic throes of capitalism in the early 1990s, there has been an assertion of 'new' Russian ethnic identity. This is felt particularly among the younger generation who have been 'politically socialised in post-communist Russia and identify themselves with the country within its present borders' (ibid., p. 72). Thus the awareness of 'grand purpose' has subsided, and the 'phantom of the Soviet Union' weakened (ibid., p. 73). Such changes in mindset are occurring in conjunction with compositional changes in the population, comprising a decline in the absolute number of ethnic

Russians and an increase in immigration from Central Asia and China. In this context Solovei notes a rise in xenophobic tendencies, which has typically been manifested through verbal denigration but is now increasingly taking the form of physical assault. Ethnic intolerance is most vehemently expressed by the liberal union of right forces, who are the supporters of radical market reform, and has been directed particularly at Chechens from the North Caucasus region and gypsies.

The assimilation of foreign citizens into Russian economic and social structures has emerged as high on the political agenda as Russia has become more tightly involved in the international division of labour (Krasinets, 2005). As the ILO (2006) points out, since the early 1990s, the Russian Federation has been the biggest receiving, sending and transit country for migrant workers in Eastern Europe and Central Asia. The ILO estimates that Russia will need between 800,000 and 1.5 million migrant workers each year to compensate for a shrinking labour force and to maintain economic growth. Such a burgeoning demand for labour has been met with a supply of migrants from Russia's poorer former Soviet neighbouring countries, and from more distant regions including Vietnam and Africa. According to the ILO, at least one out of three households in countries such as Tajikistan and Moldova contain a migrant worker in Russia sending home an average of US$100 per month. Economic migrants confront a difficult situation as Russian law obliges them to register at the place of their temporary stay within three days of arrival and they are not permitted to stay in Russia for more than one year. The Federal Migration Service (FMS) estimates that there are around 500,000 legal migrants and up to 1.5 million undocumented migrants in Russia constituting between 5 and 7 per cent of the working population. Migrants typically occupy unskilled and semi-skilled positions such as driving and work in construction and agriculture. Such low-paid activity, frequently involving poor and potentially hazardous conditions, has not been popular among potential Russian workers.

In a study of 224 illegal migrants in the Rostov Oblast region, supplemented by observations of experts and employers of foreign labour, Krasinets (2005) reveals the following:

- The majority of undocumented migrants originated from the Transcaucasus region and Central Asia, with high potential for migration from Ukraine, Azerbaijan, Armenia and Tajikistan. From further abroad, migrants tended to come from China, Vietnam and Afghanistan.
- Illegal migrants tended to be males in their mid-30s who had not adapted to conditions of transformation in their homeland.

Individuals had generally occupied previous employment in agriculture, trade or construction, or had been engaged in occasional work or been unemployed.

- On arrival in Russia the majority worked in trade or services, in unskilled blue- or white-collar work or in construction. A high proportion obtained work in the non-state sector, particularly in small businesses with considerable involvement in the shadow economy.
- The primary motivational factor for undocumented migrants was to earn higher wages and to improve their material conditions, with the acquisition of Russian citizenship, obtaining domicile in Russia and using Russia for transit purposes representing secondary factors.
- Employers' incentives to employ illegal migrant labour related primarily to their desire to reduce production costs by paying lower wages and evading taxes, and also as migrants placed fewer demands on social and medical care and were willing to work at jobs that are hard and dangerous and to work longer hours. Such jobs tended to be necessary ones but not attractive to the local population. Employers, as well as migrants themselves, were deterred by the bureaucracy associated with the granting of official status to foreign labourers.

Labour migration in Russia has received political attention at both national and international levels, particularly in the light of reports of racially motivated attacks against migrant workers. In 2005, the National Security Council addressed the issue, and concerned ministries were asked to develop a national migration policy concept. In 2005, the FMS organised an amnesty for migrant workers in nine pilot regions, in Russia, granting some 7,000 migrants legal status (ILO, 2006). Such developments have occurred in conjunction with a review of legislation, particularly the Law on the Legal Status of Foreign Citizens. In a move in April 2007, the government banned individuals not holding Russian passports from working in indoor and outdoor clothing markets and in roadside kiosks (Osborn, 2007). Such a development is emblematic of the recognition by the authorities that, while labour migrants perform vital work for economic growth, this is at the cost of contribution to social funds through lost taxation. It is acknowledged also that migrants are facilitating the expansion of the shadow economy, exerting a downward influence on pay and conditions particularly at the lower end of official employment structures, and contributing to local unemployment. While the Kremlin appears to be embarking upon an assertive approach to dispel migrant labour, other bodies have called for greater sensitivity in policy formulation. The ILO (2006) has stressed the need for an adaptation of regulations and working conditions for migrants, including the granting of amnesty, while the UN Committee on the Elimination of Racial Discrimination and Amnesty International (2003), have demanded that the Kremlin should take unequivocal action to counteract racial abuse. According to Amnesty International, actions taken by the police and other law enforcement agencies have tended to reflect the discriminatory attitudes of society rather than counteracting them. The UN has urged Russia to protect labour migrants who are subject to exploitation, and to punish officials and law enforcement officers who discriminate against ethnic minorities.

Conclusion

This chapter has demonstrated that the emergence of a new, liberalised, economic order in Russia has been associated with growing segmentation of the labour force and significant disparities in occupational and earnings status. Women, who are frequently as well or better qualified than their male counterparts, have found their specialist skills downgraded as 'neo-familial' values have emerged, and as men have come to dominate the most prestigious and highly rewarded occupations. In observing the changing status of women in communist and post-communist times, our study broadly reflects the contemporary theoretical notion in diversity management that socio-demographic characteristics may not be regarded as employees' 'fixed essence' (Janssens and Zanoni, 2005), but rather that 'diversity is always deeply embedded in the power-laden relations of production between management and employees' (ibid., p. 314). Migrant workers, who are generally poorly qualified, effectively constitute an underclass, concentrated in the informal economy, whose work has nevertheless provided the raw labour resources for economic growth. While women and migrant labourers have experienced different manifestations of discrimination it may be argued that, in a deregulated labour market setting, the extremely impoverished conditions of (mainly male) migrant workers in the shadow economy has exerted a detrimental and undermining effect on pay and conditions of women who tend to occupy the lower-status occupations in the formal economy, as well as needing to compete for informal employment. Accordingly, official policy to legitimise the status of migrant workers to act against their exploitation may have a benign 'knock-on' effect on indigenous Russian workers who have become most displaced and downgraded by economic liberalisation. Indeed it may be argued, in line with ILO and similar conventions, that in treading a path of economic reform, the government could be more expeditious in ensuring that reserves of human capital are utilised in a civilised, as well as productive, fashion. Affirmative public policy and legislation in the field of diversity is most likely to provide the catalyst for change in formal and informal norms and behaviours which have persisted in the 'new' Russia, and which have tended to perpetuate discrimination and inequality.

References

Ahlander, A.M.S. (2001), 'Women's and men's work in transitional Russia: legacies of the Soviet system', *Post-Soviet Affairs*, **17**, 56–80.

Amnesty International (2003), *Dokumenty; Discrimination on Grounds of Race in the Russian Federation*, London: Amnesty International Publications.

Antonova, V.K. (2005), 'The state of multiculturalism in Russia', *Essex Graduate Journal of Sociology*, **5**, February: 46–55.

Ashwin, S. (2002), 'The influence of the Soviet gender order on employment behavior in contemporary Russia', *Sociological Research*, **41**, 21–37.

Ashwin, S. (2006a), 'Dealing with devastation in Russia. Men and women compared', in Ashwin (ed.), *Adapting to Russia's New Labour Market: Gender and Employment Behaviour*, London and New York: Routledge, pp. 1–31.

Ashwin, S. (2006b), 'The post-Soviet gender order. Imperatives and implications', in Ashwin (ed.), *Adapting to Russia's New Labour Market: Gender and Employment Behaviour*, London and New York: Routledge, pp. 32–56.

BBC (2008), 'Medvedev "to continue Putin work"', available at: http://news.bbc.co.uk/1/hi/world/europe/7274001.stm (accessed 3 March 2008).

Blagov, S. (2000), 'Equal opportunities remain a pipedream', *Asia Times Online*, 10 March.

Camiah, N. and G. Hollinshead (2003), 'Assessing the potential for effective cross-cultural working between "new" Russian managers and Western expatriates', *Journal of World Business*, **38**, 245–61.

CIA (2008), 'The World Factbook 2008, Russia', available at: https://www.cia.gov/library/publications/the-world-factbook/print/rs.html (accessed 10 October 2008).

Clark, C.L. and M.P. Sachs (2004), 'A view from below: industrial re-structuring and women's employment at four Russian enterprises', *Communist and Post-Communist Studies*, **37**, 523–45.

Datamonitor (2004) *Country Profile, Russia*, February.

Degtiar. L. (2000) 'The transformation process and the status of women', *Problems in Economic Transition*, **43** (7), 7–19.

Domsch, Michel E. and Tatjana Lidokhover (eds) (2007a), *Human Resource Management in Russia*, Aldershot, UK and Burlington, VT, USA: Ashgate.

Domsch, Michel E. and Tatjana Lidokhover (2007b), 'Introduction', in Domsch and Lidokhover (eds), pp. 1–22.

Gerasimova, E. (2006), 'Fallen icon: the worker in postcommunist Russia', lecture at the International Forum for Democratic Studies, Washington, DC, 1 July.

Gerber, T.P. (2000), 'Membership benefits or satisfaction effects? Why former Communist party members do better in post-Soviet Russia', *Social Science Research*, **29**, 25–50.

Gerber, T.P. (2001), 'The selection theory of Communist Party advantage: more evidence and implications', *Social Science Research*, **30**, 653–71.

Gerber, T.P. and O. Mayorova (2006), 'Dynamic gender differences in a post- socialist labor market: Russia, 1991–1997', *Social Forces*, **84** (4), 2047–75.

Hollinshead, Graham (2007), 'Pay in Russia', in Domsch and Lidokhover (eds), pp. 227–41.

International Labour Organization (ILO) (2000), *Russia and other CIS Countries, A Break with the Past*, Geneva: ILO.

International Labour Organization (ILO) (2004), ILO SRO-Budapest Newsletter, 2–94.

International Labour Organization (ILO) (2006), *Russia Needs Migrant Workers to Support Economic Growth*, Geneva: ILO.

Janssens, M. and P. Zanoni (2005), 'Many diversities for many services; theorizing diversity (management) in service companies', *Human Relations*, **58** (3), 311–40.

Kendall, B. (2007), 'Russians face up to prosperous reality', BBC News, available at: http://news.bbc.co.uk/1/hi/business/6696427.stm (accessed 31 September 2008).

Krasinets, E.S. (2005), 'Illegal migration in Russia, factors, consequences and problems of regulation', *Sociological Research*, **44** (1), 7–25.

LaFont, S. (2001), 'One step forward, two steps back: women in the communist and post-communist states', *Post Communist Studies*, **34**, 203–20.

Ledeneva, A. (2001), *Unwritten Rules, How Russia Really Works*, London: Centre for European Reform.

Levada Center (2006), 'Trends in the Phenomenon of Poverty Report', Moscow.

May, Ruth C. and Donna E. Ledgerwood (2007), 'One step forward, two steps back: negative consequences of national policy on human resource management practices in Russia', Domsch and Lidokhover (eds), pp. 25–42.

Nee, V. (1996), 'The emergence of a market society: changing mechanisms of stratification in China', *American Journal of Sociology*, **101**, 908–49.

New York Times (2005), 'In Russia's boom, riches and rags', 15 April.

Oglobin, C.G. (1999), 'The gender earnings differential in the Russian transition economy', *Industrial and Labor Relations Review*, **52**, 602–27.

Oglobin, C.G. (2005), 'The gender earnings differential in Russia after a decade of economic transition', *Applied Econometrics and International Development*, **5** (3), 602–27.

Osborn, A. (2007), 'Russia bans foreign workers from retail jobs', *The Independent*, available at: http://www.independent.co.uk/news/world/europe/russia-bans-foreign-workers-from-retail-jobs-442963.html (accessed 3 October 2008).

Round, J., C.C. Williams and P. Rodgers (2008), 'Corruption in the post-Soviet workplace: the experiences of recent graduates in contemporary Ukraine', *Work, Employment and Society*, **22** (1), 149–66.

Sakwa, Richard (2008), *Putin, Russia's Choice*, 2nd edn, London and New York: Routledge.

Snezhkova, I.A. (2004), 'Ethnic aspects of gender social inequality', *Sociological Research*, **43** (3), 85–96.

Solovei, V.D. (2008), 'The revolution of Russian identity – Russia for the Russians?', *Sociological Research*, **47** (3), 56–79.

Stiglitz, Joseph E. (2002), *Globalization and Its Discontents*, London and New York: Penguin Group.

Teplova, T. (2007), 'Welfare state transformation, childcare, and women's work in Russia', Social Politics: International Studies in Gender, State and Society, **14** (3), 284–322.

van der Lippe, T. and E. Fodor (1998), 'Changes in gender inequality in six Eastern European countries', *Acta Sociologica*, **41**, 131–49.

Vestnik statistiki (1992a), **1**: 65.

Vestnik statistiki (1992b), **1**: 53.

Volkov, V. and A. Peters (2004), 'Russia, Putin lays siege to social benefits', World Socialist Web.

White, S. (2000), *Russia's New Politics; The Management of a Postcommunist Society*, Cambridge: Cambridge University Press.

World Bank (2003), *World Development Indicators*, Washington, DC: World Bank.

World Bank (2004), *World Development Indicators*, Washington, DC: World Bank.

8 The main problems of cultural diversity management in Turkish companies which operate in Central Asian countries
Beliz Dereli

Introduction

The changing face of organisations, and an increasingly competitive and globalised world economy are posing great challenges to management (Johnston and Packer, 1987 cited in Ayoko and Härtel, 2006, p. 345). The business world is becoming more diverse, more technical, more global, and at the same time more dependent than ever on productive working relationships. The workplace is changing dramatically, with minorities moving into all types of executive, managerial, technical and professional jobs. Business relationships are more diverse than ever, and various groups have different issues that are important to them; business leaders should build and practise their multicultural skills when they create a multicultural work environment. Diversity can be the greatest source of a company's power, and it can also be the source of its disintegration as a culture (Carr-Ruffino, 1996, p. 27).

Cultural diversity management is a very important tool for international human resource (HR) management. Managing diversity means establishing a heterogeneous workforce to perform to its potential in an equitable work environment in which no one group enjoys an advantage or suffers a disadvantage. At least five factors account for the increasing attention that companies are paying to diversity: (i) the shift from a manufacturing to a service economy; (ii) the globalisation of markets; (iii) new business strategies that require more teamwork; (iv) mergers and alliances that require different corporate cultures to work together; and (v) the changing labour market. Each of these factors can represent opportunities for firms whose managers and employees understand what culture is and the cultural differences among other employees and managers, and especially the firm's market (Cascio, 1995, p. 83).

Managing a diverse workforce to derive the benefits it is capable of producing depends on communication among the diverse cultures that makes it possible for each culture to understand the perspectives engendered by others and thereby to become comfortable with perspectives different from one's own. Rather than suppress cultural difference at work, managers are being taught how to respect them and how to work with them to maximise the contribution of each employee. Not only do managers need to learn about various cultures, they also have to be aware of differences within a culture and also about personal idiosyncrasies and preferences (Cascio, 1995, p. 82).

This chapter will examine the concepts of diversity management and in particular cultural diversity management, and present the results of the research related to cultural diversity management problems in Turkish companies which operate in Central Asian countries. There are various reasons for choosing this region, one of them being the common historical, racial, linguistic, religious and cultural ties between Turkey and Central Asian countries. Cultural relations operate in parallel with commercial and political relations, and as from 1995, Turkish companies started to make investments in the region. Another reason relates to the strong force that Russia exerts on some former Soviet Republics (Uslu, 2003), which gives rise to some ethnic national and religious conflicts between the Russians and the citizens of Central Asian countries. Similar conflicts also occur among the citizens of Central Asian countries. In the light of this discussion, and with reference to how these conflicts are reflected in the working environment, the research part of this chapter will investigate the potential problems of cultural diversity management in Turkish companies which operate in Central Asian countries and their HR management approaches.

Diversity management
In order to define cultural diversity management and examine the organisation's culture to measure the effects of diversity within that particular organisation, the term 'diversity' should be defined. Generally, it may be defined as the presence of differences among members of a social group or unit. Cox (1993, cited in Choy, 2007, p. 11) defines diversity as 'the representation, in one social system, of people with distinctly different group affiliations of cultural significance'. Ferdman (1995, cited in Choy, 2007, p. 11) emphasised the fact that membership in social groups distinguishes one person from another not only in name but also in their view of the world, in their construction of meanings, and in their behavioural and attitudinal preferences, and other patterns of values, beliefs and norms (Choy, 2007, p. 11).

The most important dimension of diversity relates to the increasing globalisation of many companies. As companies become more global, diversity must be defined in global and not just Western terms. Defining diversity in global terms means looking at all people and everything that makes them different from one another, as well as the things that make them similiar. Differentiating factors often go beyond race and language and may include such things as values and customs (Trenka, 2006, pp. 17–18). Global diversity management can be defined as the planning, coordination and implementation of a set of management strategies, policies, initiatives, and training and development activities that seek to transcend national differences in diversity management policies and practices in organisations with an international, multinational, global, transnational workforce (Özbilgin, 2008).

Daft (2003, cited in Seymen, 2006, pp. 297–8) examines diversity in both a basic and a secondary dimension, that is, recognising a dual differentiation. For Daft, the basic dimensions – race, ethnicity, gender, physical or cognitive capability – are those that depict differences which are inborn or have an influence on individuals throughout their lives; in other words, the qualities acquired later on and usually changeable. Some specifications such as individual beliefs, marital status, languages, socio-economic status, education level and business experience add new dimensions both to identify oneself and to be identified by others (Seymen, 2006, p. 298).

'Diversity means many things to many people' is now a common caveat that precedes many discussions on the topic. This is one of the main stumbling blocks achieving effective management of diversity. At the organisational level, diversity management suffers from individualisation of its definition, with different organisations adopting diversity initiatives in a pick and mix fashion, selecting aspects of diversity management that are too ambiguous to monitor and which present the organisation in a positive light, such as valuing diversity of opinions and ignoring other aspects such as ethnic and gender diversity which require capital investment or significant changes in corporate practices (Özbilgin, 2008).

Workplace diversity is not limited to international business. Global demographic trends are diversifying the domestic labour force in most countries of the world. Therefore, an understanding of different heritages between as well as within national boundaries is important for successfully managing diversity (Haq, 2004, p. 277). Managing diversity involves creating an environment that allows all employees to contribute to organisational goals and experience personal growth. This requires the company to encourage employees to be comfortable in working with others from a wide variety of ethnic, racial and religious backgrounds (Hollenbeck and Wright, 1997).

The three predominant traditional HR approaches for managing diversity are diversity enlargement, diversity sensitivity and cultural audits. *Diversity enlargement* approaches increase the representation of individuals of different ethnic and cultural backgrounds in an organisation. The goal of this strategy is to create diversity in a firm by changing an organisation's demographic composition and increasing the number of people from different races.

Diversity sensitivity approaches acknowledge the existence of cultural distance and attempt to teach individual members about cultural differences via training programmes (Ferdman, 1989 cited in Kossek and Lobel, 1996, p. 4). Training sessions are often held to help sensitise employees to stereotyped differences of various employee racio-ethnic and gender groups. The goal is to promote communication and understanding, and to build relationships among members of different backgrounds (Kossek and Lobel, 1996). Diversity-based training programmes include: improving interpersonal skills; understanding and valuing cultural differences; improving technical skills; socialising employees into a corporate culture; indoctrinating workers from different cultures or different backgrounds with the domestic work ethic; mentoring; and improving language proficiency and bilingual skills (Dessler, 2002, p. 202).

A *cultural audit* generally tries to determine what is blocking progress. A consultant collects data via focus groups or surveys. These data are analysed to assess various demographic groups' identification of the major obstacles they face in the current culture (Morrison et al., 1993). Members from diverse backgrounds may be asked to talk about how the current culture, which is generally viewed as favouring males, negatively affects the performance of women and those from racio-ethnic minorities. Cultural audits should not only focus on the differences between groups, but also identify the similarities between groups that the culture and supportive HR systems can reinforce to achieve organisational objectives. Finally, cultural audits tend to rely largely on cross-sectional data (Kossek and Lobel, 1996).

Cultural diversity management

While 'diversity' may refer to many kinds of heterogeneity, one of the most challenging dimensions for many workplaces is cultural diversity, including racial and ethnic background. Cultural diversity refers to identities such as race, ethnicity, nationality, religion, gender, and other dimensions of difference derived from membership in groups that are socio-culturally distinct, that is, they 'collectively share certain norms, values or traditions that are different from those of other groups' (Cox, 1993, pp. 5–6).

The concept of globalisation increases the importance and the role of workforce diversity in terms of 'culture'. The subject of cultural diversity in all organisations serving in an unlimited area in respect of activation fields has been addressed more frequently in recent studies. Cultural workforce diversity, foreseen to greatly influence the twenty-first-century business world, is extensively effective in management styles of organisations, behaviour forms, communication styles and, in general, work relations among individuals. Thus, it is necessary to understand the organisational and managerial dimensions of cultural diversity (Seymen, 2006, p. 310).

In multinational or global businesses, a director's awareness of cultural diversity and its effective management can be summed up as follows: providing for richness, perspective and a spectrum of alternative ways of thinking, creativity and innovation; ensuring organisational flexibility; enriching the HR potential; recognising the needs of different markets; stimulating job satisfaction; stimulating learning through doing; providing the basis for specialisation which is imperative in today's complex business scenarios; and diminishing costs by reducing the workforce turnover rate (Harung and Harung, 1995, from Seymen, 2006, p. 302; Özkalp and Kırel, 2000).

It is widely acknowledged that the effective management of diversity implies changes in mindsets, attitudes, behaviours, organisational practices and structure (Kossek and Lobel, 1996 in Sippola, 1997; Tayeb, 1996; Kandola and Fullerton, 1998; Dass and Parker, 1999; Lorbiecki, 2001; Litvin, 2002; Kirton and Greene, 2005) and aims to modify organisation standards, procedures and management practices that hinder creativity, productivity and advancement of all employees (Elmuti, 1996). As shown in Figure 8.1, 'managing diversity' refers to a variety of management issues and activities related to the hiring and effective utilisation of personnel from different cultural backgrounds.

Greater diversity will create certain specific challenges but also make some important contributions. Communication problems are certain to occur, including misunderstandings among employees and managers as well as the need to translate verbal and written material into several languages. Solutions to these problems will necessitate additional training involving work in basic skills such as problem writing and problem solving. In addition to creating the above challenges, greater diversity presents new opportunities. Diversity contributes to creating an organisation culture that is more tolerant of different behavioural styles and wider views. This often leads to better business decisions (Trenka, 2006, p. 19).

Cultural diversity management can have both positive and negative effects on organisations. If the cultural diversity is well managed, organisations can easily attract, retain and motivate people from diverse cultural backgrounds and may gain a competitive advantage in creativity, problem solving and flexible adaptation to change. These kinds of organisations' specific features are as follows: (i) pluralism: reciprocal acculturation where all cultural groups respect, value and learn from one another; (ii) full structural integration of all cultural groups so that they are well represented at all levels of the organisation; (iii) full integration of minorities;

Source: Cox and Blake (1991).

Figure 8.1 Spheres of activity in management of cultural diversity

(iv) an absence of prejudice and discrimination; (v) equal identification of minority and majority group members with the goals of the organisation, and with opportunity for alignment of organisational and personal career goal achievement; and (vi) a minimum of inter-group conflict based on race, gender, nationality or any other identity groups of organisation members (Cox and Blake, 1991, p. 52).

On the other hand, if the cultural diversity is mismanaged, this situation causes some problems such as ineffective cultural communication, lack of group cohesiveness, race and sex discrimination, class stratification, backlash sentiments towards diversity (Stockdale and Cao, 2004, p. 304), conflicts among the employees, and so on.

Adler (1980, cited in Choy, 2007, pp. 14–15) strongly emphasised the fact that cultural synergy as an approach in managing workplace diversity, involves a process whereby managers establish organisational policies, strategies, structures and practices according to the unique characteristics of staff members and clients. To ensure that organisational staff are able to cope effectively at the macro level of the organisational system, management should develop organisational policies and training programmes that: (i) create awareness and increase social consciousness; (ii) emphasise the importance of organisational culture, management responsibility and accountability, and programme content in diversity education in the workplace; (iii) reduce the sense of alienation experienced by minority group employees within the company; (iv) actively ensure the incorporation of diversity management as an integral part of overall organisational development and change process; (v) empower management and employees so that they are more involved in the process of institutionalising diversity in the workplace; (vi) review corporate infrastructure, systems and policies that promote diversity; and (vii) create internal support systems that encourage diversity of thought and actions of staff from different socio-cultural backgrounds (Choy, 2007). In addition, four other areas require attention: (i) stereotypes and their associated assumptions; (ii) actual cultural differences; (iii) the exclusivity of the 'white male club' and its associated access to important organisation information and relationships; (iv) unwritten rules and double standards for success that are often unknown to minorities and women (Henderson, 1994, p. 10).

Regional information and national identity of Central Asia

The need for the acceptance of a communicated national identity within a nation is vital. However, many academics argue that national identity is contested because of social and cultural differences such as gender, class, language and ethnicity. National identity building in post-communist contexts highlights, in particular, ethnic differences. Bingöl (2004, cited in Palmer, 2007, p. 646) argues that ethnic nationalism has now succeeded communism. Horowitz (1993, cited in Palmer, 2007, p. 646) remarks that in ethnically divided societies the determination of social, economic and political inclusion and exclusion is dependent upon clear identification of ethnic identity. For Central Asia, Soviet national delimitation simplistically positioned ethnic identity in terms of titular (that is, core group or native ethnic group) versus non-titular (Aydıngün, 2002) ethnic groupings. With respect to post-Soviet nation-building activities, Kolossov (1999, cited in Palmer, 2007) argues that the state has to simultaneously 'glue together' the titular people and a nation consisting of many other ethnic groups. Thus, it has to identify its priorities and strategy and decide whether it will primarily support the nation as a whole or concentrate on the titular people (its 'core group'). Gachechiladze (1997, cited in Palmer, 2007) observes the division of Soviet nationalities into 'native' (titular population) and 'non-native' (non-titular population) and claims that

Source: Available at: http://centralasia.imb.org/map.htm (accessed 12 December 2007).

Figure 8.2 *Central Asia*

non-native citizens rarely possessed a patriotic feeling towards their Union Republic of residence (Palmer, 2007, p. 646).

Central Asia is a large area, roughly twice that of the European continent (4 million km^2); but its population is relatively small (57 million) and it is in a geo-strategically important location neighbouring Russia, China and Afghanistan (Akıncı, 2006; Figure 8.2). Central Asia comprises five countries – Kazakhstan, Uzbekistan, Turkmenistan, Tajikistan and Kyrgyzstan – that gained independence following the collapse of the Soviet Union in 1991. It is bordered by Russia to the north, Iran and Afghanistan to the south, and China to the east; the landlocked Caspian Sea to the west separates it from the Caucasian isthmus. Central Asia's geography and climate have determined the livelihood of its peoples. The Turkmen, whose homeland is dry, were staunchly nomadic until Soviet times; the Kazakhs and their closest ethnolinguistic 'cousins', the Kyrgyz, were also traditionally pastoral nomads. The Uzbeks, based between the Amu Darya (Oxus) and the Syr Darya (Jaxartes) rivers, became slightly more amenable to agriculture over the years. The Tajiks have the oldest sedentary tradition in the region. But in addition to these peoples, countless tribes have competed for influence across the Central Asian steppes for more than two millennia ('Where is Central Asia?', 2000).

None of the nation-states existed in the centuries before Russian conquest, and substantial transmigration of ethnic groups has characterised the region. As a result, major concentrations of ethnic minorities reside within countries other than their titular nation, because artificial, 'divide and conquer' boundaries, established during the Stalinist era, deliberately cut across nationalities (Smith, 1996).

All Central Asian countries have minorities that give rise to concern and tension in intra-regional relations, for example, Russians mostly in Kazakhstan, Uzbeks in Kyrgyzstan, Tajikistan and Kazakhstan, and Tajiks in Uzbekistan. An ethnic mix of former Soviet states and the tradition inherited from the Soviet 'Nationalities Policy' which favoured lesser ethnic groups against larger ones made nation building difficult and encouraged separatism. Moreover, the discrepancies between ethnic and political boundaries carried the danger of conflict. Although countries of the region share the same geography, a common history and similar cultural traits, they do not constitute a monolithic entity. They differ markedly in size of territory, population, ethnic characteristics, levels of development, per capita GDP, defence capability and resource endowment (Akıncı, 2006).

As Soviet power receded in Central Asia, national movements became more powerful, but they were quite different in scope and support from nationalist movements in the Baltics, Ukraine, Georgia, Armenia and Azerbaijan. In Central Asia, these were largely movements for cultural autonomy, political reform (such as the Democratic Front in Tajikistan), or most importantly, religious revival (such as the Islamic Renaissance Party in Tajikistan and Uzbekistan). Central Asia's various diasporas and minority populations, such as the Uzbeks and Russians of Kazakhstan, seem to have engaged in little ethnic redefinition. Stalin-era ethnic designations still predominate in most parts of Central Asia. Ethnic Russians living in Kazakhstan, for example, view themselves as Russians, not Kazakhs, even if their families have been rooted for generations on Kazakh soil. All minority communities create potential faultlines in a society, but the region's Russians have the potential support of what Rogers Brubaker termed the 'homeland nationalism' of Russia (Olcott, 2000, pp. 52–4).

Russia's participation in Central Asian affairs is also encouraged by the presence of Russians in Central Asia. In order to increase its hold on the region, the Soviet Union had encouraged the emigration of ethnic Russians to Central Asia. After independence, Russians made up approximately 10 per cent of the population in Tajikistan and Uzbekistan, 22 per cent in Kyrgyzstan and nearly 40 per cent in Kazakhstan. These Russians were never assimilated into the population, and most have not learned the local language. Instead, they continue to think of themselves as Russians, a notion encouraged by Moscow. As long as a sizable Russian population remains in Central Asia, the Russian government will consider its welfare an extension of domestic policy (Ebon, 2001).

The policies of national consolidation chosen by the five Central Asian states have not been driven by the aspirations of their people, most of whom have yet to speak out. None of these states has undergone genuine nationalist experiences, and none is a real democracy by Western standards. Nor are they headed by bona fide nationalists, leaders who gained popular credibility through their role in a liberation struggle. Instead, all are still headed by men produced by the old Soviet system. Almost without exception, each of these men is trying to define an agenda for national consolidation that will meet the nationalist aspirations of the population without empowering them to change the political regime (Olcott, 2000, p. 54).

The political, economic and religious frame of Central Asia
Kazakhstan, Kyrgyzstan, Tajikistan, Turkmenistan and Uzbekistan share a number of common characteristics, including the inheritance of the structures, culture, educational success and so on of the Soviet Union (including the more liberal legacy of the late 1980s), the experience of de facto post-colonialism, developing new national, political and cultural identities, the economic (and social) problems of transition economies, and the infrastructure underpinning effective environmental management is also poor compared with Western countries. However, it is also important to ensure that key differences between the five republics, which will affect the development of socially and environmentally sustainable societies, are also recognised. These include the following (Farmer and Farmer, 2001, p. 137):

- widespread differences in a commitment to a pluralistic democracy, from a relatively open Kyrgyzstan to a more 'repressive' Turkmenistan and Uzbekistan;
- different ethnic (and therefore cultural compositions), with four republics being Turkic, while Tajikistan is 'Persian' and Kazakhstan retains a large Russian minority;
- differing security problems, from the uneasy end of civil war in Tajikistan to local disturbances in Kyrgyzstan and Uzbekistan; and
- differing economic prospects based on natural resources, with Kazakhstan and Turkmenistan having extensive reserves of oil, gas and other minerals.

Since 1998, however, the threat of Islamic militancy in Central Asia has decidedly strengthened diplomatic and military relations between Russia and Kyrgyzstan, Uzbekistan, Kazakhstan and Tajikistan. The Islamic insurgency in Central Asia is an opportunity for Russia to intervene and further its own interests in the region (Ebon, 2001).

All five republics have suffered sharp economic dislocation since gaining independence. They were suddenly cut off from the centralised command economy that directed their resource allocation, long-range planning, investment funding and management. Exploitation of rich natural energy and mineral resources has been stalled. No longer a part of the Soviet Union, the five republics are all landlocked, and goods must transit through a second nation via transport networks that do not yet exist (other than through Russia). Migration of ethnic Slavs to Russia has cost the republics a large cadre of skilled technicians and managers; migration of ethnic Germans has cost them the group most responsible for culti-vated agriculture. At the same time, population growth has produced an underclass of poor, unemployed or underemployed, less-educated workers whose dissatisfaction in the 1980s often provoked the riots leading up to independence (Smith, 1996).

Demarcation of state borders is ongoing between these republics and sometimes gives rise to tension. The unresolved legal status of the Caspian Sea, which is vital for the exploitation and transportation of energy resources, constitutes yet another cause for dispute. Disputes exist over water and energy resources and mutual dependence as regards water resources, and energy is another source of instability. Kyrgyzstan and Tajikistan are rich in water resources, while Uzbekistan, Kazakhstan and Turkmenistan are rich in oil and natural gas. Uzbekistan is dependent upon Tajikistan and Kyrgyzstan for water supplies, while Tajikistan and Kyrgyzstan are dependent upon Uzbekistan for natural gas. Regional countries do not hesi-tate to cut supplies if a dispute arises over payments. Distribution of natural resources, water supplies, transport systems and so on dictate unhindered economic cooperation among these states (Akıncı, 2006).

A good portion of the world's religions were incubated in Central Asia: Zoroastrianism, Buddhism, Nestorian Christianity, Manichaeism and Islam have all played major roles in the history of the region. The lan-guages of Central Asia reflect the Turkic, Mongol and Iranian mixture of its peoples ('Where is Central Asia?', 2000). On the other hand, religious extremism is considered as one of the major threats to security in Central Asia by some scholars, especially after the rise of 'Islamic' terrorism in the last few years. These fears were based both on the internal dynamics within the Central Asian republics and on the influence from the countries situ-ated in the south and southwest of the region. However, there is no serious religious extremist threat in Central Asia, perhaps with the exception of the Ferghana Valley of Uzbekistan. The Central Asian governments are all secular and the leadership is sensitive towards religious extremism. As a matter of fact, all the people in Central Asia follow the Sunni sect of Islam. Propaganda could not take any root even in Azerbaijan, a Caucasian

Turkish state where most of the population is shi'ite. This is due to the interpretation of the Islamic religion by the Turkish people which has never been fundamentalist. Following their acceptance of Islam in the ninth century, Turks combined their shamanistic traditions with Islamic teaching. Therefore, the way they practise religion does not accomodate fundamentalist approaches. In Tajikistan, where people speak Dari, the same language (Persian: Farsi) of Iran, religious extremism could not be disseminated. Therefore, religious extremism is not an issue for Central Asian states (Akıncı, 2006).

Jason Strakes examines the three Central Asian cases of Kazakhstan, Uzbekistan and Turkmenistan, all petrol-rich states (as opposed to Kyrgyzstan and Tajikistan, which in their present condition can be categorised as hydro-rich). He finds differences in the degree to which the independent variables of natural resource endowment and informal social structures serve as determinants for the strength of political management. Among his three case studies, Strakes finds that today's Kazakh leadership has the most success in establishing a concrete national identity, the Uzbek leadership resorting to violent repression, and the Turkmen state relying on a highly artificial nationalism, one with unlikely sustainable long-term prospects (cited in Yavuz and Foroughi; 2006, p. 6).

Turkey's economic relations with Central Asian countries
In the short story of relations after the disintegration of the Soviet Union, there was an uncertain period in Turkey, as in the whole world, about the methods and dimensions of the relations with the new independent countries of the Caucasus and Central Asia. Nonetheless, Turkey was the first country to officially recognise their independence (Kaya, 2006). Turkey's trade and economic ties with these countries far outweigh its place in world trade as a whole. For instance, Turkey is the third investor country in Kyrgyzstan and Kazakhstan. Turkish companies contribute to 10 per cent of Turkmenistan's GDP. Some 60 per cent of construction in Astana, the new capital of Kazakhstan, is attributed to Turkish firms. Turkey is the third trade partner of Azerbaijan and is among the primary trade partners of Uzbekistan. Furthermore the grand project of the early 1990s, the Baku–Tbilisi–Ceyhan pipeline, has been completed (Akıncı, 2006).

In the beginning of the 1990s, relations that had begun with mutual visits with the regional countries started to gain a corporate frame with bilateral agreements in various fields. In this context, in 1992 Turkey established the Turkish Cooperation and Development Agency (TİKA) in Ankara in order to conduct its regional policy from one centre. TİKA has implemented various education, technical assistance and cultural projects in the region, and it has representative offices in all the region's countries.

Relations that had begun officially then gained a new dimension when small and medium-sized enterprises (SMEs) began to establish economic relations. They assigned an important role to the people of the region, survivors of the communist era, in understanding the logic of free trade and the establishment of private companies. As from 1995, large-scale companies followed the SMEs, and Turkish companies started to make investments throughout the region. Turkish companies have a presence in the fields of food, agriculture, livestock, textiles, energy, mining, market chains, transport, banking and tourism (Kaya, 2006).

Kazakhstan is an important economic partner of Turkey. Turkish companies have been investing in industries such as food and beverages, oil, banking, retailing and tourism. In *Kyrgyzstan*, Turkish companies have worked with local businesses and helped them to acquire a greater share in the privatisation process. Turkish companies are operating in the hotel, food and beverages, banking and construction sectors. The Business Council supports the companies in their operations in Kyrgyzstan and also organises training programnes as well as investment seminars. *Turkmenistan* has been one of the most attractive investment destinations for Turkish companies investing heavily in the textile industry, undertaking major projects such as the construction of Ashgabat Airport and the Turkmenbasi Refinery as well as hotels, administrative and business complexes. New investments in healthcare, food and agro-industries are underway. *Uzbekistan* has also been one of the most attractive destinations for Turkish investment. The Business Council has formed sectoral committees (a light industry group – textiles and so on – a food industry group, a construction and construction materials group, an industry group) in order to help to improve economic relations between the two countries (DEIK, 2007). The Republic of *Tajikistan* is slowly but surely reviving from the political, social and economic crises of recent years. All sections of society feel the necessity to look for ways to intensify the mobilisation of domestic resources and foreign investments for the efficient reconstruction and sustainable development of the country. The capital inflow is very limited because of the economic instability. Turkish companies in Tajikistan are operating mostly in the construction and textile sectors (UNTJ, 2007).

Turkey is striving to foster a more peaceful environment in Central Asia and the Caucasus, which would ensure the promotion and expansion of the Turkish economic sector. Currently, Turkish businesses have contributed greatly to the successful launch of Migros supermarkets in Kazakhstan; primary schools in the deserts of Turkmenistan and Uzbekistan; the first five-star hotels in Turkmenistan and Kazakhstan; the Coca-Cola factories in Kazakhstan and Kyrgyzstan; and sophisticated textile conglomerates in Turkmenistan and Uzbekistan. The activities of Turkish companies in the region have raised the standard of living, creating a modern environment suitable for international business development and preparing the ground for further Western advances (Moustakis and Ackerman, 2002, p. 433).

Cultural relations are executed in parallel with commercial and political relations. Turkish companies have a big advantage in that except for Georgia, the Turkish language is spoken throughout the region, and they can integrate quickly with the people of the region. In addition, Turkey has placed great importance on the value of education. Turkey's cultural and educational initiatives in the regional states are likely to contribute to the improvement of multilateral relations (Uslu, 2003). Throughout both the public and the private sectors, over 10 thousand students have been educated in Turkish universities. Most of the graduates return to their own country and are given preferential treatment by Turkish companies. These well-educated personnel can also obtain employment in international companies and institutions (Kaya, 2006).

From the perspective of the Central Asian states, friendship with Turkey has had even greater importance in strengthening their ties with the West. In other words, Turkey serves as an agent in helping them to obtain capital, technology and friendship from the West. Turkey's active policies at the beginning caused unease to some states who were also taking an interest in the region. Russia's extension of its nuclear umbrella to some states of the region could be interpreted as a veiled warning to Turkey, an attempt to dissuade it from becoming too involved in the region. As Turkey increased its initiatives, Russia and Iran became more formidable rivals and they have begun to take measures against Turkish efforts. However the Turkish policy of deepening its economic relations with the Central Asian republics and launching large-scale investments in these countries will help them to become more self-sufficient. Moreover, if Turkey plays an active role in the initiatives of regional cooperation, especially in those that are related to Turkish interests, this will strengthen regional solidarity and will ultimately serve Turkish interests. As a country that is geographically close to the region and has historical and cultural ties with it, it is in Turkey's interest to become one of the most influential powers in the region (Uslu, 2003).

Research

The aim of the study

In this study the research aimed to identify the cultural diversity problems in Turkish companies which operate in Central Asian countries and examine their HR management approaches and methods to combat these problems.

Methodology

First, information was obtained from the Foreign Economic Relations Board (DEIK) and the Turkish Commercial Counsellors regarding an updated list of Turkish companies that operate in Central Asian countries. In the next stage of the study, a questionnaire was prepared to investigate the main cultural diversity problems in Turkish companies and to examine their HR management approaches or methods to solve or minimise these problems.

Then the questionnaires were sent by email to the HR managers of the Turkish companies, which were selected randomly. According to the data from the updated list, the number of companies that operate in Uzbekistan, Turkmenistan and Kazakhstan is greater than the number of companies operating in Kyrgyzstan and Tajikistan. Therefore most of the questionnaires were sent to Turkish companies in Uzbekistan, Turkmenistan and Kazakhstan. In total, 442 questionnaires were distributed to companies that are operating in different sectors such as the food industry, construction, construction materials, the oil industry, and textiles, in all five republics. However the actual sample size (that is, usable returned and completed questionnaires) was only 135, with a response rate of 30.7 per cent.

Table 8.1 shows the number of distributed and answered questionnaires and the percentage of feedback for each country.

Findings and results

Although the questionnaires were distributed to Turkish companies in each of the five countries, they were returned only from companies that are located in Turkmenistan, Uzbekistan and Kazakhstan. The percentage dispersal of employees according to their status and country (home country, host country or other) where they come from is shown in Table 8.2.

The table shows that the companies mostly employed top-level managers from Turkey, the home country (84 per cent). On the other hand, department managers, staff and workers were largely employees from the host countries (Turkmenistan, Uzbekistan and Kazakhstan) (62 per cent for department managers, 75 per cent staff and 88 per cent for workers). Compared with the employees from home and host countries, the percentage of employees from other countries is very low (13 per cent for department managers, 16 per cent staff and 8 per cent for workers). Companies employed top-level managers from Turkey because the management trusted the superiority of the Turkish managers' technical knowledge and managerial experience more than that of the host country's managers. Also, the management believed that Turkish top-level managers are more effective in organisational coordination and control in the host country.

Table 8.1   Number of distributed questionnaires and feedback (%)

Country	Distributed questionnaires	Answered questionnaires	Feedback (%)
Turkmenistan	158	37	23.4
Kazakhstan	154	52	33.7
Kyrgyzstan	4	–	–
Uzbekistan	123	46	37.4
Tajikistan	3	–	–

Table 8.2   Dispersal of employees according to status and country (%)

Status	Home country (%)	Host country (%)	Other (%)
Top-level manager (general manager, vice-general manager, general coordinator)	84	14	2
Department manager	25	62	13
Staff (specialist, secretary, engineer, officer, etc.)	9	75	16
Worker	4	88	8

On the other hand, companies mostly prefer employees from the host country for department manager, staff and worker status. According to HR managers, the main reason for this preference is the host country employees' familiarity with the local language and culture, which is an advantage to Turkish companies in their relations with the local government and the environment. Another reason for this preference is related to the companies' aim of achieving effective cultural diversity management among its employees. If the department managers come from a similar culture as the staff and workers, communication and managerial problems in the company are minimised. The last reason is related to the labour cost – especially with regard to staff and workers, employing the host country's citizens constitutes a labour cost advantage since their wages and salaries are very low in comparison with those of employees from the home or other countries.

The other finding of the study concerns the cultural diversity problems of the Turkish companies. In preparing the questionnaires, following the literature review, three main problems arose concerning cultural differences: ethnicity, language and religion. Among these ethnicity is seen as a considerable problem (52 per cent), followed by religion (35 per cent),

Table 8.3   Cultural diversity problems in Turkish companies (%)

Main cultural diversity problem	(%)
Ethnicity	52
Language	13
Religion	35

and then language, which rates very low (13 per cent) in comparison with the other two cultural diversity problems. Table 8.3 shows the percentage dispersal of these problems.

The ethnic and religious problems are mostly seen between two different groups: (i) between Russian employees and the employees from Central Asian countries (the Turkmen, Kazakh or Uzbek employees). Many Russians, as long-time representatives of the majority culture, feel a sense of displacement living in a minority community. They fear discrimination and do not want to live as second-class citizens. On the other hand, after the collapse of the Soviet Union, Central Asian countries gained their independence after a fierce struggle and they are very averse to any dependency on Russia. Consequently, this affects their relations with Russians in the workplace. In particular, if the Turkmen, Kazakh or Uzbek employees work under Russian managers, a power conflict is likely to erupt; and (ii) between employees from other countries (especially Vietnam and Korea) and employees from Central Asian countries (the Turkmen, Kazakh or Uzbek employees).

In addition to ethnic and religious problems, there are tensions regarding salaries and job position. Some of the Turkmen, Kazakh or Uzbek employees (especially Uzbek employees) have very strong feelings about the promotion of employees (especially Vietnamese or Korean employees) from other countries. In some Turkish companies the salary or wage of employees from other countries can be more than that of the host country employees because of the technical knowledge or work experience of the former – but sometimes this situation is described by some of the Turkmen, Kazakh or Uzbek employees as discrimination.

HR managers note that Turkish managers and employees have fewer ethnic, religious and language problems with the Turkmen, Uzbek and Kazakh managers and employees, for two reasons: the first concerns the longstanding historical, cultural, linguistic and ethnic ties between Turkey and these Central Asian countries; and the second is related to the Turkish-based educational background of the host country employees. Some of the Turkmen, Uzbek and Kazakh department managers and staff were educated in Turkish universities and they subsequently take up

*Table 8.4   Utilisation of methods applied by Turkish companies for
dealing with cultural diversity management problems (%)*

Methods	Application of methods (%)
To provide diversity training (cultural information training, empathy training, sensitivity training etc.) for managers	20
To provide diversity training for employees	9
To provide a language training programme to all levels of employees within the company	43
To organise social activities to enable employees to become closer to one another	28

a position in a Turkish company with a knowledge of Turkish culture and the ability to speak Turkish. These reasons are very effective in keeping the cultural diversity problems between Turkish employees and employees from the host country to a minimum.

The study's last finding concerns the Turkish companies' approaches and methods for dealing with the cultural diversity problems. In the questionnaire, four different methods were mentioned. Among these, three are related to the training programmes that are provided by the Turkish companies' management. Table 8.4 shows these approaches and their application by Turkish companies.

Most of the Turkish companies use language training programmes (43 per cent) in addition to other methods or training programmes to alleviate cultural diversity problems. Generally the formal or business language in Turkish companies is English, so the language similarity between the Turkish and the Central Asian countries is of little advantage in organizational communication.

The second most commonly used method is with regard to social activities (28 per cent) such as birthday parties, sports tournaments (especially football), dinner parties, picnics and so on, organised by the Turkish companies' management to build strong communication and cooperation among the employees.

The other method was a 'diversity management' training programme for managers (20 per cent) and for employees (9 per cent). But there is a big difference between the application percentages of the diversity training programmes. According to the HR managers, there are various reasons for this difference. The main reason is related to the high cost of the diversity training programme – providing the programme to a limited number of managers rather than to all employees is very cost effective. Also in most of the companies the managers who attend the programme are expected by the top management to share their knowledge with employees through the internal training programme. The other reason is related to the priority of the training programmes for employees. According to the HR managers, the employees need a language training programme more than a diversity training programme. The last reason is related to the top managements' approach to effective cultural diversity management – they think that the managers' competency regarding diversity management is very important in preventing cultural diversity problems and managing cultural diversity effectively. For this reason, the top management of the companies gives priority to the managers to undertake diversity training.

Conclusion

Turkey is a country that has many industrial outlets in Central Asian countries (Kazakhstan, Uzbekistan, Kyrgyzstan, Tajikistan and Turkmenistan). As from 1995, commercial relations have been executed in parallel with cultural relations – Turkish companies began to invest in all production fields in these countries. Drawing upon the cultural diversity management literature, the cultural diversity management problems of these companies and their approaches and methods for effective cultural diversity management were investigated.

According to the research results, ethnicity is the most commonly rated cultural diversity problem. After the collapse of the Soviet Union, Central Asian countries gained their independence by hard-won struggles; they are very averse to any dependence on Russia, and this affects their relations with Russians in the workplace. In particular, if the Turkmen, Kazakh or Uzbek employees work under Russian managers, the power conflict is apparent. On the other hand, ethnic problems also arise between employees from other countries (especially Vietnam and Korea) and those from Central Asian countries (the Turkmen, Kazakhs or Uzbeks). There are also issues of salary and job position. In some Turkish companies the salary or wage of employees from other countries can be higher than that of the host country employees, because of their superior technical knowledge or work experience – sometimes described by some of the Turkmen, Kazakh or Uzbek employees as a discrimination problem.

Ethnicity along with religion, ranked first and second, respectively, affect cultural diversity management. It is known that the top management of these companies are usually Turkish or Russian, and management styles can differ according to cultural identity along with the other variables. This can be because Russian managers come from a more individualistic culture than their Turkish counterparts and also because a different religion is practised.

Language is the last main problem, created by cultural differences. Furthermore, managers and the employees from diverse cultures may prefer to use their own native language. In addition, 'business English' which is a foreign language for both managers and employees, is compulsory. To prevent or to minimise these problems, Turkish companies arrange diversity and language training programmes and organise social activities for their employees and managers. Other results indicate that the companies provide diversity training programmes for a certain number of managers and employees – far more for the former, than for the latter. The diversity training programme is a very important tool for harmonising a wide range of people and developing their perception of diversity. Turkish companies should increase the number of diversity training programmes for both managers and employees.

This study had some limitations. First, the participation rate of Turkish companies in the research was low. On the other hand, this study focused on the cultural diversity problems and the methods applied by the companies to prevent or to minimise such problems. In future research, the cultural diversity problems should be investigated in each Central Asian country separately and the interview method could be used in order to obtain comprehensive information. Also, future research could focus on the benefits of cultural diversity in the Turkish companies which operate in Central Asian countries.

References

Akıncı, Halil (2006), 'Turkey's relations with Central Asian countries', December, available at: http://www.usiofindia.org/article_Oct_Dec06_2.html (accessed 25 November 2007).

Aydıngün, A. (2002), 'Creating, recreating and redefining ethnic identity: Ahiska/Meskhetian Turks in Soviet and post-Soviet contexts', *Central Asian Survey*, **21** (2), 185–97.

Ayoko, Oluremi B. and Härtel, Charmine E.J (2006), 'Cultural diversity and leadership – a conceptual model of leader intervention in conflict events in culturally heterogeneous workgroups', *Cross Cultural Management: An International Journal*, **13** (4), 345–60.

Carr-Ruffino, Norma (1996), *Managing Diversity: People Skills for a Multicultural Workplace*, Cincinnati, OH: Thomson Executive Press.

Cascio, F. Wayne (1995), *Managing Human Resources Productivity, Quality of Work Life, Profits*, New York: McGraw-Hill.

Choy, William K.W. (2007), 'Globalisation and Workforce Diversity: HRM Implications for Multinational Corporations in Singapore', *Singapore Management Review*, **29** (11), 1–20.

Cox, T.H. (1993), *Cultural Diversity in Organizations: Theory, Research and Practice*, San Francisco, CA: Berrett-Koehler.

Cox, Taylor H., Jr. and Blake, Stacy (1991), 'Managing cultural diversity: implications for organizational competitiveness', *The Executive*, **5** (3), August, 45–57.

Dass, P. and Parker, B. (1999), 'Strategies for managing human resource diversity: from resistance to learning', *Academy of Management Executive*, **13** (2), 68–80.

DEIK (2007), 'The aim of the Turkish–Kazakh Business Council', available at : http://www.deik.org.tr/Pages/EN/IK_AnaSayfa.aspx?IKID=30 (accessed 23 November, 2007).

Dessler, Gary (2002), *Human Resource Management*, Englewood Cliffs, NJ: Prentice-Hall.

Ebon, Lee (2001), 'Central Asia's balancing', *Harvard International Review*, **23** (2), Summer, 30–34.

Elmuti, Dean (1996), 'Revising affirmative action and managing cultural diversity challenge in corporate America', *Equal Opportunities International*, **15** (6/7), 1–16.

Farmer, Andrew M. and Farmer, Alma A. (2001), 'Developing sustainability: environmental non-governmental organizations in former Soviet Central Asia', *Sustainable Development*, **9** (3), August, 136–48.

Haq, Rana (2004), 'International perspectives on workplace diversity', in Margaret S. Stockdale and Faye J. Crosby (eds), *The Psychology and Management of Workplace Diversity*, Malden, MA: Blackwell, pp. 277–98.

Harung, H.S. and Harung, L.M. (1995), 'Enhancing organizational performance by strengthening diversity and unity', *The Learning Organization*, **2** (3), 9–21.

Henderson, George (1994), *Cultural Diversity in the Workplace*, Westport, CT: Quorum Books.

Hollenbeck, Noe and Wright, Gerhart (1997), *Human Resources Management: Gaining A Competitive Advantage*, New York: McGraw-Hill.

Kandola, R. and Fullerton, J. (1998), *Managing the Mosaic: Diversity in Action*, 2nd edn, London: Institute of Personnel Development.

Kaya, Kemal (2006), 'Impact of Turkey's membership to EU over Caucasus and Central Asia', available at http://www.eastweststudies.org/makale_detail.php?tur =221&makale=231 (accessed 25 November 2007).

Kirton, G. and Greene, A. (2005), *The Dynamics of Managing Diversity: A Critical Approach*, Oxford: Elsevier Butterworth-Heinemann.

Kossek, Ellen Erst and Lobel, Sharon A. (1996), *Managing Diversity: Human Resource Strategies for Transforming the Workplace*, Oxford: Blackwell.

Litvin, D. (2002), 'The business case for diversity and the "iron cage"', in B. Czarniawska and H. Höpfl (eds), *Casting the Other: The Production and Maintenance of Inequalities in Work Organizations*, London: Routledge, pp. 160–84.

Lorbiecki, A. (2001), 'Changing views on diversity management', *Management Learning*, **32** (3), 345–61.

Morrison, A., Ruderman, M. and Hughes-James, M. (1993), *Making Diversity Happen: Controversies and Solutions*, Greensboro, NC: Center for Creative Leadership.

Moustakis, Fotios and Ackerman, Ella (2002), 'September 11: a dynamic for Russo-Turkish co-operation or conflict?', *Central Asian Survey*, **21** (4), 423–34.

Olcott, Martha (2000), 'National consolidation', *Harvard International Review*, **22** (1), Winter/Spring, 50–54.

Özbilgin, M. (2008), 'Global diversity management', in Peter B. Smith, Mark F. Peterson and David C. Thomas (eds), *Handbook of Cross Cultural Management Research*, Newbury Park, CA: Sage, pp. 379–96.

Özkalp, E. and Kırel, Ç. (2000), '*Globalleşen örgütler ve örgütsel davranışın bu süreçteki yeri ve yeni ilgi alanları*', (Globalized organisations and the importance of organizational behaviour and its sphere of new interests in this process), 8. *Ulusal Yönetim ve Organizasyon Kongresi Bildiriler* (Proceedings of the 8th National Management and Organization Congress), Nevşehir, 25–27 May, pp. 447–62.

Palmer, Nicola (2007), 'Ethnic equality, national identity and selective cultural representation in tourism promotion: Kyrgyzstan, Central Asia', *Journal of Sustainable Tourism*, **5**, (6), 645–62.

Seymen, Oya Aytemiz (2006), 'The cultural diversity phenomenon in organisations and different approaches for effective cultural diversity management: a literary review', *Cross Cultural Management: An International Journal*, **13** (4), 296–315.

Sippola, Aulikki (2007), 'Developing culturally diverse organizations: a participative and empowerment-based method', *Women in Management Review*, **22** (4), 253–73.

Smith, Dianne L (1996), 'Central Asia: a new great game?', *Asian Affairs: An American Review*, **23** (3), Fall, 147–75.

Stockdale, Margaret S. and Cao, Feng (2004), 'Looking back and heading forward: major themes of the psychology and management of workplace diversity', in Margaret S. Stockdale and Faye J. Crosby (eds), *The Psychology and Management of Workplace Diversity*, Oxford: Blackwell, pp. 299–316.

Tayeb, M.H. (1996), *The Management of a Multicultural Workforce*, Chichester: Wiley.

Trenka, Johannes (2006), 'Diversity in the workforce: challenges for employers', *SuperVision*, **67** (10), October, 17–21.

UNTJ (United Nations in Tajikistan) (2007), 'Tajikistan Human Development Report 2000', available at: http://www.untj.org/files/reports/NationL%20Human%20Development%20 Report%202000.pdf (accessed 27 November 2007).

Uslu, Nasuh (2003), 'The Russian, Caucasian and Central Asian aspects of Turkish foreign policy in the post Cold War period', *Alternatives: Turkish Journal of International Relations*, **2** (3–4), Fall/Winter, 164–87.

'Where is Central Asia?' (2000), *Harvard International Review*, **22** (1), Winter/Spring, p. 49.

Yavuz, Hakan and Foroughi, Payam (2006), 'State, society and Islam in Central Asia: Introduction to the Special Issue', *Journal of Muslim Minority Affairs*, **26** (1), 3–8.

9 Caste-based quotas: India's reservations policies
Rana Haq

Introduction

The 2001 Census of India recorded that India had crossed the one billion population mark, making it the second most populated country in the world, after China (Census of India, 2001). Both these countries have experienced unprecedented growth as a result of recent economic reforms and the removal of trade barriers. Consequently, they are increasingly drawing businesses from around the globe eager to tap into these booming consumer markets. Scholars too are interested in this growing phenomenon. However, Western business and management concepts are often challenged within the Asian context. The people of India are diverse in language, culture and religion since there are 28 states and seven Union Territories (Government of India, 2008) each with a distinct history, culture, cuisine, customs, official language, multiple dialects, religious beliefs and festivals.

India's diversity issues are primarily based upon intra-racial differences, unlike most Western countries, with high immigration patterns, which have workplace diversity issues based on inter-racial differences (Haq, 2004). For example, the hyphenated-American labels such as the African-Americans, the Latin-Americans and the Asian-Americans, in the US, do not fit diversity concerns outside of the US context (Nishii and Özbilgin, 2007). Diversity issues in India are primarily based on religion. India's affirmative action policies, commonly known as 'reservations', were established in the 1950 constitution as a temporary corrective process of compensatory positive discrimination to address centuries of past injustices and repression based on class and status arising from the traditional Hindu caste system. The importance of understanding the impact of the centuries-old caste system is critical in assessing the inequalities in human capital formation, opportunity structures and wage determination in India even today (Deshpande, 2001; Scoville, 2003; Freitas, 2006).

Estimates put the start of the caste system anywhere between 3000 BC and 1000 BC. Even today it remains an important issue for Indian society with the Indian government's proposals for caste based job quotas in the private sector and increases in caste based reservations at institutions of higher learning. It is still an important determinant of people's economic choices. . . . With the widespread criticism the institution currently faces the persistence of this system of social stratification for 3000 years during periods of changing economic and social environments is puzzling. (Freitas, 2006: 2)

This chapter will highlight cross-national differences in the target groups protected by diversity policies and explore the key drivers that underpin the reservations context, practices and outcomes in the realm of India's complex workforce diversity challenges. For more information and different perspectives on managing diversity in India, also see the contributions by Patel (ch. 13) and Robinson and Ensign (ch. 15), as well as Härtel et al. (ch. 10) in this book. The focus of this chapter is to provide a discussion on the socio-economic and political influences on the reservations policies, thus contributing to the global discussion on diversity management by examining the antecedents, interventions and outcomes of India's reservations policies. The primary aim is to extend India's reservations issues into the cross-national conversations on managing diversity by informing, educating and raising the awareness of readers, scholars and practitioners unfamiliar with the Indian diversity management context.

Diversity dilemma

For the past few decades, there has been an ongoing debate among workforce diversity scholars, policy makers and practitioners as to the goals of diversity programs and what the diversity construct specifically does and does not encompass. Scholars who advocate defining diversity along historical lines of oppression argue that the goal of diversity initiatives is to identify and remove power imbalances and level the playing field for certain groups historically marginalized in the workplace (Abella, 1984). The richness of the debate over how to define the diversity construct and achieve diversity goals emphasizes the fact that diversity is a socially, politically and emotionally charged topic in most countries across the world. This is certainly true in the context of the reservations policies in India.

Griggs (1995) classified diversity into two sets: primary and secondary dimensions. The six primary dimensions are those which human beings are born into and cannot change, such as, age, ethnicity, gender, mental/ physical abilities, race and sexual orientation. These primary dimensions represent personal characteristics that influence each individual's socialization and social identity. Workplace discrimination on primary dimensions has traditionally led to the marginalization of certain minority groups in the workforce, consequently legal protections have been sought for these designated groups. The next set includes several secondary dimensions which can be changed because individuals have some control over these features throughout their lives, such as, education, income, geographic location, language, marital status, parental status, religion, occupation, work style, work experience, behavioural style, life experiences and so on. Other researchers (Morrison 1992; Thomas, 1992; Gardenswartz and Rowe, 1993; Tomervik, 1994; Wilson, 1996; Bell et al., 2004) also offer a broader diversity definition by including obesity, values, personality characteristics, physical appearance, lifestyle, beliefs and background characteristics such as geographic origin, tenure with the organization, role in functional departments, power, class and economic status. However, these broader approaches are seen by some as an attempt to weaken the legitimate concerns of the narrowly defined designated groups and a watering down of the protections afforded them through hard-fought legislation. Caudron and Hayes (1997) raise the concern that it diverts attention from the issue of actually disadvantaged groups because the additional groups added by a broader definition do not face equal prejudice or similar hostile conditions in the workplace. Abella (1984) argues that since the systemic barriers within organizations are based on values, beliefs and attitudes towards certain groups, they become historically entrenched organizational policies and practices. These attributes become salient because, collectively, they stymie the entry and progress of individual and group members and their participation within organizations. Therefore, it is necessary to re-evaluate past practices and replace them with inclusionary policies and practices through organizational development and culture change strategies.

Diversity is universally accepted, in the West, as a North American construct that has been conceptualized in a variety of different ways by the public in general and by researchers, practitioners and policy makers in particular. Employment equity (EE) in Canada and South Africa, equal opportunity (EO) in the UK and Australia, equal employment opportunity (EEO) and affirmative action (AA) in the US, are terms used to indicate legislation-driven programs towards leveling the playing field for certain protected groups which have traditionally been marginalized in the workplace based on their primary dimensions of diversity. Although inspired by each other to some extent, there is no unifying term to describe these protective legal programs for the identified groups which are, in fact, quite unique to each country, arising from their historical and cultural context. Notably, women are the consistent primary focus of equality programs across most countries. Globally, diversity management remains a complex construct on several fronts including the definition of the terminology, the legally required versus voluntary programs, the inclusivity or exclusivity issues, as well as the necessary extent of accommodations, positive measures, or affirmative action. Consequently, the perception, awareness, acceptance, interpretation and implementation of diversity policies differs in most countries across the world, resulting in major constraints on straightforward applications and cross-national comparisons (Nishii and Özbilgin, 2007).

In Canada, the Employment Equity Act (EEA) legislation requires organizations to, at minimum, review their employment practices and remove systemic barriers faced by the four designated groups: Aboriginal Peoples, Persons with Disabilities, Visible Minorities, and Women as set out in the federal Act and Regulations (EEA, 1986). The goal of this act is outcome based requiring federally regulated Canadian organizations to become proportionally reflective of the communities they serve by meeting the Census-documented workforce availability data in their employee representation within all occupational hierarchies of their workforce. The EEA regulates the federal public service and public organizations in four main federal sectors: Banking, Transportation, Communications and Other (mostly natural resources and services based) with more than 100 employees. Private organizations are regulated under this act via the Federal Contractor's Program (FCP) which requires companies with 100 or more employees and with contracts over $200,000 CDN with the federal government, to implement EE (See Haq and Ng, 2010 for more details).

In the US, the equal opportunity policies rose out of the Black African-American anti-discrimination movement resulting in the 1964 Civil Rights Act, requiring government agencies to redress the under-representation and occupational segregation of minorities and women in their work-force. Notably, the US Supreme Court had historically sanctioned legal racial segregation by passing laws towards maintaining and nurturing the separation of races in many spheres of life, such as establishing seg-regated schools for White and Coloured children, segregation in the use of public services such as transportation, toilets, beaches, restaurants and so on leading to attitudes of White supremacy and a life of violence, intimidation and lynch terror for the Black African-Americans even after the abolition of slavery. 'If one race be inferior to the other socially, the Constitution of the United States cannot put them up on the same plane' (Boston and Nair-Reichert, 2003: 4, citing Birnbaum and Taylor, 2000: 166–7) was the position of the US Supreme Court in its 1896 decision on *Plessy v. Ferguson*, where 'the court held with deadpan gall that racially segregated railway cars were both constitutional and reasonable and did not violate the rights of the Blacks' (Boston and Nair-Reichert, 2003: 4). It was President Lyndon Johnson who first used the term 'affirmative action' to persuade the US Congress to pass the 1964 Civil Rights Act authorizing the Attorney General to enforce the 100-year-old Fourteenth Amendment to the Constitution to end the state-sanctioned racial segregation. In 1965, the Executive Order 11246 and its amendment empowered the federal government and recipients of federal contracts over $50,000 USD to implement AA plans to remove discrimination in employment for minorities and women (Boston and Nair-Reichert, 2003).

Interestingly, there has been much backlash in both these countries, Canada and the US, from the mainstream opposed to these policies by terming them as 'reverse discrimination'. In the US, the state of California held a public ballot Proposition 209 in 1996, opposing affirmative action by prohibiting public institutions from implementing this reverse discrimination on the basis of race, sex and ethnicity. Although opposed by pro-affirmative action groups, Proposition 209 was voted into law with a 54 per cent majority. In 2006, the state election of Michigan followed suit and passed the Michigan Civil Rights Initiative via public ballot. In Canada, Ontario's provincial elections were used as a platform by the Conservative party of Premier Mike Harris for discrediting the incumbent Liberal party's newly implemented Employment Equity Act of Ontario (EEAO) in 1994, as reverse discrimination. The Conservative government came into power on the promise to repeal Ontario's EEA upon their successful election to power in June 1995. As a result of the repeal, organizations in Ontario preparing to implement the EEAO promptly put a stop to their initial diversity efforts, especially the collection of self-identifying workforce data which became illegal under the new rules and, in fact, had to be destroyed by many organizations. This was the same year that the federal Canadian government revised and strengthened its EEA of 1986, resulting in federally regulated organizations stepping up their EEA efforts. This dichotomy is a clear indication that political and legal pressures are the primary catalyst to diversity policies in most North American organizations.

By comparison, the Indian diversity debate predates the North American diversity construct. In India, it is largely the secondary set of diversity dimensions that form the basis for discrimination and are the focus of its constitutional reservations policies. The 1950 constitution of independent India established the world's first and oldest system of positive discrimination and affirmative action towards its marginalized minorities. It enshrines India's reservations policies requiring public organizations to set quotas for the three main identified groups: Scheduled Castes (SCs), Scheduled Tribes (STs) and Other Backward Classes (OBCs). Despite these protections, discrimination against these groups persists due to the caste system which has continued to remain pervasive in India, even in today's modern context. Moreover, the discrimination is not limited only to workplace issues but pervades every aspect of life from birth, in education, in jobs, in marriage, in housing, in temples, in death, and even after death in cremation rights, especially in the rural parts of the country.

Members of the lowest caste and the outcaste continue to face discrimination in all aspects of life although the practice of labeling people as 'Untouchables' was outlawed by the Indian constitution in 1950. India's non-governmental organizations lobbied for many years to bring the issue of caste to the forefront while the Indian government argued that, because of its uniqueness, the caste issue was not to be held at par with the international definition of racial discrimination. It was only at the 2001 UN Conference on Race in Durban, South Africa, that caste discrimination was internationally recognized to be equivalently as serious as racism. The term 'Untouchables' has now been replaced by the term '*Dalits*' which translates as 'the oppressed' in the Indian Marathi language. According to a Dalit Solidarity Network report of 2006, *dalit* children are forced to sit in the back of the classroom in more than half of Indian schools, are bullied, assaulted and humiliated, leading to a government reported *dalit* dropout rate of 73 per cent.

> Upper class teachers, who send their own children to private schools, are often accused of discriminating against lower caste students by refusing to pick them for leadership roles and using them for menial chores, including sweeping and cleaning latrines – the kind of occupations that are traditionally the only ones available to the students' parents. (Wax, 2008)

Background context of India's reservations issues
The simple Black–White divide in the US is a stark contrast to the complexity of the Indian caste system which is grouped into four *varnas*: *Brahmanas* (priests, philosophers and scholars), *Kshatriyas* (rulers and warriors), *Vaisyas* (merchants), *Sudras* (artisans and peasants) and a fifth catchall 'Outcastes' (Nesiah, 1997). Caste, or *jati* in Sanskrit, is determined upon the birth of a child based on perceptions of purity and pollution of the family profession which is generally identified through the family name and remains unaltered over the generations. The *Rig Veda*, dated approximately the second millennium BC, and the *Manu Smriti*, dated between the second and fifth century BC, are the two ancient Hindu religious texts that are the primary sources of the Hindu caste system. These quotes from the *Manu Smriti* explain:

> But in order to protect this universe He, the most resplendent one, assigned separate duties and occupations to those who sprang from his mouth, arms, thighs and feet. To *Brahmanas* he assigned teaching and studying [the *Veda*], sacrificing for their own benefit and for others, giving and accepting [of alms]. The Kshatriyas he commanded to protect the people, to bestow gifts, to offer sacrifices, to study [the *Veda*], and to abstain from attaching themselves to sensual pleasures; The *Vaisyas* to tend to cattle, to bestow gifts, to offer sacrifices, to study [the *Veda*], to trade, to lend money, and to cultivate land. One

occupation only the lord prescribed to the *Sudras*, to serve meekly even these [other] three castes. (Buehler, 1886: Chapter 1, Verses 87–91)

No collection of wealth must be made by a *Sudra*, even though he be able; for a *Sudra* who has acquired wealth, gives pain to *Brahmanas*. (Ibid.: Chapter 10, Verse 129: 430)

A fifth category included all the outcaste, mostly the people involved in occupations such as janitorial and sanitation, generally regarded as the unclean and polluting professions, and were thus called the Untouchables, or 'non-persons' outside the caste system. The Untouchables were required to maintain a physical distance from 'caste Hindus' as even their shadow was believed to be polluting and any breach of this code often resulted in individual and collective acts of violence against the offender. Despite the ban on the term 'Untouchable' and the protections under the 1950 constitution, discrimination, persecution and violence against the Untouchables continue to be prevalent, particularly in rural India:

It should be emphasized that at its core, the treatment of SC/ST persons by Hindus is predicated on the belief that SC/ST persons are inferior to 'caste' Hindus. Not to put too fine a point on it, such treatment is predicated on a devaluation of their worth as human beings. This, then has considerable resource implications for SC/ST families: in villages, it is not uncommon for them to be denied access to Hindu wells; in village schools, their children are often made to sit away from caste Hindu children and are routinely referred to as *Bhangis* ['latrine cleaners' in Hindi]; their women are frequently humiliated and violated; and their houses are located in the low-lying (and therefore, most liable to flooding) parts of villages. Consequently, SC/ST persons, compared to [upper-caste] Hindus, are more likely to be ill, less likely to be adequately educated, more likely to cultivate marginal land and more likely to live in a climate of fear and oppression. (Borooah, 2005: 412)

Osborne (2001) explains that the caste system is distinct from the *varna* hierarchy in that each Hindu is born into a *jati* or caste which in turn belongs to a *varna* or the broader superstructure of traditional Hindu social ordering. (See Srinivas, 1962 for further discussion on *varnas* and caste.) Thus, one's occupation was predetermined at birth since each caste traditionally had an obligation to perform certain services to the community based on their traditional role in the complex network of relationships, formally known as the *jajmani* system, to exchange services without a conventional monetary economy. As a form of barter system, they drew on the services from members of other castes employed in performing their own hereditary occupations in the service of the community. Therefore, it was the *jatis*, rather than the *varnas* that determined the details of the caste system.

While the term 'caste' is hard to define, it is clearly different from the concept of race, class, ethnic groups and tribes (Freitas, 2006). Several authors (Ghurye, 1961; Dutt, 1965; Hutton, 1981; Klass, 1993) use common features to define caste, similar to Freitas (2006: 7) who defines it as having five distinct characteristics:

1. *Occupational specialization* The caste usually had a monopoly over an occupation and its subsets that are followed by that caste's members. Restrictions were limited to occupations that they could *not* follow.
2. *Purity scale* Occupations were ranked on a purity scale of clean and unclean.
3. *Hierarchy* An individual's status was determined by the rank of his caste.
4. *Commensality* Restrictions on eating and drinking with members of other castes based on their hierarchy within the caste system.
5. *Ascriptiveness* A person's caste was determined by birth and membership could be taken away upon violation of the caste rules and marriage was restricted to within members of the same caste.

Dumont (1980) explains caste as separating purity from impurity based on any contact between a higher and lower caste member because the three higher *varnas* Brahmins, Kshatryas and Vaisyas, are believed to be 'twice born' (*dwij*) or entitled to a rebirth at the end of life while the Shudras and the *dalits* are not. The most common discrimination practices include:

(1) the denial of access to public facilities, wells, schools, post offices and courts; (2) prohibitions against entering Hindu temples; (3) exclusion from professional occupations; (4) residential segregation; (5) denial of access to restaurants, theatres and barber shops; (6) prohibition from using horses, bicycles, umbrellas, or wearing jewelry; (7) restrictions involving maintaining prescribed distance from persons of higher caste while on roads and streets. The untouchables were not allowed to touch people from the four Varnas, enter homes of the higher Varnas or the temples or use the same wells used by members of the higher castes. During public occasions they were seated at a distance from the four Varnas. (Boston and Nair-Reichert, 2003: 6)

In pre-independence India, *Mahatama*, meaning 'great soul' in Hindi, Mohandas Karamchand Gandhi, the great Indian leader, renamed the Untouchables as '*Harijans*', meaning 'People of God' in Hindi. He regularly interacted with them, including eating their food and drinking their water and sleeping at their homes, to bring down the walls of discrimination based on pollution, impurity and caste hierarchy. Despite his efforts and six decades of the constitutional abolition of these discriminatory practices, the social stigma to being an Untouchable remains stronger than ever in the Indian psyche. Religious discrimination is still prevalent in the personal, professional, social and economic lives of the people in this largely rural country. While the urban areas have apparently become less stringent about these customs and are seeing more mobility between professions and more inter-marriages between the castes, discrimination remains a current issue in India. Recently, the *Globe and Mail* newspaper of Toronto reported (Pepper, 2008: A3) that a law suit was filed with the Delhi High Court against four New Delhi municipal agencies by a *dalit* rights group – the National Campaign for the Dignity and Rights of Sewage and Allied Workers. 'If you see, the engineers and officers are all from the upper castes of Indian society' said Hemlata Kansotia, Social Activist and Campaign Chair (ibid.: A3). Because of discrimination and lack of education as well as opportunities, the *dalits* work in some of the dirtiest and most dangerous jobs in the sub-continent, such as sewage cleaning. Of the 8,000 sewage cleaners in New Delhi, 1,000 have died in the past seven years from gas asphyxiation, drowning in excreta, tuberculosis, hepatitis, and others suffer from diseases such as skin rashes, respiratory and liver problems in this hazardous job working without boots, masks, gloves and other safety equipment. In ship breaking, *dalits* are used for dismantling ships containing dangerous materials, such as asbestos, without any protective gear. In manual scavenging, about one million *dalits* are responsible for digging village graves, lifting dead bodies onto the funeral pyres, lighting those fires and collecting the cooled ashes afterwards. They also dispose of the carcasses of dead animals. India has to face the challenge of competing in the global economy with its labour force still deeply divided by religion, caste and traditional customs.

India's reservations policies

The four key principles for the rationale behind India's reservations policies are: (i) compensation for past injustices; (ii) protection of the weak; (iii) proportional equality; and (iv) social justice (Sivaramayya, 1984: 51). The private sector is not bound by the reservations policies and has taken no voluntary measures to support affirmative action although there are increasing demands to do so and these pressures are expected to continue into the future. For the purposes of affirmative action, the Indian government publishes lists of the Scheduled Castes, the Scheduled Tribes and Other Backward Classes as the only designated groups. Census 2001 documented 1,221 SCs accounting for over 166 million people or 16.2 per cent of the Indian population; and 664 STs accounting for over 84 million people or 8.2 per cent of the Indian population (Census of India, 2001). The STs are India's tribal indigenous or aboriginal peoples known as *adivasis*, meaning 'original inhabitants' in Hindi. Eighty-seven per cent of these identify themselves as Hindus, about 7 per cent as Christians, and about 5 per cent exclusively practice traditional tribal religious beliefs and customs (ibid.).

Led by Mahatma Gandhi's non-violent movement of passive resistance, India won its independence from the British Raj on 15 August 1947. The Constitution of India was drafted by the Constituent Assembly which appointed a drafting committee under the chairmanship of Dr B.R. Ambedkar, a Harvard-educated lawyer, who was India's greatest champion for the *dalits*, being himself of the same caste. The Indian constitution came into effect on 26 January 1950. Articles 15, 16 and 17 (see Table 9.1) of the 1950 Constitution of Independent India, prohibit discrimination, promote equality of opportunity in public employment, and abolish 'Untouchability'. Articles 29, 45 and 46 protect minorities, provide free and compulsory education up to the age of 14 years, and further protect the economic and educational needs of the SCs and STs. Articles 340, 341 and 342 empowered the president of India to establish lists of these three groups for the affirmative action purposes of reservations.

While there is reasonable consensus among Indians on establishing reservations for the SCs and the STs, there is vehement disagreement on the definition, need and extent of reservations for the 'socially and educationally backward classes' (commonly known as the Other Backward Classes) as the term itself has not been clearly explained in the constitution. Shortly after independence, the government appointed Kaka Saheb Kalelkar in 1953 to list the OBCs, choosing not to create a nationwide list but allowing each state to determine its own list of backward classes. Twenty-six years later, on 1 January 1979, a second OBC commission was set up by the president, chaired by B.P. Mandal (see Table 9.2 for comparative details on these two OBC commissions). In 1990, when the V.P. Singh government finally implemented the Mandal Commission's recommendations for caste-based reservations of government jobs and educational institutions, there were large-scale anti-Mandal demonstrations all over the country, especially by upper caste student groups supporting the merit system over reservations in government jobs and educational opportunities (Kader, 2004). As the states experimented with over-and under-inclusion issues based on different formulae to determine caste identity and backwardness, the Supreme Court ruled in 1992 that the central government and all state governments must create a permanent body for recommending inclusion in the OBC lists, with the exclusion of the 'creamy layer' of affluent OBC members not in need of reservations, and the total reservations should not exceed 50 per cent of the Indian population.

Table 9.1   Relevant articles from the Constitution of India (1950)

Article	Description
Article 15 Prohibition of discrimination on grounds of religion, race, caste, sex, or place of birth	(1) The State shall not discriminate against any citizen on grounds only of religion, race, caste, sex, place of birth or any of them. (2) No citizen shall on grounds only of religion, race, caste, sex, place of birth or any of them, be subject to any disability, liability, restriction or condition with regard to – (a) access to shops, public restaurants, hotels and places of public entertainment; or (b) the use of wells, tanks, bathing ghats, roads and places of public resort maintained wholly or partly out of State funds or dedicated to the use of the general public. (3) Nothing in this article shall prevent the State from making any special provision for women and children. (4) Nothing in this article or in clause (2) or article 29 shall prevent the State from making any special provision for the advancement of any socially and educationally backward classes of citizens or for the Scheduled Castes and the Scheduled Tribes
Article 16 Equality of opportunity in matters of public employment	(1) There shall be equality of opportunity for all citizens in matters of employment or appointment to any office under the State. (2) No citizen shall, on grounds only of religion, race, caste, sex, descent, place of birth, residence or any of them, be ineligible for, or discriminated against in respect of, any employment or office under the State. (3) Nothing in this article shall prevent Parliament from making any law prescribing, in regard to a class or classes of employment or appointment to an office under the Government of, or any local or other authority within, a State or Union territory, any requirement as to residence within that State or Union territory prior to such employment or appointment. (4) Nothing in this article shall prevent the State from making any provision for the reservation of appointments or posts in favour of any backward class of citizens which, in the opinion of the State, is not adequately represented in the services under the State. (4A) Nothing in this article shall prevent the State from making any provision for reservation in matters of promotion to any classes of posts in the services under the State in favour of the Scheduled Castes and the Scheduled Tribes which, in the opinion of the State, are not adequately represented in the services under the State. (5) Nothing in this article shall affect the operation of any law which provides that the incumbent of an office in connection with the affairs of any religious or denominational institution or any member of the governing

Table 9.1   (continued)

Article	Description
	body thereof shall be a person of a particular religion or belonging to a particular denomination
Article 17 Abolition of Untouchability	'Untouchability' is abolished and its practice in any form is forbidden. The enforcement of any disability arising out of 'Untouchability' shall be an offence punishable in accordance with the law
Article 45 Education for children	The State shall endeavour to provide, within a period of ten years from the commencement of this Constitution, for free and compulsory education for all children until they complete the age of fourteen years
Article 46 SC, ST & other weaker sections	The State shall promote with special care the education and economic interests of the weaker sections of the people, and in particular, of the Scheduled Castes and the Scheduled Tribes, and shall protect them from social injustice and all forms of exploitation
Article 341 Scheduled Castes (SCs) & Article 342 Scheduled Tribes (STs)	(1) The President may with respect to any State or Union territory and where it is a State, after consultation with the Governor thereof by public notification specify the castes or tribes or parts of or groups within castes, races or tribes which shall for the purposes of this Constitution be deemed to be Scheduled Castes in relation to that State or Union territory, as the case may be. (2) Parliament may by law include or exclude from the list of Scheduled Castes specified in a notification issued under clause (1) any caste, race or tribe or part of or group within any caste, race or tribe, but save as aforesaid a notification issued under the said clause shall not be waived by any subsequent notification Article 342 reads similarly, as above, for the Scheduled Tribes
Article 340 Special Provision	Appointment of a Commission to investigate the conditions of backward classes (1) the President may by order appoint a Commission consisting of such persons as he thinks fit to investigate the conditions of socially and educationally backward classes within the territory of India and the difficulties under which they labour and to make recommendations as to the steps that should be taken by the Union or any State to remove such difficulties and to improve their condition and as to the grants that should be made for the purpose by the Union or any State and the conditions subject to which such grants should be made, and the order appointing such Commission shall define the procedure to be followed by the Commission

Table 9.2 A comparison of two OBC commissions for identifying 'socially and educationally backward classes' under Article 340 of the Indian Constitution

	FIRST OBC COMMISSION	SECOND OBC COMMISSION
ESTABLISHED:	January 29, 1953	January 1, 1979
REPORTED:	March 30, 1955	December 1980
CHAIR:	Kaka Kalelkar	B. P. Mandal
TERMS OF REFERENCE:	(a) determine the criteria to be adopted in considering whether any sections of the people in the territory of India in addition to the SCs and STs as socially and educationally backward classes, using such criteria it was to prepare a list of such classes setting out their approximate members & distribution; (b) investigate the conditions of all such socially and educationally backward classes & the differences under which they labour & make recommendations as to (i) the steps that should be taken by the union or any state to remove such difficulties or to improve their economic condition, and (ii) the grants that should be made by the union or state and the conditions subject to which such grants should be made; (c) investigate such other matters as the president may hereafter refer to them; (d) present a report setting out the facts as found by them and make recommendations.	(1) determine the criteria for defining the socially and educationally backward classes; (2) recommend the steps to be taken for their advancement; (3) examine the desirability or otherwise for making any provision for the reservation of appointments or posts in their favour; (4) present a report setting out the facts found by the commission.

CRITERIA:

(1) Low social position in the traditional caste hierarchy of Hindu society.

(2) Lack of general educational advancement among the major section of a caste or community.

(3) Inadequate or no representation in government services.

(4) Inadequate representation in the field of trade, commerce and industry.

The commission prepared three questionnaires: for the state government, the central ministries and the general public. A socio-educational field survey was organized under a panel of experts, to include caste studies, analysis of data, village monographs and legal and constitutional issues.

- Adopted 11 criteria grouped under three major headings for assessing castes/classes: **Social** (i) which were considered as socially backward by others; (ii) which depend on manual labour for livelihood; (iii) where at least 25% females & 10% males above state average marry at age below 17 years in rural areas (10% females & 5% males for urban areas). (iv) where participation of females in work is at least 2% above the state average. **Educational** (v) where the number of children in the age group of 5–15 years who never attended school is at least 25% above the state average; (vi) where the rate of student drop-outs in the age group of 5–15 years is at least 25% above the state average; (vii) where the proportion of matriculates is at least 25% below the state average. **Economic** (viii) castes/classes where the average value of family assets is at least 25% below the state average; (ix) where the number of families living in 'kuccha' [raw] houses is at least 25% above the state average; (x) where the source of drinking water is beyond half a km for > 50% of the households. (xi) where the number of households with loans is at least 25% above the state average.

- A weight of 3 points each was given to all the social indicators; 2 points each to educational indicators; and one point to each economic indicator.

- In addition to social and educational, economic indicators were considered important as they directly flowed from social and educational backwardness mainly to highlight the fact that socially and educationally backward classes are economically backward also. Total added up to 22. These 11 indicators were applied to all criteria of the castes covered by the survey for a particular state. All castes with a score of 50% (i.e., 11 points) or above while applying the weight were listed as socially and educationally backward and the rest were treated as 'advanced'.

Table 9.2 (continued)

	FIRST OBC COMMISSION	SECOND OBC COMMISSION
RESULTS: Prepared a list of 2,399 backward castes or communities for the entire country, of which 837	Using the above-mentioned criteria, the commission identified 3,743 caste groups as OBC. Figures of caste-wise population were not available beyond 1931. So the commission used 1931 census data to calculate the number of OBCs. The population of Hindu OBCs was derived by subtracting from the total population of Hindus, the population of SCs and STs and that of forward Hindu castes and communities, and it worked out to be 52%. Assuming that roughly	
were classified the 'most backward'	the proportion of OBCs among non-Hindus was of the same order as among the Hindus, the population of non-Hindu OBCs was also considered as 52% of the actual proportion of their population of 16.16% or 8.40%. The total population of Hindu and non-Hindu OBCs therefore added up to 52% of the country's population.	
MAIN RECOMMENDATION: Caste as the criteria to determine backwardness	The population of OBCs, which includes both Hindus and non-Hindus, was around 52% of the total population. However, only 27% of reservation was recommended owing to the legal constraint that the total quantum of reservation should not exceed 50%. The already existing reservation for SCs and STs is in tune with their proportion to total population (i.e., 15% for SCs and 7.2% for STs) and together amounting to 22.5% is to be taken into account, while counting the total percentage of reservation. States which had already introduced reservation for OBCs exceeding 27% were not to be affected.	
OTHER RECOMMENDATIONS: (i) undertaking caste-wise enumeration of population in the census of 1961;	(1) OBC candidates recruited on basis of merit in an open competition should not be adjusted against their reservation quota of 27%. (2) The above reservation should also be made applicable to promotion quota at all levels.	

(ii) relating social backwardness of a class to its low position in the traditional caste hierarchy of Hindus

(iii) all women as a class of 'backward'

(iv) reservation of 70% seats in all technical and professional institutions for qualified OBC students

(v) minimum reservation of vacancies in all government services & local bodies for OBC. Scale: class I = 25%, class II = 33⅓%, class III & IV = 40%

OUTCOME:

Report was not accepted by the government, who feared that the backward classes excluded from the caste and communities selected by the commission would not be considered and the really needy would be swamped by the multitude for receiving special attention.

(3) Reserved quota remaining unfilled should be carried forward for a period of 3 years then de-reserved.

(4) Relaxation in the upper age limit for direct recruitment extended to the OBC candidates in the same manner as for SCs and STs.

(5) A roster system for each category of posts be adopted by the concerned authorities as presently done for SC and ST candidates.

Recommendations applicable to recruitment in the public sector both under the central and state governments, & nationalized banks. All private sector undertakings which have received financial assistance from the government in one form or another should also be obliged to recruit personnel on the aforesaid basis. All universities and affiliated colleges should also be covered by the above scheme of reservation.

Note: Educational reform was not within the terms of reference of this commission which was expected to suggest palliative measures within the existing framework.

It suggested a review of the entire implementation of its recommendations after 20 years.

In 1990, the V.P. Singh government finally implemented the Mandal Commission's recommendations for caste-based reservations of government jobs and educational institutions. There were large-scale anti-Mandal demonstrations all over the country, especially by upper caste student groups supporting the merit system over reservations in government jobs and educational opportunities.

Social scientists and intellectuals opposed the Mandal Commission's recommendations on the grounds that there were many technical errors in the methodology adopted for identifying the educationally and socially backward people and that the justification for reserving 27% of government jobs for OBCs was not valid.

Source: Based on Ramaiah (1992).

Clearly there remain many gray areas, such as which ones are the well-off 'creamy layers' within the lower castes and the OBCs and whether they should be included or excluded from the reservations quotas and how that determination should be made. Ghosh (2006) proposes several methods of dealing with the creamy layer, such as an economic cut-off above which there would be no eligibility for a reserved seat, allowing only two or three generations of a family to benefit from the reservation, and so on which are easily administered and would ensure that the system is just, fair and time limited. But these disagreements have resulted in actually reinforcing and strengthening the caste, education, economic class and backwardness identities of people trying to take advantage of the reservations benefits and have led to greater stratification along these divisive labels with individuals and groups vying for protective coverage.

Reservations for other religions
Constitutionally, India is a secular nation with equal respect for all religions and there are no reservations based on religion *per se*. The 2001 Census of India reports 80.5 per cent (over 827 million) out of 1,028 million population as followers of the Hindu religion, 13.4 per cent (over 138 million) as Muslims or the followers of Islam, 2.3 per cent (over 24 million) as Christians, 1.9 per cent (over 19 million) as Sikhs, 0.80 per cent (over 8 million) as Buddhists and 0.4 per cent (over 4 million) as followers of the Jain religion. In addition, over 6 million respondents reported professing other religions and faiths, including tribal religions, different from six main religions (Census of India, 2001).

Historically, India's diversity challenges were based on caste distinctions grounded in the Hindu religion. In reality, however, the Sikhs and the Buddhists were also successful in challenging the reservations policy and became included, in 1956 and 1990, respectively, under the Scheduled Castes. Muslims and Christian were not included in the reservations as these two religions did not officially recognize the caste system. Therefore, any conversion of *dalits* from Hinduism to Islam or Christianity legally disqualified them from the reservations benefits as they were no longer protected under the constitution since they were now officially Muslims or Christians and not Hindu 'SC'. Interestingly, the majority of the Christians in India are *dalits* who converted into Christianity hoping for equality through the church for escaping from their 'Untouchable' label. But they were doubly unsuccessful because they lost their SC protection and even after the conversion they continued to be treated as *dalits* based on deep societal beliefs on one's birth into religion and caste. It was a similar situation for the majority of the Indian Muslims who were descendents of Untouchable or low caste converts. Only a small minority of Indian Muslims can trace their roots to Persian and Mughal conquerors and rulers of India. Muslims with pure bloodlines of foreign descent are known as a*shraf* or 'noble' while Muslim descendents of indigenous converts are contemptuously known as *ajlaf* or 'lowly' (Anwar, 2001). The low caste converted Muslims continue to be ill-treated by the *ashraf* Muslims, similar to the Hindu *dalits*, and are now raising reservations demands for '*dalit* Muslims'. Consequently, the caste issue has now become an overall Indian issue having extended beyond the bounds of the Hindu religion, as *dalit* Christians and Muslims are now demanding the removal of religion from reservation policies.

While the origin of the caste/*jati* system is from Hindu practices, today the caste system is a universal 'Indian' problem pervasive across religions including Islam, Sikhism, Buddhism, Jainism, Christianity and so on that traditionally do not recognize a formal caste system. More recently, Muslims and Christians in the states of Kerala, Tamil Nadu and Karnataka have been provided reservation protections as OBCs. In the state of Kerala, where Muslims account for 22 per cent of the population, now 12 per cent of government jobs are reserved for Muslims. In Tamil Nadu, Muslims are entitled to 30 per cent of reservation, and 4 per cent in Karnataka. The 1993 and 2000 National Sample Survey reported that Muslims faced greater deprivation in education and employment than any other religious minority in India and were under-represented in all areas of private, public and government jobs as well as in the legislature (Hassan, 2005).

Political, social and economic outcomes
In North America, the diversity debate has now moved from the legally protected designated groups towards a broader concept of voluntary programs for managing diversity. Critics argue that it has been transformed from a moral and ethical issue of the need for removing discrimination into a business strategy issue for gaining a competitive advantage. The reservations policies in India, however, have not evolved that far and remain at the initial and very controversial stage of who exactly should or should not be included under the reservations policies. Moreover, instead of integrating the castes into the mainstream in the spirit of the Indian constitution, it has actually re-institutionalized the caste divisions and strengthened caste identities among lower as well as upper caste members. Reservations reinforce the maintaining of one's caste identity even for those 'creamy layers' who are financially and economically well off. The 1992 Supreme Court ruling, in *Indra Sawhney v. Union of India*, upheld job reservations for the OBCs but limited total reservations to no more than 50 per cent of the population and excluded the creamy layer of the OBCs who were not disadvantaged (Borooah et al., 2007).

The transformation has been political by removing the marginalization of Hindu caste-based occupational distinctions into a broader political issue, beyond religious boundaries, and making it a vote-grabbing strategy. Many authors (Lynch, 1968; Basu, 1996; Osborne, 2001) note that caste, ethnicity and tribal identity are becoming more important in national and state-level politics in India, the largest democracy in the world, by being leveraged for votes, coalitions, political power and increased reservations. Consequently, the proportion of Indians eligible for reservations has expanded dramatically since independence and there are continued pressures, by this substantial electoral force, on increasing the reservations quotas. Today, potentially 50 per cent or half the positions in education and public employment are subject to the reservations policy. These levels of reservations are the highest found anywhere in the world! In the state of Tamil Nadu, 68 per cent of the public university seats are reserved, in Karnataka, 90 per cent of the population is eligible for reservations, and in Uttar Pradesh the OBC list includes 'everyone who is not twice born plus some who are' (Osborne, 2001: 671).

Even the political parties reflect their key supporters in terms of caste. The Congress party is the most balanced or secular of all, while the Bharatiya Janata party (BJP) is significantly supported by the upper castes, and the Bahujan Samaj party (BSP) is primarily a lower caste political party. But there is also increasing violence and opposition to reservations in India. Caste-based violence over the increase in quotas are common as upper caste students engage in public demonstrations, burning effigies and self-immolating in protest.

With the dramatic economic liberalization of India since the 1980s, foreign investments have been on the increase, price controls have decreased, and many state enterprises have been privatized, making market forces more influential. Many multinational corporations (MNCs) have entered the Indian market and established branch offices in India, bringing with them Western human resource practices. Urbanization and migration for better educational and job opportunities have made the traditional caste system less prominent for occupational specialization in urban cities. While the family name of a person can easily identify their caste or *jati*, few actually pursue it as it is now possible for people to transcend their ancestral occupation for more lucrative opportunities in the cities. This phenomenon is seen largely in the information technology industry and in other private sector service and managerial jobs.

Yet, based on data from 28,922 households, Borooah (2005) showed that at least one-third of the average income difference between upper caste Hindu and SC/ST households was as a result of caste-based discrimination. This is compared to Cowell and Jenkins's (1995) findings of

the four factors – age, sex, race and employment status – which collectively explained less than one-quater of the overall US income inequality.
Borooah recommends the empowering of SC/ST persons through affirmative action in education and jobs to force higher redistribution of resources
towards these disadvantaged groups.

Cunningham (1999) uses Glenn Loury's economic theory distinguishing between 'human capital' and 'social capital' where the former refers to
an individual's own characteristics valued by the labour market and the
latter refers to value from membership in a community, such as access to
information networks, mentoring, reciprocal favours and so on. 'Potential
human capital can be augmented or stunted depending on available social
capital' (ibid.: 22). This economic model is useful in explaining how labour
market discrimination has perpetuated huge differences in social capital
between upper and lower caste communities over generations as a result
of segregated social structures. Cunningham urges increasing individual
human potential by unblocking their access to social capital in order to
eliminate the lingering effects of generations of discrimination.

Reservations for women

In Canada, the 'double disadvantage' (Abella, 1984) is defined as the discrimination faced by individuals belonging to more than one designated
group under the Employment Equity Act. For example, a person could
be both an Aboriginal and a Woman, or a Visible Minority and a Person
with a Disability, and so on. In the US, Nkomo and Cox (1989) also
present this as the concept of the 'doublewhammy' effect proposing that
African-American and other minority women may experience a double
disadvantage in the workplace due to their race and gender. In Australia,
the concept of the dual disadvantage faced by 'the other woman' has
been suggested by Syed (2007) distinguishing minority women from the
mainstream Anglo-Celtic women. In India, women are not fully protected
under the reservations policies as quotas for women are still being negotiated in the various Indian states. Moreover, because of the caste system,
dalit women face dual discrimination as they are still tormented with
sub-human treatment due to their lower caste and female gender (Niazi,
2008). In addition, women face multiple disadvantages resulting from the
traditional burden of dowry. As a patriarchal society, the preferential
treatment of the male child over the female continues despite laws such
as the Pre-Natal Diagnostic Techniques Regulation Act (1994) preventing the use of amniocentesis and sonogram tests for sex determination
during pregnancy which were being deliberately misused for terminating a
disproportionate number of female fetuses resulting in a significant under-
population ratio of women to men in certain parts of India. If a girl child

is born, poverty and limited access to resources often result in the parents giving priority to the healthcare, nutrition, education and skills development of the male child over the female child. Undoubtedly, women in India face multi-discrimination.

Although the 1950 Constitution of Independent India promises equal rights for all Indians, in Article 15 prohibiting discrimination on the grounds of sex, allowing special measures for women and children and Article 16 guaranteeing equal opportunity in employment prohibiting discrimination in employment on the basis of sex, women are not as yet formally included under all the reservations policies. In February 2001, the Committee on the Elimination of Discrimination against Women (CEDAW) of the United Nations Commission on Human Rights (UNCHR) recommended an extensive range of legal reforms and government affirmative action to eliminate gender inequality. Several laws have already been enacted to protect women in India: the Sati-Widow Burning Act (1829), the Widow Re-marriage Act (1856), the Child Marriage Restraint Act (1929) to age 14 and (1976) raised age to18, the Constitution of Independent India (1948), the Dowry Prohibition Act (1961), the Equal Remuneration Act (1976), the Immoral Traffic (Prevention) Act (1956), the Family Courts Act (1984), the Indian Divorce Act (1869), the Pre-Natal Diagnostic Techniques Regulation Act (1994), the Protection from Domestic Violence Bill (2001), the Hindu Succession Act (1956), and so on. However, women continue to face discrimination and unequal treatment as the government is unable to enforce these laws given the deep-rooted traditions, especially in the rural areas.

In the political arena, Pratibha Patil became the first female president of India in July 2007. India is also well known for the political leadership of Prime Minister Indira Gandhi, daughter of the first Prime Minister of Independent India, Jawahar Lal Nehru. But women generally have not done well in the political arena despite reservations for doubly-disadvantaged SC and ST women provided in the Indian constitution under Part IV – The Panchayats, defined as an institution of self-government for rural areas:

> Article 243D – reservation of seats (1) Seats shall be reserved for (a) the Scheduled Castes and (b) the Scheduled Tribes, in every Panchayat and the number of seats so reserved shall bear, as nearly as many as may be, the same proportion to the total number of seats to be filled by direct election in that Panchayat as the population of the Scheduled Castes in the Panchayat area or of the Scheduled Tribes in that Panchayat area bears to the total population of that area and such seats may be allotted by rotation to different constituencies in a Panchayat. (2) Not less than one-third of the total number of seats reserved under clause (1) shall be reserved for women belonging to the Scheduled Castes or, as the case may be, the Scheduled Tribes. (3) Not less than one-third

(including the number of seats reserved for women belonging to the Scheduled Castes and the Scheduled Tribes) of the total number of seats to be filled by direct election in every Panchayat shall be reserved for women and such seats may be allotted by rotation to different constituencies in a Panchayat. (4) The offices of the Chairpersons in the Panchayats at the village or any other level shall be reserved for the Scheduled Castes, the Scheduled Tribes and women in such manner as the Legislature of a State may, by law provide. (Constitution of India, 1950)

In 1993, India passed the Panchayati Raj, a constitutional amendment reserving 30 per cent of the elected seats in the village councils for women. This was a significant step in bringing almost 1 million women into the political system at the grassroots level. Panchayats are elected village councils in every Indian village. They have a five-year tenure and are responsible for the local administration ranging from agriculture, fisheries and forestry, to health and education and so on. Despite these measures, women remain under-represented in government parliament seats, at less than 8 per cent; cabinet positions, at less than 6 per cent; and the High Court and Supreme Court seats, at less than 4 per cent (Kumar and Menon-Sen, 2001). Women in the technical and professional workforce are only at 20 per cent compared to 45 per cent in China (Hafkin and Taggart, 2001). Prejudices remain ingrained, as seen in Uttar Pradesh, India's largest state, which elected a *dalit* woman, Mayawati Kumari, as its chief minister for the second time. Meanwhile, in the same state, upper caste students refused to eat their school lunches cooked by a *dalit* woman.

On the literacy front, the 2001 Census reports that as a result of the concerted efforts by the government, the male literacy rate crossed the 75 per cent mark but the female rate was only at 53 per cent. However, the absolute number of female illiterates in the country fell from 200 million in 1991 to 193 million in the 2001 Census, with the urban female literacy rate at almost 73 per cent but the rural female literacy rate at only 46 per cent. Among the total number of literates, the proportion of those educated up to primary level was about 55.6 per cent. Surprisingly, there were at least 2,351 villages in the country with a population of over 100 persons without even a single female literate in the village (Census of India, 2001), despite constitutional commitment to education until age 14.

Discussion

India is the oldest country with constitutional provisions, established in 1950, for the reserved protection of its unique marginalized minorities: the Scheduled Castes, the Scheduled Tribes, and the Other Backward Classes. However, the jury's verdict on the success of India's reservations policies is still out and depends largely on who the jury is. The Indian people are still divided on how successful their country's reservations policies have been in addressing past injustices and achieving its goals as set out in the constitution. Meanwhile, the total number of people protected under the SC, ST and OBC labels has grown phenomenally as more groups demand inclusion in order to benefit from these protections. After India's independence from the British Raj, the first prime minister, Jawahar Lal Nehru, and other leading members of the Congress party had envisaged the reservations policy as a temporary means to eradicating the caste system from India. They were confident that in creating a secular constitution and providing these protective measures for the weakest groups, SCs, STs, and OBCs, in the political and economic participation of the country, the caste system would eventually disappear. Ambedkar, one of the founders of Independent India and chair of the Drafting Committee for the Indian Constitution was a champion of the *dalits*, believing that affirmative action reservations were necessary for them to get equal opportunities in a free India. Yet, nearly 70 years later, while there is acceptance of reservations for the SCs/STs there is still no consensus on the reservation levels for the OBCs and women, and their quota levels are being negotiated in various states. Demands for extending the reservations into the private sector are also increasing.

While caste-based work specialization is becoming relatively less important in terms of economic activities in an increasingly urbanized and technologically advanced India, Osborne (2001) reports that an analysis of recent Indian elections confirms that caste is becoming more important in national and state politics. Moving away from a previously national agenda into a 'communal' agenda has strengthened political parties based on representing these SC, ST and OBC factions. Meanwhile, clashes between those for and against reservations still continue as does the grim reality of social economic and religious discrimination against the SCs, STs and the OBCs.

As for women, 'India Inc. is still largely a men's club. But an increasingly large number of companies are taking steps to make it more gender-diverse' (Agrawal, 2006: 88). MNCs, bringing their affirmative action and diversity management practices within their operations in India, have improved the employment opportunities for women, reaching around 20 per cent of the MNC workforce via diversity initiatives. For example, GE's Women's Network (GEWN) launched in 2002, Coca-Cola's Women Operational Trainees (WOTEs), Motorola's Country Diversity Council for India, Cisco's 18 per cent female workforce, Pepsi's flexible work–life balance initiatives and so on, have all made it respectable, and quite a status symbol, for Indian women to seek paid employment outside the home. However, there are no data available on the SC, ST, and OBC employees of these MNCs. Clearly, with regard to reservations policies, there are different forces operating on the public and private organizations in India.

Conclusion

In India, the reservations policies are primarily targeted to the SCs, the STs and OBCs in three areas: higher education, public employment and legislative representation. Moreover, the diversity issues in India are very different from those of the North American context where they are primarily a consequence of the increased immigration population and demands for gender equity, whereas in India the diversity concerns are primarily the discrimination and marginalization of native Indians as a result of attitudes ingrained within the country's caste-based social and religious traditions. The over 3,000 year-old bias against the lower castes still persists in India and has become a vote-grabbing pawn in this world's largest democratic nation.

Currently, the existing diversity literature reflects the concepts and research primarily designed upon the Western model. Interestingly, broader definitions of diversity such as sexual orientation do not qualify under India's reservations policies. As the Asian market grows and more Western organizations are attracted to conducting business in Asia, there will undoubtedly be the challenge of understanding and maneuvering within India's traditional societal rituals, beliefs and practices. This chapter provides business scholars and practitioners with insights into understanding the Indian religious, social and cultural barriers to equity and equality in the workplace and its impact on the socio-politico-economic practices in the country. It contributes in highlighting the international implications of the comparative approaches and outcomes of managing workforce diversity and competitive advantage in this global economy. The comparison of Indian diversity context with Western diversity issues will add to the knowledge of diversity construct and strategies beneficial to both academics and practitioners worldwide. It will be useful for future comparative diversity studies and has a rich potential for diversity theory development and contribution to diversity practitioners, educators, and policy makers both nationally and internationally.

References

Abella, R.S. (1984), *Report of the Commission on Equality in Employment*, Ottawa: Canadian Government Publishing Centre.

Agrawal, Shaleen (2006), 'Women rising', *Business Today*, New Delhi, 12 March, 88.

Anwar, Ali (2001), *Masawat ki jung: Pasemanzar; Bihar ka Pasmanda Musalman* (in Hindi), New Delhi: Vani Prakashan.

Basu, Amrita (1996), 'Caste and class: the rise of Hindu nationalism in India', *Harvard International Review*, **18** (3) Summer: 28–31.

Bell, M.P., M.E. McLaughlin and J.M. Sequeira (2004), 'Age, disability, and obesity: similarities, differences, and common threads', in M.S. Stockdale and F.J. Crosby (eds), *The Psychology and Management of Workplace Diversity*, Oxford, Blackwell, pp. 191–205.

Birnbaum, Jonathan and Clarence Taylor (2000), *Civil Rights since 1787*, New York: New York University Press.

Borooah, Vani (2005), 'Caste, inequality and poverty in India', *Review of Development Economics*, **9** (3): 399–414.

Borooah, V., A. Dubey and S. Iyer (2007), 'The effectiveness of jobs reservation: caste, religion and economic status in India', *Economic Development and Cultural Change*, **38** (3), May: 423–45.

Boston, Thomas and Usha Nair-Reichert (2003), 'Affirmative action: perspectives from the United States, India and Brazil', *Western Journal of Black Studies*, **27** (1), Spring: 3–12, InfoTrac Diversity Studies eCollection, Gale, Laurentian University–J.N. Demarais Lib, available at: http://find.galegroup.com/itx/start.do?prodld=SPJ.SP05 (accessed 20 December 2007).

Buehler, G. (1886), *The Sacred Books of the East. Volume 25: The Laws of Manu, Translated with extracts from seven commentaries by G. Buehler*, Oxford: Clarendon Press, CXXXVlll: 620pp.

Caudron, S. and C. Hayes (1997), 'Are diversity programs benefiting African Americans?', *Black Enterprise*, **27**: 121–32.

Census of India (2001), available at: http://www.censusindia.gov.in (accessed 2 December 2007).

Constitution of India (1950), available at: http://www.constitution.org/cons/india/p16338.html (accessed 2 December 2007).

Cowell, F. and S. Jenkins (1995), 'How much inequality can we explain? A methodology and an application to the United States', *The Economic Journal*, **105**: 421–30.

Cunningham, C.D. (1999), 'Affirmative action: India's example', *Civil Rights Journal*, **4** (1), Fall: 22–7.

Deshpande, A. (2001), 'Caste at birth? Redefining disparity in India', *Review of Development Economics*, **5** (1): 130–44.

Dumont, Louis (1980), *Homo Hierarchius: The Caste System and its Implications*, trans. Mark Sainsbury, Louis Dumont, Basia Gulati, 2nd edn, Chicago, IL: University of Chicago Press.

Dutt, N.K. (1965), *Origin and Growth of Caste in India, Vol. II: Castes in Bengal*, Calcutta: Firma L. Mukhopadhyay.

Freitas, Kripa (2006), 'The Indian caste system as a means of contract enforcement', available at: http://www.depot.northwestern.edu/kmf579/papers/freitas_jobmkt.pdf (accessed 2 December 2007).

Gardenswartz, L. and A. Rowe (1993), *Managing Diversity: A Complete Desk Reference and Planning Guide*, Burr Ridge, IL: Irwin.

Ghosh, Jayati (2006), 'Case for caste-based quotas in higher education', *Economic and Political Weekly*, 17 June: 2408–32.

Ghurye, G.S. (1961), *Caste, Class, and Occupation*, Bombay: Popular Book Depot.

Government of India (2008), available at: http://india.gov.in (accessed 10 November 2008).

Griggs, L.B. (1995), 'Valuing diversity: where from. . . where to?', in L.B. Griggs and L.L. Louw (eds), *Valuing Diversity: New Tools for a New Reality*, New York: McGraw-Hill.

Hafkin, N. and N. Taggart (2001), 'Gender, information technology, and developing countries: An analytical study', available at http://ict.aed.org/infocenter/gender.htm and http://www.comminit.com/en/node/1861 (accessed December 2009).

Haq, R. (2004), 'International perspectives on workplace diversity', in M.S. Stockdale and F.J. Crosby (eds) *The Psychology and Management of Workplace Diversity*, Oxford: Blackwell, pp. 277–98.

Haq, R. and Ed Ng (2010), 'Employment equity in Canada', in Alain Klarsfeld (ed.),

Intenational Handbook on Diversity Management at Work, Cheltenham, UK and Northampton, MA, USA: Edward Elgar (forthcoming).

Hassan, Zoya (2005), 'Reservation for Muslims', available at www.india-seminar. com/2005/. . ./549% 20zoya% 20hassan.htm (accessed December 2009).

Hutton, J.H. (1981), *Caste in India*, Oxford: Oxford University Press.

Kader, Salil (2004), 'Social stratification among Muslims in India', 15 June, available at http://www.countercurrents.org/ (accessed 2 December 2007).

Klass, M. (1993), *Caste: The Emergence of the South Asian Social System*, New Delhi: Manohar.

Kumar, A.K. and K. Menon-Sen (2001), *Women in India: How Free? How Equal?*, New Delhi: United Nations Development Assistance Framework.

Lynch, O. (1968), 'The politics of untouchability: a case from Agra, India', in S. Milton and B. Cohn (eds), *Structure and Change in Indian Society*, Chicago: Aldine.

Morrison, A.M. (1992), *The New Leaders: Guidelines for Diversity Leadership in America*, San Francisco, CA: Jossey-Bass.

Nesiah, D. (1997), *Discrimination with reason? The policy of reservations in the United States, India and Malaysia*, Delhi: Oxford University Press.

Niazi, Shuriah (2008), 'Central India: Caste Difference Contributes to Violence Against Dalit Women', Women's News Network, January, available at: http://womensnewsnetwork. net/2008/01/27/caste (accessed 20 February 2008).

Nishii, Lisa H. and Mustafa F. Özbilgin (2007), 'Global diversity management: towards a conceptual framework', *International Journal of Human Resource Management*, **18** (11): 1883–94.

Nkomo, S.M. and T. Cox (1989), 'Gender differences in the upward mobility of Black managers: double whammy or double advantage?', *Sex Roles*, **21**: 825–39.

Osborne, Evan (2001), 'Culture, development and government: reservations in India', *Economic Development and Cultural Change*, **49** (3), April: 659–85, ABI-Inform Global.

Pepper, Daniel (2008), 'India's dirty secret–life at the bottom of a caste ridden country', *The Globe and Mail*, 29 January: A3.

Ramaiah, A. (1992), 'Identifying other backward classes', *Economic and Political Weekly*, 6 June: 1203–7.

Scoville, J.G. (2003), 'Discarding facts: the economics of caste', *Review of Development Economics*, **7** (3): 378–91.

Sivaramayya, B. (1984), 'Affirmative action: the schedule castes and scheduled tribes', *International Perspectives on Affirmative Action*, New York: Rockerfeller Foundation.

Srinivas, M.N. (ed.) (1962), 'Varna and Caste', in *Caste in Modern India and Other Essays*, Bombay: Asia Publishing House, pp. 63–9.

Syed, Jawad (2007), '"The other woman" and the question of equal opportunity in Australian organizations', *The International Journal of Human Resource Management*, **18** (11): 1954–78.

Thomas, R.R., Jr. (1992), 'Managing diversity: a conceptual framework', in S.E. Jackson and M. Ruderman (eds), *Diversity in Work Teams: Research Paradigm for a Changing Workplace*, Washington, DC: American Psychological Association, pp. 306–18.

Tomervik, K. (1994), 'Workforce diversity in Fortune 500 corporations headquartered in Minnesota: concepts and practices', unpublished doctoral dissertation, University of Minnesota, St. Paul, MO.

Wax, Emily (2008), 'Overcoming caste: for those working to build an integrated India, hope starts and ends with the schools', *Washington Post Foreign Service*, 20 January: A01.

Wilson, T. (1996), *Diversity at Work: The Business Case for Equity*, Toronto: John Wiley.

10 Intercultural competencies across cultures: same or different?
Charmine E.J. Härtel, Shannon Lloyd and Divya Singhal

Introduction
Although the movement of people across geographic borders and engagement in international business activities has occurred for centuries, the significant changes that took place in the latter part of the twentieth century have led to a dramatic increase in both the number of organizations working in foreign markets and the overall diversity of the global workforce. As a result, engaging in intercultural business interactions is now almost a part of daily life for employees in many organizations. Nonetheless, the business environment seems to be littered with examples of business objectives becoming the casualty of intercultural interactions going awry (Bartel-Radic, 2006).

Differences in national culture mean that today's employees are often confronted with unfamiliar language rules and communication norms. As the culture one is brought up in shapes one's notion of appropriate communication and interaction behaviors, it is unsurprising that intercultural interactions are often beset with confusion, misunderstandings and conflict. For these reasons, organizational scholars are increasingly emphasizing the importance of intercultural competence for people working in intercultural settings.

Intercultural competence refers to being able to understand the differences which may arise as a result of different cultural backgrounds and to communicate and integrate across these differences (Iles, 1995). Individuals who are interculturally competent tend not to judge those who have different attitudes and behaviors to themselves, are better at evaluating how their own behavior is affecting those they are interacting with and are generally more effective communicators than individuals lacking intercultural competence (Shaw and Barrett-Power, 1998). While a myriad of intercultural competencies have been proposed in the management literature (Leiba-O'Sullivan, 1999), as yet, there is a lack of research which seeks to identify if there are core competencies that are effective across cultures and, if there are, what are they and is the relative emphasis on these competencies the same in different cultures? For this reason, in this chapter, we present the findings of preliminary research which seeks to address these questions through a comparative survey study undertaken in India and Australia.

To set the backdrop for the chapter, we begin by reviewing literature addressing the impact of culture on interactions between people from different cultural backgrounds. Next, we link these findings with the intercultural competencies identified in the literature and identify the importance of determining whether or not the same competencies are important across cultures. Then, we describe our study, which undertook to examine the full range of core intercultural competencies identified in the taxonomy derived by the first two authors from a comprehensive literature review (see Lloyd et al., 2004). We conclude the chapter by first discussing the contributions the findings make to the available literature on intercultural competencies in India and Australia, respectively, and then discussing the implications of the research for the understanding of intercultural competencies generally.

The impact of culture on interactions: an overview
'Culture' can be defined as 'the collective programming of the mind that distinguishes the members of one group or category of people from another' (Hofstede, 2001, p. 9). Thus, 'cultural group' refers to 'an affiliation of people who collectively share certain norms, values, or traditions that are different from those of other groups' (Cox, 1993, p. 5). While we are often unaware of the influence that our cultural background has on us, it plays a critical role in shaping who we are and how we see the world. In addition, culture affects communication in a variety of ways (Vuckovic, 2008, p. 49). While there are a plethora of ways in which the term 'communication' has been used (Lustig and Koester, 1999, p. 25), most scholarly definitions of communication recognize that (a) communication is symbolic, (b) communication is a transactional process and (c) communication involves shared meanings.

Gudykunst and Ting-Toomey (1988) identified four dimensions upon which the style of verbal communication can differ for people from different cultural backgrounds. The first of these, direct versus indirect communication, refers to the extent to which people explicitly state or identify their intentions. The second dimension, elaborate versus succinct communication, refers to the differences in the amount of information that is communicated. The third dimension, personal versus contextual communication, refers to the assumption of similarity and equality versus the focus on maintaining the social context through 'formal elements that reflect the social and organizational differences between people' (Scachaf, 2005, p. 49). The fourth dimension, instrumental versus affective communication, refers to the degree to which communication is sender versus receiver oriented.

When interacting with people from a different cultural background, we are often confronted with language, rules and norms that are unknown to us, which can lead to confusion, breakdown in communication and ultimately relationship collapse. In the context of business, the lack of awareness and skills for dealing with intercultural differences in communication often results in a breakdown in communication between people from different cultural backgrounds, and consequently, a failure to achieve organizational goals and objectives.

In this chapter, we contrast the use of intercultural competencies in India and Australia, two quite different cultural contexts. Australia represents a low-context culture, where communication norms include getting straight to the point, saying no when one thinks something is not possible or they are not happy with a situation (Lloyd et al., 2004, p. 58). In contrast, India is a high-context culture, where communication norms include being reluctant to say no so as not to damage an ongoing relationship (for an expanded discussion on cultural features of India, see Ali (2010) and the chapters in this volume by Rana Haq, ch. 9; Taran Patel, ch. 13; and Nurit Zaidman and Ayala Malach Pines, ch. 23).

As identified in the introduction, in order to try to overcome problems and ensure effective interactions when communicating with people using different cultural communication norms, management scholars are increasingly emphasizing the importance of intercultural competence. This concept is explored in more detail in the next section.

Intercultural competence
Bartel-Radic (2006) indicates that intercultural competence includes a number of cognitive, affective and behavioral components which come together to enable a person to understand the meaning of intercultural interactions and provide them with the ability to adapt their behavior to these meanings to ensure effective interactions. In line with this definition of intercultural competence, the first two authors developed a taxonomy of intercultural competencies based on a comprehensive review of the literature. A key motivation for developing this taxonomy was to overcome the difficulty presented by the myriad of competencies put forward by management scholars that frequently refer to the same construct. The taxonomy offers a coherent set of variables that represent the core competencies identified in the literature as fostering positive working relationships between people from different cultural backgrounds (see Lloyd et al., 2004). The cognitive competencies included in the taxonomy are cognitive complexity and goal orientation; the affective competencies included in the

taxonomy are dissimilarity openness, tolerance for ambiguity and cultural empathy, while the behavioral competencies included in the taxonomy are intercultural communication competence, emotion management skills and conflict management skills (ibid.).

Cognitive complexity

Individuals from culturally diverse backgrounds have different ways of processing the information that they receive as well as different cognitive styles (the ways in which we structure our beliefs and attitudes and respond to incoming information) (Gudykunst and Kim, 1997). As such, cultural diversity impacts the extent to which individuals use similar cognitive styles and attribute the causes of behavior to similar factors (Milliken and Martins, 1996). To overcome the difficulties that may be created by this, it is important that people working with others from culturally diverse backgrounds are cognitively complex.

An individual is said to exhibit cognitive complexity when they are able to make fine-grained interpersonal discriminations (Dodd, 1987). The concept of cognitive complexity comprises two primary components: differentiation and integration. 'Differentiation, refers to the number of dimensions used by individuals to perceive environmental stimuli [while] integration, refers to the complexity of rules used by individuals in organizing the differentiated dimensions' (Wang and Chan, 1995, p. 35). In line with the argument that individuals who are cognitively complex have a number of frameworks they can draw upon to evaluate a situation (see Gudykunst and Kim, 1997), research shows that the greater an individual's cognitive complexity, the greater his/her capacity to develop an understanding of different cultures (Yum, 1982). In addition, individuals 'tend to have very differentiated and detailed information and knowledge schemes with regard to cultural information. They are able to think deeply and more meaningfully about related concept and challenges. From an intercultural perspective, this means that they have a sophisticated, well-developed understanding of how culture might affect behavior' (Karim, 2003, p. 36). According to Kagan (1992), a significant but often overlooked benefit of cognitive complexity is the ability to communicate and interact more effectively with others. She suggested that research in this area indicates that 'individuals who think complexly appear to adapt and to modify their verbal communication to the needs of listeners, reflecting the ability to anticipate the thinking and perceptions of others' (p. 290). This further indicates that cognitive complexity will play a role in the success of interactions between culturally diverse individuals.

Goal orientation

Goal orientation theory, which developed from educational psychology and the child development literature, is a useful theory for understanding people's need to engage in social comparisons and intergroup distinctions. Initially goal orientation was proposed as a two-factor model by Elliott and Dweck (1988), who defined these dimensions as performance and learning goals. Overall, individuals with a performance goal orientation strive to maintain positive assessments regarding their skills and capabilities and to show their superiority over others (Vrugt et al., 2002). Due to their high level of concern regarding how they are perceived by others they frequently engage in social comparison (Skaalvik, 1997), which often results in intergroup distinctions being made and negative feelings being elicited. People with learning goals on the other hand focus on task mastery and the development of new skills (Vrugt et al., 2002). They place a high value on learning, understanding and problem solving and are willing to collaborate with others in order to satisfy this orientation (Skaalvik, 1997). As a consequence, people who have a learning orientation are likely to communicate with others in a less threatening way and to strive to engage in interactions with others in a cooperative manner in order to reach their goals, positively facilitating intercultural interactions.

Dissimilarity openness

According to similarity attraction theory, individuals will be attracted to those people that they perceive to be similar to themselves (Byrne, 1971). This similarity may be either in the form of readily detectable attributes such as race or ethnicity or in the form of underlying attributes such as values, attitudes or beliefs. While perceived similarity is said to create interpersonal attraction between individuals (Triandis et al., 1994), increasing the likelihood of positively biased evaluations and decisions between these people (Härtel et al., 1999b; Härtel and Fujimoto, 2000), it can also lead to increased conflict with and the exclusion of dissimilar others. However, this is not always the case as, according to the perceived dissimilarity–openness moderator model developed by Härtel and Fujimoto, individuals who are open to dissimilarity are less likely to make negative intergroup distinctions based on such things as cultural differences than those who are closed to dissimilarity. Specifically, Härtel and Fujimoto argue that similarity attraction may be moderated by an individual's openness to dissimilar others (ibid.). Individuals high on dissimilarity openness tend to be more receptive and open to learning from dissimilar others, and are more likely to incorporate differences into work processes in a positive way and make an effort to see things from the point of view of the people they are working with, than people who are low on dissimilarity openness.

In recent years, a number of studies have emerged that have looked at the impact of the level of an individual's openness to dissimilarity for a team or organization. Härtel et al. (1999b) found that racial discrimination was more evident in the performance ratings of diversity closed raters than for diversity open raters. Ayoko and Härtel (2000b) found that openness to differences and other team members' opinions contributed to conflict resolution and group cohesion. They also suggested that when group leaders are open to dissimilarity this will contribute to their ability to minimize the impact of cultural differences in their work group and improve the experience of diverse employees. In addition, the results of a study by Fujimoto et al. (2000) demonstrated that employees', work groups' and organizations' openness to diversity produces positive results.

Cultural empathy
As previously indicated in this chapter, cultural background influences each individual's view of reality (Maznevski, 1994). 'Culture comprises an entire set of social norms and responses that condition people's behavior' (Rodrigues, 1997, p. 690). Subsequently, there are a vast number of cultural variables on which individuals from different cultural groups differ. It is for this reason that cultural empathy is important to intercultural interactions. 'Cultural empathy is the ability to recognize, understand and acknowledge the identity, experience and position of a culturally different person without denying one's own cultural identity' (Karim, 2003, p. 37).

Cultural empathy incorporates a number of concepts. Besides being empathetic to cultural difference, people must also be aware of and have sensitivity and flexibility towards cultural differences. In the international management literature, there is compelling evidence for the role of cultural empathy in the success of cross-cultural relations, with a number of studies showing that awareness of and sensitivity to cultural differences is a key component in the success of people engaging in cross-cultural relations (for example, Hawkes and Kealey, 1981; Abe and Wiseman, 1983; Lolla and Davis, 1991). Other factors related to cultural empathy that make a difference to intercultural interactions include the ability to relate to culturally different colleagues, understanding other cultures, and a willingness to communicate and make relationships with people from different cultures (Johnson et al., 1996).

When people are empathetic they do not have to agree with the culturally diverse others rather they have to understand the position that others take. 'The willingness to suspend judgment is based on the recognition that different does not equal deficient, and that things that are equal do not need to be the same' (Fine, 1995, p. 153). In addition, people who have cultural empathy take into consideration what is important to those they are working with, for example collectivist versus individualist values, and understanding the meanings that others ascribe to behaviors (Fine, 1995). Overall, when individuals working together from different cultural backgrounds have cultural empathy, it tends to strengthen the communication effectiveness between them and provides a foundation for trust (Johnson et al., 1996).

Intercultural communication competence
As already identified in this chapter, people's communication is influenced by the particular culture in which they are raised. Because we are generally unaware of how our culture influences the way that we communicate and behave (Gudykunst and Kim, 1997), this can result in confusion and misunderstandings when interacting with culturally dissimilar others. For this reason, the value of intercultural communication competence is increasingly being emphasized (Beamer, 1992).

Definitions of intercultural communication are similar to those of communication, with the component of culture added. Gudykunst and Kim (1997) define intercultural communication as 'a transactional, symbolic process involving the attribution of meaning between people from different cultures' (p. 19). Intercultural communication competence has also been identified as the ability to encode and decode meanings that correspond to the meanings held by culturally different others (Beamer, 1992). For intercultural communication to be effective, individuals need to have an understanding of the cultures involved to effectively encode and decode messages. Communication barriers are best minimized by increasing interactants' knowledge and understanding of cultural factors and commitment to successfully communicating across cultures (Samovar et al., 1981). Experts argue that when people acquire knowledge of different cultures, 'the influence of their cultural background on the way they process and use information will be less' (Mamman, 1995, p. 99). The reason for this is that as individuals acquire information about other cultures, they get a better understanding about the frames of reference or cultural 'map' used by people from that cultural background and hence are better able to interact and communicate with these individuals (Zakaria, 2000). For example, knowledge about the culture of a culturally diverse team member will allow an individual to 'process correctly various non-verbal signals and thus avoid many problems resulting from cultural and behavioral difference. [Furthermore] they may be able to provide proper stimuli to induce desired behaviors' (Paik and Sohn, 2004, p. 64).

Emotion management skills

The differing values, wishes and desires that people from diverse cultural backgrounds have can often lead to social and emotional conflict, however, 'the successful regulation of emotions allows individuals to refocus their own and others' attention on more important problems' (Ayoko and Härtel, 2000a, p. 83). Thus sound emotion management skills play an important role in ensuring that interactions between people from different cultural backgrounds are successful.

Research in the area of emotion management includes the literature dealing with interpersonal intelligence, social intelligence and more recently, emotional intelligence (Härtel et al., 2006). 'These areas indicate that effective emotion management involves the ability to identify, monitor, and regulate one's own and others' emotions' (Ayoko and Härtel, 2000a, p. 83). The ability to monitor one's own emotions may be regarded as a key facet of stress-management skills (Leiba-O'Sullivan, 1999). Individuals with sound emotion management skills have the ability to deal with stressful situations in a calmer more even fashion, greatly facilitating interactions with diverse others.

Jordan et al. (2002) identified four significant factors to emotional intelligence. These include dealing with one's own emotions (awareness of own emotions, control of felt emotions, display of own emotions); dealing with the emotions of others (awareness of others' emotions, ability to manage others' emotions, empathy); using emotions in decision making and using emotions in problem solving. While individuals differ in their abilities in each of the aforementioned areas (Härtel et al., 1999a), it has been argued that with effort and suitable training, emotional intelligence can be modified (Mayer and Salovey, 1994).

Conflict management

The conflict literature identifies the existence of three distinct types of conflict: relationship conflict refers to disagreements based on personal and social matters that are unrelated to work; task conflict refers to disagreements based on work issues; and process conflict refers to disagreements about how work should be conducted (Jehn and Chatman, 2000). While task and relationship conflict are proposed to provide the most crucial barriers to diverse colleagues working together effectively (Ayoko and Härtel, 2000a) and conflict is largely perceived to be damaging to work interactions, it should be noted that some forms of conflict can be beneficial, leading to such things as greater innovation (Jehn et al., 1997).

'Because individuals' dispositions are rooted in their early social and cultural experiences and because conflict is an interpretive behavior, culture shapes people's interpretation of behavior and their style of interaction with others' (Ayoko and Härtel, 2000b, p. 11). Clearly then, individuals' cultural background will have a significant role in their perception of conflict, their reaction toward conflict and the way they handle conflict (Kirchmeyer, 1993). For this reason, while 'dealing with conflict is a natural part of the daily activities of any workplace, when people with different cultural orientations are interacting, complications and misunderstandings beyond the usual tensions may arise. These misunderstandings are due to differing needs, conflict management styles, assumptions and expectation' (Brew and Cairns, 2004, p. 28). Consequently, it is often 'difficult to know what effective conflict management or problem-solving processes should look like in diverse workgroup settings, since each player might have different expectations and preferences for problem-solving approaches, as well as assumptions and realities surrounding the conflict itself' (Broome et al., 2002, p. 241).

Research has shown that individuals from different cultural backgrounds differ in their styles of dealing with and managing conflict (Rahim and Blum, 1994: Ayoko and Härtel, 2000b). For example, people from collectivist cultures tend to avoid conflict leading to passivity and a failure to voice opposing opinions or information, while people from individualistic cultures are far more assertive and self-focused in their approach to conflict (Brew and Cairns, 2004). Empirical research predominantly supports these distinctions in the way that individuals from different cultural backgrounds manage conflict (ibid.). For this reason, 'it is critical that cultural differences in attitudes and approaches to conflict management are understood in order to facilitate effective employee interactions' (ibid., p. 28) and to facilitate perceptions of inclusion and a supportive team climate.

It is preferable to use a cooperative rather than a competitive approach to dealing with conflict when working in a diverse setting (Brew and Cairns, 2004). This is because competitive approaches to conflict often involve behavior that can be perceived as intimidating and thus provoke further segregation among group members (see Lloyd et al., 2004). Furthermore, sound conflict resolution strategies will involve the ability to respond to cultural cues that prompt the need for using alternative conflict-resolution styles appropriate to the situation (Leiba-O'Sullivan, 1999).

The relative importance of competencies across cultures
The taxonomy described above identifies a coherent set of variables that represents the competencies predicted to foster positive working relationships between people from different cultural backgrounds. However, given the complexity of culture, it is possible that the relative importance that people place on each of the competencies described above may differ

based on cultural background. To date, however, as far as we are aware, no research has been undertaken examining the relative importance of intercultural competencies across different cultures to determine whether or not they are the same or different. This is the gap that this chapter seeks to address. Using data collected from individuals working in culturally diverse teams in both Australia and India, we examine the range of competencies identified in the taxonomy previously discussed to determine if the relative emphasis on the competencies is variant or invariant across different cultural settings. If the importance of these competencies does differ across cultures, it will be important to understand which are most relevant in a given cultural context so that they can be developed and fostered in people who will be working with people from that context.

Method
Data were collected in both Australia and India. In Australia, individuals working in teams in the information technology division of an organization operating in the finance and business services sector were approached to participate in the research. In India, individuals working in teams from a range of industry sectors were approached to participate in the research.

Measures
Where possible, established measures were used. Details for each variable assessed are presented next.

Independent variables Cognitive complexity was measured with an adapted scale from Chang (2002) using a six-item 7-point scale where 1 = strongly disagree and 7 = strongly agree. This measure considers how often individuals look at all the information available to them when making a decision as well as how often they look at a situation from a different point of view. The reliability of this measure was reported as exceeding the recommended level of 0.70.

Goal orientation was measured using Härtel et al.'s (2005) Task and Ego Orientation at Work (TEOWQ) scale. This 12-item measure was developed through the adaptation of Duda and Nicholls's (1992) Task and Ego Orientation in Sport Questionnaire which previous research suggests is useful for assessing the impact of one's work environment on goal orientation and motivation (Härtel et al., 2005). Respondents were asked to indicate the extent of their agreement with statements representing task and performance orientation on a 7-point scale where 1 = strongly disagree and 7 = strongly agree. Sample items include, 'I feel most successful at work when I can do better than my colleagues' and, 'I feel most successful at work when I enjoy learning something'. Task orientation was reported as consisting of two subscales (task effort and task learning) and ego orientation was reported as consisting of two subscales (being the best and being better than others). The composite reliability for 'being the best' is reported as 0.64 and 0.76 for 'being better than others' while the composite reliability for task-effort orientation is reported as 0.77 and 0.68 for task-learning orientation (ibid.).

Dissimilarity openness was measured using nine items adapted from Härtel's Openness to Perceived Dissimilarity measure (Fujimoto et al., 2000) and three items from the Acceptance of Cultural Differences subscale of Wang et al.'s (2003) Ethnocultural Empathy scale. Respondents were asked to indicate the extent of their agreement with statements related to their comfort, communication and like of interactions with dissimilar individuals on a 7-point Likert scale where 1 = strongly disagree and 7 = strongly agree. Sample items include, 'I enjoy exchanging different ideas with team members who do tasks very differently from me', 'I feel more comfortable interacting with team members whose behaviors are familiar to me than with team members who behave differently than people I usually interact with', and 'I get impatient when communicating with people from other racial or ethnic backgrounds regardless of how well they speak English'. The reported reliability of the original scales is between 0.76 and 0.91.

Tolerance for ambiguity was measured using four items from McLain's (1993) Multiple Stimulus Types Ambiguity Tolerance (MSTAT-1) scale and adapted to suit the work context. A sample item is 'I am good at managing unpredictable situations at work'. The response scale ranged from 1 = strongly disagree to 7 = strongly agree. The original 22-item scale has a reported reliability of Cronbach's alpha = 0.86.

Cultural empathy was measured using five items from the Empathetic Feeling and Expression subscale and two items from the Empathic Perspective Taking subscale of the Ethnocultural Empathy scale (Wang et al., 2003). Items were measured on a 7-point scale where 1 = strongly disagree and 7 = strongly agree. Sample items include, 'When other people struggle with racial or ethnic oppression, I share their frustration' and, 'It is difficult for me to put myself in the shoes of someone who is racially or ethnically different to me'. Reliability of the Empathetic Feeling and Expression subscale is reported as Cronbach's alpha = 0.91 while reliability of the Empathic Perspective Taking subscale is reported as Cronbach's alpha = 0.90.

Intercultural communication competence was measured using five items adapted from Hammer et al.'s (1978) widely used questionnaire designed to assess intercultural effectiveness. Using a 7-point scale where 1 = low ability and 7 = high ability, the five items adapted from the Ability to Effectively Communicate factor asked respondents to indicate how high they believe their intercultural communication ability was. Sample items include, 'Your ability to deal with communication misunderstandings between yourself and others' and, 'Your ability to adopt different communication styles when communicating with different people'.

Emotion management was measured using 25 items taken from Version 3 of Jordan et al.'s (2002) measure of work group emotional intelligence. This measure uses a 7-point scale where 1 = strongly disagree and 7 = strongly agree. It considers awareness of own emotions, ability to regulate felt emotions, ability to display own emotions, ability to recognize the emotions of others, ability to manage the emotions of others, empathetic perspective taking and ability to use own emotions to facilitate thinking. Sample items include, 'I can explain the emotions I feel to team members' and, 'When I am frustrated with fellow team members I can overcome my frustration'. The reported reliability of each of the subscales is between 0.60 and 0.86.

Conflict management was measured using four items adapted from Tjosvold's (1985) Cooperative Approach to Conflict subscale. Respondents were asked to indicate the extent of their agreement with statements regarding the way in which they deal with conflict or differences with another team member. Items were measured on a 7-point scale where 1 = strongly disagree and 7 = strongly agree. A sample item is, 'I seek a solution that will be good for all of us'. The reliability of the scale was reported as Cronbach's alpha = 0.70.

Dependent variables   The extent to which respondents trust the other members of their team was measured using a three-item, 7-point Likert scale where 1 = strongly disagree and 7 = strongly agree. The measure, adapted from Brockner et al.'s (1995) trust measure contains items such as 'I trust the other members of my team'. The reported reliability of this measure is coefficient alpha = 0.75.

While team climate is a group-level concept, it is commonly measured at the individual level. Currently there is a 'lack of availability of published validated measures of team affective climate' (Pirola-Merlo et al., 2002, p. 568). Consequently, in order to measure emotional team climate, the Workgroup Emotional Climate scale (Härtel et al., 2006) was used. This scale asks respondents questions related to the way their team works together and the feelings that team members collectively experience. A sample item is, 'My team is enthusiastic towards their work'. The response scale ranges from 1 = completely disagree to 7 = completely agree. The coefficient alpha for this scale is reported as 0.71.

As relationship conflict is the type of conflict which has the most detrimental impact upon a team (Jehn and Chatman, 2000), the four-item Relationship Conflict subscale of the Intragroup Conflict scale developed by Jehn (1994) was used. Respondents were asked to indicate the extent to which friction, personality conflicts, tension and emotional conflicts occur in their team. The response scale ranged from 1 = none to 7 = a lot. The coefficient alpha for this scale is reported as 0.87.

Control variables   A review of the diversity literature indicates that there are several forms of diversity which can impact on individual outcomes and perceptions of team climate including gender diversity, age diversity, organizational cohort diversity and information and functional diversity. Therefore, in order to ensure that any conclusions drawn from this study can be specifically attributed to cultural diversity and not another form of diversity, the following control variables were measured.

Diversity in age was measured by asking participants to write down their age in years. To control for diversity in gender, participants were asked to identify if they were male or female.

Informational and functional diversity refers to differences in such things as knowledge, skills, educational background and functional background (work experience). Accordingly, informational and functional backgrounds were measured using two items. The first item asked participants to indicate their highest level of education completed. Options ranged from completed Year 10 to doctorate. The second item asked participants to indicate in what other industries they had experience.

Two items were used to measure organizational cohort diversity. The first item asked participants to indicate the length of time they had worked in their current team and the second item asked participants to identify the length of time they had worked for their current employer.

Procedure

The procedure used to collect the data differed in Australia and India. In Australia, the survey was available online. Employees were sent an email by a human resource representative describing the research and inviting them to participate. The email included a web link to the survey if they chose to participate and advised employees that the survey would be available to complete online for a period of one month. In India, employees were given a hard copy of the survey along with a letter describing the purpose of the research and an envelope in which they could seal the survey should they choose to participate. Completed surveys were left in the sealed envelope for the researcher to collect from their place of employment.

Results

As per the recommendations of Tabachnick and Fiddel (2007), the normality of each of the scales was examined. Based on this examination, data transformation was deemed unnecessary. The reliability of each of the scales was assessed in order to ensure the consistency and accuracy of the measurement techniques adopted in the study to measure each scale. The reliability for each of the scales is shown in Table 10.1.

Examination of the correlation matrix revealed that none of the proposed control variables was significantly correlated with the dependent variables and therefore they were dropped from inclusion in the analysis. In addition, none of the independent variables had a correlation value at or above 0.7. Therefore, there was no evidence of multicollinearity.

Respondents

Eighty-eight team member surveys were completed in Australia and 25 team member surveys were completed in India, providing a total sample

Table 10.1   Measure of reliability

Scale	Cronbach's alpha
Cultural Empathy	
● Empathetic feelings/expression	0.84
● Empathetic perspective taking	0.73
Intercultural Communication	0.71
Cognitive Complexity	0.76
Goal Orientation	
● Learning orientation	0.79
● Performance orientation	0.84
Dissimilarity Openness	
● Comfort with difference	0.71
● Communication	0.72
● Like/enjoy	0.78
Tolerance for Ambiguity	0.64
Conflict Management	0.85
Emotion Management	
● Ability to recognize non-verbal emotions in others	0.86
● Ability to regulate felt emotions	0.75
● Ability to display own emotions	0.53
● Awareness of own emotions	0.65
● Ability to understand emotions in others	0.62
Trust	0.77
Emotional Team Climate	0.83
Perceptions of Conflict	0.91

Table 10.2   Survey sample respondents' religious beliefs

Religious affiliation	Australian sample	Indian sample
Christianity	58 (65.9%)	6 (24%)
Hinduism	0	17 (68%)
Islam	0	1 (4%)
Other religion	2 (2.3%)	0
No religion	28 (31.8%)	0

of 113 respondents. The gender and age ranges of the two samples were fairly similar. Of the Australian respondents, 49 were male (56 percent) and 39 were female (44 percent), while in the Indian sample, 13 were male (52 percent) and 12 were female (48 percent). The age range of respondents in the Australian sample was 21–55 years, with the mean age being 38 and the standard deviation being nine years, while in the Indian sample, the sample ranged in age from 23–62 years, with the mean age being 34 years and the standard deviation being 11 years. The two samples provided a diverse group of respondents in regard to religious beliefs. While the majority of respondents in the Australian sample were Christian, the majority of respondents in the Indian sample were Hindu. A breakdown of the religious affiliations for each sample is shown in Table 10.2.

Over half of both the Australian and Indian samples had experience working in an industry different from that in which they were currently employed. Specifically, 86.4 percent of the Australian sample had experience working in another industry while 64 percent of the Indian sample had such experience. The highest level of education completed by respondents in both samples was a Master's degree (10.2 percent of the Australian sample and 76 percent of the Indian sample) while the lowest level of education completed in the Australian sample was Year 10 (3.4 percent) and in the Indian sample the completion of Secondary school (4 percent). A breakdown of the education profile of respondents is presented in Table 10.3.

The length of respondents' tenure in their organization as well as the length of time they had worked in their current team is shown in Tables 10.4 and 10.5. While the number of respondents employed at their current organization for more than five years was much higher in the Australian sample than in the Indian sample, the number of respondents who had been in their current work team for more than five years was higher in the Indian sample.

Table 10.3 Survey sample education profile

Level of education	Australian sample	Indian sample
Completed Year 10	3 (3.4%)	0
Secondary Education	11 (12.5%)	1 (4%)
Certificate	7 (8%)	0
Diploma/Advanced Diploma	9 (10.2%)	0
Bachelors Degree	31 (35.2%)	3 (12%)
Graduate Diploma/Certificate	14 (4.5%)	2 (8%)
Honours Degree	4 (4.5%)	0
Master's Degree	9 (10.2%)	19 (76%)

Table 10.4 Organizational tenure

Tenure	Australian sample	Indian sample
Up to 6 months	3 (3.4%)	3 (12%)
6 months to 1 year	4 (4.5%)	5 (20%)
2 years	11 (12.5%)	3 (12%)
3 years	4 (4.5%)	3 (12%)
4 years	3 (3.4%)	3 (12%)
5 years	9 (10.2%)	2 (8%)
More than 5 years	54 (61.4%)	6 (24%)

Table 10.5 Team tenure

Tenure	Australian sample	Indian sample
Up to 6 months	11 (12.5%)	3 (12%)
6 months to 1 year	21 (23.9%)	5 (20%)
2 years	20 (22.7%)	3 (12%)
3 years	10 (11.4%)	3 (12%)
4 years	4 (4.5%)	3 (12%)
5 years	9 (10.2%)	2 (8%)
More than 5 years	12 (14.8%)	6 (24%)

Data analysis
Analysis of variance techniques were employed to test the hypotheses. In all the analyses, an alpha level of 0.10 was selected to determine significance.

Hypothesis testing

H1a: Cognitive complexity will be positively related to trust in both India and Australia, respectively.

A two-way between-subjects analysis of variance was conducted to evaluate the relationship between cognitive complexity and cultural background on trust in one's fellow team members. The results revealed a significant main effect for cognitive complexity on trust for the combined sample ($F(1, 108) = 6.569, p < 0.05$). The main effect for country however, was non-significant ($F(1, 108) = 0.867$, n.s.), as was the interaction effect ($F(1, 108) = 0.016$, n.s.).

H1b: Cognitive complexity will be positively related to perceptions of emotional team climate in both India and Australia, respectively.

A two-way between-subjects analysis of variance was conducted to evaluate the relationship between cognitive complexity and cultural background on perceptions of emotional team climate. Neither country ($F(1, 108) = 0.052$, n.s.) nor cognitive complexity ($F(1, 108) = 1.987$, n.s.) produced a significant main effect. Similarly, the interaction effect was non-significant ($F(1, 108) = 0.160$, n.s.).

H1c: Cognitive complexity will be positively related to perceptions of conflict within respondents' work team in both India and Australia, respectively.

A two-way between-subjects analysis of variance was conducted to evaluate the relationship between cognitive complexity and cultural background on perceptions of conflict within respondents' work team. The results revealed a significant main effect for cognitive complexity on perceptions of conflict for the combined sample ($F(1, 108) = 3.223, p < 0.10$), such that a 1-point increase in cognitive complexity was associated with a 0.587 decrease in team conflict. The main effect for country, however, was non-significant ($F(1, 108) = 0.867$, n.s.), as was the interaction effect ($F(1, 108) = 0.460$, n.s.).

H2a: The learning but not performance dimension of goal orientation will be positively related to trust in both India and Australia, respectively.

A two-way between-subjects analysis of variance was conducted to evaluate the relationship between goal orientation and cultural background on trust. The results revealed a significant main effect for learning orientation on trust for the combined sample $F(1, 106) = 4.992, p < 0.05$. The main effects for both country ($F(1, 106) = 0.792$, n.s) and performance orientation ($F(1, 106) = 2.285$, n.s.) were non-significant as were the interaction effects of country and learning orientation ($F(1, 106) = 0.331$, n.s.) and country and performance orientation ($F(1, 106) = 0.535$, n.s.).

H2b: The learning but not performance dimension of goal orientation will be positively related to perceptions of emotional team climate in both India and Australia, respectively.

A two-way between-subjects analysis of variance was conducted to evaluate the relationship between goal orientation and cultural background on trust. Although no effect on the combined sample was observed, there was a significant effect of performance orientation on emotional team climate in the Australian sample such that higher levels of performance orientation were associated with higher levels of emotional team climate ($t(106) = 2.71$, $p < 0.05$, $\eta = 0.07$).

H2c: The learning but not performance dimension of goal orientation will be positively related to perceptions of conflict within respondents' work team in both India and Australia, respectively.

A two-way between-subjects analysis of variance was conducted to evaluate the relationship between goal orientation and cultural background on perceptions of conflict. The results revealed a significant main effect for performance orientation on perceptions of conflict for the combined sample ($F(1, 105) = 4.950$, $p < 0.05$) such that higher levels of performance orientation were associated with lower levels of team conflict. The main effects for both country ($F(1, 105) = 1.112$, n.s.) and learning orientation ($F(1, 105) = 0.336$, n.s.) were non-significant. In addition, no significant interaction effects were found.

H3a: Cultural empathy will be positively related to trust in both India and Australia, respectively.

A two-way between-subjects analysis of variance was conducted to evaluate the relationship between cultural empathy and cultural background on trust in one's fellow team members. The results revealed a significant main effect for the empathetic feelings and expression subscale on trust for the combined sample ($F(1, 106) = 3.378$, $p < 0.10$) but not for the empathetic perspective taking subscale ($F(1, 106) = 0.320$, n.s.), or country ($F(1, 106) = 0.264$, n.s.). In addition, no significant interaction effects were found.

H3b: Cultural empathy will be positively related to perceptions of emotional team climate in both India and Australia, respectively.

A two-way between-subjects analysis of variance was conducted to evaluate the relationship between cultural empathy and cultural background on perceptions of emotional team climate. Neither country ($F(1, 106) = 0.111$, n.s.) nor the subscales related to cultural empathy, namely empathetic feelings/expression $F(1, 106) = 0.203$, n.s.) and empathetic perspective taking $F(1, 106) = 0.088$, n.s.), produced a significant main effect. In addition, no significant interaction effects were found.

H3c: Cultural empathy will be positively related to perceptions of conflict within respondents' work team in both India and Australia, respectively.

A two-way between-subjects analysis of variance was conducted to evaluate the relationship between cultural empathy and cultural background on perceptions of conflict within respondents' work team. Neither country ($F(1, 106) = 2.662$, n.s.) nor the subscales related to cultural empathy, namely empathetic feelings/expression $F(1, 106) = 1.942$, n.s.) and empathetic perspective taking $F(1, 106) = 0.192$, n.s.), produced a significant main effect. However, there was a significant interaction between country and the empathetic feelings/expressions' subscale ($F(1, 106) = 3.117$, $p < 0.10$) such that the relationship between empathetic feelings/expressions and perceptions of conflict in one's work team was positive for the Australian sample but negative for the Indian sample.

H4a: Dissimilarity openness will be positively related to trust in both India and Australia, respectively.

A two-way between-subjects analysis of variance was conducted to evaluate the relationship between dissimilarity openness and cultural background on trust in one's fellow team members. The results revealed a significant main effect for the communication with dissimilar others' subscale on trust for the combined sample ($F(1, 104) = 3.658$, $p < 0.10$) such that a 1-point increase in communication with dissimilar others was associated with a 0.201 increase in trust. No significant main effect was found for the dissimilarity openness subscales 'comfort with dissimilar others' ($F(1, 104) = 1.667$, n.s.) and 'like/enjoy dissimilar others' ($F(1, 104) = 1.068$, n.s.) or for country ($F(1, 106) = 0.512$, n.s.). However, a significant interaction effect was found between country and the like/enjoy dissimilar others' subscale ($F(1, 104) = 3.477$, $p < 0.10$) such that the relationship between like/enjoy dissimilar others and trust was positive in the Australian sample but negative in the Indian sample.

H4b: Dissimilarity openness will be positively related to perceptions of emotional team climate in both India and Australia, respectively.

A two-way between-subjects analysis of variance was conducted to evaluate the relationship between dissimilarity openness and cultural background on perceptions of emotional team climate. The results revealed a significant main effect for the like/enjoy dissimilar others' subscale on emotional team climate for the combined sample ($F(1, 104) = 5.539$, $p < 0.05$) such that a 1-point increase in like/enjoy dissimilar others was associated with a 0.273 increase in positive perceptions of emotional team climate. However, no significant main effect was found for the comfort with dissimilar others' ($F(1, 104) = 0.001$, n.s.) or communicate with dissimilar others' ($F(1, 104) = 1.176$, n.s.) subscales or for country ($F(1, 106) = 0.393$, n.s.). In addition, no significant interaction effects were found.

H4c: Dissimilarity openness will be positively related to perceptions of conflict within respondents' work team in both India and Australia, respectively.

A two-way between-subjects analysis of variance was conducted to evaluate the relationship between dissimilarity openness and cultural background on perceptions of conflict within respondents' work team. The results revealed a significant main effect for country on perceptions of conflict ($F(1, 104) = 3.142$, $p < 0.10$) such that significantly greater levels of team conflict were reported in the Indian sample than in the Australian sample. None of the dissimilarity subscales, namely comfort with dissimilar others ($F(1, 104) = 0.266$, n.s.), communication with dissimilar others ($F(1, 104) = 1.749$, n.s.) or like/enjoy dissimilar others ($F(1, 104) = 0.207$, n.s.) revealed significant main effects. There was, however, a significant interaction between country and the like/enjoy dissimilar others' subscale ($F(1, 104) = 3.580$, $p < 0.10$) such that the relationship between like/enjoy dissimilar others and perceptions of conflict was negative for the Australian sample but positive for the Indian sample.

H5a: Tolerance for ambiguity will be positively related to trust in both India and Australia, respectively.

A two-way between-subjects analysis of variance was conducted to evaluate the relationship between tolerance for ambiguity and cultural background on trust. Neither country ($F(1, 108) = 0.010$, n.s.) nor tolerance for ambiguity ($F(1, 108) = 0.109$, n.s.) produced a significant main effect. Similarly, the interaction effect was non-significant ($F(1, 108) = 0.975$, n.s.).

H5b: Tolerance for ambiguity will be positively related to perceptions of emotional team climate in both India and Australia, respectively.

A two-way between-subjects analysis of variance was conducted to evaluate the relationship between tolerance for ambiguity and cultural background on perceptions of emotional team climate. Neither country ($F(1, 108) = 0.165$, n.s.) nor tolerance for ambiguity ($F(1, 108) = 0.785$, n.s.) produced a significant main effect. Similarly, the interaction effect was non-significant ($F(1, 108) = 0.491$, n.s.).

H5c: Tolerance for ambiguity will be positively related to perceptions of conflict within respondents' work team in both India and Australia, respectively.

A two-way between-subjects analysis of variance was conducted to evaluate the relationship between tolerance for ambiguity and cultural background on perceptions of conflict within respondents' work team. Neither country ($F(1, 108) = 1.161$, n.s.) nor tolerance for ambiguity ($F(1, 108) = 1.303$, n.s.) produced a significant main effect. Similarly, the interaction effect was non-significant ($F(1, 108) = 0.682$, n.s.).

H6a: Intercultural communication competence will be positively related to trust in both India and Australia, respectively.

A two-way between-subjects analysis of variance was conducted to evaluate the relationship between intercultural communication competence and cultural background on trust. Neither country ($F(1, 108) = 0.007$, n.s.) nor intercultural communication competence ($F(1, 108) = 0.191$, n.s.) produced a significant main effect. Similarly, the interaction effect was non-significant ($F(1, 108) = 0.028$, n.s.).

H6b: Intercultural communication competence will be positively related to perceptions of emotional team climate in both India and Australia, respectively.

A two-way between-subjects analysis of variance was conducted to evaluate the relationship between intercultural communication competence and cultural background on perceptions of emotional team climate. Neither country ($F(1, 108) = 0.211$, n.s.) nor intercultural communication competence ($F(1, 108) = 0.017$, n.s.) produced a significant main effect. Similarly, the interaction effect was non-significant ($F(1, 108) = 0.521$, n.s.).

H6c: Intercultural communication competence will be positively related to perceptions of conflict within respondents' work team in both India and Australia, respectively.

A two-way between-subjects analysis of variance was conducted to evaluate the relationship between intercultural communication competence and cultural background on perceptions of conflict within respondents' work team. Neither country ($F(1, 108) = 0.189$, n.s.) nor intercultural communication competence ($F(1, 108) = 0.421$, n.s.) produced a significant main effect. Similarly, the interaction effect was non-significant ($F(1, 108) = 0.031$, n.s.).

H7a: Conflict management will be positively related to trust in both India and Australia, respectively.

A two-way between-subjects analysis of variance was conducted to evaluate the relationship between conflict management style and cultural background on trust. The results revealed a significant main effect for conflict management on trust ($F(1, 108) = 9.575$, $p < 0.05$) such that a 1-point increase in conflict management was associated with a 0.160 increase in trust for Australians and a 0.294 increase in trust for Indians. However, the main effect for country ($F(1, 108) = 1.096$, n.s) was non-significant as was the interaction effect ($F(1, 108) = 0.837$, n.s.).

H7b: Conflict management will be positively related to perceptions of emotional team climate in both India and Australia, respectively.

A two-way between-subjects analysis of variance was conducted to evaluate the relationship between conflict management style and cultural background perceptions of emotional team climate. The results revealed a significant main effect for conflict management on perceptions of emotional team climate for the combined sample ($F(1, 108) = 12.809$, $p < 0.05$) such that a 1-point increase in conflict management was associated with a 0.5 increase in positive perceptions of emotional team climate. However, there was no main effect for country ($F(1, 108) = 0.717$, n.s) and no interaction effect ($F(1, 108) = 1.023$, n.s.).

H7c: Conflict management will be positively related to perceptions of conflict within respondents' work team in both India and Australia, respectively.

A two-way between-subjects analysis of variance was conducted to evaluate the relationship between conflict management style and cultural background on perceptions of conflict. The results revealed a significant main effect for conflict management style on perceptions of conflict for the combined sample ($F(1, 108) = 10.237$, $p < 0.05$) such that a 1-point increase in conflict management was associated with a 0.749 decrease in perceptions of conflict. However, there was no main effect for country ($F(1, 108)$ = 2.979, n.s) and no interaction effect ($F(1, 108)$ = 2.022, n.s.).

H8a: Emotion management will be positively related to trust in both India and Australia, respectively.

A two-way between-subjects analysis of variance was conducted to evaluate the relationship between emotion management ability and cultural background on trust. Neither country ($F(1, 108)$ = 0.006, n.s.) nor any of the emotion management subscales, namely ability to recognize non-verbal emotions in others ($F(1, 100)$ = 0.667, n.s.), ability to regulate felt emotions ($F(1, 100)$ = 0.756, n.s.), ability to display own emotions ($F(1, 100)$ = 2.425, n.s.), awareness of own emotions ($F(1, 100)$ = 0.012, n.s.) and ability to understand emotions in others ($F(1, 100)$ = 0.733, n.s.) produced significant main effects. In addition, no significant interaction effects were found.

H8b: Emotion management will be positively related to perceptions of emotional team climate in both India and Australia, respectively.

A two-way between-subjects analysis of variance was conducted to evaluate the relationship between emotion management ability and cultural background on perceptions of emotional team climate. Neither country ($F(1, 108)$ = 0.186, n.s.) nor any of the emotion management subscales, namely ability to recognize non-verbal emotions in others ($F(1, 100)$ = 0.079, n.s.), ability to regulate felt emotions ($F(1, 100)$ = 2.116, n.s.), ability to display own emotions ($F(1, 100)$ = 2.214, n.s.), awareness of own emotions ($F(1, 100)$ = 0.463, n.s.) and ability to understand emotions in others ($F(1, 100)$ = 1.648, n.s.) produced significant main effects. In addition, no significant interaction effects were found. However, examination of the parameter estimates indicated a significant negative effect of ability to understand own emotions on perceptions of emotional team climate for the Australian sample such that a 1-point increase in ability to understand own emotions was associated with a 0.308 decrease in positive perceptions of emotional team climate.

H8c: Emotion management will be positively related to perceptions of conflict within respondents' work team in both India and Australia, respectively.

A two-way between-subjects analysis of variance was conducted to evaluate the relationship between emotion management and cultural background on perceptions of conflict. The results revealed a significant negative main effect for the ability to display own emotions' subscale for the combined sample on perceptions of conflict ($F(1,100) = 3.641, p < 0.10$) and a significant positive main effect for the awareness of own emotions' subscale for the combined sample on perceptions of conflict ($F(1,100) = 9.039, p < 0.05$). Specifically, a 1-point increase in ability to display own emotions was associated with a 0.571 decrease in perceptions of team conflict, whereas a 1-point increase in awareness of own emotions was associated with a 1.19 increase in perceptions of team conflict. Significant main effects were not found for the emotion management subscale's ability to recognize non-verbal emotions in others ($F(1,100) = 0.771$, n.s), ability to regulate felt emotions ($F(1,100) = 0.022$, n.s) or ability to understand emotions in others ($F(1,100) = 0.037$, n.s) or for country ($F(1,100) = 0.000$, n.s). However, there was an interaction between country and ability to regulate felt emotions ($F(1,100) = 4.588, p < 0.05$) such that ability to regulate felt emotions was negatively associated with perceptions of team conflict in the Australian sample but positively associated with perceptions of team conflict in the Indian sample. Furthermore, there was an interaction between country and ability to understand emotions in others ($F(1,100) = 3.794, p < 0.10$) with a significant positive relationship between ability to understand emotions in others and perceptions of conflict being observed in the Australian sample but not in the Indian sample.

Discussion
The aim of this chapter was to investigate whether or not the intercultural competencies that have been identified as being important for people working with colleagues from diverse cultural backgrounds carry the same relative importance across cultures. In an effort to investigate this question we conducted a comparative survey study in India and Australia. The competencies investigated in the research were those intercultural competencies identified in a taxonomy the first two authors developed from a comprehensive review of the literature. The cognitive competencies included in the taxonomy were cognitive complexity and goal orientation; the affective competencies included in the taxonomy were dissimilarity openness, tolerance for ambiguity and cultural empathy; and the behavioral competencies included in the taxonomy were intercultural communication competence, emotion management skills and conflict management.

The research provided compelling findings. While some of the intercultural competencies were identified as significantly impacting upon individuals' trust in co-workers and perceptions of emotional team climate and conflict in both Australia and India, other competencies showed a significant effect in only one of the countries, and yet others made no significant difference at all. A summary of the findings can be seen in Table 10.6.

Table 10.6 Summary of results

Hypothesis	Combined sample	Australia	India
H1a	Main effect of cognitive complexity on trust		
H1b	n.s.		
H1c	Main effect of cognitive complexity on perceptions of conflict		
H2a	Main effect of learning orientation on trust		
H2b	n.s.	Positive relationship between performance orientation and emotional team climate	
H2c	Main effect of performance orientation on perceptions of conflict		
H3a	Main effect of empathetic feelings and expression subscale on trust		
H3b	n.s.		
H3c	Main effect of communication with dissimilar others' subscale on trust	Positive interaction between country and empathetic feelings/expression on perceptions of conflict	Negative interaction between country and empathetic feelings/expression on perceptions of conflict
H4a	Main effect of communication with dissimilar others' subscale on trust	Positive interaction between country and like/enjoy dissimilar others' subscale on trust	Negative interaction between country and like/enjoy dissimilar others' subscale on trust
H4b	Main effect of like/enjoy dissimilar others' subscale on emotional team climate		

Hypothesis			
H4c	Main effect of country on perceptions of conflict	Lower levels of conflict reported than in Indian sample Negative interaction between like/enjoy dissimilar others and perceptions of conflict	Higher levels of conflict reported than in Australian sample Positive interaction between like/enjoy dissimilar others and perceptions of conflict
H5a	n.s.		
H5b	n.s.		
H5c	n.s.		
H6a	n.s.		
H6b	n.s.		
H6c	n.s.		
H7a	Main effect of conflict management on trust		
H7b	Main effect of conflict management on emotional team climate		
H7c	Main effect of conflict management on perceptions of conflict		
H8a	n.s.	Negative relationship between ability to understand own emotions and emotional team climate	
H8b	n.s.	Negative relationship between ability to regulate felt emotions and perceptions of conflict Positive relationship between ability to understand emotions in others and perceptions of conflict	
H8c	Negative main effect of ability to display own emotions on perceptions of conflict Positive main effect of awareness of own emotions on perceptions of conflict		Positive relationship between ability to regulate felt emotions and perceptions of conflict

With regard to the cognitive competencies, while cognitive complexity was found to be related to individuals' trust in co-workers and their perceptions of conflict within their team in both Australia and India, the results regarding the relationship between cognitive complexity and emotional team climate were not significant. The results regarding the relationship between goal orientation and the dependent variables were mixed. While learning goal orientation was found to be related to trust in both Australia and India, it was performance goal orientation that was found to be related to perceptions of conflict in both countries. Furthermore, performance goal orientation was related to emotional team climate, but this was only the case in the Australian sample.

The results with regard to the affective competencies were also mixed. While empathetic feelings/expressions were found to be related to trust in both Australia and India, the results regarding the relationship between cultural empathy and emotional team climate were not significant. A further interesting finding was that while empathetic feelings /expressions were found to be positively related to perceptions of conflict in the Australian sample, in the Indian sample the findings were the opposite, with a negative relationship being found. With regard to dissimilarity openness, a significant relationship was found between the communication with dissimilar others' subscale of the dissimilarity openness measure and perceptions of trust in both Australia and India. In addition, while the like/ enjoy dissimilar others' subscale of the dissimilarity openness measure was positively related to trust in the Australian sample, in the Indian sample the relationship between these two variables was negative. Furthermore, like/enjoy dissimilar others had an effect on emotional team climate in both Australia and India. With regard to dissimilarity openness and perceptions of conflict, lower levels of conflict were reported in the Australian sample than in the Indian sample. Furthermore, while a negative interaction was found between like/enjoy dissimilar others and perceptions of conflict in the Australian sample, a positive interaction was found in the Indian sample. Finally, the relationship between tolerance for ambiguity and each of the dependent variables failed to reach significance.

Like with the other competencies investigated in this study, the findings regarding the behavioral competencies were mixed. While intercultural communication competence was not related to any of the dependent variables, conflict management style was related to all of the dependent variables in both Australia and India. In addition, while the relationship between emotion management ability and trust was non-significant and it also failed to show a significant main effect on emotional team climate, there was a significant interaction between the ability to understand own emotions' subscale of the emotion management measure and emotional team climate in the Australian sample. Finally, emotion management was related to perceptions of conflict in the two samples. Specifically, ability to display own emotions had a negative effect on perceptions of conflict in both countries while awareness of own emotions had a positive effect on perceptions of conflict in both countries. Furthermore, while ability to regulate felt emotions was negatively related with perceptions of conflict in Australia, the reverse was the case in India. Lastly, ability to understand emotions in others was positively related to perceptions of conflict in the Australian sample.

Based on the findings described above, it appears that some competencies generalize across cultures while others are country specific. In particular, while dissimilarity openness and emotion management ability appear to be country specific, cognitive complexity and conflict management style influenced individuals' perceptions of their team and their colleagues in the same way in both Australia and India, indicating that they may generalize across cultures. It is important to note here that given the small size of the Indian sample, caution does need to be exercised when saying that particular competencies are country specific. Nonetheless, the differences found suggest the need for closer future examination of these competencies across cultures.

Theoretical and practical contributions

While the importance of intercultural competencies is increasingly being stressed, to date there has been a lack of empirical investigation examining whether or not the same competencies are applicable across cultures. This research has attempted to address this gap by examining the relative importance of a comprehensive set of cognitive, affective and behavioral intercultural competencies across two distinctly different cultures. The results of the research suggest that some intercultural competencies may generalize across cultures, while others may be country specific. This is a significant finding as it suggests that the importance of different competencies to intercultural communication may vary from one culture context to another.

These findings also present important practical implications for such things as selection, training, development and performance management practices. For example, given that competencies such as conflict management and cognitive complexity appear to be generalizable across cultures, training and developing these competencies in all employees regardless of cultural setting would be advisable. In terms of training and development for a specific cultural context, steps should be taken to examine those competencies which have been shown to vary between countries to determine whether they are relevant to the target context. Similarly, the relative emphasis placed on the competencies in selection decisions and perform-ance management across cultures may need to vary.

Limitations

Despite the contributions of the research undertaken in this chapter, there are a number of limitations which must be noted. First and foremost is the small sample size, particularly in relation to the Indian section of the sample. Second, the fact that respondents were reporting on their percep-tions of a situation could be a source of potential inaccuracy in the results. Third, the research undertaken was cross-sectional and for this reason is unable to provide insight into how changes in the level of individu-als' competencies over time may lead to changes in individual responses. Fourth, while the findings of the present research shed some light on the relative importance of intercultural competencies in different cultural con-texts, the research was only undertaken in two cultural settings and further research is required before definitive conclusions can be drawn as to the extent to which the identified competencies facilitate intercultural effec-tiveness across cultural contexts. In addition, this research only examined the impact that employees' intercultural competence has on individual-level outcomes yet, the level of individuals' competencies is also likely to impact on the experiences of their team members and, consequently, on team-level outcomes. For this reason it would be beneficial to investigate the relative importance of intercultural competencies across cultures using the team as the level of analysis.

Conclusion

Whether working within a single cultural setting or working across cultural settings, there is no doubt that today's workforce needs to be equipped to deal with intercultural business interactions. This makes it particularly surprising that so little research is available identifying the specific inter-cultural competencies required to work effectively with culturally diverse others. Even more problematic is the lack of cross-national comparative research examining the impact of competencies expected to facilitate inter-cultural communication. The research presented in this chapter goes some way toward broadening our understanding of how different competencies may play different roles in different cultural settings and provides prelimi-nary evidence that some intercultural competencies appear to generalize across cultures while others appear to be country specific.

References

Abe, H. and Wiseman, R.L. (1983), 'A cross-cultural confirmation of the dimensions of inter-cultural effectiveness', *International Journal of Intercultural Relations*, 7: 53–67.

Ali, F. (2010), 'A comparative study of EEO on Pakistan, India and Bangladesh', ch. 3 in M.F. Özbilgin and J. Syed (eds), *Managing Gender, Diversity in Asia: A Research Companion*, Cheltenham, UK and Northampton, MA, USA: Edward Elgar, pp. 32–53.

Ayoko, O.B. and Härtel, C.E.J. (2000a), 'Cultural differences at work: how managers deepen or lessen the cross-racial divide in their workgroups', *Queensland Review*, 7 (1): 77–87.

Ayoko, O.B. and Härtel, C.E.J. (2000b), 'Culturally heterogeneous workgroups: the effects of leader behaviors and attitudes on conflict and its relationship to task and social outcomes', paper presented at the Academy of Management Conference, August, Toronto, Canada.

Bartel-Radic, A. (2006), 'Intercultural learning in global teams', *Management International Review*, 46 (6): 647–78.

Beamer, L. (1992). 'Learning intercultural communication competence', *Journal of Business Communication*, 29 (3): 285–304.

Brew, F.P. and Cairns, D.R. (2004), 'Styles of managing interpersonal workplace conflict in relation to status and face concern: a study with Anglos and Chinese', *International Journal of Conflict Management*, 15 (1): 27–56.

Brockner, J., Wiesenfeld, B.M., Martin, C.L. (1995), 'Decision frame, procedural justice and survivors' reactions to job layoffs', *Organizational Behavior and Human Decision Processes*, 63: 59–68.

Broome, B.J., DeTurk, S., Kristjansdottir, E.S., Kanata, T. and Ganesan, P. (2002), 'Giving voice to diversity: an interactive approach to conflict management and decision-making in culturally diverse work environments', *Journal of Business and Management*, 8 (3): 239–64.

Byrne, D.E. (1971), *The Attraction Paradigm*, New York: Academic Press.

Chang, S. (2002), 'Competencies for managing multicultural work groups in Australia', Department of Management, Melbourne, Monash University.

Cox, T. (1993), *Cultural Diversity in Organizations: Theory, Research and Practice*, San Francisco, CA: Barrett-Koehler.

Dodd, C.H. (1987), 'An introduction to intercultural effectiveness skills', in C.H. Dodd and F.F. Montalvo (eds), *Intercultural Skills for Multicultural Societies*, Washington, DC: SIETAR International: 3–12.

Duda, J.L. and Nicholls, J.G. (1992), 'Dimensions of achievement motivation in schoolwork and sport', *Journal of Educational Psychology*, 84: 290–99.

Elliott, E.S., and Dweck, C.S. (1988), 'Goals: an approach to motivation and achievement', *Journal of Personality and Social Psychology*, 54: 5–12.

Fine, M.G. (1995), *Building Successful Multicultural Organizations: Challenges and Opportunities*, Westport, CI: Quorum Books.

Fujimoto, Y., Härtel, C.E.J., Härtel, G.F. and Baker, N.J. (2000), 'Openness to dissimilarity moderates the consequences of diversity in well-established groups', *Asia Pacific Journal of Human Resources*, 38 (3): 46–61.

Gudykunst, W.B. and Kim, Y.Y. (1997), *Communicating with Strangers: An Approach to Intercultural Communication*, New York: McGraw-Hill.

Gudykunst, W.B. and Ting-Toomey, S. (1988), *Culture and Interpersonal Communication*, Newbury Park, CA: Sage.

Hammer, M.R. Gudykunst, W.B. and Wiseman, R.L (1978), 'Dimensions of intercultural effectiveness', *International Journal of Intercultural Relations*, 2: 382–92.

Härtel, C.E.J. and Fujimoto, Y. (2000), 'Diversity is not a problem to be managed by organizations but openness to perceived dissimilarity is', *Journal of Australian and New Zealand Academy of Management*, 6 (1): 14–27.

Härtel, C.E.J., Barker, S. and Baker, N.J. (1999a), 'The role of emotional intelligence in service encounters: a model for predicting the effects of employee–customer interactions on consumer attitudes, intentions and behaviors', *Australian Journal of Communication*, 26 (2): 77–87.

Härtel, C.E.J., Douthitt, S.S., Härtel, G.F. and Yarbough Douthitt, S. (1999b), 'Equally qualified but unequally perceived: openness to perceived dissimilarity as a predictor of race and sex discrimination in performance judgments', *Human Resource Development Quarterly*, **10** (1): 79–89.

Härtel, C.E.J., Gough, H. and Härtel, G.F. (2006), 'Service providers' use of emotional competencies and perceived workgroup emotional climate to predict customer and providers' satisfaction with service encounters', *International Journal of Work Organization and Emotion*, **1** (3): 232–54.

Härtel, C.E.J., Hanrahan, S. and Cerin, E. (2005), 'Developing the Task And Ego Orientation at Work Questionnaire', paper presented at Australia and New Zealand Academy of Management Conference, 7–10 December, Canberra.

Hawkes, F. and Kealey, D.J. (1981), 'An empirical study of Canadian technical assistance', *International Journal of Intercultural Relations*, **5**: 239–58.

Hofstede, G. (2001), *Culture's Consequences: Comparing Values, Behaviors, Institutions and Organizations Across Nations*, Newbury Park, CA: Sage.

Iles, P. (1995), 'Learning to work with difference', *Personnel Review*, **24** (6): 44–60.

Jehn, K.A. (1994), 'Enhancing effectiveness: an investigation of advantages and disadvantages of value based intragroup conflict,' *International Journal of Conflict Management*, **5**: 223–38.

Jehn, K.A., Chadwick, C. and Thatcher, S.M.B. (1997), 'To agree or not to agree: the effects of value congruence, individual demographic dissimilarity and conflict on workgroup outcomes', *International Journal of Conflict Management*, **8** (4): 287–305.

Jehn, K.A. and Chatman, J.A. (2000), 'The influence of proportional and perceptual conflict composition on team performance', *International Journal of Conflict Management*, **11** (1): 56–73.

Johnson, J.L., Cullen, J.B., Sakano, T. and Takenouchi, H. (1996), 'Setting the stage for trust and strategic integration in Japanese–U.S. cooperative alliances', *Journal of International Business Studies*, **27** (5): 981–1004.

Jordan, P.J., Ashkanasy, N.M., Härtel, C.E.J. and Hooper, G.S. (2002), 'Workgroup emotional intelligence: scale development and relationship to team process effectiveness and goal focus', *Human Resource Management Review*, **12** (2), 195–214.

Kagan, D. (1992), 'The social implications of higher level thinking skills', *Journal of Accounting Education*, **10**: 285–95.

Karim, A.U. (2003), 'A developmental progression model for intercultural consciousness: a leadership imperative', *Journal of Education for Business* **79** (1): 34–9.

Kirchmeyer, C. (1993), 'Multicultural task groups: an account of the low contribution level of minorities', *Small Group Research*, **24** (1): 127–48.

Leiba-O'Sullivan, S. (1999), 'The distinction between stable and dynamic cross-cultural competencies: implications for expatriate trainability', *Journal of International Business Studies*, **30** (4): 709–25.

Lloyd, S.L., Härtel, C.E.J. and Youngsamart, D. (2004), 'Working abroad: competencies expatriates need to successfully cope with the intercultural experience', *Doing Business Across Borders Journal*, (Special Issue: Australian Perspectives on the Expatriate Experience), **3** (1): 54–66.

Lolla, C. and Davis, H.J. (1991), 'Cultural synergy and the multicultural workforce: bridging occidental and oriental cultures', *Advances in International and Comparative Management*, **6**: 103–25.

Lustig, M.W. and Koester, J. (1999), *Intercultural Competence: Interpersonal Communication across Cultures*, Reading, MA: Addison Wesley Longman.

Mamman, A. (1995), 'Socio-biographical antecedents of intercultural effectiveness: the neglected factors', *British Journal of Management* **6**: 97–114.

Mayer, J. and Salovey, P. (1994), 'The intelligence of emotional intelligence', *Intelligence*, **17** (4): 433–42.

Maznevski, M.L. (1994), 'Understanding our differences: performance in decision-making groups with diverse members', *Human Relations*, **47** (5): 531–52.

McLain, D.L. (1993), 'The MSTAT-I: a new measure of an individual's tolerance for ambiguity', *Educational and Psychological Measurement*, **53**: 183–9.

Milliken, F.J. and Martins, L.L. (1996), 'Searching for common threads: understanding the multiple effects of diversity in organizational groups', *Academy of Management Review*, **21** (2): 402–33.

Paik, Y. and Sohn, J.D. (2004), 'Expatriate managers and MNCs' ability to control international subsidiaries: the case of Japanese MNCs', *Journal of World Business*, **39**: 61–71.

Pirola-Merlo, A., Härtel, C.E.J., Mann, L. and Hirst, G. (2002), 'How leaders influence the impact of affective events on team climate and performance in R&D teams', *Leadership Quarterly*, **13**: 561–81.

Rahim, A. and Blum, A.A (1994), *Global Perspectives on Organizational Conflict*, Westport, CT: Praeger.

Rodrigues, C.A. (1997), 'Developing expatriates' cross-cultural sensitivity: cultures where "your culture's OK" is really not OK', *Journal of Management Development*, **16** (9): 690–702.

Samovar, L.A., Porter, R.E. and Jain, N.C. (1981), *Understanding Intercultural Communication*, Belmont, CA: Wadsworth.

Scachaf, P. (2005), 'Bridging cultural diversity through e-mail', *Journal of Global Information Technology Management*, **8** (2): 46–60.

Shaw, J.B. and Barrett-Power, E. (1998), 'The effects of diversity on small work group processes and performance', *Human Relations*, **51** (10): 1307–25.

Skaalvik, E.M. (1997), 'Self-enhancing and self-defeating ego orientation: relations with task and avoidance orientation, achievement, self-perceptions and anxiety', *Journal of Educational Psychology*, **89** (1): 71–81.

Tabachnick, B.G. and Fiddel, L.S. (2007), *Using Multivariate Statistics*, Boston, MA: Pearson/Allyn & Bacon.

Tjosvold, D. (1985), 'Implications of controversy research for management', *Journal of Management*, **11**: 21–37.

Triandis, H.C., Kurowski, L.L. and Gelfand, M.J. (1994), 'Workplace diversity', in H.C. Triandis, M.D. Dunnette and L.M. Hough (eds), *Handbook of Industrial and Organizational Psychology*, Palo Alto, CA: Consulting Psychologists: 769–815.

Vrugt, A., Oort, F.J. and Zeeberg, C. (2002), 'Goal orientation, perceived self-efficacy and study results amongst beginners and advanced students', *British Journal of Educational Psychology*, **72**: 385–97.

Vuckovic, A. (2008), 'Inter-cultural communication: a foundation of communicative action', *Multicultural Education and Technology Journal*, **2** (1): 47–59.

Wang, P. and Chan, P.S. (1995) 'Top management perception of strategic information processing in a turbulent environment', *Leadership and Organization Development Journal*, **16** (7): 33–44.

Wang, Y., Davidson, M.M., Yakushko, O.F., Savoy, H.B., Tan, J.A. and Bleier, J.K. (2003), 'The scale of ethnocultural empathy: development, validation, and reliability', *Journal of Counseling Psychology*, **50** (2): 221–34.

Yum, J.O. (1982), 'Communication diversity and information acquisition among Korean immigrants in Hawaii', *Human Communication Research*, **8**: 154–69.

Zakaria, N. (2000), 'The effects of cross-cultural training on the acculturation process of the global workforce', *International Journal of Manpower*, **21** (6): 492–510.

11 When East meets West: managing Chinese enterprise relationships through *guanxi*-based diversity management

Charmine E.J. Härtel, Ruby M.M. Ma and Sharif As-Saber

Introduction

Increasingly, the forces of globalization are leading to the necessity for organizations to operate on an international scale in order to remain viable (Deresky, 2000). While these international operations can create a number of benefits for organizations, they also introduce a whole new set of challenges which must be dealt with, not least of which is the challenge of interacting with individuals from diverse backgrounds. The problems created by a limited understanding of the diversity-related issues that can arise in international interactions are nowhere better illustrated than in the case of Sino–Western business collaboration. While China is a rising international business player, a closer examination of the international business interactions between China and the West reveals that only a small proportion of the joint ventures and negotiations undertaken by Westerners with the Chinese are successful. Consequently, there is an urgent need to understand the factors which impact upon the effectiveness of communication, negotiation and overall business relationships between Western and Chinese counterparts. It is with this focus that this chapter explores the management of diversity-related issues in the context of Sino–Western business interactions. In line with the two-dimensional conceptualizations of diversity advocated by Härtel and Fujimoto (2000), diversity will be considered in relation to both identity groups and individual differences. This approach is being adopted, rather than simply viewing diversity itself as the cause of breakdowns in communication and negotiation in Sino–Western interactions, it allows for an examination of the antecedents that lead to both positive and negative relational and business outcomes in these situations. In particular, at the group level, it allows us to illustrate the role that differences in cultural values and norms can have on the overall interaction while at the individual level, it allows us to illustrate how cognitive and affective reactions of the individuals involved in an interaction can impact on the interaction overall.

An understanding of diversity management in the context of Sino–Western business collaborations is of considerable importance for a number of reasons. First, as alluded to above, China is an emerging superpower in the world economy and is fast becoming one of the largest sources of both exports and imports for many countries around the globe. The differences between the Chinese and Western cultures are, however, great, particularly in relation to the degree to which individualism and collectivism is emphasized and the role this plays at the individual and group levels. Given that 'cross-cultural studies have revealed that, across the cultures of the world, the most important dimension of cultural differences is the relative emphasis on individualism vs collectivism' (Fujimoto and Härtel, 2006, p. 205), understanding the impact that cultural diversity plays on the way that parties from Western and Chinese organizations engage in business interactions is of critical importance. Simply put, the effective management of these differences will play a key role in the development of effective working relationships between China and the West.

In discussing this topic, we extend on the model of effective diversity management presented by Gilbert et al. (1999) which considers the most effective methods for internal diversity management to ensure favorable individual- and organizational-level outcomes. Like Gilbert et al., we focus on the more intangible aspects related to diversity management such as emotion, trust and relationship quality; however, rather than looking at their impact within an organization, we consider their impact on inter-organizational communication and negotiation. While it is known that emotions can influence cross-cultural communication and negotiation (George et al., 1998), we argue that this, along with differences that arise as a result of the influence that culture has on groups and individuals (Hall, 1976; Hofstede, 1980, 2001; Trompenaars, 1993), can impact on the success or failure of Sino–Western communication and subsequent business relationships (Ma and Härtel, 2005; Härtel and Ma, 2006). We focus in particular on the role that *guanxi*, a key to developing and maintaining relationships in the Chinese culture, plays in the success or failure of Sino–Western business enterprises. In addition, we examine how affective communication competence and differences in Chinese and Western communication patterns can impact on the probability of communication events occurring which can be perceived by the Chinese party as positive or negative affective events. We argue that these affective events can influence the moods and emotions experienced during the relationship development process, which if allowed to build up, can affect the Chinese perceptions of the quality of *guanxi* in the overall relationship. By providing inside knowledge of the intricate systems in which a key non-Western culture conducts business, this chapter serves to enhance diversity management competence within the ever-growing market niche characterized by Chinese consumers and business partners. It also provides an excellent example of the type of cross-cultural training referred to by Nishii and Özbilgin (2007) as necessary for developing global competencies.

To achieve the objectives outlined above, in this chapter a model is developed to examine the Sino–Western business relationship building process, in particular, looking at the factors affecting Chinese business partners' perception of *guanxi* and how it can influence the relationship (see Figure 11.1). The model is developed from an affective events theory perspective (Weiss and Cropanzano, 1996) by incorporating the constructs of affective communication competence; relationship quality in terms of *guanxi*; culturally founded communication patterns in terms of high and low context (Gudykunst and Ting-Toomey, 1988, 1996; Hall, 1976); George et al.'s (1998) model of affect in cross-cultural negotiations; and Griffith's (2002) model for international communication effectiveness. This model extends existing conceptualizations of the cross-cultural communication process by combining theories of emotions and research on *guanxi* and the second author's own unique understanding and experience of the Chinese perception of *guanxi*, combined with well-accepted theories of contextual, social and cognitive influences on communication and negotiation (Phatak and Habib, 1996; Risberg, 1997; Ghauri and Fang, 2001).

Before describing the model in detail, and applying it to the Sino–Western business context, we outline the choice of affective events theory as the grounding behind analyzing the events which construct relations between Chinese and Western parties. We then discuss the business relationship development process in its four phases, while acknowledging that business negotiation is a dynamic and interactive process. Next, we discuss the concept of *guanxi*, which is the core to relationship development and maintenance in Chinese culture. We explain how *guanxi* plays an important role in the informal phase of business negotiation. Then, we describe the key features of the formal phase of the business negotiation and how culturally founded communication patterns and the affective communication competence of individuals involved in the negotiation influence the elements of this phase. After that, we show how the emotions resulting from the formal phase of the business negotiation influence the affect-driven behavior of the Chinese counterpart and the perception of *guanxi* by the Chinese counterpart. Finally, we discuss how these processes impact on the post-negotiation scenario in terms of the judgment-driven behaviors of the Chinese counterpart, which in turn, determine the success of business relations with a Western partner. From a Western perspective, this understanding is crucial in the development of successful joint

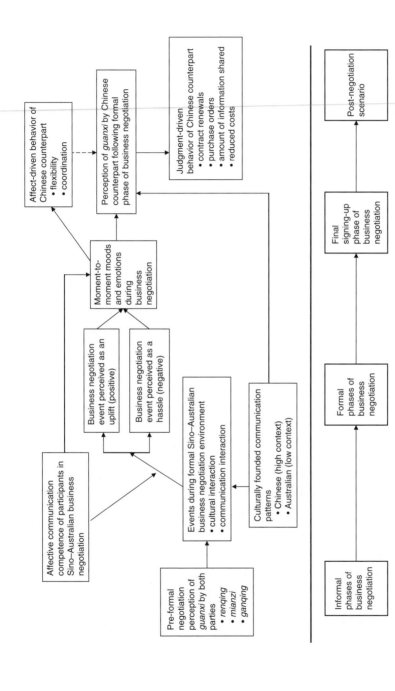

Figure 11.1   A model of factors affecting Chinese negotiators' perception of guanxi in Sino–Australian negotiations: an affective events theory perspective

227

ventures, negotiating contracts and opening up further opportunities for
doing business with the Chinese.

Affective events theory

Affective events theory (AET) is considered as an appropriate lens for
studying the outcomes of business interactions between parties from
diverse cultural backgrounds as it is an uncomplicated framework which
is logical to follow and allows researchers to look at emotions in organizations while adapting other existing concepts (Ashkanasy et al., 2002). AET
adopts a cognitive appraisal perspective of emotions, which means it takes
into account the interplay between cognition and emotion.

AET looks at the antecedents and consequences of momentary affective experience (moods and emotions) and provides a cogent theoretical
framework to study emotions in the workplace. It indicates that experiences at work can be pleasant and positive (uplift), or difficult and negative
(hassles), and they can affect the way one feels and behaves in the workplace. According to AET, daily hassles and uplifts (affective events) can
lead to expressions of positive emotions such as joy or pleasure or negative
emotions such as anger or sadness. If these emotions accumulate over
time, they can impact on people's intentions and behaviors towards their
work, which can impact upon more concrete forms of judgment-driven
behavior (Weiss and Cropanzano, 1996).

Most research to date on communication and negotiation focuses on
how contextual (Phatak and Habib, 1996; Risberg, 1997), social (Ghauri
and Fang, 2001), and cognitive (George et al., 1998) factors impact on
communication/negotiation outcomes. Researchers have only recently
begun to study how the intangible aspects of negotiation such as trust,
reputation, relationship quality, moods, emotion and cultural values
such as the Chinese concept of *guanxi* shape the processes and outcomes
of communication and negotiation in a diversity context (Griffith, 2002;
Ma and Härtel 2005; Härtel and Ma, 2006; Zhao and Krohmer, 2006).
These studies demonstrate that theories of cross-cultural business negotiation must take into account contextual and individual difference factors
from both cognitive and affective perspectives. It is these criteria which
informed our choice of AET (Weiss and Cropanzano, 1996) as the underpinning theory for the development of the model of cross-cultural business
relations development presented in this chapter.

Business relationship development in a diverse business setting

Business relationship development in general involves a process in which
participants, taking into consideration their respective goals and aspirations, strategically share information and pursue alternatives that are

mutually beneficial (Robinson and Volkov, 1998). Depending on the types of business negotiations and their cross-cultural orientations (Fuller, 1991; Oikawa and Tanner, 1992; Woo and Prud'homme, 1999; Macduff, 2006), it can be an intricate, lengthy process that involves several stages (De Moor and Weigand, 2004; Atkin and Rinehart, 2006; Mouzas, 2006), most commonly conceptualized as the informal phase, the formal phase, the final signing-up phase, and the post-negotiation phase. Each phase contributes to the ultimate course that a business negotiation will take.

The informal phase is usually the preparatory stage, which deals with information gathering about the prospective partner, environmental scanning and planning (Urban, 1996; Usunier, 1996; Atkin and Rinehart, 2006). Thus, it is important to consider a set of preparatory tasks. Richards and Walsh (1990) identified a list which includes: taking into account one's needs; checking one's assumptions about the possible outcome; being factual with one's position and ability; considering the issues relevant to the negotiation; and most important of all, remembering the needs of one's counterpart. While pre-negotiation training for negotiators may be considered appropriate at this stage (Fuller, 1991), we argue that in the context of Sino–Western business negotiations this is critical. The reason for this is that the negotiations to be undertaken will be done so in a culturally diverse context.

Cultural diversity refers to diversity as a result of dissimilarity in identities such as race and ethnicity (Foldy, 2004). 'Members of the same cultural identity group often – though not always – have similarities of background experience that shape the way they see the world' (ibid., pp. 530–31) thus influencing the way that they perceive and interpret incoming information. Furthermore, 'culture and communication are very closely connected. Culture, to a great extent, decides with whom we communicate, how we communicate, and what we communicate' (Gersten, 1990, p. 345). The manner in which people communicate is based on the language, rules and norms that they learn as they are growing up within their cultural setting. However, as these are learnt at an early age, we are generally unaware of how our culture influences the way that we communicate and the way that we behave (Gudykunst and Kim, 1997). For this reason, the key at this stage of the Sino–Western negotiation process is to provide the negotiation team with some understanding about cultural differences as well as legal issues, negotiation styles and the reactive modes that may have an influence during the formal negotiation process. In addition, activities such as getting to know people through informal gatherings (for example, trade fairs and personal invitations) can be used to build a rapport before the formal business activities take place. This is of particular importance in doing business with the Chinese, as they like to deal with people they are familiar with. It is therefore important to build a relationship (*guanxi*), to allow mutual trust (*xin*) to be established before proceeding to the more formal phase of conducting business (these concepts will be discussed in more detail later in the chapter).

The formal phase of business negotiation can be a significant determinant of the final outcome of the negotiation, establishing the terms under which business is to be conducted. Careful planning is the precondition of any negotiation success. Hence, it is important to consider the give and take around specific issues during this phase (Atkin and Rinehart, 2006). It is for this reason that the formal phase of the negotiation process should not be rushed. Both parties should be comfortable with the venue and the language used during the formal negotiation (Howarth et al., 1995; Nokatani, 2006). According to Lassere and Schütte (1995), Western negotiators require an unusually high degree of flexibility when negotiating in Asia. As to concluding a win–win outcome, mutual respect and understanding and a friendly atmosphere need to be maintained throughout the formal negotiation phase. This is even more so in the case of the Sino–Western business negotiation where the perception of a good *guanxi* is far more important to the Chinese than rushing to the signing of an agreement on paper.

In order to establish a good relationship and to ensure that the formal phase of the negotiation process runs smoothly, it is particularly important that negotiators have sound intercultural communication competence. Intercultural communication can be defined as 'a transactional, symbolic process involving the attribution of meaning between people from different cultures' (Gudykunst and Kim, 1997, p. 19). Due to differences in cultural rules and norms, the communication styles of Western and Chinese negotiators tend to be quite different. For example, while most Western negotiators tend to come from low-context cultures where people get straight to the point when communicating, China is a country which has a high-context culture and as such, when communicating, people tend to be less direct with their message (Lloyd et al., 2004). Consequently, in the Sino–Western negotiation context, it is possible that members of both sides in the negotiation could be confronted with language, rules and norms that are unfamiliar to them, which can in turn lead to such things as confusion and hostility. To prevent this from creating a problem in the negotiation process, negotiators need to have an understanding of the cultures involved in the process to effectively encode and decode messages (Beamer, 1992) and to ensure that they are communicating and behaving in a manner that will not offend the other party. To this end, 'a number of studies have shown that awareness of and sensitivity to cultural differences is a key component in cross-cultural relations' (Lloyd et al., 2004, p. 59).

The final signing-up phase of the negotiation process involves careful preparation of the documentation of the terms and conditions discussed in the formal negotiation phase. While this usually takes place as part of the formal negotiation phase, the complex nature of the preparation of documentation for the final signing of the contract, however, brings about the necessity to consider it as a separate phase. The document is prepared in accordance with the host-country legal requirements, however, it is good practice for a foreign partner to understand relevant host-country legal issues and interpret them according to the home-country law for any future legal implications (Howarth et al., 1995). This is no exception in the Sino–Western context.

The final signing-up phase generally leads to the formal conclusion of a negotiation process. The post-negotiation phase, however, is as critical as the previous phases mentioned above (Atkin and Rinehart, 2006; Mouzas, 2006) as, during this phase, parties may still change the agreed clauses to their own advantage (Mouzas, 2006). In the Sino–Western business relationship context, it is important to utilize this post-negotiation period as an ongoing process to achieve optimum benefit from the agreed outcomes. Open-mindedness and flexibility need to be exercised, as it is likely that the Chinese counterpart may feel more comfortable continuing the discussion following the formal negotiation, as part of the ongoing building of *guanxi* which is discussed next.

Understanding the impact of culture in cross-cultural interactions: theoretical background on *guanxi*

Given that individuals' cultural backgrounds shape their view of reality (Maznevski, 1994), the impact of cultural differences on interpersonal interactions can be widely seen in the management literature. Culture 'comprises an entire set of social norms and responses that condition people's behavior' (Rodrigues, 1997, p. 690). As a consequence, there are a wide variety of cultural variables on which individuals from different cultural groups can differ (Lloyd et al., 2004). However, in the context of Sino–Western interactions, it can be said that the key cultural variable that it is important to know about in order to effectively manage the relationship in this diverse setting is that of the Chinese cultural concept of '*guanxi*'.

The concept of '*guanxi*' has been widely researched (see Leung et al., 1996). *Guanxi* in Chinese literally means 'relationship' or 'relation' and it can also be translated in general as 'special relationship' or 'connections'. It is a very important part of the Chinese culture and way of life (Hutchings, 2002; Hutchings and Murray, 2002, 2003; Zhao and Krohmer, 2006) and regarded as a guiding principle of economic and social organization (Hu,

1944; Walder, 1986; Hwang, 1987; Cheng and Rosett, 1991; Fei, 1992, cited in Bian and Ang, 1997). In the Chinese context, however, *guanxi* goes much beyond the usual understanding of relationship or connection. It demands very personal interactions with other people and almost always involves reciprocal obligation (Stone, 1988, cited in Bian and Ang, 1997). It can be a set of interpersonal connections that help with the exchange of favors between people on a dyadic basis (Hwang, 1987). It is based on blood or kinship (Tong and Yong, 1998) and networks (Davies, 1995) and thus can also be defined as 'Friendship with implications of continual exchange of favors' (Chen, 1995, cited in Wong, 1998). According to Davies (1995), the *guanxi* network can consist of the social interactions with those individuals one knows and the place where the network members tend to interact (cited in Wong, 1998). It is believed that the continual favor exchanges develop trust among the members of the *guanxi* network, and this helps to reduce the risk of uncertainty. Therefore, kin or non-kin relationships do not matter, as they are the relational bases to develop *guanxi* in Chinese society.

Guanxi *and Chinese culture*

Chinese culture is strongly influenced by Confucian tradition, which defines individuals in relational terms (Yang, 1994; contrast this to Lee's discussion (ch. 12, this volume) on the influence of Confucian and Buddhist thought on Korean and Japanese culture). Confucianism relates individuals to their significant others. For example, the relationship between the father and the son, the wife and the husband in the family; between the uncle and the nephew or niece; between the grandparents and the grandchildren; between the teacher and the student; between schoolmates; and the relationship between the boss and subordinate in one's career development. It is very different from Western culture which is strongly influenced by Christianity, which puts individuals in reference to God. The significant others in the Chinese context are not, however, seen as instruments to help identify and recognize 'self', which is the fundamental point of cognitive development theory underlying the Western traditions of individualism and capitalism (Mead, 1934, as cited in Bian and Ang, 1997). Traditionally, in Chinese culture, the collective is almost always considered greater and more significant than the individual. It is suggested that self is identified, recognized and evaluated in terms of one's relations to various groups and communities where one belongs. This provides both the abstract and the concrete foundations for *guanxi* to work in Chinese societies both within and outside of China (Hsiao, 1988, as cited in Bian and Ang, 1997). It is the expectation that each one will behave according to his or her specified role according to the defined relationship in the society, that the majority of Chinese live their lives by and which has underpinned harmonious interactions between individuals over thousands of years.

Guanxi *bases*

The reality is that *guanxi* is everywhere, in modern China, and among overseas Chinese (see Nolan, 2010 for discussions of *guanxi* and gender). Tong and Yong (1998) found that the social foundations and organizational dynamics of Chinese business firms, and their tendency to include personal relationships, can impact on overall decision making. Therefore, in the Sino–Western business context, it is important to understand how *guanxi* is established and maintained, and under what conditions it deteriorates and changes. In addition, the dynamics of *guanxi* and interpersonal trust (*xin* and *xinyong*) and the reason for activating some *guanxi* bases should be noted (ibid.).

According to Tong and Yong, early emigration of Chinese people to East Asian countries such as Singapore, left them without their close family, compelling them to seek help from people from their own villages or districts in China for food, lodging and work. This form of *guanxi* base can often become mutual help associations organized according to the locality or dialect spoken. Another common Chinese practice is to look for people with the same surnames, and organize clans based on these, due to the belief that people sharing the same surname descended from the same ancestor, and therefore are *qin ren* or kinsmen (relatives). Often *renqing* (a special favor for people you like or share something in common with) is considered when dealing with people from the same village, with the same surname or who speak the same dialect. These early *guanxi* bases are organized according to fictive kinship and also take into account the locality/dialect criteria.

The Chinese also believe that one's immediate *kin* are the most trustworthy, as nothing compares to one's family. This form of kinship *guanxi* base is most important (Landa, 1983; Greenhalgh, 1984; Yoshihara, 1988, all cited in Tong and Yong). They can be sorted as agnates or affines. It is generally regarded that affinal *guanxi* is less dependable than agnatic *guanxi*, however, they are still important in helping a business person to establish a dependable *guanxi* network. Sometimes marriages are deliberately set up to bind two families together or to keep a capable employee within one's organization. This was found to be particularly important in intra-organizational relations especially in shared ownership and control of business.

Another *guanxi* base is the trade association/social club, which is again based largely on locality and dialect principles. For example, in Singapore, the rubber traders are mainly Hokkien (people from the Hokkien province who speak the Hokkien dialect); a situation arising because immigrants turned to their relatives and people from their place of origin for help. This phenomenon can serve as an entry restriction into the trade for groups from other dialects. The trade associations and social clubs actually assist with information gathering and opportunities for dealings through their social gatherings and dinner functions, and people can establish *guanxi* with potential buyers, suppliers and financiers who can provide loans. This form of *guanxi* was particularly crucial before the rise of Chinese banking.

Friendship in business transactions and dealings with the Chinese are valued, because it provides a close form of *guanxi*, which is paramount to doing business. The level of *ganqing* (loosely translated as affection and sentiment) involved depends on the quality of the friendship and the length of time over which the two parties have been able to get to know each other. Even in a law-abiding society such as Singapore, bureaucratic red tape and lengthy procedures can be prevented when dealing with friends when the person involved has a good reputation and integrity (*xinyong*) (Tong and Yong, 1998).

Xinyong *and building* guanxi *in Chinese business networks*

While the presence of a *guanxi* base can assist the building of *guanxi*, it does not equate to an actual alliance. It does, however make it easier for a person to establish a business relationship than when there is no *guanxi* base at all. The reason for this is that there is often a mentality that 'if we don't know him at all, we don't know if he has *xinyong*'. The Chinese believe in trading with someone they know well and who has established *xinyong* (credibility, integrity, reliability, or reputation). Akin to the insider and outsider mentality, this is not unique to the Chinese community. It was a particularly important notion in the days preceding legal contractual agreements where business dealings were usually based on a gentleman's word and agreement between two parties. Nonetheless, having good *guanxi* is still considered important in today's legally binding, competitive international business environment (Zhao and Krohmer, 2006). *Guanxi* is deeply rooted in the minds of the Chinese; often it is the principle of not failing friends or business counterparts with whom one has good *guanxi* and deep *ganqing* and trust (*xin*) that bind the Chinese, rather than the actual contractual agreements (Ma and Härtel, 2005; Härtel and Ma, 2006).

In the case of no commonly shared *guanxi* base, the Chinese business counterpart tends to look for intermediaries. These are often people who share common *guanxi* bases with one's self or one's preferred business contacts, to assist in establishing an alliance. Hence, personal recommendations are very important, especially the word of a trustworthy individual or an organization source with *xinyong*. In business, the Chinese typically want a long-term business relationship, tend not to put at risk a sound relationship or friendship or *xinyong* that has taken a long time to establish and are careful with whom they recommend to another party. The key to doing business with the Chinese then is to develop *ganqing*, as the stronger the *ganqing* the closer the *guanxi*. If strong *ganqing* can be developed, then *guanxi* can become closer, which also means that it is easier to ask for a favor, that is, *renqing* in Chinese, and the Chinese will give face, that is, *mianzi*. Without *ganqing*, the *guanxi* between two parties can become distant and this makes it difficult for one party to request a favor, and less likely for the other party to oblige.

Maintaining guanxi

In doing business with the Chinese, it is important to maintain your *guanxi* base or network; this often includes social interactions and functions. Sometimes gifts are exchanged, as this is regarded as a gesture of respect and facilitates the building of relationships. It is not the mere value of the gift that counts; it is more the thoughtfulness of a gift at the appropriate time that is important and for paying respect to the other party. This is a demonstration of *renqing* (a gesture due to the sentiment and affection towards the party), a unique Chinese behavioral appreciation of the *guanxi* shared between two parties. Demonstrating appreciation also gives the other party *mianzi*, showing in the presence of appropriate people that the other party is held in high regard. *Renqing* is very important for a long-term relationship with the other party as it is regarded as almost second nature that one will behave and present themselves appropriately for the occasion. *Renqing* does not always equate to gifts; often it is one's presence at an occasion, or putting in a word for someone, or paying appropriate respect to the person at the appropriate time. An inappropriate display of behavior in the name of *renqing* and causing the Chinese party to lose 'face' (*mianzi*) can be interpreted as *'bugou pengyou'*, meaning 'not enough of a friend' (Hutchings and Murray, 2002; Ma and Härtel 2005; Härtel and Ma, 2006), which can cause the feeling that one's trust was abused.

Ongoing social interactions can help to create a stronger *guanxi* base. By adding more bases to *guanxi*, a multiplex *guanxi* relation is created, which increases the opportunities for subsequent interaction. By greater sharing through such interactions, two individuals can enhance their *ganqing* and further develop *xinyong*. Multiplex *guanxi* therefore is closer and more consolidated than single-strand *guanxi* (see Jacobs, 1979, p. 262, cited in Tong and Yong, 1998).

The maintenance of *guanxi* in doing business with the Chinese depends on continuing demonstration of *xin* and *xinyong*. A good *guanxi* can change into a distant one if one breaks one's own *xinyong* and becomes unreliable or if one abuses the trust of the other party. Therefore, in order to ensure a long-term relationship in doing business with the Chinese, one has to attend to the maintenance of their *guanxi* and not risk the benefits of the trust and friendship of their Chinese counterpart for short-term gain. Once good *guanxi* is established and time and effort is taken to develop this *guanxi*, people are often unwilling to make decisions that can destroy this relationship. In the case of an objective reason such as a price difference in a business deal, so long as the difference is not too great, the party that has the *guanxi* can still get the deal (Tong and Yong, 1998). Some researchers believe the notion of *guanxi* in doing business with the Chinese helps explain why a market perspective is not the only consideration, rather one needs to consider economic actions entrenched in social relations.

The role of *guanxi* in the management of Chinese business relations
Cross-cultural communication/negotiation is a dynamic and interactive process, and this is particularly true in the case of Sino–Western negotiation (see Figure 11.1). We propose that the Chinese perceptions of the state of *guanxi* in the relationship can impact on the overall success or failure of any given Sino–Western business enterprise. This is of particular importance during the informal phase of the business negotiation as Chinese like to do business with people they know, someone they can trust (*xin*) or who has established credibility and reputation (*xinyong*), or someone who they have *guanxi* with.

As the concept of *guanxi* is deeply rooted in the minds of the Chinese due to the Confucian influence (Yang, 1994; Bian and Ang, 1997), the key to successful Sino–Western business communication/negotiation is to establish a certain level of rapport in the informal phases of business negotiation. This is what the Chinese call '*ganqing*'; the deeper the *ganqing*, the stronger the *guanxi*. As discussed earlier, if there is *guanxi* between the Western and the Chinese counterpart, the Chinese counterpart will give more *mianzi* and *renqing*, and thus give more favorable treatment to the Western counterpart than they will to parties that do not have *guanxi* or a *guanxi* of a lesser significance (Hutchings and Murray, 2002; Ma and Härtel 2005; Härtel and Ma, 2006). Returning to the focal point of the chapter, a key consideration during the formal phases of business negotiation between Western and Chinese counterparts is the impact of culture on the way in which communication unfolds in the negotiation process.

As mentioned earlier, in doing business with the Chinese the formal negotiation cannot be rushed. Give and take is necessary (Atkin and Rinehart, 2006) and the Western counterpart should show high flexibility (Lassere and Schütte, 1995). Further, as the Chinese are a high-context culture, non-verbal signals are more important than spoken and written words. This contrasts with the Anglophone culture, which is a low-context culture where spoken and written words are more important.

Mutual respect and understanding also need to be maintained throughout the formal negotiation phase as the Chinese perception of *guanxi* can sometimes be more important than the signing of an agreement on paper. This is often because the Chinese do not see the signing of the contract as the end of the negotiation process; rather they see it as just the beginning of more discussions and negotiations that can strengthen the *ganqing* between the two parties to ensure the development of a long-term business relationship. If not carefully managed, potential miscommunication can occur as a result of the different communication patterns between the Western and the Chinese counterparts. In addition, the difference in their affective competence or the capacity to accurately detect and address affective responses in communication can also have an impact on the next stage of the negotiation.

The formal phase of negotiation is usually a precondition to the success or failure of the subsequent business relationship. The affective communication competence of participants in Sino–Western business negotiation together with the difference in culturally founded communication patterns, can affect the events in the communication/negotiation environment, which can directly impact on the affective events. These events can then trigger emotions, which in turn, can impact on the negotiating parties' perception of the event as a positive event or uplift or alternatively as a negative event or hassle (see Figure 11.1). This perception further influences the negotiator's moment-to-moment moods and emotions during business negotiation, which can influence the affect-driven behavior (that is, flexibility and coordination) of the negotiators. This may cause them to either be more flexible and willing to coordinate if the business negotiation event is perceived as a positive one, or be inflexible and unwilling to coordinate during the business relationship development process if the business negotiation event is perceived as a negative one.

The business counterpart's experience of emotion, whether it be positive emotions (positive affect) or negative emotions (negative affect), can positively or negatively influence their perception regarding the quality of the relationship including perceptions of trust, commitment and satisfaction. This is of particular importance in the Chinese counterpart, as depicted in our model 'perception of *guanxi* by Chinese counterpart following formal phase of business negotiation', because the Chinese counterpart comes from a high-context culture and as such tends to rely more on non-verbal cues. In addition, due to the Chinese tendency to be high on conflict avoidance, even if their perception of *guanxi* becomes negative, they seldom speak up or display emotion. Therefore, it is highly probable that the negotiation process can actually slow down in the lead-up to the final signing phase of business negotiation without the Western counterpart understanding what is happening. In contrast, Western cultures tend to be low-context cultures, meaning that Western counterparts tend to be more explicit in their communications and due to their tendency to be lower on conflict avoidance, are more likely to speak up if they have a negative experience or perceive the relationship as strained.

Based on the foregoing, we propose that the 'perception of *guanxi* by the Chinese counterpart following the formal phase of business negotiation' can impact on the success or failure of the more concrete form of behavior, that is, judgment-driven behavior (that is, contract renewals, purchase orders, amount of information shared and reduced costs), in the post-negotiation scenario which can result in either a positive or a negative negotiation outcome. In addition, the culturally founded communication patterns of the negotiator(s) on each side of the cross-cultural communication/negotiation can also influence the perception of *guanxi* by the Chinese counterpart following the 'formal phases of business negotiation', which can again have an impact on judgment-driven behavior (see Figure 11.1).

Managing diversity in the case of Sino–Western negotiations: theoretical foundation of framework

Earlier research on communication demonstrates that it can either be explicit and direct where the intent is in the messages transmitted, termed as low-context communication, or implicit and indirect where the intent is set in the context (socio-cultural) or in the individual, termed as high-context communication (Hall, 1976, cited in Gudykunst et al., 1996). In addition, Hall argues that although people, regardless of culture, use both low- and high-context communication, on average, one dominates in its usage according to the prevailing cultural norms. Others suggest that low-context communication is predominantly used in individualistic cultures, and high-context communication is predominantly used in collectivistic cultures (Gudykunst and Ting-Toomey, 1988). Overall, the style of communication that individuals use can be different both within the same culture (within culture differences) and between different cultures (cross-cultural differences) (see Gudykunst et al., 1996).

In conducting negotiations with parties from diverse cultural backgrounds, it is important to manage cross-cultural communications effectively. If the negotiating parties lack intercultural communication competence and communications are not managed effectively, it can result in negative emotions, which if not detected and rectified, can result in a negative emotion spiral (George et al., 1998). This can lead to hard feelings and if unnoticed can actually bring a relationship to its end (Adler, 1997). It is a challenge for the negotiators to be able to get out of the negative emotion spiral successfully to prevent miscommunications due to misunderstanding. Figure 11.1 depicts the key factors proposed in this chapter to predict the probability of miscommunications occurring, and the important role that affective competence plays in moderating the course of cross-cultural communication interaction.

It is important to understand that potential problems may arise due to misunderstanding of the language used or simply misinterpreting the agendas in cross-cultural business management, which can result in the parties involved in the communication/negotiation experiencing ambiguity, mutual mistrust and confusion (Young and Post, 1993). Such events in the communication environment (see Figure 11.1) are likely to be perceived as a hassle, which can lead to negative emotions. Naturally, individuals high in affective competence are less likely to interact in ways which produce negative events and more likely to interact in ways which produce positive events, which are perceived by the other party as an uplift. In the event that a negative event occurs, the business partner high in affective competence is more likely to be able to convert a perceived potential negative event (hassle) to a positive (uplift) (see Figure 11.1). Affective competencies refer to the attitudes and personality traits which allow people to understand (and acquire) the affective patterns including emotional responses and expressions to events and behaviors that are embodied in the behavior of culturally different individuals (Gudykunst and Kim, 1997).

In this chapter, we propose that when the negative emotions and moods associated with the business negotiation are not transformed into positive or neutral emotions and moods, the proposed effect can be a reduction in the perceived *guanxi* by the Chinese counterpart following the formal phase of business negotiation. On the other hand, positive emotions and moods associated with the business negotiation process are proposed to enhance the perceived *guanxi* by the Chinese counterpart, which is particularly important in the context of Sino–Western negotiation. This aspect of the model can be verified by research examining psychological distance (PD), which shows that PD between people is decreased when positive affect is experienced (Bateman and Organ, 1983, p. 588). Conversely, negative affect leads to emotional conflict, lower interpersonal attraction, and personal and relationship issues (Ayoko and Härtel, 2002).

The communication patterns (see Figure 11.1) derived from the national and organizational culture in which one is socialized are expected to affect both the types and likelihood of negative and positive communication events as well as the formulation of *guanxi* perceptions. As discussed earlier in terms of Hall's (1976) work, China is considered a high-context culture, and as such, non-verbal or situational cues are considered significant in communication because high-context communications use implicit and indirect messages where the meaning is derived from the socio-cultural context and the person involved (Stone, 2002). On the other hand, in the West, inclusive of many low-context cultures, the focus is on time and formal documentation such as contractual agreements. This is due to the fact that low-context communications use explicit and direct messages where the meanings are mostly contained in the transmitted messages. These different orientations mean that communication is even more difficult to understand and communication mishaps more likely to occur (Risberg, 1997).

An important aspect of our theoretical framework is the demonstration of the connection between culture and emotional expression. Some cultures have been classified as affective, for example, the Western cultures; while others have been classified as neutral, for example, the Eastern cultures (Trompenaars, 1993). Past research indicates that members from more affective cultures are more likely to react in a direct way while neutral cultures are more likely to react in an indirect way, and people from affective cultures tend to express their emotions more than people from neutral cultures (ibid.).

Lessons for diversity management from the Sino–Western business relationship development context

In our refined theoretical model in which we have modified AET (see Figure 11.1), we argue that cross-cultural business communication/ negotiation is a dynamic process involving four stages (that is, informal phases of business negotiation, formal phases of negotiation, final signing-up phase of negotiation, and the post-negotiation scenario), therefore, this model should be viewed as one that is dynamic, continuous, interactive and not a static model made up of boxes and arrows.

To begin with, we propose that in any given Sino–Western business negotiation, the pre-formal negotiation perception of *guanxi* by both parties, that is, *renqing*, *mianzi* and *ganqing* can play an important role in the negotiation process, particularly on events occurring in the formal Sino–Western business negotiation environment (that is, cultural interaction and communication). As discussed earlier, it is likely that prior to the formal negotiation, there is already a perception of the quality of the relationship, in this case the *guanxi* between the Western and the Chinese counterparts due to the prior interactions that took place to initiate the business venture. The Chinese counterpart, traditionally influenced by Confucian values, will almost always see the collective as more significant than the individual. So the key to doing business with the Chinese is to show respect, by giving *mianzi* and to understand and practice *renqing.* Most importantly, *ganqing* must be developed, as the stronger the *ganqing* the closer the *guanxi*. It is also necessary for gaining *xin*, and ultimately *xinyong*. As said by Zhao and Krohmer (2006), it is better to have some *guanxi* than no *guanxi*. For reasons discussed earlier in this chapter, Chinese business persons can be sentimental (*ganqing*); they like to deal with people they know, or at least with some common shared *guanxi* base. Otherwise, the Chinese business person will search for intermediaries, which often are people with common *guanxi* bases, with a certain established level of *xinyong*. It is unlikely for the Chinese counterpart to take part in the formal phases of business negotiation without a certain level of *guanxi* established with the other party. Once good *guanxi* is established, however, with quality *ganqing* and *xingyong*, it is likely to last for a very long time. That is why the Chinese counterpart can be more willing to overlook or tolerate any potential mishaps during the business negotiation if there is good *guanxi*.

In addition, we propose that the culturally founded communications patterns of the communicators/negotiators on each side involved in the cross-cultural business relationship (for example, the Western and the Chinese counterparts) can lead to the occurrence of events in the communication environment (that is, cultural interaction and communication). The Western manager is generally more assertive, direct, outspoken, more able to confront, and lower in conflict avoidance. In contrast, the Chinese counterpart is generally less assertive, more reserved, less forthcoming with opinions, and in general higher in conflict avoidance (Morris et al., 1998). This, inevitably, can lead to events occurring in the cultural and communication interactions between Westerners and Chinese and can be interpreted by each party as either a positive or negative experience. Consequently, as indicated in the model of Gilbert et al. (1999) which looks at the management of diversity within organizations, consideration must be given to the unique differences between people of different cultural groups to ensure that communications between diverse individuals leave all parties feeling that they are valued.

In addition, the affective communication competence of participants in Sino–Western business relationships can have an influence on the events in the communication environment, which can directly impact on the affective events. This is particularly important, as miscommunication can occur if one does not show respect and understanding towards the cultural differences and the different communication patterns, which can impact adversely on the affective events. These events can then trigger emotions, which can impact on the negotiating parties' perception of the event as an uplift (a positive) or a hassle (a negative). This perception, in turn, influences the negotiator's moods and emotions during communication, which can influence the affect-driven behavior (that is, flexibility, coordination and so on) of the negotiator, compelling him/her to behave more flexibly/ willing to coordinate or more inflexibly/unwilling to coordinate during the business negotiation process. The outcome depends upon whether the negotiators experience positive emotions (positive affect) or negative emotions (negative affect) (Watson et al., 1988; Watson and Clark, 1994), which determines, in part, whether there is a positive or negative impact on the negotiator's perception of the relationship.

For these reasons, the perception of *guanxi* by the Chinese counterpart following the formal phase of business negotiation can play a very important role in Sino–Western business relationships. If the Chinese party believes that the *guanxi* between the Chinese and the Western parties is good and strong, he or she is more likely to be cooperative and willing to help due to the trust (*xin*) and sentiment or affection (*ganqing*) that exist between the Chinese and the Western parties (see Hutchings, 2002; Hutchings and Murray, 2003; Härtel and Ma, 2006). If, however, during the formal phases of negotiation, the Chinese negotiator experiences considerable negative affect which is not recognized by the Western counterpart and allowed to build up, it can impact on the perception of *guanxi*. Because the Chinese do not voice their concerns or reasons for not wanting to confront and cause conflict it is likely to impact negatively on the more concrete type of judgment-driven behavior in the relationship. It is therefore suggested that the higher or lower level of *guanxi* between the negotiating parties (quality of the *guanxi*) perceived in the negotiation can have a strong influence on the positive or negative outcome of the more concrete type of behavior, the judgment-driven behavior (that is, contract renewals, purchase orders, amount of information shared and reduced costs), which can translate into a better or worse communication or negotiation outcome (Ma and Härtel, 2005; Härtel and Ma, 2006).

The culturally founded communication patterns (that is, Chinese, high context and Western, low context) of the communicator/negotiator on each side of the cross-cultural communication/negotiation (Hall, 1976; Gudykunst and Ting-Toomey, 1988) can also influence the *guanxi* perceived by the Chinese counterpart, which can again have an influence on the more concrete judgment-driven behavior of the overall communication/negotiation outcome. This is because, if the level of trust (*xin*) is not there or the relationship is not strong enough (the quality of *ganqing* is not high), the negotiation that takes place can be meaningless and unfruitful. It could be that out of politeness and not wanting to directly confront the Western counterpart, the Chinese party gets involved in negotiation earlier in the process, and even signs some form of contractual agreement as per the request of their Western counterpart. In the eyes of the Chinese, however, this would not mean much, as in the Chinese culture it is the trust and reciprocity (*xin* and *xinyong*) or the level of desired relationship (*guanxi* and *ganqing*) that makes the Chinese bind themselves. If good *guanxi* is established, it is unlikely that they would want to let their friend down.

The situation can be very different if the Western counterpart causes the Chinese counterpart to lose face (*mianzi*) during the business negotiation possibly due to differences in communication patterns (see 'culturally founded communication patterns', that is, high or low context, in Figure 11.1). If this happens, even when there is a degree of trust and a desired level of relationship, the Chinese counterpart can still get very upset and even angry. This is because the Chinese would interpret the Western counterpart as having abused their trust and not respecting them as a friend (Hutchings, 2002; Hutchings and Murray, 2003; Ma and Härtel, 2005; Härtel and Ma, 2006), because friends should not cause the other to lose face. Therefore, the Chinese may begin to think that maybe the Western counterpart is not serious about this relationship (*guanxi*), and there is not the level of trust (*xin*) the Chinese initially believed was present, which leads the Chinese party to experience negative emotions (such as anger and humiliation) due to the loss of face (*mianzi*).

These emotions can be so overwhelming as to cause the Chinese to not want to communicate/negotiate calmly and openly during the formal phases of business negotiation, even if they are morally or legally obliged to do so. This may be due to their negative perception of the event as a hassle (see Figure 11.1), possibly due to their own cultural interpretation of the event (that is, loss of face), which may go undetected by the Western counterpart. But the moods and emotions that the Chinese are experiencing during the communication/negotiation (see moment-to-moment 'moods and emotions' in Figure 11.1) can be so strong and overwhelming as to justify a certain level of revenge in the mind of the Chinese party. They are likely to be thinking that since the Western party is *bugou pengyou*, that is 'not enough of a friend' (see Hutchings and Murray, 2002, for more details) and abused their trust, then they cannot blame the Chinese for not being a friend (*pengyou*). They may appear to drag their feet with the negotiation process due to feeling upset from losing face. Traditional Chinese cultural norms mean, however, that the Chinese are unlikely to tell the other person that he or she is upset (that is, conflict avoiding). Due to the high value placed on conformity and tradition (see Morris et al., 1998), in this situation the Chinese are unlikely to want to openly discuss mutual needs and wants, impacting on their desire to be flexible or coordinate (see 'affect-driven behavior' in Figure 11.1) in the formal negotiation process, leading up to the final signing-up phase of business negotiation. This, in turn, can result in damage to the business relationship when renewing the contract, issuing purchase orders, sharing information, and possibly reducing costs (see 'judgment-driven behaviors' in Figure 11.1). Consequently, the whole relationship can come to a stop without the Western counterparts fully understanding what really went wrong during the negotiation process (see Figure 11.1).

The diversity management imperative in Chinese relations
Research on how emotions can impact on cross-cultural communication/ negotiation is very topical and is particularly relevant to the Sino–Western business diversity management context. In this chapter, we discussed the model we developed to assess the factors affecting the Chinese perception of *guanxi* in Sino–Western negotiations, using an affective events theory perspective, to better understand the processes contributing to effective and ineffective business relationship development with the Chinese, to study the factors which may predict successful or unsuccessful business relationships and to provide an example of the type of cross-cultural train-ing that will assist in the development of global competencies. We argued that *guanxi*, as a key to relationship development and maintenance in Chinese culture, plays an important role for the success or failure of any given Sino–Western enterprise. Hence, in order to increase the chances of success in business communication, it is important to understand what *guanxi* means in the minds of the Chinese as well as how to build and maintain *guanxi* and good *ganqing* with the Chinese in order to establish *xin* and *xinyong*.

More specifically, we discussed how affective communication compe-tence and the culturally grounded communication patterns of Chinese and Western business counterparts can influence the likelihood of positive or negative communication events occurring during the negotiation. These affective events can then influence the moods and emotions experienced during the negotiation. If the Chinese perceive the event as a negative one then negative emotions are experienced, and if these negative emotions are not detected by the Western counterpart and are not converted to a positive experience, their build-up can affect the Chinese perceptions of the state of *guanxi* in the relationship. This may impact on the overall success or failure of business enterprises in the Sino–Western context and should be considered an issue worth addressing in the field of diversity management during this century of rapidly increasing Chinese economic vigor.

References

Adler, N.J. (1997), *International Dimensions of Organizational Behavior*, 3rd edn, Cincinnati, OH: Shout-Western College Publishing.

Ashkanasy, N.M., Härtel, C.E.J. and Daus, C.S. (2002), 'Advances in organizational behavior: diversity and emotions', *Journal of Management*, **28**: 307–38.

Atkin, T.S. and Rinehart, L.M. (2006), 'The effect of negotiation practices on the relationship between suppliers and customers', *Negotiation Journal*, January: 47–65.

Ayoko, O. and Härtel, C.E.J. (2002), 'Making a difference from differences: a theoretical model of the effectiveness of leader interventions in destructive conflict events in culturally heterogeneous workgroups', paper presented at the 3rd Bi-Annual Meeting of the Emotions in Organizational Life Conference, July, Gold Coast, Australia.

Bateman, T.S. and Organ, D.W. (1983), 'Job satisfaction and the good soldier: the relationship between affect and employee "citizenship"', *Academy of Management Journal*, **26**: 587–95.

Beamer, L. (1992). 'Learning intercultural communication competence', *Journal of Business Communication*, **29** (3): 285–304.

Bian, Y. and Ang, S. (1997), '*Guanxi* networks and job mobility in China and Singapore', *Social Forces*, **75** (3): 981–1005.

Cheng, L. and Rosett, A. (1991), 'Contract with a Chinese face: socially embedded factors in the transformation from hierarchy to market, 1978–1989', *Journal of Chinese Law*, **5** (2): 143–244.

Davies, H. (1995), *China Business: Context and Issues*, Hong Kong: Longman Asia Ltd.

De Moor, A. and Weigand, H. (2004), 'Business negotiation support: theory and practice', *International Negotiation*, **9**: 31–57.

Deresky, H. (2000), *International Management: Managing across Borders and Cultures*, Englewood Cliffs, NJ: Prentice-Hall.

Fei, X. (1992), *From the Soil, the Foundations of Chinese Society: A Transition of Fei Xiatong's Struggle Xiagtu Zhongguo* (with an introduction and Epilogue by Gary G. Hamilton and Wang Zheng), Berkeley, CA: University of California Press.

Foldy, E.G. (2004), 'Learning from diversity: a theoretical exploration', *Public Administration Review*, **64** (5): 529–38.

Fujimoto, Y. and Härtel, C.E.J. (2006), 'A self-representation analysis of the effects of individualist–collectivist interactions with organizations in individualistic cultures: lessons for diversity management', *Cross Cultural Management: An International Journal*, **13** (3): 204–18.

Fuller, G. (1991), *The Negotiator's Handbook*, Englewood Cliffs, NJ: Prentice-Hall.

George, J.M., Jones, G.R. and Gonzalez, J.A. (1998), 'The role of affect in cross-cultural negotiation', *Journal of International Business Studies*, **29** (4): 749–72.

Gersten, M.C. (1990), 'Intercultural competence and expatriates', *International Journal of Human Resource Management*, **1** (3): 341–62.

Ghauri, P. and Fang, T. (2001), 'Negotiating with the Chinese: a socio-cultural analysis', *Journal of World Business*, **36** (3): 303–25.

Gilbert, J.A., Stead, B.A. and Ivancevich, J.M. (1999), 'Diversity management: a new organizational paradigm', *Journal of Business Ethics*, **21**: 61–76.

Griffith, D.A. (2002), 'The role of communication competencies in international business relationship development', *Journal of World Business*, **37**: 256–65.

Gudykunst, W.B. and Kim, Y.Y. (1997), *Communicating with Strangers: An Approach to Intercultural Communication*, New York: McGraw-Hill.

Gudykunst, W. and Ting-Toomey, S. (1988), 'Culture and affective communication', *American Behavioral Scientist*, **31**: 384–400.

Gudykunst, W. and Ting-Toomey, S. (1996), 'Communication in personal relationships across cultures: an introduction', in W. Gudykunst, S. Ting-Toomey and T. Nishida (eds), *Communication in Personal Relationships across Cultures*, Thousand Oaks, CA: Sage, pp. 3–16.

Gudykunst, W., Matsumoto, Y., Ting-Toomey, S., Nishida, T., Kim, K.S. and Heyman, S. (1996), 'The influence of cultural individualism–collectivism, self construals, and individual values on communication styles across cultures', *Human Communication Research*, **22**: 510–43.

Hall, E.T. (1976), *Beyond Culture*, New York: Doubleday.

Härtel, C.E.J. and Fujimoto, Y. (2000), 'Diversity is not a problem to be managed by organisations but openness to perceived dissimilarity is', *Journal of Australian and New Zealand Academy of Management*, **6** (1): 14–27.

Härtel, C.E.J and Ma, R.M.M. (2006), 'How emotions shape the processes and outcomes of cross cultural communication and negotiation: an affective events theory perspective', paper presented at the Academy of International Business Conference, 23–26 June, Beijing, China and conference proceedings.

Hofstede, G. (1980), *Culture's Consequences: International Differences in Work-related Values*, Beverley Hills, CA: Sage.

Hofstede, G. (2001), *Culture's Consequences*, Thousand Oaks, CA: Sage.

Howarth, C., Gillin, M. and Bailey, J. (1995), *Strategic Alliances: Resource Sharing for Smart Companies*, Melbourne: Pitman.

Hu, H.C. (1944), 'The Chinese concepts of Face', *American Anthropologist*, **1**: 45–64.

Hutchings, K. (2002), 'Improving selection processes but providing marginal support: a review of cross-cultural difficulties for expatriates in Australian organizations in China', *Cross Cultural Management*, **9** (3): 32–57.

Hutchings, K. and Murray, G. (2002), 'Australian expatriates' experiences in working behind the Bamboo Curtain: an examination of *guanxi* in post-communist China', *Asian Business and Management*, **1**: 373–93.

Hutchings, K. and Murray, G. (2003), 'Family, Face, and favors: do Australians adjust to accepted business conventions in China?', *Singapore Management Review*, **25** (2): 25–49.

Hwang, K.-K. (1987), 'Face and favor: the Chinese power game', *American Journal of Sociology*, **92**: 944–74.

Lassere, P. and Schütte, H. (1995), *Strategies for Asia Pacific*, Melbourne: Macmillan.

Leung, T.K.P., Wong, Y.H. and Wong, S. (1996), 'A study of Hong Kong businessmen's perceptions of the role "*guanxi*" in the People's Republic of China', *Journal of Business Ethics*, **15** (7): 749–58.

Lloyd, S.L., Härtel, C.E.J. and Youngsamart, D. (2004), 'Working abroad: competencies expatriates need to successfully cope with the intercultural experience', *Journal of Doing Business Across Borders*, **3** (1): 54–66.

Ma, R.M.M. and Härtel, C.E.J. (2005), 'Modification of affective events theory for cross cultural communication/negotiation', paper presented at the Brisbane Emotions and Work Life Symposium, 25 November, Brisbane, Australia, and proceedings.

Macduff, I. (2006), 'Your peace or mine? Culture, time and negotiation', *Negotiation Journal*, January: 31–45.

Maznevski, M.L. (1994), 'Understanding our differences: performance in decision-making groups with diverse members', *Human Relations*, **47** (5): 531–52.

Morris, M.W., Williams, K.Y., Leung, K., Larrick, R., Mendoza, M.T., Bhatnagar, D., Li, J., Kondo, M., Luo, J. and Hu, J. (1998), 'Conflict management style: accounting for cross-national differences', *Journal of International Business Studies*, **29**, 729–48.

Mouzas, S. (2006), 'Negotiating umbrella agreements', *Negotiation Journal*, July: 279–301.

Nishii, L.H. and Özbilgin, M.F. (2007), 'Global diversity management: towards a conceptual framework', *International Journal of Human Resource Management*, **18** (11): 1883–94.

Nokatani, Y. (2006), 'Developing an oral communication strategy inventory', *Modern Language Journal*, **90** (ii): 151–68.

Nolan, J. (2010), 'Gender and equality of opportunity in China's labour market', ch. 10 in

M. Özbilgin and J. Syed (eds), *Managing Gender Diversity in Asia: A Research Companion*, Edward Elgar: Cheltenham, UK and Northampton, MA, USA: Edward Elgar, pp. 160–82.

Oikawa, N. and Tanner, Jr., J.F. (1992), 'The influence of Japanese culture on business relationships and negotiations', *Journal of Business and Industrial Marketing*, **7** (4): 55–62.

Phatak, A.V. and Habib, M.M. (1996), 'The dynamics of international business negotiations', *Business Horizons*, **39** (3): 30–38.

Richards, C. and Walsh, F. (1990), *Negotiating*, Canberra: Australian Government Publishing Service.

Risberg, A. (1997), 'Ambiguity and communication in cross-cultural acquisitions: towards a conceptual framework', *Leadership and Organization Development Journal*, **18** (5): 257–66.

Robinson, W.N. and Volkov, V. (1998), 'Supporting the negotiation life cycle', *Communications of the ACM*, **41** (5): 95–102.

Rodrigues, C.A. (1997), 'Developing expatriates' cross-cultural sensitivity: cultures where "your culture's OK" is really not OK', *Journal of Management Development*, **16** (9): 690–702.

Stone, R.J. (2002), *Human Resource Management*, Milton, Queensland: John Wiley.

Tong, C.K. and Yong, P.K. (1998), '*Guanxi* bases, *xinyong* and Chinese business networks', *British Journal of Sociology*, **49** (1): 75–96.

Trompenaars, F. (1993), *Riding the Waves of Culture: Understanding Cultural Diversity in Business*, London: Nicholas Brealey.

Urban, S. (1996), 'Negotiating international joint ventures', in P.N. Ghauri and J. Usunier (eds), *International Business Negotiations*, Oxford: Pergamon, pp. 231–51.

Usunier, J. (1996), 'The role of time in international business negotiations', in P.N. Ghauri and J. Usunier (eds), *International Business Negotiations*, Oxford: Pergamon, pp. 153–72.

Walder, A.G. (1986), *Communist Neo-Traditionalism: Work and Authority in Chinese Industry*, Berkeley, CA: University of California Press.

Watson, D. and Clark, L.A. (1994), 'Emotions, moods, traits, and temperament: conceptual distinctions and empirical findings', in P. Ekman and R.J. Davidson (eds), *The Nature of Emotion: Fundamental Questions*, New York: Oxford University Press, pp. 89–93.

Watson, D., Clark, L.A. and Carey, G. (1988), 'Positive and negative affect and their relation to anxiety and depressive disorders', *Journal of Abnormal Psychology*, **97**: 346–53.

Weiss, H.M. and Cropanzano, R. (1996), 'Affective events theory: a theoretical discussion of the structure, causes and consequences of affective experiences at work', in B.M. Staw and L.L. Cummings (eds), *Research in Organizational Behavior*, Greenwich, CT: JAI, pp. 1–74.

Wong, Y.H. (1998), 'The dynamics of *Guanxi* in China', *Singapore Management Review*, **20** (2): 25–42.

Woo, H.S. and Prud'homme, C. (1999), 'Cultural characteristics prevalent in the Chinese negotiation process', *European Business Review*, **99** (5): 313–23.

Yang, M.M. (1994), *Gifts, Favors and Banquets: The Art of Social Relationships in China*, NY: Cornell University Press.

Young, M. and Post, J.E. (1993), 'Managing to communicate, communicating to manage: how leading companies communicate with employees', *Organizational Dynamics*, **22** (1): 33–43.

Zhao, X. and Krohmer, H. (2006), 'Exploring Chinese business negotiation behaviors: having good *Guanxi* vs no *Guanxi*', paper presented at the Academy of International Business Conference, 23–26 June, Beijing, China.

12 A comparison of the Japanese and South Korean mindset: similar but different management approaches
Yang-Im Lee

Introduction

It has been suggested that diversity management is a widely interpreted area of study and that there is a need to revisit existing issues and concerns (Lorbiecki and Jack, 2000: S18). It has also been suggested that there is a need to look more closely at functional diversity in teams (Bunderson and Sutcliffe, 2002) and to comprehend more fully aspects of organizational change (Capowski, 1996). This would indicate that the different approaches used need to be synthesized so that a greater theoretical understanding emerges (Harrison and Klein, 2007: 1200–201). What is important to note, is that research needs to be undertaken into diversity management that balances cross-national and intra-national diversity so that it is possible 'to truly understand cross-cultural phenomena, and thus further improve the quality of cross-cultural research' (Tung, 2008: 41). Research undertaken by Rowley et al. (2010) into the role of women in management in a Confucian culture, proved revealing as it highlighted gender inequality due to male dominance, which was rooted in societal expectations and cultural norms. The turnover of staff is another key issue that can in part be related to gender bias, and ultimately to a firm's productivity (Robinson and Dechant, 1997: 23). The findings of such research would help those managing international business operations to devise relevant cross-cultural training programmes (Ellis and Sonnenfeld, 1994: 80), to harness the qualities of those involved in group work (Thomas and Ely, 1996) and to make sure that local management practices were developed (Newman and Nollen, 1996). Indeed, reference has been made to the level of multicultural training provision in multinational corporations (Nishii and Özbilgin, 2007: 1883) and this area of focus will no doubt be given increased attention in the years ahead, as the benefits associated with diversity management become more widely appreciated.

This chapter makes reference to the mindset of Japanese and Korean people, and provides insights into how they make management decisions. Attention is paid to Japanese and to Korean organizational culture, and this is then followed by a section on the main steps in the research. The exploratory research undertaken relating to the culture of both countries is outlined and followed by an analysis, and a number of important cultural factors are highlighted. The discussion element is divided into two: the interpretation of the Japanese exploratory research and the interpretation of the Korean exploratory research. The similarities and differences between Japanese and Korean culture are highlighted, and a conclusion is provided.

Japanese organizational culture

Managers in Japanese organizations are keen for their staff to compete with each other because this creates a survival instinct within the organization. Indeed, Mito et al. (1999: 165) have provided evidence of this and have cited staff taking work home with them and attending the office during weekends and holiday periods as such proof. Hazama (in Maruyama, 1997: 114–15) and Mito et al. (1999: 193), argue that the Japanese concept of relationship building results in strong employee–company relationships that can be viewed as people within the organization having a shared fate, which means that once an individual joins an organization, he/she becomes bonded to the other organizational members. This suggests that the fate of an individual employee is linked with the fate of all the members of the organization. Furthermore, cooperation and loyalty to the leader are seen as important personal qualities, and are valued highly by Japanese managers. Ohmae (1982: 217–27) and Abegglen and Vogel (in Bae and Chung, 1997: 81–2), have indicated that Japanese workers are committed to their job and to the organization itself, and Japanese national and socio-cultural values and beliefs (which emphasize collectivistic and paternalistic bonds) give Japanese workers a strong sense of job security. Indeed, managers in Japanese organizations are known to embrace a collectivist value system (Bigoness and Blakely, 1996), and it can be argued that the main strength of this approach is that transparent group decision making is promoted, which encourages diverse ideas and approaches, which manifests in solving recurring and unique problems.

It has been noted that Japanese people work well in a small group and meet after office hours in order to discuss problems encountered in the day. As well as facilitating communication, this interactivity is viewed as a socialization process (Ichikawa, 1992: 14–15 and 1993: 54; Okazaki-Ward, 1993: 147–50), which helps to reinforce bonding and relationship building. According to Ichikawa (1993: 55–6) and Iwata (in Maruyama, 1997: 116–17), individual employees need to form an identity within their work group, because an individual is awarded the status associated with group membership. Ichikawa (1992: 14–16) has distinguished the role of a leader from the role of management within Japanese organizations, and it is important to note that the leader has a strong influence over matters raised at a meeting.

Ichikawa (ibid.: 17–22) has argued that national and geographical factors have influenced the development of Japanese organizations and this view has been reinforced by Campbell (1994: 22). The key point to note is that open and continuous communication, as practised by Japanese managers, allows trust-based partnership arrangements to be formed (Lee, 2004a: 151) and this further strengthens organizational structures. Another point to note is that by adopting the strategic marketing approach (Aaker, 1992), managers in organizations are well able to develop training and management development programmes that allow employees to understand and relate to the organization's identity (Lee and Trim, 2008: 71–2). Referring again to the strategic marketing approach, it can be deduced that managers in Japanese organizations have embraced diversity management, because as Tung (2008: 44) indicates, 'Japan has identified itself more closely with the West than with other geographically proximate countries in east Asia'.

Korean organizational culture

Korean organizations are at the enterprise stage of development (Song, 1992: 193; Ungson et al., 1997: 63; Kim and Yi, 1998–99; 78; Shin, 1998–99: 40; Jeong, 1999: 99), and are firmly locked into South Korea's economic and political development. Song (1992: 115), Ungson et al. (1997: 71–2 and 223–4), and Kim and Yi (1998–99: 74), have pointed out that managers in South Korean organizations are required to have skills that facilitate collusion between the organization itself and the state. The logic of this can be understood when one notes that the objective is for the best-managed organizations (Kim and Yi, 1998–99: 75; Shin, 1998–99: 42) to match their aspirations with the government's desired growth development objectives. In order to do this, South Korean companies produced low-priced products and relied on imported technology; and on external financing (Kim and Yi, 1998–99: 75 and 80; Yoon, 1998–99: 45; Jeong, Porter, and Shin, cited in Jeong, 1999: 101). As a result, the chaebols were able to establish a strong domestic market position, which acted as an inducement for foreign companies to develop business relationships with them (Kim and Yi, 1998–99: 75).

Since the mid-1980s, the government has liberalized trading arrangements in South Korea, partly as a result of pressure from the International Monetary Fund (IMF), which came to the country's aid during a period of economic upheaval (Ungson et al., 1997: 222 and 224; Kim and Yi, 1998–99: 77–9; Lee, 1998–99: 26). More recently, the country's economic position has been made worse by the slowdown in the world economy, and the fact that countries such as China, Thailand and Malaysia, have become lower-wage-based economies than South Korea (Ungson et al., 1997: 225; Kim and Yi, 1998–99: 77), and this has resulted in a loss of inward investment.

The chaebols are entrepreneurial organizations that are strongly controlled by family ties (Song, 1992: 192–3; Shin, 1998–99: 40; Jeong, 1999: 99). Because of this, managers need to have a clearly defined vision about their own business activities; sophisticated political skills and appropriate knowledge (Kim and Yi, 1998–99: 71–5; Jeong, 1999: 101). According to Kim and Yi (1998–99: 75–6), it is also true to say that Korean organizations exhibit a military-style bureaucratic system that incorporates a highly centralized control system, and this means that ultimate responsibility for decision making rests in the hands of a few people only.

With reference to the relationship between the state and South Korean companies, and the influence of family control, Confucian social ethical thought is evident and influences the decision-making process. In particular, the authoritarian elements of Confucianism can be seen in the hierarchical order and unconditional obedience that characterize Korean Films. (Song, 1992: 193–4; Lee, 1998–99: 29–30). Korean culture promotes group benefits as opposed to individual self-interest. Managers ensure that staff are well trained and competent, and that the strategic marketing approach outlined by Aaker (1992) is adopted and results in a clearly defined organizational identity being established (Lee and Trim, 2008: 72–4).

Ungson et al. (1997: 69–70) are right to suggest that chaebols' managerial style is 'paternalistic' in orientation, because control comes from the centre, as a result of the founder's sense of duty and feeling of responsibility for the company's performance and consequently, the welfare of the employees. According to Song (1992: 192) and Kim and Yi (1998–99: 76), Korean organizational cultural values are based on Confucian values and this is supported by the fact that Lee Byung-Chul, the founder of Samsung, and Chung Ju-Young, the founder of Hyundai, incorporated Confucian ethics into their organizations' culture. Although traditional culture has been influenced by the country's industrialization (Kim and Yi, 1998–99: 78; Lee, 1998–99: 26 and 30), Confucian thought remains predominant and so does the concept of mutuality. It is the concept of mutuality and its reinforcement that is partly responsible for the emergence of new business models in South Korea (Lee, 2004b). Bearing this in mind, it can be deduced that managers embrace diverse views and are prepared to adapt accordingly. This suggests that they react to and absorb the various influences that Nemetz and Christensen (1996) outline as important with respect to managing diversity within a multicultural setting. Indeed, managing cultural diversity effectively has resulted in Korean organizations becoming as Cox and Blake (1991: 52) suggest, more fluid and adaptable.

The main steps in the research

The author of this chapter attended a conference at the Korea Institute, Harvard University in order to present a paper entitled: 'Organizational culture from a Korean perspective'. Those present formed a critical friendship group. The author also used the occasion to undertake a number of in-depth interviews with specialists in both Korean and Japanese culture; and this necessitated the use of a structured questionnaire. The same questionnaire was sent to various people for them to complete and return to the researcher.

Primary data collection relating to Japanese culture

With respect to interviewing Japanese people about their culture, the author used the same standardized, open-end questionnaire (see below), which was also used to collect data from the Koreans, and explained matters accordingly (the purpose of the research, the type of research, and how the data collected were to be used). The exploratory questionnaire is featured below:

(1)   How can Japanese culture be defined?
(2)   What are the characteristics of Japanese culture?
(3)   How important are relationships in Japanese culture?
(4)   How important is the concept of loyalty in Japanese culture?
(5)   What role does trust play in the development of a relationship?
(6)   How important is cooperation in Japanese culture? (for example, teamwork in a class/in a company).
(7)   When is conflict appropriate in Japanese culture?
       Age: Gender:
Work experience (in years)
Level of education attained (BA/Master's degree/PhD)
Where were you born? (in Japan? Y/N)
please indicate where you were born
How many years have you lived outside Japan?
(a)   less than 1 year
(b)   1 to 2 years
(c)   2 years plus (please indicate the number of years).

A number of undergraduates, postgraduates, research students and academics participated in the research. They were based at Harvard University, Cambridge, MA; Birkbeck College, University of London; and Stirling University, Scotland.

Observations of the Japanese group in the UK

It is evident from the data collection exercise that the Japanese preferred to respond in written form as opposed to being interviewed and tape-recorded. This implies that Japanese people tend to take time to think and formulate their ideas and/or prefer not to do so in the presence of the interviewer. They also want to retain their influence/control/power when they introduce one person to another, although those who are introduced can make own decisions.

Primary data collection relating to Korean culture in the USA

The researcher attended a talk entitled 'Beyond dichotomy; perspectives, criteria, and methodology' given by Dr. Myung-Lim Park at Harvard University, and at the same time met a professor from South Korea, who agreed to meet the author to discuss her research.

The senior academic from the university in South Korea suggested that small group interviews or in-depth interviews with students, timed to last between 40 and 60 minutes would be appropriate for data collection. The senior academic then made arrangements for the researcher to collect data from a group of Korean academics and researchers/practitioners on sabbatical at the Korea Institute (Yenching Institute) at Harvard University. The exploratory questionnaire is featured below:

(1) How can Korean culture be defined?
(2) What are the characteristics of Korean culture?
(3) How important are relationships in Korean culture?
(4) How important is the concept of loyalty in Korean culture?
(5) What role does trust play in the development of a relationship?
(6) How important is cooperation in Korean culture? (for example teamwork in a class/in a company).
(7) When is conflict appropriate in Korean culture?
       Age: Gender:
Work experience (in years)
Level of education attained (BA/Master's degree/PhD)
Where were you born? (in Korea? Y/N)
please indicate where you were born
How many years have you lived outside Korea?
(a) less than 1 year
(b) 1 to 2 years
(c) 2 years plus (please indicate the number of years).

Observations of the Harvard-Korean group

The following observations were made by the researcher during the conversation with the professor from South Korea and the small group interview that followed the conversation:

1. The Koreans needed everything to be clearly defined to avoid any ambiguity; they worried that they might not provide accurate and relevant answers.
2. The Koreans were reluctant to provide answers when they found the

subject matter unclear. Words such as 'inductive' versus 'deductive' needed to be adequately defined and broad questions avoided.

3.   The Koreans could be highly critical and tended not to listen to other people's views, or they tried to impose their own view on other people.
4.   If a senior member of the group made a critical comment, this discouraged the junior members from participating in the discussions.
5.   If one of the members of the group was strongly critical and disagreed with the researcher's approach, other members of the group tended to hold back and be unwilling to provide information (in the interest of group harmony).
6.   Some members found the questionnaire ambiguous as they saw it as highly personal; they were concerned that their answers might not be placed in context.

The following conclusions were drawn: interviewees should be selected carefully as Koreans do not necessarily view themselves as being homogeneous; the subject matter should be clearly explained and actual examples provided; the data collection exercise should not be rushed as it is necessary to explain why the research is being conducted, how it is being conducted, and why it is conducted in the way that it is; good relations should be maintained with the gatekeeper, who can provide further assistance and access to the same or different respondents; there is no need to be apprehensive about receiving critical appraisal; and when necessary, the logic and purpose of the exercise should be clearly explained.

The fact that the researcher presented a paper at the Korea Institute was beneficial because the critical friendship group was an excellent means for exploring, critiquing and justifying the research strategy adopted by the researcher. A key issue explored was the Korean management model, which is now in a process of transformation (Lee, 2004b).

Primary data collection exercise in the UK relating to Korean culture
On returning to London, the author visited an academic at the School of Oriental and African Studies (SOAS), University of London, whom she had met prior to going to the United States to attend the annual conference at the Korea Institute. The Korean academic arranged for the researcher to meet other Korean academics who were visiting SOAS, and the researcher undertook interviews with three Korean academics and two Korean postgraduate students who studied there (known as the 'London-Korean' group).

The members of the London-Korean group were each interviewed for an average of 50 minutes and each interview was tape-recorded. The researcher explained each time what the purpose of the research was, the type of research being conducted and how the data collected would be used. During the interview, the researcher explained each question when required to do so and used the sound 'um-um' in order to show the interviewee that the researcher was listening to him/her and wanted to encourage the interviewee. When the researcher interviewed the visiting Korean academics, the researcher went to their office at the appropriate time. The researcher interviewed the Korean postgraduate students in a room at Birkbeck College. The interviews were conducted at an appropriate time previously agreed with the interviewees.

Observations of the London-Korean group
The following observations were made by the researcher and relate to the London-Korean group:

1. The Koreans worried about whether they had provided the right answer or an answer that the researcher expected (although the researcher had explained at the beginning of the interview that there was no standard answer).
2. Although the Koreans had a good knowledge of English, they seemed to have some difficulty understanding what was being asked. So the questions had to be translated into Korean by the researcher to ensure that they were fully understood.
3. The Koreans were concerned about age and status, and were careful about how they expressed their opinions.

The researcher felt that the London-Korean group had welcomed her. One of the visiting Korean academics suggested that if the researcher needed to contact more Koreans, that would be possible.

A summary of the observations relating to the Harvard-Korean and London-Korean groups
A summary of the characteristics of the two groups is listed below.

1. *Attitude toward uncertainty*   Both groups were worried about providing the correct answer.
2. *Behaviour of junior people*   Juniors behave in a set manner in front of their seniors. They tend to listen to what the seniors say, but do not seem to challenge them, and do not always provide their own views.
3. *Conceptual understanding*   Koreans seem to have different perceptions from Westerners (trust, loyalty and teamwork are viewed differently, for example).

Analysis of the exploratory research: Japanese and Korean culture

Japanese culture

The evidence in Table 12.1 shows that the Japanese have a clear identity (67 per cent response), which is based on lineage, language, customs, a sense of beauty, the tea ceremony and flower arranging. Some of these have been strongly influenced by other Asian cultures and philosophies (Confucian and Buddhist thought). However, Japan's process of industrialization had been influenced by Western culture. Japanese life revolves around the practice of collectivism, and adaptation is viewed as important. Keeping the peace with others through cooperating with them is important (22 per cent). Politeness and strong in practice (that is, applying knowledge in a practical context) were also cited.

Table 12.2 shows a broad range of characteristics which are simplicity and solitariness/quietness (39 per cent); cooperation/harmony (29 per cent); traditionalism (18 per cent); humility and imitation, each of which received a response rate of 14 per cent followed by minimalism/functionalism, and adaptation, each of which received a response rate of 11 per cent. A sense of belonging/harmony and a collectivist mentality are important and so are law abiding, real and professed intention, planning in advance, and self-reflection.

The evidence in Table 12.3 suggests that building strong relationships is very important (71 per cent) and is fundamental in Japanese society. Relationships also need to be placed in a hierarchical context (25 per cent); and harmony is viewed as important. Other important elements include: equality, a sense of belonging to a group, and networking (and communication). Furthermore, improving knowledge, cooperation, discipline, maintaining private space, good teamwork, trustworthy behaviour and adaptability are also important elements for building relationships.

It is interesting to note from Table 12.4 that although the Japanese consider the concept of loyalty to be very important (64 per cent), a high percentage of people indicated that people need to change from seniority to elitism or individualistic behaviour (46 per cent). It is significant that the word 'seniority' appeared 7 times (25 per cent). Also, loyalty is viewed as not important by 21 per cent of the respondents and loyalty is perceived as a sense of beauty (11 per cent). Furthermore, respect, humanity and diligence/hard work were highlighted.

Table 12.5 shows that trust plays a crucial role in relationship building (86 per cent). Building relationships is very important (61 per cent) and so too is belonging to a group (11 per cent). Exchanging information, fairness, cooperation and harmony are all recognized as important.

The evidence in Table 12.6 strongly suggests that cooperation in

Table 12.1   Japanese culture defined

Characteristics	Frequency	%
Identity (language, sense of beauty, tea ceremony and so on)	18	67
Influence from Asian culture (China, Korea and so on)	13	48
Influence from Western culture	9	33
Collectivism	9	33
Retain old values and adapt	7	26
Keep the peace with others (cooperation)/harmonious relations	6	22
Politeness	3	11
Strong in practice	1	4

Note: $N = 27$.

Table 12.2   Characteristics of Japanese culture

Characteristics	Frequency	%
Simplicity and solitariness/quietness	11	39
Cooperation/harmony	8	29
Traditionalism	5	18
Humility (modesty, reverence and humbleness)	4	14
Imitation	4	14
Minimalism/functionalism	3	11
Sense of belonging	3	11
Adaptation	3	11
Collectivist mentality	2	7
Law abiding	1	4
Real intention and professed intention	1	4
Planning in advance	1	4
Self-reflection	1	4

Note: $N = 28$.

Japanese culture is very important (86 per cent). This is because if people work together, the results achieved are greater than the results achieved by an individual, hence the concept of mutual goal accomplishment. Harmony is viewed as a key concept for cooperation and received a response rate of 21 per cent. However, even though individualism received a low response rate (14 per cent), it is important to note that individualism

Table 12.3   The important elements for relationships in Japanese culture

Characteristics	Frequency	%
Building strong relationships	20	71
Knowing one's position in the hierarchy (seniority)	7	25
Harmonious relationships	7	25
Networking (and communication)	3	11
Equality	3	11
Belonging to a group	3	11
Improving knowledge	2	7
Cooperation	2	7
Discipline	1	4
Private distance/space	1	4
Good teamwork	1	4
Trustworthy behaviour	1	4
Adaptability	1	4

Note: N = 28.

Table 12.4   The importance of the concept of loyalty in Japanese culture

Characteristics	Frequency	%
Very important	18	64
Need to change from seniority to elitism/individualism	13	46
Seniority	7	25
Loyalty is not important today	6	21
Loyalty is perceived as a sense of beauty	3	11
Respect	2	7
Humanity	2	7
Diligence/hard work	1	4

Note: N = 28.

is becoming recognized as an important element in Japanese culture. The Japanese believe that cooperation provides an opportunity to create a good relationship and this leads to a good group work.

It is clear from Table 12.7 that the Japanese tend to avoid conflict situations, although conflicts do arise and are viewed as appropriate (58 per cent of the respondents answered 'occasionally'). Conflict can result in improvements, reform/advancement, and can be utilized to achieve a good result, and in some cases to protect an idea/privacy and to prove a point.

Table 12.5   The role of trust in the development of relationships in Japanese culture

Characteristics	Frequency	%
Trust is crucial	24	86
Building relationships	17	61
Belonging to a group	3	11
Exchanging information	2	7
Fairness	1	4
Cooperation	1	4
Harmony	1	4

Note: N = 28.

Table 12.6   The importance of cooperation in Japanese culture

Characteristics	Frequency	%
Cooperation is important (greater than individual ability, to achieve (mutual) goal)	24	86
Harmony is a key concept	6	21
Individualism	4	14
Group work	4	14
Creating a good relationship	3	11

Note: N = 28.

Table 12.7   When is conflict appropriate in Japanese culture?

Characteristics	Frequency	%
Occasionally	15	58
For improvement, reform/advancement	9	35
To achieve a good result	8	31
Protection (own idea)	4	15
To prove a point	3	12

Note: N = 26.

Korean culture

The evidence from Table 12.8 suggests that Koreans have a clearly defined identity that is based on a specific value system (76 per cent). Koreans have been heavily influenced by Confucianism and Buddhism (both of which penetrated Korea from China) (67 per cent), but the Japanese

Table 12.8   Korean culture defined

Characteristics	Frequency	%
Identity = Korean value system	16	76
Influence from China = Confucianism and Buddhism	14	67
Western influence	6	29
Japanese influence	4	19
Korean culture has influenced other cultures	2	10
Noncommittal	1	5

Note: N = 21.

Table 12.9   Characteristics of Korean culture

Characteristics	Frequency	%
Resistance to change (slow to adapt new/approaches)	7	35
Respect for elders and obedient behaviour	6	30
Spirituality (non-materialism)	6	30
Perseverance	5	25
Family oriented	4	20
Humanity	4	20
Peace-loving	3	15
Cooperation	3	15
Speedy behaviour	2	10
Creativity	1	5
Self-orientation	1	5
Aggression	1	5
Adaptive behaviour	1	5
Homogeneity	1	5
Practical orientation	1	5
Fashion orientation	1	5
Loyalty ties	1	5

Note: N = 20.

occupation of Korea has had little impact on the Korean value system and in a modern-day context, Western influence is evident, but not strongly so (only in the context of industrialization). It was noted that Korean culture has influenced other cultures and Koreans can be noncommittal.

The evidence in Table 12.9 shows that the Korean characteristics are resistance to change (35 per cent); respect for their elders and obedience; and spirituality as opposed to materialistic behaviour. Koreans are known to persevere; are family oriented; exercise humanity; are peace-loving

Table 12.10   The important elements for relationships in Korean culture

Characteristics	Frequency	%
Personal relationship (blood, area, background and which school)	17	81
A clearly defined relationship	11	52
Sense of belonging / humane–humanity	11	52
Trustworthiness	1	5
Age	1	5

Note: N = 21.

Table 12.11   The importance of the concept of loyalty in Korean culture

Characteristics	Frequency	%
To own group (boss/company) (to generate a strong sense of belonging, homogeneity)	12	67
Very important	11	61
Underpins relationship building	5	28
Family commitment	3	17

Note: N = 18.

and cooperative; and can act speedily. There is evidence of creativity, but this is low. Other characteristics cited were: self-orientation, aggression, adaptive behaviour, homogeneity, practical and fashion orientation and loyalty ties.

Table 12.10 is interesting because it suggests that personal relationships, based on blood, area (where one is born), and school/university (from which a person graduated) is fundamentally important (81 per cent). A clearly defined relationship is also very important in the sense of family ties and place within society (and within a company). The sense of belonging/humane–humanity is also an important element and refers to spiritual understanding; it can be interrelated with the element of trustworthiness. Age was cited by one respondent only.

The evidence in Table 12.11 shows that it is important for Koreans to be loyal to their own group; the group can be a company and this suggests that there is pressure from the top for members to maintain their commitment to the group so that it benefits and remains strongly homogeneous. Hence a strong sense of belonging is evident. Loyalty is said to underpin relationship building, and family commitment was also cited.

Table 12.12 indicates that the role of trust in developing a relationship

Table 12.12   The role of trust in the development of relationships in Korean culture

Characteristics	Frequency	%
The role of trust is important	20	95
Continuous	16	76
Responsibility	5	24
Cultural understanding	4	19
Mutuality	3	14
Humanity	3	14

Note: N = 21.

Table 12.13   The importance of cooperation in Korean culture

Characteristics	Frequency	%
Important for better performance	11	52
More individualistic than Japanese	8	38
Peer support	4	19
Network building	3	14
Personal sacrifice for the group's goals	3	14
More important (because the workload is increasing)	2	10
Within reason (does not kill individual ability/ motivation)	2	10
Not always	1	5

Note: N = 21.

is perceived as important and should be viewed as continuous; that people should be responsible for their actions; that Koreans are keen to have cultural understanding; and that they exercise mutuality and exhibit humanity.

The evidence in Table 12.13 shows that cooperation is important in order to achieve a better performance (52 per cent), but Koreans believe that they are more individualistic than the Japanese (38 per cent). Peer support, network building and making personal sacrifices in order for the group to achieve its goals are considered important. Also, the evidence shows that there are two opposite perspectives relating to the importance of cooperation; one view suggests that it is becoming more important and needs to be managed positively due to the increasing workload; however, on the other hand, an alternative view suggests that the degree of cooperation needs to be placed in a specific context so that each individual is able

Table 12.14   When is conflict appropriate in Korean culture?

Characteristics	Frequency	%
Conflict is not appropriate	10	56
Conflict is appropriate for change	5	28
To protect / safeguard something	4	22
To implement change within society	2	11
Importance of negotiation	2	11

Note: $N = 18$.

to strengthen his/her own capability without losing individual motivation. Some Koreans think that cooperation is not always important in modern society.

It is interesting to note from Table 12.14 that 10 out of 18 people (56 per cent of the respondents) considered that conflict is not appropriate in order to solve a problem whereas 5 out of the 18 (28 per cent) felt that conflict is appropriate to change something. Conflict is perceived as necessary to implement change within society and to protect or safeguard something. It can also be noted that negotiation is viewed as a way to solve a problem. If people do not engage in conflicts, then a stalemate may arise, and this might have negative consequences in the long term.

Discussion

Interpretation of the Japanese exploratory research

Japanese culture defined (Table 12.1)   Japanese culture has been influenced by other Asian cultures (China and Korea proved influential through Buddhism and Confucianism). This point has been recognized by Umehara (1992: 28–41) and Meyer (1993). The Japanese have their own identity, and this is because Shintoism was forced by Buddhism to become a distinct form of religion (Yanaga, 1976: 539). The Japanese believe that their identity is based on certain ideas and a certain commonality as identified in their language, sense of beauty, the tea ceremony, and flower arranging, which stem from Buddhist ceremonies (Osumi, 1992: 27) and customs. This implies that the Japanese absorb ideas from other cultures and are steeped in ceremony (the tea ceremony and flower arranging, for example). Japanese culture adapts to and absorbs cultural influences via the change process that is evident in society, and this is achieved without causing conflict between the new and the old cultures. This also implies that the people value harmonious relationships as they believe in maintaining a peaceful environment; this is attributed to the fact that Shintoism and Buddhism were merged (Osumi, 1992) and as a result produced a harmonious value system.

Characteristics of Japanese culture (Table 12.2)   The characteristics of Japanese culture are heavily influenced by Buddhism as opposed to Confucianism as has been explained by Umehara (1992: 28–41) and Meyer (1993). This is because (as the evidence in Table 12.2 shows), the characteristics of simplicity and solitariness/quietness, minimalism/functionalism and imitation, are derived from Buddhism (the environment of Buddhists and how Buddhists have been trained).

Some characteristics such as cooperation/harmony, humility, a sense of belonging, adaptation, a collectivist mentality, and real and professed intention one can argue, are mixed in the sense that they contain influences of Buddhism, Japanese local customs and a degree of Confucian thought. Furthermore, the humility characteristic, as Lee (1996) has argued, reflects how the Japanese use their language to express politeness, and this form of expression is different from how Koreans use their language to express politeness, although both languages contain a polite element.

The characteristics of 'traditionalism' are related to Japanese old culture (not local customs). This means that when the Japanese identify with their own cultural characteristics, they tend to think from their traditional cultural perspective (rather than current culture), which is influenced by Buddhism, Confucianism and Japanese customs. This is due to the historical context itself, political ideologies that shape national identity, and can also be linked with the Japanese educational system (Adams and Gottlieb, 1993: 5; Ouston, 1998).

The important elements for relationships in Japanese culture (Table 12.3)   In Japanese society, building strong relationships is fundamentally important. In order for individuals to build a strong relationship with others, they must know their own position and how they should place themselves in a hierarchical structure. This has been recognized by Ichikawa (1993: 55) and Mito et al. (1999: 164–5) who have written about relationship-building characteristics and linked them to Japanese national characteristics. They also need to be able to maintain harmonious relationships and this suggests that relationships are long term (Nagatani, 1998: 371–2). Therefore, in order for an individual to be valued in society and/or improve a relationship further, he/she needs to have a good network, good communication skills and be fair to everybody. The individual should also improve his/her own individual knowledge (both directly and indirectly related subject matter), and this is important from the perspective of Japanese leadership styles. In order to achieve this, the individual must be disciplined and be adaptable, and be perceived as trustworthy. This last point can be linked with an individual belonging to a group/company during his/her lifetime (Sasajima, 1993: 40; Hanaoka, 1997: 147; Hazama in Maruyama, 1997: 114).

The importance of the concept of loyalty in Japanese culture (Table 12.4) Although the Japanese still view loyalty as important, the evidence in Table 12.4 shows that they feel that change is needed so that the concept of individualism is accepted and respected. This implies that they recognize and value individual ability/capability and are less concerned with the concept of status and hierarchy, especially in an organization. This can be attributed to two factors: (i) Japanese organizations can no longer guarantee lifetime employment (the result of problems in the business environment), and the pressures exerted by society (Okazaki-Ward, 1993; Sano, 1993: 11–13; Sasajima, 1993: 31–2 and 39); and (ii) the educational system is undergoing reform and is promoting the concept of individualism (Ouston, 1998).

The evidence in Table 12.4 shows that the concept of seniority is important, however, this includes respect and humanity, and needs to be placed in a social as opposed to a hierarchical context within an organization. This is because in order for an individual to be loyal, he/she needs to identify with a group/individual, for example. So the senior members of staff within an organization can be the subject of loyalty for junior members; however, Table 12.4 shows that some perceive the concept of loyalty today as unimportant, and see a sense of beauty, respect and humanity as being important. This implies that the Japanese respect the elderly; they think that it is important that there is a certain order in society, and this leads to a feeling of well-being. These characteristics are influenced by Buddhism and Confucianism (Osumi, 1992; Meyer, 1993). Furthermore, the reason why the Japanese believe that the concept of loyalty is less important can be explained through the present situation whereby many companies are making employees redundant (the commitment to the concept of lifetime employment is no longer evident); on the other hand, the younger generation are influenced by Western culture (individualism) whereas their parents (the previous generation) were not. These last points have been noted in the above (Okazaki-Ward, 1993; Sano, 1993: 11–13; Sasajima, 1993: 31–2 and 39; Ouston, 1998).

The role of trust in the development of relationships in Japanese culture (Table 12.5) The role of trust is fundamentally important with respect to building relationships and, according to Ichikawa (1993: 51–2), this process is evident and carried on within the organization. Lincoln et al.

(1998: 245) have indicated that staff in Japanese organizations need to constantly update themselves by learning from others, and this determines how individual staff members are valued and rewarded. The point relating to acquiring additional skills has also been noted by Ouston (1998). It also relates to the 'sense of belonging to a group'. This means that if an individual is trusted by a group of people, that individual is accepted by the group and is allowed to exchange information with members of the group. In order to be trusted, an individual needs to be perceived as fair, cooperative and harmonious.

The importance of cooperation in Japanese culture (Table 12.6) Cooperation is perceived as important in order to achieve a better performance and is necessary with respect to achieving mutual benefits. In order for cooperation to take place, harmonious behaviour is viewed as the key concept, and this has also been highlighted by Umehara (1992) and Meyer (1993). Therefore, when an individual is perceived as cooperating with others, he/she can influence others and can help the change process by creating a good relationship with others/the group. It is important to note that individualism is considered important as highlighted by Ouston (1998). This means that although the Japanese understand that cooperation is important in order to achieve better results, they also recognize that in order to achieve a better performance, they need to respect an individual's ability as well, and this could lead to good group work.

When is conflict appropriate in Japanese culture? (Table 12.7)   Although the Japanese do not like to be in a conflict situation, they do accept that conflict is necessary in order to improve or reform something. Conflict can leads to a good result. Also, a conflict can arise in order to protect an individual's idea and/or to prove a point. Although this point is not always dealt with adequately in the literature, it can be explained in the sense that individualism can give rise to competitive behaviour both within the education system and within an organization.

Interpretation of the Korean exploratory research

Korean culture defined (Table 12.8)   Koreans have a strong sense of identity that underpins their value system. The system has been influenced by Chinese culture (Buddhism and especially Confucianism) as can be seen in Tables 12.9 and 12.10. This has been recognized by Nahm (1988). Although Japan invaded Korea and occupied the country for a long period, Japanese culture did not influence the Korean value system. This is because the Japanese occupiers of Korea did not allow the Koreans to advance themselves academically (Adams and Gottlieb, 1993: 14–17). Koreans consider themselves to be noncommittal, and this may be the result of geographical conditions (Korea is a peninsula), and historical and political factors. There are complex issues here relating to the period of Japanese occupation and Western (American) influence, as well as the policy of the Korean government as regards education policy.

From the time when Korea underwent industrialization, Western culture began to influence the Korean value system, albeit gradually, as noted by Kim and Yi (1998–99: 78) and Lee (1998–99: 26–30). On the other hand, Korean culture has influenced other Asian cultures through the process of disseminating Buddhism and Confucianism to other countries as highlighted by Meyer (1993).

Characteristics of Korean culture (Table 12.9)   The characteristics of Korean culture indicate that Koreans are resistant to change or are slow to adapt to change (a new/approach, for example). This could be because they are strongly family oriented and respect their elders (not only within the family but also the elderly within society). This is because society is viewed as an expanded family and obedience to elders is paramount. This underpins the fact that Confucianism has strongly influenced the Korean value system (Nahm, 1988; Song, 1992: 192; Ungson et al., 1997: 228; Kim and Yi, 1998–99: 76; Lee, 1998–99: 27; Whang, 1998–99: 22–3). One could argue that this is why Koreans value spirituality as opposed to materialism in their relationships with other people. This indicates that Buddhism has had a strong influence on Korea (Weems, 1966: 243; Nahm, 1988: 95; Deuchler, 1992: 90). Characteristics such as humanity, a love of peace, cooperation and loyalty can be seen as examples of how the concept of spirituality is embedded in Korean culture.

The traditional value system has been strongly influenced by Confucianism, which has had more influence than Buddhism, but the characteristics of personal relationship building (see Table 12.10) are fundamental with respect to building a relationship (see comments made with respect to Table 12.9). Characteristics such as speedy behaviour, self-, practical- and fashion-oriented behaviour, which it could be argued represent change in Korean society/culture (since Korea has undergone industrialization), require people to act promptly in order to survive. Therefore, it can be assumed that conflict *vis-à-vis* the traditional Korean value system will be evident. Factors such as individual self-expressionism are influential here (Song, 1992: 189–90; Kim and Yi, 1998–99: 76).

Important elements for relationships in Korean culture (Table 12.10)   With respect to the important elements for relationships in Korean culture, one can think in terms of personal relationships based on blood relationships, and other factors such as where an individual was born, his/her status and background, for example. This can be placed in the context of organizational recruitment; people are hired based on the concept of *Yong-go* (which is part of the *Gong-che*) and key considerations are blood links, family ties, school ties and place of birth, for example (Ungson et al., 1997: 192–3; Lee, 1998–99: 30–31). This is because the concepts of the sense of belonging and humane–humanity are viewed as important. To understand the degree of sense of belonging it is necessary to understand the importance of trustworthiness and why clearly defined relationships are valued in terms of how Korean people develop and maintain their relationships.

The importance of the concept of loyalty in Korean culture (Table 12.11)   The concept of loyalty is paramount; and in order for an individual to be perceived as loyal to his/her own group (which can be the boss one works for or the company itself), an individual needs to express a strong sense of belonging. Group behaviour is underpinned by homogeneity and a person needs to be viewed as committed and must not exhibit noncommittal behaviour. When individuals demonstrate their loyalty to the group, they can build a strong relationship with other members of the group. All these points have been explained by Ungson et al. (1997: 64–73 and 223–4), who have indicated that in a Korean organization, the following factors are key elements: a close relationship between the organization and the state; entrepreneurism; control based on family ties; central government; and strong paternalistic leadership. A number of authors agree with this interpretation (Chen, 1995: 155; Kim, 1997: 88; Kim and Yi, 1998–99: 74–5; Shin, 1998–99: 42; Woo in Kim and Yi, 1998–99: 74–5; Jeong, 1999: 89).

The role of trust in the development of relationships in Korean culture (Table 12.12)   In order to develop a relationship, the role of trust is perceived as basic, because it allows an individual to communicate and discuss a subject thoroughly and this leads to a further/deeper level of relationship building. Trust-oriented behaviour includes such issues as responsibility for an individual's actions, and cultural understanding (between two or more people and/or groups); furthermore, it should be the basis of and result in mutual benefit and humanity. Koreans are strongly motivated and adhere to the concept of mutuality (Dacin et al., 1997: 12).

The importance of cooperation in Korean culture (Table 12.13)   The importance of cooperation is highlighted; although Koreans admit that they are more individualistic compared to the Japanese, they agree that cooperation is important in order to achieve a better performance (which requires peer support and a good network). It is recognized that an increasing workload and a degree of complexity associated with solving problems in a short period, are key considerations.

However, in order to facilitate the process of cooperation, each member of a group should not lose his/her own motivation level and should improve his/her own ability/skills or appraise the ability and skills of others (colleagues). This can also be interpreted from the point of view that organizational employees are expected to have special skills and knowledge (Ungson et al., 1997: 193; Lee, 1998–99: 36–7).

This interpretation can be linked with the answer that cooperation is 'not always' important. It should be noted that this aspect can be contradictory in the sense that in order to stimulate cooperation, an individual may need to sacrifice his/her personal goals for the goals of the group. One can conclude that Korean society is in a process of transformation, a factor that has been recognized by Moran (1998: 25) and Mathews (1998: 748).

When is conflict appropriate in Korean culture? (Table 12.14) Koreans do not think that conflict is appropriate to solve a problem; however, when a situation needs to be changed, they will accept that conflict is sometimes necessary in order to protect or safeguard something and/or implement changes within society. This has been recognized by Lee (1998–99: 34) and Trim and Lee (2000: 121). Koreans are willing to negotiate and recognize its benefits in order to resolve a conflict situation, and this suggests that they are committed to finding a positive solution as and when required. Indeed, this is evidence of the fact that group harmony is important (Ungson et al., 1997; Lee, 1998–99).

Similarities and differences between Japanese and Korean cultures

The results of the analysis and interpretation of the exploratory research relating to Japanese and Korean culture has allowed the author to identify the similarities and differences between the two cultures. This is a valuable contribution to the body of knowledge as it can help to explain the Japanese and Korean mindsets to managers of non-Asian companies who are contemplating managing/entering into a strategic alliance and/or partnership arrangement with either a Japanese or a Korean company or both. This is because the research findings allow senior managers to manage local staff without affecting the motivation level of such staff/employees; therefore, staff/employees should remain loyal to the (senior) manager/ the company. The importance of managing subcultures has been highlighted by Hofstede (1997), Bryant (1998: 8–9), Harris (1998: 368–9) and

Morden (1999: 20). In order to understand changes in a society, it is necessary to have an appreciation of what organizational culture is and how it evolves and develops through time (Allaire and Firsirotu: 1984: 210). Furthermore, by reflecting on the complexity of diversity management, it is possible to appreciate the fact that economic arguments predominate *vis-à-vis* a moral rationale (Lorbiecki and Jack, 2000: S21) and that diversity can be viewed from the perspective of net added value that results in a competitive advantage (Cox and Blake, 1991: 45–6). The evidence of the research findings is that change is apparent in both societies. A deeper understanding requires that knowledge relating to comparative national culture and comparative organizational culture is developed (Olie, 1994: 386–7; Hofstede, 1997: 11–19). This is because an organization is an extension of society, and the way people relate to other people is mirrored by how people in a society relate to one another (Ulrich, 1998; Tsoukas, 1998: 294). An organization's culture needs to be modified through time, so that senior managers can formulate strategy better and implement it more effectively (Dawson, 1992: 140; Schein, 1992: 209–18; Morgan, 1997: 137; Andersen, 2000: 2281–3).

Similarities between Japanese and Korean cultures
Some similar characteristics can be identified between Japanese and Korean cultures:

1. Both have been influenced by Chinese culture through Buddhism and Confucianism.
2. Accordingly, it can argued that both the Japanese and the Koreans have absorbed ideas into their national culture and applied the ideas into their own way of doing things over a long period.
3. Since both Japan and Korea have undergone industrialization, the people of both countries have been influenced by Western culture.
4. Both the Japanese and the Koreans value cooperation/harmony and humanity, have a distinct form of behaviour and are polite. The nature of their behaviour can be different due to the fact that Japanese society was strongly influenced by Buddhism, which merged with Shintoism, whereas the Koreans were influenced more by Confucian as opposed to Buddhist thought.
5. Both the Japanese and the Koreans perceive building relationships as fundamentally important, which, once developed, need to be maintained. Therefore, in order to build a strong relationship, each individual needs to understand his/her position in the hierarchical structure as this dictates how the relationship is developed and maintained.
6. In order for an individual to be valued in society (in both Japan and

Korea), he/she should have a good knowledge of direct and related subject matter.

7. Although there is some degree of difference as to the concept of loyalty, it can be noted that both the Japanese and the Koreans value loyalty.
8. Both the Japanese and the Koreans view trust as a basic ingredient of building further relationships, and trust underpins the sense of belonging to a group.
9. Both the Japanese and the Koreans understand that cooperation is important to achieve a better performance.
10. With respect to point (9), both the Japanese and the Koreans recognize that in order to facilitate cooperation, the ability, skills and experiences of each individual in the group must be respected, so that the group can achieve better results without losing the motivation of each individual within the group.
11. Although the concept of conflict is perceived differently, both the Japanese and the Koreans prefer to avoid a conflict situation.

Differences between Japanese and Korean cultures
In order to understand the Japanese and the Koreans better, it is important to understand what the differences are between the cultures and how and/or where the differences arise. This is because Japan and Korea have both been influenced by Buddhism and Confucianism (Lee and Trim, 1999; Trim and Lee, 2000). The behaviour of the Japanese is different from that of the Koreans in that:

1. Buddhism in Japan merged with Shintoism and provided a distinct religious form.
2. Relating to point (1), it can be argued that the Japanese adopted a harmonious value system. They identify themselves through certain ideas, and commonality such as their language, sense of beauty, the tea ceremony and various other customs.
3. Korean society has been influenced more strongly by Confucian thought compared with Japanese society, and this has influenced the Korean value system.
4. The Koreans inherited a noncommittal approach through geographical location, historical and political events that have had an impact on the country.
5. The Japanese characteristic of observing other cultures is different from how the Koreans observe other cultures. For example, Japanese characteristics (see Table 12.2), such as simplicity and solitariness/quietness, minimalism/functionalism and imitation stem from the Buddhist environment.

6. As Table 12.9 shows, Koreans have developed their cultural value system based on blood links/relations, school ties and place of birth, which are rooted in Confucianism.
7. Although both the Japanese and the Koreans share the same view relating to building strong relationships, the approach is different in the sense that the Japanese approach the issue from the stance of how an individual is valued in society and why certain attitudes/skills are necessary. Koreans have indicated that the important elements for building a relationship are the concept of sense of belonging and humane–humanity.
8. With respect to the view of loyalty, although both the Japanese and the Koreans view this as important, the Japanese appear to recognize the necessity of changing the concept of loyalty, and how there appears to be an acceptance and respect for the concept of individualism. Koreans relate the concept of loyalty firmly to building a strong relationship.
9. As regards trust, the Japanese relate the role of trust to building a relationship; trust, therefore, is underpinned by a continuing commitment to improve individual knowledge and skill enhancement, whereas the Koreans indicated that trust-oriented behaviour is important in order for them to build mutually beneficial and harmonious relationships.
10. The view of cooperation is different between the two cultures as the Japanese see it as a chance to create a good relationship with others (and this implies that in order for an individual to build a good relationship in society, the behaviour of an individual is more important than the relationship based on blood links, school ties and place of birth), whereas Koreans see cooperation as a process or mechanism for change. The degree of cooperation can also be related to the nature of change (workload, level of complexity and how it can be facilitated, for example).
11. The view of why conflict is accepted in Japanese society is different from how it is accepted in Korean society. For example, the Japanese accept conflict when they need to protect an idea or when they want to prove a point, whereas Koreans view conflict as necessary in order to protect or safeguard something and/or implement changes in society. However, Koreans prefer to use negotiation to resolve a conflict situation.

Placing the similarities and differences in context
The exploratory data research process allowed the researcher to identify the similarities and differences between Japanese and Korean cultures, and as a consequence she was able to explain why Japanese characteristics are

different from Korean characteristics. Basically, Japanese and Korean cultures have been influenced by Buddhism and Confucianism; both cultures have their own identity; as a result of industrialization (Western culture has influenced both cultures); both cultures value cooperation/harmony and humanity, and this is responsible for people wanting and achieving a better performance; relationship building is perceived as important in both cultures and is underpinned by the concept of trust; a good level of knowledge is required in both cultures; loyalty is valued by both the Japanese and the Koreans, and the concept of loyalty results in commitment to a group and the success of the group; and both the Japanese and the Koreans prefer to avoid conflict.

The differences between the Japanese and the Koreans stem in part from the fact that Buddhism influenced Japanese society more heavily whereas Confucianism influenced Korean society more heavily. Furthermore, the Koreans are known to be more noncommittal than the Japanese, and as a consequence the latter identify with certain ideas more so than the former; Koreans have developed a cultural value system based on a specific group identity (blood links/relations, school ties and place of birth), whereas the Japanese have a group identity that is based on certain attitudes/skills, and may include a degree of individualism; trust is perceived as important in both cultures, but the Koreans are committed to the concept of mutuality whereas the Japanese consider that trust can be obtained via continual improvement *vis-à-vis* increasing individual knowledge, skill enhancement and fair behaviour; the concept of cooperation is viewed differently because the Japanese view it as a way of creating a good relationship with others whereas the Koreans see it as a process or mechanism for change; and although both the Japanese and the Koreans prefer to avoid a conflict situation, it can be said that the former will engage in a conflict in order to protect an idea or to prove a point, whereas the latter view conflict from the stance of protecting or safeguarding something. Figure 12.1 depicts the similarities and differences between the Japanese and the Koreans, and their cultural characteristics are highlighted.

Conclusion

There are a number of implications for managers based in international organizations that want to do business with Japanese and Korean organizations. For example, as well as embracing diversity management, it can be suggested that future employees should be drawn from various cultural backgrounds (Ellis and Sonnenfeld, 1994: 81) and that existing employees need to be made aware of the fact that functional diversity can underpin team effectiveness (Bunderson and Sutcliffe, 2002: 875). By embracing the strategic marketing approach (Aaker, 1992) and requiring that managers

Japanese characteristics	Korean characteristics
1. Buddhism has a stronger influence than Confucianism	1. Confucianism has a stronger influence than Buddhism
2. People identify with certain ideas	2. People are noncommittal
3. A group identity exists based on a certain attitude/skills	3. A cultural value system based on a specific group identity (blood links/relations, school ties and place of birth)
4. Trust can be obtained by constantly improving one's level of knowledge and skills	4. The concept of trust is based on mutuality
5. Cooperation results in a good relationship	5. Cooperation is a process or mechanism achieving mutuality
6. Conflict is acceptable if one needs to protect an idea/prove a point	6. Conflict is acceptable in order to protect or safeguard something

Circle in centre:
1. Influenced by Buddhism and Confucianism
2. Have own identity
3. Influenced by Western culture
4. Cooperation/harmony is valued and humanity leads to achieving a better performance
5. Relationships are important and are underpinned by trust
6. Loyalty to a group is important (based on commitment)
7. Prefer to avoid conflict

Note: The circle in the centre represents the similar characteristics between Japanese and Korean culture; the area outside the circle represents the differences.

Figure 12.1   Japanese and Korean cultural characteristics: similarities and differences

think in terms of transformational management, it should be possible to manage diversity and organizational cultural change simultaneously (Capowski, 1996: 16). This should have the advantage of forcing managers to view diversity from '*the varied perspectives and approaches to work that members of different identity groups bring*' (Thomas and Ely, 1996: 80, original italics). A key point to note is that by adopting the strategic marketing approach (Aaker, 1992), it should be possible for managers operating in various parts of the world to adapt the organization's management practices to local management practices (Newman and Nollen, 1996), and as a result, ensure that diversity management is fully embraced. This should result in organizational identity being linked with corporate identity (Lee and Trim, 2008: 74–5) and the implementation of a corporate strategy that results in a sustainable competitive advantage being achieved.

References

Aaker, D.A. (1992), *Strategic Market Management*, Chichester: John Wiley.
Adams, D. and E.E. Gottlieb (1993), *Education and Social Change in Korea*, New York: Garland.

Allaire, Y. and M. Firsirotu (1984), 'Theories of organisational culture', *Organisational Studies*, **5** (3), 193–226.

Andersen, J.A. (2000), 'Leadership and leadership research', in S.B. Dahiya (ed.), *The Current State of Business Disciplines*, vol. 5, Rohtak: Spellbound Publications, pp. 2267–87.

Bae, K. and C. Chung (1997), 'Cultural values and work attitudes of Korean industrial workers in comparison with those of the United States and Japan', *Work and Occupations*, **24** (1), 80–96.

Bigoness, W.J. and G.L. Blakely (1996), 'A cross-national study of managerial values', *Journal of International Business Studies*, **27** (4), 739–52.

Bryant, M.T. (1998), 'Cross-cultural understandings of leadership: themes from native American interviews', *Educational Management and Administration*, **26** (1) (January), 7–20.

Bunderson, J.S. and K.M. Sutcliffe (2002), 'Comparing alternative conceptualizations of functional diversity in management teams: process and performance effects', *Academy of Management Journal*, **45** (5), 875–93.

Campbell, N. (1994), 'The role of Japan's top managers', *Journal of General Management*, **20** (2) (Winter), 20–28.

Capowski, G. (1996), 'Managing diversity', *Management Review*, (June), 12–19.

Chen, M. (1995), *Asian Management Systems: Chinese, Japanese and Korean Styles of Business*, London and New York: Routledge.

Cox, T.H. and S. Blake (1991), 'Managing cultural diversity: implications for organizational competitiveness', *Academy of Management Executive*, **5** (3), 45–56.

Dacin, M.T., M.A. Hitt and E. Levtas (1997), 'Selecting partners for successful international alliance: examination of US and Korean firms', *Journal of World Business*, **32** (1) (Spring), 3–16.

Dawson, S. (1992), *Analysis Organisation*, London: Macmillan.

Deuchler, M. (1992), *The Confucian Transformation of Korea: A Study of Society and Ideology*, Boston, MA: Harvard University Press.

Ellis, C. and J.A. Sonnenfeld (1994), 'Diverse approaches to managing diversity', *Human Resource Management*, **33** (1), 79–109.

Hanaoka, M. (1997), 'The characteristics of Japanese style human resource management', in *Global Studies in Management: A Japanese Perspective*, Tokyo: Institute of Business Research, Daito Bunka University, pp. 45–177.

Harris, L.C. (1998), 'Cultural domination: the key to market-oriented culture', *European Journal of Marketing*, **32** (3/4), 354–73.

Harrison, D.A. and K.J. Klein (2007), 'What's the difference? Diversity constructs as separation, variety, or disparity in organizations', *Academy of Management Review*, **32** (4), 1199–228.

Hofstede, G. (1997), *Culture and Organisations: Software of the Mind Intercultural Cooperation and Its Importance for Survival*, New York: McGraw-Hill.

Ichikawa, A. (1992), 'Leadership and culture: the present and future of leadership in Japanese society', *Research for Strategic Management*, **16** (2), 12–22.

Ichikawa, A. (1993), 'Relationships between strategic management and Japanese culture, an interaction: characteristics and base of Japanese management', *Research for Strategic Management*, **18** (1), 50–65.

Jeong, J. (1999), 'Personnel management policies for workplace restructuring and their implications for industrial relations: a case in Korea from a comparative perspective', *International Journal of Human Resource Management*, **10** (1) (February), 89–107.

Kim, L. (1997), 'The dynamics of Samsung's technological learning in semiconductors', *California Management Review*, **39** (3) (Spring), 86–100.

Kim, L. and G. Yi (1998–99), 'Reinventing Korea's national management system', *International Studies of Management and Organization*, **28** (4) (Winter), 73–83.

Lee, H.-C. (1998–99), 'Transformation of employment practices in Korean businesses', *International Studies of Management and Organization*, **28** (4) (Winter), 26–39.

Lee, Y.-I. (1996), 'A Comparison of the Polite Speaking Way in Japanese and Korean', unpublished dissertation, Hokkaiguen University, Sapporo, Japan (in Japanese).

Lee, Y.-I. (2004a), 'Factors to consider when entering into a partnership arrangement in Japan', *Strategic Change*, **13** (3), 151–8.

Lee, Y.-I. (2004b), 'South Korean companies in transition: an evolving strategic management style', *Strategic Change*, **13** (1), 29–35.

Lee, Y.-I., and P.R.J. Trim (1999), 'Teaching Japanese and Korean students using case studies and group work: cultural differences and similarities', paper presented at the Simulations and Games for Transition and Change SAGESET Annual Conference, University of Glamorgan, Glamorgan, 27–29 July.

Lee, Y.-I. and P.R.J. Trim (2008), 'The link between cultural value systems and strategic marketing: unlocking the mindset of Japanese and South Korean managers', *Cross Cultural Management: An International Journal*, **15** (1), 62–80.

Lincoln, J.R., C.L. Ahmadjian and E. Mason (1998), 'Organizational learning and purchase–supply relations in Japan: Hitachi, Matsushita, and Toyota compared', *California Management Review*, **40** (3) (Spring), 241–64.

Lorbiecki, A. and G. Jack (2000), 'Critical turns in the evolution of diversity management', *British Journal of Management*, **11** (Special Issue/September), S17–S31.

Maruyama, K. (1997), 'A comparative study of the Japanese management theories of four scholars: Masumi Tsuda, Hiroshi Hazama, Ryushi Iwata and Kiniyoshi Urabe', in *Global Studies in Management: A Japanese Perspective*. Tokyo: Institute of Business Research, Dait Bunka University, pp. 111–25.

Mathews, J.A. (1998), 'Fashioning a Korean model out of the crisis: the rebuilding of institutional capabilities', *Cambridge Journal of Economics*, **22** (6), 747–59.

Meyer, M.W. (1993), *Japan: A Concise History*, Lanham, MD: Rowman & Littlefield.

Mito, H., H. Ikenouchi and N. Katsube (1999), *Theory of Organisation*, Tokyo, Japan: Ubikaku-Arma (in Japanese).

Moran, J. (1998), 'The role of the security services in democratization: an analysis of South Korea's Agency for National Security Planning', *Intelligence and National Security*, **13** (4) (Winter), 1–32.

Morden, T. (1999), 'Models of national culture: a management review', *Crosscultural Management*, **6** (1), 19–44.

Morgan, G. (1997), *Images of Organisation*, Newbury Park, CA: Sage.

Nagatani, K. (1998), 'Economics and culture', *International Journal of Development Planning Literature*, **13** (4) (October–December), 367–75.

Nahm, A.C. (1988), *Korea: Tradition and Transformation: A History of the Korean People*, Elizabeth, NJ: Hollym International Corp.

Nemetz, P.L. and S.L. Christensen (1996), 'The challenge of cultural diversity: harnessing a diversity of views to understand multiculturalism', *Academy of Management Review*, **21** (2), 434–62.

Newman, K.L. and S.D. Nollen (1996), 'Culture and congruence: the fit between management practices and national culture', *Journal of International Business Studies*, **27** (4), 753–79.

Nishii, L.H. and M.F. Özbilgin (2007), 'Global diversity management: towards a conceptual framework', *International Journal of Human Resource Management*, **18** (11), 1883–94.

Ohmae, K. (1982), *The Mind of the Strategist: The Art of Japanese Business*, New York: McGraw-Hill.

Okazaki-Ward, L. (1993), *Management Education and Training in Japan*, London: Graham & Trotman.

Olie, R. (1994), 'Shades of culture and institutions in international mergers', *Organisational Studies*, **15** (3), 381–405.

Osumi, K. (1992), 'Religion in Japan: the interweaving of Shinto and Buddhism', in *Essays on the Japanese from Japan*, Tokyo: Maruzen, pp. 14–27 (in Japanese).

Ouston, J. (1998), 'Educational reform in Japan: some reflections from England', *Management in Education*, **12** (5), 15–19.

Robinson, G. and K. Dechant (1997), 'Building a business case for diversity', *Academy of Management Executive*, **11** (3), 21–31.

Rowley, C. and V. Yukongdi and J.Q. Wei (2010), 'Managing diversity: women managers in Asia', ch. 11 in M. Özbilgin and J. Syed (eds), *Managing Gender Diversity in Asia: A Research Companion*, Cheltenham, UK and Northampton, MA, USA: Edward Elgar, pp. 183–209.

Sano, Y. (1993), 'Changes and continued stability in Japanese HRM system: choice in the shared economy', *International Journal of Human Resource Management*, **4** (1) (February), 11–27.

Sasajima, Y. (1993), 'Changes in labour supply and their impacts in human resource management: the case of Japan', *International Journal of Human Resource Management*, **4** (1) (February), 29–44.

Schein, E.H. (1992), *Organisational Culture and Leadership*, San Francisco, CA: Jossey-Bass.

Shin, Y.K. (1998–99), 'The traits and leadership styles of CEOs in Korean companies', *International Studies of Management and Organization*, **28** (4) (Winter), 40–48.

Song, B.-N. (1992), *The Rise of the Korean Economy*, Hong Kong: Oxford University Press.

Thomas, D.A. and R.J. Ely (1996), 'Making differences matter: a new paradigm for managing diversity', *Harvard Business Review*, (September–October), 79–90.

Trim, P. and Y.-I. Lee (2000), 'Insights from teaching Japanese and Korean students using group work and case studies', in D. Saunders and N. Smalley (eds), *The International Simulation and Gaming Research Yearbook Volume 8, Simulations and Games for Transition and Change*, London: Kogan Page, pp. 113–25.

Tsoukas, H. (1998), 'Introduction: chaos, complexity and organization theory', *Organization*, **5** (3), 291–313.

Tung, R.L. (2008), 'The cross-cultural research imperative: the need to balance cross-national and intra-national diversity', *Journal of International Business Studies*, **39** (1), 41–46.

Ulrich, D. (1998), 'A new mandate for human resources', *Harvard Business Review*, (January–February), 124–34.

Umehara, T. (1992), 'The Constitution of Seventeen Articles and the spirit of "Wa"', in *Essays on the Japanese from Japan*, Tokyo: Maruzen, pp. 28–41 (in Japanese).

Ungson, G.R., R.M. Steers and S.-H. Park (1997), *Korean Enterprise: The Quest for Globalization*, Boston, MA: Harvard Business School Press.

Weems, C.N. (1966), 'Korea', *Encyclopedia International*, vol. 10, New York: Grolier, pp. 239–46.

Whang, I.-C. (1998–99), 'Awareness of social responsibility by Korean managers in marketing practices', *International Studies of Management and Organization*, **28** (4) (Winter), 19–25.

Yanaga, C. (1976), 'Japan', *Encyclopaedia International*, vol. 9, New York: Grolier, pp. 532–54.

Yoon, S.-C. (1998–1999), 'A successful strategy of follow the leader combined with cultural adaptation: a food company case', *International Studies of Management and Organization*, **28** (4) (Winter), 40–48.

13 Confronting discrimination through affirmative action in India: playing the right music with the wrong instrument?
Taran Patel

> Muniyammal Krishnan, a small round 45 year old from Kunvathur, a village near Chennai (formerly Madras) in Southeastern India, has worked as a 'human scavenger' since she was a little girl, cleaning the latrines of upper caste villagers. Before there was running water in Kunvathur, she carried away human excrement in a bucket on her head. By birth it is incumbent upon Krishnan to handle feces for a living because, like more than 150 million Indians, she is an untouchable and belongs to the bottom of the Hindu caste hierarchy.
>
> (Giry, 2004)

Introduction

The story of Muniyammal Krishnan, recounted by Stephanie Giry, although shocking, is a reality for over 150 million Indians who are commonly referred to as 'untouchables'. Despite the outstanding economic development of India in recent years it seems that the benefits of this economic boom have silently circumvented these underprivileged sections of Indian society.

In this conceptual chapter we explore some of the discrimination-related issues that plague India today. The first part of this chapter addresses the discussion at the national level. We expose some of the discrimination-related issues faced by different minority groups such as members of the lower castes of the Hindu religion, minority religions particularly the Muslims who constitute about 12 percent of the Indian population, women, homosexuals and transgenders. Then we discuss the history of the evolution of affirmative action in India and expose its current status in India today. We also expose some of the challenges that Indian society currently faces in implementing affirmative action. In the second part of this chapter, we address the diversity debate at the corporate level. We provide examples of some diversity-related issues that international managers may have to cope with while working in India. Finally, after comparing India's approach to addressing its diversity with those of other nations such as France, Canada and the United States, we suggest some solutions to resolve some of the current challenges that India faces in this field.

While issues such as gender inequality and religious intolerance are common to many developing and developed countries of the world (see also Ali, 2010), issues such as casteism make the diversity debate in India unique and complex. Also, while certain diversity-related issues such as casteism and gender disparity are openly discussed in India, other issues such as discrimination towards homosexuals and transgenders are still taboo. This chapter distinguishes itself from past research in the field by addressing some of these taboo issues. In addition to addressing the caste, religious and gender-related issues (see also Haq, ch. 9, this volume), we also focus our attention on some minority groups which as of today have no protection against discrimination according to the Indian affirmative action and equality laws, that is, the homosexuals and transgenders. Other than these broad contributions to past literature, this study also answers a question that is central to the current diversity discourse in India.

The Indian government has recently increased the reservations for lower castes in universities from 22 to 50 percent. Further, half the jobs in the private sector have also been reserved for lower castes. This has caused an uproar in the country (Kripalani, 2006). While proponents cite 3,000 years of exclusion and deprivation as the argument to support the new measures, opponents claim that such reservations will dilute the quality of output from the country's top educational establishments. They also argue that reducing educational and career possibilities for a section of the country's youth only increases the problem of brain drain (ibid.). Using secondary literature and sources of information, we attempt to answer the following question: will the Indian government's move to increase affirmative actions or quotas improve the situation of minority communities in India? Will it reduce discrimination against them and provide them opportunities to live a better life?

Diversity and demographic trends

India is the world's largest democracy and the earliest proponent of affirmative action (AA) in the world. India is also one of the most diverse countries in the world. This diversity stems from the coexistence of many different religions, cultural groups, physical features, festivals and food habits in its different states. India is also a country of many languages. It has 18 constitutionally recognized languages, in addition to around 1,600 other languages and dialects. Although there is no single language which is spoken by all Indians, Hindi is the official national language. However, contrary to popular belief, less than 40 percent of the people speak or understand Hindi. For most business purposes, English serves as a second mother tongue to Indians, since most educational programs and business activities are conducted in English. Yet, it would be naive to assume that every person on the street is equally fluent in English. Linguistic diversity is not the only kind of diversity found in India, which is also home to several religions, castes, tribes and so on. With an 82 percent Hindu population, it is also home to a large Muslim population (12 percent of this population is Muslim), making it the largest minority in India, exceeding the total population of Pakistan. The remaining 6 percent of India's population includes people following different religions such as Christianity (4 percent), Sikhism, Jainism, Zoroastrianism, Buddhism, Judaism and some lesser known religions such as Baha'ism. It is commonly believed about India that it is such a diverse country that whatever you say of it, the opposite is equally true (Ratnam and Chandra, 1996).

India is also a nation where demographic trends are evolving rapidly. Comparing the demographic statistics over a 90-year period (1901–91), Ratnam and Chandra have highlighted that these 90 years have seen a decrease in the proportion of women in the population. While the birth rate has dropped, so has the death rate. These authors also point out that while the trend is shifting from large families to nuclear families in urban India, there is nonetheless an increasing interaction between rural and urban Indians due to increasing migration of rural relatives to cities in search of a livelihood. Ratnam and Chandra also point out that more and more younger people are entering the workforce, creating issues of redundancy.

This vast diversity in India has given rise to certain chronic problems. None is more complicated than the caste system of the Hindu society. Most past literature addressing diversity management in India acknowledges castes as being at the core of the discrimination debate. The complex system of castes is one of the elements that make this country a unique case study in diversity management.

Caste and tribe-based discrimination

Caste can be defined as a small and named group of persons characterized by marriage within a group, hereditary mentalities and a specific lifestyle such as rituals, status or a particular occupation (Beteille, 1996). Bougle (1958) explains that the caste system divides the whole society into a large number of hereditary groups, distinguished from one another and connected by three characteristics: separation in matters of marriage and contact; division of labor, each group having a profession from which their members can depart only within certain limits; and finally hierarchy, which ranks the groups as relatively superior or inferior to one another. The caste system in the Hindu religion is born out of the four divisions of the Hindu society: (i) *Brahmins* (priests and scholars) (ii) *Kshatryas* (rulers and soldiers) (iii) *Vaishyas* (traders and merchants) and (iv) *Shudras* (agriculturalists) (Zwart, 2000). Zwart warns that these *varnas* are not actual groups but ideological schemes, used by people 'as a handy gross classification of others' (Mandelbaum, 1970: 13). Zwart adds that the current approach (see Cohn, 1968, 1987; Dumont, 1970; Geertz, 1973) to caste rejects its treatment as an ancient 'given' and prefers to treat it as a construction that originated largely in British times as a means of exercising political and administrative control.

Since it is the *Shudras* who are at the bottom rung of the Hindu caste ladder, they suffer most from caste-based discrimination. Jaffrelot (2006) describes the *Shudras* (and *ati-shudras*), also referred to as 'untouchables', as being that segment of the Hindu society that has been excluded from the mainstream of society for several generations due to their 'supposed impurity'. Other members of the society believed that they would be 'polluted' through their contact with the untouchables. The untouchables have been marginalized for several generations and have had little occupational choice other than those functions which other castes did not wish to indulge in. These involved menial tasks, domestic labor, barbers, butchering of dead animals, handling human dead and excreta, cheap labor and so on (see also Banerjee and Knight, 1985). Kijima (2006) explains that traditionally, only members of the upper castes possessed land and power. Since lower castes mostly existed to serve the needs of the other dominant castes, they tended to be poor. Further, there was a social rejection of untouchables. They did not have access to public wells, schools, or shops owned by higher castes and could not participate in village festivals! Kijima points out that despite laws and affirmative actions, there are indications that there is still caste-related division of labor in India. People from one caste might help other members of their caste to find a job. However, low caste people tend to find a job even today in low-paid positions (Munshi and Rosenzweig, 2003). Jaffrelot (2006) maintains that even today, despite reservations and quotas for jobs in the government sector, untouchables mostly fill public sanitation posts, although now they wear government uniforms and have a civil servant status.

Other than the lower castes of the Hindu system, there is another section of the population which has been targeted for protection against discrimination through affirmative action laws: the scheduled tribes often referred to as STs. Kijima (2006) explains that the tribal community of India is composed of over 50 million people and these are distinct from the Hindu caste society in term of religion, lifestyle and languages (see also Bhengra et al., 1999; Dev, 2004). Before the British colonization of India, these tribes lived in the hill and forest regions and were self-governing. Since their lands were rich in natural resources, the British started occupying them and their suppression began (Bhengra et al., 1999). Although after AA and quotas were created, some members of STs have gained access to parliament and educational institutions, the average attendance rate in schools and literacy rates still remains low (Chakrabarty and Ghosh, 2000, cited by Kijima, 2006). This can be explained by geographical inaccessibility of schools in the far-flung areas where these tribes choose to live (Raza et al., 1985), by language and cultural differences (Heredia, 1995) and by low access to well-paid jobs for STs after formal schooling (Kijima, 2006).

The story of Muniyammal Krishnan presented at the beginning of this chapter highlights the plight of being a low-caste Hindu in modern India. Her case is not helped by the fact that in addition to being a low-caste Hindu, she is also a woman. Gender roles are rigidly defined in India and breaking free from these rigid categorizations based on gender might be just as difficult as breaking the caste barrier.

Gender-based discrimination

In 1950, the Indian constitution granted the adult franchise and property rights, equal access to education and equal right to run for public office to women (Ratnam and Chandra, 1996). Although the law clearly establishes equality between the genders, the reality seen in the workforce and society is different. On the social front, the girl child continues to suffer. Female infanticide is still common. Until two decades ago it was also common to hear of 'Dowry Deaths'. Dowry was a practice common to Hindu (and non-Hindu) families, where the bride's family was expected to give money or gifts to the groom. This was part of an implicit deal and was perceived as gift given to ensure the well-being of the bride in her new family. Failing to give the gift (dowry) often led to ill-treatment or even murder of the bride by the groom and/or his family. A law banning dowry came into force in 1961. Subsequent amendments to the law were enacted in 1986 to make it easier for victims to seek redress from potential harassment by the husband's family.

A recent report by the United Nations Population Fund (2004) states that in the past decade the women:men ratio in India has dipped considerably. From 945 girls per 1,000 boys in 1991 it has dropped to 927 girls in 2007. In the worst-affected states such as Punjab, Haryana, Himachal Pradesh and Gujarat, the ratio is as low as 800 women to 1,000 men. Female infanticide and abortion of female foetuses is still common. The report explains that people believe that it is the male child that ensures the continuity of the family, takes care of aging parents and the family business, performs religious rites and so on. Such beliefs lead them to favor the male child. Whatever the reason, if this trend continues unabated, India might be faced with the problem of an imbalanced male:female ratio in coming years.

Other articles in the popular press (see *The Economist*, 2007a) outline the pathetic condition of many of India's Hindu widows, who continue to be unwanted baggage and live lives of exclusion, devoid of pleasures and social company. They are not allowed to remarry and are often abandoned by their families. Many of these widows spend their lives singing prayers in the many temples of Vrindavan where they get paid meager sums of money in return. Many of the 45 million widows of India were married at a very young age and were widowed even before their mid-twenties.

Although in many ways the situation of Indian women is unique, in many other ways it is a reflection of the problems faced by women all over the world (see, for example, Özbilgin and Woodward, 2004; Kusk et al., 2007). The current debate in India and the continuing resistance to the Women's Reservation Bill (WRB) echoes similar discussions in Europe regarding reserving seats for women in parliament. Despite the differences in the contexts, there are similar concerns that such measures might not prove to be effective. Observers suggest that if such reservations are made obligatory, political parties will be obliged to nominate women but they will consciously do so only in those constituencies where they are sure that these female candidates will lose. Narasimha (2002) has explored the resistance to the WRB, also referred to as the Eighty Fifth Amendment Bill in India, in some depth. She explains that the WRB seeks to reserve 33 percent of seats in the parliament/state legislature for women, with the aim of promoting gender equity. Although the bill has been introduced in parliament every year since 1996, it has been met with resistance by a small group of male members, who claim that this bill would not be in the interest of the nation. They insist that the only way to get the bill accepted is to reserve 20 percent of the 33 percent seats for women from other backward classes (OBCs). They argue that without this sub-quota, the reserved seats will be occupied by elite women who will not promote the interests of women from schedule castes (SCs), STs and OBCs.

Narasimha (ibid.) is not convinced of the credibility of such arguments. She explains that despite the fact that there has been an overall improvement in the situation of Indian women and that women now occupy 9 percent of seats in the Lower House as compared to 2.8 percent seats in 1952, India's economic liberalization in the past 15 years has only led to a feminization of poverty. She points out that 94 percent of women in the workforce are in unorganized sectors. These have been marginalized by forces of globalization and cuts in state allocation of health, education and water. Narasimha points out that past efforts to reserve seats for women at the local administration level have proved to be fruitful. She highlights the positive results of the Seventy Third and Seventy Fourth constitutional amendments, which reserved 37 percent of seats in local administration (village and district levels) for women. One-third of these seats were reserved for women from SCs and STs. She explains that despite being illiterate, less experienced and subject to societal gender roles attribution, some of these women have demonstrated impressive self-confidence and have rapidly assumed their new responsibilities. She sees the implementation of the WRB as a repetition of the same exercise, albeit at the state and national levels and hence does not agree with those that resist the WRB.

Despite the continuing discrimination against women, their situation is not completely without hope. Young women have plenty of role models they can look up to. Indira Gandhi, Sonia Gandhi and Pratibha Patil are examples from politics while Kiran Majumdar Shaw is an example of an outstanding woman corporate leader in India. Further, recent statistics from the International Labour Organization (ILO) show that there has been a steady increase in the percentage of working women in India in the past decade, rising from 26.6 percent in 1995 to 37.4 percent in 2003 (*India Country Profile*, 2008). Although these numbers are promising, careers for women still continue to be treated as secondary to those of their husbands (Ratnam and Chandra, 1996). We believe that gender-based vertical and horizontal segregation of women continues in India. Women are still under-represented in certain sectors that have been male dominated. Women are generally concentrated in those professions which fit with the gender-role definition of Indian society at large. These include nursing, childcare, healthcare, hospitality, education and so on. Women continue to remain under-represented in engineering, the armed forces, the police and top managerial roles (see also Rowley et al., 2010). Recent protests by policewomen against their 'second-citizen status' in the force support our argument. A recent report by the human resource firm Redileon reveals the extent of gender discrimination in India (Shrivastava, 2007), and confirms the existence of a glass ceiling. Less than 1 percent of CEOs are women. Out of 9,000 board members in 1,500 listed companies, only 465 were women. The study also revealed that women earned 40 percent less than men and 90 percent of the women surveyed felt that they were under-paid. Table 13.1 provides more information on the proportion of women in senior management positions across sectors.

Ratnam and Chandra (1996) express dissatisfaction with the current state of affairs regarding gender equality in India. Giving the example of the State Electricity Board, the authors explain that recruitment in this state government undertaking is based on marks in the qualifying exam, seniority in the employment exchange register and position in the caste roster. The interviews and medical tests are merely formalities. By

Table 13.1 Proportion of women in senior management positions across sectors in India

Sector	Proportion of women in senior management positions
Information technology	8
ITES/BPO	14
Retail	12
Financial services	40
Telecom	7
FMCG	11
Manufacturing	6
Hospitality/travel	45

Notes: ITES = IT Enabled Services; BPO = Business Process Outsourcing; FMCG = Fast Moving Consumer Goods.

Source: Shrivastava (2007).

following the quota system, several women have been recruited in the past years. However, this is not the end of the problem for female employees. Even after being recruited, these women find the working conditions unsuitable. It is difficult to find accommodation in rural areas since single women are not positively perceived in rural communities. Also they do not feel 'safe' visiting far-off sites or working late-night shifts. Thus although quotas for women have led to their recruitment in this public sector company, a lot remains to be done to make the workplace a female-friendly environment. Similarly the representation of women in the public sector, that is, in Doordarshan (the public service broadcaster of India owned by Prasar Bharti and founded by the government) and All India Radio (AIR) is far from satisfactory. Despite some improvements in the case of Doordarshan, there is still substantial gender-based job segregation in both Doordarshan and AIR, with women's jobs being relegated to lower-level 'feminine' positions, while most top executive positions are occupied by men (Patel, 1994). Reverting to the private sector, Ratnam and Chandra (1996) report a general dominance of males in sales-related jobs in many companies. They do, however, point out some exceptions such as the Mumbai-based pharmaceutical firm USV Ltd, which recruits only middle-aged mothers wanting to return to the workforce for part-time sales jobs. The firm invites women in the 35–45-year age group to return to flexible part-time sales jobs requiring no traveling and the possibility of working at their convenience. However, such examples are rare, both in the public and private sectors.

Women are not the only minority group to feel that they are being treated unfairly. Many of the members of religious minorities also complain about discrimination. The Muslims make up the largest minority community, yet this is also the group that is exploited as a vote bank by competing political parties.

Religion-based discrimination

India is home to several different religions, such as Hinduism, Christianity, Islam, Jainism, Zoroastrianism, Bahai'sm, Buddhism, Sikhism and Judaism. Being a *secular* democratic republic, the Indian constitution specifies that every religion will be treated with equal respect. It is worth noting that different countries define *secularism* differently. For example, while the French concept of secularism (*laicité*) implies a complete separation of religion (which is considered a personal and individual choice) from public spheres of activity (including work and education), the Indian concept means that all religions will be treated as equal. The Indian idea of secularism does not demand a separation of religion from public life. Despite the supposed 'secular' nature of society, India has witnessed some of the bloodiest communal and religious riots, such as those seen in 1993 in Mumbai and the communal riots between the Sikhs and the Hindus in 1984 following the assassination of Indira Gandhi by her Sikh bodyguard.

As Ratnam and Chandra point out, the bloody partition of India in 1947 has left its legacy. Since independence, the Indian Muslims have been charged with the stigma of dismembering India (Farooqui, 2007). They struggle with illiteracy and poverty, often perceiving themselves as a victimized group. According to a 2001 census, the Muslim population is growing at twice the rate of the Hindu majority (ibid.). The reasons behind this are believed to be the disproportionately low literacy levels among Muslim women. A recent popular press article (*The Economist*, 2006) explores why India's 150 million Muslims are missing out on the country's economic growth. There are two answers to this question: (i) low levels of literacy especially among Muslim girls and (ii) less representation of Muslims in top positions in the public sector. The article explains that the problem of illiteracy is rampant among Indian Muslims. Part of the explanation can be provided by the fact that Muslim populations are found living in the old quarters of cities which are not so well-off. In rural areas as well, young children are required to travel long distances to get to school. In states like Uttar Pradesh, home to one-fifth of the Muslim population, schools are not easily accessible to children. With increasing difficulty in accessing educational establishments, attendance drops, especially for young girls. The situation is much better in the southern state of Kerela. The low presence of Muslims at higher positions in the public sector is attributed partly to discrimination and partly to the fact that Muslim students do not stay in school long enough to acquire the level of qualification expected in these positions.

Farooqui (2007) points out that many Muslims are dissatisfied by the efforts of the government in providing them reservations or quotas as the largest religious minority. Opponents argue that being a secular and democratic nation, India cannot allow reservations based on religion. Nonetheless, as in the case of low-caste Hindus, politicians continue to exploit the Muslim population in order to attract the vote bank. They try to appease the Muslim population through concessions and promises, which have no impact on the long-term improvement in their conditions. Notwithstanding these hardships, the Muslim community has produced several leaders in various domains, for example, the recent Indian President, Dr A.P.J Abdul Kalam, cricketer Mohammad Azirruddin, several film stars, politicians, academics and thinkers. Farooqui (p. 29) states that the Muslim community in India is a peaceful community, that has 'a centuries old history of coexistence to draw on and no insecurity can shake a longstanding belief that they are the salt that brings together the many disparate dishes that make up India'.

Unfortunately not everyone shares such feelings. India has witnessed a number of bloody communal riots. Such riots understandably have an impact on local economies. Since religions and castes are often closely related to professional choices, at times of communal riots, people from the affected castes or communities cannot come to work (Ratnam and Chandra, 1996). For example, during the Mumbai riots in 1993, certain shops were closed for long periods and certain skills were unavailable. Ratnam and Chandra further point out that in private businesses owned by Hindus, there are few Muslims in the top positions. Since India is a secular nation, businesses are required to make allowances for the religious beliefs and practices of their employees. For example, in industries with many Muslim employees, prayer breaks are necessary. Managers and owners from other communities sometimes lack the sensitivity to allow for such religious practices in the workplace.

Many states (such as Uttar Pradesh) have started including Muslims into the backward classes deserving reservation (*The Economist*, 1994b). The government of Karnataka has a special quota for Muslim butchers (Blank, 1995). There is some thought concerning extending this to other classes and other states, but this is complicated because Indian Muslims (like Indian Hindus) often behave in a segmented fashion. Poorer sections of the community that already benefit from quotas do not wish to share them with their relatively richer brethren. Further, there are conflicts among different sections of the Muslim society, notably between the Shiites and the Sunnis (ibid.).

In the previous sections of this chapter, we have discussed some of the discrimination-related challenges in India, specifically discrimination based on caste, gender and religious differences. Discrimination also occurs due to age differences, although this is not as serious an issue in India as it is in European nations.

Age-based discrimination

One of the major preoccupations of European policy makers at the present time is the aging European workforce. Age-based discrimination in Europe seems to impede both young and old employees: while people over 50–55 years of age experience discrimination during recruitment, training and promotion, younger people get fewer job opportunities due to limited exposure and experience. Fortunately, this is less serious in India as compared to European nations. Despite being a very old civilization, India is a surprisingly young country, with a median age of 24. Around 40 percent of its population falls in the range of 20–44 years (India Country Profile). Commenting on the demographic changes in India over a 90-year period (1901–91), Ratnam and Chandra (1996) highlight that in these years, both the birth rate and the death rate have dropped in India. Life expectancy has increased from less than 24 years in 1901 to over 57 in 1991. They point out that more young people are now entering the workforce, creating issues of redundancy. The retirement age is 55 years in the private sector and 58 in the public sector with the absolute limit set at 60 years, although there have been attempts by state governments and the private sector to reduce the retirement age.

As in other parts of the world, there is considerable difference in the attitudes and values of the younger versus the older generation. The younger generation that has not been exposed to India's struggle for independence, the bloodshed of the world wars and the pain and anguish of India's partition, is much more confident and ambitious and has more liberal and consumerist values than the older generation. This recent change in the country's demographics has major implications for changes in the cultural values and behaviors of the workforce and consumers.

A much more sensitive matter than age-based discrimination is the discrimination against homosexuals, transgenders (commonly referred to as '*hijras*') and people infected with AIDS.

Discrimination based on sexuality and sexual orientation

Although discrimination due to religious, caste and gender differences is commonly discussed in the context of India, relatively less attention has been paid in past literature to discrimination resulting from different sexual orientations. The transgenders (*hijras*) are also an important minority group in India, which suffers from discrimination, ridicule, ill-treatment and exclusion from society. Nonetheless very few studies focus on their problems. The same is true for people infected with AIDS.

Parekh (2003) states that the idea of homosexuality is not new to India. The writings of the *Kama Sutra* and the sculptures in the ancient temples of Khajuraho, Konark and Modhera often depict scenes of sexual relations between people of the same sex. The author further provides examples from Hindu epics of sexual relations between women. He states that under the Muslim rule (eighteenth and early nineteenth centuries) homosexuality, especially between men, was a common practice in Delhi, Faizabad and Lukhnow. In contemporary India the number of homosexual men varies between 12.5 million and 37.4 million (Chan et al., 1998). Although homosexuality has never been completely accepted, no one has yet been persecuted for it (Vanita and Kidwai, 2000). Reactions to it might vary from dislike, to insult, fear and even physical attacks. Until recently, the media preferred to steer clear of the topic of homosexuality. The first case that came forward was of two women constables in Madhya Pradesh who wished to get married. They were fired for 'unauthorized absence from work', although one might suspect that the real reason was their sexual orientation (Jaising, 1988). Today there is a gradually increasing awareness about gay rights and their health concerns. Several gay interest groups are being created: for example, the Humsafar Trust based in Mumbai, the Lakshya Trust based in the state of Gujarat and the ABVA (AIDS Bhedbhav Virodhi Andolan, roughly translated as AIDS Antidiscrimination Movement). The ABVA is a non-governmental organization, working for the welfare of AIDS victims, AIDS awareness and gay rights. It has recently filed a petition in the Supreme Court to legalize same-sex marriages and to challenge the Indian Penal Code's (IPC) section 377, which defines what it calls 'unnatural offences' as 'whoever voluntarily has carnal intercourse against the order of nature with any man, woman or animal, shall be punished with imprisonment for a term which may extend to ten years and shall be liable to a fine'.

Another category of people that deserve a special mention in our discussion of discrimination in India is the community of people called *hijras*. They are variously referred to in Indian society as eunuchs, androgynes, as people who are intersexed, transgendered, effeminate and impotent (Lal, 1999). Lal comments that the *hijras* themselves distinguish between those that are born that way, that is, with ambiguous genitals, and those that choose to become *hijras* through castration. These are mostly men who identify themselves as females and hence choose to dress like women.

Although they live at the fringes of Indian society, they continue to be tolerated and even feared, because they are believed to have the power to confer fertility on others. These supposed powers give them a unique role to play in Indian society. They often turn up in groups at a wedding party or a celebration for the birth of a child. Although no one ever invites them, people are generally happy to give them some money in return for blessings to the married couple or the newborn child. Those *hijras* who do not earn a living through such activities, generally end up begging or engaging in prostitution.

Hijras are often subject to ridicule, humiliation and exclusion. Although they number over 500,000, they continue to live in their separate colonies, often on the outskirts of cities and in filthy conditions, shunned by family members. Very few have the means to acquire a decent level of education. The few that do are not accepted into the workforce and so have no recourse but to turn to begging or prostitution. Recently, there have been some attempts to improve their lot through the creation of *hijra* organizations such as the All India Eunuch's Welfare Association, the Dai Welfare Society and the Hijra Kalyan Sabha. These organizations work towards creating better conditions for the *hijra* community and towards creating awareness about AIDS. In recent times, many *hijras* have entered into politics. Shabnam Mausi was elected India's first *hijra* Member of the Legislative Assembly (MLA) in 1999. Although India granted voting rights to men and women immediately after independence, the *hijras* attained their right to vote only in 1994. In 2000, Asha Devi, a *hijra*, was elected mayor of Gorakhpur in a post that was reserved for a woman. She was unseated when a court decided that she was a man. However, she was later reinstated. Despite the proliferation of the vast number of categories that benefit from reservations or quotas, there is no law protecting the homosexuals and the *hijras* from discrimination and social exclusion. Other than in politics, there is little discussion on integrating *hijras* into the mainstream of the workforce. Furthermore, there is little reference to this discriminated group in diversity-based literature.

The previous sections of this chapter have focused on how members of different minority groups experience discrimination in India. The government has adopted a hard approach against discrimination. This means that unlike other countries, it has opted to use a system of reservations and quotas for different minority groups. Although this system of reservations predates India's independence, it has still not had the impact one would have expected on society. In order to understand the reasons behind this near failure, it is important to first explore the history of affirmative action.

A historical review of affirmative action (AA)

It is often wrongly believed that the quota system was the creation of the post-independence government. However, Tummala (1999) comments that affirmative actions or quotas existed even in feudal kingdoms and in British legislatures, although the objective in the latter case was to pit the majority Hindu community against the minority Muslims, an exercise which eventually led to the partition of India. As Jaffrelot (2006: 174) points out, 'The British census rigidified the contours of Indian society by outlining the three main groups [of the Hindu society]. These groups no doubt pre-existed, but their frontiers were fuzzy until then and certainly had never been quantified'. The British rulers also made efforts to improve the lot of the untouchables. Jaffrelot comments that in 1892, the British set up schools for untouchables, who were not allowed into schools for children of the higher castes. By 1921, the literacy levels had been brought up to 6.7 percent for boys and 4.8 percent for girls. In 1944, a five-year budget of 300,000 rupees was put aside to provide scholarships to children from these classes.

In subsequent years, the British expanded reservations from the sector of education to that of public services. In 1934, 8.5 percent of civil service posts were reserved for untouchables, a figure which was raised to 12.5 percent in 1946 (ibid.). Prior (1996) confirms that reservations were used in India in public employment and universities during British rule. Public service posts were also reserved for Muslims, Christians, Anglo-Indians and other such groups. Quotas were limited only to recruitment and did not influence promotion-related decisions. There were several reasons for putting into place such reservation systems. One of the aims was to adjust the political balance between different caste and religious groups. The other objective was to appease the minorities. Many critiques of the British rule in India view the quota system as Britain's strategy of 'divide and rule'.

Many of the leaders involved in India's struggle for independence were conscious of issues relating to discrimination, not just the one they were fighting against, but also one that plagued Hindu society and continued to impede India's growth and development. Leaders such as Mahatma Gandhi were very sensitive to the condition of untouchables. Gandhi fondly referred to untouchables as *Harijans* (roughly translated as God's people). He was also very sensitive to the condition of Indian women. Gandhi once said that the condition of a nation can be best judged by the condition of its women. He was also a firm believer that India would never be able to achieve its full potential unless 50 percent of the population, namely the women, were allowed to contribute. Although Gandhi was a strong supporter of the lower castes and of other minority categories, he nonetheless preferred a conservative or 'soft' stance (Jaffrelot, 2006). While he crusaded to improve the situation of the untouchables, he believed in doing so by reforming the mentalities to better integrate them into the mainstream of society, rather than by the creation of quotas, which he believed would accentuate the differences between the castes rather than eliminate them.

Tummala (1999) explains that India's independence from the British in 1947 was followed by a debate among Indian leaders regarding preferential treatment for minority groups through the creation of quotas, and how this stood in light of 'equality', which had become a watchword for all democracies of the world. Most leaders agreed that the lower castes had been deprived for over 3,000 years and hence preferential treatment towards them only helped to redress this injustice and did not contradict the idea of equality. It was therefore decided to set up affirmative actions or quotas in government positions (direct recruitment) through open competitive exams: a quota of 15 percent for SCs and 7.5 percent for STs was set up roughly in proportion of their population. State governments were also to have similar quotas with minor changes in the ratios. At that time the private sector was not obliged to respect similar quotas. Also, at that time no reservations were envisaged for the 'socially and economically backward classes' (OBCs) by the central government although nearly half the Indian population fell under this category (Zwart, 2000). The reason behind not setting up OBC quotas was the ambiguity regarding those that constituted this group. Each state government was free to set OBC quotas as it saw fit. This has changed today: the central government now reserves 27 percent of government jobs and seats in higher educational institutions for OBCs. Most states also follow this policy, and some have an even higher percentage of reservation.

Current status of affirmative action and equality programs
Prior (1996) states that coinciding with India's independence, the Constituent Assembly was formed in 1946. It attempted to obtain a political balance by reserving seats in the state legislatives and the House of People for SC and ST. In addition to this, Article 15 of the Indian constitution prohibited discrimination on the basis of other criteria such as religion, race, caste, sex or place of birth. There was, however, no mention of the protection of homosexuals, transgenders or other similar categories from discrimination.

Articles 4–18 of the Indian constitution list the rights of equality, which are inspired by the Universal Human Rights Charter (Ratnam and Chandra, 1996). Article 17, in particular, abolishes untouchability. Prior (1996) points out that although this made millions of untouchables equal in the eyes of the law, on the social front, they are still not equal to other segments of Hindu society. This is why past decades have seen a movement among untouchables towards changing their religious orientations from Hinduism to Christianity, Buddhism and Islam, that is, towards those religions that do not propagate caste-based classifications. Even this desperate attempt by members of the low castes has met with only partial success. Ratnam and Chandra (1996) point out that the caste identification and network is so strongly entrenched in the Indian mindset that even a change of religious affiliations does not succeed in breaking it. For example, there has been a recent demand to create reservations for '*dalit*' (underprivileged) Christians. This shows that despite a change of religion, these people have still not managed to break free from their classification as *dalits*. The same has been observed in the case of conversions to other religions. We shall explore this topic in subsequent sections of this chapter.

Prior (1996) explains that although immediately after India's independence, SCs and STs were provided reservations by the Constituent Assembly, the OBCs did not benefit from the same because this category was not easy to define. Therefore, in order to determine the criteria for identifying socially and educationally backward classes, the government appointed the first Backward Classes Commission in 1953, which identified 2,399 groups which it considered backward, based on trade and occupation, security of employment, level of education, representation in government positions and position in the Hindu caste hierarchy. The recommendations of this commission were rejected by parliament due to accusations of methodological flaws and internal contradictions. Hence, a second Backward Classes Commission was created in 1978 which was headed by a member of parliament, B.P. Mandal. The second commission handed in its report to the prime minister on 31 December 1980. The Mandal Commission recommended that a total of 22.5 percent of reservation were made for SCs and STs and another 27.5 percent for OBCs. The original recommendation of the commission was to set aside 52 percent of government posts for OBCs who made up to 52 percent of the population. However, this clashed with the Supreme Court order that set a ceiling on reservations at just below 50 percent. Hence the original recommendation of the commission was modified to respect the Supreme Court verdict.

Despite the government's generous albeit badly implemented AA plans, untouchables are still economically very weak compared to other Indians. More than 20 million are bonded labor. Only 7 percent have access to basic amenities such as electricity, drinking water and toilets. As Narula and Macwan (2001) state, it is not by chance that the untouchables are disproportionately poor: 'Poverty is manufactured to maintain the status quo'. Although the AA plans have pushed forward some leaders of backward caste origin into prominent positions (for example, President K.R. Narayanan, B.R. Ambedkar, the first law minister of independent India and the creator of the Indian constitution), the effects in other areas are less spectacular. For example, seats reserved for lower castes in higher educational establishments and civil services often remain vacant. Further, although the police and the judicial structures are in the best position to enforce quotas, they rarely bother because they are not subject to AA policies.

Since the law has had little impact on improving the condition of lower castes, people from these classes have resorted to conversion to other religions that do not have castes. In 1956, Dr Ambedkar led the conversion of half a million untouchables to Buddhism, an act copied by three million other untouchables. Other untouchables have converted to Christianity, while still others have chosen Islam. This spate of conversion to religions other than Hinduism has caused some hardliners to feel insecure about the future of Hindusim. Therefore, during the rule of the Bharatia Janata Party (BJP) government from 1998 to 2004, there was a law banning such conversions, asserting that these were often carried out by promising people material gains if they converted to another religion. However, conversions back to Hinduism were allowed by the new law. Proponents explained that this was not a religious conversion at all since the convertees were Hindus to begin with. Besides, conversions have not really changed the lives of these untouchables. They continue to be treated as Dalit Christians, Dalit Sikhs and so on. Recent amendments of the law allow AA protection to Dalit Sikhs and Dalit Buddhists, stating that Sikhism and Buddhism are actually offshoots of the Hindu religion. However, Dalit Christians and Dalit Muslims do not benefit from similar protection.

In subsequent years, further amendments were made to AA laws to include other minority categories such as the disabled, ex-army personnel and so on in education and employment in the government sector. As Ratnam and Chandra (1996) point out, in recent decades, several attempts have been made by state governments to increase quotas for some of these groups, all of which have been thwarted by the Supreme Court which insists that the total percentage of reservations should not exceed 50 percent. More recently the central government has tried to increase the quotas for SCs, STs and OBCs in universities and public sector positions, a move which has been met with violent protests from students and other sections of society. The government is also trying to make reservations obligatory in the private sector. This suggestion has met with strong resistance from different groups of stakeholders (*The Economist*, 2004). In the western state of Maharashtra, the richest state in India, some businesses have even threatened to quit the state if the state government goes ahead with implementing the plan. Opponents of this new scheme provide several arguments against the move: (i) AA policies are already being misused in the public sector; (ii) these days people can purchase a caste certificate to benefit from the reservations of backward castes; (iii) such stringent measures will only lead to reverse discrimination; (iv) the quotas will impose new constraints on the autonomy to hire and fire employees, in a country with already stringent labor laws; (v) AA policies have led to the mushrooming of power-broker politicians, who use their position to manipulate different minority groups and to play one against the other (ibid.).

Independent thinkers such as Amit Mitra from the Federation of Indian Chambers of Commerce and Industry believe that rather than impose more reservations, the government should use a softer approach similar to the ones used by the Canadian government. He suggests that the Indian government should encourage voluntary efforts by companies and reward such firms through tax incentives or rebates (ibid.). The government on the other hand feels it is time that the private sector took its share of responsibility in redressing this wrong.

In this section we have outlined the current status of AA programs in India. The purpose of such laws is to improve the condition of the members of minority communities. The opening story of this chapter which describes the life of Muniyammal Krishnan shows that equality might still be a distant dream for many low-caste Indians. The situation of Muniyammal Krishnan also highlights the significant impact of the overlap of minority categories. Being a member of a lower caste in India is bad enough, but being a woman from a lower caste is even worse! Have the AA policies and equality laws succeeded in bringing us any closer to the ideal of equality in the past six decades?

The outcome of affirmative action programs
While some believe that reservations or quotas were put into place to provide special support to underprivileged castes eventually leading to equality between the different segments of the population, others (see Raman, 1999) believe that by taking caste into account, the government may have accentuated the divide between people rather than eliminating them. 'What originally was a well-intentioned policy of integrating long oppressed ethnic minorities into the national politics, has over 50 years, been perverted into means of promoting ethnic particularism' (ibid.: 34). Raman believes that the AA program is an abysmal failure (see also Dhesi, 1998; Jaffrelot, 2006). He highlights that the only reason there was no resistance to the initial proposal of quotas for SCs and STs was that decision

makers and leaders of independent India, including Ambedekar believed that this was a temporary measure. Raman points out that problems arose when similar reservations were institutionalized for OBCs. Although, it is true that many of the OBCs were indeed socially and economically oppressed, there were also Hindus of high castes who worked as priests and who led impoverished lives. Hindus of lower castes engaged in trade and were economically better off. So the real issue is the identification of who is classified among the OBCs. The central government delegated this important task to different state governments. This resulted in political parties at state level using the caste card to attract the maximum adherents and to get votes. Currently over 3,700 castes have been identified as OBCs and in some states such as Tamil Nadu, 69 percent of government jobs go to SCs, STs and OBCs, despite clear instructions from the Supreme Court that reservations should not surpass the 50 percent ceiling.

The viewpoint that the AA program has failed is also supported by Dhesi (1998), who believes that there is sufficient evidence to support that even today, despite six decades of reservations and quotas, discrimination continues to be perpetrated in education as well as in the labor market against certain social categories. He stresses that these categories do not have equal access to sources for human capital acquisition. This reinforces their inequalities in the labor market. Like many others before him, he emphasizes that there is an overlap between caste–religion discrimination and class discrimination. Despite the ideals of secularism and democracy, the traditional caste differences still exercise a strong influence in people's day-to-day lives. Similar viewpoints are also supported in recent articles in the popular press (see *The Economist*, 2007b). These reports claim that although people from lower castes are getting richer, this is happening at the same rate as the rest of the population. This means that reservations have not had any measurable impact on improving the well-being of members of lower castes.

Ratnam and Chandra (1996) are slightly more optimistic than other scholars about the results of affirmative actions. Providing the example of trade unions, they explain that the leadership of trade unions is now moving into the hands of people from lower castes, while in the past these were dominated by members of the upper castes. They also point out that despite continuing discrimination, more and more women and minority categories are being employed in jobs that were earlier beyond their reach. Notwithstanding this optimism, even these authors acknowledge that much remains to be done to improve the lot of minority groups. Like our predecessors, we are also not convinced about the positive outcome of reservations. We believe that discrimination continues and is even encouraged for political reasons. Affirmative action has become a way of appealing to the different groups of people and vote banks, thereby perpetuating a 'divide and rule' policy. Similar trends are also being observed in other countries that have adopted affirmative action or quotas as a response to their discrimination problems. Perhaps a systematic comparison between the approaches taken by India and those of other countries to overcome such problems might provide us with an insight into how India can solve some of its own.

Comparing diversity measures in India, the USA, France and Canada

As has been mentioned in previous sections (see also *The Economist*, 1994a, b) we believe that the government's AA program, although well-intentioned, has not eliminated but further deepened discrimination-related issues. Since the lower castes form a vast majority of the population, politicians lure them with promises of a better life. Politics has become more and more polarized across caste lines (*The Economist*, 2007b). The high-caste members ignored by one group of politicians are then wooed by another group of politicians. Religious minorities such as the Sikhs, Christians and Muslims are also involved in the caste debate when this suits the vested interests of competing political parties. By engaging with the caste issue, past governments have only accentuated the caste problem. This raises questions regarding the effectiveness of the implementation of the quota system. Further, the existing AA and equality laws do not pay sufficient attention towards all the minorities in Indian society (for example, homosexuals and *hijras*).

The term 'affirmative action' was introduced to the world when the Indian representative to the International Covenant on Economic, Social and Cultural Rights (ICESCR) proposed 'special measures for advancement of any socially and educationally backward sections of society [which] shall not be construed as "distinction"'. It soon became the catchphrase in many countries around the world. The Americans were quick to adopt the concept. President Lyndon Johnson defended his decision to impose quotas for minorities in the US in 1965 saying, 'You do not take a person who has been hobbled by chains and liberate him and then say, "You are free to compete with others", and still believe that you are being fair'. Although the adoption of AA was rapid by the Americans, other nations were more cautious.

Canada, for example, preferred a softer approach to ensure equal opportunity for its citizens. Instead of imposing quotas for minorities, it encourages its companies to respect diversity in lieu of tax rebates. As Saha et al. (2008) state, Canada enforces anti-discrimination laws and permits special programs to remedy past or present discriminatory practices. The Federal Employment Equity Act (1986) applies to Federal Crown corporations and federally regulated private sector employers with 100 or more employees, and the federal public service. Instead of imposing a quota system, the act requires that each organization's employment equity plan contain 'an effective enforcement mechanism', the design of which is left to the employer. This has caused minimal backlash, either because organizations, instead of being compelled to fill quotas, are allowed to develop a system that best suits their needs or because such measures are seen as having very little impact (see ibid. for details).

France is another country that has historically opposed the hard approach to combat discrimination. The French principles of *'liberté, égalité et fraternité'* are well known. *Égalité* implies that all human beings irrespective of their ethnic origins, religious affiliations or skin color are equal. This has interesting manifestations. For example the principle of *égalité* bars any questions about ethnic origin, religion and so on at all times. This implies that since asking questions about minority criteria is illegal, there are no official measures of the different minority groups living in France. One might venture to say that France has chosen not to engage in the measurement of minority groups, precisely because it wishes to avoid treating them as 'minorities' (because this could reinforce the inequality). This approach is in line with Litvin's (1997) arguments that the very use of categories of persons, for example, men, women, the aged, and ethnic minorities/majorities, as repositories of difference are divisive. The French way of addressing diversity is very different from the stand taken by the Indian government after the country's independence. Although India's leaders at the time of independence started off with the same guiding principle of equality, they chose to impose quotas to redress past wrongs. However, not limiting these actions to a specific duration of time has led them to become ineffective. Further, the proliferation of categories to be included in the reservation system has only led to diluting the effect of the outcomes. Rather than eliminating the system of quotas once minority groups have benefited enough from it, the present system has led to a rush among other segments of Indian society to be included in the reservation system. This is contrary to the French approach. The only minority group that has been accorded quotas in the French system is that of people with disabilities. French companies with over 100 employees are required to recruit at least 6 percent disabled employees. Companies not respecting this law are required to pay a penalty. The reality is that despite these laws, very few companies actually employ disabled people. They find paying the penalty to be a much easier option. Although France and India have used very different approaches to confront discrimination, both have met with very limited success. Let us now explore how the other early adopter of AA has fared over the past decades.

In the US, many experts are now questioning the usefulness of affirmative action. Myers (2007) shows that in the US, while minorities and women made gains in the labor market in the 1970s and 1980s, it is not clear what portion of this was due to affirmative action and what portion was due to other influences. Myers's findings suggest that AA programs in the context of her study (in California) were either indifferent or had been effective while in place but had failed to create lasting change in employers' prejudicial attitudes. Many states in the US are now in the process of repealing their AA policies. Like California (in 1996), in Washington and Michigan, affirmative action has also been repealed from public universities and colleges. When California banned affirmative action in 1996, admissions among black freshmen dropped from 50 percent (1995–97) to 20 percent (1998–2001). Many experts use such figures to assert that affirmative action has had a strong impact in the US and that it should be continued. Those that support the decision to AAs demand an optimistic era where people are not judged by their skin color or by who they are, but by their merit (Richardson, 2007). Proponents of this recent move claim that AA policies or quotas were never meant to be permanent; rather, they were meant to provide support to minority groups until such groups achieved the same level of skills and opportunities as majority groups.

Now that we have a broader picture of the diversity debate in some other countries, we shall revert back to our discussion of diversity policies in India. Considering that reservations over the past 60 years of independence have produced only partial improvements, one might wish to reflect on the implementation and the duration of these measures. As Ambedekar said, these measures were meant to be temporary (see *The Economist*, 2007b). Although we agree that millennia of oppression of minority communities cannot be expected to be erased in six decades, we nonetheless believe that continuing and indeed strengthening current measures may only deepen the fragmentation of Indian society. We do not recommend that nothing should be done for members of minority groups, only that the current measures of reservations are not the most appropriate. Although the goals are noble, the instruments used to achieve the goal have proved to be ineffective so far. It is therefore time to realize that we might be playing the right music with the wrong instrument in this case! We recommend that more supportive measures rather than affirmative action be used to improve the conditions of minority groups. We believe that providing support measures such as scholarships, subsidized accommodation, free school lunches, free books and so on for students from underprivileged backgrounds might be a better solution than reserving seats for them in educational institutions. If needy and meritorious students irrespective of their caste or class are provided such support measures, this will foster a spirit of brotherhood and healthy competition rather than the hostility and reverse discrimination that we see today. In the same way, understanding the challenges faced by working women and providing them with training, mentorship and a positive working environment is a better solution than reserving seats or quotas for them.

Notwithstanding the limited outcome of the AA plans, one can safely assume that the diversity in Indian society is not going away. Managers continue to encounter it everyday in their workplace. The challenge of managing diverse people is complex for managers. The complexity increases hugely for the expatriate manager. In the subsequent part of this chapter we address diversity at the corporate level. We also provide examples of diversity management measures by local and international companies.

Managing diversity in corporate India

For the sake of simplicity, in this chapter, we have focused on only some of the sources of diversity in India. We have discussed diversity arising from different religions, castes, tribes, gender, age, sexual orientation and sexuality. It is, however, beyond the scope of the chapter to elaborate on cultural diversity. Despite this limitation, it is safe to assume that this diversity has an impact on the way businesses should be conducted. Besides, perceived discrimination is believed to have a stronger impact on the outcome of employees than other workplace stressors (Sanchez and Brock, 1996). Hence, gradually an increasing number of companies are engaging in voluntary and proactive measures to enhance the inclusion and engagement of those individuals who had hitherto remained underrepresented (Gilbert et al., 1999).

Lorbiecki and Gavin (2000) provide many different definitions of diversity management. One of the definitions which strikes us as being particularly pertinent is the following:

> The basic concept of managing diversity accepts that the workforce consists of a diverse population of people. The diversity consists of visible and non-visible differences which will include factors such as sex, age, background, race, disability, personality and work style. It is founded on the premise that harnessing these differences will create a productive environment in which everyone feels valued, where their talents are being fully utilised and in which organisational goals are met. (Kandola and Fullerton, 1998: 8)

Our earlier examples of the Doordarshan and All India Radio expose the gender-based discrimination in these public sector companies. Also, past years have seen several gender-based discrimination cases in Indian courts (Ratnam and Chandra, 1996) dealing with issues such as unequal remuneration for male and female employees performing the same job (Jain and Ratnam, 1996). How can Indian companies better manage their gender-based diversity? Some experts (see Bhargava and Herr, 1996) suggest that the (mostly male) top management should get rid of its inherent prejudice against women, they should accept maternity as a fact of life and support female employees through it, they should root out masculine intimidation by establishing redressal forums, offer both female and male managers flexible working hours and work-from-home options and treat female managers as a long-term investment. Although well-meaning, these suggestions are too prescriptive to be effective. Since their usefulness depends on managers making the right choice, it is heavily incumbent upon managers' values and beliefs. Since values and beliefs are deep-seated, these are difficult to change. This is a time-consuming exercise and requires creating awareness through training and education. This involves commitment from the top management and resource allocation for this purpose. Further, the top management needs to create policies regarding flexible work time, and special training and mentorship programs to support women.

While international managers might be exposed to gender-based diversity issues even in their own country, the Indian caste system can be difficult for them to comprehend. We learnt of some experiences of expatriate managers during the course of our earlier studies conducted in the south of India (see Patel, 2007a and b for details). The French human resource director of an Indo-French joint venture complained about never being able to organize meetings at noon. It took him a long time to understand that 12.00 noon was considered as an 'inauspicious time' by the Hindus in the south of India. This meant that any meeting organized around that time was bound to start late. Being a European he was not familiar with such beliefs. The same manager related another incident which reveals the extent to which the caste and community identity is still entrenched in the Indian mindset. The manager had become aware over time of escalating tension between the telephone operators and a group of engineers in his company. When he attempted to discover the source of this tension, he felt as if he had come to a dead end. He was merely scratching at the surface without being able to uncover the real issues. Meanwhile the situation escalated, with workers threatening to go on strike. Our respondent then requested one of his Indian colleagues to act as the mediator between the two conflicting parties. The reality was then revealed to him: all the telephone operators came from the same caste, in fact from the same village in the south of India, while the engineers came from another caste and another village. Over the past years, the telephone operators had been recruited upon recommendation from existing telephone operators. The same was the case with the engineers. Without the human resource director's knowledge, two groups based on caste and village affiliations had come into being in the company. Over time, it had become a numbers game. More adherents to one group meant that the other party had to 'boost its numbers' as well. What had begun originally as a simple act of providing 'support to a member of one's caste' had transformed into a gang rivalry. International managers need to be very vigilant not to inadvertently set the stage for a caste- or community-based conflict in their company.

Authors such as Ratnam and Chandra (1996) also provide examples of the challenges foreign companies have had to encounter in managing diversity in India. They observe that although it was India who introduced affirmative action to the world, for many Indians this is an American concept. International managers also had difficulty convincing their Indian collaborators that diversity management was indeed a necessity in India! Ratnam and Chandra provide the example of a British hotel chain in which the management had to grapple with caste-based groupism among the workforce. The groups were so cohesive that any action that indirectly favored one group of employees was seen as an attack on the other. People from so-called 'higher' castes would not eat in the same canteen as those from 'lower' castes. The company took a stand towards putting a stop to all these discriminatory practices. They created a common canteen for all castes. Initially this led to resistance from the higher castes who boycotted the canteen, but in time they accepted the management's decision. This example shows that foreign companies, like Indian ones, need to take a stand against discrimination and need to enforce simple but firm measures to counter it within their premises (for more examples of diversity management measures by multinational companies in India, see Robinson and Ensign, ch. 15 in this volume). It is not AA laws, but a commitment to equality that they need so as to put a stop to discrimination.

Conclusion

This chapter reveals the inherent complexity of confronting discrimination in India. There are several key points which make India's diversity problems unique as compared to other countries. The caste issue is the first of these. In addition to scheduled castes and tribes, other minority groups in India such as women, disabled people, homosexuals and *hijras* also experience discrimination. It is also true that some minority groups such as the *hijras* and the homosexuals experience much more discrimination than others. They are stigmatized and experience social exclusion and isolation. The situation of these minority groups is much worse as compared to other nations such as France and Holland, where homosexuals are not only accepted at par with heterosexuals but also continue to play prominent roles in society. For example, the current mayor of the city of Paris, Bertrand Delanoe, is openly homosexual.

The polarization of politics based on caste and religion is the second characteristic that makes the Indian situation unique as compared to other countries. It is true that minority communities represent vote banks in many countries. However, in recent decades India has seen instances where this polarization has almost cost it its secularism. How else can one justify the attempts of the previous BJP government to create laws to prevent people from choosing to change their religion? Since when did democracy become an excuse for controlling individual choices? The polarization of Indian politics coupled with the ineffective implementation of AA measures have resulted in what Tummala (1999) has aptly described as a polarized society. Citing Steele (1990), Tummala explains that in such a society the norm appears to be the 'politics of difference' defined as 'a troubling, volatile politics in which each group justifies itself, its sense of worth and its pursuit of power, through difference alone' (Steele, 1990: 132). Tummala (1999: 504) explains that in such a society 'every victory of one group would lead its enemies to arms'. By reinforcing reservations, the present Indian government may be contributing to further polarizing the society. We believe that it is time to put an end to this trend and to focus on a more integrative collaborative approach. Reinforcing affirmative actions, as the government has recently suggested, is not the solution to the country's diversity problem. This will only lead to increased discrimination and a backlash against minority groups.

As the opening quotation suggests, there is a hierarchy of minorities in India and some minority members might be unfortunate enough to be caught up in an overlap of these categories. This hierarchy makes the diversity scenario all the more complex and unique. It is already unfortunate if one is born in a low caste, but if one happens to be a woman as well or a disabled person, then the future does not hold much in store for such a person in a country like India. While most women including those in developed countries face some form of vertical and horizontal segregation in the workplace, it is only in India where they are doubly damned if they happen to be widows. This categorization of different minority groups and the implicit hierarchy between these categories is strongly grounded in social beliefs and values. Since these are the products of uneducated and uninformed minds, there is little that laws can do to change them. The only hope lies in educating the masses, and in the younger generations of the country who can change the perceptions of future generations. As Prakash Ambedekar (grandson of Dr B.R. Ambedekar) insists, the solution lies in changing attitudes, not numbers, 'No set regulations can take the place of grass root action. We do not need crutches. Equality is a notion, not a law. If true change comes at all, it will come not from the politicians, but from the people' (Blank, 1995, p. 1; see also Saha et al., 2008).

While being such a diverse nation, India continues to be a democratic, secular republic. It is a pluralistic nation and has always insisted on nurturing its heterogeneity. Being such a diverse nation means that its pluralism can often be chaotic and difficult to manage. Yet, maintaining and valuing this plurality is the only way it can survive (see also Marriott, 1976).

References

Ali, F. (2010), 'A comparative study of EEO in Pakistan, India and Bangladesh', ch. 3 in M. Özbilgin and J. Syed (eds), *Managing Gender Diversity in Asia: A Research Companion*, Cheltenham, UK and Northampton, MA, USA: Edward Elgar, pp. 32–53.

Banerjee, B. and Knight, J. (1985), 'Caste discrimination in the Indian urban labour market', *Journal of Development Economics*, **17** (1): 277–307.

Beteille, A. (1996), *Caste, Class and Power: Changing Patterns of Stratification in a Tanjore Village*, Delhi: Oxford University Press.

Bhargava, S. and Herr, H. (1996), 'How to manage gender bias', *Business Today*, 7–21 January: 154–7.

Bhengra, R., Bijoy, C. and Luithui, S. (1999), 'The Adivasis of India', MRG International Report 98/1, Minority Rights Group International, London.

Blank, J. (1995), 'Quotas that are cast in stone', *US News and World Report*, **118** (12).

Bougle, C. (1958), 'Essais sur le Régime des Castes', English translation of the Introduction in *Contributions to Indian Sociology*, II, p. 4.

Chakrabarty, G. and Ghosh, P. (2000), 'Human Development Profile of Scheduled Castes and Tribes in Selected States: A Benchmark Survey', Report no. 4, National Council of Applied Economic Research, New Delhi.

Chan, R., Row Kavi, A., Carl, G., Khan, S., Oetomo, D., Tan, M. and Brown, T. (1998), 'HIV and men who have sex with men: perspectives from selected Asian countries', *AIDS*, **12** (Supp/B): 559–68.

Cohn, B. (1968), 'Notes on the history and study of Indian society and culture', in M. Singer and B.S. Cohn (eds), *Structure and Change in Indian Society*, Chicago, IL: Aldine, pp. 3–28.

Cohn, B. (1987), 'The census, social structure and objectivation in South Asia', in B.S. Cohn (ed.), *An Anthropologist Among the Historians and Other Essays*, Delhi: Oxford University Press.

Dev, R. (2004), 'Human rights, relativism and minorities in North-East India', *Economic and Political Weekly*, October 23.

Dhesi, A. (1998), 'Caste, class synergies and discrimination in India', *International Journal of Social Economics*, **25** (6/7/8), 1030–48.

Dumont, L. (1970), *Homo Hierarchicus: The Caste System and Its Implications*, Chicago, IL: University of Chicago Press.

Farooqui, M. (2007), 'Minority Report', *New Statesman*, 6 August: 28–9.

Geertz, C. (1973), *The Interpretation of Cultures*, New York: Basic Books.

Gilbert, J., Stead, B. and Ivancevich, J. (1999), 'Diversity management: a new paradigm', *Journal of Business Ethics*, **21**: 61–76.

Giry, S. (2004), 'Chennai Dispatch', *The New Republic*, April 16.

Heredia, R. (1995), 'Tribal education for development: need for a liberative pedagogy for social transformation', *Economic and Political Weekly*, **30** (16): 891–97.

India Country Profile (2008), www.datamonitor.com.

Jaffrelot, C. (2006), 'The impact of affirmative action in India: more political than socioeconomic', *India Review*, **5** (2): 173–89.

Jain, H. and Ratnam, C. Venkata (1996), 'The working of the Equal Remuneration Act in India', mimeo, McMaster University, Hamilton.

Jaising, I. (1988), 'Gay rights', *The Lawyers*, February–March: 24–5.

Johnson, L. (1965), 'To fulfill these rights', Commencement Address at Howard University, available at: http://www.lbjlib.utexas.edu/johnson/archives.hom/speeches.hom/650604.asp (accessed 27 January 2010).

Kandola, R. and Fullerton, J. (1998), *Diversity in Action: Managing the Mosaic*, 2nd edn, London: Chartered Institute of Personal Development.

Kijima, Y. (2006), 'Caste and tribe inequality: evidence from India, 1983–1999', *Economic Development and Cultural Change*, Chicago, IL: University of Chicago Press, pp. 369–404.

Kripalani, M. (2006), 'India's affirmative action rocks the boat', *Business Week*, 00077135, May 22, 2006.

Kusk, F., Özbilgin, M. and Ozkale, L. (2007), 'Against the tide: gendered prejudice and disadvantage in engineering', *Gender, Work and Organization*, **14** (2): 109–29.

Lal, V. (1999), 'Not this, not that: the hijras of india and the cultural politics of sexuality', *Social Text*, **17** (4): 119–40.

Litvin, D. (1997), 'The discourse of diversity: from biology to management', *Organization*, **4** (2): 187–210.

Lorbiecki, A. and Gavin, J. (2000), 'Critical turns in the evolution of diversity management', *British Journal of Management*, **11** (Special Issue): S17–S31.

Mandelbaum, D. (1970), *Society in India* (two volumes), Berkeley, Los Angeles, CA and London: University of California Press.

Marriott, M. (1976), 'Hindu transactions: diversity without dualism in B. Kapferer (ed.), *Transaction and Meaning: Directions in the Anthropology of Exchange and Symbolic Behavior*, Philadelphia, PA: Institute for the Study of Human Issues, pp. 109–42.

Munshi, K. and Rosenzweig, M. (2003), 'Traditional institutions meet the modern world: caste, gender and schooling choice in a globalizing economy', Working Paper 038, Bureau for Research in Economic Analysis of Development, Harvard University.

Myers, C. (2007), 'A cure for discrimination? Affirmative action and the case of California's proposition 209', *Industrial and Labour Relations Review*, **60** (3): 379–96.

Narasimha, S. (2002), 'Gender, class and caste schisms in affirmative action policies: the curious case of India's Women's Reservation Bill', *Feminist Economics*, **8** (2): 183–90.

Narula, S. and Macwan, M. (2001), 'Untouchability: the economic exclusion of Dalits in India', paper presented at the International Council on Human Rights Policy, January, Geneva, Switzerland.

Özbilgin, M. and Woodward, D. (2004), '"Belonging" and "Otherness": sex equality in banking in Turkey and Britain', *Gender, Work and Organization*, **11** (6): 668–88.

Parekh, S. (2003), 'Homosexuality in India', *Journal of Gay and Lesbian Psychotherapy*, **7** (1/2): 145–64.

Patel, I. (1994), *Gender Differences in Employment Patterns of Doordarshan and All India Radio*, New Delhi: Media Advocacy Group and Friedrich Ebert Stiftung.

Patel, T. (2007a), 'Using cultural theory to explain the viability of international strategic alliances: a focus on Indo-French alliances', *Management Decisions*, **45** (10): 1532–59.

Patel, T. (2007b), *Stereotypes of Intercultural Management*, Delft: Eburon.

Prior, E. (1996), 'Constitutional fairness or fraud of the constitution? Compensatory discrimination in India', *Case Western Reserve Journal of International Law*, **28** (1): 63–100.

Raman, S. (1999), 'Caste in stone: consequences of India's affirmative action policies', *Harvard International Review*, Fall, 30–34.

Raza, M., Aijazuddin, A. and Sheel Chand, N. (1985), 'Tribal literacy in India: the regional dimension', Occasional Paper 9, National Institute of Educational Planning and Administration, New Delhi.

Richardson, N. (2007), 'Diversity watch: nationwide attacks on affirmative action', *Black Enterprise*, Graves Ventures, LLC, p. 29.

Rowley, C., Yukongdi, V. and Wei, J. (2010), 'Managing diversity: women managers in

Asia', ch. 11 in M. Özbilgin and J. Syed (eds), *Managing Gender Diversity in Asia: A Research Companion*, Cheltenham, UK and Northampton, MA, USA: Edward Elgar, pp. 189–209.

Saha, S., Patel, T., O'Donnell, D. and Heneghan, J. (2008), 'A study of individual values and employment equity in Canada, France and Ireland', *Equal Opportunities International*, **27** (7), November: 629–45.

Sanchez, J. and Brock, P. (1996), 'Outcomes of perceived discrimination among Hispanic employees: is diversity management a luxury or a necessity?', *Academy of Management Journal*, **39** (3): 704–19.

Shrivastava, P. (2007), 'Exposed: glass ceiling at India Inc', *Business Today*, 23 September, 30.

Steele, S. (1990), *The Content of Our Character*, New York: St. Martin's Press.

The Economist (1994a), 'Casting the first stone', **333** (7864).

The Economist (1994b), 'The hills are ablaze', **333** (7884).

The Economist (2004), 'A backward cast of mind?', **373** (8401).

The Economist (2006), 'Don't blame it on the scriptures. India's Muslims: Why India's 150 m Muslims are missing out on the country's rise?', **381** (8506).

The Economist (2007a), 'Singing for supper: India's widows: abandoned women but at least they are paid to pray', **384** (8542).

The Economist (2007b), 'Untouchables and unthinkable', **385** (8549).

Tummala, K. (1999), 'Policy of preference: lessons from India, the United States, and South Africa', *Public Administration Review*, **59** (6): 496–508.

United Nations Population Fund (2004), 'India's disappearing females: mapping the adverse child sex ratio in India', New York. Published in *The Futurist*, available at: www.unfpa. org (accessed 15 March 2008).

Vanita, R. and Kidwai, S. (eds) (2000), *Same-Sex Love in India: Readings from Literature and History*, Delhi: Macmillan India Ltd and New York: St. Martin's Press.

Ratnam, C. Venkata and Chandra, V. (1996), 'Sources of diversity and the challenge before human resource management in India', *International Journal of Manpower*, **17** (4/5): 76–107.

Zwart, F. (2000), 'The logic of affirmative action: caste, class and quotas in India', *Acta Sociologica*, **43**, 235–49.

14 Demographic profile of economic resources and environment in South Asia
Jalandhar Pradhan

Introduction

South Asia is known to constitute one of the critical regions in the world primarily due to the fact that most of the Asian states are engrossed in varying degrees of interstate disputes and conflicts. Also, the South Asian region – Afghanistan, Bangladesh, Bhutan, India, Maldives, Pakistan, Nepal and Sri Lanka – possesses an extraordinary diversity in land forms and climatic regimes ranging from the highest mountains, hottest plains, wettest and driest places and dissected valleys to coral islands. With a total population of 1,379.8 million (World Bank, 2003), the major concern of the region has been the deepening nature of poverty and its impact on the process of environmental degradation. With 22 per cent of the world's population, and a high density rate, it is plagued by high levels of illiteracy, prevalence of poor health conditions and a low GNP. The extent of human deprivation in South Asia is also colossal. About 260 million people lack access to even rudimentary health facilities, 337 million lack safe drinking water, 830 million have no access to basic sanitation facilities, and over 400 million go hungry each day. Despite all this, South Asia is one of the most militarized regions in the world. The widespread human deprivation contrasts sharply with large armies, modern weapons and expanding military budgets. Indeed, two of the largest armies in the world are in South Asia and it is also the only region where military spending (as a proportion of GNP) has gone up since 1987; it declined substantially in all other parts of the world after the end of the Cold War. Historically, the region has been the profitable hinterland for several colonial powers, which perhaps remained as major reasons for backwardness in all sectors from education to health, from agriculture to industry and so on.

On the other hand, the potentials of the region are quite good. In fact, the region is rich in terms of natural resources, which, if harnessed appropriately, could perhaps change the entire scenario. However, this is the particular area where there is a tremendous flaw despite the available opportunities.

It is true that there is great amount of disparity in the distribution of economic resources in the region. It is also true that all the countries in the region are striving to accumulate as much physical and human capital as they can to achieve and accelerate their economic development. Against this backdrop and particularly in the face of growing competition in global trade, economy and investment, concerted cooperation among the countries of the region has become imperative. The process of globalization has also spearheaded the concept and practice of interdependence. Economic and trade liberalization policies enforce stronger bilateral and multilateral cooperation. This has infused the trend for regional and subregional cooperation in many parts of the world and, as we have been seeing, such moves resulted in substantial benefits. The case in point could be the various alliances, such as the Association of South East Asian Nations (ASEAN), the European Union (EU), the South Asian Association for Regional Cooperation (SAARC), the South Asia Free Trade Area (SAFTA), the North American Free Trade Area (NAFTA) and so on.

There have also been several attempts in the region to stage such co-operative endeavours. But regrettably nothing has worked well so far and the situation tends to remain as gloomy as ever. The need for a strong regional or more specifically subregional cooperation has always been well orchestrated, but real work on the issue has never surfaced.

The development of regional or subregional cooperative endeavours is indeed imperative when resources are shared by the concerned countries, and more so when opportunities for accumulating common benefits are in place. While we should not ignore the possibilities of benefit from such cooperation, we must also ensure that these endeavours are based on natural and due advantages for each and every participating country. In this context the countries of the region need to examine carefully the development option available to them, and cooperate in designing strategies that promote sustainable development. This chapter is organized as follows. The first part deals with the state of the South Asian economy and environment. It begins with an overview of the main structural features of the region as a whole and thereafter examines the national trends. This is followed by an analysis of the emerging environmental problem, the demographic profile of the region and the situation relating to human resources, including the development of human capital and the incidence of poverty. The second part examines a few likely scenarios of long-term economic growth, foreign investment, and demographic change and their implications for regional economic relationships on the one hand and the sustainability of regional ecosystems on the other.

Sources of data

For this study, the data have been extracted from the World Bank's *World Development Report* (2003, 2007a) and *World Development Indicators*

(2007b); the UNDP's *Human Development Report* (2000, 2004, 2007–08); the Mahbub ul Haq Development Center's *Human Development in South Asia* (2001, 2003, 2005); Esty et al.'s *Environmental Sustainability Index* (2005); and the Asian Development Bank's *Asian Development Outlook* (2001, 2003, 2004, 2009).

Macro aspects of South Asian countries

The human development index (HDI), the gender related development index (GDI) and the human poverty index (HPI), provide summary information about human development in a country. Table 14.1 shows the various indices of human development or deprivation in the countries of the South Asian region. In terms of HDI, Sri Lanka ranked first followed by Maldives and India. However, in terms of GDI, Maldives is on the top followed by Sri Lanka. Massive poverty is a common feature among South Asian countries. Bangladesh is characterized by a high level of poverty, followed by Bhutan and Nepal, and it is lowest for Maldives (17.0 per cent).

Structural features

The share of GNI, GDP and external debt reveals the economic status of any country. The national proportion of GNI, GDP and total external debt for South Asia as a whole is shown in Table 14.2.

On the economic front, Maldives is placed first among the South Asian countries. In GNI and GDP Maldives has performed well, followed by Sri Lanka. Bhutan's GNI is better than its GDP. Pakistan, Bangladesh and Nepal rate lower than the average of South Asia both in terms of GNI

Table 14.1   Comparison of human development indices

South Asian countries	Human development index (HDI)	Gender development index (GDI)	Gender empowerment measure (GEM)	Human poverty index (HPI-1), (%)
India	0.619	0.600	–	31.3
Pakistan	0.551	0.525	0.377	36.2
Bangladesh	0.547	0.539	0.379	40.5
Sri Lanka	0.743	0.735	0.369	17.8
Nepal	0.534	0.520	0.351	38.1
Maldives	0.741	0.744	0.437	17.0
Bhutan	0.579	–	–	38.9

Source: UNDP (2007–08).

Table 14.2   GNI and GDP per capita

Regions	GNI per capita US$ 2003	GDP per capita (PPP US$ 2003)	Total external debt (US$ bn) 2003
South Asia	525	2682	182
India	540	2892	113.47 (62.08)
Pakistan	520	2097	36.35 (19.97)
Bangladesh	400	1770	18.78 (10.31)
Sri Lanka	930	3778	10.24 (5.62)
Nepal	240	1420	3.20 (1.75)
Maldives	2350	4798	–
Bhutan	630	1969	–

Note: Percentage in parenthesis.

Source: Mahbub ul Haq Human Development Center (2005).

Table 14.3   Growth of output

	GDP average annual % growth		Agriculture average annual % growth		Industry average annual % growth		Manufacturing average annual % growth		Services average annual % growth	
	1990–2000	2000–2005	1990–2000	2000–2005	1990–2000	2000–2005	1990–2000	2000–2005	1990–2000	2000–2005
Afghanistan	–	12.0	–	0.4	–	21.1	–	13.8	–	21.9
Bangladesh	4.8	5.4	2.9	2.5	7.3	7.3	7.2	6.7	4.5	5.6
India	6.0	7.0	3.0	2.5	6.3	7.5	7.0	6.9	8.0	8.5
Nepal	4.9	2.8	2.4	3.2	7.2	1.1	8.9	−0.6	6.4	2.8
Pakistan	3.8	4.8	4.4	2.3	4.1	6.5	3.8	9.1	4.4	5.4
Sri Lanka	5.3	4.2	1.8	0.7	6.9	3.3	8.1	2.9	5.7	5.8

Source: World Bank (2007b).

and GDP. The external debt is high in India, with a 62.08 per cent share of the debt.

The analysis on the growth of output shows that developing economies grew faster over the last decade, 1995–2005 (World Bank, 2007b). South Asia has grown from 6 per cent in 1995 to 8 per cent in 2005. The country-wise detail is given in Table 14.3.

The average annual growth percentage in South Asian countries is quite impressive despite the low contribution of agriculture to GDP. There is enormous growth in the services sector, particularly in India. The recent

Table 14.4   Selected economic indicators

Regions	GDP 2009	Inflation	Current account balance
Afghanistan	9.0	6.0	−3.5
Bangladesh	5.6	7.0	0.2
Bhutan	5.5	3.5	5.5
India	5.0	3.5	−1.5
Maldives	1.0	4.5	−30.0
Nepal	3.0	10.0	1.5
Pakistan	2.8	20.0	−6.0
Sri Lanka	4.5	8.0	−7.5

Source: Asian Development Bank (2009).

financial crisis has also affected this region, but only slightly. The Asian Development Bank (2009) states that in the year 2009, Afghanistan, Bangladesh, Bhutan and India will have more than 5 per cent of GDP where as Maldives, Nepal and Pakistan will account for less than 3 per cent. The socio-political unrest in Nepal may account for the drastic decline. The projection on inflation is also high in Pakistan (20) and Nepal (10). These are depicted clearly in Table 14.4, including the current account balance of the South Asian countries.

Trends in saving and investment
The South Asian region as a whole was able to achieve reasonably high average rates of economic growth during the 1990s. Although these were lower than the more dynamic economies of East and South East Asia, the economic performance of South Asian economies was creditable considering the economic condition of many African and Latin American countries, where rates of economic growth were much lower or negative. The process that contributed to the dynamic growth of East and South East Asia derived from their international competitiveness, gained through their macroeconomic policies and the dynamic structural adjustments of their economies to the shift in comparative advantage. South Asian economies were just beginning to emerge from the inward-looking state-regulated economic system in the early 1980s, with Sri Lanka taking the lead in the process of liberalization. However, the main economic aggregates of saving and investment had begun to rise significantly in almost all countries (Table 14.5).

In the largest economy, India, domestic saving had fallen from about 25 per cent in 1995 to 23 per cent in 2001. The corresponding figures for

Table 14.5   Trends in saving and investment

Regions	Gross domestic saving		Gross domestic investment	
	1995	2001	1995	2001
India	25.1	22.8	26.8	23.8
Pakistan	14.2	11.6	18.3	15.5
Bangladesh	16.7	21.8	19.1	23.3
Sri Lanka	15.3	18.9	25.7	27.0
Nepal	16.3	–	25.2	–
Maldives	–	–	–	–
Bhutan	43.9	19.0	48.7	44.1

Source: Asian Development Bank (2001).

Pakistan were 14 and 11 per cent, for Bhutan 44 and 19 per cent and for Bangladesh 17 and 22 per cent. Investment had not increased as significantly as the proportion of GDP during the recent past. Gross domestic investment had declined from 27 per cent in 1995 to 24 per cent (2001) in India. The same trend is also revealed in Pakistan and Bhutan.

Structural change
The structures of economies have also been changing significantly, with the share of agriculture decreasing and that of industry increasing. Table 14.6 shows the percentage share of GDP contributed from various sectors among South Asian countries. The rate of structural change, measured by the rates of decline of the share of agriculture and rates of increase of the share of industry has been relatively high for the 1970–2000 period. In the Indian economy, which accounts for 78 per cent of South Asian GDP, the share of agriculture declined from 44.5 per cent in 1970 to 24 per cent in 2000, the share of industry increased from 23.9 to 27.1 per cent and the services sector rose from 31.6 to 48.9 per cent for the corresponding period. All the countries in South Asia have experienced this trend. This structural change, which leads to accelerated industrialization and urbanization, will have a far-reaching impact on the environment of the individual countries and the region as a whole, with major consequences for the political and economic relationships.

The prospect of sustaining the South Asian growth effort that has been evident in the recent past will depend on a number of critical preconditions. The first among these are regional political stability and peace along with stability and order within the nation. The related political issues lie outside the scope of this chapter. These issues, however, are relevant to

Table 14.6   Structural change, sectoral share of GDP

Regions	Agriculture				Industry				Services			
	1970	1980	2000	2002	1970	1980	2000	2002	1970	1980	2000	2002
India	44.5	38.1	24.0	22.0	23.9	25.9	27.1	27.2	31.6	36.0	48.9	50.8
Pakistan	40.1	30.6	26.2	23.9	19.6	25.6	24.9	25.6	40.3	43.8	48.9	50.6
Bangladesh	–	49.4	24.3	24.0	–	14.8	24.7	26.7	–	35.8	51.0	49.3
Sri Lanka	30.7	26.6	20.6	19.8	27.1	27.2	27.3	26.6	42.2	46.2	52.1	53.6
Nepal	–	61.8	38.8	39.0	–	11.9	20.7	22.8	–	26.3	40.5	38.2
Maldives	–	–	9.5	10.0	–	–	15.5	15.0	–	–	75.0	75.0
Bhutan	–	56.7	32.5	31.7	–	12.2	32.4	34.9	–	31.1	35.1	33.4

Source: Asian Development Bank (2004).

the extent that economic growth will increase income and employment and alleviate poverty. This will help to reduce internal tensions, which fuel unrest and sharpen ethno-religious conflicts that spill over into intergovernmental relations.

Apart from the political preconditions, the prospects of sustaining economic growth depend crucially on the macroeconomic 'fundamentals', the pursuit of a set of consistent macroeconomic policies that control fiscal deficits, reduce the international competition, prevent the overvaluation of the local currencies, contral inflation, privatize the public sector and create an economic environment that can attract foreign investment. Table 14.7 presents two key indications of macroeconomic performance for the countries – the state of the current account deficits in the balance of payments and the fiscal deficit. All the countries have substantial deficits in the current accounts of their balance of payments as well as in their government budgets. Domestic borrowing and external assistance and loans meet the major part of these deficits. Although, as discussed earlier, investment has increased, these increases are heavily dependent on net external resource flows.

South Asia also holds the dubious distinction of lacking the economic incentives for regional cooperation. History shows that regional economic integration can be successful only if the countries concerned establish a commonality of political purpose. Levels of trade between India and its neighbours are low because their economies do not complement each other in resource availability, the structure and content of production, the supply of services, and cut-throat competitiveness. For example, Bangladesh, India and Nepal compete with their jute products in the UK, the EU and Japan. India, Sri Lanka and Bangladesh compete with tea in the UK and the EU. Similarly, there is bitter rivalry between India,

Table 14.7   Macroeconomic indicators

Regions	Balance of payments on current account ($ million)		Balance of payments on current account (% of GDP)	
	1995	2000	1995	2000
South Asia	−10,495	−9155	−2.2	−1.9
India	−5910	−6509	−1.7	−1.3
Pakistan	−2484	−977	−4.1	−1.6
Bangladesh	−920	−442	−2.4	−1.0
Sri Lanka	−786	−989	−6.0	−6.0
Nepal	−343	−82	−8.1	−1.5
Maldives	−18	−29	−4.5	−4.6
Bhutan	−34	−127	−12.1	−28.5

Source: Asian Development Bank (2001).

Pakistan and Bangladesh over the export of textiles to the US and the EU, which has been compounded in recent years by complex rules and regulations regarding textiles in the international trading system. Trade between SAARC countries amounts to a dismal 3.4 per cent of their total global trade. The corresponding figures for ASEAN, the EU, and NAFTA are 27, 70, and 19 per cent, respectively. In contrast, all the SAARC members have attempted to diversify their trade relations away from India over the last few years. This trend is far more pronounced in the case of Indo–Nepal and Indo–Pakistan trade.

The state of environment
The richness and the diversity of both the physical and the human environment of South Asia hold the promise of significant growth possibilities for the region. But the absence of social vision, political leadership and enlightened economic policies, together with the presence of a huge population base and burgeoning poverty, continue to hamper South Asia's progress.

The region is sufficiently endowed with natural resources, although their distribution is skewed countrywise. In terms of mineral resources, India's reserves are extensive and diversified, Bangladesh has huge reserves of natural gas and coal, while Pakistan has reserves of coal, natural gas and crude oil. Natural resources such as rubber, bauxite and marble are found in Nepal, Bhutan and Sri Lanka. Forest resources, which cover 19 per cent of the total area, are scattered throughout the subcontinent. But of the total land area, the forest area covers 8 per cent of the land area in Bangladesh, 35 per cent in Nepal, 59 per cent in Bhutan and 22 per cent in India. The region is also rich in biodiversity.

Environmental issues

There are a plethora of environmental problems facing the region, among which are destruction of forest, soil, aquifers, reefs, fisheries and biological species; pollution of air, land, subterranean and marine resources through human and industrial activities; and unsustainable environments caused by both anthropogenic activities and natural disasters (Table 14.8).

Among the principal causes of environmental degradation in the subcontinent are: demographic pressure, which has worsened the man–land ratio, causing severe strain on the ecological support base; developmental activities, which have resulted in indiscriminate attacks on the natural resource base; absence of adequate environmental legislation or the failure to implement such legislation to guarantee minimum protection to the environment; and natural disasters, whose frequency and ferocity appear to have increased in recent decades. The impact of any one of these factors is bad enough but the cumulative effect is proving to be disastrous. Table 14.8 shows that, although South Asian economies are characterized by the predominance of the agricultural sector, the percentage of irrigated land is somewhat less, except for Pakistan (81 per cent). The impact of the greenhouse effect on the availability of croplands, cropping patterns, crop productivity, human settlement, rainfall and its special distribution, to name just a few, will become a major concern for all the countries of the region. Finally, most of these environmental problems link up with the desperate poverty of the people in South Asia; for want of any viable alternatives for sustaining their livelihoods, they have no choice but to denude and destroy the very land, forests and water resources that they live on –little realizing that these resources are not everlasting ('South Asia and the United States', 1994).

Rapid economic growth in the region over the past decade has created unprecedented opportunities for poverty reduction. From a global change mitigation perspective, rapid economic growth fuelled by coal poses an obvious challenge and in particular India is now the world's fourth largest emitter of CO_2. Between 1990 and 2004, emissions increased by 97 per cent (UNDP, 2007–08). The carbon stock in the forest biomass is huge in India (Table 14.9).

The emission of CO_2 is a major cause for climate change and it results in unsustainability of the environment which threatens the existence of all living beings, indeed the earth itself. Hence, the UN Millennium Development Goals (MDGs) include an environmental sustainability measure as an important goal to achieve. South Asia, which has a peculiar topography and biodiversity, should consider this issue seriously. Maldives, an island nation, will be one of the first to be affected, with rising sea levels, and the possibility of becoming environmental refugees

Table 14.8 State of the environment

	Afghanistan	Bangladesh	Bhutan	India	Maldives	Nepal	Pakistan	Sri Lanka
Land area 000 sq.km 2005	652.1	130.2	–	2973.2	–	143.0	770.9	64.6
Forest area								
1990	2.0	6.8	–	21.5	–	33.7	3.3	36.4
2005	1.3	6.7	–	22.8	–	25.4	2.5	29.9
Arable land								
1990	12.1	30.1	–	54.8	–	16.0	26.6	13.5
2005	12.1	26.3	–	53.7	–	16.5	27.6	14.2
Agicultural land % of land area								
1990–92	58.3	73.5	–	60.9	–	29.0	33.7	36.2
2003–05	58.3	69.3	–	60.6	–	29.5	35.2	36.5
Irrigated land % of crop land								
1990–92	33.9	33.8	–	28.3	–	43.0	78.5	28.0
2001–03	33.8	54.3	–	32.7	–	47.2	81.1	34.4
Average annual deforestation % 1990–2005	2.3	0.1	–	–0.4	–	1.6	1.6	1.2

Source: World Bank (2007b).

Table 14.9 *Carbon dioxide emissions and stocks*

	Afghanistan	Bangladesh	Bhutan	India	Maldives	Nepal	Pakistan	Sri Lanka
Total (Mt CO_2)								
1990	–	15.4	0.1	681.7	0.2	0.6	68.0	3.8
2004	–	37.1	1.4	1342.1	0.7	3.0	125.6	11.5
Annual change %, 1990–2004	–	10.1	15.9	6.9	26.5	27.3	6.0	14.8
Share of world total %								
1990	–	0.1	–	3.0	–	–	0.3	–
2004	–	0.1	–	4.6	–	–	0.4	–
Carbon intensity of energy								
1990	–	1.20	–	1.89	–	0.11	1.57	0.68
2004	–	1.63	–	2.34	–	0.34	1.69	1.22
Carbon intensity of growth								
1990	–	0.12	–	0.48	–	0.03	0.39	0.09
2004	–	0.15	–	0.44	–	0.08	0.41	0.15
CO_2 emissions from forest biomass, 1990–2005	–	1.2	-7.3	-40.8	–	-26.9	22.2	3.2
Carbon stocks in forest biomass, 2005	–	31.0	345.0	2343.0	–	485.0	259.0	40.0

Source: UNDP (2007–08).

Table 14.10   Environmental sustainability index (ESI) scores and ranking

	ESI rank	ESI score
Afghanistan	–	–
Bangladesh	114	44.1
Bhutan	43.1	53.5
India	101	45.2
Maldives	–	–
Nepal	85	47.7
Pakistan	131	39.9
Sri Lanka	79	48.5

Source: Esty et al. (2005).

is high. The environment sustainability index (ESI), prepared with the help of Yale University in 2005, reveals some of the critical determinants of environmental performance. In Table 14.10 the ESI scores and rank of South Asian countries is given. The ESI score quantifies the likelihood that a country will be able to preserve valuable environmental resources effectively over a period of several decades. It evaluates a country's potential to avoid major environmental deterioration. The Himalayan country, Bhutan is the only country in South Asia that has a score above 50, and Pakistan, with less than 40, has the lowest score. These scores help us to compare the environmental systems with regard to reducing environmental stress and human vulnerability to environmental stress, societal and institutional capacity to respond to environmental challenges, and global stewardship. Based on this analysis it can be inferred that Bhutan and Nepal have a moderate environmental system and stress, high vulnerability and low capacity, and above-average stewardship; Bangladesh, India, Pakistan and Sri Lanka have a low system score: moderate stress, vulnerability, capacity and stewardship (Esty et al., 2005).

Demographic profile
Table 14.11 gives the demographic profile for the South Asian countries, which provides both a long- and a short-term process of development. High levels of fertility characterize the South Asian regions. The crude birth rate (CBR) has declined, but only marginally. The total fertility rate (TFR) was higher than replacement levels of fertility, that is, TFR = 2.1. There is no significant change in the growth rate of the labour force in the region with the exception of Sri Lanka. Most of the countries are characterized by an agrarian economy. At the current growth rate, the population of India will double by 2047, Pakistan by 2038, Bangladesh by

Table 14.11 Demographic profile

	India	Pakistan	Bangladesh	Nepal	Sri Lanka	Bhutan	Maldives	South Asia (weighted average)
Population (in millions)								
1960	442	50	51	9	10	1.0	0.1	563
2001	1,071	152	137	26	20	2.1	0.3	1,408
Population doubling date (at current growth rate) 2003	2047	2038	2039	2036	2080	2035	2031	2047
Crude birth rate (per 1000 live births)								
1970	40	43	46	42	29	42	40	41
2003	24	36	29	33	16	35	36	26
% decline (1970–2003)	40	16	37	21	45	17	10	37
Crude death rate (per 1000 live births)								
1970	17	18	21	22	8	22	17	17
2003	8	10	8	10	7	9	6	8
% decline (1970–2003)	53	44	62	55	13	59	65	52
Total fertility rate								
1960	6.0	7.0	6.7	6.0	5.4	6.0	7.0	6.1
2003	3.0	5.0	3.4	4.2	2.0	5.0	5.3	3.3
% decline (1960–2003)	50	29	49	30	63	17	24	46
Life expectancy at birth (in year)								
1960	44	43	40	38	62	37	44	44
2003	63	63	63	62	74	63	67	63

319

Table 14.11 (continued)

	India	Pakistan	Bangladesh	Nepal	Sri Lanka	Bhutan	Maldives	South Asia (weighted average)
Infant mortality rate								
1970	127	117	145	165	65	156	157	144
2003	63	81	46	61	13	70	55	63
Under-five mortality (per 1000 live births)								
1970	202	181	239	250	100	267	255	235
2003	87	103	69	82	15	85	72	86
Maternal mortality ratio reported (per 100,000 live births) 2000	540	500	380	740	92	420	110	516
Total labour force (in millions)								
1980	300	29	40	7	5	–	–	382
2003	473	56	71	12	9	–	–	620
Female labour force (% of labour force), 2003	154	17	31	5	3	–	–	210
% annual growth in labour force, 1990–2003	2.1	2.7	2.1	2.2	2.0	–	–	2.2

Source: Mahbub ul Haq Human Development Center (2005).

2039, Nepal by 2036, Sri Lanka by 2080, Bhutan by 2035, and Maldives by 2031.

The demographic scenario that unfolds is therefore forbidding in the magnitudes that emerge. The new high-yielding varieties that are likely to be developed and the second green revolution, which is being predicted on the basis of ongoing international research, would suggest that these yield levels could well be within the reach of these countries. But almost all these increases will have to come from increases in the productivity of already cultivated land. This would imply more-intensive farming, higher inputs of agro-chemicals and more irrigation, all of which will lead to environmental stresses of various types.

Another consequence of the rapidly growing population is the corresponding increase in the economically active population and the large cohorts of new entrants to the workforce. If all countries of the region are unable to achieve and sustain high rates of economic growth sufficient to absorb the growing workforce in gainful employment in each of their economies, not only will there be social unrest and instability in the country itself but also the movement of population across national borders which has already became a problem in the region, is likely to intensify and become a serious destabilizing factor. The rate of economic growth of 6–7 per cent should be quite sufficient to absorb a workforce that is growing at the rate of 2.1 per cent (India), 2.7 per cent (Pakistan), 2.1 per cent (Bangladesh), 2.2 per cent (Nepal) and 2.0 per cent (Sri Lanka), allowing for the increases in the productivity of labour and the rise in real wages.

Life expectancy at birth shows the levels of the long-term development process. It varies within the region, with the highest of 74 (Sri Lanka) to the lowest of 62 (Nepal). The infant mortality rate is the highest in Pakistan (81) and the lowest in Sri Lanka (13). The under-five mortality ranges from 103 in Pakistan to 15 in Sri Lanka, compared to the regional average of 86. The maternal mortality ratio shows the dynamics of health services in the society. It is highest in Nepal (740) and India (540) compared to the lowest figure of 92 in Sri Lanka.

Education and health profiles
Tables 14.12 and 14.13 present the education and health profiles. With the exception of Sri Lanka, the other countries indicate one major deficiency in the foundation of basic human capital required for development – the relatively poor level of health and education. In South Asian countries, other than Sri Lanka, this component can have a critical impact in accelerating the demographic transition and development; in general, female literacy is well below the average for low-income countries. Enrolment in primary and secondary schools is not satisfactory in countries such as

Table 14.12 Education profile

	India	Pakistan	Bangladesh	Nepal	Sri Lanka	Bhutan	Maldives	South Asia (weighted average)
Adult literacy rate %								
1970	34	21	24	13	77	–	91	32
2003	61	49	41	49	90	47	97	58
Male literacy rate (% age 15 and above)								
1970	47	40	47	22	86	–	–	47
2003	73	62	50	63	92	61	97	70
Female literacy rate (% age 15 and above)								
1970	19	5	9	3	68	–	–	17
2003	48	35	31	35	89	34	97	45
Combined enrolment for all level (%)								
1980	40	19	30	28	58	7	–	37
2002/03	60	35	53	61	69	49	75	57
Public expenditure in education (as % of GNP)								
1960	2.3	1.1	0.6	0.4	3.8	–	–	2.0
2000–02	4.1	1.8	2.4	3.4	1.3	5.2	3.9	3.6

Source: Mahbub Ul Haq Human Development Center (2005).

Table 14.13   Health profiles

	India	Pakistan	Bangladesh	Nepal	Sri Lanka	Bhutan	Maldives	South Asia (weighted average)
Population with access to safe water (%)								
1990–96	81	60	84	44	46	58	96	78
2002	86	90	75	84	78	62	84	85
Population access to sanitation (%)								
1990–96	16	30	35	6	52	70	66	22
2002	30	54	48	27	91	70	58	35
Population per doctor (in thousands), 1990–2004	51	66	23	5	43	5	78	49
Public expenditure on health (as % of GDP), 2000	0.9	0.9	1.5	1.6	1.8	3.7	6.3	1.0
Birth attended by trained health personnel (%), 1995–2003	43	23	14	11	97	24	70	38

Table 14.13 (continued)

	India	Pakistan	Bangladesh	Nepal	Sri Lanka	Bhutan	Maldives	South Asia (weighted average)
Child immunization rate (% of children under age one)								
Measles 2003	67	61	77	75	99	88	96	68
DPT 2001	70	67	85	78	99	95	98	72
Low birth weight infants (%), 1998–2003	43	23	14	11	97	24	70	38
Prevalence of anaemia in pregnant women (%), 1980–2000	52	37	53	65	39	30	–	50
People living with HIV/AIDS adult (% age 15–49), 2003	0.9	0.1	<0.20	0.3	<0.10	–	–	–

Source: Mahbub ul Haq Human Development Center (2005).

Pakistan (35), and Bhutan (49). The expenditure pattern in the educational sector is also not satisfactory – with the exception of Bhutan, all countries are spending 2–4 per cent of GNP on education.

The health profile (Table 14.13) is also not good, although there has been a significant improvement from the late 1990s to early 2000. Access to sanitation is very low in Nepal (27 per cent) and India (30 per cent) compared with the other countries. Population per doctor and nurse indirectly shows the health status of the country. Anaemia status of the women plays a crucial role for the survival status of the children. As per the table, pregnant women aged 15–48 with anaemia is higher in India, that is, 52 per cent. The attainment of health-related MDGs in South Asia is not satisfactory, and the accessibility and availability of health services generally in the region is quite poor.

Poverty and income distribution

Human resource development has to be seen in the context of the high incidence of absolute poverty in South Asia. As a whole the region has nearly 500 million people who live in absolute poverty, that is, about 40 per cent of the world's poor. Table 14.14 provides some relevant indicators for the countries of the region. With the process of development, Sri Lanka has achieved a significant level of poverty reduction. Table 14.14 also shows that there was a drastic variation between urban and rural poverty levels. The international standard also shows the same trend.

Trends in resource flow to South Asia

Over the last decade, the flow of private capital to South Asia has changed markedly (Table 14.15). In contrast to the beginning of the 1990s, when private debt flows comprised the majority of total private capital to the region, non-debt flows accounted for over 70 per cent by the end of the decade. A primary component of these non-debt flows has been foreign direct investments. Empirical evidence has shown that FDI has a positive impact on the economic growth of host countries, more so than other types of extreme flows and domestic investment, as a result of various inter-related factors including improvements in productivity, technology transfer and promotion of exports.

In response to these measures and owing to improving macroeconomic fundamentals more generally, the flow of FDI to South Asian countries has increased over the past decades. Most of these flows have originated from either the developed countries or the newly industrialized countries of East and South East Asia. The United States and Europe have been the main providers of FDI to India and Pakistan during the 1990s, while Japan, Hong Kong, Korea and Malaysia have made an impact in

Table 14.14   *Poverty and income distribution*

Region	National poverty line				International poverty line				
	Survey year	Rural	Urban	National	Survey year	Population below $1 per day	Poverty gap at $1 a day, %	Population below $2 per day	Poverty gap at $2 a day, %
India	1999–2000	30.2	24.7	28.6	1999–2000	34.7	8.2	79.9	35.3
Pakistan	1998–1999	35.9	24.2	32.6	2004	17.0	3.1	73.6	26.1
Bangladesh	2000	53.0	36.6	49.8	2000	36.0	8.1	82.8	36.3
Sri Lanka	1995–96	27.0	15.0	25.0	2002	5.6	0.8	41.6	11.9
Nepal	2003–04	34.6	9.6	30.9	2003–04	24.1	5.4	68.5	26.8

Source: World Bank (2008).

Table 14.15   *Foreign direct investment (US$ million)*

	Net inflows		Net outflows	
	1990	2005	1990	2005
Afghanistan	–	–	–	–
Bangladesh	0.0	1.3	0.0	0.0
India	0.1	0.8	0.0	0.2
Nepal	0.2	0.0	0.0	–
Pakistan	0.6	2.0	0.0	0.1
Sri Lanka	0.5	1.2	0.0	0.0

Source: World Bank (2007b).

Bangladesh and Sri Lanka (World Bank, 1997). Annual average growth rates were also among the fastest in the developing world, increasing from 25 per cent per year to 31 per cent over the last two decades, attesting to increasing and rapid financial integration. In relative terms, however, the increase in FDI to South Asia has been more modest, accounting for less than half of a per cent of regional GDP during the 1990s, compared to 2.7 per cent for East Asia, 1.9 per cent for Latin America and 7.4 per cent for Sub-Saharan Africa.

Trends in exchange rate in relation to the dollar (US$)
Over a period of time the value of the dollar has increased against the currencies of other countries, with the exception of Maldives. The exchange rate between the rufiyaa and the dollar has remained constant for a long period. The flow exchange rate between the dollar and other currencies is shown in Table 14.16. The table indicates that there is a devaluation of currencies among the South Asian countries, which is partly responsible for the slower pace of economic development.

Conclusions
This chapter has examined the regional dimensions of the linkage that has implications for either conflict or cooperation among South Asian countries. The current economic trends indicate that the countries are at a turning point that can take them on a path leading to a 7 to 8 per cent growth rate. The outlook for the short term appears to confirm these trends. The economic reforms on which all these countries are embarking depend on the macroeconomic foundations. Nevertheless, a poor social infrastructure and the low level of human resource development in all the countries with the exception of Sri Lanka will impose severe constraints.

Table 14.16   Exchange rates to the dollar (annual average)

Regions	Currency	1995	1996	1997	1998	1999	2000	2001	2002	2003
India	Indian Rupee (Rs/Re)	33.4	35.5	37.1	42.5	43.3	45.8	47.7	48.4	46.1
Pakistan	Pakistan Rupee (PRe/PRs)	31.5	35.9	40.9	44.9	49.1	50.1	58.4	61.4	58.5
Bangladesh	Taka (Tk)	40.2	40.9	42.7	45.4	47.8	50.3	54.0	57.4	57.9
Bhutan	Ngultrum (Nu)	31.4	34.3	35.8	38.4	42.6	43.6	46.4	48.2	47.9
Maldives	Rufiyaa (Rf)	11.8	11.8	11.8	11.8	11.8	11.8	12.2	12.8	12.8
Nepal	Nepalese Rupee (Ne/NRs)	51.9	56.7	58.0	66.0	68.2	68.8	73.7	76.7	77.9
Sri Lanka	SL Rupee (SLRe/SLRs)	51.3	55.3	59.0	64.6	70.4	75.9	89.4	95.7	96.5

Source: Asian Development Bank (2003).

Absolute poverty is still high in all countries. Demographically, population growth will be high to moderate in most countries, again with the exception of Sri Lanka, resulting in continuing pressure of population on scarce resources and environment, which is already under great stress. This creates conditions which if they persist without rapid amelioration can result in political instability and social unrest within countries, spilling over to the region as a whole.

The state of the environment in South Asia resembles the familiar features of a poor region in which the population is burgeoning and low-income livelihoods in increasing number are being supported using technologies that are at low levels of productivity. The combination is leading to environmental degradation of a high order. The degradation of these ecosystems is causing serious economic and environmental problems for all these countries. The resulting poverty and economic deprivation are partly responsible for the cross-border migration.

The South Asian region has the capability to improve on its current economic performance and reach and sustain the highest rates of economic growth in the region of 7 per cent and above. Such a growth rate will lead to a rapid alleviation of poverty and more than quadruple per capita income by the end of three decades. The social and economic improvements that result from such a process of growth will contribute to political and social stability within the nations, promote trade and economic exchange among the countries, and create conditions conducive to intraregional peace and stability.

In sum, rapid economic growth for South Asia as a whole is an essential condition for peace and stability in the region. Achieving and sustaining

high rates of growth require a high level of regional economic cooperation, which in turn can transform the present conflict-ridden inter-country
relations.

References

Asian Development Bank (2001), *Asian Development Outlook 2001*, Oxford: Oxford
University Press.
Asian Development Bank (2003), *Asian Development Outlook 2003*, Oxford: Oxford
University Press.
Asian Development Bank (2004), *Asian Development Outlook 2004*, Oxford: Oxford
University Press.
Asian Development Bank (2009), *Asian Development Outlook 2009*, Oxford: Oxford
University Press.
Esty, Daniel, M. Levy, T. Srebotnjak and A. de Sherbinin (2005), *Environmental
Sustainability Index: Benchmarking National Environmental Stewardship*, New Haven, CT:
Yale Center for Environmental Law and Policy.
Mahbub ul Haq Development Center (2001), *Human Development in South Asia 2001*,
Oxford: Oxford University Press.
Mahbub ul Haq Development Center (2003), *Human Development in South Asia 2003*,
Oxford: Oxford University Press.
Mahbub ul Haq Human Development Center (2005), *Human Development in South Asia
2005*, Oxford: Oxford University Press.
South Asia and the United States (1994), *After the Cold War: A Study Mission Report*, New
York: Asia Society.
UNDP (United Nations Development Programme) (2000), *Human Development Report
2000*, Oxford: Oxford University Press.
UNDP (United Nations Development Programme) (2004), *Human Development Report
2004*, Oxford: Oxford University Press.
UNDP (United Nations Development Programme) (2007–08), *Human Development Report
2008*, Oxford: Oxford University Press.
World Bank (1997), *World Development Report 1997: The State in a Changing World*,
Washington, DC: World Bank.
World Bank (2003), *World Development Report 2003*, Oxford: Oxford University Press and
Washington, DC: World Bank.
World Bank (2007a), *World Development Report 2007*, Oxford: Oxford University Press and
Washington, DC: World Bank.
World Bank (2007b), *World Development Indicators 2007*, Washington, DC: World Bank.
World Bank (2008), *World Development Report 2008*, Oxford: Oxford University Press and
Washington, DC: World Bank.

15 Transplanting the meritocracy in India: creating a shared corporate vision at the local and global levels
Nicholas P. Robinson and Prescott C. Ensign

Introduction

In 1492 Christopher Columbus, himself thought to be of Jewish descent, navigated the Atlantic Ocean to become the first Western European to step foot in the Americas (Vizenor, 1992). With technology developed by Muslims to navigate the seas in previously Islamic Spain in hand, and a crew of sailors from the Mediterranean region, a crossroads of sorts for Western cultures, he successfully undertook one of history's most momentous journeys. It is unsurprising to the modern diversity management scholar that Columbus came from Spain, a country that had benefited from hundreds of years of diversity before the tyrannical Spanish inquisition began. In fact, throughout human civilization the interaction of people of different races, religious creeds, cultures, nationalities and even sexes has allowed humankind to hurtle beyond previous highs and accomplish greater feats. Like Islamic Spain, the precursor to Columbus's Spain, a place where three major world religions (Judaism, Islam and Christianity) melded and meshed, India today is entering its golden age – Hindus, Muslims, Sikhs, and even notable Christian and Jewish minorities work together in one of the world's most ethnically, linguistically and culturally diverse regions.

If India is to benefit from this diversity the country must, like Islamic Spain, harness its differences and emphasize its common traits in order to succeed. Indian companies, in particular, are faced with the surmountable challenge of overcoming prevailing caste, racial, religious and linguistic differences in order to sell India to the world. The challenge at hand is to minimize the inhibitive effect that these divisions have on companies in the subcontinent while developing a common vision that can turn caste, religious, ethnic and even linguistic divisions into sources of creativity and managerial prowess. This means overcoming class prejudice, racism, linguistic preferences and even religious biases to produce an organization that is rooted in meritocracy. If managed effectively, Indian companies may be faced with the opportunity of the century – an opportunity to show the world how corporate diversity can be translated into ingenuity, and how difference can translate into opportunity.

Much has already been written about the miracle of the modern Indian Republic's government – a bureaucracy that manages and mitigates the diversity of the Indian nation. India has survived fifty years, despite separatist movements and ethnic and religious conflict, given the strength of the nation's constitution and institutions. The vision of Mahatma Gandhi, a man who sought to eliminate the caste system and unite feuding factions into one state, has been a rallying point for India. Indeed, a strong national vision is the cornerstone of a strong nation – likewise corporations require strong corporate visions if they wish to endure organizational changes and manage diversity.

Few studies have examined how multinational corporations (MNCs) operating in India can manage these differences and create visions that create a level of consistency between individual, organizational and societal values (De Anca and Vazquez, 2007). It is the argument of this chapter that the values embraced by the Indian government (through its constitution, policies and institutions) are a good starting point for organizations that wish to overcome the friction created by prejudice in the subcontinent. In fact, MNCs must draft vision statements that are consistent with the values of the Indian Republic in order to achieve consistency among the three levels (individual, organizational and societal) of stakeholders (ibid.). The values elaborated in the Indian constitution can be viewed as an example of the societal aspirations of Indians and must therefore be studied carefully.

In the first part of this chapter a demographic survey of India will be conducted in order to illustrate that diversity in India is multi-layered; the benefits of this diversity will then be discussed. Unlike the United States where diversity is largely a question of race, or Europe where diversity has traditionally been largely a question of language and culture, India's diversity is racial, religious, linguistic and even class based all at once. Further, the breadth and range of diversity is greater than one would find in many other countries given that people who are polar opposites in one sense or another work side by side. Then, the chapter will analyse and discuss some of the innovations of the Indian constitution and reasons for these innovations. The constitution was drafted in order to ensure that India succeeded in its quest to become a cohesive modern nation. Greater attention will be paid to issues identified by this document and other sources that illustrate practices and social divisions that were perceived as being particularly problematic. Finally, a discussion of how an MNC might want to go about drafting an enduring vision statement that can assist in achieving corporate goals will be offered, along with some examples of past problems faced by MNCs in India. Designing a corporate vision, and a vision as to how the company will manage Indian diversity, is essential to long-term success.

Practitioners and academics alike will benefit from a greater understanding of the problems and opportunities posed by diversity in India, and will learn how to draft a simple vision statement that can unify an Indian subsidiary and mitigate the friction caused by differences in the workplace. Case studies, corporate vision statements and other policy statements, and academic research will be meshed to illustrate how diversity in the theoretical realm is linked to diversity in the practical realm. Finally, the chapter will discuss the past successes of Indian diversity and the hope that the world has for India's experiment in managing cultural difference. Like Islamic Spain, the successful harnessing of India's diversity can be a source of inspiration to the world and an asset to profit-driven corporations with operations in the subcontinent.

Benefits of diversity

Talent, technology and tolerance. Creativity guru Richard Florida of the University of Toronto perhaps puts it best when he describes these characteristics as the 3 Ts of creative places (Florida, 2002, p. 292). Florida, himself a proponent of workplace diversity, has spent years analysing the effect that diversity has on creativity and has concluded that creative adaptable companies are also companies that value diversity and thrive on change. Diversity, according to Florida, is something that highly skilled creative people 'value in all its manifestations' and members of the creative class, those professionals and intellectuals who turn ordinary companies into extraordinary centres of best practices, 'strongly favour organizations and environments in which they feel that anyone can fit in and can get ahead' (p. 79). In order to attract and retain the best and brightest, companies must attract talented people – people who 'defy classification based on race, ethnicity, gender, sexual preference or appearance' – while creating an environment that is 'open to differences' (p. 79). Diversity, according to Florida, is just one indicator to skilled professionals and other creative workers that a meritocracy, a system that rewards those who deserve to be rewarded, is in place (p. 79).

This being said, it is little wonder why a country like Canada, with its large immigrant population and reputation for tolerance, ranks 11th in Florida's creativity index and scores correspondingly high in terms of tolerance, while India, on the other hand, scores a meagre 41st in global creativity on the same scale (Florida 2005, pp. 275–7). Despite the nation's incredible diversity, ethnic, linguistic, religious and even caste-based divisions have hampered creativity in the subcontinent and stand as a potential barrier to the country's drive to become the next economic superpower. Outside of India, Indian engineers and professionals thrive and continue to make invaluable contributions to the economies of many Western countries, including Canada and the United States. Most notably, Indo-Canadians and Indo-Americans have taken a lead in the software industry (Florida, 2002, p. 80). In fact, 'the movement of talented people from India to the United States during the 1990s represented a financial transfer to the United States equivalent to 'one-third of current Indian tax receipts' (Florida, 2005, p. 84). Similarly, in India itself the software industry has become a booming business accounting for 'more than 25$ billion in software exports in 2003' and internationally renowned information technology clusters have developed in cities like Bangalore (ibid., pp. 178–9; Ramachandran and Sougata, 2005). Further, Westernized Indians are returning to build meritocratic software firms similar to those that can be found in Silicon Valley, California, Waterloo, Ontario and Cambridge, Massachusetts. 'India's budding class of entrepreneurs and high-tech businesses is simultaneously modernizing the culture, bringing Silicon Valley business norms and lifestyles to a once-traditional environment' (Florida, 2005, pp. 178–9). This transplantation of business values is an important element of India's future success, given that some traditional norms could be considered inhibitive to the development of a meritocratic business culture that rewards excellence. In order for India to compete globally, the nation will have to move away from some cultural practices that may be inhibitive to economic development and build more organizations that hold the same meritocratic values as Indo-Americans in the Silicon Valley have enjoyed. According to Florida, this transformation has already begun:

> By establishing high-tech companies back home, returning immigrants bring modern business techniques and cultural practices to their home countries. As in the United States and elsewhere, this causes much chafing on the part of established social and economic interests. But it's hard to see how economic and therefore human development can take place without it. My colleagues from India tell me that new software firms in Bangalore are helping to break the old castelike system of social relations and establish more democratic and egalitarian business and social cultures. (2005, p. 109)

The gradual erosion (or subordination) of cultural values that are problematic to the creation of a meritocracy is therefore a critical element of economic and social development and should factor in as an important goal for MNCs that wish to transform themselves into centres of excellence (Ensign et al., 2000). In the case of India, the nation's diversity, as defined by religion, ethnicity, caste and language, poses a challenge as cultural norms might make cooperation between certain groups difficult. The issue of caste is particularly problematic and can be likened to the issue of race in the United States. Like in the US, Indian companies are faced with the challenge of creating a cohesive workforce because of prevailing cultural perceptions.

These perceptions pose a serious challenge because one 'must work effectively with people who are different from you' in order to succeed in the marketplace (Gomez-Mejia et al. 2001 [2004], p. 102). Diversity in the workforce, with described characteristics such as 'race, ethnicity, and gender has important effects on how people relate to one another' (ibid., p. 109). It is vital to 'recognize that, for the most part, these categories of diversity are important not because of intrinsic differences between these groups and other people, but rather because of attributed differences' (ibid., p. 110). The perceptions that people have of other individuals inform their opinions and affect their behaviour towards them. The challenge is 'learning how to take advantage of this diversity while fostering cooperation and cohesiveness among dissimilar employees' (ibid., p. 102). Given that 'people with different experiences may interpret reality very differently', the manager must understand the factors that influence perceptions and interfere with the creation of a cohesive workforce (ibid., p. 102). Learning to manage 'workforce diversity in a way that both respects the employee and promotes a shared sense of corporate identity and vision is one of the greatest human resource challenges facing organizations today' (ibid., p. 102).

This is equally true of immigrant societies, such as those of the Americas, as well as those regions that are inherently diverse, such as in Europe or the Indian subcontinent. The fact that both Europe and India enjoy immense diversity in close proximity has yielded comparisons between the two regions. In contrast to the United States, 'India and the European countries share, every few hundred kilometres, a new border, a new language, a new set of laws and regulations, new cultural identities and new habits' (Ulrich et al., 2000, p. 181). The diversity found in both India and Europe could be either an advantage or a disadvantage depending on whether these regions are able to utilize their 'multiplicity to its advantage' (ibid., p. 181). Similarly, some authors argue that with 'the increasing differentiation of the worldwide markets, the multiplicity should translate into strength . . . due to the trend of decentralizing functions and resources of corporations to economically favourable locations' (ibid., p. 181). In other words, a diverse workforce may be better equipped to solve novel problems and work in a globalized world. In fact, taking actions to develop a diverse workforce can be justified with at least three business arguments: (i) globalization will demand a more diverse workforce that can approach problems with a more international perspective; (ii) local markets can be better served through a diverse workforce than with a uniform work-force; and (iii) increased diversity leads to greater creativity, improves organizational problem solving, and increases the organization's flexibility (Gomez-Mejia et al., 2001 [2004], p. 106). These three possible benefits have corresponding challenges that must also be addressed. Challenges such as 'appropriately valuing employee diversity, balancing individual needs with group fairness, coping with resistance to change, dealing with backlash, ensuring open communication channels, avoiding employee resentment, retaining valued performers, and managing competition for opportunities' must be addressed (ibid., p. 106).

Diversity itself has to be understood in terms of the effects that it has on employees and their behaviours. In fact, in order to approach any of the challenges described above one must understand how stakeholders relate to one another in a diverse setting. This means understanding the characteristics of those in the office and their perceptions. Diversity consists both of 'individual characteristics over which a person has little or no control' including 'biologically determined characteristics such as race, sex, age, and certain physical attributes, as well as the family and society into which we are born' (ibid., p. 103). Second, diversity consists of 'characteristics that people can adopt, drop, or modify during their lives through conscious choice and deliberate efforts' such as 'work background, income, marital status, political beliefs, geographic location, and education' (ibid., p. 103). Companies (and even societies) that learn to look beyond these characteristics and 'treat people as individuals, not as representatives of a group' are better able to accommodate diversity and use it for the benefit of the organization (ibid., p. 103).

If diversity is not effectively managed, 'the presence of diversity among employees may have a negative impact on work performance by creating misunderstandings, ill feelings, and a breakdown of productive teamwork' and possibly even 'overt or subtle discrimination' (ibid., p. 104). Further, 'excluding certain people from full participation in an organization because of their group membership is not only illegal, it is counterproductive because it prevents capable and motivated people from making a contribution' (ibid., p. 104). In order to better accommodate management practices that are more geared towards the individual rather than the group many Asian firms are moving towards 'the US-oriented individualistic' approach to human resources management (Zhu et al., 2007, p. 763). Characteristics of this approach such as 'individual fixed-term contracts, individual performance evaluation, individual career development, downsizing and retrenchment, freedom to hire and fire' have become increasingly popular as more communitarian type human resource management styles prove more difficult when dealing with a diverse workforce (ibid., p. 763). This being said, the popularity of more authoritarian management styles in South Asia may stand as a barrier to accommodative diversity management techniques (Miah and Bird, 2007, p. 919). Other authors state that India's unique 'ability to openly accommodate new influences is the basic platform for success' (Ulrich et al., 2000, p. 183). The ability of India's people and businesses to improvise and 'make the best out of often scarce resources, to cope with limited, restricted and very diverse situations is' one of the nation's skills 'par excellence' (ibid., p. 183). The same authors point out that India has already masterfully used diversity management to its benefit with 'its union of states and a vast population composed of diverse cultures, religions and social segments living together' in relative stability (ibid., p. 184). Provided that Indian companies can reproduce the success of the Indian national project, the country's 'diversity-oriented business culture can translate into new business opportunities' and transform India into an example for the world (ibid., p. 185).

Diversity in India
Rapid social, demographic and economic changes are transforming Indian society and changing the nature of diversity in Indian corporations. However, this being said, Indian companies are still faced with the same challenges as always. The 'weaknesses' of Indian societal diversity, such as caste, 'are superimposed on its businesses and industrial organizations and exacerbated' creating an important challenge for Indian business leaders that wish to limit the extent to which factional prejudices might hinder the performance of their firms (Ratnam and Chandra, 1996, p. 76). The approach adopted in tackling this challenge can be 'difficult and easy depending on how diversity is viewed and used' (ibid., p. 76). Eroding existing societal norms that are problematic may be an impervious task while working with existing norms to satisfy organizational stakeholders may be more achievable. In this light, in order to understand the complexities of Indian diversity one must understand diversity in India itself. This diversity is the result of the nation's rich heritage – both colonial and pre-colonial – and is the product of centuries of 'customs and practices' (ibid., p. 76). Caste, language, religion, ethnicity and sex are just some of the markers that define diversity in India.

Caste
Over the course of India's rich and varied history, the caste system (a socio-religious philosophy of sorts), which developed as a result of the interaction of Aryan invaders with Dravidians, evolved (Marquardt et al., 2004, p. 247). The caste system was 'originally conceived as a division of

labour based on ability and included four main *varnas*, or groups: *Brahmin* (priests, teachers), *Kshatriya* (warriors, rulers), *Vaishya* (traders, craftsmen, farmers) and *Shudra* (menial workers and servants) . . . untouchables (also referred to as dalits) were those at the very bottom of this social ladder (Gundling et al., 2007, p. 100). It has been argued that this system is different from a typical class system given that one's caste influences their occupation and other elements of their lifestyle. Further caste divisions have made it difficult for lower-caste members to intermingle and this consequently poses a problem for multinationals that aim to reward the best and brightest. Gandhi, among others, believed that the caste system was obstructive and sought to relieve the untouchables of their suffering by instead referring to them as 'Harijan or "children of God"' (ibid., p. 100). Successive invading Arabs, Turks and Afghans did little to alter the system that renders each person only as worthwhile as their station in life (Marquardt et al., 2004, p. 247).

In the modern Indian corporation, caste still poses a serious barrier to creating a meritocracy as 'the nexus between caste and occupation' still exists and are 'superimposed on the organizational structures in the modern corporation' (Ratnam and Chandra, 1996, p. 82). Ratnam and Chandra state that four broad levels of caste-based hierarchy continue to exist, including senior managers, middle and junior managers, clerical and skilled production and non-production workers, and finally unskilled production workers such as janitors (p. 82). In a sense, the caste system has been transposed onto the modern Indian corporation and remains an important barrier to mobility among workers within those corporations. In fact, there is a 'certain amount of occupational segmentation in some parts of India on religious and caste lines which creates difficulties for commerce and business' and has even hurt local economies in times of border disputes between Indian states (ibid., p. 84).

Beyond this, the caste system has produced a situation where countless people have limited opportunities on the basis of the caste. This has spurred on the debate as to whether 'caste is synonymous with class because of the intricate nexus between economic backwardness and social backwardness' (ibid., p. 85). Numerous scholars argue that the caste system itself is not just a source of backwardness but aggravates the nation's poverty (ibid., p. 86). Indian nationalists have historically 'condemned the evils of caste and caste practices, and advocated social reform and the "uplift" of the untouchable castes, which were then called the Depressed Classes' (Jayal, 2006, p. 58). The system is especially cruel given that even conversion to another religion (for example, Islam, a religion that stresses equality and to some extent condemns caste-based behaviour) does not relieve the individual of the stigma of his/her caste.

Sex
Between 1971 and 1991 the percentage of women in the Indian workforce increased from 14 to nearly 23 per cent (Ratnam and Chandra, 1996, p. 90). This increase is just one indicator of the growing participation of women in the Indian labour market. Despite this, the ratio of females to males has declined over the last century while 'the average family size among urban educated households' has declined, shifting towards the 'nuclear family consisting of wife, husband and immediate children' (ibid., p. 77). Further, 'though women constitute roughly half the population the literacy rate among women is much less than that for men in most states' (ibid., p. 88). Additionally, women perpetuate some of the discrimination that other women suffer as 'mothers-in-law often discriminate viciously against their daughters-in-law' (ibid., p. 88). This being said, low work-force participation rates and societal norms that infrequently place women in management positions make the Indian marketplace very different from that of Western Europe or North America.

Religion
India is perhaps the most religiously diverse state on the planet. Despite being a majority Hindu state (at roughly 80.5 per cent of the population), a notable Muslim minority (at 13.4 per cent of the population) exists along-side 'Christians (2.3 per cent), Sikhs (1.9 per cent), Buddhists (0.8 per cent) and Jains (0.4 per cent)' (Gundling et al., 2007, p. 93). Despite the partition of the subcontinent specifically to accommodate a Muslim state (namely Pakistan and Bangladesh), India currently has more Muslims than either of those countries (Ratnam and Chandra, 1996, p. 83). Tensions between religious groups, especially Sikhs, Muslims and Hindus, often run high and 'the border dispute between' India and Pakistan over 'Kashmir occasionally leads to religious riots in some parts of India' (ibid., p. 83). More importantly, religion plays an important role in the lives of Indians at work. 'In private firms owned by Hindus it is unusual to find Muslims in senior managerial positions' (ibid., p. 84). Further, the principles espoused by Hinduism and Islam dictate lifestyle and influence conduct at work. For Hindus, 'dharma is more than a religion . . . it is a way of life, a guide to individual and social conduct' (Ulrich et al., 2000, p. 9). Likewise, for Muslims the Quran and Sunna (the lifestyle of the Prophet) guide the behaviour of the faithful. In some cases employers will choose to serve neither beef nor pork to employees at the company cafeteria 'because beef is forbidden for Hindus and pork for Muslims' (Gundling et al., 2007, p. 97). Further, to accommodate religious holidays and events, employees are normally entitled to '10 scheduled holidays of their choice in addition to the three national holidays' (ibid., p. 98).

Language

India is a nation of profound linguistic diversity. With '22 official languages' contained within '29 states each with their own distinct traditions and character' the level of linguistic diversity found in India can be compared to the entirety of Europe (ibid., p. 78). 'However, in India this diversity is contained within the boundaries of a single nation' (ibid., p. 78). Local languages, regional dialects and accents further complicate India's linguistic milieu, with 25 languages having 'only 50,000 speakers each in a country with over 900 million population' (Ratnam and Chandra, 1996, p. 93). In fact, strong regional accents even produce difficulty among speakers of the same language when conversing (Gundling et al., 2007, p. 78).

'The 1961 and 1971 censuses listed 1,652 languages as mother tongues spoken in India. These were grouped by linguists into 180 languages that evolved from the following six different ethnic groups that entered India since the dawn of civilization: Negroid, Austric, Sino-Tibetan, Dravidian, Indo-Aryan and others' (Ratnam and Chandra, 1996, p. 91). So contentious is the issue of language in India that the nation's constitution pays considerable attention to the issue. India's constitution provides that the 'the official language of the country is Hindi, but English could be used in communications for a period of 15 years after Independence' (ibid., p. 92).

In fact, the nation's linguistic diversity has been 'politically contentious in chiefly two types of situations: first, when it was proposed that Hindi (spoken by 40% of the population) be designated as the official or national language . . . and second, in the reorganization of the states of the federation on the basis of language' (Jayal, 2006, p. 43). Modern India has seen its states reorganized several times in order to accommodate the nation's linguistic diversity. Most notably, 'Bombay state, where Marathi and Gujarati were the two dominant languages, was split into the two states of Gujarat and Maharashtra' in order to satisfy local interests (Gundling et al., 2007, p. 82). Understandably, English has taken on a particularly important role in India given its status both as an 'important associate language recognized by the Indian constitution' and the second language of a large proportion of the Indian population (ibid., p. 79). The position of English as a language that is not associated with any one particular ethnic or religious group makes it a politically ideal choice as it is perceived as being neutral. For this reason, 'State High Courts and the Central Supreme Court use English only for their proceedings as well as in all documents' (ibid., p. 84). In addition, English is widely used in business and sometimes used exclusively by MNCs operating in India. The role of English as a 'common language' makes it particularly useful when different linguistic groups need to work together in an office setting (ibid., p. 85).

This being said, Indians are educated both in English and in their mother tongue. 'The National Education Movement, sponsored by the Congress . . . endorsed the idea that while the learning of English would be compulsory, it was important for students to be versed in the language and literary traditions of their mother-tongues' (Jayal, 2006, p. 42). Regional languages continue to flourish with, for example, Urdu, the former language of the Indian upper class, enjoying official language status in the state of Jammu and Kashmir, the only majority-Muslim state (ibid., p. 53).

General demographic trends
The impact of government policies that set standards for employment equity (known as affirmative action in the United States) and the Indian education system have slowly begun to transform Indian society. Increasing literacy rates have correlated with higher incidences of unemployment among the 'relatively young (15–29 years of age) and the educated rather than the uneducated' (Ratnam and Chandra, 1996, p. 81). Further, it is argued that 'literacy, industrialization, modernization and affirmative programmes (reservations in education and employment for backward and depressed classes) also contributed to breaking the nexus between caste and occupation' (ibid., p. 87).

India's constitution – a reflection of India's societal aspirations
The Constitution of India presents a unique image of the aspirations of the Indian people and the challenges posed by the nation's diverse population. India, by all accounts, has taken an active approach to managing its diversity by reserving positions in government and the bureaucracy for specific disadvantaged groups (Jayal, 2006, p. 71). Safeguards for members of disadvantaged groups include fixed seats in 'legislative bodies, public employment and public education' and the constitution even requires a watchdog, 'originally called the Special Officer for the Scheduled Castes and Scheduled Tribes, to oversee implementation of safeguards' (ibid., p. 71). More recent amendments to the Indian constitution have produced reservations (known in the United States as affirmative action and in other countries as employment equity) for women, and have decentralized the national government, giving greater power to the states (ibid., p. 71).

Further, the constitution also recognizes the principle of 'legal equality as a basic individual right' (under Articles 4–18) and Article 15 prohibits 'discrimination on the grounds of religion, sex, caste or place of birth' (Ratnam and Chandra, 1996, p. 85). Other articles prohibit the cruel practice of untouchability that effectively ostracizes this caste of people from the rest of Indian society and seek to erode the effect of the caste system on Indian society (ibid., p. 85). Multinationals dealing with caste politics in India have experienced resistance from employees in complying with India's prohibition of the rules on caste discrimination, but have been compelled by the fact that caste-based discrimination is against the law (ibid., p. 99). Additional provisions exist in the constitution 'for the advancement of any socially and educationally backward classes of citizens', including certain tribal groups and others (Jayal, 2006, p. 63). However, the government has abandoned the idea of allotting electoral seats for specific religious minorities such as Muslims, Sikhs and Christians (ibid., p. 48). Much like Israel and other multi-religious states, India 'decided to allow religious minorities to follow their separate personal laws in matters relating to marriage, divorce, inheritance and so on' (ibid., p. 49). This being said, compromise and accommodation for religious minorities on the part of the government is a crucial element of India's national philosophy.

Despite India's smorgasbord of languages, the nation's constitution only recognizes 22 official languages, most of which have their own literary tradition (ibid., p. 17; Gundling et al., 2007, p. 78). Indo-Arayan (for example, Sindhi), Dravidian, Austro-Asiatic, Tibeto-Burman and Andamanese languages can all be found in India and are a testament to the country's past influences from the orient, Persia and other civilizations (Jayal, 2006, p. 18). Past attempts to 'promote the spread of the Hindi language' as the national language have created tensions and English has been widely accepted given that 'National unity is more important than the language issue' (ibid., p. 19). India's position on languages therefore represents an important compromise – English is a middle of the road solution that favours no one group. Articles 29 and 30 of the constitution, however, give the right to educational institutions in the language of choice and protect linguistic minorities (ibid., p. 49). Further, the government advances the interests of minority groups through its control of spending programmes and a vast array of state-owned and-managed enterprises (Kimber and Lipton, 2005, p. 192).

India's constitution is an example of improvisation and accommodation in the face of diversity. It is therefore an important model for companies that wish to create a true meritocracy in the face of diversity. Multinational firms in India can leverage their practices internationally in managing diverse workforces in other parts of the world.

Creating a common vision

According to Arredondo, designing a clear and consistent vision of the MNC's values and the role that a diverse workforce will play within that organization is 'fundamental to arriving at a state of multicultural actualization' (Arredondo, 1996, p. 65). A transparent and bold vision can help to align the organization's values with those of the society in which the organization operates and the individuals who define the organization. In other words, the vision must be agreeable to stakeholders at the individual, organizational, and even societal levels in order to succeed (De Anca and Vazquez, 2007). This means attempting to create consistency, as much as possible, between these levels. Differences between cultures and other factors will necessitate that the vision articulated will vary to some degree depending on the place of operations, but certain core values will still have to unite the entire organization at the global level. Further, the values articulated may actually attempt to correct values at any one of the three levels (individual, organizational and societal) that are problematic to the advancement of the MNC's objectives.

The vision statement must be 'plausible', 'aligned with a business rationale' and 'must speak to and about all the primary stakeholders' (Arredondo, 1996, p. 72). Understanding the values and aspirations of Indian society, as defined by the constitution, and understanding the persistence of certain cultural practices that may negatively impact the ability of the corporation to succeed locally are necessary prerequisites. The vision statement should communicate the 'interdependence of people and the viability of a business' while 'articulating the values, purpose, and desired outcomes of an organization' and providing a 'rationale' for action (ibid., p. 68).

In other words, the vision statement must espouse values that provide the impetus for action and stand as the basis for any decision to oppose practices or perceptions that stand in the way of creating a meritocratic work environment. At the same time, the company's local vision must be consistent with the corporation's global vision. The vision statement must communicate the 'importance of human resources and the relationship between people and the success of an organization' (ibid., p. 65). The vision statement can act as an 'anchor' for strategies for change and can catalyse stakeholders towards creating a 'new identity' for the organization (ibid., p. 66). It must elaborate the organization's 'guiding principles' (also known as core beliefs and values) and be a statement of 'hope, optimism and direction' (ibid., p. 67). In order to emphasize the importance of diversity to the organization, the vision statement must go beyond simply tolerating diversity and instead encourage the engagement of 'diversity and integrate it into the work of the organization' (Awbrey, 2007, p. 26). In other words, 'assimilation and separatism do not engage diversity in ways that allow employees to fully contribute their talents' and organizations should therefore attempt to produce vision statements that 'foster a learning perspective on diversity by expanding the potential space that allows interpersonal inquiry to take place between people' (ibid., p.

26). Ensign (2002, p. 156) has concluded that cultural perceptions leading to one having a negative perception of co-workers influence employee expectations, breed distrust and ultimately interfere with the ability of co-workers to engage in interpersonal inquiry and learn from one another. Similarly, other scholars note that closer collaboration between MNC subsidiaries and MNC parent companies is needed to succeed locally and globally (Choy, 2007, p. 15). In this regard, 'there is greater need for management to align organizational development with a more culturally responsive orientation, to enhance effective international human resource management' (ibid., p. 15). This means that organizations and societies will have to seek 'unity in diversity' by learning to not just tolerate differences but use differences to achieve 'broader strategic objectives' (Ratnam and Chandra, 1996, p. 102). In other words, a company must align its corporate vision with that of its individual stakeholders, the broader global organization itself, and the society in which it operates. In Third World nations this is particularly difficult given the 'divergence between the organizational environment and social environment of the community in which the employees live and spend a greater part of their worklife' (ibid., p. 101). For instance, in India though the government may officially condemn caste-based discrimination and outlaw untouchability, the attitudes that are the foundation of these practices are widespread among individual Indians and therefore still pose a challenge for companies that wish to encourage change in this regard.

Foreign headquartered MNCs may influence the local environment 'through their FDI activities' and encourage new management practices (Zhu et al., 2007, pp. 763–4). The US particularly 'plays the so-called leadership role on influencing and forming management philosophies, policies, programmes, practices and processes' and in many nations such as India, US companies can act as catalysts for social change through corporate visions that oppose discriminatory or destructive behaviours (ibid., pp. 763–4). This being said, even a strong vision that is put into practice can encounter a great deal of resistance. According to many management scholars, 'the human capacity to protect diversity and enshrine regional and local interests seems likely to minimize rapid change, especially in the Small and Medium Enterprise (SME) and national corporation arena' (Kimber and Lipton, 2005, p. 205). It is therefore not surprising that many local and foreign MNCs have experienced difficulty in implementing visions that are consistent with the spirit of the Indian constitution – that is, visions that condemn caste, religious and linguistic discrimination and aim to create a meritocratic organization. In this light it would be unreasonable to expect a complete convergence in terms of diversity management practices, but some convergence is desirable (Rowley and Warner, 2006, pp. 400–401). That has not prevented MNCs from developing visions that emphasize meritocracy. Lehman Brothers, for instance, has stated that their vision was to create 'an environment where everybody feels that they can be their best; an organization where employees walk through the doors and feel proud of who they're working for' (Chinnery and Bothwick, 2005, p. 18). Further, one Microsoft management guru has cited developing a vision that creates 'an us versus them mentality' – where 'them' is industry competitors – as one key element of the goal-driven organization (Thielen, 2001). Having an *us versus us* mentality – where employees discriminate among themselves – on the other hand is incredibly problematic and needs to be addressed by the corporate vision statement.

Foreign MNCs entering the Indian market need to address problematic practices and attitudes that are inhibitive to growth and success. For employees it is particularly difficult given that 'on the one hand, they have to adapt to western practices in their current workplaces because of their everyday interaction with overseas counterparts; on the other hand, they are pressured by their families and society to adhere to their Indian roots and traditions' (Gundling et al., 2007, p. 110). The vision statement must therefore perform a balancing act by accounting for individual, organizational and societal values and creating consistency, wherever possible, among these levels. Before drafting a vision statement the organization, including stakeholders at all levels, should ask the following series of questions:

- What organizational *goals* does the MNC wish to achieve?
  Responses:

    1. Corporate profitability and the creation of shareholder value is an important consideration.
    2. Utilize diversity to advance and not hinder corporate objectives.
    3. Healthy relations between all levels of the company and between stakeholders is also important.

- What *values* are necessary in order to achieve those organizational goals?
  Responses:

    1. Value teamwork; a cohesive and motivated workforce will be better able to achieve profit objectives.
    2. For the organization that wishes to accommodate and benefit from diversity, values such as tolerance, inclusiveness,

participation of minority groups, and rewarding those who merit it are all important.
3. Respect and even encourage differences among co-workers.

- What *actions* can be taken to transform those values into a reality?
  Responses:

  1. Offering tailored incentives to those who achieve organizational profit objectives, while disciplining those employees and stakeholders that perpetuate potentially problematic attitudes that are damaging to organizational cohesiveness.
  2. Use affirmative action programmes or reservation programmes to ensure that under-represented groups (for instance women and lower-caste members) that are able to complete certain jobs are awarded positions.
  3. Foster an environment that leads to interaction and intercultural exchanges between groups that would otherwise segregate themselves, for instance through common dining facilities or group activities.

- Are these values *consistent* with the broader values of the society in which the organization operates (in this case India), those of the individual employees and other stakeholders, and those of the entire organization (that is, the head office)?
  Responses:

  1. The MNC's parent is likely most interested in the subsidiary's profitability making this value consistent with its objectives; societal stakeholders are likely keen to see the organization succeed provided it benefits society on the whole; the success of individual stakeholders is intertwined with the success of the organization broadly, but the impact is less direct.
  2. In India resistance should be expected when individual norms clash with corporate and societal norms that stress non-discrimination. Communal spaces designed to accommodate individual employees from all castes, religious and linguistic groups might lead to resistance from upper-caste employees. However, such actions are necessary to create consistency between India's societal objectives (eliminating discrimination, as elaborated in the Indian constitution) and organizational objectives.
  3. Not only is eliminating discrimination and creating a meritorious organization an important priority but it is often also

essential if local subsidiaries are to be in line with the policies of the entire MNC. Discrimination at the local level could produce a public relations nightmare internationally for the company.

Consider both Tata Group, an Indian-based MNC with operations in industries as varied as consulting to tea and automobile manufacturing, and Microsoft Corporation, the US-based software giant with development activities in India. Both of these companies have produced visions that emphasize diversity and draw a connection between it and broader corporate goals such as satisfying stakeholders. Further, both have created a relatively consistent strategy that aligns societal, organizational and individual values. Where problematic individual values – such as those related to racial, caste, linguistic or religious discrimination – conflict with the values of the society and the organization at large, both companies have taken a stand. Microsoft and Tata have made a point of identifying and opposing problematic attitudes in order to improve the chances of creating a true meritocracy (Table 15.1 and 15.2).

Drafting a vision statement that supports an organization's efforts to create a merit-based organization may be simple, but implementing such a vision is often challenging – both to local and foreign MNCs in India. For instance, a British-based MNC with five star hotels operating in India faced a serious problem when trying to treat employees from different groups equitably in accordance with their position at the hotel:

> [S]everal people belonging to a dominant community in the region were hired for junior positions as well. The hotel faced immense problems in making such employees undertake certain tasks considered to be menial. Also, disciplining such employees became a problem because any action against an employee belonging to a dominant community was considered as aggression on the community itself . . . (Ratnam and Chandra, 1996, p. 99)

In other scenarios, simply creating a communal space where employees of different castes could interact proved difficult for an MNC operating in India. When the company chose to offer common cafeteria facilities employees rebelled and some members of higher castes insisted upon being served by the lower castes (ibid., p. 99). In light of this, management took a firm position that 'the hotel could not tolerate discrimination any longer because they not only conflicted with the value system that the hotel wanted to encourage but it was also unlawful' (ibid., p. 96). Similarly, some Indian companies have seen discriminatory practices introduced in lunchrooms. One employee in such a firm was noted as saying that '"the white [US] Sahibs did not mind having lunch with us, but the native, brown [Indian] Sahibs have an aura of superiority about themselves"'

Table 15.1   Tata Group's vision statement and diversity policies

	Corporate vision at Tata Group
Goals	'Our purpose is to improve the quality of life of the communities we serve . . . through leadership in sectors of national economic significance' Tata Group's corporate vision emphasizes the importance of making a contribution to local communities through the company's business activities
Values	'Integrity, understanding, unity, excellence, and responsibility' are Tata's cardinal values. The company elaborates on understanding as 'caring' and showing respect for others and states that unity is involved in creating a cohesive team
Actions	'A Tata company shall provide equal opportunities to all its employees and all qualified applicants for employment without regard to their race, *caste*, religion, colour, ancestry, marital status, sex, age, nationality, disability and veteran status . . . . Human resource policies should promote diversity and equity in the workplace . . . Employee policies and practices shall be administered in a manner that would ensure that in all matters equal opportunity is provided to those eligible and the decisions are merit-based' The company employs practices that encourage employment equity and identifies the barriers that it wishes to eliminate through its policies
Consistency	'Comply with all labour laws and international best practices . . . in accordance with Tata policies' Tata's policies create consistency between the societal goals of eliminating discrimination on the basis of caste, religion, and linguistic group, and the organizational need to develop a meritocratic company that rewards excellence. At the individual level the company's policies are likely a source of friction for employees who wish to impose their cultural and social beliefs on the corporate identity. Caste-conscious Indians would likely pose some resistance to Tata's corporate vision. This being said, individuals in other regions where the company has operations could also resist the policies. Inconsistency may be necessary in order to achieve the company's principle goal of advancing the welfare of the communities in which it operates.

Source: Tata Corporation (2008a and b).

Table 15 2   Microsoft Corporation's vision statement and diversity policies

	Corporate vision at Microsoft Corporation
Goals	'Accountable to our customers, shareholders, partners, and employees by honouring our commitments, providing results, and striving for the highest quality' and 'Thinking and acting globally. Microsoft employs a multicultural workforce that generates innovative decision-making for diverse customers and partners'
	Microsoft envisages a company that works to meet not just shareholder needs, but the needs of all stakeholders including product users and employees. The company aims to provide the best possible service to customers and partners through a multicultural workforce
Values	'As a company, and as individuals, we value integrity, honesty, openness, personal excellence, constructive self-criticism, continual self-improvement, and mutual respect'
	Respect, honesty and openness are all essential to the development of a multicultural workforce that can engage in cross-cultural learning
Actions	'Project Bhasha, a program aimed at accelerating local language computing in India . . .' and 'Attracting, developing, and retaining a diverse workforce . . . Creating a culture and climate of respect and inclusion'
	In India, Microsoft has already begun to develop centres of excellence where Indian software engineers develop products for local and international markets. Through Microsoft's diverse workforce the company can better address the needs of what will one day be the world's largest software market. Further, the company actively recruits the best and brightest from India's universities to work for it in Bangalore and other locations
Consistency	Microsoft's values of respect and openness are consistent with the organization's vision of multicultural offices that can address and respond to global demands. The value of openness may run up against individual cultural values in some Asian countries, even in India, that place more emphasis on authoritarian management styles. Further, respect is a necessary precursor for organizational diversity and this value is consistent with India's societal vision. Again, respect for differences could be in conflict with individual values (against specific castes, linguistic and religious groups) that could be considered discriminatory.

Source: Microsoft Corporation (2008a, b and c).

(ibid., p. 96). Resistance to changes that are considered socially trans-formative are both natural and expected. As with Microsoft and Tata, corporate visions that attempt to eliminate longstanding prejudices and barriers to meritocracy will be confronted with opposition. Successfully implementing such visions is well worth any dissent that may erupt given the enormous benefits, both at the societal and organizational levels, to creating a more equitable workplace. In this light, it can be argued that MNCs have a responsibility to promote values that alleviate the plight of India's most beleaguered communities.

Conclusion

India is a nation with a rich and varied history and a population that is arguably more diverse than that of Europe. Linguistic, religious, caste, and even ethnic considerations define a nation that has over 1 billion people and may some day be the world's largest consumer market. For this reason, MNCs have placed considerable emphasis on succeeding in the Indian market – both because India represents an invaluable source of skilled human resources, as Microsoft and other high-tech firms know, and because it is an important market for selling their wares. India's eco-nomic importance, and the importance of Asia more generally as a driving force of global economic growth, make its study critical to future business leaders. However, succeeding in India will require a better understand-ing of the nation's unique demographics and the barriers that traditional Indian society has imposed. Discrimination on the basis of caste, religion, and even language has had an indelible impact on India's political history and has even had profound influence on the nation's constitution, a docu-ment that can be viewed as representative of India's problems and societal aspirations.

In this light, similar to how India's government has had to navigate traditional barriers to create a vision that attempts to unify a fragmented nation, MNCs operating within India must develop a strong vision that encourages rewarding excellence over community politics. This means introducing and implementing a vision and policies that oppose prob-lematic cultural norms that lead to discrimination and make it difficult for the best and brightest to rise through company ranks. Further, it also means creating a vision that, whenever possible, produces consistency between the values of individual stakeholders such as employees, society at large and the organization's global goals. In other words, the challenge is to eliminate prejudice and discriminatory practices while building a multicultural organization that aims to satisfy stakeholders at all levels (individual, organizational and societal). This chapter proposes that by understanding India's concern for equitable treatment of disadvantaged groups and introducing a vision that plays on these concerns, MNCs can produce the meritocratic culture that is necessary for success in the global marketplace. Further, in many cases foreign parent companies would require merit-based practices, making the decision to impose such policies necessary to meet the organization's demands. MNCs can therefore act as agents of social change by encouraging merit-based practices and opposing discrimination. This attitude is of great benefit both to the company and to local stakeholders – especially considering that these same values are enshrined in India's constitution. Merit-based organizations, according to Richard Florida, attract the best and brightest and are generally more creative (2002, p. 79). Fostering an environment that subordinates discriminatory practices in favour of intercultural exchange and learning may be what India needs to become the next economic superpower.

References

Arredondo, Patricia (1996), *Successful Diversity Management Initiatives: A Blueprint for Planning and Implementation*, London: Sage.

Awbrey, Susan M. (2007), 'The dynamics of vertical and horizontal diversity in organization and society', *Human Resource Development Review*, **6** (1), 7–32.

Chinnery, Christine and Fleur Bothwick (2005), 'Sharing a diversity initiative at Lehman Brothers', *Strategic Communication Management*, **9** (4), 18–21.

Choy, William K.W. (2007), 'Globalisation and workforce diversity: HRM implications for multinational corporations in Singapore', *Singapore Management Review*, **29** (2), 1–19.

De Anca, Celia and Antonio Vazquez (2007), *Managing Diversity in the Global Organization: Creating New Business Values*, New York: Palgrave Macmillan.

Ensign, Prescott C. (2002), 'Reputation and technological knowledge sharing among R&D scientists in the multidivisional, multinational firm', unpublished dissertation, University of Montreal.

Ensign, Prescott C., Julian M. Birkinshaw and Tony S. Frost (2000), 'R&D centres of excellence in Canada', in Ulf Holm and Torben Pedersen (eds), *The Emergence and Impact of MNC Centres of Excellence: A Subsidiary Perspective*, London: Palgrave Macmillan, pp. 131–53.

Florida, Richard (2002), *The Rise of the Creative Class*, New York: HarperCollins.

Florida, Richard (2005), *The Flight of the Creative Class*, New York: HarperCollins.

Gomez-Mejia, Luis R., David B. Balkin, Robert L. Cardy, David E. Dimick and Andrew J. Templer (2001), *Managing Human Resources*, 3rd Canadian edn, (2004), Toronto, ON: Pearson Education Canada.

Gundling, Ernest, Anita Zanchettin and Aperian Global (2007), *Global Diversity: Winning Customers and Engaging Employees within World Markets*, Boston, MA: Nicholas Brealey International.

Jayal, Niraja Gopal (2006), *Representing India: Ethnic Diversity and the Governance of Public Institutions*, New York, NY: Palgrave Macmillan.

Kimber, David and Phillip Lipton (2005), 'Corporate governance and business ethics in the Asia-Pacific region', *Business and Society*, **44** (2), 178–210.

Marquardt, Michael, Nancy Berger and Peter Loan (2004), *HRD in the Age of Globalization: A Practical Guide to Workplace Learning in the Third Millennium*, New York: Basic Books.

Miah, M. Khasro and Allan Bird (2007), 'The impact of culture on HRM styles and firm performance: evidence from Japanese parents, Japanese subsidiaries/joint ventures and

South Asian local companies', *International Journal of Human Resource Management*, **18** (5), 908–23.

Microsoft Corporation (2008a), *Our Mission*, available at: http://www.microsoft.com/about/default.mspx#values (accessed January 30, 2008).

Microsoft Corporation (2008b), *Fostering Local Innovation*, available at: http://www.microsoft.com/india/msindia/unlimited_potential_innovation.aspx (accessed January 30, 2008).

Microsoft Corporation (2008c), *Diversity and Inclusion: Vision and Strategy*, available at: http://www.microsoft.com/about/diversity/vision.mspx (accessed January 30, 2008).

Ramachandran, Kavil and Ray Sougata (2005), 'Creating information technology industrial clusters: learning from strategies of the early and late movers', in Tojo Thatchenkery and Roger R. Stough (eds), *Information Communication Technology and Economic Development: Learning from the Indian Experience*, Chellenham, UK and Northampton, MA, USA: Edward Elgar, pp. 149–66.

Ratnam, C.S. Venkata and V. Chandra (1996), 'Sources of diversity and the challenge before human resource management in India', *International Journal of Manpower*, **17** (4/5), 76–108.

Rowley, Chris and Malcolm Warner (2006), 'Business and management in South East Asia: studies in diversity and dynamism', *Asia Pacific Business Review*, **12** (4), 389–401.

Tata Corporation (2008a), *Tata Code of Conduct 2008*, available at: http://www.tatamail.com/0_our_commitment/corporate_governance/code_of_conduct.htm (accessed January 30, 2008).

Tata Corporation (2008b), *About Us: Values and Purpose*, available at: http://www.tata.com/0_about_us/values_purpose.htm (accessed January 30, 2008).

Thielen, David (2001), 'Ultimate management secrets from former Microsoft superstar', Boardroom Inc., available at: http://www.bottomlinesecrets.com/blpnet/article.html?article_id=14013 (accessed January 30, 2008).

Ulrich, Karl, R.S. Chaudhry and Kishan S. Rana (2000), *Managing Corporate Culture: Leveraging Diversity to Give India a Global Competitive Edge*, New Delhi: Macmillan India.

Vizenor, Gerald (1992), 'Christopher Columbus: lost havens in the ruins of representation', *American Indian Quarterly*, Special Issue: Shamans and Preachers, Color Symbolism and Commercial Evangelism: Reflections on Early Mid-Atlantic Religious Encounter in Light of the Columbian Quincentennial, **16** (4), 521–32.

Zhu, Ying, Malcolm Warner and Chris Rowley (2007), 'Human resource management with "Asian" characteristics: a hybrid people-management system in East Asia', *International Journal of Human Resource Management*, **18** (5), 745–68.

16 Workforce diversity in Iran: some case study evidence of private sector organisations*
Ebrahim Soltani, Hugh Scullion and David Collings

Introduction

From Bach's (2005) point of view, human resource management (HRM) is unitarist (employer and employee interests should coincide) with an emphasis on organisational effectiveness. To enhance organisational effectiveness, HR managers are responsible for overseeing the functions relating to recruitment of capable, flexible and committed people, managing and rewarding their performance and developing their key competencies. While such tasks are far from easy in developed countries, the demand for a highly skilled workforce in developing countries raises a particular dilemma. While developed countries benefit from an inflow of highly trained and educated workers from the developing nations in terms of sustaining both prosperity and economic growth, developing countries suffer from brain drain or the outflow of their skilled labour force. This is particularly the case for the Middle Eastern countries and a significant issue in Iran. In a recent survey of 90 countries by the International Monetary Fund, Iran appeared to have the highest rate of brain drain (Harrison, 2006). Furthermore, the costs associated with such migration of skilled workers have been estimated to be over $50 billion every year (Thomas, 2006).

While a thorough discussion of the reasons for such a high rate of brain drain is beyond the scope of this chapter, one thing is clear-cut: the current Iranian management's approach to managing organisations has resulted in a considerable underinvestment in human resources compared with major neighbouring countries (see Ali and Amirshahi, 2002; Javidan and Dastmalchian, 2003; House et al., 2004; Latifi, 2006; Namazie and Tayeb, 2006; Namazie and Frame, 2007). In this chapter we present an alternative and more nuanced account of the management of human resources in Iran which has a specific explicit focus on the operation of equality of opportunity policies in recruiting and managing diverse work groups in the organisations. In our view, this issue is of growing importance for several reasons. First, approximately 61 per cent of the population are under 30 years old (*Middle East Times*, 2007) making Iran the world's second youngest country after Jordan (*Iran Daily*, 2005); second, Iran is a multicultural state where Fars, Kurds, Arabs, Turks, Azaris, Turkemens and Baluchis also live with different linguistic, ethnic and cultural characteristics. Given these facts, it can be suggested that effective management of such diverse pool of young workforce is a key litmus test of the reality of the adoption of equal opportunity (EO) policies within Iranian organisations. Clearly, if diversity of the workforce is not afforded high priority on the management's agenda, it is suggested that the key strategic HR problem of the brain drain will continue.

This chapter draws on the notion of 'diversity management', in the sense used by Cox (1994, p. 246), which implies the representation of people with distinctive group affiliations such as race, gender, religion and even personality and political party affiliation. In a similar vein, Ivancevich and Gilbert (2000, p. 77) define the term as the organisation's commitment to 'recruit, retain, reward and promote a heterogeneous mix of productive, motivated and committed workers' with the mix referring to race/ethnicity, gender and physical abilities. The chapter seeks to address the situation that little (with the exception of a recent special issue of Tayeb, 1997; Robertson et al., 2001; IJHRM, 2007) is known about managing human resources and HRM processes within the Middle Eastern region. It also builds on the work of Budhwar and Mellahi (2007), who highlight the need for more empirical work in the area of HRM in the Middle East (see Keep, 1989; Pye and Pettigrew, 2005). Finally, as the Iranian government seeks to diversify the economy and to reduce its reliance on oil and gas revenues (Iran is the world's fourth biggest oil exporter and has the world's second biggest gas reserves), investment in human resources and upgrading their skills will be a key challenge in implementing this new strategy.

The underlying foundation of this study is that while there exists a comprehensive labour law in Iran, it is open (to quote Keep, 1989, p. 124) 'to manipulation and distortion by those who enforce it' with the consequence of ineffective utilisation of all human resources, or as Dickens (1995, p. 253) put it, 'wasted resources'. This chapter begins by reviewing the literature pertinent to diversity management (effective management of a diverse workforce) in general and its status in the context of Iranian labour law in particular. The following section discusses the qualitative research methodology adopted for this study. The study adopts a multiple case study design, comparing six organisations from two different but related sectors: construction and manufacturing (brick-making/burning). The next section reports the research findings. The central argument of this section is that the presence of equality of opportunities in employment in the labour law does not necessarily indicate an intention to be enforced. It can be seen, rather, to echo Dickens's (ibid., p. 279) words, 'as a declaration or symbolic ratification of current practice', or as Young (1987, p. 98) put it, 'an affirmation that customary behaviour conforms to the canons of acceptability'. The final section concludes with some brief remarks about the reality of diversity management in Iran, its implications for effective management of human resources, and the need for further research on the factors that impede its spread among Iranian organisations.

Human resource management and workforce diversity[1]
Depending on how it is defined, HRM appears to have moved in and out of fashion over the last 50 years, both as a managerial function and as a subject of study, reflecting the centrality of the workforce to the long-term organisational survival. Views about what has been happening to HRM turn on a number of separate but related perspectives. On the one hand, the early version of HRM owed much to the circumstances of the 1960s and 1970s: low organisational productivity. For Storey (1989), this view conforms to 'hard' HRM in that the emphasis is on the resource side of human resources, on the costs in the form of 'headcount', and on the managerial control over the workforce. Accordingly, in order to increase organisational/workforce productivity, the manager's role is to manage numbers effectively, keeping the workforce closely matched with requirements in terms of both bodies and behaviour. In the 1980s, on the other hand, labour productivity was seen to be high and therefore there were more products available in the market. Despite such oversupply of products, product sales revenues decreased significantly. One explanation for this was the availability of cheap products of low quality in the market. In order to increase the product and service quality, a range of quality management initiatives was adopted to positively and directly affect the customer perceived quality outcome. Despite the surge of interest in quality management initiatives, there has been much concern among practitioners and academia alike as to the high rate of quality management failure (see Wilkinson et al., 1998; Mak, 2000; Soltani et al., 2005, 2007). One generally accepted explanation for this was seen to be low organisational commitment and a reduced investment in human resources (see, for example, MSC/NEDO, 1986). In other words, the main challenge to management was therefore likely to come from the human resources. As a consequence, recent theoretical work has begun to shed light on the importance of human resources and on the management's approach and attitudes towards employees (Fombrun et al., 1984; Schuler and Jackson, 1987; Arthur, 1994; Sisson, 1994; Huselid, 1995; Legge, 1995; Becker et al., 2001; Bach, 2005). The new approach to human resources is consistent with

the notions of 'soft' HRM, human resource capital, strategic HRM and talent management. In more elaborate language, human aspects of HRM should be given higher priority, human resources contribute to determining and realising strategic objectives of the organisation, and a systemised approach for making a linkage between organisation excellence and effective people management is critical to organisational continuity (Berger and Berger, 2003). For Legge (1989), the organisation's 'human resources' are valued assets, not a variable cost, and the commitment of employees can be regarded as a source of competitive advantage (see Storey, 1989; Bratton and Gold, 1999, p. 17). For others (for example, Berger and Berger, 2003), alignment of a company's people with the current and future needs of the organisation by placing employees in positions that maximise their value is closely associated with higher productivity and organisational performance (see also Michaels et al., 2001). As a consequence, all those activities and practices which affect the behaviour of individuals in their efforts to formulate and implement the strategic needs of business should be taken into account (Schuler, 1992; Purcell et al. 2003). One such practice is the existence of EO in employment for all organisational members regardless of their background.

An important corollary of the above discussion is that there should be an appropriate set of HRM policies, built on individual employee differences or employee diversity, to ensure effective recruitment and management of people who are diverse in terms of gender, culture, race, age, religion, language and nationality (see Syed, 2010). Such a diverse workforce, it is argued, requires an effective diversity management approach. This management approach is characterised by capitalising on the benefits of a diverse workforce. With regard to the Middle Eastern region and in particular Iran, this issue is of paramount importance to tackle the region's slow economic developments. According to Abed (2003), the region can be characterised by its lagging political reforms, dominant public sector, underdeveloped financial markets, high trade restrictiveness and inappropriate exchange regime. For others (Talib, 1996 cited in Budhwar and Mellahi, 2007, p. 2; Mellahi and Al-Hinai, 2000; Looney, 2003; Yousef, 2004), why the Middle Eastern countries are increasingly said to be dysfunctional in their socio-economical systems relates to the lack of integration into the global economy, cultural and religious conflicts (see Dereli, ch. 8, this volume), growing unemployment rates, closed economies, overdominance on the oil sector, lack of privatisation and the weakness of local entrepreneurial cultures. This line of argument begs the question as to how such longstanding problems can be overcome. This brings us to our attempt to discuss diversity management and how such a diverse workforce is recruited, trained, motivated and disciplined.

Within the context of Iran, effective management of the diverse workforce is deemed to be especially important. On the one hand, the government's intention to privatise most state industries and the rise of foreign direct investment in Iran imply that there is a need on the part of management of both domestic and Iranian-based multinational organisations to attract and recruit the most talented people from a pool of diverse workforce. Such a diversity-driven approach towards recruiting a range of qualified candidates for Iranian organisations is needed not least because of the country's diverse population (Box 16.1).

BOX 16.1   FACT-BASED EVIDENCE ON IRAN'S SOCIO-ECONOMIC, CULTURAL AND POLITICAL CONTEXTS

Ethnic groups: Persians (51 per cent), Azeris (24 per cent), Gilaki and Mazandarani (8 per cent), Kurds (7 per cent), Arabs (3 per cent), Baluchi (2 per cent), Lurs (2 per cent), Turkmens (2 per cent), Others (1 per cent).

Religion: Islam (the official state religion), 90 per cent Shi'a branch of Islam, 8 per cent Sunni (mainly Kurds and Iran's Balochi Sunni), 2 per cent are non-Muslim religious minorities (Zoroastrians, Jews, Christians and others).

Language: Persian (Farsi) is the official language. However, ethnic groups speak their own language.

Culture: a predominant culture of the Middle East and Central Asia; strong emphasis on cultural institutions such as religion and family; individualism; strong in-group collectivism; high power distance; high performance orientation; high male orientation; family orientation; strong influence of Islamic principles on management.

The birth of modern Iran: (i) rise of the Safavid Empire (1501–1920), (ii) from the Pahlavi era to the Iranian revolution (1921–79), (iii) Iranian Revolution and Iran–Iraq War (1979–88). Most modern and Westernized country in 1979 versus a fundamentalist Islamic country after 1979.

Population: 70 million.

Geography: 30 provinces.

Economy: state ownership of oil and other large enterprises. Iran's major commercial partners are China, Germany, South Korea, France, Japan, Russia and Italy. Foreign investment hit a record $10.2 billion in mid-2007 from $4.2 billion in 2005 and $2 million in 1994.

Energy: Iran ranks second in the world in natural gas reserves and third in oil reserves.

Inflation: 17 per cent (mid-2007).

Unemployment: 15 per cent (mid-2007).

Labour force: 26.2 million (of which women accounted for 33 per cent) – one-quarter of the workforce is engaged in manufacturing and construction, one-fifth is engaged in agriculture, and the remainder are divided almost evenly between occupations in services, transportation and communication, and finance.

Sources: Khajehpour (2001); Menashri (2001); Yasin et al. (2002); Javidan and Dastmalchian (2003); House et al. (2004); *Iran Economics Magazine* (2005); CIA World Factbook (2007); *Middle East Times* (2007); Namazie and Frame (2007); Wikipedia (2007).

On the other hand, achieving multiple objectives of Iran's 20-Year Vision[2] implies that it is not the country's sole reliance on the oil or near total reliance on imported technology from the West or even foreign/domestic cheap labour which determine organisational profitability and competitiveness, but the effective merit-based recruitment of the workforce and enhancing their interpersonal and work-related skills regardless of gender, culture, race, age, disability and language – to name but a few.

This study aims to shed new light on the extent to which diversity management may contribute to the effectiveness of the workforce in a major Islamic country. The analysis is grounded on multiple case research in six organisations operating in construction and manufacturing (brick-making) sectors. The underlying feature common to all these cases is that they have a range of diverse workforces, both local and foreign,[3] different in terms of gender, working experience, language, education, physical ability/disability and indeed religion. We also highlight the increasing pressure on HR managers to recruit the best people for the right jobs in the context of the Iranian economy.

Method

The research approach adopted for the present study conforms to qualitative methodology. To this end, a multiple case study design was applied. It consisted of six cases in two different but related private sectors: (i) construction and (ii) manufacturing (brick-making/burning). The selection of the two private sectors was partly based on the authors' familiarity with the labour market in Iran and also was in line with the current evidence where the construction and manufacturing (including brick-making) sectors were seen to attract nearly one-quarter of Iran's labour force and over three-quarters of foreign workers in Iran (see Wickramasekara et al., 2006). The six cases were chosen from the Directory of Iran Industries Info Base and the Iranian Golden Pages, representing as Goldthorpe et al. (1968–69) put it, 'critical cases' for our research not least because of their higher annual turnover, long experience with recruiting foreign and diverse pool of workers, long-established HRM departments, and large establishment size. Semi-structured interview and analysis of documentary evidence were utilised to examine the extent and nature of diversity management from both managers' and workers' point of view. A total of 76 interviews (11–14 per case) were conducted with senior HR managers, middle/supervisory managers, and workers (both local and foreign). Both managers and workers were asked to think about the nature and extent of diversity management and its associated practices as their organisations pursue various cost reduction strategies and endeavour to achieve a suitable integration of business policy and personnel practices. The main interview topics were as follows:

- to examine the rationale for and commitment to diversity practices;
- to unfold the meaning of workers' experiences with diversity management;
- to evoke information on the status of foreign workers in comparison to local workers in terms of equal opportunities in employment; and
- to find out whether diversity arrangements fulfil the immediate needs of both the organisation and the workers.

The selection of research participants from both management and non-managerial employees conforms to the notion of 'multiple perspectives' of qualitative research methods (Strauss and Gorbin, 1994, p. 280; Taylor and Bogdan, 1984). Table 16.1 provides descriptive statistics on interviewees in the two sectors and in each case. All interviews were of circa one and a half to two hours. With the interviewees' consent, the interviews were tape-recorded and transcribed verbatim. To analyse the collected data and sift through the large volumes of interviewees' responses, Miles and Huberman's (1994) four stages of qualitative methodology were used: data collection, data reduction, data display and conclusion drawing/verification. The qualitative examination of the specified characteristics of the interviewees' responses across the two industries is outlined below.

Table 16.1 Descriptive statistics on interviewees

	Construction			Manufacturing (brick-making/burning)		
	Case 1	Case 2	Case 3	Case 1	Case 2	Case 3
Number of interviews: senior/middle (supervisory) workers	3(4)6	4(3)7	4(3)6	3(3)5	2(4)6	4(4)5
Tenure with company: managers (workers)	12(16.20)	13.30(17)	15(18)	11.50(14.20)	12.10(11.60)	16.20(17.10)
Gender mix: male (female)	12(1)	12(2)	10(3)	10(1)	9(3)	11(2)
Nationality – Iranian (foreigner):						
Managers	7(0)	7(0)	7(0)	6(0)	4(0)	8(0)
Workers	2(4)	2(5)	3(3)	1(4)	2(4)	1(4)
Average age (years): managers (workers)	39.30(41.40)	42.50(39.50)	37.80(44.60)	44.60(43.60)	40.30(42.50)	45.30(43.60)
Education – university degree (diploma or less):						
Managers	6(1)	5(2)	6(1)	4(2)	3(3)	6(2)
Workers	0(6)	0(7)	0(6)	0(5)	0(6)	0(5)
Full-time employment based on contract:						
Managers: Yes (No)	7(0)	7(0)	7(0)	6(0)	6(0)	8(0)
Workers: Yes (No)	2(4)	2(5)	1(5)	2(3)	2(4)	1(4)
Total number of interviews in each case	13	14	13	11	12	13

Note: Total number of interviews = 76.

Industry context

Due to the post-war reconstruction of Iran, both construction and manufacturing (brick-making/burning) sectors went through a significant period of restructuring. Accordingly, their markets experienced significant growth due to an increase in national and international investments in the post-war reconstruction period. While as a result of the 8-year Iran–Iraq war, many of the country's plants were seriously damaged, the war stimulated the growth of the whole economy followed by reconstruction of many small- and large-scale construction and manufacturing projects. As a consequence, not only did the share of Iran's construction and manufacturing sectors in the GDP increase, but also construction was reported to be the largest in the Middle Eastern region (*Iran Daily*, 2007). In this respect, there are two closely related features of the construction industry in Iran which are important in contextualising the employer–employee relationship later. First, the shareholding of some 98 per cent of the industry remained with private sector investment. Second, as a result, mass development projects were launched, resulting in foreign firms (mainly Chinese and European) establishing agents or partnerships with domestic companies. For example, brick-making/burning is now one of the most important and thriving high export sectors in Iran, and construction accounts for approximately 35 per cent of the total private investment. The implication of such fast-paced project execution accompanied by the use of new technology, technological advances and application of new construction materials in the two sectors impacted on employment in the sector, and the need on the part of management to recruit a diverse and multi-skilled workforce in response to such a rapidly growing market.

Results and discussion

The rationale for diversity practices and its implications for the workforce commitment

Managers in the construction and brick-making companies were seen to consider diversity practices mainly with regard to their own self-interests and to a lesser extent the workers'. Across senior and middle management levels there was a high mention of managerial and organisational self-interests and a low mention of worker self-interest as the main drivers behind the diversity initiatives. In a similar vein, supervisory level managers provided particularly strong evidence of how senior management self-interest shaped and dominated the current diversity-related practices and overrode both the organisation's and the workers' self-interest. The highly male orientation of the privately owned organisations compounded by the existence of high power distance of Iranian managers led many supervisory managers and workers to describe their senior management's willingness to adopt diversity practices as being driven by a 'cost–benefit regime'. When pressed for evidence of the existence of such a regime, one supervisory manager commented: 'Cost minimisation at any price is one important measure to differentiate effective from ineffective management across the whole industry'.

Our observation of the workers' employment records also showed that some workers had no social protection or proper working contracts and therefore there was strong evidence on the part of management to avoid the associated costs of their employment. Indeed, we found the cost-reduction impact of such contractual arrangements for both the organisation and to a lesser extent the blue-collar workers to be substantial. For example, a review of the labour and tax laws shows that employers are required to not only pay income tax but also to contribute to the State Social Security Fund and the Employment Fund. In this respect, both the employer and the employee have to contribute to social security and unemployment insurance 23 and 7 per cent of the worker's salary, respectively (plus 3 per cent as the state's contribution). Interestingly, not only did a majority of the workers have no written employment contracts but also in all six cases across the two sectors the foreign workers as well as diverse work groups outnumbered local workforce and homogeneous work groups. While in both sectors workforce diversity was a reality, the appropriate diversity arrangements as a means to capitalise on various individual and organisational benefits of a diverse workforce (see Cox and Blake, 1991) were seen to be the missing link in the senior management thinking on the diverse workforce. Even two middle managers who had policy-making roles in the two sectors acknowledged that their diversity initiatives were not running very deep. In one middle manager's words, 'My impression is that diversity in the workforce always results in reducing the importance of some groups of workers'.

Other rationales for adopting diversity initiatives appeared to lie in apparent compliance with labour legislation. 'We encourage people from different backgrounds to apply for our vacancies' was one of the most frequent comments about the reality of diversity management, an indication of compliance with the labour legislation and an equal opportunity employer. However, we found less evidence that managers attempted to integrate diversity practices with HR policies, and if they did, it was a short-term response to the governmental interim monitoring. The major way in which HR policies and diversity initiatives were integrated was through the initial company's job advertisement in which potential job applicants were given a fair chance to apply for the job regardless of unrelated job factors such as race, sex, nationality or age. However, as one supervisory manager commented, 'the existence of equality of employment opportunities was only limited to manual and low-levels jobs'. Although on the surface management appeared to embrace diversity management as evidenced through encouraging a diverse range of applications in recruitment and indeed selecting a diverse range of employees, especially for blue-collar roles, it appeared that management took advantage of the relatively insecure position which many of these employees enjoyed in the labour market to reduce the cost of production. Specifically, they paid these employees lower levels of remuneration and forced them to work longer hours with lower levels of terms and conditions, and indeed did not fulfil their obligations in terms of obtaining work permits for them or making tax payments on their behalf.

The evidence highlighted the centrality of cost reduction and of the managerial and organisational benefits that were attendant upon EO for low-level and low-paid positions. As a result of such compulsory compliance with government equality legislation (they appear to do this only on recruitment, but once in they seem to fail to take any account of legislative requirements), there was an explicit cost–benefit or solid economic rationale for the uptake of EO policies. Such a managerial approach to adopting EO practices and government legislation can be termed 'equal opportunity for Taylorism' not least because the workers were carefully selected for the low-level and low-paid jobs (see Taylor, 1911). Unfortunately, despite such marginalisation of the workers in the labour market, and offering them only blue-collar jobs, the six case organisations were reaping immense financial rewards from employing the cheap diverse work groups. Accordingly, a majority of the workers from the two industries mentioned the alignment of the organisation's strategic objectives with diversity management practices (that is, fulfilment of the workers' self-interest) less frequently and less positively. Furthermore, there was an extremely *negative* feeling for the benefits of effective diversity management for the workers:

> We have all been abused by our managers in terms of working long hours and poor working conditions. We are also paid less for the same jobs. They say it is your choice. If you are unhappy you can go. Our working status has never been monitored by external bodies. Since there is no respect for the law, they view us as those who are cheap and easy to exploit.

Further analysis of the workers' responses yielded a different version of organisational commitment. For the majority of the workers there was little attention paid to career development because they believed that the current HRM policies were to improve the motivation and effectiveness of white-collar staff. Job security was the dominant concern and this was the basis of their 'job satisfaction' as opposed to commitment. In order to achieve this, there was a strong emphasis on the need to establish a close relationship with their supervisors. In such circumstances there is clearly no need on the part of management to establish a true commitment to diversity practices. 'Working hard enough so as not to get fired', was one of the most frequent comments about the reality of organisational life and a major concern of the blue-collar workers. As a result of differences in language, age, culture, nationality and much more, specifically the high unemployment rate of the economy, workers were seen to be forced to be in full compliance with their supervisory managers by working long and beyond their contracted hours, under poor working conditions. This had the effect of limiting workers' commitment and involvement (Beer, 2003). In one worker's words, 'we are afraid of speaking out freely for fear of losing our jobs'.

Workers' perceptions of diversity management
For the majority of workers, EO practices were promoted as being in the best interests of the management. As a result, blue-collar workers were regarded as, in one worker's words, a 'disadvantaged group' not least because they were unlikely to receive training, to get promotion, to receive recognition or even to get fair pay. Specifically, there was an extremely high negative mention of direct discrimination and being treated as refugees – as opposed to employees. From the workers' perspective, therefore, it would appear that equal opportunities in terms of treating workers as valued assets have been too few or have failed and fallen short of promises in practice. One explanation for this and an impediment to the implementation of EO policies appeared to lie in the conflict between management and employee self-interests. In both industries, all companies were seen to make a good profit by hiring diverse groups of workers for low-level and low-paid jobs. At the same time, recruiting such a diverse workforce was claimed to be a sign of compliance with the labour law, social justice, and ethical and human rights (see Wilson, 1996; McDougall, 1996), an indication of the so-called 'equal opportunity employer':

> We are a company with a very ethnically diverse workforce with different background and age groups. Each working group has its own culture, language and social values. Frankly speaking, the company's profitability depends on how diverse the workforce is. This in itself creates a competition in that each working group tries to perform better than the others. That's what our managers want. They want us to work harder.

In effect, recruitment of a diverse workforce was seen to be a mechanism to fit only the management priorities and initiatives in relation to the needs of the management. In one worker's words, 'Diversity management practices are all tools for effecting management's own interests and organisational priorities. I do not think there is anything positive in it for us [workers]'.

Across the two industries, there was a strong underlying preference for low-skilled workers from the neighbouring countries (for example, Afghanistan), driven by management's desire to intensify the control of capital over diverse work groups rather than seeking to use the advantages of a diverse workforce (Bartz et al., 1990) and recruiting the best talents (Ross and Schneider, 1992). In both industries, foreign workers were seen to outnumber the local workers. A large number of these workers shared a language (Dari) and religion (Shia Islam) with the Iranians. Despite their large size and such similarities, senior management deliberately adopted a 'hands-off' approach to managing these workers (see Peel and Boxall, 2005) and as a result, they were disadvantaged in terms of, among others, accident or unemployment insurance or even paid annual or sick leave – let alone access to training, taking unfair dismissal claims, pay schemes and fringe benefits or future career prospects. Comments such as 'The jobs we take are unattractive to local people because of low pay and poor working conditions', 'We are not in a position to set any precondi-tions prior to our employment' and 'We do not receive any support from our employer with regard to work permits and legal residence status' were examples of the extent and nature of equal employment opportunity to the foreign workers, an indication of direct or overt discrimination against the foreign workers. Due to the nature of the jobs in the two industries, there was a marked divergence in the labour force participa-tion rates among male and female employees. In all cases we observed, women were seen to receive lower pay and to take lower-level jobs with low levels of responsibility (see Metcalfe, 2010). As a consequence, for a majority of workers, diversity practices or equal employment opportuni-ties were regarded as of such insignificance that it did not contribute to fulfilling their basic employment needs. In the construction industry, for example, oral contracts or even no contract were seen to be an accepted practice.

In the two industries and in particular brick-making/burning compa-nies, foreign workers were long-serving employees with relatively high levels of technical skills, but a weak labour market position. They typically chose to accept 'no written contract' work in order to be able to survive. Their choice of employment was not optional and therefore they had to do those manual jobs which were unattractive to the local workforce. As a result of their illegal status in the country and therefore a lack of a work permit, their working arrangements – whether written or oral – were seen to be unfair. For example, their average wage was lower than that of local workers; they were not entitled to any work benefits or to receive social security insurance. In one foreign worker's words,

> The only thing I have learned is to work hard to survive, to keep quiet and do what I am told to do. I cannot recall a single occasion when I made a complaint within the last 14 years. We are constrained by a threat of unemployment as well as being deported. I have never received any support regarding my status or even work permit. The cheaper you are the higher the chance of employment you have.

As previously mentioned, in all six cases across the two sectors, diverse work groups and in particular foreign workers outnumbered homogeneous and local work groups. Our observation of the workers' employment records showed that they varied significantly in terms of age, language, education, work experience, religion and nationality. However, it appeared that such differences remained unrecognized in managing the workforce. In one foreign worker's words, 'I have worked here for over 23 years and I am now over 60 years old. Compared to the past and despite my old age, I have to work harder'.

For a majority of the employers in our research, foreign workers were regarded as refugees not least because of their illegal status. In one worker's words, 'No matter how long we have been here and how hard we have worked, we have always been treated as refugees'. While this status disadvantaged foreign workers as a cheap and variable labour force, it had substantial cost–benefit implications for the employers.

The overall impact of diversity practices: manager/organisation versus workers
In all of the cases, the apparent diversity practices were often in response to increasing labour costs. To the majority of managers, the use of foreign workers rather than hiring a local workforce offered greater flexibility not least because all HR-related policies such as workers' compensation claims, fringe benefits, tax compliance, working hours and termination of contract remained under the control of the employers. While some supervisory managers were critical of the HR policies with regard to unfair treatment of blue-collar workers, senior managers were seen to appreciate the freedom and power to exercise control over the workers with regard to the ability to hire and fire, to adjust wages, and to consult and negotiate their employment. These issues are consistent with the arguments of labour market theorists and with the recognition of equal opportunity as merely a label or public declaration, and apparent evidence of no unfair discrimination. Part of the argument that these workers were highly committed to their work and their organisations was that the workers' tenure with the companies ranged from approximately 12 to 18 years (see Table

16.1), and that they had rarely filed complaints against either their managers or even peer workers. As one senior manager stated: 'A large number of our workers have been with us for over 16 years. This indicates the presence of high employee morale, good managerial attitudes towards the workforce, good working conditions and strong loyalty and commitments towards their jobs'.

However, whether such long-term employment relationships or unwillingness to complain about the working conditions can be attributed to the existence of equal opportunity practices is questionable. One the one hand, the long employment relationship with a specific company could be attributed to the considerable restrictions imposed by the government on the physical movement of foreign workers and therefore government permits were required for travel within the country (see Strand et al., 2004). On the other hand, the good intention of effective diversity management was seen to be neutralised through managerial and organisational self-interest considerations which in most cases appeared to run counter to, rather than support, diversity management practices. For a majority of workers, in particular foreign ones, the mere presence of diverse work groups was a matter of compliance with the labour law. However, as previous research found (see Dickens, 1995), such compliance with the letter of the equality law did not take the organisations far along the EO path. The nature of the work in the two industries naturally implied a strong need on the part of management for those employees who were interested in blue-collar jobs, who had fewer or no working expectations, who could work under poor working conditions, who could work without any written contract, and finally who would have no objection to whether EO practices were firmly on management agendas in their organisations.

In respect of the impact of diversity practices on the workers, the analysis of the managers' and workers' responses revealed one important factor influencing their impression towards EO practices: the importance of mutuality of matching the needs of the worker with the needs of the manager and the organisation. For the workers in both industries, there was no prospect of receiving training, getting promotion, receiving recognition and getting higher pay. However, a long-term relationship with the employers (without a written contract) and avoiding paying tax on their earnings were seen to be the positive side of their employment. Unfortunately, there was no attempt on the part of management to resolve their working status in terms of work permits and other employment-related arrangements required by the law. Comments such as, 'what matters most to me is to have a job regardless of how much I get. I am happy to work more to earn more' and 'I do not want to put my whole life and hopes in jeopardy. Although they do not help us get a working visa, they still want us to work. This is more than enough for me', were some of the most frequent comments about the impact of EO practices on the workers' organisational life. In both industries, managers chose foreign and to a lesser extent unskilled local workers, as an opportunity to exert more power and control and reduce their labour costs. In a similar vein, while employers were obliged to contribute to the social security and unemployment insurance of the workers, due to a lack of written contracts for some 73 per cent of the workers, they managed to avoid their obligations in these matters.

Conclusions

This chapter presents a picture of diversity management in Iran based on the data of six case studies from two different but related sectors: construction and manufacturing (brick-making/burning). Across the six cases, the reality and existence of diversity management or any related initiatives seems to be more influenced by first, managerial self-interest and second organisational self-interest. Based on our analysis of the data, the implications of the current management's approach towards managing the diverse workforce and the related EO policies can be summarised in Figure 16.1.

The research findings suggest one dominant path of management's approach: it leads to a more short-term approach to managing a diverse workforce which apparently ensures fair and equitable employment of diverse work groups regardless of nationality, age, language, culture and religion – to name but a few. As the figure shows, however, such managerial orientations towards diverse work groups stop at the point of 'selection'. This implies that the current management of the six cases fails to appreciate the wider implications of individual differences after 'selection' and to

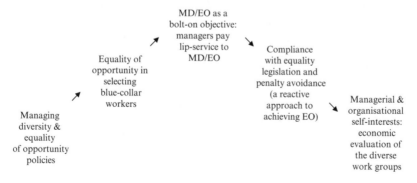

Figure 16.1   Management's orientations towards diverse work groups and EO practices and its resultant implications

value and respect the differences among employees 'as an asset to work being done more efficiently and effectively' (Bartz et al., 1990, p. 321). One characteristic of such lip-service to managing a diverse workforce is that it only focuses on eliminating discriminatory practices imposed by the state legislation rather than using the individual differences as a means to 'person–organisation fit' (Chatman, 1989) so that both the organisation's and individual's needs, desires and preferences are fulfilled (Kristof, 1996). Furthermore, the impacts of initial EO policies in selecting low-skilled employees appeared to be more significant not least because they were viewed as an opportunity to achieve cost-effectiveness and improve profitability. However, as we discussed earlier, such a limited form of a legally backed selection of the workforce is not without its shortcomings. Focusing on the reasons why the labour law and its associated legislation may be being translated inadequately into practice suggested several issues which deserve further attention. First, EO policies motivated by the Iranian labour law for both employees and organisational benefits would deliberately change their focus in practice to reflect only management needs. Second, there is no reliable source for disadvantaged groups to push their demands and exert pressure for equality. In Iran, unions historically do not have a good record in tackling discrimination. Although Iranian workers have, in theory, the right to form labour unions, there is, in actuality, no union system in the country. Workers are represented ostensibly by a state-sponsored institution that nevertheless attempts to challenge some state policies. Furthermore, the right of workers to strike in any form is generally not respected by the state (see 'Labour and tax laws in Iran', 2007). Finally, the ineffectiveness or failure of EO policies can be attributed to the senior management's orientation towards equality of opportunities in employment for diverse work groups. Management in Iran, as previous research confirms (Mortazavi and Salehi, 1992; Latifi, 1997; Namazie, 2003), represents a hybrid of Western, ancient and Islamic styles (Kiani and Latifi, 1995). It values the Islamic notions of equality, justice and protection and support for subordinates and workers; it follows the traditions and respects the norms of the 6000-year-old ancient Iranian culture with a particular focus on power and control as the main recipe for good management; it tries to adapt to the Western management style by focusing on flexibility, low power orientation, preparedness to take risks, low rule orientation (Pant et al., 1996) and also tends to apply those Western managerial techniques aimed at enhancing productivity and quality. While all these appear to be positive, promising, appropriate and valuable, the dominant paternalistic culture of Iranian organisations tends to create independent managers. For Levinson (1968), such paternalism has close affinity with ancient clans and kingdoms that needed to sustain their soldiers' loyalty. As we observed, however, such paternalistic managers were seen to be very bitter towards any feedback by their subordinates or as Aronoff and Ward (1993) argued, sap employee initiative and creativity, and can even eat away at responsibility as organisational members learn that 'The Boss' will take care of things.

The overriding managerial implications arising out of the research evidence is that there is a fundamental need for senior management to reconsider their role and adjust their approach and attitude towards meeting the needs of the workforce, organisation and customers in a long-term horizon. In respect of implications for future research, there appears to be a need to extend the current research by understanding the extent to which the government (labour law) can help to protect the workers and promote diversity-related practices. Research could also explore the current state of diversity management in publicly owned organisations. Further, it would be interesting to explore management's orientations towards EO and diversity policies within multinational corporations in Iran to find the extent and nature of diversity-related practice and any associated impediments (in progress).

Notes

* This chapter is a short and revised version of a research project on managing diverse work groups in Iran which was earlier accepted by IJHRM (**21**(1), 84–108). The authors would like to thank S. Yousefi who helped with data collection and analysis.
1. In this chapter, the terms 'equal opportunity' (EO) and 'diversity management' (DM) are interchangeable and are often used as such throughout.
2. Iran's Outlook for the Next 20 Years: the plan envisages Iran as a developed country with a leading position in the economic, scientific and technological domains of the Middle Eastern region by March 2026.
3. By foreign workers we mean those workers who are mainly from neighbouring countries, and involved in least-skilled blue-collar jobs

References

Abed, G.T. (2003), 'Unfulfilled promise', available at: www.imf.org/external/pubs/ft/fandd/2003/03/abed.htm (accessed 15 October 2007).

Ali, A.J. and Amirshahi, M. (2002), 'The Iranian manager: work values and orientations', *Journal of Business Ethics*, **40** (2), 133–43.

Aronoff, C.E. and Ward, J.L. (1993), 'The high cost of paternalism', *Nation's Business*, May, 61–2.

Arthur, J.B. (1994), 'Effects of human resource systems on manufacturing performance and turnover', *Academy of Management Journal*, **14**, 33–46.

Bach, S. (2005), 'Personnel management in transition', in Bach (ed.), *Managing Human Resources: Personnel Management in Transition*, 4th edn, Oxford: Blackwell, pp. 3–44.

Bartz, D.E., Hillman L.W., Lehrer, S. and Mayhugh, G.M. (1990), 'A model for managing workforce diversity', *Management Education and Development*, **21** (5), 321–6.

Becker, B.E., Huselid, M.A. and Ulrich, D. (2001), *The HR Scorecard: Linking People, Strategy and Performance*, Boston, MA: Harvard Business School Press.

Beer, M. (2003), 'Why total quality management programs do not persist: the role of management quality and implications for leading a TQM transformation', *Decision Sciences*, **34** (4), 623–42.

Berger, L.A. and Berger, D.R. (2003), *The Talent Management Handbook: Creating Organizational Excellence by Identifying, Developing and Positioning Your Best People*, New York: McGraw-Hill.

Bratton, J. and Gold, J. (1999), *Human Resource Management: Theory and Practice*, 2nd edn, London: Macmillan.

Budhwar, P. and Mellahi, K. (2007), 'Introduction: human resource management in the Middle East', *International Journal of Human Resource Management*, **18** (1), 2–10.

Chatman, J. (1989), 'Improving interactional organisational research: a model of person-organisation fit', *Academy of Management Review*, **14** (2), 333–49.

CIA World Factbook (2007), *The World Factbook*, April, available at: https://www.cia.gov/news-information/press-releases-statements/press-release-archive-2006/pr04052006.htm (accessed 15 October 2007).

Cox T. (1994), *Cultural Diversity in Organizations*, San Francisco, CA: Berrett-Koehler.

Cox T. and Blake, S. (1991), 'Managing cultural diversity: implications for organizational competitiveness', *Academy of Management Executive*, **5** (3), 45–56.

Dickens, L. (1995), 'Wasted resources? Equal opportunities in employment', in Sisson, K. (ed.), *Personnel Management: A Comprehensive Guide to Theory and Practice*, 2nd edn, Oxford: Blackwell, pp. 253–96.

Fombrun, C., Tichy, N. and Devanna, M. (1984), *Strategic Human Resource Management*, New York: John Wiley.

Goldthorpe, J., Lockwood, D., Beckhofer, F. and Platt, J. (1968–69), *The Affluent Worker*, vols 1–3, Cambridge: Cambridge University Press.

Harrison, F. (2006), 'Huge cost of Iranian brain drain', available at: http://news.bbc.co.uk/1/hi/world/middle_east/6240287.stm (accessed 14 October 2007).

House, R.J., Hanges, P.J., Javidan, M., Dorfman, P.W. and Gupta, V. (2004), *Culture, Leadership and Organisations: The GLOBE Study of 62 Societies*, London: Sage.

Huselid, M. (1995), 'The impact of human resource management practices on turnover, productivity and corporate financial performance', *Academy of Management Journal*, **38** (3), 635–73.

IJHRM (2007), *International Journal of Human Resource Management*, special issue, **18** (1), January, 1–171.

Iran Daily (2005), 'Iran: second youngest nation', 22 June, available at: http://iran-daily.com/1383/2225/html/panorama.htm#47448 (accessed 14 October 2007).

Iran Daily (2007), 'Domestic economy', 9 April, available at: http://iran-daily.com/1386/2812/html/economy.htm (accessed 15 October 2007).

Iran Economics Magazine (2005), 23 October, available at: http://www.iraneconomics.net/fa/index.asp (accessed 9 October 2007).

Ivancevich, J.M. and Gilbert, J.A. (2000), 'Diversity management: time for a new approach', *Public Personnel Management*, **29** (1), 75–92.

Javidan, M. and Dastmalchian, A. (2003), 'Culture and leadership in Iran: the land of individual achievers, strong family ties and powerful elite', *Academy of Management Executive*, **17** (4), 127–42.

Keep, E. (1989), 'Corporate training strategy: the vital component', in Storey, J (ed.), *New Perspectives on Human Resource Management*, London: Routledge, pp. 109–25.

Khajehpour, B. (2001), 'Iran's economy: 20 years after the Islamic revolution', in Esposito, J.L. and Ramazani, R.K. (eds), *Iran at the Crossroads*, Basingstoke: Palgrave, pp. 98–122.

Kiani, R. and Latifi, F. (1995), 'The impact of ancient, Islamic and western culture in Iran's work-related values', EIASM Workshop: Cross-Cultural Perspectives: Comparative Management and Organisation, Henley Management College, Henley-on-Thames.

Kristof, A.L. (1996), 'Person–organization fit: an integrative review of its conceptualizations, measurement, and implications', *Personnel Psychology*, **49**, 1–49.

'Labour and tax laws in Iran' (2007), available at: http://www.mefa.gov.ir/ (accessed 15 October 2007).

Latifi, F. (1997), 'Management learning in national context', PhD thesis, Henley Management College, Henley-on-Thames.

Latifi, F. (2006), 'A dynamic model interpreting work-related values of multi-faceted cultures: the case of Iran', *International Journal of Human Resource Management*, **17** (12), 2055–73.

Legge, K. (1989), 'Human resource management: a critical analysis', in Storey, J (ed.), *New Perspectives on Human Resource Management*, London: Routledge, pp. 19–40.

Legge, K. (1995), *Human Resource Management: Rhetorics and Realities*, Basingstoke: Macmillan.

Levinson, H. (1968), *The Exceptional Executive*, Cambridge, MA: Harvard University Press.

Looney, R. (2003), 'The Gulf Co-operation Council's cautious approach to economic integration', *Journal of Economic Cooperation*, **24** (2), 137–60.

Mak, W.M. (2000), 'The Tao of people-based management', *Total Quality Management*, **11** (4–6), 537–43.

McDougall, M. (1996), 'Equal opportunities versus managing diversity: another challenge for public sector management?', *International Journal of Public Sector Management*, **9** (5/6), 62–72.

Mellahi, K. and Al-Hinai, S. (2000), 'Local workers in Gulf co-operation countries: assets or liabilities?', *Middle Eastern Studies*, **26** (3), 177–91.

Menashri, D. (2001), *Post-Revolutionary Politics in Iran*, London: Routledge.

Metcalfe, B. (2010), 'Reflections on difference: women, Islamic feminism and development in the Middle East', ch. 9 in Özbilgin, M. and Syed, J. (eds), *Managing Gender Diversity in Asia: A Research Companion*, Cheltenham, UK, Northampton, MA, USA: Edward Elgar, pp. 140–59.

Michaels, E., Handfield-Jones, H. and Axelrod, B. (2001), *The War for Talent*, Boston, MA: Harvard Business School Press.

Middle East Times (2007), Iran's population tops 70mn, 15 May, available at: http://www.metimes.com/storyview.php?StoryID=20070515-084703-7413r (accessed 14 October 2007).

Miles, M.B. and Huberman, A.M. (1994), *Qualitative Data Analysis*, 2nd edn, Thousand Oaks, CA: Sage.

Mortazavi, S. and Salehi, A. (1992), 'Organisational culture, paternalistic leadership and job satisfaction in Iran', paper presented at the 22nd International Congress of Applied Psychology, 22–27 August, Hove: Lawrence Erlbaum Associates.

MSC/NEDO (1986), *A Challenge to Complacency: Changing Attitudes to Training*, Sheffield: Manpower Services Commission.

Namazie, P. (2003), 'Factors affecting the transferability of HRM practices in joint ventures based in Iran', *Career Development International*, **8** (7), 357–66.

Namazie, P. and Frame, P. (2007), 'Developments in human resource management in Iran', *International Journal of Human Resource Management*, **18** (1), 159–71.

Namazie, P. and Tayeb, M.H. (2006), 'HRM in Iran', in Budhwar, P. and Mellahi, K. (eds), *Managing Human Resources in the Middle East*, London: Routledge, pp. 20–39.

Pant, D., Allinson, C. and Hayes, J. (1996), 'Transferring the Western model of project organisation to a bureaucratic culture: the case of Nepal', *International Journal of Project Management*, **14** (1), 53–7.

Peel, S. and Boxall, P. (2005), 'When is contracting preferable to employment? An exploration of management and worker perspectives', *Journal of Management Studies*, **42**, 1675–97.

Purcell, J., Kinnie, N., Hutchinson, S., Rayton, B. and Swart, J. (2003), *Understanding the People and Performance Link: Unlocking the Black Box*, London: CIPD.

Pye, A.J., and Pettigrew, A.M. (2005), 'Studying board context, process and dynamics: some challenges for the future', *British Journal of Management*, **16**, 27–38.

Robertson, C., Al-Habib, M., Al-Khatib, J. and Lanoue, D. (2001), 'Beliefs about work in the Middle East and the convergence versus divergence of values', *Journal of World Business*, **36** (13), 223–35.

Ross, R. and Schneider, R. (1992), *From Equality to Diversity: A Business Case for Equal Opportunities*, London: Pitman.

Schuler, R.S (1992), 'Strategic human resource management: linking people with the strategic needs of the business', *Organizational Dynamics*, **21** (1), 18–32.

Schuler, R. and Jackson, S.E. (1987), 'Linking competitive strategies with human resource management practices', *Academy of Management Executive*, **1**, 207–19.

Sisson, K. (1994), *Personnel Management*, Oxford: Blackwell.

Soltani, E., Lai, P. and Mahmoudi, V. (2007), 'Managing change initiatives: fantasy or reality? The case of public sector organisations', *Total Quality Management and Business Excellence*, **18** (1–2), 153–79.

Soltani, E., van der Meer, R.B., Williams, T.M. and Lai, P. (2005), 'A contextually appropriate performance appraisal for TQM', in Sunder, K. Shyam (ed.), *Measuring HRM's Effectiveness: An Introduction*, Andhra Pradesh, India: Le Magnus University Press, pp. 21–60.

Storey, J. (1989), 'Introduction: from personnel management to human resource management', in Storey, *New Perspectives on Human Resource Management*, London: Routledge, pp. 1–18.

Strand, A., Suhruke, A. and Harpviken, K.B. (2004), 'Afghan refugees in Iran: from refugee emergency to migration management', CM1/PR10, available at: http://www.cmi.no/pdf/?file=/afghanistan/doc/CM10-PR10-AfghanRefugeesInIran.pdf (accessed 7 October 2007).

Strauss, A. and Gorbin, J. (1994), 'Grounded theory methodology: an overview', in Denzin, N. and Lincoln, Y. (eds), *Handbook of Qualitative Research*, Thousand Oaks, CA: Sage, pp. 273–85.

Syed, J. (2010), 'From gender empowerment to gender diversity: measuring the gender gap in Muslim majority countries', ch. 12 in Özbilgin, M. and Syed, J. (eds), *Managing Gender Diversity in Asia: A Research Companion*, Cheltenham, UK and Northampton, MA, USA: Edward Elgar, pp. 120–26.

Talib, Y. (1996), 'Privatization: a review of policy and implementation in selected Arab countries', *International Journal of Public Sector Management*, **9** (3), 3–21.

Tayeb, M. (1997), 'Islamic revival in Asia and human resource management', *Employee Relations*, **19** (4), 352–64.

Taylor, F.W. (1911), *The Principles of Scientific Management*, New York: Harper & Brothers.

Taylor, S.T. and Bogdan, R. (1984), *Introduction to Qualitative Methods: The Search for Meanings*, 2nd edn, New York: John Wiley.

Thomas, J. (2006), 'The dynamics of globalisation and the uncertain future of Iran: an examination of Iranians in Dubai', *Al Nkhlah*, Fall: 3.

Wickramasekara, P., Sehgal, J., Mehran, F., Noroozi, L. and Eisazadeh, S. (2006), 'Afghan households in Iran: profile and impact' (final report), available at: http://www.unhcr.org/cgi-bin/texis/vtx/home/opendoc.pdf?tbl=SUBSITES&page=SUBSITES&id=455835d92 (accessed 15 October 2007).

Wikipedia (2007), 'Iranian oil bourse', available at: http://en.wikipedia.org/wiki/Iranian_Oil_Bourse (accessed 28 September 2007).

Wilkinson, A., Redman, T., Snape, E. and Marchington, M. (1998), *Managing with Total Quality Management: Theory and Practice*, London: Macmillan.

Wilson, E. (1996), 'Managing diversity and HRD', in Stewart, J. and McGoldrick, J. (eds), *HRD Perspectives, Strategies and Practice*, London: Pitman, pp. 158–79.

Yasin, M.Y., Alavi, J. and Zimmerer, T. (2002), 'An examination of the impact of economic variables and cultural values on Iranian business organisations', *Cross Cultural Management*, **9** (1), 3–18.

Young, K. (1987), 'The space between words: local authorities and the concept of equal opportunities', in Jenkins, R and Solomos, J. (eds), *Racism and Equal Opportunity Policies in the 1980s*, Cambridge: Cambridge University Press, pp. 93–109.

Yousef, T.M. (2004), 'Growth and policy reform in the Middle East and North Africa since 1950', *Journal of Economic Perspectives*, **18** (3), 91–114.

17 Is diversity management relevant for Turkey? Evaluation of some factors leading to diversity management in the context of Turkey

Olca Sürgevil

Introduction

Today, the changing workforce is one of the most significant challenges that many organizations face. According to Wentling (2000, p. 435), 'Workforce diversity is a demographic phenomenon playing upon not only the US organizations but also multinational corporations and institutions in other countries around the world (Littlefield, 1995; Morosini, 1998). In addition, other business forces, such as global competition and the need to remain competitive, are driving diversity into organizations regardless of their geographical location'.

Diversity describes the many unique internal and external qualities and characteristics that make a person similar to or different from others. Diversity means difference or variety, and diverse workforce refers to the workers with a variety of different characteristics such as gender, disability, culture, ethnicity, religion, experience, body size, sexual orientation, language, social class, skills and so on (Mujtaba, 2007, pp. 5, 13; Weir, ch. 18, this volume).

Some scholars categorize these characteristics as surface- and deep-level diversities (Harrison et al., 1998), readily detectable and less observable diversities (Milliken and Martins, 1996), and highly and less job-related diversities (Pelled, 1996; Pelled et al., 1999; Simons et al., 1999).

Harrison and Klein (2007, p. 1200) state that the meaning of diversity is not very clear and use the term 'to describe the distribution of differences among the members of a unit with respect to a common attribute, X, such as tenure, ethnicity, conscientiousness, task attitude, or pay'.

Diversity management emerged as a management discourse and practice in the 1990s in the United States (Özbilgin and Tatli, 2008, p. 3). According to McMillan-Capehart (2003, p. 22), 'The United States has been culturally diverse for many hundreds of years. In fact, diversity dates back to the colonization of America. Colonialism and immigration are two major means by which culturally diverse populations develop'.

In addition, the Civil Rights Act in 1964 contributed to the increased diversity in the workplace:

> The Civil Rights Act and Equal Employment Opportunity Commission (EEOC) of 1964 and the Affirmative Action Plan proposed by Kennedy all opened the door for culturally diverse individuals in the workplace. Organizations were required to not discriminate against anyone; inform people that they did not discriminate; treat those who applied for jobs without discrimination; and seek out those who might not apply for jobs in that organization (Glazer, 1975). (McMillan-Capehart, 2003, p. 28)

At that time, there was no study about the impact of diversity in management literature. Diversity management has been studied as an academic subject since the 1990s (ibid., p. 28).

Thomas (1991, p. 10) defined diversity management as 'a comprehensive managerial process for developing an environment that works for all employees' and Hays-Thomas (2004, p. 10) stated that 'effective diversity management does not benefit one group over others'.

The concern of diversity management is quite new for Turkey. There are some studies on equal employment opportunity, diversity management and discrimination in the context of Turkey (Woodward and Özbilgin, 1999; Aytac, 2000; Özbilgin, 2000, 2002; Özbilgin and Healy, 2004; Özbilgin and Woodward, 2004; Healy et al., 2005; Aliefendioglu and Özbilgin, 2006; Bereket and Adam, 2006; Kara, 2006; Bulutlar, 2007; Kamasak and Yucelen, 2007; Kusku et al., 2007; Özgener, 2007; Sural Özer, 2007; Uzuncarsili and Uzuncarsili Soydas, 2007; Budak, 2008; Sürgevil, 2008; Dereli, ch. 8, this volume).

The following questions and issues are discussed in the coming pages: whether diversity management is a valid concept in Turkey, and how diversity appears and whether it is relevant for Turkey. Country-specific studies should be carried out in order to discover whether diversity management programmes and applications work well in different countries and in different circumstances. In line with this argument, it is necessary to assess the Turkish context in order to highlight the applicability of diversity management in that country. This chapter aims to contribute to the previous diversity studies by examining the conditions of Turkey in terms of diversity.

Modern workplace trends have created an impetus for a focus on diversity and diversity management. First, diversity management has become a concern because of real and perceived changes in the demographic make-up of the workforce. Second, factors such as globalization, growth of the service sector, increased use of electronic technology especially within the communication area, increase in knowledge work, teamwork approaches, organizational mergers and increase in contingent employment are of relevance in the context of diversity management (Ashkanasy et al., 2002, p. 308; Hays-Thomas, 2004, p. 3). Some of these factors are explained below and evaluated in the Turkish context.

For this purpose, in this study, the concept of diversity management is briefly explained and the factors that make the diversity management concept important in the domain of science and the business world are evaluated in the Turkish context. In the evaluation process, secondary statistical data are used, published by the Turkish Statistical Institute (TUIK), the Turkish Enterprise and Business Confederation (TURKONFED) and the Turkish Confederation of Employers' Union (TISK).

Evaluation of the factors leading to diversity management
The workplace, the way people work together and what they do throughout the world are changing. Minority groups are moving into managerial, executive, technical and professional careers. People with disabilities are trying to find ways to use the many abilities that they have and become productive employees. Many gay people no longer try to hide their sexual preferences. Older people want to have the right to refuse mandatory retirement and work as long as they are productive (Carr-Ruffino, 1998, p. 2). An inability to understand demographic and other differences and the expectations of people can lead to discrimination.

The results of a field study conducted by Özgener (2007) on diversity management, its impacts and the dimensions of discrimination occurring due to demographic differences, show that demographic characteristics, socio-cultural structure, managerial policy and behaviours, union tendency and regional differences, and political opinions have an influence on discrimination. According to the results, discrimination has been mostly observed in job processes such as promotions and appointments, recruitment and selection, especially employment examination and interviews, and performance appraisal.

According to the results of a study conducted by Kasimoglu and Halici (2000), political opinions, religious beliefs, local community, gender and age differences are influential in discrimination.

In a study which analyses diversity management practices in the Ottoman Empire, Katrinli et al. found that although the Ottoman Empire exhibited characteristics of Cox's (1991) plural organization type, the main characteristics and implementations are of a multicultural type:

> Diversity in the Ottoman Empire was due to many different factors, like ethnicity (Arabs, Kurds, Laz, Tcherkess, Greeks, Albanians), language (Arabic, Kurdish, Turkish, Greek, Bulgarian, Armenian, Albanian, Serbian) and religion

(Orthodox, Gregorian, Jewish, Catholic) (Mardin, 1977). However major criteria for defining different groups was religion. Different groups were formed on the basis of religion rather than ethnicity or geography. Basically the society is classified as Muslims and non-Muslims and the Muslims formed about 80 per cent of the population, thus constituting the majority (Guler, 1995). Non-Muslims enjoyed the same liberty and rights like privacy of residence, liberty of religion and thought, liberty of education, right to have access to public utilities and employment right as Muslims (Erdemir, 2001). (Katrinli et al., 2004, p. 8)

This situation has continued in the Republic of Turkey. There is a common belief that none of the minority groups has become a target for discrimination. Turkey is committed to a philosophy of being a nation-state; tolerance is a major belief system and this helps to prevent most types of discrimination.

Diversity management has gained legitimacy worldwide as an important subject for academicians and practitioners. However, the same cannot be said for the Turkish context. In other words, practitioners and academicians have only started to give importance to the subject during the last few years. There is a belief that there are no major differences between the people (Kamasak and Yucelen, 2007, p. 41) and Turkey's discrimination position is in line with this belief.

The International Management Development Institute's 2006 World Competition Power research ranks discrimination as a criterion. Estonia (1.89 points) and Finland (1.91 points) score the lowest points in discrimination. The countries with the highest points are Romania (5.54), Korea (5.23) and France (5.23). Turkey, with 2.98 points, holds a very good position among European countries, and likewise compared with the USA (3.71), Japan (4.74), China (3.73), India (4.00) and Russia (4.92) (TISK, 2007, pp. 161–2).

Turkey is part of a globalized world and cannot ignore the issues of diversity management. Although the country enjoys a good position on discrimination and positive standing due to its nation-state philosophy, it is still essential to pay attention to diversity management issues. Turkish companies must work towards employing workers with different talents, knowledge and expertise, thereby gaining a competitive advantage in the global arena. As the service sector expands, the number of contingent workers, foreign investments and multinational companies will increase. Furthermore, companies must start to address social responsibility issues and begin to conform to the SA 8000 Standard (Social Accountability Standard).

Turkey has a strategic advantage because of the conjunction of the European and Asian continents. According to Usluata and Bal (2007, pp. 98–9), because of this conjunction:

Turkey has been a historical gateway of commerce and culture between East and West, North and South. As a result, the society is characterized as one of 'diverse dynamics [whose] communicative practices reflect external (Western) influences and global trends on the one hand, and Turkish norms and values on the other' (Akar, 2002, p.1). In business life, as private holding companies that are run by family members are getting more dominant, state economic enterprises are decreasing in number.

As a secular country that is open to cross-cultural interactions, Turkey has a unique position in the global world, attracting an increasing number of multinational corporations and considerable foreign investment (Usluata and Bal, 2007, p. 99).

Diversity management is a concept that is rapidly being deployed worldwide. However, as some scholars argue, 'there is a need for context specific frames to understand how diversity management may work across different cultural and economic settings' (Özbilgin and Tatli, 2008, pp. xii, 3). Thus, diversity management approaches of one national context may not be appropriate for others (Nishii and Özbilgin, 2007, p. 1885). In line with this notion, this study aims to evaluate the Turkish context by examining the conditions in the country.

Turkish companies' concern about diversity management is quite new, and diversity issues have only recently been considered important. Workers are far from equally distributed on demographic dimensions such as race/ethnicity, age and disability (Özgener, 2007, p. 621).

Before we proceed to an evaluation of diversity in the workplace, general information about Turkey's population and demographic structure is given, assuming that workplace demography reflects the whole population and demographic structure of a country.

Population and demographic structure
Evaluation of the information about the population and its annual growth rate for the years 1927–2000 shows that the annual growth rates of the population are high. The population was estimated as 13,648,270 in the first census of 1927, and 20,947,188 in 1950, 40,347,719 in 1975, and 67,803,927 in 2000. In 2007 it was estimated to be 73,805,000, and it is projected to rise to 76,505,000 in 2010 (TUIK, 2008, p. 7). According to these data, the population has grown quickly and, according to some projections, will go on growing.

The number of males per 100 females was 92.65 in 1927, 101.91 in 1950, 105.82 in 1975 and 102.66 in 2000 (ibid., p. 31). Thus, when the population is evaluated by sex, the number of men is slightly higher than the number of women.

The median age of the population was 21.21 (19.11 for males and 23.40

for females) in 1935 and 24.83 (24.41 for males and 25.30 for females) for the year 2000. The median age is increasing for both males and females, especially in the last decades (it has increased continuously from 1970) (ibid., p. 31). These statistics show that the population is becoming older.

The percentage of older people in the world population is increasing and is seen as a problem by many countries; in particular, the average age of people in EU countries is increasing, as it is in Turkey. Future projections show that the population of EU countries will decrease in terms of number but will increase in terms of average age until the year 2050. The EU Commission reports that the working population (approximately 48 million) in the EU will decrease by 16 per cent and the senior population (over 65) will increase by 77 per cent. The reason for this elderly population seems to be the low fertility rate in these countries. This rate reflects the average number of live births that a woman would have during her reproductive life, assumed to be between 15 and 49 years of age. This rate was 2.66 decades ago but has now decreased to 1.48. The current rate of the EU shows that the number of young people will decrease to half the level in every two generations (TISK, 2007, p. 54). The fertility rate was 2.17 for Turkey in 2007 but is estimated to decrease to 1.79 by 2050. Thus Turkey's future would appear to be the same as European countries with regard to a young population.

If the population is evaluated according to marital status, the proportion of married people is always more than it is for those who never married, or are widowed or divorced. By the year 2000, the proportion of married people was 60 per cent (59.5 per cent for males and 61.8 per cent for females), which was more than the proportion of those who had never married (43.07 per cent), were widowed (4.40 per cent) or divorced (1.09 per cent) combined. The proportion of those who are married increases after the age of 25 for males and 20 for females compared to other age periods (TUIK, 2008, p. 38). In view of the relatively high marriage rate, companies should take marital status into account during policy making with regard to employees.

Migration from village to city is another important issue that creates a form of diversification. In the year 1990, the general population was 56,473,035, and 33,656,275 people lived in cities while the remaining 22,816,760 lived in villages. These figures were 44,006,274 for cities and 23,797,653 for villages in year 2000. The annual growth rate of the whole population was 18.28 per cent, the annual growth rate of the city population was 26.81 per cent, and the annual growth rate of the village population was 4.21 per cent (ibid., 2008 p. 33).

These numbers show that the growth rate in cities is higher than in villages. This also means that the number of people with different backgrounds is increasing. As a result of the policies of the 1980s, migration to cities climbed to high levels and was maintained in the following years.

Obviously, the population and its demographic structure are constantly changing, and since the workforce reflects the characteristics of the whole population, companies should have a general understanding of population statistics. The following subsections explain the changing structure of the workforce as well as the employment status of the population.

Employment

Unemployment is one of the major economic and social problems in developing countries as well as in developed countries, and Turkey considers unemployment as a major problem. The problem stems from economic crises, unsustainable growth rates, low competition power among international markets and no significant policies to improve a skilled workforce. Some 20 per cent of the population is unemployed and, according to the trend in population growth, this rate will be higher in the near future. The working population (aged 15–64) is estimated to show a high growth rate for the coming 30 years (TISK, 2007, p. 107). Unemployment rates are shown in Table 17.1.

The table shows that by the year 2006, the population of males who could work was 25,601,000, and the population of females was 26,070,000. When those who are unable to work for any reason are deducted from the population, these numbers become 18,297,000 for males and 6,480,000 for females. Thus, the rate of active participation in the workforce is 71.5 per cent for males and 24.9 per cent for females. These rates show that there is a huge gap between males and females in terms of participation in the workforce.

In addition, by 2006, there were 7,304,000 males and 19,588,000 females not included in the workforce. These data also support the important differences between the genders. Why people were not included in the workforce was investigated and the results indicated the following reasons for males: being retired, being a student, and being disabled, old or ill. The most important reason for females was being a housewife (TUIK 2008, p. 156). The differences between males and females will be elucidated below.

According to TUIK data, the educational status of the employed workforce in 2006 shows that the rate of those completing higher education among the workforce was 13 per cent, high school 20 per cent, secondary education 11 per cent, and primary education 46 per cent. The non-literate workforce was 5 per cent and the literate but unschooled workforce was 5 per cent. These rates show that the education status of the workforce is not high.

Table 17.1   Labour force status of non-institutional civilian population (age ≥ 15; thousands)

	2002	2003	2004	2005	2006
Turkey					
Total population	68,393	69,479	70,556	71,611	72,606
Population (age ≥ 15)	48,041	48,912	49,906	50,826	51,668
Labour force	23,818	23,640	24,289	24,565	24,776
Labour force participation rate (%)	49.6	48.3	48.7	48.3	48
Employed	21,354	21,147	21,791	22,046	22,330
Unemployed	2,464	2,493	2,498	2,519	2,446
Unemployment rate (%)	10.3	10.5	10.3	10.3	9.9
Not in labour force	24,223	25,272	25,616	26,260	26,892
Males					
Total population	34,154	34,692	35,226	35,747	36,214
Population (age ≥ 15)	23,827	24,260	24,755	25,209	25,601
Labour force	17,058	17,086	17,902	18,213	18,297
Labour force participation rate (%)	71.6	70.4	72.3	72.2	71.5
Employed	15,232	15,256	16,023	16,346	16,520
Unemployed	1,826	1,830	1,878	1,867	1,777
Unemployment rate (%)	10.7	10.7	10.5	10.3	9.7
Not in labour force	6,768	7,174	6,854	6,996	7,304
Females					
Total population	34,239	34,787	35,330	35,864	36,392
Population (age ≥ 15)	24,214	24,652	25,150	25,617	26,070
Labour force	6,760	6,555	6,388	6,352	6,480
Labour force participation rate (%)	27.9	26.6	25.4	24.8	24.9
Employed	6,122	5,891	5,768	5,700	5,810
Unemployed	638	663	620	652	670
Unemployment rate (%)	9.4	10.1	9.7	10.3	10.3
Not in labour force	17,455	18,098	18,763	19,264	19,588

Source: TUIK (2008, p. 154).

In the following subsection, employment conditions are evaluated in terms of basic diversity dimensions. These include employment of young people, women and the disabled.

Employment of young people   Unemployed youth is a common problem for all countries worldwide. According to the International Labour Organization (ILO) (2006), 400 million job opportunities must be created to use the full potential of the young population. According to ILO research ('Global approaches to youth employment, 2006'), the youth unemployment rate is 13.5 per cent, far above the overall rate of 4.5 per cent. Almost 50 per cent of unemployed workers in the world are young. The best-performing countries in youth employment are the Netherlands (65.2 per cent), Denmark (62.3 per cent) and the UK (54 per cent). Countries with a poor performance in youth employment are Poland (36.9 per cent), Slovakia (30.1 per cent) and Greece (26 per cent) (TISK, 2007, p. 165).

Turkey has very similar results to the rest of the world. According to the 2006 numbers, the youth unemployment rate is 18.7 per cent, rising to 21.5 per cent in the big cities. One out of four young people is unemployed in Turkey (ibid., p. 165), indicating that there is a problem in this area.

Most of the EU countries apply different incentive plans for youth employment and education. These plans include financial subsidies, tax reductions and reductions in social security payments (ibid., p. 158). Since there is no significant incentive plan in Turkey, although similar problems exist, there is a need to establish these kinds of practices in the country.

Employment of women   The female employment rate in Turkey is relatively low compared to other countries. In other words, Turkey fails to use its female workforce in the economic and social development process. In the process of harmonization with the EU, the regulatory framework is well structured but has failed to encourage women to participate in the workforce. The problems faced by women are not legally based, but appear to be economically and socially based (ibid., p. 154).

The unemployment problem is common for both males and females, but the rate of unemployed females is significantly higher than that for males (TURKONFED, 2007, p. 79).

According to the Global Sexual Equality 2006 Report presented in the World Economic Forum, Turkey's position regarding general conditions is 105th among 115 countries. Turkey rank's 110th in terms of female employment, 106th in having female parliamentarians, 105th in having female ministers and 95th in having female civil servants. These poor rankings show that the country needs to address the issue of sexual equality (TISK, 2007, p. 163).

According to the Human Development Report of the United Nations Development Programme, Turkey is rated 92nd on the Gender Development Index. The report indicates that females are paid less for the same job compared to males. The income difference in the marketplace in Turkey stems primarily from this fact (TURKONFED, 2007, p. 27).

Compared to EU countries, Turkey has the lowest rate (23.8 per cent) of females in the workforce. According to TUIK statistics, the female workforce rate was 34.1 per cent in 1990 and decreased to 24.9 per cent in 2006. Women are employed primarily in the agriculture sector. A low level of education and being unskilled are the main reasons for unemployment among women (TISK, 2007, pp. 155–7).

Flexible working conditions, which normally lead to an increase in the number of women in the workforce, are not widespread in the country. The role of women in society and cultural dimensions also discourages them from working. The laws and regulations concerning the protection of women in employment are very conservative, and increase the cost of having a female workforce; this is one of the reasons why companies hesitate to employ women (ibid., p. 161).

The rate of female attendance in the workforce is one-third that of males. Some 48 per cent of employed women work in the agriculture sector, 14 per cent in production, 10 per cent in trade, 6 per cent in education, 5 per cent in the healthcare sector, and 5 per cent in the other services sector. Social and family pressure (16 per cent) is the biggest barrier for women. Others are marriage, low confidence level, injustice about wages and difficulties in the workplace (TURKONFED, 2007, pp. 23, 27).

Discrimination against women, whether implicit or explicit, has the effect of reducing their participation in the workforce. As of 2006, 16,520,000 men worked in every economic area (agriculture, forestry, hunting and fishing; mining and quarrying; manufacturing; electricity, gas and water; construction; the wholesale and retail trade, restaurants and hotels; transportation, communication and storage; finance, insurance, real estate and business services; community, social and personal services). In contrast, 5,810,000 women worked only in agriculture (2,816,000) and community, social and personal services (1,091,000). In other words, women have no adequate representation in other economic areas. In the year 2006, of the 2,816,000 females employed in the agriculture sector, 2,092,000 were unpaid. Of the males who were employed in the sector (3,272,000) in the year 2006, 2,167,000 were self-employed (TUIK, 2008, pp. 157–9).

Sexual discrimination also shows itself in other professions. Some professions are considered women's work and others are seen as men's work. When the 2006 data are analysed, men are represented in most areas (legislators, executives, officials and managers, professionals, technicians, clerks, service workers and shop and market sales workers, skilled agricultural and fishery workers, craft and related trades workers, plant and machine operators and assemblers, and so on); although many women also worked in the agriculture sector, they were not well represented as legislators, seniors, officials and managers, plant and machine operators and assemblers (TUIK, 2008, p. 158). As the above data show, there are significant problems in terms of gender equality. Among these, prejudice towards women may be the most important.

Although the economic activity rates of women are very low, the proportion of female academics who achieve professorial status is very high (Özbilgin and Healy, 2004). Healy et al. (2005, p. 252) state: 'there are many possible reasons for Turkish women's academic achievements, many rooted in specific historical, social and economic contexts'.

Some research indicates that in spite of laws and regulations related to individual choices of female employees, conditions for women in the workplace remain poor. For example, when women give birth they usually leave their job, whereas men who become fathers continue to work. Women are perceived as suffering from more ill health, and because they leave their job for marriage and children, employers often regard them as a poor economic risk. This means that work–family conflict is of more importance to women than to men. In fact, women are very similar to men in terms of psychological attitudes and reactions in the workplace (Thomas et al., 2004, pp. 37–8).

Inequality in terms of gender is observed not just in Turkey, but also in most countries of the world. For example, Syed (2010) states that women have limited employment opportunities in Saudi Arabia, and Calveley and Hollinshead (ch. 7, this volume) point out that a significant number of women face inequality in the Russian workplace. They demonstrate that in Russia 'women and migrant workers are most likely to be at the lower end of the economic stratum and find themselves in the position of competing for lower-paid work'. Also, women have problems attaining a managerial position in Lebanon (Al Ariss, ch. 4, this volume).

Employment of disabled people   The proportion of disability in Turkey was 12 per cent (11 per cent for males and 13 per cent for females) in 2002. The proportion of people who have orthopaedic, visual, hearing, speaking and mental disabilities is 2.58 per cent (3.05 per cent for males and 2.12 per cent for females). Some 9.70 per cent of the disabled population have chronic illnesses (8.05 per cent for males and 11.33 per cent for females). These data were collected from the Turkey Disability Survey that was carried out in 2002 (TUIK, 2008, p. 89).

Employment of disabled people, their education and social rights are written in to Turkish constitutional law. These rights are also included in other laws and regulations, but implementation causes some problems, and employment of disabled people is one of these (TISK, 2007, p. 171).

The labour force participation rate of disabled people in Turkey is 21.71 per cent, the unemployment rate is 15.46 per cent and the rate of unemployment is 78.29 per cent. The labour force participation rate of people with chronic illnesses is 22.87 per cent, the unemployment rate is 10.77 per cent and the rate of those with chronic illnesses not employed is 77.13 per cent (TUIK, 2008, p. 91).

In spite of the social principle in Turkish constitutional law, employment of the disabled is primarily left to the quota system and the responsibility is transferred to employers (TISK, 2007, p. 171). According to this, when disabled people's expectations from their organizations are evaluated, they mostly expect financial support from the organizations (61.2 per cent). The other expectations can be listed as help in finding a job (9.55 per cent), having treatment and care services by health personnel at home (4.12 per cent), defence in legal rights (3.51 per cent) and creation of educational opportunities (3.31 per cent).

According to Thomas et al. (2004, p. 42),

> One common assumption about physically disabled workers is the belief that physical limitations cause them to miss more work than do non-disabled workers, produce poorer quality work, and drive up the costs of healthcare premiums. Cox (1994: 90) elaborates by suggesting that 'employers have traditionally resisted hiring persons with disabilities partly because of the belief that they pose safety risks, increase health care costs, have higher absence, and lower productive capacity than non-disabled workers.' In actuality, disabled workers can be major assets to an organization's workforce. Workers with disabilities are often most loyal to their employers, thus saving organizations money from turnover costs (Hughes and Kleiner, 1995; Mergenhagen, 1997).

Finally, to improve the situation of disadvantaged groups, the governments must adopt the ILO's conventions on equal treatment and non-discrimination (Özgener, 2007, p. 629).

Social developments

The equality principle, a discourse used worldwide as well as in Turkey, makes diversity management a must for organizations (Booth, 2006, p. 50). For a good working economic and social life, it is necessary to eliminate discrimination by age, sexuality, race and apply the principle of equal opportunity (TISK, 2007, p. 161).

The concept of equality is on the agenda of some communities, governments, organizations and individuals for specific reasons. One of the most important is that women's desire to participate in the workforce is increasing daily. It is probable that there will be more part-time work; some sectors, such as paid home-care services, childcare, institutional care and care of the elderly will grow because of the increasing rate of women's participation in the workforce (Booth, 2006, p. 50).

In addition to this development, e-learning and the establishment of information societies are other changes necessitating diversity management. These conditions have also raised the concept of knowledge workers. The increasing number of such workers is another of the factors necessitating effective diversity management. Management practices that encourage innovation and a high performance and learning culture that embraces all workers are needed in organizations where employees' knowledge, skills, abilities and attitudes are important. Diversity management holds the potential for contributing to such goals (Ashkanasy et al., 2002, p. 308).

Growth in the service sector

The service sector is defined as the fastest-growing industry in the economies of countries all over the world, and it will increase even more (ibid., p. 308). Although manufacturing is often carried out at a distance by people who never see the customers using their products, when services are provided there is direct interaction between the provider and the consumer of services. Therefore, the needs and satisfaction of customers are very important to providers. In this context, efficient diversity management is very important in the service sector since, in particular, cultural differences between provider and customer may impair communication (Hays-Thomas, 2004, pp. 15–16).

According to the 2007 TUIK data, when employment in sectors is evaluated, 27 per cent are employed in the low-effective low-value-added agriculture sector. The other sector proportions are 20 per cent for production, 6 per cent for construction and 47 per cent for services (TISK, 2007, pp. 110–12). The service sector rate is higher when compared to other sectors and it increases yearly (43 per cent for the year 2004, 46 per cent for the year 2005 and 47 per cent for the year 2006).

Increase in the number of contingent workers

Contingent work is defined as 'borrowed work', and refers to the temporary transfer of workers from one employer to another. This kind of work is encouraged and regulated by laws in the EU, and the primary reason is the need for flexibility; one of the benefits is creating employment for the unemployed, women, young and old people (ibid., pp. 175–76).

The increase in contingent workers is another change affecting diversity initiatives. Despite the fact that some contingent employees are long-term workers, the increase in the proportion of these workers' attachment to their employers has been dramatic. Greater diversity in the identities and the very presence of the individuals who are at work from day to day is the inevitable result. Furthermore, policies of companies, wage scales and benefit structures related to every kind of employee may vary (Hays-Thomas, 2004, p. 17).

Globalization, international businesses and mergers
The global economy has moved diversity and diversity management to the top of the agenda (Mor Barak, 2005, p. 2). According to Rowntree et al. (2003, p. 1):

> The most important challenges facing the world in the twenty-first century are associated with globalization, the increasing interconnectedness of people and places through converging processes of economic, political and cultural change. . . . Many observers specify that globalization is the most fundamental reorganization of the planet's socio-economic structure since the Industrial Revolution.

In spite of the influence of industry or of geographic location on the level of diversity, organizations also depend on demographic changes and globalization (Agars and Kottke, 2004, p. 55). The world is increasingly experiencing globalization (Al Ariss, ch. 4, this volume). As globalization becomes commonplace in multinational corporations, free trade agreements and joint ventures cause individuals from very different races to come into close contact within organizations (Bhadury et al., 2000, p. 144).

Because international business is one of the most remarkable factors in valuing diversity, management is essential for success. It is very important to develop and implement initiatives for multinational corporations since, because of these initiatives, they capture and retain diverse customer bases. Furthermore, multinational corporations need to recruit a diverse workforce in order to respond to the requirements of a diverse market (Wentling, 2000, p. 435).

The number of mergers among companies has increased in recent years. This combination causes different cultures, technologies and ways of working to pose challenges to management and to employees. In this context, dealing effectively with differences enables companies to achieve their aims (Hays-Thomas, 2004, pp. 16–7).

In conjunction with the increase of mergers and acquisitions, diversity in the workforce will become the most important subject for organizations and people will have more definite ideas about what diversities are and how they can be managed in the future (Mavin and Girling, 2000, p. 420). But workplace diversity is not limited to mergers and acquisitions or international businesses. According to Dereli (ch. 8, this volume), 'Global demographic trends are diversifying the domestic labour force in most countries of the world'.

Sustainable development is a result of globalization and the competition brought by globalization, and sustained economic growth goes hand in hand with social harmony and environmental protection. The need for sustainable development leads companies to consider their position and role in the community. Corporate social responsibility is a major component of these discussions and globalization, corporate transparency, accountability and an information-based economy have triggered this major component. The common point of all corporate social responsibility definitions is a willingness in these affairs rather than an enforcement of regulations (TISK, 2007, pp. 41, 43).

Laws and regulations

Law is one of the factors leading us to address organizational diversity issues. The roots of diversity have taken place in the civil rights legislation and policies of the 1960s and the changes in the legal climate that have resulted from politics, elections and the development of case law (Hays-Thomas, 2004, pp. 11, 17).

The US Civil Rights Act of 1964 was arguably the most important influence in diversity-related concerns and practices in the USA. As Hag (2004) states, legal structures shape diversity practices in nations around the world. Engaging in pro-diversity practices enables many organizations to avoid breaking the law and having to submit to costly penalties. In other words, legal structures are very important in helping diversity practices in nations around the world (Stockdale and Cao, 2004, pp. 300–01).

Various regulations and laws that help to improve the practice of diversity management in the United States and the UK are listed below (Hays-Thomas, 2004, p. 18; Hubbard, 2004, pp. 41–3; US GAO, 2005, pp. 33–4). The United States has the Civil Rights Act, Affirmative Action, Equal Employment Opportunity, Sexual Harassment, American with Disabilities Act, the Rehabilitation Act, the Age Discrimination in Employment Act and the Equal Pay Act. The UK has the Sex Discrimination Act, the Race Relations Act, the Race Relations Amendment, the Human Rights Act, the Disability Discrimination Act, the Equal Pay Act, the Rehabilitation of Offenders Act, the Fair Employment Act, Criminal Justice and Public Order, the Employment Rights Act, the Asylum and Immigration Act, and rights relating to religion and beliefs and sexual orientation.

Laws that can be thought of as related to diversity management in Turkey are classified below.

According to Article 49 of the constitution of the Republic of Turkey, dealing with 'the right and duty to work':

> Everyone has the right and duty to work. The State shall take the necessary measures to raise the standard of living of workers, and to protect workers and the unemployed in order to improve the general conditions of labour, to promote labour, to create suitable economic conditions for the prevention of unemployment and to secure labour peace.

On the other hand, equality related to this working right is set out Articles 10 and 70. According to Article 10:

> All individuals are equal without any discrimination before the law, irrespective of language, race, colour, sex, political opinion, philosophical belief, religion and sect, or any such considerations . . . men and women have equal rights. The State shall have the obligation to ensure that this equality exists in practice . . . No privilege shall be granted to any individual, family, group or class . . . State organs and administrative authorities shall act in compliance with the principle of equality before the law in all their proceedings.

According to Article 70: 'Every Turk has the right to enter public service . . . No criteria other than the qualifications for the office concerned shall be taken into consideration for recruitment into public service'.

The equality principle and the prohibition of discrimination in the workplace are usually added to the agenda in terms of gender. However, this is not the only dimension. The equality principle encompasses language, religion, class, political thinking, union attendance, disability and age. Discrimination in these areas is forbidden by the law (Balci, 2007, p. 110).

According to the New Labour Law, 4857, which came into force in 2003, Article 5 states: 'No discrimination based on language, race, sex, political opinion, philosophical belief, religion and sex or similar reasons is permissible in the employment relationship'. Thus, Turkey has come into line with EU legal standards. However, some improvements are needed in practice.

Turkey has also signed international conventions and declarations such as the Universal Declaration of Human Rights, the European Human Rights Declaration, the European Convention of Human Rights and Fundamental Freedoms, the International Convention on the Elimination of All Forms of Racial Discrimination (ICERD), the Declaration on the Elimination of All Forms of Intolerance and of Discrimination Based on Religion or Belief, the Declaration on the Rights of Persons Belonging to National or Ethnic, Religious or Linguistic Minorities, and the Convention on the Elimination of All Forms of Discrimination against Women (CEDAW). Thus, the issue of diversity management should now be supported more by legal regulations.

In addition,

> The Directorate General on the Status and Problems of Women was established in the late 1980s to encourage and support women's active participation in politics and employment in Turkey. Although this organization was equivalent to the Equal Opportunities Commission in Britain, it has not yet established a comparable reputation as a public service agency in Turkey. Although there are

institutions and groups working towards equality in Turkey, they largely lack legislative power to act against discriminatory practices and their programs fail to reach rural areas in Turkey. Therefore, the policing of sex discrimination in employment is largely left to the good will of employers at the point of recruitment and selection. (Özbilgin, 2000, p. 48; Woodward and Özbilgin, 1999, p. 327)

Conclusion

The Turkish population has grown quickly and, according to some projections, will go on growing. The median age of the population is increasing and the population is becoming older. The fertility rate is decreasing, which means that the young population will diminish. Because of the high marriage rate, companies have to consider marital status during policy making with regard to employees. The population growth rate in cities is higher than in villages, which means that the number of people with different backgrounds is getting higher. Thus, the population and demographic structure of Turkey is constantly changing.

Age, gender and disability are thought to be the basic dimensions of diversity in Turkey. Not surprisingly, they feature in laws. The working population is estimated to show a high growth rate for the coming 30 years but there is a huge gap between males and females in terms of participation in the workforce. The problem of unemployment is common for both men and women, but the number of unemployed women is significantly higher than that for men. The low education rate and the lack of skills are seen as the main reasons for unemployment among women, but other reasons exist, such as nonexistent flexible working conditions, the role of women in society and cultural dimensions, social and family pressure, marriage, low confidence level, unjust wages and difficulties in the workplace. In addition, the proportion of disability in Turkey is very high. Although there are some regulations in the law, there continue to be problems with implementation.

According to Özgener (2007, p. 621): 'Workforce diversity is an international phenomenon in developed and developing countries. . . . Many countries such as Turkey, China, Mexico, Brazil, India and Russia have diverse ethnic, linguistic and religious groups (Jain and Verma, 1996; Leme and Fleury, 1999)'. This is also emphasized by the studies of April and Smit (ch. 5, this volume), Calveley and Hollinshead (ch. 7, this volume) and indeed in almost every chapter in this book. In their study which is conducted in the context of China, April and Smit state: 'China can be seen as a cluster of cultures from different regions'. Calveley and Hollinshead comment: 'the Russian case offers unique insights into the field of diversity'.

As well as having diverse groups, internationalization and globalization of the economy means that businesses have to work in multinational and multicultural markets, and gives importance to diversity issues (Özgener, 2007, p. 621). For these reasons, diversity management is becoming an important area of consideration for businesses and managers in Turkey as well as in other countries worldwide.

In line with this, the concept of diversity management in Turkey should be investigated with field studies. Diversity management implications in Turkish companies, the process of these practices and effects of these approaches on the outcomes of the companies can be a starting point for future research studies. These kinds of empirical studies will contribute to the Turkish diversity management literature.

References

Agars, Mark D. and Janet L. Kottke (2004), 'Models and practice of diversity management: a historical review and presentation of a new integration theory', in Margaret S. Stockdale and Faye J. Crosby (eds), *The Psychology and Management of Workplace Diversity*, Cambridge, MA: Blackwell, pp. 55–77.

Aliefendioglu, H. and M.F. Özbilgin (2006), 'Kadin-erkek esitligi politikalari uzerine bir degerlendirme: Turkiye ve Britanya Karsilastirmasi' (An evaluation of institutional policies of sex equality in Britain and Turkey), *Kadin Arastirmalari Dergisi* (Journal for Women Studies), **9**, 1–19.

Ashkanasy, N.M., C.E.J. Härtel and C.S. Daus (2002), 'Diversity and emotion: the new frontiers in organizational behavior research', *Journal of Management*, **28** (3), 307–38.

Aytac, S. (2000), 'Ozurlulerin rehabilitasyonunun artan onemi' (The importance of rehabilitation of disabled people), *Dokuz Eylul Universitesi Sosyal Bilimler Enstitusu Dergisi* (Dokuz Eylul University Journal of Social Sciences), **2** (2), 54–79.

Balci, Sebnem (2007), 'Turk is ve sosyal guvenlik hukukunda esitlik ilkesi ve ayrimcilik yasagi' (Equality principle and prohibition of discrimination in Turkish Labour and Social Security Law), in Beliz Dereli (ed.), *Isgucunde Farkliliklarin Yonetimi* (Managing workforce diversity), Istanbul: Beta Basim, pp. 109–26.

Bereket, T. and B.D. Adam (2006), 'The emergence of gay identities in contemporary Turkey', *Sexualities*, **9** (2), 131–51.

Bhadury, J., E.J. Mighty and H. Damar (2000), 'Maximizing workforce diversity in project teams: a network flow approach', *International Journal of Management Science*, **28**, 143–53.

Booth, C. (2006), 'Managing diversity and mainstreaming equality: reflections on initiatives in the Planning Inspectorate', *Planning Theory and Practice*, **7** (1), 47–62.

Budak, G. (2008), *Yetkinlige Dayali insan Kaynaklari Yönetimi* (competency-based human resource management), Izmir: Baris Yayinlari.

Bulutlar, Fusun (2007), 'Isgucu farkliligi, performans degerlendirmesi ve duygular' (Workforce diversity, performance evaluation and emotions), in Beliz Dereli (ed.), *Isgucunde Farkliliklarin Yonetimi* (Managing workforce diversity), Istanbul: Beta Basim, pp. 163–83.

Carr-Ruffino, N. (1998), *Managing Diversity, People Skills for a Multicultural Workplace*, New York: Simon & Schuster.

Cox, T.H. Jr (1991), 'The multicultural organization', *Academy of Management Executive*, **5** (2), 34–47.

Hag, R. (2004), 'International perspectives on workplace diversity' in Margaret S. Stockdale and Faye J. Crosby (eds), *The Psychology and Management of Workplace Diversity*, Cambridge, MA: Blackwell, pp. 277–98.

Harrison, D.A., K.H. Price and M.P. Bell (1998), 'Beyond relational demography: time and the effects of surface- and deep-level diversity on work group cohesion', *Academy of Management Journal*, **41** (1), 96–107.

Harrison, D.A. and K.J. Klein (2007), 'What's the difference? Diversity constructs as separation, variety, or disparity in organizations', *Academy of Management Review*, **32** (4), 1199–228.

Hays-Thomas, Rosemary (2004), 'Why now? The contemporary focus on managing diversity', in Margaret S. Stockdale and Faye J. Crosby (eds), *The Psychology and Management of Workplace Diversity*, Cambridge, MA: Blackwell, pp. 3–30.

Healy, G., M. Özbilgin and H. Aliefendioglu (2005), 'Academic employment and gender: a Turkish challenge to vertical sex segregation', *European Journal of Industrial Relations*, **11** (2), 247–64.

Hubbard, Edward E. (2004), *The Manager's Pocket Guide to Diversity Management*, Amherst, MA: HRD Press.

International Labour Organization (ILO) (2006), 'Global employment trends for youth', Report, Geneva: ILO, available at: http://www.ilo.org/global/What_we_do/Publications/Officialdocuments/lang--en/docName--WCMS_077664/index.htm (accessed 10 June 2009).

Kamasak, Rifat and Murat Yucelen (2007), 'Farklılıkların etkin yonetimi: calisanlarin farklilik algisi ve ampirik bir arastirma' (Effective diversity management: the perception of diversity of employees and an empirical study), in Beliz Dereli (ed.), *Isgucunde Farkliliklarin Yonetimi* (Managing workforce diversity), Istanbul: Beta Basim, pp. 31–57.

Kara, O. (2006), 'Occupational gender wage discrimination in Turkey', *Journal of Economic Studies*, **33** (2), 130–43.

Kasimoglu, M. and A. Halici (2000), 'Insan kaynaklarına yonelik ayrimciliga iliskin olcek gelistirmesi' (Scale development related to the discrimination against human resources), Proceedings of the 8th National Management and Organization Conference, 25–27 May, Nevsehir, pp. 373–85.

Katrinli, A., J. Kesken, G. Atabay, and G. Gunay (2004), 'History that embraces diversity', Proceedings of the 9th bi-annual conference of the International Society for the Study of Work and Organizational Values (ISSWOV), CD-rom, New Orleans.

Kusku, F., M.F. Özbilgin and L. Özkale (2007), 'Against the tide: gendered prejudice and disadvantage in engineering study from a comparative perspective', *Gender, Work and Organization*, **14** (2), 109–29.

Mavin, S. and G. Girling (2000), 'What is managing diversity and why does it matter?', *Human Resource Development International*, **3** (4), 419–33.

McMillan-Capehart, A. (2003), 'Hundreds of years of diversity: what took us so long?', *Equal Opportunities International*, **22** (8), 20–37.

Milliken, F.J. and L.L. Martins (1996), 'Searching for common threads: understanding the multiple effects of diversity in organizational groups', *Academy of Management Review*, **21** (2), 402–33.

Mor Barak, Michalle E. (2005), *Managing Diversity, Toward a Globally Inclusive Workplace*, Newbury Park, CA: Sage.

Mujtaba, B.G. (2007), *Workforce Diversity Management, Challenges, Competencies, and Strategies*, Fort Lauderdale, FL: Llumina Press.

Nishii, L.H. and M.F. Özbilgin (2007), 'Global diversity management: towards a conceptual framework', *International Journal of Human Resource Management*, **18** (11), 1883–94.

Özbilgin, M.F. (2000), 'Is the practice of equal opportunities management keeping pace with theory? Management of sex equality in the financial services sector in Britain and Turkey', *Human Resource Development International*, **3** (1), 43–67.

Özbilgin, M.F. (2002), 'The way forward for equal opportunities by sex in employment in Turkey and Britain', *Management International*, **7** (1), 55–65.

Özbilgin, M. and G. Healy (2004), 'The gendered nature of career development of university professors: the case of Turkey', *Journal of Vocational Behavior*, **64**, 358–71.

Özbilgin, Mustafa F. and Ahu Tatli (2008), *Global Diversity Management, An Evidence-Based Approach*, New York: Palgrave Macmillan.

Özbilgin, M.F. and D. Woodward (2004), 'Belonging and otherness: sex equality in banking in Turkey and Britain', *Gender, Work and Organization*, **11** (6), 668–88.

Özgener, S. (2007), 'Diversity management and demographic differences-based discrimination: the case of Turkish manufacturing industry', *Journal of Business Ethics*, **82** (3), 621–31.

Pelled, L.H. (1996), 'Demographic diversity, conflict, and work group outcomes: an intervening process theory', *Organization Science*, **7** (6), 615–31.

Pelled, L.H., K.M. Eisenhardt and K.R. Xin (1999), 'Exploring the black box: an analysis of work group diversity, conflict, and performance', *Administrative Science Quarterly*, **44** (1), 1–28.

Rowntree, Les, Martin Lewis, Marie Price and William Wyckoff (2003), *Diversity Amid Globalization*, Englewood Cliffs, NJ: Prentice Hall.

Simons, T., L.H. Pelled and K.A. Smith (1999), 'Making use of difference: diversity, debate, and decision comprehensiveness in top management teams', *Academy of Management Journal*, **42** (6), 662–73.

Stockdale, Margaret S. and Feng Cao (2004), 'Looking back and heading forward: major themes of the psychology and management of workplace diversity', in Margaret S. Stockdale and Faye J. Crosby (eds), *The Psychology and Management of Workplace Diversity*, Cambridge, MA: Blackwell, pp. 299–316.

Sural Özer, Pinar (2007), 'Cesitliligi yeniden dusunmek ve cesitliliklerin yonetimi' (Rethink of diversity and diversity management), in Mustafa Kurt and Serkan Bayraktaroglu (eds), *Turkiye'de isletmecilikte yeni perspektifler* (New perspectives of business in Turkey), Ankara: Gazi Kitapevi, pp. 97–122.

Sürgevil, Olca (2008), 'Diversity and an analytic approach to workforce diversity management', PhD thesis, Dokuz Eylul University, Turkey.

Syed, Jawad (2010), 'From gender empowerment to gender diversity: measuring the gender gap in Muslim majority countries', ch. 12 in Mustafa Özbilgin and Jawad Syed (eds), *Managing Gender Diversity in Asia: A Research Companion*, Cheltenham, UK and Northampton, MA, USA: Edward Elgar, pp. 210–26.

Thomas, Kecia M., Dan A. Mack and Amelie Montagliani (2004), 'The arguments against diversity: are they valid?', in Margaret S. Stockdale and Faye J. Crosby (eds), *The Psychology and Management of Workplace Diversity*, Cambridge, MA: Blackwell, pp. 31–51.

Thomas, R.R., Jr. (1991), *Beyond Race and Gender: Unleashing the Power of Your Total Workforce by Managing Diversity*, New York, AMACOM.

TISK – Türkiye Isveren Sendikaları Konfederasyonu 23. Genel Kurul Calisma Raporu (Turkish Confederation of Employers' Union, Labour Report) (2007), Ankara.

TUIK (Turkish Statistical Institute) (2008), *Turkey's Statistical Yearbook, 2007*, Ankara.

TURKONFED – Türk Girisim ve Is Dunyasi Konfederasyonu, Is Dunyasinda Kadin Raporu (Turkish Enterprise and Business Confederation, Women in Business Report) (2007), Istanbul.

United States Government Accountability Office (US GAO) (2005), 'Diversity Management: Expert-Identified Leading Practices and Agency Examples', Report to the Ranking Minority Member, Committee on Homeland Security and Governmental Affairs, US Senate, GAO-05-90, available at: www.gao.gov/cgi-bin/getrpt?GAO-05-90 (accessed 10 June 2009).

Usluata, A. and E.A. Bal (2007), 'The meaning of diversity in a Turkish company: an interview with Mehmet Oner', *Business Communication Quarterly*, **70**, 98–102.

Uzuncarsili, Ulku and Ayda Uzuncarsili Soydas (2007), 'Farkliliklarin yonetimi ve cinsiyet ayrimciligi: is dunyasinda kadin olmak' (Diversity management and gender discrimination: to be a woman in a business world), in Beliz Dereli (ed.), *Isgucunde Farkliliklarin Yonetimi* (Managing workforce diversity), Istanbul: Beta Basim, pp. 59–107.

Wentling, R.M. (2000), 'Evaluation of diversity initiatives in multinational corporations', *Human Resource Development International*, **3** (4), 435–50.

Woodward, D. and M. Özbilgin (1999), 'Sex equality in the financial services sector in Turkey and the UK', *Women in Management Review*, **14** (8), 325–32.

18 Ethical and cultural aspects of diversity and unicity in the Arab Middle East: managing diverse knowledge in a culturally unicist environment
*David Weir**

Cultural background to diversity management philosophies in Europe and the UK

There is a common philosophical thread to most discussions of equality and diversity in Western European countries that relates also to notions of equality and legal status enshrined explicitly in both the American and French constitutions. Thus 'equality' under the law normally includes notions of fairness backed by legislation to ensure as far as possible systems and processes in which all citizens can participate to ensure that as individuals their rights under law are protected, and in which relevant opportunities to develop their individual capabilities are maximised. These notions of equality may be expressed either in absolute or processual terms but are in some interpretations taken almost as emblematic of the post-Enlightenment 'modern' condition (Berlin, 1964, 1988).

These notions of diversity stem from a perception that individual capabilities spring from differing cultural roots. Consequently in the corporate environment it may be seen as organisationally advantageous for institutions to encourage complexity as a system value to ensure that opportunities to learn for the organisation and its members are not diminished by the hegemony of one pattern of thought. These understandings have in the European context been supported by a political discourse that sees the member states of the European Union as implicated in specific histories and that explicitly recalls the potential for conflict that has occurred historically when one state or one belief pattern has sought to impose hegemonic cultural domination, be it under Napoleonic, Hitlerian or Stalinist leadership.

As the United States has appeared to become ethnically and organisationally more diverse, largely through recognition of historic injustices that were faced by both indigeneous Americans and African Americans but also by a continuing influx of Hispanic-origin immigrants, a discourse of diversity has also more recently impacted on managerial thinking.

Sometimes in management texts this has been supported by a perception that failure to recognise the inherent diversities of workforces and of their members can impair organisational functioning and jeopardise business success.

A comprehensive account of the bases for diversity would involve ethnicity, religion, gender, sexual orientation, region, language, social class, education, age, ability and personal beliefs, and we have not the space to review all these here.

In managerial terms as for example in 'best practice' manuals and training materials published by such organisations as the Chartered Institute of Personnel and Development (CIPD) in the UK, there is a general formulation that implies assent to notions that all humans are intrinsically different in some substantial ways (CIPD, 2009). Moreover, research in the field supports the claim that the recognition within systems of organisational management that these differences represent a benefit rather than a threat can improve the chances of organisational success through effective performance (Tatli et al., 2007).

The contemporary managerial discourse of diversity in Western countries differentiates itself from an earlier discourse of 'equal opportunity'. This can sometimes be expressed in terms of metaphoric analogy seeing, for example, the former as rooted in a 'melting pot' model and the latter as a 'stir fry' in which the separate ingredients maintain their individual flavour after the cooking process.

The driving forces of the diversity discourse are typically rooted in legislative imperatives and in the changing nature of the external and internal labour markets and the increasingly global scale of operations, especially of business organisations operating in diverse contexts on a global scale. Often these arguments are related to theories of impending skill shortages and limited bases of 'talent' available to employers.

Another driving force in the recognition of diversity as a central aspect of modern management has come from the growing recognition of the importance of cultural aspects of organisation.

An even more fundamental theoretical focus on diversity as a determining aspect of post-modern social organisation has come from the continuing philosophical concern with the 'other'. This has ranged from Levinas's call for ethics to be regarded as first philosophy, prior to ontological and epistemological concerns to Schutz's elaboration of the nature of social understanding (Levinas, 1969; Schutz, 1949; see also Barber, 1989). These are not issues that in day-to-day life resonate much with operational managers: nonetheless there is continuing intellectual concern with these topics, exemplified most recently perhaps in the continuing theme in Charles Taylor's work to bridge the Anglo-Saxon and the European approaches to these themes (Taylor, 1992) and these fundamental analyses form an underpinning backdrop to our concerns.

Diversity in Islamic culture and philosophy
While there is a growing body of empirical research on management in the Arab Middle East, nonetheless much contemporary literature suffers from an attempt to explain the organisational practices of this milieu in terms of Western models and modes of explanation that are inappropriate to the physical and spatial structures as well as the cultural framework (see Said, 1997; Weir, 1998). This critique applies equally to diversity management, where implicitly it is the Western models of diversity that may underpin explanations. A similar point is made by Yükleyen (ch. 20, this volume) and also by Metcalfe (2010). Lewis (2002) goes further and finds that differences of this kind provide evidence for the conclusion that in these respects as in others, Arab society in particular has 'failed'.

It has been argued that considerations of this kind underpin, as much as does the experienced reality of terrorism, the characterisation of the Arab world in particular as 'dangerous' (Weir, 2005).

Empirical research shows that the practice of management is indeed different in the Arab Middle East from the West. The dual pull of tradition and modernity is evident in the characteristic responses of Arab managers to the problems of managing authority and relationships in organisations. We have previously identified these practices as together constituting a 'fourth paradigm' of management values, styles and behaviours (Weir, 1998, 2000).

Al-Rasheed has compared managerial practices and organisation systems in comparable Western and Arab situations, finding that in the Arab contexts the personalised concept of power leads to feelings of uncertainty and loss of autonomy among lower-level organisational participants. Conversely, when problems occur, they tend to be ascribed to personal failure rather than to organisational or administrative shortcomings (Al-Rasheed, 1994).

Management, leadership, decision-making and followership issues relate to complex phenomena in Arab organisations and are closely tied up with notions of shame and reputation. Other cultures of the Mediterranean regions have been characterised as 'shame cultures' rather than 'guilt cultures': thus if a senior person fails to provide hospitality for a guest, this may be seen as shameful. A good leader is thus one who arranges matters so as to protect dependants, whether in organisations or family, from shame (Peristiany, 1966).

These regions have been characterised in many ways, as zones of cultural backwardness (Banfield, 1958) and of cultural cauldrons in which geo-morphological, economic, ethnic and historical influences have typically been potentiated in conflict (Braudel, 1949). In a series of publications both fictional and historical, Maalouf has characterised the history of these conflicts in terms framed by the discourse of identity, and his French tract on identity calls on the modern reader to recognise that these diverse identities can become murderous if the search for overarching singularity in matters of identity is carried to extremes (Maalouf, 1984, 1988, 2000, 2002; see also Badin, 2002).

The management of essential differences is therefore a fundamental aspect of life in the Middle Eastern and North African world, but its connotations therefore are not necessarily the same as those in the West.

In Islamic tradition, much weight is placed on the concept of the 'just ruler', and this emphasis on how the ruler exerts authority takes precedence over considerations of how the power and position were obtained and whether this can be defended as legitimate according to general rules of decision (Sachedina, 1988). Thus the discourse of 'democracy' may not be as significant as the discourse of 'justice'.

The ways in which power is exercised within the organisation may also not be explicable according to models imported from practice in other types of society. Thus Western discourse of organisational authority tends to follow Max Weber in stating that there are three ways by which leadership can be exerted in the modern organisation: (i) control through charisma; (ii) control through close supervision and compliance with organised systems of procedure (expressed by Weber as 'bureaucratic'); and (iii) control through culture (expressed by Weber as 'traditional'). It is often presumed that the third of these modes is incompatible either with good management practice or with the expectations of workers, but this is not necessarily the case in the Arab world.

A study of Palestinian companies indicates that the most common model is control through close supervision. Thus plant managers go to considerable lengths to demonstrate that they are highly active in supervising the behaviour of employees who in their opinion cannot be trusted to act responsibly of their own accord (Nahas et al., 1995). The Islamic conception of the importance of the conservation of wealth as compared to earnings emphasises the stewardship of resources exercised over relatively long time spans as more significant in accounting for the perceived legitimacy of managerial authority than the maximisation of returns on assets.

The classic study based on empirical research into behaviour and attitudes among Arab managers is *The Arab Executive* (Muna, 1980). Muna claimed that the typical form of decision making in Arab organisations is consultative, and found that delegation was the least widely used technique. Loyalty is prized above all other organisational values, even efficiency and this can be guaranteed by surrounding the executive with trustworthy subordinates.

Arab managers have a more flexible interpretation of time than Western management, and they can often run several meetings, perhaps on quite unrelated topics, simultaneously. The basic rule of business with Arab managers is to establish the relationship first and only come to the heart of the intended business at a later meeting, once trust has been achieved. This process may and often does take considerable time. Verbal contracts are absolute and an individual's word is his bond. Failure to meet verbally agreed obligations may be visited with dire penalties and will certainly lead to a termination of a business relationship. Nonetheless, the Arab world is essentially a trading world, governed by an implicit and extensive understanding of the requirements of commercial activity and implicit understandings of interpersonal relations.

Al-Faleh (1987) identifies status, position and seniority as more important than ability and performance. The central control of organisations is associated with a low level of delegation. Decision making is located in the upper reaches of the hierarchy, and authoritarian management styles predominate. Subordinates are deferential and obedient, especially in public in the presence of their hierarchical superiors. Consultation occurs on a one-to-one, rather than a team or group, basis. Decisions tend to emerge rather than to be located in a formal process. Prior affiliation and existing obligation are more influential than explicit performance objectives.

Ali (1985) contrast Saudi-Arabian with North American managerial styles, reinforcing the general finding that Arab managers prefer consultative styles and are unhappy with delegation. However, they point to the experience of political instability and to the growing fragmentation of traditional kinship structures as the origins of an ongoing conflict between authoritarian and consultative styles, and the need for Arab managers to resolve this conflict by developing a pseudo-consultative style in order to create a supportive and cohesive environment among themselves. Their value systems are described by Ali as 'outer-directed', tribalistic, conformist and socio-centric, compared to the 'inner-directed', egocentric, manipulative and existentialist perspectives of the North Americans.

Ali finds that whereas American organisations are tall, relatively decentralised and characterised by clear relationships, Saudi organisations are flat, authority relationships are vague, but decision making is centralised. In the West staffing and recruitment proceed on principles which are perceived or can be defended as objective, based on comparability of standards, qualifications and experience. In Saudi organisations, on the other hand, selection may be highly subjective, depending on personal contacts, nepotism, regionalism and family name. Performance evaluation in Saudi may be informal, with few systematic controls and established criteria, and the planning function is typically undeveloped and not highly regarded (Ali and Al-Shakhis, 1989).

But cohort differences mean that the younger generation of managers who are often Western-trained may hold different expectations. Al-Hashemi and Najjar (1989) were among the first to document the emergence of a managerial class in Bahrain in a series of publications which draw a picture of a well-educated and sophisticated cadre of professional managers who may not be able to find the fulfilment that their Western counterparts would seek in their work, because of the tight constraints of organisational and administrative structures.

The matrix of management in the Arab Middle East is provided by the historical culture of Islam (Arnold and Guillaume, 1968; Hitti, 1970). That is by no means to claim that all management systems in the region are officially 'Islamic' or even 'Muslim' in their bases, but that it is impossible to understand the prevailing tendencies, historical evolution or areas of contestation without first understanding the widespread and pervasive impact of Islam into all areas of public life in this region. Abuznaid (1994) provides a schematic overview of the principles of Islam as relevant to business and management.

Islam, like Christianity is intrinsically an expansionist religion claiming universal application; but while Christianity emerged in the context of a pre-existing state system that itself claimed universal hegemony – the Roman empire – and therefore from the outset had to develop a theory of its sphere of influence in the context of a definite and separate political power, Islam, in contrast developed in the context of an ethnic and regional unification that was both cultural and political and can be viewed as itself the seminal element in a novel political order (Landau, 2000). Historically, Islam in practice suffered schism, split and conflict, but the essential core belief pattern has remained strongly unicist. Adamson and Taylor provide an essential overview of the development of Arab philosophy, and go into detail that is not possible in this brief study (Adamson and Taylor, 2005).

Within Islamic philosophical tradition, a special place is accorded to a theory of knowledge that is intrinsically different from that which obtains in Western philosophy. The Arabic word for knowledge is *'ilm*. Knowledge in the Western world since the time of Descartes has in the over-riding discourses of science-based explanation come to be limited to the scientific knowledge that can be subjected to some test of verification and is typically distinguished from the concept of 'belief'. However, this distinction does not have the same force in Islamic thinking and knowledge is therefore not restricted to information about something, divine or corporeal, and *'ilm* is an all-embracing term covering theory, action and education. This distinction has implications for the practice of management.

If the near-universal matrix of explanation within the Arab Middle Eastern region derives from the religion of Islam, it is essential to understand Islam itself as a diverse phenomenon with many subcategories, but with distinctive central features. We distinguish within contemporary Islam between *ijtihad* or individual interpretation and *taqlid*; the reliance on the interpretation of authorities. The notion of 'fundamentalism' that comes originally from the Christian eschatological tradition does not really define any trend in contemporary Islam especially well. There is a sense in which all Muslims or none are 'fundamentalist'. In relation to concepts of diversity all Muslims are, in terms of the Ummah, 'brothers' (although in certain contexts non-Muslims may also be counted as members of the Ummah).

The Islamic cultural matrix infuses the management patterns in countries that are Islamic but not Arabic like Indonesia, Malaysia, Pakistan and Bangladesh as well as in several places in which Muslims are a small minority, for instance increasingly in Southern Africa. But in fact not everyone even in the core Arab Middle Eastern region is a Muslim, and other cultural traditions have created diversity. Many countries, for example, Lebanon, Palestine and Iran, present multi-stranded histories of organisational practice, including varieties of Christianity relatively insignificant in the West that have coexisted for centuries cheek-by-jowl with Islam. Nonetheless, Islam is a religion that claims universal applicability, and Muslims in principle have no conceptual issues about ethical universalism.

Islam may be described briefly and summarily as a religion of practice and observance rather than of dogma. The basic principles are simple and easily codified, consisting of an obligation to pray five times daily, to undertake the pilgrimage to the Holy places, the Hajj once at least in a lifetime, to publicly claim that there is one God and that his prophet is Mohammed, to undertake Zakat to share worldly riches with the poor and to follow the way of life understood to be that of Islam. The word 'Islam' itself means 'submission' (Rahman, 1966).

It is in its universality and simplicity that the behavioural and conceptual power of Islam lies, and it infuses the practices of management as it does all other aspects of culture. This is not necessarily to imply that Islamic principles compel tightly structured and intractable obligations to manage in a specific way, but rather that the diversity of behaviours and practices that do exist in these regions have to be explicable within this framework.

Science, law, interpersonal behaviours and obligations to others are all understood to be aspects of a fundamental reality that has to be understood as far as it is practicable, and knowledge and the bearers of knowledge, the scholars, are themselves highly regarded. Knowledge is an obligation. And the realities of social and political obligation are to be respected. Rulers are to be obeyed and duties to be undertaken. Trust is central to all relations, including those of business and trade. The prophet Mohammed, who was a successful businessman, was renowned for his integrity, holding the title, 'al-Amin' the Trustworthy One.

In principle, there is in Islam no inevitable conflict between religion and science as exists currently between creationists and Darwinists as represented, for instance, in the work of Dawkins (1986). Islam positions itself as a final revelation of a continuous tradition that embraces the other religions of 'the book', that is the Judaic and Christian revelations. The followers of these faiths are to be accepted as 'people of the book', and Moses and Jesus are alike respected as prophets in Islam.

This philosophy has emerged historically through the collective experience of surviving hardship and of maintaining social value through periods of threat and challenge in threatening environments, rather than privileging the calculus of individual choice under conditions of affluence. It is also relatively indifferent to political considerations that are construed as having temporary impact.

The master social structures that support Islam are those of the web of family and kin obligations. These are networked societies (Hutchings and Weir, 2006), but Arabic society is by no means the only one to be structured in this way and many societies bordering the Mediterranean share similar elements (Peristiany, 1966). These structures frame life in city and town alike and are powerful elements in family, business and political experience. Works of fiction like the 'Cairo Trilogy' of the Egyptian novelist Naguib Mahfouz trace the interpenetration of family and kin obligations through periods of radical political change, the end of colonialism and the upheavals of nationalism (Mahfouz, 1992).

In this region, political boundaries and the managerial philosophies of governments are in some respects regarded as surface phenomena compared to the deeper infrastructures of belief, family, kin and obligation (Esposito, 1988).

There is in this system of philosophy no fundamental polarisation of the economic and ethical realms for 'the particularity of Islamic directives in economic matters is the total, permanent and inclusive link that exists between this sphere and the moral point of reference' (Ramadan, 2001, p. 130).

The moral comprises the existential in this philosophy for as Ramadan (p. 130) argues:

[C]ommercial and financial transactions among men are . . . encompassed and nourished by the foundation of *tawhid* or the principle of the unicity of God . . . It is impossible here to conceive of man as resembling part of a machine and defined, outside of any ethical quality . . . and whose norm of action is solely quantitative . . . In fact, the most frequent, simple and natural economic fact is always identifiable by its moral quality . . . it is from the moral quality that man derives his value and not, in the first place, from his performance in terms of productivity, profitability or profit in the broader sense.

These practical obligations contain the structural foundations of the ethical basis of all behaviour for a believer, including the beliefs and practices of management and business life.

While they may be detailed and specified by subsequent interpretations, behaviours that are incompatible with these foundations cannot be '*halal*' or acceptable; they are '*haram*', that is to say, unacceptable. The strength of this complex of beliefs and attitudes is in their simplicity and incorrigibility as they are universally adhered to by all believers, and thus they condition the content of belief and practice in all areas of life. The distinction made in Western philosophy between the 'secular' and the 'sacred' does not obtain in these societies, for in principle there is understood to be a common texture to all social life. The realms of science, economics and organisational management are not exempt from these restraints.

The antecedents of some of the theories and philosophies that affect the practice of management in the Arab Middle East therefore are not in practice drawn exclusively, if at all, from the classical Western traditions. Some concepts that at first sight appear to carry the same implications as in Western usage derive from different intellectual contexts. Mubarak (1998) has shown how even such a familiar concept as 'motivation' can be traced to the corpus of Islamic scholarship and located in the writings of Abu Hamid Al-Ghazali and Ibn Khaldun as well as Abraham Maslow, Frederick Herzberg and Frederick Taylor. So even where words like 'motivation', 'leadership', 'incentives', 'management' and so on are used in discourse, the context and connotation are different from Western usage.

A growing corpus of researches report on the impact of Islamic imperatives, some of them formally embodied in law, on the practice of business and management. A specialised subset of these concerns is represented by the studies of Islamic banking and financial institutions. These are characterised by differing accounting and financial concepts from those that form the basis of Western financial and accounting theory; in particular, the avoidance of interest on financial capital, rooted in a basic moral concern to avoid usury (a conception that was shared with Christian business thinking until the Renaissance).

A fundamental ethical feature of Islamic finance is that of profit and loss sharing so that the banking and financial systems may take responsibility for the conduct of the enterprise, not just for the security of their own investment in it. The rate of interest concept which entitles the original owners of financial capital to earn, regardless of the economic success or otherwise of the enterprise in which they are investing, is regarded as improper in Islam. A general ethical principle enjoins all believers that wealth, which can only be created by God, must not be diminished by human agency (Al-Sadr, 2000).

The role of management, therefore, involves the notion of stewardship, and the role of the financial structures includes that of maintaining intrinsic value and minimising waste of resources. This in turn impacts on financial and managerial concepts of risk, which leads to a greater involvement of financial institutions in the business affairs of their customers and depositors and thus approximates more closely to the German or Japanese model of long-term joint involvement in economic affairs, rather than the Anglo-Saxon concept of short-termism and optimisation of purely financial returns. It also, when it works efficiently, involves banks and financial institutions in the realities of commercial and industrial enterprise (see, for example, Al-Janahi and Weir, 2005a and b).

It is impossible to do justice in a short outline to the immense range of Islamic theories of the economy or to the very diverse range of interpretations that are visible in practice, and there are many sources of this knowledge (see, for example, An-Nabhani, 1990; Ramadan, 2001). Ali (2005) provides a very thorough review of the cultural principles underpinning the development of business and management in Islam.

The theories we are discussing are not vestiges of some 'traditional' or legacy system that is being eroded and bypassed by more orthodox Western theories and practices. Rather, Islamic finance and economics is a very recent development and practically everything that has been published about it has been written since the late 1940s.

These theories are finding an increasingly positive reception in the 'real' worlds of global finance and banking. The Islamic Finance Forum, founded in 2000, is a growing forum for bankers and financiers, and Islamic finance is of growing significance in Western and non-Islamic developing economies.

The growth of Islamic economics has much to do with an increasing self-consciousness about the Muslim and Arab experience relating to the central significance of being Muslim, sharing a common culture and consciousness of cultural difference in their core practice. Arab managers are conscious, sometimes pointedly so, that the generic depictions of the essential lineaments of 'management' and the ethical positions embodied in the Western ways of doing business do not fit their life-spaces at all points but this is not to be construed as 'anti-Americanism' or 'anti-business values' or of an atavistic 'traditionalism' as it is sometimes characterised. Contemporary Islam is a contested terrain of diverse interpretations and practices.

Nonetheless, this basis for organisational practice is a religion that claims extensive and intensive universality, and is expressed as a pattern of thought that claims to be comprehensive and coherent. Elsewhere we have attempted an overall account of the philosophical and sociological underpinnings of management practice in this milieu (Weir, 2004).

Moreover, the unity of Islamic involvement is expressed in the concept of the 'Ummah'. This identifies the community of all believers who are in practice joined as they touch the ground during prayer. The Ummah is universal and indivisible, representing in a real sense a 'body' in which the individuals who believe inhere. Thus to attack the Ummah at any one point implies damaging all of it. This idea clearly posits a different positioning for individuals in relation to other individuals in a collectivity compared to the Western conceptualisation of individuals as ends of moral actions in their own right. Value comes from participation in the Ummah, rather than from individual essence or original rights. This conceptualisation impacts quite directly on the presuppositions which underlie the differing bases of economic science in the West and in the Islamic worlds. Economics is treated in the former as a division of positive science in which the units, the economic actors, are individuals; it is they who have tastes, wants, desires and can express demand and offer supply; it is these specific actions which can be particularised and identified as 'economic'. In the latter, economic actions are governed by the implacable philosophy of Islam, which applies to all social behaviour; some actions are permitted and are 'halal', others are not permitted and are stigmatised as 'haram'. The Ummah constitutes all who are constrained by these obligations.

Islam is a societistic religion and both the revelations of the Qur'an and Islamic tradition stress the social life of humanity and the ethics and mechanics of human society. But this societistic focus is not secular; for it is by ordering society along the ethical lines prescribed in revelation that human beings can enter into a more proper relation with God.

While only believers are *necessarily* part of the Ummah, admission into this community is available to all human beings. Theoretically, then, all human beings are potential members of the community. Admission into the Islamic community carries with it obligations to follow the Islamic sacred law, or Shari'ah, and also confers certain privileges, such as immunity from the tax imposed on non-believers in Islamic states.

In Islamic social theory, the Ummah is formed from the threefold consensus of its members: consensus of the mind, consensus of the heart and consensus of arms. The Ummah is formed from the consensus of minds in that all the members of the society share the same view of reality. It is formed from the consensus of hearts in that all members share the same values. It is formed from the consensus of arms in that all members exert themselves to actualise or realise their values. While Islamic social theory holds that all communities are formed in this way, the Qur'an states clearly that the Islamic Ummah is the best of all human communities given to humanity by God.

The antithesis to the Dar al-Islam is the Dar al-Harb, the 'House of Warfare,' or the non-Islamic world. This is the world of non-believers and must be struggled against by the faithful until either it is Islamicised or it allows for the free practice of Islam and the free commerce in ideas and values (Hooker, 2005).

It seems that the 'other' in Islam is in principle quite well defined as the occupants of the Dar al-Harb; but it is not quite so straightforward. In prayer, when the faithful physically participate in the Ummah, the believers claim:

> [W]e believe in God and in the Revelation given to us, and to Abraham, Ishmael, Isaac Jacob and the Tribes. We believe in the Revelation that was sent to Moses, Jesus and all other Prophets from their Lord. We make no distinction between them, and to Him we surrender. (3:83; 2:136)

Furthermore it is written:

> He has revealed to you (O Muhammad) the scripture with truth, confirming that which was revealed before it even as He revealed the Torah and the Gospel before as a guide to mankind and has revealed the Criterion (for judging between right and wrong). All of them called humanity to the way of the Lord, the way of submission to God. All of them gave the same message, and all of them stood for the same cause: Islam. (3:3–4)

Abdullah (ch. 2, this volume) explains the broader, more inclusive structure of Hadhari as capable of promoting 'an alignment between Islam, modernity and local culture'. The principles of Islam in this more inclusive formulation, Abdullah states, are: 'faith and piety in Allah, a just and trustworthy government, a free and independent people, mastery of knowledge, balanced and comprehensive economic development, a good quality of life, protection of the rights of minority groups and women, cultural and moral integrity, safeguarding the environment, and strong defences'.

None of the above implies any privileging by the author of these ways of managing or these cultures of business, or (and it should not need to be said) any statement of preference for one way of managing over another, whether justified by criteria of efficiency, productivity or any other measure of business performance, still less in any comparative calculus of moral virtue. But nor should it be taken as licence for the imputation that the Arab world or that of Islam conceived more broadly are incapable of self-critique. Sharabi (1988), Dadfar (1993), Said (1997), Ramadan (2001) and Ali (2005) are among many internal critics whose contributions are vital to understanding the internal vitality and diversity of these traditions. But we should know more about them before we indulge in the generalisations about 'diversity' that emanate from consideration of only one model of modernism. The iron laws of economics are always mediated by culture, and specific histories are manifested in diverse practices.

Contemporary practice

It follows from all of the above arguments that ideas of 'diversity' in management are likely to imply quite different conceptual and practical consequences from those of 'diversity' in Western culture. This has important implications for the discourse of diversity management in relation to the strategic options open to multinational organisations.

Strategy is the most general level of organisational functioning and it is at this level that multinational organisations make their most far-reaching decisions, implicating actually or potentially the whole of their systems and subsystems. To the business vocabularies of market, competition, cost, price and efficiency, the strategic decision makers, in attempting to frame a discourse of diversity, need to come to turns with the difficult concepts of culture, complexity and knowledge management. When in addition they propose to operate in new domains such as the Arab Middle East in which they have not built up an organisational history and experience, it is not surprising that they may sometimes appear to be overwhelmed at the magnitude of the task. But the dictates of some of the current thinking and theorising about globalisation imply that some business strategies ought to possess universal validity. But this frame of reference needs to have a subtle understanding of 'culture'.

The musician Brian Eno once said 'Culture is everything you don't have to do', and the very ubiquity of this suggestion demands that we limit our discourse in some ways, but almost all of the current discourse of diversity proposes or implies a similar level of generality. The concepts of culture, complexity, universalism, globalisation and knowledge management are ideas that are easier to use than to define. None of the above concepts is exactly new, but the 'post-modern turn' has put a specific gloss upon them. What is striking about the present situation is that there is an emerging and overlapping sense that the scientific and humanistic frames of reference are equally implicated in them.

Sociologists and anthropologists have long lost their original hegemony over the definition of culture, and the definition offered by Stuart Hall resonates in the fields of literary studies and philosophy also. Hall (1980, p. 24) writes:

> 'Culture' is not a practice; nor is it simply the descriptive sum of the 'mores and folkways' of societies . . . It is threaded through all social practices and is the sum of their inter-relationship . . . The 'culture' is those patterns of organisation . . . which can be discovered as revealing themselves, in 'unexpected identities and correspondences' as well as 'in discontinuities of an unexpected kind', within or underlying all social practices.

This definition of culture is useful for managers because it draws attention to the contextual universality and implicative nature of culture. It is concerned with practice, not just with abstracted knowledge and with generic social practice within communities, rather than with the interests of specific groups like the intelligentsia.

'Globalisation' is another word that is more written about than precisely defined. Cole (2002, p. 338) writes:

> Globalization is an enormously, interactive, social process, in which people, albeit often unwittingly, increasingly interrelate through complex international financial and investment institutions, extensive trade and production networks, sophisticated modes of communication, all within changing global cultural and ethical parameters.

This process is increasingly relevant because

> [T]oday . . . more people than ever are caught up in the process of cooperation and exchange involved in the production and distribution of every sort of commodity in a system that is global in scale [breaking] down national and sectoral constraints on the circulation of commodities and capital, creating one interdependent market and production unit. (Petras and Veltmeyer, 2001, p. 156)

But, despite these caveats it is the case that the dominant cultural paradigms of this very large MENA region of the Middle East and North Africa are linked by a common set of cultural beliefs and practices. The concept of the business relationship is therefore a longlasting or permanent one. This has implications for the way the banking system, for example, deals with its clients (Al-Janahi and Weir, 2005a and b).

The most significant characteristic of the business and management cultures of this region, however, are that they are rooted in philosophies of life, society and action that claim a universal validity. Islam as a collective basis for social organisation admits no limitations on its potential application. In respect of the analyses proposed in the previous section, and as we argued in previous publications, there are some grounds for expecting that the business practices and management styles typically found in this region will at least not be hostile to the new ideas about knowledge management and that certain elements, in particular the fact that these are highly networked societies, would be positively supportive and provide supportive social frameworks.

A widely used argument for the importance of diversity is that it is through diverse elements in the workforce that the knowledge available to the organisation can be maximised. So let us examine the likely dimensions of the emerging economic patterns of the twenty-first century through this lens. The economy of the world is moving from an industry- to an information-based format: large economies on the pattern of the former Soviet Union or even of the USA are not necessarily advantaged compared to the flexibilities, adaptiveness and fluidities of smaller economies, probably based on the city-region models of Singapore, Hong Kong, Concordia and *par excellence* the Gulf Cooperation Council (GCC) economies which are mainly of this city-region model.

Whereas in the past the economy was more dependent on physical power, equipment and raw material, in a knowledge-based society the value of a product increases through knowledge and not via physical effort.

Enterprise structures are moving from the command organisations, with their persistent and obstructive hierarchies, to the smaller, networked organisations, with both latent and active elements, based on the familial models which are prevalent in the Arab world rather than on juridical composites linked by shareholder and stakeholder obligations that generate purely legal obligations and an army of corporate lawyers to soak up the intermittent profit streams.

Knowledge economies depend on educated and trained entrepreneurs rather than on conformant management cadres, and it is in this respect that much work still needs to be done in the Arab economies. Centralist state control is not the obvious answer to creating social wealth through business activity, but nor, probably, is the ethic of selfish individualism. The success of the growth poles of the European economy, like the Emilia Romagna as well as in the Far East, indicates that it is the common bonds of family, kinship, clan and tribe, naturally existing as potential bases for capital, skills and commitment, that provide the most reliable motor for sustained economic growth.

Decision making follows different rules in the network economy of the information society to the imposition down the hierarchy of the strategic judgements of highly paid executives remote from customers and suppliers on unwilling or ill-informed operatives. If it is informed consent that will be required, perhaps it is the Middle Eastern decision-making model of the family *diwaniah* or *majlis*, with its balance of consultative and auto-cratic phases, that provides a better guide than the corporate boardroom to the 'loose–tight' properties of effective decision making in this context. The countries of the Arab world have generations of hard-won expertise in the operational adaptation to the needs of trading partners in Europe, Africa, the Indian subcontinent and the Americas and, in the case of many family-based enterprises, of creating networks, alliances and partnerships in these markets.

Banking and financial systems also need to adapt to the requirements of new forms of enterprise. This need not mean merely the adoption of high-risk strategies and financial manipulation. But the techniques of corporate recovery, portfolio-balancing and organisational support are not alien to the new generation of bankers in the region. Islamic models of financing for house purchase, assurance and investment are compatible with sus-tainable enterprise growth.

There are issues about the use to which expensively trained and highly educated young managerial talent is put. There is an almost tangible frus-tration among many young managers throughout the region at not being called upon to utilise their hard-won state-of-the-art skills in the service of enterprise. Inflated state bureaucracies offer too easy a route for the absorption of energies rather than the creation of social wealth.

The overall characterisation of management in the MENA region presents a mixed and on the whole somewhat depressing picture in terms of economic development. This region is in many ways the product of its recent history and of the failure of its contemporary attempts to escape its past. The population is growing and living standards are on average not rising. There are more educated people than ever before but poverty and unemployment is on the increase. Some 80 million people in the region or 30 per cent of the population live below a UN poverty line of less than two dollars a day. Unemployment affects 15 to 20 per cent of people in some countries in the region and this figure includes a disproportionate number of young graduates. Women's labour force participation rates are so low that in some statistics they are not entered into the calculation of unem-ployment rates. These statistics relate to longstanding inequalities and employment structures and, as Al-Dajani (2010) perceptively notes: 'in the meantime however, their employment trends and causal factors need to be addressed *vis-à-vis* their overall socio-political status'.

The authoritative UNDP report on social indicators concluded that on a wide range of social measures the MENA region showed signs of concern. In terms of life expectancy, school enrolment and adult literacy as well as in per capita income, the MENA region rates at or near the bottom of the league tables. But it also has the largest proportion of young people, and 38 per cent of Arabs are under 14. The UNDP report concludes that these statistical shortfalls are associated with the three deficits, in civic and social freedoms, in the involvement of women in economic society and in knowledge itself. While adult illiteracy has declined it is still high, with 65 million Arab adults illiterate, almost two-thirds of them women. Investment in R&D is one-seventh of the global average and internet access and personal computer use well below global norms (Arab Human Resource Development Report, 2003).

Lack of enthusiasm for education *per se* does not appear to be the main concern in this region, for these depressing outcome figures must be set against a backdrop of on average a higher percentage of GDP spent on education than is the case in developing countries in other regions, and a generally improving pattern of literacy and enrolment rates over the last two decades. Overall, more than 90 per cent of males in these countries and almost 75 per cent of females are enrolled in primary school; in secondary-level education the enrolment rates were 60 per cent for males and 50 per cent for females; and at the tertiary level, male and female enrolment in Arab countries is higher than in all developing regions except for Latin America. Education in the Middle East is still behind in terms of quality. The same source claims that the production of knowledge in the Arab world is manipulated by fear and increased protection. This has led to weak decision-making skills within families and has deprived children of their rights to independence and initiative (ibid.).

Images of diversity are on the whole lacking in this environment because the media in the Arab world suffer from lack of freedom of expression, and in many Middle Eastern countries the freedom of the press is still manipulated by boycott and closure. Some 70 per cent of TV channels in the Arab world are government owned (ibid.). The same source has indicated that in the Arab world the percentage of media channels to the number of inhabitants is low, in that there are 53 newspapers to every 1,000 inhabitants as compared to 285 newspapers to every 1,000 inhabitants in typical Western modern countries.

Translation of texts from other cultures is another challenge in the Middle East. Translation is another key to knowledge of other cultures of management, yet translation is still weak. Despite the fact that the number of translated books rose from 175 titles between 1975 and 1990 to nearly 330 in 2000–05, the total number of books translated in the Arab world at the present time amounts to 10,000. This number equals the number of books translated in Spain, for example, in one year.

The World Bank study concludes that the 'extraordinary dynamism of early Arab and Muslim civilisation, that had as its foundation the ability to absorb, enrich, and disseminate the knowledge that was developing at that time' must be *re*-discovered because 'efficient use of knowledge and innovation throughout economies and societies is the only way to restore high economic growth and create the 40 million jobs needed over the coming decade' (Aubert and Reiffers, 2003, p. 63).

Elsewhere we have considered some of the reasons for this 'knowledge economy deficit' in the MENA region (Weir, 2003). For instance, it is necessary to consider whether the deficiencies revealed in the World Bank study are to be attributed solely to a weakness in political and social organisation. Is there a wide-ranging 'democratic deficit' that impairs the spread of understanding of diversity and its potential organisational advantages? Is it these phenomena that have led to a failure to develop a Western-style appreciation of what may be required for a management agenda that can comprise a more relevant approach to diversity management?

Our characteristic Western narratives of modernity seem to imply that with economic globalisation and the force of political liberation exercised through Western military might, democratic ideals and practice would become universalised and with them different conceptions of diversity, but even from within the discourses of the Arab diaspora scholars like Hisham Sharabi have contributed to characterisations of Arab society that position the contemporary Arab experience as problematic in terms of core Western values of democracy, openness and equality, especially of gender (see Sharabi, 1988).

Western scholars operate typically with taxonomies that relate to market scale and interdependencies, in which the presumed end-point is the 'global economy'. But there is remarkably little empirical research on which to base the judgements that the economies of the Western world are placed typically at opposite ends of these presumed behavioural continua between underdevelopment and globalisation than are those of the Arab Middle East. A priori there is much to recommend the inference that Arab businesspeople are well-attuned and have been for several generations to the requirements of a global economy linked by bonds of trade and family connection.

But yet this does not seem to be happening. The evident pleasure in using new technologies of communication that is visible in the consumer-oriented city-states of Dubai and Bahrain has not translated into the business practices of the knowledge economy that in principle are available. The current situation in relation to the knowledge economy as evidenced by most objective statistical and comparative reports is not good. Aubert and Reiffers (2003, p. 2) conclude:

> [T]he MENA region's readiness for the knowledge economy is low, although a number of governments have begun to adapt their economies to meet the new

challenges. Compared to other parts of the developing world, the region trails East Asia, Eastern Europe, Central Asia, and Latin America. It is somewhat ahead of South Asia and Sub-Saharan Africa. In general terms, the MENA countries' knowledge economy is somewhat lower than their overall level of economic development as measured by gross domestic product (GDP).

Jean-Louis Sarbib, Vice-President of the World Bank, has commented of the MENA region that despite the reverence officially paid to education and the objectively high share it takes of national budgets,

> [Y]et there is little evidence that education has contributed to economic growth. This is paradoxical at a time when literate, educated human capital has become critical to gaining competitivity in a global economy driven by advances in knowledge and technology and when developing countries with an educated labour force such as Korea and Brazil are raising their economies' share of high value-added productive activities. By contrast, Arab countries' share of international outsourcing – which has fuelled the transfer of technology and employment to developing countries in Asia and Latin America – has been negligible. (Sarbib 2002, p. 63)

The issue of education in general is even more indistinct, and in some respects the current situation is counterintuitive. Of course, the economic picture is not the same throughout the whole region. Aubert and Reiffers show that the range of dispersion is in fact greatest of all the regions surveyed by the World Bank, with three distinct groupings of countries. Jordan and Kuwait show above the MENA average in the World Bank benchmarking exercise; Tunisia, Morocco, Egypt, Saudi Arabia, Iran and Algeria are in the middle; while Syria and Yemen fall below. All countries in the region except Jordan show a pattern in which their GDP per head ranks relatively better than their performance in knowledge-economy-related activities.

A striking feature of all the studies undertaken on economic aspects of movement towards the knowledge economy is that it is not necessarily the oil-rich states that have made the greatest strides. But it is often remarked that in these respects it is states like Jordan, a resource-poor state with significant problems over the last two decades in relation to its involvement in the geo-political scene and Dubai, the only one of the United Arab Emirates without a strong natural resource base in oil and gas, that have moved forward.

Within the knowledge-based sectors of secondary and especially higher education, the systems again work imperfectly. These processes effectively hinder the development of the 'learning economy' (Lundvall and Borràs, 1999). Higher learning is perceived and managed in terms of ascription rather than achievement. It is impossible to obtain a position in a university or a college without possession of a doctoral diploma; but after appointment there are no consistent pressures to publish, and promotion is likely to be based in large part on seniority rather than output. Professors on the whole do not publish to anything like the levels even of European, let alone North American, professors. Empirical research is undertaken for doctoral qualification and then often not returned to after the first two or three papers. This goes quite counter to the basic precepts of diversity management thinking which are that the actual stock of knowledge matters less than its renewal, and the generation of systems for knowledge sharing.

Although we earlier eschewed simplistic culturalist explanations of lack of progress, there is in fact little evidence from the global scene as a whole of wholesale cultural convergence in business matters, especially as these are having an effect on the role of cultural factors or social networks in impacting on business processes. So as technology advances it will not necessarily bring adherence to Western norms of business behaviour. Indeed, there is some evidence of an increasing divergence and of an increasingly diverse cultural framework for business. In other words, globalisation may operate to increase rather than to diminish complexity. This is by no means to infer or imply that the effective management of cultural differences is in any way unimportant for the post-modern organisation in the Middle East or anywhere. Cleland (1988) is among many who see this competence as the distinctive and criterial dimension of good management in the global society. Mubarak (1998) reminds us that it is possible to arrive at similar practical positions on such central management concerns as motivation from an understanding of quite distinct historical antecedents. But within this more complex framework of consideration of where our ideas about diversity come from and where they may lead to, it is conceivable that network models may be more promising than structural arrangements based on the command and control patterns, and the current Western-based models of diversity management may themselves become increasingly more contestable.

It is worth considering whether there can emerge a more generic and inclusive basis for management as a professional practice that can be disengaged from its specific historical and cultural roots (Weir, 2000 and 2008) and that it may be within this framework that a more inclusive conception of diversity can be framed.

Note

*   The author thanks all who have assisted in the creation of this chapter, especially all my friends, students and colleagues in the Middle East and North Africa region. The mistakes are all my own work.

Bibliography

Abuznaid, S. (1994), 'Islam and management', in M. Alwani and D. Weir (eds), *Proceedings of the Second Arab Management Conference*, Bradford: University of Bradford Management Centre.

Adamson, P. and Taylor, R.C. (2005), *The Cambridge Companion to Arabic Philosophy*, Cambridge: Cambridge University Press.

Al-Dajani, H. (2010), 'Diversity and inequality among women in employment in the Arab Middle East Region: a new research agenda', ch. 2 in M. Özbilgin and J. Syed (eds), *Managing Gender Diversity in Asia: A Research Companion*, Cheltenham, UK and Northampton, MA, USA: Edward Elgar, pp. 8–31.

Al-Faleh, M. (1987), 'Cultural influences on Arab managerial development', *Journal of Management Development*, **6** (3): 19–33.

Al-Hashemi, I. and Najjar, G. (1989), 'Strategic choices in management education: the Bahraini experience', in J. Davies, M. Easterby-Smith and S. Mann (eds), *The Challenge to Western Management Development*, London: Routledge.

Al-Janahi, A. and Weir, D.T.H. (2005a), 'Alternative financial rationalities in managing corporate failure', *Managerial Finance*, **31** (4): 34–5.

Al-Janahi, A. and Weir, D.T.H. (2005b), 'How Islamic banks deal with problem business situations: Islamic banking as a potential model for emerging markets', *Thunderbird International Business Review*, **47** (4), July–August: 429–45.

Al-Rasheed, A.M. (1994), 'Traditional Arab management: evidence from empirical comparative research', in M. Alwani and D. Weir (eds), *Proceedings of the Second Arab Management Conference*, Bradford: University of Bradford Management Centre.

Al-Sadr, M. Baquir (2000), *Our Economics*, trans. Kadom Shubber, London: Book Extra.

Ali, A. (1985), 'The relationship between managerial success and value systems', *Proceedings: Midwest Business Administration Association Management Division*, **1** (1): 8–59.

Ali, Abbas J. (2005), *Islamic Perspectives on Management and Organisation*, Cheltenham, UK and Northampton, MA, USA: Edward Elgar.

Ali, A. and Al-Shakhis, M. (1989), 'Managerial beliefs about work in two Arab states', *Organization in Studies*, **10** (2): 169–86.

An-Nabhani Taqiuddin (1990), *The Economic System in Islam*, London: Al-Quilafah Publications.

Arab Human Resource Development Report (2003), *Building a Knowledge Society*, New York: UNDP.

Arnold, Sir Thomas and Guillaume, A. (eds) (1968), *The Legacy of Islam*, Oxford: Oxford University Press.

Aubert, Jean-Eric and Reiffers, Jean-Louis (2003), *Knowledge Economies in the Middle East and North Africa: Towards New Development Strategies*, Washington, DC: World Bank.

Badin, Sandra J. (2002), 'Review of Maalouf, A. *In the Name of Identity: Violence and the Need to Belong*', *Harvard Human Rights Journal*, **15**, Spring: 341–2.

Banfield, Edward (1958), *The Moral Basis of a Backward Society*, New York: Free Press of Glencoe.

Barber, M.D. (1989), *Social Typifications and the Elusive Other: The Place of Sociology of Knowledge in Alfred Schutz's Phenomenology*, Lewisburg: Bucknell University Press and London and Toronto: Associated University Presses.

Berlin, Isaiah (1964), *Herder and the Enlightenment*, Baltimore, MD: Johns Hopkins University Press, quoted in Berlin (1997).

Berlin, Isaiah (1988), *On the Pursuit of the Ideal*, Turin: Agnelli Foundation.

Berlin, Isaiah (1997), *The Proper Study of Mankind: An Anthology of Essays*, edited by H. Hardy and R. Hausheer, London: Chatto & Windus.

Braudel, F. (1949), *La Méditérranée et le Monde Méditérranéean à l'epoque de Philip II*, Paris: Armand Colin, trans. Sian Reynolds: London: William Collins, 1972.

CIPD (Chartered Institute of Personnel and Development) (2009), available at: http://www. cipd.co.uk/research/_divarw.htm (accessed 10 June 2009).

Cleland, D.I. (1988), 'The cultural ambience of the Matrix Organisation', in D.I. Cleland and

W.R. King (eds), *Project Management Handbook*, New York: Van Nostrand Reinhold, pp. 981–9.

Cole, K. (2002), 'Globalization: understanding complexity', working paper, School of Development Studies, University of East Anglia, Norwich.

Dadfar, H. (1993), 'In search of Arab management, direction and identity', in M. Alwani and D. Weir (eds), *Proceedings of the First Arab Management Conference*, Bradford: University of Bradford Management Centre.

Dawkins, R. (1986), *The Blind Watchmaker*, Harmondsworth: Penguin Books.

Esposito, J. (1988), *Islam: The Straight Path*, New York and Oxford: Oxford University Press.

Hall, S. (1980), 'Cultural studies: two paradigms: media, culture and society', in T. Bennett, *Culture, History and Social Process*, Milton Keynes: Open University Press, pp. 22–49.

Hitti, P. K. (1970), *History of the Arabs*, 10th edn, New York: St. Martin's Press.

Hooker, R. (2005), 'Ummah: Community', available at: http://www.wsu.edu:8080/~dee/GLOSSARY/UMMAH.HTM (accessed 10 June 2009).

Hutchings, K. and Weir, D.T.H. (2006), '*Guanxi* and *Wasta*: a review of traditional ways of networking in China and the Arab world and their implications for international business', *Thunderbird International Business Review*, Special Issue: Journeys on the Silk Road, **48** (1), 141–56.

Landau, R. (2000), *The Arab Heritage of Western Civilization*, New York: League of Arab States, Arab Information Center.

Levinas, E. (1969), *Totality and Infinity: An Essay on Exteriority*, Pittsburgh, PA: Duquesne University Press.

Lewis, Bernard (2002), *What Went Wrong?*, London: Weidenfeld & Nicholson.

Lundvall, B.-Å. and Borràs, S. (1999), *The Globalising Learning Economy: Implications for Innovation Policy*, Brussels: DG XII.

Maalouf, Amin (1984), *The Crusades Through Arab Eyes*, New York: Schocken Books.

Maalouf Amin (1988), *Leo the African*, London: Abacus.

Maalouf, Amin (2000), *In the Name of Identity: Violence and the Need to Belong*, trans. Barbara Bray, New York: Arcade.

Maalouf, Amin (2002), *Balthasar's Odyssey*, London: Harvill.

Mahfouz, N. (1992), *Palace Walks, Sugar Street, The Palace of Desire* (The Cairo Trilogy), New York: Anchor.

Metcalfe, B. (2010), 'Reflections on difference: women, Islamic feminism and development in the Middle East', in M. Özbilgin and J. Syed (eds), *Managing Gender Diversity in Asia: A Research Companion*, Cheltenham, UK and Northampton, MA, USA: Edward Elgar, pp. 140–59.

Mubarak, A. (1998), 'Motivation in Islamic and Western management philosophy', PhD thesis, Bradford University.

Muna, F.A. (1980), *The Arab Executive*, London: Macmillan.

Nahas, F.V., Ritchie, J.B., Dyer, W.G. and Nakashian, S. (1995), 'The internal dynamics of Palestinian family business', *Proceedings of the Third Arab Management Conference*, Bradford: University of Bradford Management Centre.

Peristiany, J.G. (1966), *Honour and Shame: The Values of Mediterranean Society*, Chicago, IL: University of Chicago Press.

Petras, J. and Veltmeyer, H. (2001), *Globalization Unmasked: Imperialism in the 21st Century*, London: Zed Books.

Rahman, F. (1966), *Islam*, Chicago, IL: University of Chicago Press.

Ramadan, Tariq (2001), *Islam, the West and the Challenges of Modernity: The Islamic Foundation*, Leicester: Markenfield.

Sachedina, A. (1988), *The Just Ruler in Shi'ite Islam: The Comprehensive Authority of the Jurist in Imamite Jurisprudence*, New York: Oxford University Press.

Said, E. (1997), *Covering Islam*, New York and London: Random House.

Sarbib, J.-L. (2002), 'Building knowledge societies in the Middle East and North Africa', Marseilles Forum on Knowledge in Middle East and North Africa, Marseille, 9–12

September, World Bank, Washington, DC, accessed at: http://www.worldbank.org/k4dmarseille (accessed 4 January 2010).

Schutz, A. (1949), 'The problem of rationality in the social world', reprinted in Schutz, A. (1964), *Collected Papers*, vol. 2, Amsterdam: Martinus Nijhoff, pp. 64–88.

Sharabi, Hisham (1988), *Neo-Patriarchy: A Theory of Distorted Change in Arab Society*, Oxford: Oxford University Press.

Tatli, A., Mulholland, G., Özbilgin, M. and Worman, D. (2007), *Managing Diversity in Practice: Supporting Business Goals*, London: Chartered Institute of Personnel and Development.

Taylor, C. (1992), *Sources of the Self: The Making of Modern Identity*, Cambridge, MA: Harvard University Press.

Weir, D.T.H. (1997), 'The ethical basis of management', in E.H. Marshall, D. Jenkins, D. Weir, Zaki Badawi and S. Howes (eds), *Business Ethics: The Religious Dimension*, Bradford: Bradford University Management Centre, pp. 2–8.

Weir, D.T.H. (1998), 'The Fourth Paradigm', in A.A. Shamali and J. Denton (eds), *Business Management in the Arab Middle East*, Kuwait: Gulf Management Centre.

Weir, D.T.H. (2000), 'Management in the Arab world', in M. Warner (ed.), *Management in Emerging Countries: Regional Encyclopedia of Business and Management*, London: Business Press/Thomson Learning, pp. 291–300.

Weir, D.T.H. (2003), 'Human resource development in the Arab world', in Monica Lee (ed.), *Human Resource Development in a Complex World*, London: Taylor & Francis, pp. 69–82.

Weir, D.T.H. (2004), 'Some sociological, philosophical and ethical underpinnings of an Islamic management model: an alternative paradigm', *Journal of Management, Philosophy and Spirituality*, **1** (2).

Weir, D.T.H. (2005), 'The Arab as dangerous other', paper presented at the Track on Post-colonialism: CMS4 Critical Management Studies Conference, 4–6 July, Cambridge University.

Weir, D.T.H. (2008), 'Can there be a universal ethical basis for professional management?', Inaugural Lecture, 28 May, Liverpool Hope University.

19 Diversity management in Thailand
Daungdauwn Youngsamart, Greg Fisher and Charmine E.J. Härtel

Introduction

Diversity management literature emerged first in the United States and initially spread to other economically developed countries. The underlying emphasis of this literature has been on organization-level issues faced by groups historically marginalized in employment opportunity or career progression, on the basis of gender, age, race and ethnicity, or religion. More recently, newly industrialized and economically emerging nations have begun to be a focus of diversity management research. The overwhelming emphasis of the research in these contexts has been gender diversity, though there is some coverage of race and ethnicity, or religion.

In such fields as political science and development administration there has also been research on gender, race and ethnicity and religion, with a particular focus on migrant workers moving from rural- to industrial- or city-based employment. This research has concentrated on societal-level issues such as poverty, corruption, exploitation, slave labor, and lack of political representation. There is little focus in this literature on organization-level management issues.

Although culture and institution issues, such as the quality and enforcement of workplace-related legislation are common in diversity management, political science and development administration literature, these domains have essentially developed separately.

It could also be argued that research into the expatriate experience is a form of diversity management research. However, the underlying emphasis of this literature is on management-level expatriates from developed countries, working in developing countries. These expatriates are generally in positions of relative organizational power. As such, this turns the notion of diversity management on its head. While there is an emerging focus on the challenges faced by Western female expatriates, generally the emphasis had not been on addressing historical disadvantage, and there is often an ethnocentric assumption that they will face stronger discrimination in non-Western nations than they do in their home countries. When dealing with differences resulting from race, ethnicity and religion, it is the adjustment to the cultural context by the expatriate, and the subsequent performance of the expatriate, that are the dominant themes.

In this chapter we provide a review of the literature on the management of diversity in Thailand and report findings that are relevant to the domain of diversity management drawn from previously unpublished results of four convergent interview-based studies conducted over a 12-year period from 1996 to 2008. While the main focus of each of these studies was not diversity management, each study dealt in some way with culture, race, ethnicity, religion and management issues in Thailand. In quantitative research, a statistical meta-analysis is sometimes used to draw together disparate research on a topic from a number of prior studies. In this chapter we use incidental results from a number of qualitative studies, to explore and explain the nature of diversity management in the Thai business context.

From this discussion, we suggest areas for future study, make practical suggestions on how to manage diversity issues in the Thai business contexts, and comment on the applicability of the 'Western' theoretical perspective of diversity management to Thailand. We do not pretend that this provides a comprehensive or definitive position. Rather it builds on the first steps in research into diversity management in Thailand.

Consistent with literature that deals with other research that deals with management in organizations in Thailand, we suggest that social class and patron–client relationships are stronger influences on the career outcomes of women, ethnically diverse and religiously diverse employees (Fisher and Hutchings, 1997; Hutchings and Fisher, 1998; Hutchings, 2000; Fisher and Härtel, 2003; van der Boon, 2003). Education enables individuals to move through class barriers, and receive career benefits. The fluidity of the patronage system creates the opportunity for individuals to develop advantageous relationships, which may be beneficial for those individuals, but overall does not align with the Western concepts of equity in the workplace.

There has been political and military conflict in several of the nations bordering Thailand. This has resulted in the arrival of refugees. In the 1970s, Vietnamese refugees arrived in the north-east, and camps still exist. Since the 1990s, the Karen people and other Burmese refugees have continued to flee the military regime in Myanmar. Some, particularly in the north-west, have temporary working permits, while others work illegally. More recently in the south there have been arrivals and expulsions of Muslim refugees from Myanmar. There are other stateless people such as the Hill tribes and Hmong, who have always lived in parts of what is now Thailand, but are not always considered citizens. And of course there are also issues related to the sale or kidnapping of rural adults and children to work in the fishing, construction or sex industries. In this chapter, we have elected not to deal with these groups. This is not because we believe that such issues are unimportant. Rather it is because there is already extensive information available from the United Nations High Commissioner for Refugees, non-governmental organizations, the media, and scholarly research in the international relations and development administrations disciplines.

Why Thailand is an important context in which to study diversity management

The social and cultural environment of Thailand is unique in South-East Asia. Unlike its neighbors, Thailand has never been colonized. It has been a constitutional monarchy since 1932, and its governments for most of the period since then could best be described as military authoritarian or semi-democratic, with power balanced between three elite groups in society: the military elite, the bureaucratic elite and the business elite. Its government has changed by bloodless *coups d'état* more times than through elections, with the most recent of these being in 2006. This military government stayed in power only a short period before calling democratic elections in line with a revised constitution, but political instability has continued due to perceptions in different parts of Thai society of lack of legitimacy of subsequent coalition governments. We have also seen in the last 10 years the emergence of 'wedge' politics, in which sections of the ruling elite have adopted policies and electoral rhetoric to create the image of a Bangkok urban elite who are both uncaring of the poorer northern and eastern rural provinces, and too supportive of southern provinces, including people from the three, largely Muslim provinces on the Thai–Malaysia border.

Thailand is religiously homogeneous, with 95 percent of the population identifying as Buddhist (Lekhakul, 1996). The Buddhism practiced is Therevada Buddhism, which teaches that Buddha was a man, rather than Mahayana Buddhism, common in China, Japan and Tibet, which ascribes a level of divinity to Buddha. Its second largest religious group are Islamic, who are relatively evenly distributed across all provinces in Thailand, with a great concentration in the south. Overall they constitute 2–3 percent of the population.

The large 'Chinese-Thai' community is largely integrated into Thai society. Unlike neighboring countries such as Indonesia and Malaysia, they have a long history of involvement in the civil service, political parties of all persuasions, and the military. Furthermore, they have not faced barriers to access to education or employment, or systematic race-based violence, which has occurred in some other South-East Asian countries. While many are actively involved in small and large business, they are no more likely to be part of the business elite than similarly qualified and experienced 'Thai-Thai'. This differentiates Thailand from Singapore, Taiwan and the Penang province in Malaysia, where the Chinese business community is dominant. Indeed it could be suggested that the differentiation between Thai-Thai and Chinese-Thai is now largely artificial in Bangkok and larger cities, and frequently foreigners are told, in jest, that the only way to tell them apart is through their preferences for different brands of Japanese and European cars.

Prior to the creation of a constitutional monarchy in 1932, Thailand was an absolute monarchy. Underlying the power of the King was a system of patron–client relationships, known as the *sakdina* system. This defined the status of individuals within Thai society. Unlike rigid, family-based patron–client relationship practices in other Asian countries, individuals could move up (or down) in society based on the relative and non-relative patron–client relationships they held. While the formal system no longer exists, the influence of *sakdina* can still be felt at all levels of society (Bunnak, 1990, 1991; Pornpitakpan, 2000). Contemporary relationships tend to have three components: a patron and a client agree to exchange benefits; the benefits are personal and direct in nature; and, as the agreement is based on personal benefit, as distinct from principle, the continuity of the relationship is uncertain (Girling, 1981; Bunnak, 1991). If the current relationship is not providing them with the benefits they desire, clients seek patrons with more status, seniority and personal connections to enable them to achieve their goals (Samudavanija, 1995; Girling, 1981). Such relationships are often used to circumvent formal rules and procedures that nominally govern the behavior of individuals and organizations in Thailand. From a Western perspective, these relationships can be seen as discriminatory or inequitable. However, from a traditional Thai cultural perspective, they are the way that relationships are maintained and developed, and business is done, in Thai society.

The legal framework
The main pieces of legislation in Thailand that address employment issues are the Labor Protection Act (1998), the Labor Relations Act (1975), the Workers' Compensation Act (1994) and the Social Security Act (1980). Labor disputes are dealt with in Labor Courts, which in turn are governed by the Act on Establishment of Labor Courts and Labor Court Procedures (1979). In addition, the Civil and Commercial Code on contracts relating to the hire of services may also impact on labor hire agreements. The responsibility for enforcing the law, and for inspecting workplaces rests with the Ministry of Labor and Social Welfare.

The laws cover minimum wages, which vary by the level of development of provinces, maximum work hours, termination processes and severance pay, workers' compensation, employee record keeping, social security contribution and recruitment and employment transfer. The basic, albeit limited, protections, are applicable to all workers, and there are no specific provisions related to gender, ethnicity, religion, sexual orientation or age. The labor laws are not evenly enforced, in part, due to poor funding of the relevant ministry, and in part due to cultural issues discussed earlier in this chapter.

Employers are free to state age, gender, marital status and other criteria in job advertisements and select staff on the basis of the criteria specified. Employers also have the freedom to develop their own policies for broad or narrow retrenchment of workers, based on a simple justification of adverse business conditions. Employment contracts need to specify a period of notice of termination, and where they do not, termination occurs in the next pay period. Thus, a person on the common monthly pay period, could be advised of his/her termination on the last day of the month, effective from the first day of the next month. In addition, there are a broad range of justifications available for a worker to be dismissed without notice.

In the public sector and government business enterprises, unions and staff associations were effectively abolished in the early 1990s, though in typical Thai style many still exist informally, and at times include relatively senior management. Private sector unionization is weak and arguably ineffective.

There are no antidiscrimination laws that provide for equal employment opportunity regardless of ethnicity, gender, sexual orientation, religion or age. Further, the provision of affirmative action programs may contravene regulations of the Ministry of Labor and Social Welfare, though it is unclear what enforcement penalties would arise from such an interpretation. As such, the Thai institutional environment is largely mute on race, gender and religious discrimination, and makes no attempt to provide legislative support for diversity.

Method

There are two parts to the research conducted for this chapter. The first component is essentially a literature search and review, supported by a small number (9) of exploratory strategic interviews with senior academics and managers in Thailand. These activities were conducted in 2008. As we felt it was important to access Thai language research on diversity management, we initially undertook a literature search using Thai language journal databases, and university library catalogues at Thammasat University. We supplemented this with visits to university bookshops, and access to publishers' websites. We understand that to some Western readers, this will seem an old-fashioned and possibly less comprehensive way of undertaking a literature review. However, while Thai universities have access to all the major international journal databases, the Thai language databases are less developed, and as such a more labor-intensive method was prudent.

We identified a number of journal articles and books that dealt with diversity issues including gender, ethnicity and religion. However, on reading the articles and books that we identified, it became clear that they did not cover the issues related to diversity management. Rather they dealt predominantly with equal treatment for women in property and political rights; and political violence in the three 'Muslim majority' provinces in Thailand. As such, they were not directly related to the issue of diversity management in Thai organizations.

As we are experienced researchers and former academics at universities in Thailand, the lack of Thai language research did not come as a surprise. However, to further ensure that we were not imposing our own bias, we approached business, management and political science academics at a number of universities and asked them if there was important Thai language research that we had missed. No further Thai language papers were identified through this process, though several of our informants did refer to English language research which we subsequently obtained through our English language database search.

In Thailand we conducted our English language database search using the individual databases ScienceDirect, EBSCO Business Premier and Emerald Insight. We also searched the library catalogue, and visited university bookshops to identify English language research published in Thailand. On our return to Australia, we repeated the database search and expanded the databases to include Blackwell, Wiley and Ingenta, supplemented by the Find-It catalogue and e-resources search aggregator available through the RMIT library. We also used Google Scholar and library catalogues to identify books and book chapters.

Similar to our Thai search, we found many articles that dealt with political and societal issues of gender, racial and religious diversity. However, we also found articles and book chapters that dealt directly with issues of the management of gender diversity, ethnicity, religious diversity in Thai organizational contexts. It is this research that we document in the following sections.

The second component of this research draws from a number of focus groups and interviews conducted in Thailand between 1997 and 2006. These were part of separate programs of research into aspects of human resource management in Thailand. Although the major research questioned varied in the different studies, all the studies included issues related to culture, ethnicity, religion age and gender.

The sample for the first project comprised 25 Thai managers, professionals, consultants and academics (involved in business or consulting) working in Bangkok. There were slightly more female than male respondents. Information on the religion of the respondents was not collected. This sample was drawn from the Australia Thai Chamber of Commerce and the Thai Civil Service Commission. The data were collected in 1997 and 1998. All interviews and focus groups were conducted in English.

The sample for the second project comprised 68 Thai managers and professionals evenly split between males and females. All were working in middle or senior management positions and worked for foreign and domestic banks and financial institutions. All described themselves as Thai or Chinese-Thai. Four self-identified as Muslim and one as Christian, with the balance being Buddhist. This research was conducted in 1999, 2000 and 2002.

The sample for the third project comprised 10 public sector managers, who held senior accounting or auditing roles in Thai government agencies. Again there was an even number of males and females. Information on the respondents' religion was not collected. These interviews occurred in 2003 and 2004. All interviews were conducted in Thai.

The sample for the fourth project comprised eight company secretaries and corporate consultants. There were four males and four females in this group. All described their ethnicity as Thai. While the respondents were not directly asked about their religion, we are aware that two of the respondents identified as Muslim. This research was conducted in 2005 and 2006. All interviews in this project were conducted predominantly in English, with some clarifying and probing questions conducted in Thai.

Although the main research question in these projects varied, all dealt in some way with human resource issues including gender, ethnicity, religion and age. In all studies the data were collected using a convergent interviewing process (Dick, 1990, 1998). Convergent interviewing has the advantage of being both inductive and deductive. The broad structure of the interview process remains consistent across interviews, but within interviews the probing questions asked are informed by previous participants' responses. The aim of the convergent interviewing process is to identify areas of agreement among interviewees, exceptions to those agreements, and areas of disagreement. As such, it is also a useful technique with which to draw together information from a number of thematically similar, but distinct research projects.

Gender

The literature on gender discrimination in South-East Asia clearly indicates that they are often the most marginalized groups within these societies (Copeland, 1987; Dwyer and Bruce, 1988; Standing, 1992). In organizations they are more likely to be part-time or casual employees and to have less opportunity for career development than their male co-workers (Carny and O'Kelly, 1987; Duffy and Pupo, 1992). Lim (1993), Stockman et al. (1995) and Hutchings (1996) highlight their limited access to human resource development and training programs. Frequently, this discrimination is attributed to the patriarchal nature of the South-East Asian societies (Bradley, 1989; Walby, 1986).

However, much of this research focuses on unskilled and semi-skilled workers. When discussing female managers and professionals in Asia, a more diverse range of outcomes are evident (Fisher et al., 2000a). On one hand is a body of literature that supports the argument that female managers face high levels of discrimination. In China they have fewer opportunities for employment and job mobility (Hidebrandt and Liu, 1988). In Singapore they have less job satisfaction, career success and emotional well-being than comparably qualified and experienced Canadian women (Burke et al., 1997), are less likely to hold middle- and upper-level managerial and professional roles (Luke, 1998), and in part due to government policies aimed at reinforcing the traditional homemaker roles of women (Koh, 1996; Lan and Lee, 1997), have low workforce participation rates (Lan and Lee, 1997) and reduced opportunities for promotion (Koh, 1996). Organizations in Hong Kong did not practice female- or family-friendly human resource management (Chui and Ng, 1999).

In contrast to the above, Horton (1999) indicates that women in newly industrialized countries are increasingly represented in higher-paid professional and white-collar jobs, and that the wages of these women have risen faster in Asia than in the United States. Similarly, van der Boon (2003) notes that Thailand, Singapore and the Philippines rank well ahead of the Netherlands, France and Germany in terms of the percentage of women in management and administrative roles. In Japanese companies, the representation of women on company boards is more than four times greater than it is in Dutch or British firms (Bolger, 1997). In addition, women are accepted at higher levels of management (Frazee, 1996). Women in Asia are seen as empowered leaders (O'Shea, 1997), who have reached top positions without affirmative action programs (van der Boon, 2003). An explanation provided by several authors for this phenomenon is that class, linked to access to education, rather than gender, is the most important determining demographic factor in career opportunity in Asia (Fisher and Hutchings, 1997; Hutchings and Fisher, 1998, Hutchings, 2000; Fisher and Hartel, 2003; van der Boon 2003). Narrowing the focus to Thailand, there is even stronger evidence that this is the case (Fisher and Hutchings, 1997; Fisher et al., 2000a).

There is, however, support for the argument that women in Thailand are less marginalized in their access to managerial positions (Sheehan, 1995; Luke, 1998), and that class, rather than gender, may be the main determinant of access to these positions (Dunn and Sheehan, 1993; Fisher and Hutchings, 1997; Hutchings and Fisher, 1998; Hutchings, 2000). Appold et al. (1998) identified that there was a greater representation of women in top management positions in Thailand than in either Japan or the USA. Luke (1998) suggested that a similar situation exists when comparing the representation of women as education managers in Thailand and other Asian countries. Female managers have also been identified as key contributors to the nation's economic success (Hoffarth, 1989). Fisher and Härtel (1998) found that gender was not an important issue in relation to management effectiveness, as long as education was perceived as appropriate. In a later quantitative study that focused only on expatriate managers, gender was found not to contribute to perceived management effectiveness (Fisher et al., 2000b). Further, Appold et al. (1998) found that employing female managers did not limit the performance of the organization.

Beckmann et al. (2008) argued that the 46.4 percent female representation of financial managers and professionals in their sample reflected the nature of the Thai funds management industry, even though this was four times greater than their US and German samples, and double their Italian sample.

Van der Boon (2003) notes that senior female managers interviewed in her research did not perceive that they had been discriminated against, and concluded that social class, rather than gender, created career opportunities. Unlike Fisher and Hutchings (1997) she did identify age as a barrier to career advancement. Research conducted by Fisher et al. (2000a) in a multi-organization study concluded that female Thai middle and senior managers did not feel disadvantaged in access to a range of career development activities, nor in terms of reward or promotion. Respondents in the same study suggested the possibility that Western managers and academics may be imposing their own perceptions of gender relationships as distinct as the reality of the relationship in Thailand.

The key findings related to the research on gender are listed in Table 19.1. There was no notable difference in the responses to any of the questions for either male or female managers in either consensus or dissenting and qualifying views.

The consensus view was that both social class and education were more

Table 19.1   Gender

Topic	Consensus view	Dissenting or qualifying view
What is the role of education?	Education is more important to your career than gender It is lack of education or skills that stop lower-level employees from being promoted regardless of gender	Poorly educated women are often poorly rewarded, unless they are beautiful
What is the role of social class?	Social class is more important to a career than gender	Lower-class women are often exploited, but then so are lower-class men
Is discrimination different in foreign companies from Thai companies?	There is no difference whether the company is foreign or Thai owned.	Female managers who work for Western multinationals are more likely to be discriminated against on the basis of gender, but the discrimination comes from Western managers. In some Chinese-Thai family companies it's better to be a Chinese-Thai man
Are there differences in compensation?	There is little difference between the remuneration packages of male and female managers. Compensation for the same job can vary greatly from company to company	Men tend to get more non-salary benefits than women
Are there barriers to promotion for women in the public sector?	It's a myth that there are no senior female managers in the public service	Social class and patronage influence promotion. In some organizations you are more likely to be promoted if you are a man
Has the situation changed in the public sector?	No. Senior female public sector managers are not a new thing	Yes. The further we get away from military government, the more women are promoted
Are there barriers to women in engineering?	It is true there are not a lot of female engineers. But there are a lot of female	Women don't want to study engineering. It's the same everywhere in the world

Table 19.1   (continued)

Topic	Consensus view	Dissenting or qualifying view
	project managers, CEOs and company directors in charge of engineering companies	
Are there barriers to women in academia?	There are many female professors and deans. Being a woman is not a disadvantage	A lot of women academics see it as a career. A lot of male academics concentrate on consultancy or other business activities. So of course there are more opportunities for women to be promoted
Are there barriers to women in finance?	There are many senior women in finance, including CEOs, company secretaries and board members	It's based on education and patronage, but some companies are more likely to promote men
Are these changes new?	There are more jobs for women since the Asia crisis	No clear dissenting view expressed

important than gender, in terms of all aspects of employment. Low education acted as a barrier to promotion. Social class was also more important than gender, in part because it enabled access to education. However, education was also seen as a way to change one's social class. Both lower-class men and lower-class women have the potential to be exploited, but possibly in different ways.

The salaries paid for the same job in different companies varied widely, and there was little difference in the salaries paid to women or to men. A dissenting view was that women receive lower salaries in foreign companies, and in some Chinese-Thai family companies. A minority view was that men are always paid more than women for the same job.

The consensus view was that there were no real barriers to promotion based on gender, and that there were female senior managers in the public sector, the professions, and academia, though there were few female engineers. Both social class and patronage were seen as having an influence on the likelihood of promotion in the public sector and in the financial professions.

Race and ethnicity

Earlier in the chapter we noted that there was little literature dealing with racial or ethnic diversity in Thai organizations. Indeed, Lawler (1996) noted that the Thai workforce is largely homogeneous, and infers that there are limited opportunities for discrimination. Lawler specifically states that the employment discrimination against people of Chinese ethnicity that appears in neighboring countries is largely absent in Thailand. In addition, it is noted that most other ethnic minorities, such as Indian and Malay, are very small, and tend to be located in a limited number of provinces.

The largest ethnic minority are the people from the Isan region in northwest Thailand. Lawler indicates that this group, while Thai, have similar characteristics to the people of the adjacent country of Laos. The area is a source of low-skilled labor, and its people are the poorest and least educated in Thailand. As such, an explanation for the perception that the jobs they hold are at lower levels than those for the broader Thai population may be based on educational barriers rather than discrimination based on ethnicity.

The key findings related to the research on race and ethnicity are listed in Table 19.2. While the consensus view was that there was little bias based on ethnicity or race if the individual was Chinese-Thai, there was clear evidence of bias towards Isan people, albeit moderated by educational attainment, and there was a clear perception that Isan people were of a lower social class. Some bias was also expressed against poorly educated Chinese, and people of African American–Thai dissent. The latter was partly attributed to perceptions of the children of American GIs and Thai prostitutes, and may therefore be based in perceptions of social class in addition to perceptions of race.

Religion

Over 95 percent of Thai people identify themselves as Buddhist, and the largest ethnic minority is located in the three predominantly Muslim southern provinces that are situated on the Malaysian border. Lawler (ibid.) notes that it is almost impossible to obtain hard data on the employment outcomes of religious minorities, and asserts that the majority of Muslims who live in and around Bangkok are involved in factory work. While this assertion may be true, the authors note the relative ease with which we were able to identify managers and professionals in our research who professed to be Islamic, and the prominence of Muslims in high-profile business, government and military roles, as a counterpoint to this assertion.

The consensus view of our respondents was that there was little

Table 19.2   Race and ethnicity

Topic	Consensus view	Dissenting or qualifying view
Does race and ethnicity matter to a person's career opportunities overall?	It does not matter if you are Thai-Thai or Chinese-Thai: you are just Thai. Sometimes people assume that if you have darker skin you are less educated. But when they realize you are qualified, there is no problem	Some Chinese are *Djek* – a slang term for untrustworthy lower-class Chinese.[1] Thai people think that foreign Thais and foreigners are rich and have all the benefits. So they are often biased against us[2]
Does it matter which part of Thailand you come from?	It is more likely that you will be low class or uneducated if you come from Isan or somewhere else upcountry.[3] So of course you are not going to have as good a job if you have less education[4]	A lot of people in Bangkok are biased against the people in the north. Note that this view was more frequently expressed by respondents in research projects conducted in the 2000s than in the 1990s
Does race influence access to training and staff development	No	No dissenting views expressed
Does race influence how much you are paid?	No, it's education, performance, your position and your network that count	Not everyone wants to get ahead. If your company wants to train people, and you want training, you can probably get it
Does race influence your chance of being promoted?	No, if you have good relationships you will be promoted	Some international companies don't want to promote Thais. They want *farang*.
Does race influence whether you get a job or not?	No, though there are some companies that might want local people	If you are African and Thai some people will be scared of you, so you might not get employed

Notes
1. Note that this view was stated by people who identified as Thai, as Thai-Thai and as Chinese-Thai.
2. View stated by foreign-born and some foreign-educated Thai.
3. 'Upcountry' is the term used by Thailand to apply to people from northern and north-eastern rural Thai provinces: this includes the Isan region.
4. Note comment about skin color in previous question.

Table 19.3 Religion

Topic	Consensus view	Dissenting view
Are there barriers to private sector careers based on religion?	People get promoted on their personal connections or on their performance. There are plenty of middle and senior managers who are Muslim	No dissenting views expressed
Are there barriers to public sector careers based on religion?	No. There are generals, professors, and managers who are Muslim. Muslims are not a big part of the population, but they are well represented at all levels	Under recent governments (2000s) it was a disadvantage, because they were anti-Muslim
Religious stereotypes	Most Thai are Buddhist, and just want to get along with people. In the south there are people who just do not have a good work ethic. There are a lot of Muslims in the south	No dissenting views expressed

discrimination against Muslim managers and professionals. However, it was noted that some recent governments had been anti-Muslim. Personal connections and patron–client relationships were also emphasized. The key findings related to religion are listed in Table 19.3.

Conclusion, limitations, implications and opportunities for future research
There is a strong body of research that emphasizes the importance of social class, education and patron–client relationships over gender as determinants of career success in Thai public and private sector organizations at managerial and professional levels. The research in this chapter supports this contention. Further, our findings support the argument that the same forces play a similar role with regard to both racial and ethnic diversity, and religious diversity in Thai organizations. Again, this finding is most appropriately applied only to managers and professionals, rather than the broader Thai workforce. Given the limited amount of prior research conducted in this area, this finding is an important contribution to the study of diversity in Thai organizations.

However, there was relatively clear evidence of bias against the ethnic minority from Isan. Further research is necessary to identify if this bias is indeed based on ethnicity, or is attributable to education and social class issues. Given the wedge politics being played out in Thailand, and the apparent 'rural–urban' divide that has emerged, at least in the media coverage of this political issue, research to identify the source of this bias and possible solutions based on educational access could make a positive contribution to the performance of Thai organizations, and the broader society as a whole.

Also interesting is the finding that discrimination is seen to be greater towards women in foreign organizations operating in Thailand, than it is in Thai organizations. This would indicate that the gender bias is being imported as part of foreign organizations' culture. If this is a widespread perception, it has practical implications for recruitment and selection, as foreign companies may be perceived as less attractive to female managers and professionals than Thai companies.

There are clear limitations in the research we have conducted. None of the studies we have reported to support our findings had a key goal of investigating racial, ethnic or religious diversity in Thai organizations. Rather, these were incidental to research dealing with other issues in management. Our sample size, though comparable with previous studies, and our sample profile, limited to managers and professionals, do not necessarily lead to the generalizability of our findings across the broader Thai organizational settings. Further, our findings are limited to the perceptions of Thai managers and professionals who have already achieved middle- and senior-level positions, in an environment where patronage supports promotion. There may be a self-serving bias in place. These limitations could be addressed in future research, using a broader sample of employees, managers and professionals.

References

Appold, S.J., Siengthai, S. and Kasarda, J.D. (1998), 'The employment of women managers and professionals in an emerging economy: gender inequality as an organizational practice', *Administrative Science Quarterly*, **43** (3): 538–66.

Beckmann, D., Menkhoff, L. and Suto, M. (2008), 'Does culture influence asset managers' views and behavior?', *Journal of Economic Behaviour and Organisation*, **67**: 634–43.

Bolger, A. (1997), 'Segregated by sex; women all over the world are excluded from top jobs', *Financial Times*, London, 11 December.

Bradley, H. (1989), *Men's Work. Women's Work. A Sociological History of the Sexual Division of Labour in Employment*, Oxford: Polity Press.

Bunnak, P. (1990), *Non-relative Patron–Client Relationship*, Bangkok: Chulalongkorn University Press.

Bunnak, P. (1991), *The Patron–Client System in the Evolution of Thai Politics*, Bangkok: Sukhothaithammathirat.

Burke, R., Peng, K.Y. and McKeen, C.A. (1997), 'Experiences of professional women in Canada and Singapore', *The Asian Manager*, **10** (6): 78–83.

Carny, L.S. and O'Kelly, C.G. (1987), 'Barriers and constraints to the recruitment and mobility of female managers in the Japanese labour force', *Human Resource Management*, **26** (2): 193–216.

Chui, W.C.K. and Ng, C.W. (1999), 'Women-friendly HRM and organisational commitment: a study among women and men in organizations in Hong Kong', *Journal of Occupational and Organisational Psychology*, **72** (4): 485–502.

Copeland, M.S. (1987), 'The interaction of racism, sexism and classism in women's exploitation', in E.S. Fiorenza and A. Carr (eds), *Women, Work and Policy*, Edinburgh: T and T Clark, pp. 19–27.

Dick, B. (1990), *Convergent Interviewing*, Chapel Hill, Qld: Interchange.

Dick, B. (1998), 'Convergent interviewing: a technique for qualitative data collection', available at: http://www.scu.edu.au/schools/sawd/arr/iview.html (accessed 1 January 2008).

Duffy, A. and Pupo, N. (1992), *Part-Time Paradox: Connecting Gender, Work and Family*, Toronto: McClelland & Stewart.

Dunn, L. and Sheehan, B. (1993), 'Women in management in Thailand – report on a small survey', unpublished working paper, Rungsit University, Bangkok.

Dwyer, D. and Bruce, J. (1988), *A Home Divided: Women and Income in the Third World*, Stanford, CA: Stanford University Press.

Fisher, G., Bibo, M., Youngsamart, D. and Chomjunroone, S. (2000a), 'Gender equity and human resource management practices in Thailand: some exploratory findings', *International Issues in Human Resource Management*, **1** (1): 1–18.

Fisher, G. and Härtel, C.E.J. (1998), 'Culture, characteristics and performance: an examination of effectiveness of western managers operating in intercultural teams in Thailand', paper presented at the 12th ANZAM International Conference, Refereed Proceedings, 6–9 December, Australia and New Zealand Academy of Management, Adelaide.

Fisher, G.B. and Härtel, C.E.J. (2003), 'Cross-cultural effectiveness of Western expatriate–Thai client interactions: lessons learned for IHRM research and theory', *Cross-Cultural Management: An International Journal*, **10** (4): 4–28.

Fisher, G.B., Härtel, C.E.J. and Bibo, M. (2000b), 'Does task and contextual performance measurement apply across cultures? An empirical study of Thai and Western managers and professionals', in *Proceedings of the Transcending Boundaries Conference*, 6–8 September, Brisbane, Griffith University.

Fisher, G. and Hutchings, K. (1997), 'Divergent in a positive way? Class, gender and the human resource management practices in multinational corporations', paper presented, Thailand, Refereed Proceedings of AIRAANZ, 10 January–1 February, Brisbane: Association of Industrial Relations Academics Australia and New Zealand.

Frazee, V. (1996), 'Keeping up on Chinese culture', *Personnel Journal*, **1**: 16–17.

Girling, J. (1981), *Thailand: Society and Politics*, Ithaca, NY: Cornell University Press.

Hidebrandt, H.W. and Liu, J. (1988), 'Chinese women managers: a comparison with their U.S. and Asian counterparts', *Human Resource Management*, **27** (3): 291–314.

Hoffarth, V. (1989), *Corporate Women Managers in Southeast Asia*, Singapore: Asian Institute of Management.

Horton, S. (1999), 'Marginalization revisited: women's market work and pay, an economic development', *World Development*, **27** (3): 571–82.

Hutchings, K. (1996), 'Workplace practices of Japanese and Australian multinational corporations operating in Singapore, Malaysia and Indonesia', *Human Resource Management Journal*, **6** (2): 58–71.

Hutchings, K. (2000), 'Class and gender influences on employment practices in Thailand: an examination of equity policy and practice', *Women in Management Review*, **15** (8): 385–403.

Hutchings, K. and Fisher, G. (1998), 'It is not fashionable here so why do it? A re-examination of IR and HR practices in Southeast Asia', paper presented, refereed Proceedings of AIRAANZ, 3–5 February, Wellington: Academics Australia and New Zealand.

Koh, T.A. (1996), 'Wandering through the minefield; leading who, where to and for what?', *Awareness*, **3**: 23–30.

Lan, L. and Lee, J. (1997), 'Force-field analysis on policies affecting working women in Singapore', *Journal of Management Development*, **16** (1): 43–53.

Lawler J.J. (1996), 'Diversity issues in South-East Asia: the case of Thailand', *International Journal of Manpower*, **17** (4/5): 152–67.

Lekhakul, K. (1996), *The Personality of Thailand*, Bangkok: Aarnsutha Press.

Lim, L.L. (1993), 'The feminization of labour in the Asia-Pacific Rim countries: from contributing to economic dynamism to bearing the brunt of structural adjustments', in N. Ogawa, G.W Jones and J.G. Williamson (eds), *Human Resources in Development along the Asia-Pacific Rim*, Singapore: Oxford University Press.

Luke, C. (1998), 'Cultural politics and women in Singapore higher education management', *Gender and Education*, **10**: 245–64.

O'Shea, L. (1997), 'Up close and personal', *Asian Business*, **33** (12): 22.

Pornpitakpan, C. (2000), 'Trade in Thailand: a three-way cultural comparison', *Journal of Business Horizons*, **43** (2): 61–70.

Samudavanija, L. (1995), *Politics and Thai Society*, Bangkok: Thai Wattanapanit.

Sheehan, B. (1995), *Thailand: An Introduction to Thailand, Its People, Trade and Business Activity*, 3rd edn, Bangkok: National Institute of Development Administration.

Standing, H. (1992), 'Employment', in L. Ostergaard (ed.), *Gender and Development: A Practical Guide*, London: Routledge, pp. 57–75.

Stockman, N., Bonney, N. and Sheng, X. (1995), *Women's Work in East and West: The Dual Burden of Employment and Family Life*, London: UCL Press.

van der Boon, M. (2003), 'Women in international management: an international perspective on women's ways of leadership', *Women in Management Review*, **18** (3): 132–46.

Walby, S. (1986), *Patriarchy at Work: Patriarchal and Capitalist Relations in Employment*, Cambridge: Polity.

20 Islamic civil society and social capital in
Turkey: the Gülen community
Ahmet Yükleyen

Introduction

Theoretical discussion on the interaction of globalization and national diversity management has concentrated on the tension between the particularities of the context and the universal homogenization of Anglo-American standards. This chapter suggests two ways to expand the discussion on diversity management. First, it applies lessons from Western-oriented globalization on the relationship of diversity and development in the cultural context of Turkey, which is often presented as a 'bridge between East and West'. The role of civic culture in promoting democratization has re-emerged in Western scholarship, which could be useful to examine political and economic development in the 'non-Western' context.[1] The cultural diversity within each country has to be studied to draw lessons on the global scale.[2] Turkey's presumed in-between identity indicates that the context of each country regardless of its subjection to occidental or oriental discourse creates particular conditions and approaches to manage diversity.

Second, diversity management literature's level of analysis primarily focuses on the company, national or multinational. The goal of increasing market efficiency and respecting human dignity through the recognition of ethnic, racial, gender, religious and other identity within companies could have implications for state–society relations as well. On the one hand, the national context in each country significantly shapes the diversity management strategy in each company.[3] On the other, lessons of cultural diversity management could fruitfully be applied to state–society interaction. The public (un)recognition of emerging group identities could challenge or facilitate the economic development of a country, depending on how cultural diversity is politically managed. This chapter focuses on how the secular Turkish state is (mis)managing the rising Islamic identity within the civil society through the case of a moderate Islamic movement.

The source of Turkish cultural diversity has been the modernization process, which predates the Republican period, as a state-driven project. This has resulted in the dominance of state-oriented approaches to understanding ethnic and religious diversity in Turkey, which are the two major challenges to the secular nation-state. Nevertheless, some scholars have recently suggested new theoretical approaches, which are in dialogue with the traditional modernization and dependency schools, but also offer a novel state-in-society perspective.[4] These new theoretical directions go beyond 'bringing the state back in' by studying states in their social setting and concentrating on the mutually transforming quality of state–society relations. States mold the society, but they are also molded by the societies within which they are embedded.

There are two claims of this state-in-society approach that are at the center of my analysis. One of these claims is that states must be disaggregated. If states have to be viewed in their social context, it is important to study not only the elite social groups or organizations at the center of the polity, but also state–society interactions at the periphery. Components of the state encounter the same pushes and pulls from the scattered elements of society and the blurring boundaries between state and society increase the role of these social organizations.

Turkish social scientists writing on state–society relations have long talked about a dominant center and a weak periphery, which dates back to the Ottoman period.[5] However, the shift from the center–periphery analysis is significant to understanding the context in which Turkish civil society has developed. This center–periphery analysis is based on a state-versus-society approach, in which the center is defined as the dominant social and political groups, such as the educated elite class (*ilmiyye*), the military (*askeriyye*), the judges (*kadı*) and the clerics in the bureaucracy of the state. During the Ottoman rule these groups dictated the content of law, education and public policy in religious terms, and in the Republican period in secular terms. The interests of these groups were promoted either in Islamic or secular terms through the coercive (*ceberrut*) state conception. These self-interested groups have used this coercive state system, which had the bureaucratic tradition behind it, as a strong apparatus against the periphery when their interests clashed.

The periphery refers to the majority of the society, such as the middle-class merchants, city dwellers, religious and ethnic minorities, and the rural population. These groups were not organized enough to challenge the center and demand accountability. Moreover, the center is perennially suspicious of the civic associations of civil society, which it tries to control and suppress. The state is strong in this sense, as a powerful, legitimate apparatus in the hands of these elite, privileged groups, which do not allow the formation of a societal consensus that might merge as a social force in their attempts to gain autonomy from their authoritarian rule.

The tension between the state and civil society is still central in the Turkish political context. I argue that in order to talk about a vibrant civil society there are rights and obligations to be expected from both sides. The state is supposed to provide a liberal constitutional democratic regime, and in return civil society is required to be 'at peace' with the state. Although, these obligations are not totally fulfilled, there are improvements on both sides. This argument will be pursued further in the discussion on the development of civil society in Turkey.

The second claim is that states and other social forces, such as civil society, can be mutually empowering, if cultural diversity is politically recognized as a resource rather than a threat to the existing polity. This asks scholars to eschew a state-versus-society perspective that rests on a view of power as a zero-sum conflict between the state and society. Although for some social groups this is indeed an accurate rendering of the nature of their interactions with the state, some interactions between state and civil society can create more power for both.

I argue that there is a mutually empowering relationship between the state and civil society in Turkish economic and political development. A vibrant civil society provides 'social capital' for the system to invest in economic development for the society.[6] The state empowers civil society in return by providing economic development, which allows more room and power for the nurture of civil society. The economic transformation in the 1980s by the total subscription to neoclassical models empowered Turkish civil society. This transformation allowed the emerging bourgeoisie to finance and organize civil society formations for commercial or public purposes.[7]

Thus, the state-in-society approach points to the increasing role of civil society as an analytical tool to study development issues. The *Nur* movement is a religio-social movement, which has been very influential in the religious revivalism, but also managed to be at peace with the Kemalist state elite. This case indicates that a state-in-society perspective is more helpful to study the role of civil society in the economic and political development. In this analysis the social contribution of this movement to development will be studied through the 'social capital' argument as put forth by Robert Putnam.[8] He has done studies on civic life in Italy where he illustrated how social capital, which is produced primarily by the civic associations, matters in the development of societies. His most recent study concludes the following:

> In the short run, however, immigration and ethnic diversity tend to reduce social solidarity and social capital. New evidence from the US suggests that in ethnically diverse neighbourhoods residents of all races tend to 'hunker down'. Trust (even of one's own race) is lower, altruism and community cooperation rarer, friends fewer. In the long run, however, successful immigrant societies have overcome such fragmentation by creating new, cross-cutting forms of social solidarity and more encompassing identities.[9]

This indicates that despite the difficulties of managing diversity in the short run, it benefits the society through the increase of social capital in the long run. In non-immigration countries the challenges of managing diversity could rise from the indigenous cultural identities as organized in civil society. Cultural diversity with either native or immigrant origin produces social capital when state and civil society develops a trust-based relationship in respecting their respective boundaries. Next, I expand on this relationship and its implications for development. Then, I shall turn to the Turkish development context and the case study on the Gülen community.

Civil society and development

The main problem of civil society as a theoretical tool is that there is no consensus on the definition. This presents a danger that the concept will lose its usefulness because of the ambiguity of its boundaries. There are competing definitions of civil society, some of which include the market and/or political parties, while others do not. Although there is disagreement about the borders of civil society, most definitions agree that civil society is autonomous from the state and the family. Lehning proposes an analytical definition of civil society to use for developmental issues:

> A space or arena between households and the state which affords possibilities of concerted action and social organization . . . civil society occupies the middle ground between government and the private sector. It is the space we occupy when we are engaged with neither government activities (voting, paying taxes) nor in commerce (working, producing, shopping, and consuming).[10]

Although there has been an ambiguity in the definition of civil society, there has also been an increasing interest in it. There are four principal reasons for the explosion of interest in civil society as suggested by Galston.[11] First, events in the former Soviet-bloc nations of Central Europe dramatized the ways in which civil associations could serve as effective sources of resistance to oppressive governments. Foley and Edwards emphasize this function of civil society. They even make a distinction between civil society that is independent of the state and is capable of energizing resistance to a tyrannical regime and civil society that only promotes habits of association to foster patterns of civility in the actions of citizens in a democratic polity.[12] Second, a plethora of non-governmental organizations (NGOs) emerged throughout the world addressing transnational issues like the environment, population, and the status of women, human rights, and even disarmament. Third, the concept of civil society as a realm of non-privatized collective action that is voluntary, rather than compulsory, and persuasive rather than coercive, provided a third basis for discussion of development. Finally, civil society is seen as a solution to the anxiety of the Western developed nations that the traditional sources of socialization, solidarity and active citizenship were becoming weak. Putnam's 'Bowling alone' touched precisely this concern, sparking a conceptual, empirical, and political debate that is continuing.[13] This chapter is inspired by the last two reasons, which focus on civil society in development and more specifically, social capital.

The increasing interest in civil society in development is as a potential tool to overcome theoretical and political problems by providing novel social policies. The liberal approach asks for less state involvement in economic development and a larger space for the private sector, whereas statists claim a greater role for the state as the driving force in development. If we want to break this binary relationship between state and/or government and the private sector, civil society can be conceived as a space where citizens rule themselves. This suggests a three-celled model in which civil society intermediates between the government and the private sector. This civic space, third sphere if you will, can work as glue between the individual and the state. This conception of civil society serves as a locus of the cultural and social aspects of development. Civil society tells us about the cultural and political context within which economic development takes place.

Some scholars have described the relationship between democracy and economic development as a trade-off or a 'cruel dilemma'. However, the state-in-society approach sees this relationship not as a trade-off but rather as a 'virtuous circle', meaning a circle in which the elements promote one another.[14] This third way can solve the dichotomy by establishing a virtuous circle between economic and political development. In this third model, democratic regimes empower civil society and in return civil society provides social capital, which is needed along with physical and human capital for economic development. The interaction between Turkish civil society and economic development provides an imperfect example of this virtuous circle.

Social capital and development

Putnam's argument on social capital suggests a mutual relationship between economic and social development.[15] His approach challenges the utility-maximizing individual argument, which is at the core of the neoclassical economic development model. According to neoclassical economic principles, as everyone pursues his or her individual interest, the society develops as a whole. However, Putnam gives examples where people do not collaborate for collective action despite their self-interest. Parents in communities everywhere want better educational opportunities, but collaborative efforts to improve public schools falter. Poor farmers in the Third World need more effective irrigation and marketing schemes, but cooperation to these ends proves fragile. Social scientists have explained this phenomenon in a variety of ways – the tragedy of the commons, the logic of the collective, public goods, the prisoners' dilemma. A novel approach to this longstanding dilemma is offered through the concept of 'social capital', which refers to 'features of social organization, such as networks, norms and trust that can improve the efficiency of society by facilitating coordinated actions'.[16] 'Social capital enhances the benefits of investment in physical and human capital'.[17] One of the argument's premises is that social capital is a prerequisite for human and physical capital to be transferred into development.

Putnam developed his argument based on his research in Italy in his *Making Democracy Work: Civic Traditions in Modern Italy*.[18] He explains how networks of civic engagement promote values of reciprocity, trust, and collaboration and transmute into financial capital. In 'Bowling alone', Putnam offers the diagnosis that social capital in the United States is on the decline. Since social capital refers to networks of civic engagement, the way to promote it encourages us to consider the role of civil society more seriously. If social capital is important, classical social policy, which is designated to enhance the opportunities of individuals, has a partially misplaced emphasis. Instead, the argument follows, 'we must focus on community development, allowing space for religious organizations, and choral societies, and Little Leagues that may seem to have little relevance to politics and economics'.[19]

My case study is crucial exactly because of the emphasis of the social capital argument on community development. In the modernization model of Turkey, the so-called 'Westernization', the leading role of social change and development is ascribed to the state, this time not for Islamic, but for secular causes. The state apparatus was used to transform an Islamic, traditional, and multi-ethnic community into a secular nation-state. This development model caused the state to disregard and suppress the demands of society regarding public life and especially religious freedoms, which are still considered a threat to the secular state. This state-led development model disregarded the contributive aspects of Turkish civil society, including religious organizations, which are not only suppressed, but also disparaged as impediments of development. After these theoretical linkages between social capital, civil society, and development, I turn to the case study, which illustrates that Islamic organizations within Turkish civil society can contribute to development and cooperate with the state.

Turkish civil society

The state-in-society perspective develops the first part of my argument, which is about the mutual obligations of civil society and state. Civil society is generally defined as the sphere between state and family. This reference to state in the definition refers to the logical conclusion that if there is no state, we are not able to identify the existence of civil society. Most of the scholars of civil society in the Middle East, including Augustus Richard Norton, who has led the largest civil society research project in the Middle East, see this as a crucial component of civil society. Norton calls this one of the three normative criteria to identify civil society, namely citizenship. The other two are associability, which entails a spirit of cooperation, and civility, which refers to tolerance for groups with different or opposing worldviews. However, the citizenship criterion is a crucial component:

> [It] underpins civil society. To be a part of the whole is a precondition for the whole to be a sum of its parts. Otherwise, society has no coherence; it is just a vessel filled with shards and fragments. Thus, the individual in civil society is granted rights by the state, but, in return, acquires duties to the states.[20]

Simply because an organization does not employ violent tactics does not necessarily mean that it respects 'others' or plays by the 'rules of the game'. That is to say, those whose ultimate goal is to overthrow or replace the existing regime cannot be considered part of civil society. The issue, as Norton suggests, is behavioral and not psychological. Thus, what matters is not how people feel about others, but how they act toward them. In short, the principle of citizenship characterizes civil society *vis-à-vis* the role of the state in the society.

This component is especially important for the study of civil society in the Middle East, because Islamic organizations in forms of communities, movements and orders have become the most effective members of civil society in the Middle East, more often through the provision of basic social services than through violent means.[21] There have been many discussions on the Gülen community, because on one hand, the liberal and moderate elements in Gülen's Islamic discourse made it difficult to categorize them as 'fundamentalists' (*irticacı*), while on the other, the religious emphasis alerted the secular state elite. According to scholars who have analyzed the Gülen community in Turkey, they work towards the goal of promoting religious consciousness and faith within the 'rules of the game'. In other words they operate as a 'moderate' religious community within civil society without posing tangible threats to the Turkish state.[22] These studies indicate that the Gülen community fulfills this important requirement of civil society.

The state-in-society perspective considers it the duty of the state to provide a liberal constitutional democratic regime in which civil society can flourish. In this respect, although the Turkish state has made great progress, there is a long way to go to establish such a regime. However, it is not possible to conclude that Turkish civil society genuinely enjoys all the freedoms of a liberal constitutional democracy. This is apparent when it comes to religious freedoms of individuals. Islamist women are not allowed to wear a veil in public institutions, most notably universities, which deprive some of them of their right for higher education. Any Islamic organization is approached with suspicion by the state as being against the state system.

Nevertheless, a brief survey on the historical development of civil society from the late Ottoman period to the contemporary Turkish Republic provides a summary of the progress that the civil society has made. Although democratic and human rights questions continue, the country is seen as less authoritarian compared to the strong state systems in the region, and the emergence of civil society is recognized.[23] Ironically, in the literature, there has not been sufficient attention to civil society in Turkey.

The strong state system of the Ottomans allowed them to rule multi-ethnic, multi-religious groups under one polity. Despite the fact that there were examples of civil society formations such as the *loncas* and *vakıf* system,[24] the strong, centralized state establishment did not leave the civil society sphere. Nevertheless, the Ottoman *millet system*, which divided the society along religious lines, allowed the representation of non-Muslims in public life and workspace. This can explain the low levels of discrimination against religious minorities in the Turkish Republican period after 1923.[25]

With the collapse of the Ottoman state, there was an era of authoritarianism with a state-led transformation to a secular, modern nation-state under one party rule until the 1950s. Considering the massive social change from top to bottom and the unstable international security ambience, there was little room for civil society. The 1960s and 1970s were years in which polarization in politics resulted in violence, and hence the interference of the military in civil life.

In 1983, Turgut Özal established the first elected government after the military intervention in 1980 by General Kenan Evren, who became the president. Evren was in charge of security issues, while Özal managed the economy. However, Özal gradually increased his sphere of influence to include the civil bureaucracy in other institutions of the government. He started dismantling the state by policies of decentralization, privatization of state economic enterprises, and orientation towards a market economy. These policies captured the aspirations of the lower and middle urban classes with a provincial conservative background, the small entrepreneurial bourgeoisie and young professionals.[26] The media, cultural and educational interests of this emerging middle class embody an authentic counter-elite that is the representative of the majority of Anatolian Turkish Sunni Muslim population.[27] In short, Özal's policies allowed the emerging bourgeoisie to finance and organize civil society formations for commercial or public purposes.

New legislation allowed collective bargaining and strikes, public meetings and demonstrations, the right to form associations and to make collective petitions – all of which were illegal in 1980. Moreover, the restrictions on forming new political parties were lifted. The government also replaced the military liaison appointees in each ministry with civilian ones. The removal of laws such as 163, 141 and 142, which were used to prosecute any organization for an ideological or religious cause, led to the reemergence of ideological and religious orders.

In terms of state–society relations, the relative autonomy of civil–societal elements from the center in the 1980s has been a turning point in Turkish political development. Political debates in the post-1980s era have shifted from questioning the legitimacy of the regime and ideology to more specific public policy issues.[28] In these debates two issues were raised: the consolidation of democracy and the function of this emerging civil society, and Islamic revivalism in both civil society and politics. The Gülen community was one of the emerging religious groups in this era of Özal's government.

To sum up, in this first part of the circular relationship between the obligations and rights of the state and civil society there are deficiencies on both sides. On one hand, there are organizations that use the civil society paradigm to pursue their goals of getting rid of the state or changing the democratic system. On the other, although the Turkish state system has made progress from revolutionary nationalism to a liberal democracy, there are problems of human rights that impede the development of a vibrant civil society.[29]

Socio-economic development
The first circle of the relationship between the state and civil society was about the obligations of these entities to one another. The second circle is about the benefits they can provide to each other. As civil society contributes to the creation of social capital for the system, the state can turn this capital, along with human and physical capital, into economic development, strengthening civil society. This state-in-society perspective is more helpful in studying the relation between society and the state in Turkish development, which has adopted a specific model of modernization, namely Westernization. After giving the background of Westernization

efforts, I shall turn to the Gülen community to analyze how this NGO creates social capital.

Development is a complex phenomenon in which one of the main issues is modernity. What is it to be modern? Modernization theories are generally understood as a dichotomous relationship between 'traditional' and 'modern', and the transition from the former to the latter is called 'modernization'. Although, there have been critiques of modernization theory, the fundamental goal of Turkish development efforts is to modernize the society in the image of the industrialized countries of the West.

Although modernization efforts date back to the Ottoman period, it was only after 1923 that the historical connection between Islam and the state was broken and a particular Western, secular model of development was envisaged for Turkey. The founder of the Republic, Mustafa Kemal Atatürk, was both the father of this Westernization model and the leader of revolutionary nationalism. This model has been followed as a creed up to today and glorified with his name, the so-called 'Kemalism'. This is why modernization, Westernization and Kemalism are considered similar, if not synonymous, notions of development. The Westernization model is incorporated as the 'state ideology', which explains Turkey's ultimate development goal, which is to become a part of the European Union.

Westernization was based on a top-to-bottom model of development. The state and the ruling elite, who internalized this transformation from an Islamic to a Western culture, would be the engine of development in society and would spread these ideas to the masses. The role of the state as the engine of development was not only in political and social, but also economic affairs. The transformation of an Islamic society into a Western one necessarily involved a drastic change, and hence measures of forceful imposition at times. The resulting authoritarian role of the state was seen as necessary for the transformation of a religious, traditional society into a modern secular one. Although Westernization did succeed at the elite level, it was not as readily accepted by the masses. For the majority of the rural population, Islam is still seen as a dominant force of social life.

After Independence and the First World War, the state system was the only organization that could start such a project. All economic development projects were planned through the state system, which was highly centralized. This centralized economy actually improved economic growth through the Five Year Development Plans in the inter-war period, but in the 1980s the shift to a market economy began to change the economic system and reduce the role of the state. Turkey went through a great structural change. Confronted with socio-economic and political problems, the last civilian government of the 1970s adopted a policy package on January 24, 1980, aimed at massive restructuring of the economy. The main thrust of the program was the implementation of export-oriented growth strategies. These policies were implemented in the 1980s under the military government and later under Özal, who was considered one of the biggest reformers of Turkish political and economic development. Özal embarked on a mission to integrate Turkey into the world capitalist market. Thus the decade of the 1980s was defined as the period of economic austerity and restructuring. The role of the state was severely curtailed in economic development through structural adjustment policies.

This relative reduction in the role of the state in development encouraged the rise of the private sector and revival of civil society. The rise of civil society together with religious revivalism has raised concerns among the state elite. Although the rise of religious civic engagements heated discussions on Islam and politics, the strengthening of civil society can also contribute to Turkey's economic development. As the state initiated the economic reforms in which civil society flourished, civil society provides the social capital needed for development. The social capital argument connects the increase in civic engagements with economic development. My case study indicates that this contribution is possible, and that the mutually beneficial circle between the state and civil society can be established.

Case study: the Gülen community and social capital

Corrupt leaders and the constant manipulation of religious and ethnic fears that the Turkish state is in danger marked the political arena of Turkey in the 1990s. The rise of the Welfare Party (WP), the party representing political Islam, into government in 1995 has especially signified the religious revivalism in Turkey. Although the incapacity of other parties to solve longstanding policy problems has played an important role in the success of the party, the WP government is an indicator of religious revivalism. Nevertheless, the WP caused political polarization along religious lines, through using religion for political purposes. This attitude was also exaggerated by the media, which resulted in the soft military intervention on January 16, 1998.[30]

In this environment Gülen, who has absorbed a global language of democracy, tolerance, and dialogue played a pivotal role by limiting polarization and opening new channels of dialogue.[31] This kind of a conciliatory role was unexpected from a religious community, which has been perceived as the source of confrontation and polarization.

The Gülen community has its theoretical foundations in the work of Said Nursi (1876–1960), an ethnic Kurd, who authored several volumes of exegesis on the Qur'an known as the *Risale-i Nur* (Epistle of Light). He was the founder of the most powerful text-based faith movement in Turkey.

This strong movement has attracted some scholars such as Şerif Mardin, with his background in sociology, who has made the first extensive scholarly study on the Nursi movement and the role of social change and religion in Turkey.[32] Nursi wrote one of the most sophisticated and appealing interpretations of the Qur'an (*tefsir*) with the goal of raising religious consciousness through education and reason. To concentrate on promoting faith in God and individual practice of Islamic precepts, Nursi's main concern was to use scientific laws to illustrate the existence of an order in nature, and then present this order as a sign of God's existence and reflections of his name and attributes. Religion was in no way in contradiction with science because Qur'an was the direct revelation of God's attribute of being able to talk, whereas nature was the revelation of the other names. Thus, study of science is in a way a search for God in this account.

Although Nursi believed that politics with its corrupted nature cannot be a way to serve religion, he discussed social and political matters in his early writings, before writing *Risale-i Nur* in 1925. He names that stage of his life as *Eski Said* (Old Said). Some reflections on social and political matters can also be found in *Risale-i Nur*. He argued that democracy and Islam are not contradictory and that democracy and freedom are necessary conditions for a just society.[33] In one of his early works, *Münazarat* (1911), he treats freedom as an integral part of faith because the individual needs freedom to realize the power of God and, through this realization, the individual will be free from man-made oppression.[34] In his speech to the Grand National Assembly in 1922, Nursi stressed the importance of popular democracy and asked the parliamentarians to institute the rule of law.

In the early 1970s, the *Nur* movement experienced profound fragmentation due to different interpretations on applying Nursi theoretical work. Some groups concentrated on the early period of Nursi, the Old Said, and followed a method that involved party politics. Others adopted a method of following Nursi by only reading, printing, and studying *Risale-i Nur*. Gülen, however, focused on the application of his ideas in educational activities. As with Nursi, Gülen's writings and worldview create a marriage between religion and science, and between tradition and modernity. The method of focusing on education has proven to be the most appealing method, and Gülen appeared as the strongest leader of this movement by the 1980s.

Fethullah Gülen was born in 1938, in Erzurum, an important city in the east of Turkey, but worked most of his life as a preacher and teacher in Izmir, a modern harbor city on the Aegean coast. He did not limit himself to *Risale-i Nur*, but also read the books of national and Western intellectuals – as he refers to them in his writings and interviews.[35] With his personal capacity and appeal, he managed to form a network of followers in Izmir in a short period. After the first establishment of student dormitories, the first three private schools were founded in 1982 in the major cities. The necessity for a better education and the appeal of the modern, individualistic, civic interpretation of Islam increased the number of followers of Gülen. It is estimated that the number of adherents ranges from two to six million.[36] Although it is difficult to give an exact figure, the Gülen community is seen as the engine behind the construction of a 'new' Islam in Turkey. To carry out his mission of shaping the next generation, Gülen meets with Christian and Jewish community leaders, high-level politicians, including presidents, advises the establishment with regard to more educational institutions including schools, courses and universities, and promotes media such as TV and radio broadcasting, weeklies and daily papers to spread his ideas.

Gülen has initiated the largest private-led social mobility of Turkish society in educational affairs on the national level, which is gaining a transnational dimension as well. There are 236 high schools and language schools, five universities, and 21 student dorms on five continents including countries such as Cambodia, the United States, Australia, Denmark, Tanzania and Vietnam. Although these schools have been established worldwide, they are concentrated in the former USSR and Central Asian republics. The first school in Central Asia was founded in 1992. There are 182 high schools, more than 100 university entrance examination preparatory courses and 240 student dormitories.[37] All of these schools are registered under the Turkish Educational Ministry, and operate according to standard state regulations. The graduates have been dominating the university entrance examination in Turkey with their superior results. The schools have been financially supported by donations from Gülen adherents, and the teachers sent to the schools are mostly young graduates who identify themselves with the ideals of Gülen. Not only Turkish Muslims, but also members of other minority groups such as the Turkish Jewish community, have associated and financially supported Gülen's educational efforts.[38] The attraction of this large and eclectic organization lies in Gülen's commitment to education as a way of social development and reconciliation of religion with science. Gülen has high levels of associability to all Turkish citizens, Muslim or not, in the establishment of these educational institutions, which provide the most comprehensive and important activities in the community.

The Gülen community and social capital
This background information on the potential and the accomplishments of the community indicates that this organization has established a social network at the grassroots level, showing that the social capital created by

the community is substantial enough to provide a case study on the creation of social capital in Turkey.

There are three main components of social capital: trust, networks and norms. Together they facilitate coordination and cooperation for mutual benefit. I shall begin with trust as one of the components of social capital produced by this community.

Trust

This component of social capital has been studied in detail in *Trust and Modern Societies* by Barbara Misztal.[39] In Turkish society, trust in Islamic groups has varied, because some groups have used religious discourse for political purposes. These groups raised skepticism about any Islamic organization in the public spheres and the masses were becoming polarized on the issues of Islam, secularism and Kemalism. During the term of the WP government, the Kemalists started a protest that involved turning the lights off in the evening for one minute. This visual protest divides the society between Kemalists and Islamists. The resulting polarization not only excludes the large number in society that stand in between, but also decreases the trust in devoted Muslims, who have a private sense of Islam. The Gülen community represents those Muslims who do not approve of the politicization of Islam, but also as devoted Muslims want to practice their religion in the public sphere.

The biggest contribution of this community has been their campaign for tolerance and dialogue to establish connections between Islamic and secular circles. The campaign was organized by the Foundation of Journalists and Writers, which was pioneered by Gülen, whose aim is to promote interfaith dialogue and mutual respect among all strata of the society on national and international levels. They have organized meetings where religious leaders, scholars and journalists of different backgrounds get together. In these gatherings they advocate tolerance and dialogue and preach multiculturalism.

Along these lines, the Foundation of Journalists and Writers organized Abant meetings, in which intellectuals, scholars and leaders of different opinions gather to discuss issues of secularism, political Islam, the state and civil society. These gatherings gave both sides a chance to understand each other and recognize the variety of views among other groups as well as their own, and the ideas spread through media coverage to the society. These attempts proved to be the first steps to break the ice between different opinions and build bridges among different religious, social and political groups. Interfaith dialogue activities in particular contribute to religious diversity management, which is critical for building trust in religiously diverse societies.[40]

These dialogue efforts of the Gülen community have increased the awareness in society that although there are differences among them, there are ways to establish dialogue and cooperation, or at least peaceful coexistence. Social and political stability are very important for economic development. The biggest social cleavage in Turkish society is about the role of Islam in social life, and the community works to build trust and encourage dialogue among the society, and show the ways in which these differences can be accommodated in a democratic, tolerant environment.

Social networks

The schools that the community has established around the world function as a transnational system of networking, not only for the community, but also for Turkish businessmen. In particular, in Central Asia and the Balkans, the community has established a strong basis of networking with the schools. Turkish businessmen liaise with them, and the schools have already formed a strong relationship with the local authorities and people. The trust and connections thus established turn into social capital for the Turkish businessmen. Especially in the Central Asian republics where power is centralized, the trust gained by the schools serves as a credit to Turkish business and diversity management in these countries.[41]

These networks not only provide trust and connections, but also a flow of specialized information. Those who are abroad become specialized individuals who know the language, culture and economy of the country or the region in which they live. The dissemination of this information provides a good resource of social capital for domestic information flow to Turkey.

The networks of the Gülen community increase the social capital of Turkish immigrant workers, mainly in Europe, who are often organized through these grassroots organizations.[42] These immigrants work together for better education for the younger generations in Europe, and the organizations allow them to express their cultural identity collectively. The younger generations who are directly exposed to Western culture have the chance to learn and to enjoy an identity outside their family.

Communitarian norms

The third feature of social capital is represented in the norms that promote cooperation in the public interest, which I call 'communitarian norms'. The norms preached in the writings of Gülen and Nursi are more communitarian than individualistic, and altruism and self-sacrifice for the society are among the most prevalent of them. The interest of the individual is defined in terms of the benefit to the Turkish and Muslim community, which can be useful to ameliorate the negative correlation between nationalism and altruism in multinational workplaces.[43] This vision is epitomized in the words of Nursi: 'The faith of my nation is in danger . . . If I see the [Islamic] faith of Turkish people in safety, I am willing to burn in the hell fire, because while I am burning my heart will be as if in heavens'.[44]

However, it is not only the writings, but also the lives of these leaders that promote norms of altruism and self-sacrifice. Some scholars even call Gülen's personal life a 'heroic lifestyle', with its total abstinence from the material comforts of life including marriage. Living his life in order to contribute to others' lives has been his personal motto: 'See your happiness in other people's happiness'.[45]

Some of the schools are established in unstable, unsafe and very poor regions or countries such as Cambodia, Albania, Northern Iraq or Siberia, where weather conditions can be very harsh. The members of this community have internalized the teachings of Gülen on altruism and self-sacrifice, and by their own behavior have shown that they have fully embraced Gülen's communitarian ideals.

Self-respect and self-esteem are some of the other norms promulgated by this movement over a period of 20 years. Turkish society has not been so mobilized for a public cause at the transnational level since the Independence War in 1923. The subordination to Western culture over the last two centuries has created a lack of confidence among the Turks. They have lost faith in their cultural heritage as the source of mobilization and development. However, the Gülen community has provided the social mobilization to make society realize that it is possible to activate Turkish social capital to make a difference to the lives of other people as well as their own.

The internalization of the Gülen community also faces contradictions and problems. First, Gülen mentions the importance of individualism, in his words 'the blossoming of the individual'.[46] However, there is an inherent contradiction between individualism and collective action. On the one hand, individuals who associate themselves with the framework of *Risale-i Nur* and Gülen's discourse should be free of any constraints to develop an original persona; on the other, followers of a movement should identify themselves with the collective identity and internalize the discourse. This problem is manageable if the Gülen collective identity provides enough space for individuality, but also maintains its collectivity. Otherwise fragmentation is inevitable.

Second, there are issues related to gender equality. Although, Gülen's discourse promotes the status of women in society, his followers are deeply embedded in the patriarchal Turko-Islamic background. The fact that there are no women in the higher organizational positions of the Gülen community has been subject to criticism.[47]

Finally, there is concern about the ability of this vast media and educational organization to transfer from civil to political society. Although this would be contrary to Nursi's apolitical framework, the strong inclinations emanating from the organizational capacity and a desire for power will be a great challenge for the movement. I argue that they should stay in the civil society sphere and in return, the state should accommodate the development and representation of this collective identity in the public space. In this way, the movement can reflect the views of the Turkish-Muslim population and find answers for its identity crisis, if the state provides a Western-style secularist democracy.

Thus, there is potential in the movement to construct a hybrid of modernity and Islam, which will be contingent on the change of Turkish state–society interaction from an authoritarian to a more democratic relationship. The scholars who study the emergence of the Gülen community should also be aware of this complex web of social relations and remind themselves that their contributions will also constitute another brick in the social construction of a 'new' identity.

Conclusion

The Gülen movement is an example of how the traditional state-versus-society framework can be challenged and moreover, a mutually empowering relationship can be established. The state–society relationship during the Ottoman and Turkish political development has been studied through center–periphery relations. This view has led to a state-versus-society approach, which established an adversarial relationship between the state and civil society, which resulted in the misrecognition of cultural diversity.

The modernization project adopted in Turkey also confirmed the central role of the state in the apparatus of development and social change, which was based on a top-to-bottom model. This specific model, the so-called 'Westernization project', focused on secularization, which evolved into an anti-Islamic stance. This further increased the tension between the secularist state and the traditional, religious masses.

The religious revivalism after the 1980s indicated that the Westernization project did not accomplish the goal of secularizing the deeply embedded Islamic culture of the masses. As political development in the project through democratization was established, civic engagements in society proliferated. Although there is a long way to go until Turkey attains a stable, constitutional, democratic regime where human rights questions are addressed, there is increasing scope for civil society.

The economic and political liberalization in the 1980s accelerated the formation and expansion of Islamic groups that have used the civil society sphere to attract culturally and economically excluded groups. For example, deregulation of broadcasting has empowered Islamic voices to express themselves on diverse radio stations and television channels, and in magazines and newspapers. Moreover, a growing Anatolian bourgeoisie has formed its own business associations such as MUSIAD (Independent Industrialists' and Businessmen's Association). New alternative spaces, such as MUSIAD and the new TV stations have served to empower Islamic groups. Although, the secular basis of the system is firmly established, the state in the 1990s felt threatened by the rise of religious revivalism in the public sphere. If the state-versus-society is replaced with the state-in-society approach, not only can different civil society groups coexist peacefully, but they can also contribute to development by increasing social capital. For instance, in 2000, the prime minister and leader of the Democratic Left Party, Bülent Ecevit promoted the Gülen community as an NGO and as evidence of civic engagement within and outside of Turkey to promote privatization projects.[48]

In conclusion, if the Gülen community manages to construct a new Turkish-Muslim identity in Turkey in which multi-religious, multi-ethnic groups can coexist peacefully, where religious freedoms are respected and Islam is not abused for political purposes, then Turkey can make a great leap forward toward to being a more democratic, modern and secular country. The role of this community is a moderating force between religious radicalism in the name of Islam and authoritarianism in the name of state security. This can provide a solution for religiously devoted Turks who want to live their lives under a secular, modern and democratic regime.

Notes

1. Alexis de Tocqueville, *Democracy in America*, trans. and ed., Harvey C. Mansfield and Delba Winthrop, Chicago, IL: University of Chicago Press, 2000; Robert D. Putnam, *Making Democracy Work: Civic Traditions in Modern Italy*, Princeton, NJ: Princeton University Press, 1993.
2. K. Au and M.W.L. Cheung, 'Intra-cultural job variation and job autonomy in 42 countries', *Organization Studies*, **25**(8), 2004, 1339–62.
3. Mustafa Özbilgin and Ahu Tatli, *Global Diversity Management*, ch. 2, Basingstoke: Palgrave Macmillan, 2008.
4. Atul Kohli, Joel S. Migdal and Vivienne Sue, *State Power and Social Forces*, Cambridge: Cambridge University Press, 1994. In this book the authors give examples of this state-in-society perspective in their case studies from different parts of the world including the Ottoman Empire, China, Africa and Brazil.
5. See, for example, Şerif Mardin, 'Center–periphery relations: a key to Turkish politics?', *Daedalus*, Winter 1973, 169–90. Also see Metin Heper, 'Center and periphery in the Ottoman Empire with special reference to the 19th century', *International Political Science Review*, **1**, 1980, 81–105.
6. 'Social capital' refers to the features of social organization, such as networks, norms and trust that facilitate coordination and cooperation for mutual benefit. Robert

Putnam gives this definition in 'The prosperous community: social capital and public life', *The American Prospect*, no. 13, Spring 1993, 35–42.

7. Nilüfer Göle, 'Authoritarian secularism and Islamist politics: the case of Turkey', in Augustus Richard Norton (ed.), *Civil Society in the Middle East*, vol. 2, Leiden: E.J. Brill, 1996, pp. 17–43.

8. Putnam, *Making Democracy Work* (see note 1).

9. Robert D. Putnam, '*E Pluribus Unum*: diversity and community in the twenty-first century', 2006 Johan Skytte Prize Lecture, *Scandinavian Political Studies*, **30** (2), 2007, 137–74, p. 137.

10. Percy B. Lehning, 'Towards a multi-cultural civil society: the role of social capital and democratic citizenship', in A. Bernerd, H. Helmich and P.B. Lehning (eds), *Civil Society and International Development*, Paris: OECD, 1998, pp. 27–42, p. 28.

11. W.A. Galston, 'Civil society and the "art of association"', *Journal of Democracy*, **11** (1), 2000, 64–70.

12. M.W. Foley and B. Edwards, 'The paradox of civil society', *Journal of Democracy*, **7** (3), 1996, 38–52.

13. Robert D. Putnam, 'Bowling alone: decline of social capital in American society', *Journal of Democracy*, **6** (1), January 1995, 65–78.

14. Jagdish Bhagwati, 'The new thinking on development', *Journal of Democracy*, **6** (4), 1995, 50–64.

15. Putnam, 'The prosperous community' (see n. 6).

16. Putnam, *Making Democracy Work* (see n. 1), p. 165.

17. Putnam, 'The prosperous community' (see n. 6), p. 2.

18. Putnam, *Making Democracy Work* (see n. 1)

19. Putnam, 'The prosperous community' (see n. 6), p. 65.

20. Augustus Richard Norton, *Civil Society in the Middle East*, vol. 1, Leiden: E.J. Brill, 1996, p. 12.

21. Jillian Schwedler, *Toward Civil Society in the Middle East*, Boulder, CO: Lynne Rienner, 1995.

22. Hakan Yavuz, 'Towards an Islamic liberalism? The Nurcu movement and Fethullah Gülen', *Middle East Journal*, Autumn 1999, 585–603. Resat Kasaba, 'Cohabitation? Islamist and secular groups in modern Turkey', in Robert W. Hefner (ed.), *Democratic Civility: The History and Cross-Cultural Possibility of a Modern Political Ideal*, New Brunswick, NJ: Transaction Books, 1998, pp. 265–82.

23. John Entelis, 'Book review of *Political Islam* by Dale Eickelman and James Piscatori', *MESA Bulletin*, no. 30, 1996, pp. 165–9.

24. Mardin emphasizes the historical specificity of civil society and its roots in the West. Norton argues that empirically that is not true, alluding to the relatively rapid emergence of civil society in Turkey, where democracy did not really begin until 1950.

25. Oka Sürgevil, ch. 17, this volume.

26. Göle, 'Authoritarian secularism and Islamist politics' (see n. 7), p. 17.

27. Hakan Yavuz, 'Search for a new social contract in Turkey: Fethullah Gulen, the Virtue Party, and the Kurds', *SAIS Review*, **19** (1), 1999, 114–43.

28. Göle, 'Authoritarian Secularism and Islamic politics' (see n. 7).

29. For human rights violations in Turkey, see the American Annual Reports on Human Rights, available at: http://www.state.gov/www/global/human_rights/1998_hrp_report/turkey.html (accessed 2 March 1999).

30. For the legal reasoning, see the decision of the Constitutional Court in *Resmi Gazete*, February 22, 1998 and Mustafa Erdogan, *Rejim Sorunu*, Ankara: Vadi, 1998, pp. 84–93.

31. Yavuz, 'Towards an Islamic Liberalism?' (see n. 22).

32. Şerif Mardin, *Religion and Social Change in Turkey: The Case of Bediuzzaman Said Nursi*, Binghamton, NY: State University of New York, 1989.

33. For more on Nursi's ideas on democracy, see Said Nursi, *Risale-i Nur Kulliyatı I–II*, Istanbul: Yeni Asya Yayınları, 1996.

34. Yavuz, 'Search for a new social contract in Turkey' (see n. 27), p. 125.
35. For Gülen's intellectual evaluation, see Erdogan and his interviews in *Ufuk Turu*, Istanbul: 1996.
36. Yavuz, 'Search for a new social contract in Turkey; (see n. 27), p. 125.
37. Ayse Ozkan, 'Hani Okullar Devredilecekti?', *Milliyet Newspaper*, June 2 1999.
38. See Jefi Kamhi, 'Gulen'e Kalbden bir Alkis', (An applause from the heart to Gulen) *Zaman Newspaper*, November 3, 1998.
39. Barbara Misztal, *Trust in Modern Societies*, Cambridge, UK: Polity Press, 1996.
40. Akram Al Ariss, ch. 4, this volume.
41. Beliz Dereli, ch. 8, this volume.
42. There are about 2 million Turkish immigrant workers in Europe, and the majority of them have a conservative background. This facilitates their interaction with Islamic organizations such as the Gülen community. There are 24 *dershanes* (reading circles promulgating Nursi's ideas) in Germany, four in Holland, four in Austria, two in Belgium and one in Sarajevo. In Yavuz, 'Towards an Islamic liberalism?', (see n. 22).
43. Pınar Acar, ch. 3, this volume.
44. Said Nursi, *Risale-i Nur Külliyati*, Volume 2, IStanbul: Nesil Yayınları, 2001, p. 2206.
45. For his books and a review of his ideas, see www.fethullahgulen.org.
46. Nevval Sevindi, *New York Sohbeti*, Istanbul: Sabah Yayınları, 1997.
47. Yavuz, 'Towards an Islamic liberalism?' (see n. 22), p. 602.
48. 'NGO Gülen', in *Hürriyet Newspaper*, January 27, 2000.

21 Asian and other immigrant entrepreneurs in the United States
Robert W. Fairlie

Introduction

The entrepreneurial success of immigrants is well known. For example, business ownership is higher among the foreign-born than the native-born in many developed countries such as the United States, the United Kingdom, Canada and Australia (Borjas, 1986; Schuetze and Antecol, 2006; and Fairlie et al., 2010). Businesses owned by some immigrant groups are also very successful with higher incomes and employment than native-owned businesses. For example, firms owned by Asian immigrants have higher sales, profits and employment, and are less likely to close than are white-owned firms (Fairlie and Robb, 2008). In an attempt to attract immigrant entrepreneurs, many developed countries have created special visas and entry requirements for immigrant entrepreneurs (Schuetze and Antecol, 2006). Although currently only a small program, the United States gives special preferences for admission to immigrants who invest $1 million in businesses that create at least 10 new full-time jobs (US Immigration and Naturalization Service, 2006).

Recently, much attention has been drawn to the contributions of immigrant entrepreneurs to the technology and engineering sectors of the economy. Twenty-five percent of engineering and technology companies started in the past decade were founded by immigrants (Wadhwa et al., 2007). These firms had $52 billion in sales and hired 450,000 workers in 2005 in the United States. Previous research also indicates that immigrant entrepreneurs have made important contributions to high-tech areas such as Silicon Valley (Saxenian, 1999, 2000). Engineers from China and India run roughly one-quarter of all technology businesses started in Silicon Valley. These firms have created substantial wealth and many high-tech jobs in the area. High rates of immigrant entrepreneurship also contribute to overall business creation in Silicon Valley (Fairlie, 2007).

Although many previous studies examine immigrant business ownership, we know very little about business formation rates and business performance among immigrants. Previous research examining the contribution of immigrant entrepreneurs generally focuses on specific sectors of the economy or regions of the country. A broader understanding of immigrant entrepreneurship at the national level and for all sectors is needed. The lack of data availability on immigrant entrepreneurs has been a major hindrance for research in this area. Limited evidence is available on how many new businesses are created by immigrants and the types of businesses created by these immigrants. There is also limited evidence on the countries of origin for these immigrant entrepreneurs, which could be especially important for immigrants coming from Asian countries. Thus, the contribution of immigrant entrepreneurs to the total US economy is not well understood.

In this study, the contribution of immigrants to business ownership, formation and performance is examined using three large, nationally representative datasets – the Census 5% PUMS Sample, the Current Population Survey (CPS), and the Characteristics of Business Owners (CBO). The Census 5% PUMS Sample is the only nationally representative dataset with large enough sample sizes to examine business ownership among detailed immigrant groups, and the CBO is the only business-level dataset with information on a large sample of immigrants. To address the absence of longitudinal data with large immigrant samples to study business formation, I create longitudinal data from matching consecutive months of the CPS.[1] The matched CPS data allow for a detailed analysis of rates of business creation among the foreign-born.

Using Census, CPS and CBO data, several key questions about immigrant entrepreneurship are explored. First, I estimate how much immigrant groups contribute to total business ownership in the United States. Do immigrants have higher business ownership rates than non-immigrants and what percent of all businesses are owned by immigrants? Second, I examine which countries immigrant business owners come from and whether immigrant businesses contribute more to specific sectors of the US economy. The contribution of immigrant entrepreneurs to new business starts in the United States is also examined. Are business formation rates higher among immigrants and do immigrants start a disproportionate share of businesses in certain skill levels, industries and states? Finally, what is the contribution of immigrant businesses to total business income, sales and employment in the United States? What industries and parts of the country do immigrants generate a large share of total business income in the United States? The goal of this study is to provide a comprehensive analysis of immigrant entrepreneurship characterizing the contribution of immigrants to the US economy. Of special interest for this study are the contributions from immigrant entrepreneurs from Asian countries.

Data

The only nationally representative and publicly available datasets with large enough samples to study immigrant business owners in detail are the Census 5% PUMS Sample and the Current Population Survey. These datasets do not include panel data, thus making it impossible to examine patterns of business formation. Following Fairlie (2008), however, consecutive months of the CPS can be matched creating monthly panel data.[2] These data allow for the creation of a measure of entrepreneurship that captures the rate of business formation at the individual-owner level. The combination of 2000 Census microdata and matched CPS data allows for a detailed study of immigrant entrepreneurship. Published estimates from the Characteristics of Business Owners provide further evidence on the contribution of immigrant entrepreneurs.[3]

Census
The Census 2000 data are described first. The primary sample used to examine immigrant business ownership and net business income is the Public Use Microdata (PUMS) 5-Percent Samples of the 2000 US Census of Population. The Census microdata include over 8 million observations for working-age adults. Even after conditioning on business ownership, the sample size is very large, allowing one to explore the causes of differences in net business incomes. The Census is also large enough to examine regional, industry and country of origin differences across immigrant-owned businesses.

Using the Census, business ownership is measured based on the class of worker question referring to the respondent's main job or business activity (that is, activity with the most hours) at the time of the interview. Business owners are those individuals who report (i) 'self-employed in own not incorporated business, professional practice, or farm', or (ii) 'self-employed in own incorporated business, professional practice, or farm'. This definition includes owners of all types of businesses – incorporated, unincorporated, employer and non-employer firms. The samples used in this analysis include all business owners aged 20 and over who work 15 or more hours in their businesses. Only business owners with 15 or more hours worked are included to rule out very small-scale businesses, disguised unemployment or casually selling goods and services. Note that self-employed business ownership is defined for the individual's main job activity, thus removing the potential for counting side businesses owned by wage and salary workers.

Matched Current Population Survey
Although research on entrepreneurship is growing rapidly, there are very few national datasets that provide information on recent trends in business formation. Using matched data from the 1996–2007 current population surveys, I use a relatively new measure of entrepreneurship to

study immigrant entrepreneurship. The new measure of entrepreneurship captures the rate of business creation at the individual owner level. The underlying datasets that are used to create the entrepreneurship measure are the basic monthly files to the CPS. By linking the CPS files over time, longitudinal data can be created, which allows for the examination of business creations. These surveys, conducted monthly by the US Bureau of the Census and the US Bureau of Labor Statistics, are representative of the entire US population and contain observations for more than 130,000 people. Combining the 1996 to 2007 monthly data creates a sample size of more than 8 million adult observations.

Households in the CPS are interviewed each month over a 4-month period. Eight months later they are re-interviewed in each month of a second 4-month period. Thus, individuals who are interviewed in January, February, March and April of one year are interviewed again in January, February, March and April of the following year. The rotation pattern of the CPS thus allows for matching information on individuals monthly for 75 percent of all respondents to each survey. To match these data, I use the household and individual identifiers provided by the CPS and remove false matches by comparing race, sex and age codes from the two months. All non-unique matches are also removed from the dataset. Monthly match rates are generally between 94 and 96 percent, and false positive rates are very low.

Potential measures of the number of existing business owners or businesses are readily available from several nationally representative government datasets. For example, the Economic Census: Survey of Business Owners provides estimates of the total number of businesses every 5 years, and the CPS provides estimates of the total number of self-employed business owners every month.[4] Typical measures of business ownership based on these data, however, do not capture the dynamic nature that is generally implied when defining entrepreneurship. In particular, they do not measure business formation at the time the business is created.[5]

To estimate the entrepreneurship rate, I first identify all individuals who do not own a business as their main job in the first survey month. By matching CPS files, I then identify whether they own a business as their main job with 15 or more usual hours worked in the following survey month. The entrepreneurship rate is thus defined as the percent of the population of non-business owners that start a business each month. To identify whether they are business owners in each month I use information on their main job, defined as the one with the most hours worked. Thus, individuals who start side or casual businesses will not be counted if they are working more hours on a wage and salary job. A disadvantage of commonly used sources of data based on tax records, such as the Survey of

Business Owners and non-employer business statistics, is that a large share of businesses are very small scale and do not represent the primary work activity of the owner.

A measure of business starts that has been commonly used in the previous literature is employer firm births from the Statistics of US Businesses (SUSB) created by the US Census Bureau.[6] Reports presenting results for detailed geographical areas have been published recently, such as Advanced Research Technologies, LLC (2005), report to the US Small Business Administration (SBA) and Burton: Center for American Progress (2005). The exclusion of non-employer firms, however, is likely to lead to a substantial undercount of the rate of entrepreneurship because non-employer firms represent 75 percent of all firms (US SBA, 2001; Headd, 2005) and a significant number of new employer firms start as non-employer firms (Davis et al., 2006). Estimates of business formation from the CPS do not suffer from this problem because they include all new employer and non-employer firms. These data are now available for downloading from http://www.kauffman.org/kauffmanindex/.

Characteristics of business owners
Estimates of business ownership and formation rates, and net business income of owners are available using Census and CPS microdata, but another approach to examining the question is to use business-level data. The business instead of the owner is the focus of the analysis. The main advantage of these data is that they typically provide more information on business performance than individual-level data, but the main disadvantage is that they do not include information on the demographic characteristics of the owner (see Headd and Saade, 2008 and Fairlie and Robb, 2008 for more discussion on the comparison between individual- and business-level data on entrepreneurship). Unfortunately, the only large, nationally representative business-level data in which the immigrant status of the owner is known is the 1992 Characteristics of Business Owners.[7] Because the CBO microdata are confidential and restricted access, I present and discuss published estimates (US Census Bureau, 1997).

Business ownership
Using microdata from the Census and Matched CPS, business ownership rates, business formation rates and business performance among immigrants are examined. What is the contribution of immigrants to the stock of business owners in the United States? What is the immigrant contribution to the number of new business starts? How much total business income do businesses owned by the foreign-born generate? Focusing on business formation separate from business performance is important for

providing a comprehensive view of the state of immigrant business owner-ship. Demographic disparities in business formation and business longev-ity are the underlying causes of differences in business ownership.

An important question is what is the contribution of immigrants to the total entrepreneurial economy? One method of answering this question is to examine the total number of immigrant business owners and compare that to the total number of all business owners in the United States. Table 21.1

Table 21.1   Number of business owners by immigrant group, Census 2000

Group	Business owners		Total workforce		Business ownership rate	Sample size
	Number	US total (%)	Number	US total (%)		
US total	11,521,910	100.00	121,440,670	100.00	9.5%	5,967,675
US-born total	10,085,500	87.53	106,659,270	87.83	9.5%	5,287,360
Immigrant total	1,436,410	12.47	14,781,400	12.17	9.7%	680,315
Mexico	255,300	2.22	3,944,740	3.25	6.5%	189,412
Korea	90,280	0.78	400,110	0.33	22.6%	17,977
India	60,210	0.52	596,010	0.49	10.1%	26,229
China	57,590	0.50	610,540	0.50	9.4%	27,465
Vietnam	51,720	0.45	523,460	0.43	9.9%	23,938
Canada	50,400	0.44	388,480	0.32	13.0%	18,443
Cuba	49,090	0.43	379,650	0.31	12.9%	17,746
Germany	41,430	0.36	315,710	0.26	13.1%	15,155
Philippines	36,860	0.32	785,170	0.65	4.7%	36,901
Italy	34,520	0.30	190,700	0.16	18.1%	8,768
Iran	33,570	0.29	156,310	0.13	21.5%	7,185
El Salvador	31,180	0.27	411,450	0.34	7.6%	19,311
Poland	30,810	0.27	226,730	0.19	13.6%	10,004
England	27,530	0.24	222,730	0.18	12.4%	10,481
Colombia	25,760	0.22	243,560	0.20	10.6%	10,973
Taiwan	23,480	0.20	176,840	0.15	13.3%	8,206
Greece	20,730	0.18	79,750	0.07	26.0%	3,613
Dominican Republic	19,960	0.17	271,450	0.22	7.4%	11,837
Jamaica	18,980	0.16	316,070	0.26	6.0%	13,749
Guatemala	18,710	0.16	231,500	0.19	8.1%	10,730

Notes
1. The sample includes all workers with 15 or more hours worked per usual week.
2. The reported immigrant groups represent the largest 20 groups based on the number of business owners.

reports estimates of the total number of immigrant business owners from the 2000 Census. The estimates indicate that there are nearly 1.5 million immigrant business owners, representing 12.5 percent of all business owners. There are a total of 11.5 million business owners.

The immigrant share of all business owners compares favorably to the immigrant share of the workforce. Immigrants comprise 12.2 percent of the total US workforce, implying a higher business ownership rate than the US-born rate. Indeed, 9.7 percent of immigrants own a business compared to 9.5 percent of the US-born workforce. This finding is consistent with the previous literature that documents higher business ownership rates among immigrants (see Schuetze and Antecol, 2006, for example).

Is the higher rate of business ownership among immigrants due to favorable characteristics, such as education, age, marital status, region and other demographic characteristics? This question is investigated by estimating multivariate regressions that control for detailed demographic characteristics of the workforce. The detailed demographic information available in the Census microdata makes it possible to control for many important determinants of business ownership.

Table 21.2 reports marginal effects estimates from a probit regression for the probability of business ownership using Census data.[8] The probit regressions include immigrant status, and controls for broad racial/ethnic categories, female, age, marital status, children, and region. The probit estimates indicate that African-Americans, Latinos, Asians and Native Americans are less likely to own a business after controlling for other factors. Women are found to be much less likely to own a business than are men. Similar to previous research, I generally find a positive relationship between education and business ownership (see van der Sluis et al., 2004 and Moutray, 2007 for recent reviews of the literature). The relationship between business ownership and age is generally positive. Being married and having children are both associated with business ownership. Overall, these findings from 2000 Census microdata are consistent with findings from the previous literature on the determinants of business ownership (see Parker, 2004 and Fairlie and Robb, 2008 for recent reviews of the literature on the determinants of business ownership).

The key coefficient of interest in this analysis is immigrant status. After controlling for racial, gender, education, family and regional differences, I find that immigrants are more likely to own a business than non-immigrants. The marginal effect estimate is 0.018, implying that immigrants are 1.8 percentage points more likely to own a business than are the US-born. This is substantially larger than the raw difference in business ownership rates reported in Table 21.1 of 0.3 percentage points,

Table 21.2   Probit and linear regressions for business ownership, formation and income, Census (2000) and Matched Current Population Survey (1996–2007)

Explanatory variables	(1)	(2)	(3)
Dependant variable data source	Business Ownership Census	Business Formation CPS	Business Income Census
Immigrant	0.0180	0.0009	0.0201
	(0.0005)	(0.0001)	(0.0069)
Black	−0.0677	−0.0012	−0.1651
	(0.0005)	(0.0001)	(0.0090)
Latino	−0.0464	−0.0004	−0.1380
	(0.0005)	(0.0001)	(0.0086)
Asian	−0.0267	−0.0013	−0.0360
	(0.0007)	(0.0001)	(0.0109)
Native American	−0.0324	−0.0005	−0.3209
	(0.0015)	(0.0002)	(0.0251)
Female	−0.0495	−0.0021	−0.7106
	(0.0002)	(0.0000)	(0.0039)
Age	0.0054	0.0003	0.0925
	(0.0001)	(0.0000)	(0.0009)
Age squared	0.0000	0.0000	−0.0010
	(0.0000)	(0.0000)	(0.0000)
High school graduate	−0.0049	0.0003	0.1620
	(0.0004)	(0.0001)	(0.0064)
Some college	−0.0053	0.0006	0.3052
	(0.0004)	(0.0001)	(0.0064)
College graduate	0.0019	0.0011	0.8501
	(0.0004)	(0.0001)	(0.0063)
Mean of dependent variable	0.0949	0.0028	10.0569
Sample size	5,967,675	7,789,698	596,385

Notes
1. The sample includes all workers with 15 or more hours worked per usual week in Specification 1, all non-business owners in the first survey month in Specification 2, and all business owners with 15 or more hours worked per usual week in Specification 3.
2. Marginal effects and their standard errors are reported.
3. In addition to the reported independent variables, Specifications 1 and 3 include controls for martial status, children and region, and Specification 2 includes controls for marital status, region, urbanicity and year of survey.

suggesting that immigrants would have even higher business ownership rates if they had characteristics that were more similar to the US-born.

Asian immigrants and other source countries

What are the main source countries of immigrant business owners in the United States? In addition to the immigrant total contribution, Table 21.1 also reports estimates of the number of business owners by source country for the top-20 countries. The largest contributing country is Mexico with 255,300 business owners representing 2.22 percent of all business owners. Korean immigrant business owners make up the next largest share of business owners with 0.78 percent or 90,280. Indian, Chinese, and Vietnamese have the next three largest shares of business owners. There are 60,210 Indian immigrant business owners, 57,590 Chinese immigrant business owners, and 51,720 Vietnamese immigrant business owners. Canadian and Cuban immigrants also represent relatively large shares of immigrant business owners. Additional, Asian groups making the top 20 list are immigrants from the Philippines (36,860 business owners) and Taiwan (23,480 business owners).

Of the largest contributing groups, Mexican immigrants have a rate of business ownership substantially below the national average (6.5 percent compared to 9.5 percent). In contrast, 22.6 percent of Korean immigrants own a business. Indian, Vietnamese, and Taiwanese immigrants have higher business ownership rates than the national average, whereas Chinese immigrants have a similar rate and Filipino immigrants have a lower rate.

Overall, immigrants contribute substantially to the number of business owners. These businesses are also quite diverse, with Mexican immigrants being the only group representing more than 10 percent of the total immigrant share of business owners. Business owners in the United States come from countries located around the world, although Asian countries represent four of the top five contributing groups.

Education, industry and state contributions

Immigrant business owners comprise a large share of all business owners, but what about their contribution to different parts of the US economy? For example, immigrant business owners may contribute differently to high-skilled businesses, industries and states. I first examine whether immigrant businesses contribute differently by skill level. Skill levels are proxied for by education levels in the Census data. Table 21.3 reports estimates of the number of immigrant businesses by education level. Immigrant business owners make up the largest share of least-educated business owners. Slightly more than 28 percent of all business owners with

Table 21.3   Number of immigrant business owners by education level, Census 2000

Industry	Immigrant business owners			All business owners	
	Number	Immigrant total (%)	US education total (%)	Number	US total (%)
All education levels	1,436,420	100.0	12.5	11,521,920	100.0
Less than high school	390,690	27.2	28.4	1,376,540	11.9
High school graduate	285,710	19.9	9.6	2,977,700	25.8
Some college	310,100	21.6	9.1	3,399,700	29.5
College graduate	449,920	31.3	11.9	3,767,980	32.7

Note: The sample includes all business owners with 15 or more hours worked per usual week.

less than a high school degree are immigrants. But, this educational group represents only 27.2 percent of all immigrant business owners. The largest educational group among immigrants is college graduates comprising 31.3 percent of all immigrant business owners. This group makes a large contribution to the US business total for college graduates. Immigrant business owners represent 11.9 percent of business owners with a college education. Interestingly, immigrant business owners contribute much less to the middle of the educational distribution.

Similar to the analysis by skill level, it is useful to examine how immigrant businesses contribute to specific industries. Table 21.4 reports the number of immigrant business owners by major industry. Immigrant businesses make notable contributions to the US economy in several industries. First, I find that more than one-fifth of all businesses in the arts, entertainment and recreation industry are owned by immigrants. This is nearly double the immigrant contribution to all industries of 12.5 percent. Immigrant businesses also contribute substantially to other services (17.6 percent), transportation (16.9 percent), wholesale trade (15.9 percent) and retail trade (15.5 percent).

Immigrants are heavily concentrated in California, Texas, New York and Florida (US Immigration and Naturalization Service, 2006). Immigrant business owners may contribute more to the economies of these states than others. Table 21.5 reports estimates of the number of immigrant business owners by state. California has by far the largest number of immigrant business owners with 427,580. These immigrant business owners represent

Table 21.4   Number of immigrant business owners by industry, Census 2000

Industry	Immigrant business owners			All business owners	
	Number	Immigrant total (%)	US industry total (%)	Number	US total (%)
All industries	1,436,410	100.0	12.5	11,521,910	100.0
Agriculture and mining	26,740	1.9	3.7	730,800	6.3
Construction	187,030	13.0	9.6	1,945,910	16.9
Manufacturing	73,070	5.1	13.6	535,550	4.6
Wholesale trade	60,900	4.2	15.9	383,370	3.3
Retail trade	182,850	12.7	15.5	1,176,230	10.2
Transportation	71,470	5.0	16.9	423,320	3.7
Information	16,330	1.1	9.2	177,290	1.5
Finance, insurance and real estate	76,900	5.4	8.6	889,800	7.7
Professional services	219,830	15.3	10.4	2,115,610	18.4
Education, health and social services	157,740	11.0	13.0	1,213,620	10.5
Arts, entertainment and recreation	144,240	10.0	21.1	683,390	5.9
Other services	219,320	15.3	17.6	1,247,020	10.8

Note: The sample includes all business owners with 15 or more hours worked per usual week.

a very large share of all business owners in the state. Nearly 30 percent of all business owners in California are immigrants. New York is not far behind. Roughly one-quarter of all business owners in New York were born outside of the United States. In New Jersey, Florida and Hawaii more than one-fifth of all business owners are foreign-born. All of these states have immigrant contributions to business ownership that are substantially higher than the national average of 12.5 percent.

Business formation
Business ownership captures the stock of entrepreneurs in the economy at a given point in time, but does not capture the dynamic nature of

Table 21.5 Number of immigrant business owners by state, Census 2000

Industry	Immigrant business owners			All business owners	
	Number	Immigrant total (%)	State total (%)	Number	US total (%)
US total	1,436,410	100.0	12.5	11,521,910	100.0
Alabama	4,361	0.3	2.7	159,460	1.4
Alaska	1,946	0.1	7.5	25,990	0.2
Arizona	24,357	1.7	12.1	200,900	1.7
Arkansas	2,327	0.2	1.9	122,150	1.1
California	427,580	29.8	28.7	1,490,590	12.9
Colorado	15,875	1.1	6.6	241,150	2.1
Connecticut	19,741	1.4	13.2	149,810	1.3
Delaware	2,044	0.1	7.2	28,330	0.2
District of Columbia	2,787	0.2	16.2	17,230	0.1
Florida	146,039	10.2	20.6	710,530	6.2
Georgia	25,883	1.8	7.7	334,140	2.9
Hawaii	10,780	0.8	20.7	51,970	0.5
Idaho	2,390	0.2	3.4	70,280	0.6
Illinois	65,178	4.5	14.5	448,600	3.9
Indiana	7,351	0.5	3.3	219,980	1.9
Iowa	2,448	0.2	1.7	147,780	1.3
Kansas	4,305	0.3	3.4	128,360	1.1
Kentucky	3,331	0.2	2.1	154,960	1.3
Louisiana	7,940	0.6	5.0	159,200	1.4
Maine	2,421	0.2	3.3	74,180	0.6
Maryland	29,500	2.1	14.6	201,920	1.8
Massachusetts	33,372	2.3	12.6	265,850	2.3
Michigan	22,714	1.6	6.4	356,250	3.1
Minnesota	6,640	0.5	2.8	241,440	2.1
Mississippi	2,310	0.2	2.3	99,430	0.9
Missouri	7,151	0.5	3.0	236,350	2.1
Montana	950	0.1	1.5	64,600	0.6
Nebraska	1,356	0.1	1.4	97,270	0.8
Nevada	8,265	0.6	13.1	62,920	0.5
New Hampshire	3,442	0.2	5.5	63,010	0.5
New Jersey	68,870	4.8	21.4	321,310	2.8
New Mexico	6,816	0.5	8.6	79,700	0.7
New York	175,834	12.2	24.7	710,560	6.2
North Carolina	15,906	1.1	4.8	334,090	2.9

Table 21.5 (continued)

Industry	Immigrant business owners			All business owners	
	Number	Immigrant total (%)	State total (%)	Number	US total (%)
North Dakota	552	0.0	1.4	38,440	0.3
Ohio	16,341	1.1	4.1	395,450	3.4
Oklahoma	4,972	0.3	3.2	155,890	1.4
Oregon	13,786	1.0	7.4	187,050	1.6
Pennsylvania	26,519	1.8	6.1	435,390	3.8
Rhode Island	3,697	0.3	9.3	39,820	0.3
South Carolina	4,776	0.3	3.3	144,600	1.3
South Dakota	667	0.0	1.4	47,660	0.4
Tennessee	7,523	0.5	3.3	230,830	2.0
Texas	125,184	8.7	15.3	817,270	7.1
Utah	4,546	0.3	5.2	87,710	0.8
Vermont	1,479	0.1	3.6	41,170	0.4
Virginia	29,155	2.0	11.0	265,520	2.3
Washington	26,895	1.9	10.2	263,590	2.3
West Virginia	1,588	0.1	3.1	51,410	0.4
Wisconsin	5,907	0.4	2.7	222,320	1.9
Wyoming	615	0.0	2.2	27,500	0.2

Note: The sample includes all business owners with 15 or more hours worked per usual week.

entrepreneurship. In this section, I examine business formation among immigrants. In particular, I estimate the number of new business starts by immigrants and make comparisons to the total number of business starts. This analysis captures how immigrants contribute to the flow of businesses in the US economy. New businesses are often associated with economic growth, innovation, and the creation of jobs.

For the analysis of business formation, panel data are needed. I use the Matched CPS (1996–2007) microdata because it is the only dataset in which entrepreneurship or business creation can be examined for immigrants because of the need for very large sample sizes and panel data. Table 21.6 reports estimates of the number of new businesses created by immigrants. Immigrants start 81,000 businesses per month. This represents 16.7 percent of all new businesses created, which is higher than the share for all business owners or the workforce. Indeed, immigrants are found to create businesses at a faster rate than are non-immigrants. The

Table 21.6   *Number of new business owners per month by immigrant group, Matched Current Population Survey (1996–2007)*

Group	New business owners		Business formation rate	Sample size
	Number per month	US total (%)		
US total	484,864	100.00	0.28	7,789,698
US-born total	403,763	83.27	0.27	6,882,897
Immigrant total	81,100	16.73	0.35	906,801
Mexico	23,094	4.76	0.34	243,167
El Salvador	3,178	0.66	0.47	26,366
Cuba	3,098	0.64	0.42	25,465
Korea	2,870	0.59	0.57	20,372
India	2,619	0.54	0.29	33,411
Dominican Republic	2,417	0.50	0.47	20,790
Guatemala	1,758	0.36	0.52	13,917
Jamaica	1,691	0.35	0.40	15,204
Vietnam	1,678	0.35	0.24	24,586
Canada	1,652	0.34	0.35	23,377

Notes
1. The sample includes non-business owners who do not own a business in the first survey month.
2. Business formation is defined as those individuals who report starting a business in the second survey month with 15 or more hours worked per week.
3. The reported immigrant groups represent the largest 10 groups based on the number of new businesses.

business formation rate per month among immigrants is 0.35 percent, implying that 350 out of 100,000 immigrant non-business owners start a business each month. This rate of business formation or entrepreneurship is higher than the non-immigrant rate of 0.27 percent or 270 out of 100,000 US-born non-business owners per month. Although higher rates of business ownership have been documented extensively in the previous literature, the finding of substantially higher immigrant business creation rates is a relatively new and important finding. Combined with the previous finding of slightly higher business ownership rates among immigrants relative to non-immigrants, it indicates that immigrants move into and out of business ownership at much higher rates than non-immigrants.[9]

Are these higher rates of business formation among immigrants due to differences in education and other demographic characteristics? Table 21.2 (see above) reports estimates from probit regressions for the probability of starting a business each month. All non-business owners in the first survey month in the matched CPS data are included in the sample. The dependent variable equals 1 if the individual reports owning a business in the second survey month. The estimates indicate that African-Americans, Latinos, Asians and Native-Americans are less likely to start a business after controlling for other factors. Women are also less likely to start a business. Business creation generally increases with age and strongly increases with education. College graduates have a 0.11 percentage point higher rate of business creation per month than those with less than a high school education. This difference represents 39 percent of the mean rate of business creation of 0.28 percent.

The probit estimates indicate that immigrants are much more likely to start businesses after controlling for education and other factors. The coefficient estimates imply that immigrants are 0.09 percent more likely to start a business than the US-born, representing 32 percent of the sample mean. The regression-adjusted difference is slightly higher than the unadjusted difference of 0.07 percent. Clearly, business creation rates are much higher among immigrants and the difference is not due to advantageous demographic characteristics.

Table 21.6 also reports estimates of the number of immigrant business starts by source country.[10] The largest number of new businesses is created by immigrants from Mexico, representing 4.8 percent of all business starts. Business starts are distributed across many other immigrant groups. Among Asian countries, a relatively large number are started by immigrants from Korea, India and Vietnam.

Education, industry and state contributions
Immigrants may contribute differently to business creation in various sectors of the US economy. For example, Wadhwa et al. (2007) find that 25 percent of engineering and technology companies started in the past decade were founded by immigrants. To investigate this question further, Table 21.7 reports estimates of immigrant business formation by education level. The largest contribution of new businesses is among immigrants who have lower than a high school education. These businesses started by immigrants represent 35.8 percent of all businesses created by this skill group. Among college graduates, immigrants start 14.8 percent of all new businesses.

Among major industries, the highest representation of immigrant business starts is in the wholesale and retail trade, and transportation and utilities industries. Table 21.8 reports estimates of the number of new immigrant businesses by industry. Immigrant entrepreneurs represent 23.1 percent of all entrepreneurs in transportation and utilities and represent 22.7 percent of all entrepreneurs in wholesale and retail trade. Immigrants also own more than one-fifth of all business starts in the leisure and hospitality, and other services industries.

*Table 21.7   Number of immigrant businesses created per month by
education level, Matched Current Population Survey
(1996–2007)*

Industry	Immigrant business owners			All business owners	
	Number	Immigrant total (%)	US education total (%)	Number	US total (%)
All education levels	81,100	100.0	16.7	484,864	100.0
Less than high school	28,001	34.5	35.8	78,195	16.1
High school graduate	20,686	25.5	13.8	149,824	30.9
Some college	13,281	16.4	10.4	127,928	26.4
College graduate	19,132	23.6	14.8	128,916	26.6

Notes
1. The sample includes non-business owners who do not own a business in the first survey month.
2. Business formation is defined as those individuals who report starting a business in the second survey month with 15 or more hours worked per week.

Immigrants make very large contributions to business creation in several states (see Table 21.9). The foreign-born start 34.2 percent of all businesses in California, which is consistent with previous findings on the importance of immigrants in California and Silicon Valley (Saxenian, 1999, 2000, and Wadhwa et al., 2007). Roughly 5 percent of all new businesses created in the United States are by immigrants in California. Immigrant business creation is also substantial in other states; nearly 30 percent of all businesses created in New York, Florida and Texas are created by immigrant entrepreneurs. These representations are substantially higher than the national average of 16.7 percent. The top-10 states in terms of the number of businesses started by immigrants are reported in the table. In the remaining states, immigrants represent only 6.3 percent of all business starts, attesting to the geographical concentration of immigrants across the country.

Immigrants contribute substantially to business starts in certain sectors and locations of the US economy. The most notable contributions are geographic. In the four largest states, immigrants start 30.6 percent of all new businesses. They also start roughly one-quarter of all firms in the transportation and utilities, and wholesale and retail trade industries.

Business income, sales and employment
The next question is how much immigrant-owned businesses contribute to total business income. Instead of focusing on the total number of businesses owned or created by immigrants, I focus on how much value they

Table 21.8   Number of immigrant businesses created per month by industry, Matched Current Population Survey (1996–2007)

Industry	Immigrant business owners			All business owners	
	Number	Immigrant total (%)	US industry total (%)	Number	US total (%)
All industries	80,659	100.0	16.7	483,743	100.0
Agriculture and mining	1,484	1.8	3.3	44,624	9.2
Construction	14,987	18.6	17.3	86,781	17.9
Manufacturing	2,367	2.9	15.1	15,664	3.2
Wholesale and retail trade	12,927	16.0	22.7	56,988	11.8
Transportation and utilities	4,254	5.3	23.1	18,439	3.8
Information	1,085	1.3	10.1	10,717	2.2
Financial activities	3,913	4.9	12.9	30,311	6.3
Professional and business services	14,864	18.4	15.7	94,484	19.5
Educational and health services	11,890	14.7	19.1	62,379	12.9
Leisure and hospitality	5,628	7.0	20.6	27,263	5.6
Other services	7,260	9.0	20.1	36,092	7.5

Notes
1. The sample includes non-business owners who do not own a business in the first survey month.
2. Business formation is defined as those individuals who report starting a business in the second survey month with 15 or more hours worked per week.

create for the US economy. This is a difficult question to answer, and measurement issues are important. I take two approaches to addressing this question. First, I start with the individual business owner. The 2000 Census includes information on business income net of all expenses reported by the owner. The extremely large sample size of the Census is necessary to examine this question and to allow for examination of immigrant contributions by source country, education level, industry and state. Second, I use the only large, nationally representative *business-level* dataset that provides information on immigrant status, the 1992 CBO, to examine the sales and employment of immigrant-owned businesses.[11] These data are useful because they provide information on the sales and employment of immigrant-owned businesses.

Table 21.9   Number of immigrant businesses created per month by state,
Matched Current Population Survey (1996–2007)

Industry	Immigrant business owners			All business owners	
	Number	Immigrant total (%)	State total (%)	Number	US total (%)
US total	81,100	100.0	16.7	484,864	100.0
California	23,331	28.8	34.2	68,133	14.1
Texas	11,633	14.3	27.7	42,045	8.7
New York	8,953	11.0	28.7	31,169	6.4
Florida	8,026	9.9	28.4	28,214	5.8
Illinois	3,453	4.3	18.9	18,273	3.8
Georgia	3,023	3.7	19.1	15,786	3.3
Michigan	2,276	2.8	15.8	14,362	3.0
New Jersey	2,156	2.7	18.3	11,783	2.4
Arizona	2,000	2.5	18.9	10,584	2.2
Maryland	1,342	1.7	14.3	9,367	1.9
All other states	14,908	18.4	6.3	235,146	48.5

Notes
1. The sample includes non-business owners who do not own a business in the first survey month.
2. Business formation is defined as those individuals who report starting a business in the second survey month with 15 or more hours worked per week.
3. The reported states represent the largest 10 states based on the number of new businesses.

Table 21.10 reports estimates from the 2000 Census on total business income for immigrant business owners. The total business income for immigrants is $67 billion, representing 11.6 percent of all business income, which is $577 billion. The immigrant representation of total business income is lower than the representation of the total number of business owners, suggesting that immigrant businesses have lower average incomes. Indeed, estimates of average business income reported in Table 21.10 indicate that immigrant business owners have lower levels of income. Immigrant business income is $46,614 on average compared to $50,643 for non-immigrants.

Immigrant businesses are also found to have lower levels of business income measured in logs. The log difference is around 3 percent. To check whether this business income disparity is due to differences in education and other demographic characteristics, I estimate a log business income regression, which is reported in Table 21.2, above. The estimates indicate that African-Americans, Latinos and Native-American business owners

Table 21.10   Total business income by immigrant group, Census 2000

Group	Net business income			Sample size
	Total (000s) ($)	US total (%)	Average per owner ($)	
US total	577,714,338	100.0	50,141	596,550
US-born total	510,757,703	88.4	50,643	529,197
Immigrant total	66,956,635	11.6	46,614	67,353
Mexico	6,890,546	1.2	26,990	12,323
Korea	4,289,510	0.7	47,514	4,136
India	4,999,076	0.9	83,023	2,794
China	2,612,293	0.5	45,360	2,621
Vietnam	1,786,430	0.3	34,540	2,349
Canada	3,272,177	0.6	64,924	2,516
Cuba	2,421,547	0.4	49,334	2,305
Germany	2,322,318	0.4	56,054	2,061
Philippines	2,179,736	0.4	59,142	1,749
Italy	1,760,395	0.3	51,004	1,637
Iran	2,559,450	0.4	76,251	1,583
El Salvador	823,997	0.1	26,431	1,504
Poland	1,341,773	0.2	43,549	1,380
England	1,580,912	0.3	57,427	1,365
Colombia	883,144	0.2	34,284	1,191
Taiwan	1,367,917	0.2	58,266	1,117
Greece	1,253,056	0.2	60,441	948
Dominican Republic	536,080	0.1	26,880	879
Jamaica	672,985	0.1	35,448	842
Guatemala	422,663	0.1	25,588	858

Notes
1. The sample includes all business owners with 15 or more hours worked per usual week.
2. The reported immigrant groups represent the largest 20 groups based on the number of business owners.

each have substantially lower levels of business income than white business owners, and Asian-American business owners have slightly lower business income.[12] Similar to previous results, female business owners are found to have substantially lower business income than male owners (Gatewood et al., 2003; Lowrey, 2006; Fairlie and Robb, 2008). Business income generally increases with the age of the owner, and is strongly related to the owner's education level. The general and specific knowledge and skills acquired through formal education may be useful for running a successful business. The owner's level of education may also serve as a proxy for his/her overall ability or as a positive signal to potential customers, lenders or other businesses.

The immigrant coefficient is positive and statistically significant, but very small. The coefficient estimate implies that after controlling for education and other demographic characteristics, immigrants are predicted to have business incomes that are roughly 2 percent higher than the US-born. The difference is negligible and suggests that immigrant businesses have similar business incomes when measured in logs.

Asian immigrants and other source countries
Immigrants from Mexico provide the largest contribution to total US business income at 1.2 percent, representing nearly $7 billion. The next two contributing groups are Indian ($5.0 billion) and Korean ($4.3 billion) businesses. Those that are owned by Chinese ($2.6 billion), Filipino ($2.2 billion), Vietnamese ($1.8 billion) and Taiwanese ($1.4 billion) immigrants also contribute substantially to total US business income. Overall, however, the estimates reported in Table 21.10 indicate that immigrant contributions to total business income are spread across a very large number of immigrant groups, with no major groups dominating.

One large difference across groups, however, is average business income per owner. Indian immigrant business owners earn $83,023 per year on average. This is substantially higher than for Mexican immigrants at $26,990. Filipino and Taiwanese immigrant owners also have very high business incomes at $59,142 and $58,266, respectively, relative to the national average of $50,141.

Education, industry and states
Unsurprisingly, the majority of total business income for both immigrants and the broader economy is produced by the most-educated business owners. Table 21.11 reports estimates of immigrant business income by education level. Among immigrants, the total business income of college graduate business owners represents 52.1 percent of all immigrant business income. Similarly, for all business owners, college graduates produce 51.9 percent of all business income. College-graduate immigrant business owners have $35 billion in business income. This sum represents 11.6 percent of all business income produced by college-educated business owners. Immigrant businesses also generate a large share of total US business income among the least educated.

Immigrant businesses provide large income contributions to a few industries (see Table 21.12). Immigrant businesses in the arts, entertainment and recreation industry produce 21.1 percent of all business income in this industry. The next two largest industry contributions are in the

Table 21.11 *Total net business income of immigrant business owners by education level, Census 2000*

Industry	Immigrant business owners			All business owners	
	Total business income (000s) ($)	Immigrant total	US education total (%)	Total business income ($)	US total (%)
All education levels	66,956,635	100.0	11.6	577,714,338	100.0
Less than high school	10,283,783	15.4	25.8	39,936,703	6.9
High school graduate	9,642,336	14.4	9.5	101,236,676	17.5
Some college	12,148,724	18.1	8.9	136,799,688	23.7
College graduate	34,881,793	52.1	11.6	299,741,272	51.9

Note: The sample includes all business owners with 15 or more hours worked per usual week.

education, health and social services industry (16.6 percent) and the other services industry (16.1 percent).

Similar to the contributions in the number of business owners and business starts, immigrants provide substantial contributions to total business income in the largest states. Table 21.13 reports estimates of business income by immigrant businesses, which produce nearly $20 billion per year in California alone. This total represents nearly one-quarter of all business income produced in the state and 3.3 percent of all business income in the United States. In New York, Florida and New Jersey total immigrant business income represents nearly one-fifth of all business income in these states. The contributions of immigrant businesses to the economy are clearly unevenly spread across the country.

Sales and employment

The 1992 CBO contains information on the immigrant status of businesses. Two business outcomes are examined using these data – sales and employment. Published estimates from the CBO on the sales of immigrant businesses are reported in Table 21.14 (US Census Bureau, 1997). Several sales categories are reported because only categorical information is available in the published report. Immigrant-owned businesses represent 9.4 percent of all businesses. This estimate is lower than the 12.5 percent reported for

Table 21.12   *Total net business income of immigrant business owners by industry, Census 2000*

Industry	Immigrant business owners			All business owners	
	Total business income (000s) ($)	Immigrant total (%)	US industry total (%)	Total business income ($)	US Total (%)
All industries	66,956,635	100.0	11.6	577,714,339	100.0
Agriculture and mining	863,382	1.3	3.6	23,733,994	4.1
Construction	7,270,433	10.9	8.9	81,803,394	14.2
Manufacturing	3,826,155	5.7	13.1	29,227,633	5.1
Wholesale trade	3,496,142	5.2	14.6	24,020,513	4.2
Retail trade	7,061,513	10.5	14.6	48,498,327	8.4
Transportation	2,646,458	4.0	14.0	18,956,561	3.3
Information	846,904	1.3	9.6	8,864,787	1.5
Finance, insurance and real estate	5,138,095	7.7	8.1	63,586,517	11.0
Professional services	11,018,063	16.5	8.1	135,541,200	23.5
Education, health and social services	14,327,217	21.4	16.6	86,492,345	15.0
Arts, entertainment	5,448,776	8.1	21.1	25,825,562	4.5
Other services	5,013,499	7.5	16.1	31,163,505	5.4

Note: The sample includes all business owners with 15 or more hours worked per usual week.

business owners, partly because the data are from 1992 before the large number of immigrants arrived in the 1990s. The CBO also contains a large number of small-scale businesses and consulting activities, whereas the Census and CPS data reported above only contain workers whose primary job activity is business ownership.[13] The estimate of the total number of businesses from the CBO is 17.3 million, which is considerably larger than the estimate of the number of business owners from the Census of 11.5 million. Direct evidence of the inclusion of small-scale business and consulting activities is provided by the large share (30.3 percent) of firms with less than $5,000 in revenues.[14] Immigrant businesses comprise only 6.8 percent of all businesses in the less than $5,000 in sales category. If this category is removed, immigrants represent 10.1 percent of all businesses.

Immigrants own a large share of high sales firms. For all firms with

Table 21.13   *Total net business income of immigrant business owners by state, Census 2000*

Industry	Immigrant business owners			All business owners	
	Total business income (000s) ($)	Immigrant total (%)	State total (%)	Total business income ($)	US total (%)
US total	66,956,635	100.0	11.6	577,714,338	100.0
Alabama	256,104	0.4	3.6	7,166,173	1.2
Alaska	69,040	0.1	5.7	1,212,297	0.2
Arizona	964,106	1.4	10.0	9,644,560	1.7
Arkansas	84,821	0.1	1.7	4,871,000	0.8
California	19,238,566	28.7	22.7	84,779,273	14.7
Colorado	732,304	1.1	6.1	12,001,064	2.1
Connecticut	1,109,478	1.7	10.9	10,138,100	1.8
Delaware	94,554	0.1	6.6	1,429,332	0.2
District of Columbia	174,008	0.3	12.4	1,400,518	0.2
Florida	6,649,952	9.9	18.7	35,561,024	6.2
Georgia	1,275,188	1.9	7.5	16,971,110	2.9
Hawaii	416,814	0.6	17.4	2,392,770	0.4
Idaho	89,535	0.1	3.2	2,774,498	0.5
Illinois	3,391,939	5.1	13.3	25,554,039	4.4
Indiana	463,032	0.7	4.5	10,317,542	1.8
Iowa	151,152	0.2	2.7	5,541,212	1.0
Kansas	168,809	0.3	3.1	5,476,371	0.9
Kentucky	175,571	0.3	2.7	6,385,840	1.1
Louisiana	342,347	0.5	4.6	7,430,561	1.3
Maine	106,948	0.2	3.8	2,847,483	0.5
Maryland	1,474,148	2.2	13.0	11,304,225	2.0
Massachusetts	1,571,727	2.3	10.6	14,892,847	2.6
Michigan	1,475,603	2.2	8.4	17,650,532	3.1
Minnesota	330,847	0.5	3.0	10,944,980	1.9
Mississippi	134,162	0.2	2.9	4,562,312	0.8
Missouri	395,880	0.6	4.0	9,897,877	1.7
Montana	50,158	0.1	2.5	2,046,671	0.4
Nebraska	52,780	0.1	1.5	3,520,465	0.6
Nevada	340,279	0.5	9.3	3,650,124	0.6
New Hampshire	170,711	0.3	5.8	2,928,503	0.5
New Jersey	3,793,618	5.7	18.0	21,125,412	3.7
New Mexico	218,281	0.3	7.1	3,077,300	0.5

Table 21.13   (continued)

Industry	Immigrant business owners			All business owners	
	Total business income (000s) ($)	Immigrant total (%)	State total (%)	Total business income ($)	US total (%)
New York	7,872,297	11.8	19.2	40,998,879	7.1
North Carolina	707,484	1.1	4.7	15,201,153	2.6
North Dakota	23,721	0.0	1.7	1,376,842	0.2
Ohio	1,050,359	1.6	5.5	18,989,629	3.3
Oklahoma	213,901	0.3	3.6	5,887,341	1.0
Oregon	549,137	0.8	6.9	7,930,674	1.4
Pennsylvania	1,391,227	2.1	6.6	21,092,206	3.7
Rhode Island	186,956	0.3	9.5	1,963,461	0.3
South Carolina	267,477	0.4	4.0	6,739,441	1.2
South Dakota	45,763	0.1	2.5	1,850,081	0.3
Tennessee	411,043	0.6	3.8	10,732,160	1.9
Texas	4,952,249	7.4	12.2	40,678,349	7.0
Utah	174,255	0.3	4.1	4,223,437	0.7
Vermont	84,016	0.1	5.4	1,554,292	0.3
Virginia	1,380,549	2.1	10.2	13,524,141	2.3
Washington	1,253,575	1.9	9.8	12,812,259	2.2
West Virginia	167,461	0.3	7.9	2,118,930	0.4
Wisconsin	246,080	0.4	2.6	9,505,478	1.6
Wyoming	16,625	0.0	1.6	1,039,570	0.2

Note: The sample includes all business owner with 15 or more hours worked per usual week.

$100,000 or more in sales, immigrants own 11.2 percent. They also own 9.2 percent of all firms with $1 million or more in sales.

The CBO also provides estimates of employment for several employment levels. Table 21.15 reports estimates of the number of immigrant-owned businesses for several employment categories. Immigrant firms comprise 8.9 percent of all firms with no paid employees. In comparison, immigrants own 10.8 percent of all firms with employees. Ownership shares of the largest employment classes are lower among immigrants, however. Immigrants own 6.8 percent of all firms with 50–99 employees, and 5.5 percent of all firms with 100 or more employees.

Table 21.14 *Number of immigrant-owned businesses by revenue size,*
Characteristics of Business Owners (1992)

Sales level	Immigrant-owned firms			All firms	
	Number	Immigrant total (%)	US sales total (%)	Number	US total (%)
All businesses	1,617,482	100.0	9.4	17,253,143	100.0
Less than $5,000	355,586	22.0	6.8	5,226,553	30.3
$5,000–$9,999	221,440	13.7	9.1	2,443,946	14.2
$10,000–$24,999	285,574	17.7	9.3	3,076,410	17.8
$25,000–$49,999	202,430	12.5	10.4	1,945,806	11.3
$50,000–$99,999	192,743	11.9	11.9	1,615,940	9.4
$100,000–$199,999	134,114	8.3	11.2	1,197,996	6.9
$200,000–$249,999	26,581	1.6	8.8	301,794	1.7
$250,000–$499,999	86,260	5.3	12.6	682,583	4.0
$500,000–$999,999	35,611	2.2	9.6	372,078	2.2
$1,000,000 or more	35,851	2.2	9.2	390,037	2.3

Note: The sample includes businesses that are classified by the IRS as individual proprietorships or self-employed persons, partnerships, and subchapter S corporations and that have sales of $500 or more.

Source: Published estimates from the 1992 CBO (US Census Bureau, 1997).

Conclusions

Immigrant businesses provide an important contribution to the US economy. Immigrant entrepreneurs start 16.7 percent of all new businesses in the United States and represent 12.5 percent of all business owners. The large contribution of immigrants to the number of business owners and starts is partly fueled by relatively high rates of business ownership and formation among immigrants. For example, immigrants are 30 percent more likely to start businesses each month than are non-immigrants. Immigrant business owners also contribute substantially to total US business income,

Table 21.15   Number of immigrant-owned businesses by employment size, Characteristics of Business Owners (1992)

Revenues	Immigrant-owned firms			All firms	
	Number	Immigrant total (%)	US employment total (%)	Number	US total (%)
All businesses	1,617,482	100.0	9.4	17,253,143	100.0
No paid employees	1,258,657	77.8	8.9	14,118,184	81.8
Less than 5 employees	243,335	15.0	11.3	2,151,914	12.5
5 to 9 employees	53,325	3.3	10.6	503,808	2.9
10 to 19 employees	25,388	1.6	9.9	256,110	1.5
20 to 49 employees	13,042	0.8	9.0	144,734	0.8
50 to 99 employees	3,100	0.2	6.8	45,331	0.3
100 or more employees	1,805	0.1	5.5	33,062	0.2

Note: The sample includes businesses that are classified by the IRS as individual proprietorships or self-employed persons, partnerships, and subchapter S corporations and that have sales of $500 or more.

Source: Published estimates from the 1992 CBO (US Census Bureau, 1997).

sales and employment. Of total business income, 11.6 percent is generated by immigrants. Immigrant-owned businesses comprise 11.2 percent of all US businesses, with $100,000 or more in annual sales and 10.8 percent of all firms with employees.

Immigrants from Mexico contribute the most to total US business ownership, formation and income, but several Asian immigrant groups also provide large contributions. For example, Korean business owners comprise 0.78 percent of all business owners, 0.59 percent of all new business starts, and 0.7 percent of total business income, even though they represent only 0.33 percent of the total workforce. Indian, Chinese and Vietnamese also provide large contributions to total business ownership, creation and income. Although contributions are fairly well spread across immigrants from all around the world, Asian immigrants represent some of the largest contributions for individual groups.

Immigrants are found to contribute even more to specific sectors of the US economy. Immigrant businesses comprise a large share of business ownership, starts and income in the lowest- and highest-skilled businesses, and the arts, entertainment and recreation, other services, wholesale and retail trade, and transportation industries. Most notably, however, immigrant businesses provide very large business contributions to several states in the country. Immigrants own 30 percent of all businesses in California, one-quarter of all businesses in New York and more than one-fifth of all businesses in New Jersey, Florida and Hawaii. Slightly more than a third of all new businesses in California and nearly 30 percent of all new businesses in New York, Florida and Texas are started by immigrant entrepreneurs. Finally, immigrant business owners generate nearly one-quarter of all business income in California, representing 3.3 percent of all business income in the United States. In New York, Florida and New Jersey, total immigrant business income represents nearly one-fifth of all business income in these states.

The findings from this analysis contribute to our understanding of immigrant entrepreneurship and the contribution of immigrant entrepreneurs to the US economy. These findings have implications for the ongoing debates over immigration policy. The evidence presented here indicates that immigrant entrepreneurs, especially from Mexico and several Asian countries, make large and important contributions to business ownership, formation and income in the United States. The economic contributions of immigrant entrepreneurs are also unevenly distributed across the country, with the largest contributions being located in California and other 'gateway' states.

Notes

1. Although the cross-sectional CPS data are commonly used to estimate static rates of business ownership, the matched data allow for the creation of a dynamic measure of entrepreneurship that captures the rate of business formation at the individual-owner level.
2. National estimates for several demographic groups and state-level estimates created from these microdata are reported in the Kauffman Index of Entrepreneurial Activity (Fairlie, 2008).
3. Unfortunately, the CBO microdata are confidential and restricted-access, and thus only published estimates for immigrant-owned businesses are presented here (US Census Bureau, 1997).
4. Regularly published estimates from the CPS by the US Bureau of Labor Statistics, such as those reported in *Employment and Earnings*, however, exclude incorporated business owners, which represent roughly one-third of all business owners.
5. The Total Entrepreneurial Activity (TEA) index used in the Global Entrepreneurship Monitor captures individuals who are involved in either the startup phase or managing a business that is less than 42 months old (Reynolds et al., 2003).
6. Estimates from the SUSB are reported by the Small Business Administration, Office of Advocacy (see www.sba.gov/advo/research/data.html).

7. The 2002 Survey of Business Owners does not include information on immigrant status of the owner. See Fairlie and Robb (2008) for more discussion on the availability of owner information in business-level datasets.
8. Marginal effects are estimated using the coefficient estimates and the full sample distribution. They provide an estimate of the effect of a 1 unit change in the explanatory variable on the probability of business ownership.
9. Conditional on two groups having similar business ownership rates, the only way that one group can have a higher business entry rate is if it also has a lower business exit rate (see Fairlie, 2006, for more discussion).
10. Estimates of immigrant business starts are reported only for the 10 largest immigrant groups because sample sizes are not large enough. Although the number of non-business owners is large for each source country, the number of business starts per month recorded in the data is relatively small (0.28 percent).
11. Unfortunately, as noted above the more recent version, the 2002 SBO, does not contain information on the immigrant status of owners.
12. See Lowrey (2007) and Fairlie and Robb (2008) for recent evidence on racial patterns in business performance.
13. CBO estimates of the number of businesses also differ from Census and CPS estimates of the number of business owners because of multiple owners of businesses, individuals who own multiple businesses, workers in occupations such as sales and real estate agents, the reference period for capturing business ownership, the exclusion of C-corporations, and other measurement issues (see Headd, 2005, Bjelland et al., 2006, Fairlie and Robb, 2008 and Headd and Saade, 2008 for more discussion).
14. The CBO sample consists of individuals who file an IRS form 1040 Schedule C (individual proprietorship or self-employed person), 1065 (partnership), or 1120S (subchapter S corporation), and have at least $500 or more in revenues.

References

Advanced Research Technologies, LLC (2005), 'The Innovation–Entrepreneurship NEXUS: A National Assessment of Entrepreneurship and Regional Economic Growth and Development', Office of Advocacy Report, US Small Business Administration, Washington, DC.

Bjelland, Melissa, John Haltiwanger, Kristin Sandusky and James Spletzer (2006), 'Reconciling household and administrative measures of self-employment and entrepreneurship', US Census Bureau Working Paper, Washington, DC.

Borjas, George (1986), 'The self-employment experience of immigrants', *Journal of Human Resources*, **21**, Fall: 487–506.

Burton, John A. (2005), 'Putting the Spotlight on Small Business', Center for American Progress Report, Washington, DC.

Davis, Steven J., John Haltiwanger, Ron Jarmin, C.J. Krizan, Javier Miranda, Al Nucci and Kristen Sandusky (2006), 'Measuring the dynamics of young and small businesses: integrating the employer and nonemployer universes', CES Working Paper 06-04, Center for European Studies, Harvard University, Cambridge, MA: February.

Fairlie, Robert W. (2006), 'Entrepreneurship among disadvantaged groups: women, minorities and the less educated', in Simon Parker (ed.), *The Life Cycle of Entrepreneurial Ventures: International Handbook Series on Entrepreneurship*, Vol. 3, New York: Springer, pp. 437–78.

Fairlie, Robert W. (2007), 'Entrepreneurship in Silicon Valley during the Boom and Bust', Final Report to the US Small Business Administration, Office of Advocacy, Washington, DC.

Fairlie, Robert W. (2008), *The Kauffman Index of Entrepreneurial Activity: 1996–2007*, Kansas City, KS: Kauffman Foundation.

Fairlie, R. and A. Robb (2008), *Race and Entrepreneurial Success: Black-, Asian-, and White-Owned Businesses in the United States*, Cambridge, MA: MIT Press.

Fairlie, Robert W., Julie Zissimopoulos and Harry A. Krashinsky (2010), 'The international

Asian business success story: a comparison of Chinese, Indian and other Asian businesses in the United States, Canada and United Kingdom', in Josh Lerner and Antoinette Shoar (eds), *International Differences in Entrepreneurship*, New York: National Bureau of Economic Research Press (forthcoming).

Gatewood, E.G., N.M. Carter, C.G. Brush, P.G. Greene and M.M. Hart (2003), *Women Entrepreneurs, Their Ventures, and the Venture Capital Industry: An Annotated Bibliography*, Stockholm: ESBRI.

Headd, Brian (2005), 'Business estimates from the office of advocacy: a discussion of methodology', Office of Advocacy Working Paper, US Small Business Administration, Washington, DC.

Headd, Brian and Radwan Saade (2008), 'Do business definition decisions distort small business results?' Office of Advocacy Working Paper, US Small Business Administration, Washington, DC.

Lowrey, Ying (2006), 'Women in Business, 2006. A Demographic Review of Women's Business Ownership', US Small Business Administration Report, Office of Advocacy, Washington, DC.

Lowrey, Ying (2007), 'Minorities in Business: A Demographic Review of Minority Business Ownership', US Small Business Administration Report, Office of Advocacy, Washington, DC.

Moutray, Chad (2007), 'Educational attainment and other characteristics of the self-employed: an examination using the Panel Study of Income Dynamics data', US Small Business Administration Working Paper, Office of Advocacy, Washington, DC.

Parker, Simon C. (2004), *The Economics of Self-Employment and Entrepreneurship*, Cambridge: Cambridge University Press.

Reynolds, Paul D., William D. Bygrave, and Erkko Autio (2003), *Global Entrepreneurship Monitor: 2003 Executive Report*, Wellesley, MA and London: Babson College, London Business School and the Kauffman Foundation.

Saxenian, Annalee (1999), *Silicon Valley's New Immigrant Entrepreneurs*, San Francisco, CA: Public Policy Institute of California.

Saxenian, Annalee (2000), 'Networks of immigrant entrepreneurs', in Chong-Moon Lee, William F. Miller and Henry S. Rowen (eds), *The Silicon Valley Edge: A Habitat for Innovation and Entrepreneurship*, Stanford, CA: Stanford University Press, pp. 248–75.

Schuetze, Herbert J. and Heather Antecol (2006), 'Immigration, entrepreneurship and the venture start-up process', in Simon Parker (ed.), *The Life Cycle of Entrepreneurial Ventures*, International Handbook Series on Entrepreneurship, Vol. 3, Springer: New York, pp. 107–36.

US Census Bureau (1997), *1992 Economic Census: Characteristics of Business Owners*, Washington, DC: US Government Printing Office.

US Census Bureau (2006), *2002 Economic Census, Survey of Business Owners*, Washington, DC: US Government Printing Office.

US Immigration and Naturalization Service (2006), *Yearbook of Immigration Statistics*, Washington, DC: US Government Printing Office.

US Small Business Administration (SBA), Office of Advocacy (2001), 'Private Firms, Establishments, Employment, Annual Payroll and Receipts by Firm Size, 1998–2001', table available at http://www.sba.gov/advo/stats/us_tot.pdf (accessed 9 January 2008).

van der Sluis, J., M. van Praag and W. Vijverberg (2004), 'Education and entrepreneurship in industrialized countries: a meta-analysis', Tinbergen Institute Working Paper TI 03–046/3, Tinbergen Institute, Amsterdam.

Wadhwa, Vivek, AnnaLee Saxenian, Ben Rissing and Gary Gereffi (2007), 'America's New Immigrant Entrepreneurs', Duke University Report, Durham, NC.

22 Nuzzling nuances? Asian Diaspora in New Zealand

*Edwina Pio**

> Our shared humanity gets savagely challenged when the manifold divisions in the world are unified into one allegedly dominant system of classification – in terms of religion, or community, or culture, or nation, or civilization . . . we are diversely different.
>
> (Amartya Sen, 2006, pp. xiii–xiv)

Introduction

Diasporas can be categorized in multiple ways based on characteristics such as modes of cultural reproduction, sites of engagement, reconstructions of place, as nations unbound, long-distance nationalism, as a governmental category that represents new geographies, or as irreal spaces which are between the real and imagined (Vertovec, 1999; Larner, 2007). Such in-between spaces of multiple affiliations serve as a source of economic opportunities, skill sets and knowledge which can be mobilized by governments and 'can make manifest new conceptions of governance premised on conceptions of global flows, networks and mobility' (Larner, 2007, p. 334). The Asian Diaspora in New Zealand (NZ) has a long and chequered history closely knit with the mental models of a particular epoch and the resultant outflow in legislation, public opinion, economic and social opportunities.

The broad objective of this chapter is to stimulate a critical analysis and reflection on the Asian Diaspora in NZ, through foregrounding ethnicity embedded within the socio-historical context of a particular period and country. By viewing the Asian Diaspora through the prism of postcolonalism, this chapter aims to contribute to the larger debates and scholarship on issues of otherness, governmentality and the significance of positionality in research. Hence this chapter will describe, explore and critically discuss the particular forms through which the Asian Diaspora is constituted, named and operationalized. For example, how is this group perceived and what are the opportunities and challenges they face? What are the formal and informal networks and efforts through which they manage and are managed? What are the categorical distinctions among individuals and why are they meaningful for exclusion/inclusion? Who gives legitimacy to whom? How do the relations between different groups change over the years in exploring inequality and is there a mitigation of discursive 'othering'? This chapter is presented as a rite of passage to some dimensions of understanding pertaining to Asians in NZ, though it does not pretend to be the last word or a complete representation in this complex terrain.

While there are numerous controversies as to which dimensions should assume greater or lesser significance in the management of diversity, there is consistent evidence that women and racial/ethnic minorities tend to have less authority and are in lower positions as compared to white men, and that white men engage in opportunity hoarding and social closure that benefits them at the expense of non-white and female workers (Prasad et al., 2006; DiTomaso et al., 2007). Thus this chapter will not present a review of diversity management; rather it hopes to carefully and mindfully address issues of diversity management, enfolded within a socio-economic and historic milieu, with a primary focus on work experiences of Asians in NZ. Consideration will be given to the micro and macro inequities at multiple levels in the daily experiences of ethnic minorities, while under-scoring power in its various manifestations in the context of diversity in NZ. Hence this chapter will problematize Asian as a category and present the cartography of the 'Asiatic', 'Chinaman', 'Hindoo', 'mongolid', 'race alien', 'yellow peril', 'Hindoo peril', 'coolies from Asia' and 'lower civiliza-tion' (Murphy, 2002; Ip, 2003a; Pio, 2008), in seeking to present diversity management as moving around, between, within and beyond difference. In 1991 in NZ, Asians constituted 3 per cent of the population with 99,759 individuals, in 1996 they numbered 173,502 or 5 per cent, in 2001 6.6 per cent or 238,176 individuals, and in 2006 9.2 per cent of the popula-tion or 354,549 persons (DOL, 2004; Statistics NZ, 2006; MSD, 2007). Projections indicate that the Asian population in 2011 will total 476,000; in 2016, 573,000; and in 2021, 667,000 (Ethnic Affairs, 2007; OEA, 2007).

The United Nations (2007) in their definition of Asia include the following regions: Eastern Asia (China, Hong Kong SAR – special administrative region, Macao SAR, Democratic People's Republic of Korea, Japan, Mongolia, Republic of Korea); South-Central Asia (Afghanistan, Bangladesh, Bhutan, India, Islamic Republic of Iran, Kazakhstan, Kyrgyzstan, Maldives, Nepal, Pakistan, Sri Lanka, Tajikistan, Turkmenistan, Uzbekistan); South-Eastern Asia (Brunei Darussalam, Cambodia, Indonesia, Lao People's Democratic Republic, Malaysia, Myanmar, Philippines, Singapore, Timor-Leste, Thailand, Vietnam); Western Asia (Armenia, Azerbaijan, Bahrain, Cyprus, Georgia, Iraq, Israel, Jordan, Kuwait, Lebanon, Occupied Palestinian Territory, Oman, Qatar, Saudi Arabia, Syrian Arab Republic, Turkey, United Arab

Emirates, Yemen). However in NZ, in contrast to the UN categories, Asian includes people from Eastern Asia, South-Eastern Asia and some parts of South-Central Asia.

This chapter will focus on the Chinese and Indians who form the largest Asian groups in New Zealand and have been recorded as the first Asian settlers in Aotearoa or the 'land of the long white cloud', which is the Maori (indigenous people) name for New Zealand. This chapter is organized into sections as follows: 'Ethnicity in NZ: who is Asian?'; 'Socio-historical context: race aliens?'; 'Working lives: discursive othering?'; 'Governmentality: courting Asia?'; and 'Locating oneself: performing research?'. The conclusion presents areas for future research and reflections on the theme of diversity management.

Ethnicity in NZ: who is Asian?

Ethnicity in NZ is dynamic and can change over time:

> [Ethnicity] is the ethnic group or groups that people identify with or feel they belong to. Ethnicity is a measure of cultural affiliation, as opposed to race, ancestry, nationality or citizenship. Ethnicity is self perceived, and people can belong to more than one ethnic group. (StatsNZ, 2007, p. 28)

Ethnicity responses are recorded in categories based on six level-one groupings: 1 European; 2 Maori; 3 Pacific Peoples; 4 Asian; 5 Middle Eastern/Latin American/African (MELAA); 6 Other Ethnicity. Other Ethnicity is a category where people can write in their responses and some of the responses include Indian Kiwi, Chinese New Zealander, New Zealander, Fourth generation New Zealander, as multiple responses in the 2006 census (StatsNZ, 2007). Moreover,

> [E]thnic statistics have evolved over time, reflecting changes in the demographic fabric of NZ society. Statistical measurement of ethnicity has a subjective basis . . . Changes to the standard over the past 20 years have sought to maintain the integrity of the classification while providing consistent ethnic and relevant ethnicity information. This is particularly in regard to its prime purpose of distinguishing Maori and to record populations who constitute the main ethnic minorities of ongoing public policy interest, such as Pacific Peoples, and Asian. (ibid., 2007, p. 2)

New Zealand, like Australia, Canada and the United States, has had an active immigration programme for more than a century, though in the last decade, the number of Asians has increased dramatically. Asian expatriate communities are the largest in the world, estimated at 30–40 million Chinese and 20 million Indians (Hugo, 2006). The Asian population in NZ based on the 2006 census include the following: Chinese consist of 147,570 people (this includes Chinese nfd – not further defined – Hong Kong Chinese, Cambodian Chinese, Malaysian Chinese, Singaporean Chinese, Vietnamese Chinese, Taiwanese and Chinese nec – not elsewhere classified). The Chinese are the largest ethnic minority among the Asian category, followed by the Indians who consist of 104,583 individuals (this includes Indian nfd, Bengali, Fijian Indian, Gujarati, Indian Tamil, Punjabi, Sikh, Anglo Indian and Indian nec). In the group of Asians there are also Afghani, 2,538; Bangladeshi, 1,491; Burmese, 1,344; Eurasian 1,614; Filipino 16,938; Indonesian, 3,540; Japanese, 11,910; Korean, 30,792; Laotian, 6,057; Nepalese, 654; Pakistani, 2,049; Sri Lankan 8,310 (this includes Sri Lankan nfd, Sinhalese, Sri Lankan Tamil and Sri Lankan nec); Thai, 139,728; and Tibetan 66 (StatsNZ, 2006). Asians make up 9.2 per cent of the NZ population of approximately 4.2 million people (ibid.).

However, the everyday or colloquial usage of Asian in NZ, as different from the Statistics NZ definition, primarily refers to those of Chinese ethnicity or those with 'Chinese' facial features such as the Japanese, Koreans and Vietnamese, and excludes Indians and those from the Indian subcontinent (McKinnon, 1996; Johnston et al., 2003; Rasanathan et al., 2006). Asian as a category can also be viewed as being problematic, since it subsumes diverse individuals from the huge land mass of Asia, where there exist differing histories, political regimes, wealth and poverty lines. Undoubtedly perceptions and attitudes, towards for example Chinese, also get transferred to Taiwanese and Koreans, and those for Indians to Sri Lankans and Pakistanis, as the majority culture in New Zealand may not be able to differentiate among these peoples. Such transference may perpetuate inaccurate stereotypes and behaviours which make diversity management challenging for individuals being managed and for those who construct policies to manage them. In the health domain, for example, there is concern that the diversity of the 'Asian' category with several axes of difference could result in an averaging of health indicators which may not necessarily give Asians the health services they need in NZ (Rasanathan et al., 2006). Yet in the interests of some order in the large number of ethnicities that exist in NZ, the Asian category has been considered as appropriate by the government to differentiate from ethnic categories such as European, Maori and Pacific Peoples.

It is important to note that the Maori, through the Treaty of Waitangi, signed a document with the British crown in 1840, resulting in a large number of immigrants – English, Scottish, Irish and also those from Europe, or traditional source countries – entering NZ in the nineteenth and twentieth centuries (Pio, 2007a). However during the nineteenth century there was a trickle of non-white individuals such as the Chinese, Indians

and Assyrians, as there was restrictive legislation on the entry of such individuals, in a desire to keep NZ the Britain of the south and hence primarily
a white nation (Phillips, 2007). However, with changes in the Immigration
Act in the late twentieth century, there has been a flood of individuals from
non-traditional source countries such as Chinese and Indians entering NZ.
This flood has been seen as an Asian invasion, resulting in what has been
commonly referred to as the 'great white flight' or those of European ethnicity moving to the South Island of NZ as most Asians tend to live in the
North Island with a high concentration in Auckland.

In the census figures up to 1986, the two main Asian communities,
Indians and Chinese, had a majority of NZ-born individuals, many of
whom were second, third and fourth generation, with those of Asian
ethnicity totalling 55,000. But with the 1986 Immigration Policy Review,
the number of Asians increased dramatically (McKinnon, 1996). Hence,
for example, in 1991 there were about 45,000 Chinese and 30,000 Indians,
besides Filipinos, Cambodians, Japanese and so on, and these groups
exhibited tremendous divergence both between, as well as within, the
various ethnic groups, along with a number of common characteristics with
New Zealanders. During the 1986–1996 period the fastest-growing Asian
community in percentage terms was the Korean one, which increased by
2,792 per cent, followed by the Thai (622 per cent), then the Filipinos (449
per cent), Japanese (317 per cent), Indonesians (211 per cent), Chinese
(205 per cent) and Indians (168 per cent). But Asians still formed less than
6 per cent of the NZ population despite this increase (Beal and Sos, 1999).
However, the conspicuous cohort of new Asian immigrants, primarily
the Chinese, have been 'hyper-visible in the NZ consciousness' (Ip and
Murphy, 2005, p. 14), and have been perceived as having economic privilege (Ip, 2003a) and purchasing large properties with ostentatious living
(Beal and Sos, 1999).

While NZ as a country has been proud of being among the most enlightened political and social nations who were the first to grant women the
right to suffrage in 1893, this enlightenment did not seem to extend to
Chinese and Indians over the many decades of the history of Asians in NZ.
In fact what was not similar was sought to be discarded, kept out, or seen
as not belonging in various facets of NZ life, through denial of membership, status, power and representation – in other words, exclusion rather
than inclusion. Arguably, then, it is possible that the patterns of exclusion
exhibited in contemporary times bear testimony to this early orientation
and carry forward exclusion towards individuals whose visible diversity
discriminators single them out as being 'non-white' and broadly Asian.
However only 'non-white' as a dimension of exclusion is perhaps too simplistic, for there were and are shades of in-between-ness in the extremes

of inclusion and exclusion. Indeed, in recent times with China and India emerging as economic powerhouses, there are equally powerful attempts to court these neighbours through trade and enterprise and in welcoming skilled and qualified immigrants as well as migrants with investment capacity.

Socio-historical context: race aliens?

The history of the Chinese in NZ 'is more than a documentation of hostility or its failure, for to be useful it must explain the survival of a community in a context that at times would deny this possibility' (Sedgwick, 1984, p. 44). This comment can be extended to the history of the Indians in NZ, though they were British passport holders by virtue of being part of the British Empire, hence officially it was more difficult to discriminate against them, though they too, like the Chinese were classified as race aliens.

California's gold rush of the 1840s resulted in a large number of Chinese miners from the Guangdong province migrating to the US, '*Gum Saan*' or Gold Mountain. Australia in the 1850s was *Sum Gum Saan* or New Gold Mountain, and NZ was also called by this name (Murphy, 1994). The first recorded Chinese was Appo Hocton (Wong Ah Poo Hocton, b. Canton c 1820 d. Nelson 1920), a steward on the immigrant ship *Thomas Harrison*, who jumped ship in Nelson in 1842, married a non-Chinese woman and is known to have descendants in NZ (Chan, 2007). In 1866, invited by the Dunedin Chamber of Commerce, the first organized group of Chinese arrived in NZ – they were miners from the goldfields of Australia (Murphy, 1994). But by 1881, public opinion resulted in the Chinese Immigrants Act which imposed a poll tax based on legislation in the Australian state of Victoria in 1855, which colonial countries such as Canada and NZ followed. Thus through the 1881 Chinese Immigrants Act, the government imposed a tonnage per person of 1:10 and a tax of 10 pounds, 1888 amendment, tonnage 1:100 and a tax of 10 pounds, 1896 amendment, tonnage per person 1:100 and a tax of 100 pounds. Between 1882 and 1934, the NZ government earned approximately 308,080 pounds from this tax (ibid.). Australia had repealed the poll tax in 1903 and Canada in 1923 (ibid.). In NZ from 1934, payment of the poll tax was waived and it was abolished in 1944. Although provision was made for a refund of the tax under certain circumstances embodied in the 1881 Act in sections 13, 14 and 10, very few (approximately 51 people) availed themselves of this as most could not speak, or read English, lived in remote gold fields and few had heard about the exemption (ibid.).

As the gold to mine decreased, the Chinese moved to the cities and occupations such as market gardeners, storekeepers, furniture and cabinet makers, fruit and vegetable wholesalers and retailers, merchants, operators of tearooms, restaurants and laundries as well as medical practitioners, lawyers and clergy (Chan, 2007). There were few Chinese women among the pioneer Chinese men, and few Indian women among the pioneer Indian men (Chan, 2007; Pio, 2008). There were deterrents to both Chinese and Indian women in the early settler colonies based on Chinese and Indian cultural traditions and the role of the wife in maintaining and caring for the family in the *qiaoxiang* (emigrant locality), or in the *gaav* (village) and the expense of faraway travel and uncertainty of migration (Chan, 2007; Pio, 2008). A number of the early Chinese settlers were Zengcheng from Xinjie and Xiaji villages (Chan, 2007).

The first Indian is believed to be a Bengali man who jumped ship in 1810 and married a Maori woman (Swarbrick, 2007). The earliest Indians were *sepoys* or military men and *lascars* or seamen who came to NZ on ships of the East India Company, as well as sojourners hoping to increase their prosperity in NZ (Pio, 2008). The early Indians, primarily Guajaratis and Punjabis, worked as flax cutters, bottle collectors, brick makers, drain and swamp diggers and hawkers of fruit and vegetables; they also milked cows, were chef aides and oiled railway tracks (ibid.). A number of Indians also came to NZ via Fiji (ibid.). There was much anti-Asian sentiment and the free movement of subjects of the British Empire, such as Indians, was not necessarily approved by various colonies. Thus, for many Asians, group insularity and self-reliance on their community networks represented the most effective strategy for survival (Leckie, 2007; Lee, 2007).

However, there were some mixed unions between the Maori and Chinese which were viewed as 'deeply disturbing' (Lee, 2007, p. 72). For instance, Chinese–*Pakeha* (*Pakeha* generally means European New Zealander) children were considered a 'stain to the *Pakeha* race', and Maori–Chinese unions were seen as 'an affront to the Maori people' (Lee, 2003, p. 100). Hence in 1929, the Akarana Maori Association, an Auckland urban-based Maori organization, noted that there were 54 Maori women living on Asian (including Indian) market gardens, and called for a ban on Maori females in the Asian market gardens (ibid., p. 100). Both the Chinese and the Indians were able to retain their language, religion and culture and establish strong communities in NZ, despite *Pakeha* hegemony resulting in racist attitudes which were legally enforced, along with social restrictions, as Asians were viewed as racially inferior and morally not on a par with Europeans (Ip, 1996; Lee, 2007; Pio, 2008).

In the early twentieth century, many Maori women, obliged to seek seasonal work, turned to the market gardens, particularly as this was a source of income where they could work with *whanau* (family) members, since the Maori during this time experienced widespread poverty as they were excluded from unemployment benefits (Lee, 2007; Pio, 2008). Fears about miscegenation, price-cutting by the Chinese and Indians and the 'immorality' of cohabiting with Maori women resulted in complaints and agitation (Lee, 2007). The White NZ League and National Council for Women were proponents of racial purity, and there was horror at white women consorting with Chinese men (ibid.). The White NZ League wanted the repatriation of all Asiatics, particularly Chinese and Indians, so that they could be replaced in their occupations by around 12,000 unemployed NZ males (Murphy, 1994).

Racism and sexism enabled the 'legal' intrusion of Chinese–*Pakeha* homes, physical separation of relationships, labelling of women as 'immoral' as well as allowing criminal punishment, through for example, the 1901 Opium Act and the 1927 Idle and Disorderly Persons Law (Law, 1994; Lee, 2007). A 1929 Commission of Inquiry by the Maori Member of Parliament Sir Apirana Ngata was set up to ascertain how many female Maori were living with Chinese or Hindus, whether lawfully married or not, and to determine whether it be in the interest of public morality that the employment of Maori women and girls by Chinese and Hindus should be permitted (Lee, 2007). The Commission condemned such unions, as miscegenation would result in an inferior population being produced, and recommended that Maori women must be 21 before accepting employment by Asiatics on the gardens (ibid.).

Awekotuku (1984), a Maori woman, in writing about migrants notes: 'their pains and problems, the stresses they encountered were too swiftly swallowed up by the fantasy of Godzone – the social laboratory of the world disclaiming any pressures, "colour bar", or inequality' (p. 245). And a Maori–Chinese woman, notes that she does not want her Maori–Chinese daughter 'to face the racist gaze' to which she and her father's generation have been exposed, as she wants her daughter to 'revel in being Maori–Chinese and take advantage of the endless possibilities that such a perspective allows her' (Lee, 2003, p. 110). Some 5,049 individuals identify as Maori–Chinese and 1,311 women and 1,302 men identify as Maori–Indian, based on the 2006 NZ census data (Lee, 2007; Didham, 2008).

Yet, while Asians have faced and continue to face various forms of discrimination in NZ, they continue to seek entry into the country in large numbers. This enthusiastic desire to live in NZ is in some ways evidence that despite the discursive othering or more subtle forms of discrimination, Asians find life better in NZ as compared to their own geographic origins. While most immigrants from Asia arrive legally through immigration processes, a few seek entry illegally. Hence for example, in 1999 the number of unauthorized arrivals by air and sea was recorded as follows: Chinese headed the list with 1,517 individuals, and those of Asian ethnicity included the Sino-Vietnamese 1,885, Cambodian 134, Vietnamese 108,

Bangladeshi 65, Sri Lankan 36, Pakistani 12, Indonesian 7, and 1 from Hong Kong (Talcott, 2000). Such unauthorized arrivals are expensive and often politically charged.

For many Asians, their main reason for migration to NZ is to create better opportunities for their children, and hence they are prepared to rationalize their own work–life experiences to hold onto the dream of better prosperity for the next generation. Other reasons for migration include quality of life, particularly a move away from bureaucracy, intense competitiveness, crowding and pollution in many Asian countries. Many migrant women enjoy and experience the gender equity that NZ represents, in contrast to gender experiences in their own source countries. Hence it is possible that in the analysis of rewards for entering a new country and the ensuing sacrifices, gender equity holds a high place in a migrant woman's mind and brings in a measure of equilibrium when weighed against the discrimination experienced in the workplace as an ethnic minority. This analysis and stance of determination by Asian women to make a success in NZ, is evidenced, for example, through data from the 'Global Gender Gap Report' of 2007 (WEF, 2007), which notes that the year women received the right to vote in NZ was 1893 (China in 1949, India in 1950), and NZ is ranked 5th out of 128 countries (China is ranked 73th, India is 114th).

Yet, Asian migration presents a paradox, for the very conditions which have allowed entry for Asians into NZ now create discomfort, as these Asian individuals, many of whom are highly qualified, seek to work in and through the system to gain employment, start businesses and rupture the socio-historical concept of race aliens.

Working lives: discursive othering?
The core of diversity is about difference and inclusion, within a legacy of hierarchical control systems and organizational authority in managing and valuing marginal groups and an acknowledgement of the role played by oppression and discrimination of the historically disadvantaged (Konrad et al., 2006). Diversity discourses are a reflection of micro and macro dynamics which produce management practices and research indicates that while 'diversity discourses contribute to challenging existing intergroup practices, they do not call existing management practices into question' (Zanoni and Janssens, 2003, p. 70). Furthermore, second-generation discrimination or the more subtle and hidden forms of discrimination are embedded in society and hence there is need for integration and learning perspectives along with fostering accountability in organizations (Matton and Hernandez, 2004). And in considering three dimensions of relationships among groups – power, status and numbers or composition – substantial research on inequality and workforce diversity

indicate the need to link discussions on diversity to structural relationships among groups and within society, as well as to long-term inequality with institutional structures which reproduce such systems and continue to constrain competition, so that privilege or disadvantage gets reinforced (DiTomaso et al., 2007).

In the area of business for example, 'the cultural assets that immigrants bring to the country are inadequately recognized or appreciated' and NZ companies 'appear to have been slow to recognize and utilize the cultural backgrounds of immigrant employees [which] still remain a hidden asset' (Watts et al., 2007). With reference to Indian women entrepreneurs, their trajectory into entrepreneurship is viewed as bitter-sweet, as for many of these women the *raison d'être* of entrepreneurship is because they could not find employment, though after a few years in business, they seem to reap many benefits (Pio, 2007b). However, in the case of Indian women from business castes, as well as those from second- and third-generation migrant families, they seem to have the ability to scan the environment, and set up successful businesses which have fewer teething problems than new migrants' businesses (Pio, 2007c, 2007d).

NZ seeks to implement a paradigm for equality in dealing with diversity, through the setting up of numerous agencies for migrants and refugees such as the Office of Ethnic Affairs (OEA), English for Speakers of Other Languages and Migrant Resource Centres. Such moves are important, especially since the experience of many skilled and talented migrants seems to be that NZ's immigration policy has not resulted in the social or economic integration of the recent Chinese arrivals from places like Hong Kong, Taiwan and other Chinese regions (Ip, 2003a; Hensley, 2005). Moreover 'the dismal employment-status profile of the three groups indicates that none has gained a foot hold here, let alone put down roots' (Ip, 2003a, p 138). A stream of research indicates that higher qualifications are not reflected in high-level employment, for employers function as both formal and informal gate-keepers for those who seek 'Kiwi experience' and have a passionate preference for a NZ accent and NZ/Western qualifications, and prefer not to employ individuals whose names they may not be able to pronounce (Henderson, 2003; Trlin et al., 2004; Pio, 2005, 2008).

Asian migrants often have to start their working life as a *tabula rasa* or blank slate, thus reinforcing research which shows that most groups attain power through homosocial reproduction and opportunities to perpetuate themselves (Elliott and Smith, 2004). In fact, such homosocial reproduction is a dangerous route, in the context of a country seeking to attract skilled and qualified migrants from Asia, the continent which presents the largest available pool of migrants internationally. Furthermore, Asian

migrants who get NZ qualifications in order to gain acceptable creden-
tials, do not necessarily achieve either recognition of their capital or the
key to mainstream employment in professions (Trlin et al., 2004), because
they are 'other, different, unknown strangers' (Henderson, 2003, p. 160).
Such discursive othering reiterates the tenacity of colonialism, for despite
the visible apparatus of equality (Prasad, 2006), there is the presence of
'racism: a reality that leaks into the consciousness of every inhabitant of
Aotearoa, as victim, or antagonist, acquiescent or aggressive' (Awekotuku,
1984, p. 244), expressed subversively, subtly and at times unknowingly, as
the default mode of thinking and behaviour in the present times.

Thus for example, individuals from South Korea would 'rather raise
their children in easy-going, environmentally cleaner, less expensive NZ,
with its English speaking educational system' despite the fact that 'many
heads of the households cannot find the high paying jobs they are used to
in South Korea and therefore return to Korea to work leaving their separated families behind' (Choi, 2003, p. 19).

Taiwanese migrants extol NZ's relaxed lifestyle and its natural beauty,
but 'they are yet to be fully integrated into the wider economic and social
life of NZ' (Ip, 2003b, p. 207). Taiwanese discover that there are limited
business opportunities for them and hence find it more prudent to leave
their money in the bank – they also do not obtain positions which match
their professional qualifications and many immigrants eventually move
to Australia (Beal and Sos, 1999). In fact business immigrants do not
emigrate for business reasons but for lifestyle, for they are aware of NZ's
small markets (ibid.).

The volatile movements of the Hong Kong Chinese families are a
dimension of a new global regime in which many people can expect to circulate between several locations where family members live, and work for
variable periods in those locations, with non-permanent migration replac-
ing the permanent settler migration of earlier years (Ho, 2003):

> It is crucial for NZ to recognize that this is an inevitable outcome of the con-
> temporary international migration of the highly skilled. Rather than criticising
> the transnational migrants for showing a lack of commitment and loyalty to
> their new country, policy makers should adjust to this new pattern of move-
> ment and make better use of a more mobile workforce for the wider benefit of
> the nation. (ibid., p. 181)

The instances described above are reinforced in, for example, the fact
that a significant number of Chinese and Indian females are underemployed employed, and a high percentage of self-employment among
these women could represent hindrances existing in the job market,
despite their pre-migration successful employment (Ip, 2002; Pio, 2007a).

This mismatch in occupations means that a number of highly qualified migrants work as restaurant and hotel workers, machine operators in the textile/apparel industry, teaching aides and check-out operators in super-markets. The first two years of migration present many employment challenges which tend to lower the self-esteem of Indian women (Pio, 2005). But if they persist in the employment arena, Indian women tend to reap some of the benefits that should have accrued to them much earlier in their working life trajectories, based on their migrant capital with which they gained entry into NZ (Pio, 2008).

In considering Sri Lankan migrants, the three biggest barriers to employment are seen as: lack of NZ experience, NZ employers' not understanding job applicants from other countries, and difficulties with recognition of qualifications (Basnayake, 1999). However, many Sri Lankans find work in the same profession in which they are qualified, but are employed in less senior positions, and take approximately 3 to 12 months to get their first job (ibid.).

Research on migrant settlement suggests that Asian migrants should take more interest in NZ, particularly those aspects which motivate New Zealanders, and make attempts to adapt, to mix in business, school and the arts, to work through the children, to be involved with their neighbours, to become thoroughly familiar with the English language and to try to understand the business environment (Beal and Sos, 1999).

Despite many advances that are not insignificant, race remains an important impediment to the attainment of authority in the workplace. There is a tendency for authority elites to reproduce themselves and in the process control the distribution of financial and other rewards, with robust research over two decades, recording the same issues, experienced in different degrees, through different mechanisms, despite advancements in various spheres of work and life across time and countries (Smith, 2002; Elliott and Smith, 2004; Goldman et al., 2006; Konrad et al., 2006).

Unfortunately, despite the reality of individuals being 'diversely different', research indicates that demographic diversity does not always result in positive outcomes and hence presents many challenges (Goldman et al., 2006). Although some research indicates that innovation and willingness to adopt new strategies increases when appropriately used, being different from one's superior and others in a work group may increase turnover due possibly to perceptions of discrimination. Individuals' perceptions of discrimination are dependent on how they perceive their treatment *vis-à-vis* others, and social theories are useful to understand how group affiliation may influence perceptions and actions, pertaining to ambiguous and negative events, that may be classified as discrimination (ibid.).

But 'what remains consistent for all discriminated persons is that they are required to cope in some way' (ibid., p. 804). Race does affect the desirability of applicants in organizations, and stigmatized individuals may experience reduced support and lower quality of mentorship that may jeopardize their career movements (Goldman et al., 2006; Prasad, 2006). It is important to bear in mind that there are imitations of 'paper people' and student samples for effectively eliciting information about what can happen in organizations, but this is not necessarily what does happen in organizations (Goldman et al., 2006). The Chinese, for instance, have a general strategy of placating to cope with fluctuating levels of host tolerance – predominantly *Pakeha* tolerance, and this placating involves four display elements: showing commitment, blending in, distancing and role playing used variously in different situations (Yee, 2003). Placating is seen as offering 'a mechanism whereby Chinese can survive and gain a degree of security, while the host society gains a compliant minority, which it can use to uphold the myths of egalitarianism and meritocracy' (ibid., p. 232). Strategies to cope with the unemployment/employment experiences faced by skilled Chinese and Indian migrants' include: taking whatever employment is available; becoming self-employed; studying to improve their English language ability and/or NZ qualifications; and engaging in onward migration (Trlin et al., 2004; Pio, 2008).

Extending the argument of placating, an apology was made in 2002 by the NZ Prime Minister to the Chinese community in NZ due to the hardship caused by the poll tax, and a Poll Tax Heritage Trust for research was established (OEA, 2007). While there are differing views about the apology, some Chinese believe that despite, marginalization of Asians through the poll tax and discrimination (Ip and Murphy, 2005), NZ offered a better life that that from where their ancestors had come, and for this they were grateful (Wong, 2003). Indians in NZ are also happy to live in NZ, and many of them thrive in their businesses, move to senior levels in their organizations and enjoy the quality of life that NZ offers (Pio, 2008). These individuals, over a period of time, have been able to move beyond othering, through their own efforts as well as through institutional support which seems to come into the working lives of migrants, after a few years, thus increasing the chances of mutual benefit for the migrant and the host country (Dunstan et al., 2004; DOL, 2006, 2007; Pio, 2008).

Governmentality: courting Asia?

Governmentality constitutes heterogeneous representations of knowledge and expertise resulting in particular forms for the subjects and objects of governance, with the global constituted through political rationalities and socio-technical practices which imagine and mobilize space in particular ways (Larner, 2007). The law has 'a great influence on the actions individuals, groups and organization can take with regard to employment and discrimination' (Goldman et al., 2006, p. 816). Foucault coined the term 'governmentality', and linked government (*'gouverner'*) and modes of thought (*'mentalité'*), thus underscoring the linkage of technologies of power and politics and foreshadowing the relatedness of forms of power and processes of subjectification (Foucault, 1991). Hence power can be guidance, consensual forms or coercion, reformulated as means of governance, which includes a versatile equilibrium in how individuals conduct themselves and how they are governed (Lemke, 2001). Arguably then, the lines of 'being' get redrawn, dependent on the equilibrium of individuals and the strategic crafting and implementation of government policies. Taking this line of argument a step further, it can be construed that diversity management in public life as well as in organizations, is to a large extent played out and intimately related to the nature of governmentality.

Following through on governmentality within a historical context, peacekeeping has drawn NZ service personnel to regions of South-East Asia on temporary deployments and 'accustomed NZ service men and women to working with the forces of very different states in maintaining regional security' over the last few decades (McGibbon, 2005, p. 30). NZ's relations with South-East Asia have had and continue to have an important trade element, as well as a continuance of a 'healthy aid relationship with a number of Southeast Asian countries' (Smith, 2005a, p. 4). For example, the Colombo Plan, which became a vehicle for cooperative economic development in South and South-East Asia, conceived in 1950 by the British Commonwealth foreign ministers' meeting in Colombo, and where NZ was active until the 1960s, after which education and training projects became a part of bilateral aid programmes (Rolfe, 2005). However, 'Southeast Asian institutions as exemplified by ASEAN (Association of Southeast Asian Nations founded in 1967), are just one part of the emerging wider regional multilateral architecture' (ibid., p. 50). In fact with reference to ASEAN 'from a thin appendage to an aid and defence relationship, it thickened into a substantial economic relationship involving trade, investment and a policy dialogue built on economic cooperation in a specific sense' (Hawke, 2005, p. 86), as well as sharing of intelligence on counter-terrorism (Smith, 2005b).

Closer home in NZ, in May 2001 the Office of Ethnic Affairs (OEA) was launched as a unit within the Department of Internal Affairs with a role to develop a public education profile, and involved involvement in engaging with communities to provide advice, increase the development of networks within communities (OEA provides a telephone service in 38 different languages) and enhance the development of social capital within the sector for the benefit of all New Zealanders (OEA, 2008a, 2008b). Another initiative is for learners from non-English-speaking backgrounds, who are a significant group at risk in not benefiting from educational opportunities available for them. Hence the government has established ESOL, or English for speakers of other languages, through the adult ESOL provision. There is also a spectrum of free services with regular newspaper items offering free services to migrants to mingle, share and gain skills; a request for New Zealanders to volunteer to help families assimilate; interpreters on call at hospitals and police stations; celebration of successful migrants; local libraries giving information, and providing books and pamphlets in ethnic/Asian languages, a Department of Labour (DOL) open system for feedback, inaugural Asian forums, and migrant business services with free business workshops (HRC, 2007).

Another example of governmentality is the Chinese Poll Tax Heritage Trust Deed, set up as a community trust with a government seeding grant of NZ$5 million. The Minister for Ethnic Affairs appointed the first trustees in September 2004. The role of the Trust is to fund projects which encourage understanding of the history of the Chinese in New Zealand and to promote public awareness of ethnic diversity. The trustees are direct descendants from the Poll Tax payers (OEA, 2007). Then there is the NZ Diversity action programme which connects organizations that value cultural diversity and promotes positive race relations in Aotearoa NZ, encourages individuals to identify what their organization can do to strengthen cultural diversity and operates on a partnership principle with partner organizations including local and central government, universities, business and religious organizations (HRC, 2008).

In an evaluation of the settlement services pilots, set up to provide for the settlement needs of new migrants and the resettlement of refugees, through 19 projects, the government allocated NZ$1,238,575 with money sourced from the migrant levy payable by migrants to NZ, and from crown funding for refugee services (DOL, 2002). These projects, which were started in 2001, included a wide range of services provided through organizations such as the Auckland Refugee Council, Shakti Women's Safe House, Refugee and Migrant Centre, Multicultural Learning and Support Services, Regional Chamber of Commerce, Business and Employment Link Service, Highly Qualified Migrants and the Auckland New Ventures Inc. The services reached a large number of people, and served as a mechanism for encouraging collaboration and sharing with 'particular success noted in the employment area where some projects used new technology to link people with employment. Courses were provided to inform on the NZ way of doing business and employment co-ordinators or mentors had a coaching role to support new settlers into employment' (DOL, 2002, p. 9). Hence in today's more helpful environment, as compared to previous decades, it is important that migrants access the free services and generous resources available for them.

Likewise, for employers, the other side of the coin, DOL has a number of excellent resources, with publications such as *People Power – Successful Diversity at Work* consisting of a series of case studies encouraging employers to employ diverse employees (DOL, 2004). This publication states that 'a more ethnically diverse workforce may demand different types of goods and services, and want different things from their work. The ability to work with people from other cultures will increasingly be a valuable skill' (p. 4). It is also important that employers are aware of the fact that Asian people in NZ currently have a lower prevalence of most chronic diseases (other than diabetes) compared to persons of other ethnicities, are less likely to access health services, and make up about 2 per cent of those in prison and 1 per cent of those serving community-based sentences (HRC, 2007).

NZ has ratified a number of international conventions based on elimination of discrimination and assurance of fundamental rights for all citizens such as the International Convention on the Elimination of All Forms of Racial Discrimination, the International Covenant on Civil and Political Rights, and the International Covenant on Economic Social and Cultural Rights. The principal human rights legislation in NZ is the NZ Bill of Rights Act 1990, and the Human Rights Act 1993 which disallows discrimination based for example on colour, race, ethnic or national origins (section 21). Human Rights Commission (HRC) states that racial harassment is behaviour that is racist, hurtful or offensive and is either repeated or serious enough to have a detrimental effect on a person and is unlawful when it occurs in any of the following areas of life as, for example, in employment, industrial and professional associations, qualifying and vocational training bodies and so on (HRC, 2004). Yet, legislation and agencies alone cannot bring about the changes necessary for equality, and it is a strategic imperative that the country focuses more strongly on the benefits ethnic communities bring, so that ethnic people can be seen, heard, accepted and included for community integration and global talent management (Singham, 2006).

But it is also crucial that governmentality spills over into accountability for migrants, not only for those who have problems such as abusive relationships in the home, or reported discrimination, but also for governmentality to undertake some responsibility for the subterranean layers which gird much of the otherness which Asian migrants face at work. Hence, for example, the Immigration Act Review of 2007 has four key drivers: circulation of people, competition for migrant skills, diversity with best settlement outcomes for migrants, and heightened risk and pressure on the border (DOL, 2008). Nevertheless legislation and policy frame-works cannot dictate human relationships and hence there is a call for a generosity of spirit, open-mindedness and patience from ordinary people (Singham, 2006), in the full knowledge that human beings do have a tendency to discriminate, and discrimination in some form or other, whether subtle or blatant, exists in the world of work throughout the world on a daily basis (ILO, 2003). In addition, while NZ seeks to build links with its high-skilled Diaspora, with around one million Kiwis living overseas, and has established KEA (the Kiwi Expats Association), as well as GNOK (the Global Network of Kiwis), it is imperative that governmentality brokers, leverages, connects and integrates the knowledge of skilled Asian migrants to enhance transnational commerce and goodwill.

In the context of increasing ethnic diversity in NZ, and with a projected estimation that 15 per cent of the workforce in NZ will be Asian in 2021, it is of urgent importance that policy makers, service delivery agencies, communities and individuals consider how they can respond and how they are responding to NZ's demographic changes; to consciously and with commitment play a role in respecting and valuing diversity in order to truly tap into the benefits which diversity can yield (OEA, 2008a; Statistics NZ, 2008). There is need for more action, more evaluation and additional publicity about the rewards accruing to the host country, with Asian migrants choosing to settle in NZ. It is time for more than nuzzling nuances! It is time for stronger shades and tones in order to move forward to garner and reap the benefits of carefully and mindfully crafted governmentality.

Locating oneself: performing research?
Locating oneself in one's work is integrally linked to performing research, for this encompasses how one asks questions, what the questions are and the modus operandi of the research in its conduct, interpretation and writing. Hence it is important to acknowledge one's positionality, as author-researcher in this instance, in 'working the hyphens' (Fine, 1994), in the researcher's insider–outsider status. This acknowledged reality is crucial to position the interpretation of data and the nature of questions raised (Jones et al., 2006) in this chapter. Moreover, this understanding of how one positions oneself and therefore one's standpoint, is 'a necessary element of the goodness in the research process. Goodness requires researchers to recognize themselves, their relationships with those involved in the study, and their relationship with the topic itself' (ibid., p. 107).

Thus, for example, the author of this chapter has experienced struggle, challenge, tension and conflict in writing about the Asian Diaspora, within knowledge and information that is largely a product of the West and situated within Western hegemonic spaces. But such a space presents the opportunity to 'negotiate from within existing hegemonic structures so as to disrupt narratives that circulate about South Asian women' (Gajjala, 2002, p. 189). Extending 'South Asian' to read 'Asian', the author of this chapter seeks to be an engaged agent of change through her research and writing, in the full knowledge that truth is partial and thus this writing is but one possible representation of the Asian Diaspora in NZ.

The author, of Indian ethnicity, is a new migrant and as a working woman has experienced in some measure the lived-in and lived-through realities of migrants, in the course of subtle and not-so-subtle discrimination and discursive othering, and has had to develop, like many migrants, coping strategies to survive and thrive in NZ. This shared history enables the presentation of a slice of reality from a standpoint of the author's orchestrated selves, as a scholar of colour, a new migrant, an 'other', an Indian woman, who is at home in NZ based on her urban mega-city English background with roots and branches that reach out from vestiges of the British Raj, in the Empire that was both India and NZ. Conversely, the author is an outsider with reference to the scholarship on Chinese migrants, but is an insider with reference to the work experiences of Indian women in NZ, as she is from the same ethnic community and gender. Yet from a different perspective the author is an insider for research on Asians in comparison to a NZ European/Maori or Pacific Island individual. Such polyphonic influences are at the heart of understanding the patterns and themes through which this chapter 'Nuzzling nuances' is offered.

Conclusion

'We all sit under the same stars' was the byline for Race Relations Day in 2008, encouraging individuals to keep up to date with human rights and race relations, to do something for positive race relations and to take a stand against discrimination (HRC, 2008). Thus future research could explore the changes in laws and immigration acts, their effect on organizations in terms of corporate governance and employment practices, the differences that free services have on migrants, and the career movement of skilled, qualified and experienced migrants into senior levels in organizations. NZ is a small island nation that has in the past served as a beacon for diversity rights through women's suffrage. In typical Kiwi fashion, NZ can once again present to the international stage and powerful players, the script of successful, inclusive and rewarding diversity management for Asian migrants, as well as for all peoples whom this little country accepts on its shores.

For despite the fragments, fissures and fine points of reality and rhetoric, there is always hope:

[The] hope of harmony in the contemporary world lies to a great extent in a clearer understanding of the pluralities of human identity, and in the appreciation that they cut across each other and work against a sharp separation along one single hardened line of impenetrable division . . . we have to see clearly that we have many distinct affiliations and we can interact with each other in a great many different ways . . . there is room for us to decide our priorities. (Sen, 2006, pp. xiii–xiv)

Note

*   With gratitude to: my son Isaac for his mindful and wise support, to Cherry Gordon and Claire O'Leary for proficiency and courtesy with information, to Alison Norman my cheerful and candid Maori friend, to James Woods for his unstinting help and perfect timing, to Cheryl Wright for opening doors, and finally to the editors of this book for their patience and belief in my work.

References

Awekotuku, N. (1984), 'Conclusion', in P. Spoonley, C. Macpherson, D. Pearson and C. Sedgwick (eds), *Tauiwi: Racism and Ethnicity in New Zealand*, Palmerston North: Dunmore, pp. 244–48.

Basnayake, A. (1999), *Employment Experiences of Sri Lankan Migrants in New Zealand*, Auckland: Equal Opportunities Trust.

Beal, T. and Sos, F. (1999), *Global Citizens: Taiwanese Immigration in Australasia and the Search for a New Life*, Wellington: Robert Steele.

Chan, H.D.M. (2007), 'Qiaoxiang and the diversity of Chinese settlement in Australia and New Zealand', in T. Chee-Beng (ed.), *Chinese Transnational Networks*, London: Routledge, pp. 153–71.

Choi, I. (2003), 'Korean Diaspora in the making: its current status and impact on the Korean economy', in C. F. Bergsten and I. Choi (eds), *The Korean Diaspora in the World Economy*, Special report 15, January, Institute for International Economics, Washington, DC: Peterson Institute for International Economics, pp. 9–27.

Department of Labour (DOL) (2002), *The Evaluation of the Settlement Services Pilots*, Wellington: DOL, February.

Department of Labour (DOL) (2004), *People Power: Successful Diversity at Work*, Wellington: DOL, August.

Department of Labour (DOL) (2006), *Skilled Migrants in New Zealand: Employers' Perspectives*, Wellington: DOL.

Department of Labour (DOL) (2007), *Fiscal Impacts of Immigration 2005/06*, Wellington: DOL.

Department of Labour (DOL) (2008), 'Immigration Act Review', available at: http://www.dol.govt.nz/actreview/update/final-issues.asp (accessed 14 February 2008).

Didham, R. (2008), 'Maori-Indians', Personal communication, 13 December, based on information culled from Statistics NZ 2006 census.

DiTomaso, N., Post, C. and Parks-Yancy, R. (2007), 'Workforce diversity and inequality: power, status, and numbers', *Annual Review of Sociology*, 33, 473–501.

Dunstan, S., Boyd, S. and Crichton, S. (2004), *Migrants' Experiences of New Zealand*, Wellington: NZ Immigration Service.

Elliott, J.R. and Smith, R.A. (2004), 'Race, gender and workplace power', *American Sociological Review*, 69 (3), 365–86.

Ethnic Affairs (2007), 'Projected Asian Population of NZ, 2001 (base) 2021', available at: http://www.ethnicaffairs.govt.nz/oeawebsite.nsf/wpg_url/Resources-Profiles-and-Statistics-National-Ethnic-Population-Projections/$file/table3.pdf (accessed 23 February 2008).

Fine, M. (1994), 'Working the hyphens: reinventing self and other in qualitative research', in

N. Denzin and Y. Lincoln (eds), *Handbook of Qualitative Research,* Thousand Oaks, CA: Sage, pp. 70–82.

Foucault, M. (1991), 'Governmentality', in G. Burchell, C. Gordon and P. Miller (eds), *The Foucault Effect: Studies in Governmentality,* Hemel Hempstead: Harvester Wheatsheaf, pp. 87–104.

Gajjala, R. (2002), 'An interrupted postcolonial/feminist cyberethnography: complicity and resistance in the "Cyberfield"', *Feminist Media Studies,* **2** (20), 177–93.

Goldman, B.M., Gutek, B.A., Stein, J.H. and Lewis, K. (2006), 'Employment discrimination in organizations: antecedents and consequences', *Journal of Management,* **32** (6), 786–830.

Hawke, G. (2005), 'The economic relationship', in A. Smith (ed.), *Southeast Asia and New Zealand: A History of Regional and Bilateral Relations,* Wellington: NZ Institute of International Affairs in association with Victoria University Press, pp. 57–92.

Henderson, A. (2003), 'Untapped talents: the employment and settlement experiences of skilled Chinese in NZ', in Ip (ed.) (2003a), pp. 141–64.

Hensley, G. (2005), 'Palm and pine: NZ and Singapore', in A. Smith (ed.), *Southeast Asia and New Zealand: A History of Regional and Bilateral Relations,* Wellington: NZ Institute of International Affairs in association with Victoria University Press, pp. 297–330.

Ho, E. (2003), 'Reluctant exiles or roaming transnationals? The Hong Kong Chinese in NZ', in Ip (ed.) (2003a), pp. 165–84.

Hugo, G. (2006), 'Improving statistics on international migration in Asia', *International Statistical Review,* **74** (3), 335–55.

Human Rights Commission (HRC) (2004), *Fact Sheet 9, Racial Harassment,* Auckland: HRC.

Human Rights Commission (HRC) (2007), *NZ Report to the Committee on the Elimination of Racial Discrimination,* New Zealand: HRC.

Human Rights Commission (HRC) (2008), 'Te Ngira: NZ Diversity Action Program', available at: www.hrc.co.nz/diversity (accessed 12 February 2008).

International Labour Organization (ILO) (2003), *Time for Equality at Work,* Geneva: ILO.

Ip, M. (1996), *Dragons on the Long White Cloud: The Making of Chinese New Zealanders,* Auckland: Tandem Press.

Ip, M. (2002), 'Redefining Chinese female migration: from exclusion to transnationalism', in L. Fraser and K. Pickles (eds), *Shifting Centres: Women and Migration,* Dunedin: University of Otago Press. pp. 149–65.

Ip, M. (ed.) (2003a), *Unfolding History, Evolving Identity,* Auckland: Auckland University Press.

Ip, M. (2003b), 'Seeking the last utopia: the Taiwanese in NZ', in Ip (ed.) (2003a), *Unfolding* pp. 185–210.

Ip, M. and Murphy, N. (2005), *Aliens at My Table: Asians as New Zealanders See Them,* Wellington: Penguin.

Johnston, R., Poulsen M.F. and Forrest, J. (2003), 'The ethnic geography of New Zealand: a decade of growth and change, 1991–2001', *Asia Pacific Viewpoint,* **44** (2), 109–30.

Jones, S.R., Torres, V. and Arminio, J. (2006), *Negotiating the Complexities of Qualitative Research in Higher Education: Fundamental Elements and Issues,* London: Routlege.

Konrad, A., Prasad, P. and Pringle, J. (eds) (2006), 'Examining workplace diversity', in A.M. Konrad, P. Prasad and J.K. Pringle (eds), *Handbook of Workplace Diversity,* London: Sage, pp. 1–22.

Larner, W. (2007), 'Expatriate experts and globalising governmentalities: the New Zealand diaspora strategy', *Transactions of the Institute of British Geographers,* **32** (3), 331–45.

Law, P. (1994), 'Too much yellow in the melting pot? Perceptions of the NZ Chinese 1930–1960', unpublished BA thesis, Otago University, New Zealand.

Leckie, J. (2007), *Indian Settlers: The Story of a New Zealand South Asian Community,* Dunedin: Otago University Press.

Lee, J.B.J. (2003), 'Eating pork bones and puha with chopsticks', in Ip (ed.) (2003a), pp. 94–112.

Lee, J.B.J. (2007), *Jade Taniwha*, Auckland: Rautaki.

Lemke, T. (2001), 'Foucault, governmentality, and critique', available at: http://www.thomaslemkeweb.de/publikationen/Foucault,%20Governmentality,%20and%20Critique%20IV-2.pdf (accessed 16 February 2008).

Matton, J.N. and Hernandez, C.M. (2004), 'A new study identifies the "markets and breaks" of diversity initiatives', *Journal of Organizational Excellence*, **23** (4), 47–58.

McGibbon, I. (2005), 'The defence dimension', in A. Smith (ed.), *Southeast Asia and New Zealand: A History of Regional and Bilateral Relations*. Wellington: NZ Institute of International Affairs in association with Victoria University Press, pp. 7–31.

McKinnon, M. (1996), *Immigrants and Citizens: New Zealanders and Asian Immigration in Historical Context*, Wellington: Institute of Policy Studies, Victoria University.

Ministry of Social Development (MSD) (2007), 'Ethnic composition of the population', available at: http://www.socialreport.msd.govt.nz/people/ethnic-composition-population.html (accessed 23 February 2008).

Murphy, N. (1994), 'The poll-tax in NZ: A research paper', Commissioned by the New Zealand Chinese Association.

Murphy, N. (2002), *The Poll-Tax in NZ*, 2nd edn, Wellington: Department of Internal Affairs.

Office of Ethnic Affairs (OEA) (2007), 'Consultations', available at: http://www.ethnicaffairs.govt.nz/oeawebsite.nsf/wpg_url/Advisory-Services-Consultations-Index (accessed 24 February 2008).

Office of Ethnic Affairs (OEA) (2008a), *Strength in Diversity*, Wellington: OEA.

Office of Ethnic Affairs (OEA) (2008b), *Portraits 2: Cultural Diversity*, Wellington: OEA.

Phillips, J. (2007), 'History of immigration', *Te Ara – Encyclopedia of New Zealand*, available at: http://www.TeAra.govt.nz/NewZealanders/NewZealandPeoples/HistoryOfImmigration/en (accessed 15 February 2008).

Pio, E. (2005), 'Knotted strands: working lives of Indian women migrants in New Zealand', *Human Relations,* **58** (10), 1277–99.

Pio, E. (2007a), 'Managing diversity', in L. Gill and E. Pio (eds), *Organisations and Management*, Auckland: Pearson, pp. 235–54.

Pio, E. (2007b), 'Ethnic entrepreneurship among Indian women in New Zealand: a Bittersweet process', *Gender, Work and Organisation,* **14** (5), 409–32.

Pio, E. (2007c), 'Ethnic minority migrant women entrepreneurs and the imperial imprimatur', *Women in Management Review*, **22** (8), 631–49.

Pio, E. (2007d), 'Enterprising Indian women in NZ', in L. Dana (ed.), *Handbook of Research on Ethnic Minority Entrepreneurship*, Cheltenham, UK and Northampton, MA, USA: Edward Elgar, pp. 744–53.

Pio, E. (2008), *Sari: Indian Women at Work in New Zealand*, Wellington: Dunmore.

Prasad, P. (2006), 'The jewel in the crown', in Konrad et al. (eds), pp. 121–44.

Rasanathan, K., Craig, D. and Perkins, R. (2006), 'The novel use of "Asian" as an ethnic category in the New Zealand health sector', *Ethnicity and Health*, **22** (3), 211–27.

Rolfe, J. (2005), 'Coming to terms with the regional identity', in A. Smith (ed.), *Southeast Asia and New Zealand: A History of Regional and Bilateral Relations*, Wellington: NZ Institute of International Affairs in association with Victoria University Press, pp. 32–56.

Sedgwick, C. (1984), 'The organizational dynamics of the NZ Chinese: a case of political ethnicity', in S. Spoonley, C. Macpherson, D. Pearson and C. Sedgwick (eds), *Tauiwi: Racism and Ethnicity in New Zealand*, Palmerston North: Dunmore, pp. 44–67.

Sen, A. (2006), *Identity and Violence: The Illusion of Destiny*. London: Allen Lane.

Singham, M. (2006), 'Multiculturalism in New Zealand – the need for a new paradigm', *Aotearoa Ethnic Network Journal*, **1** (1), 33–37.

Smith, A. (2005a), 'Introduction: the emergence of NZ's relationship with southeast Asia', in A. Smith (ed.), *Southeast Asia and New Zealand: A History of Regional and Bilateral*

Relations, Wellington: NZ Institute of International Affairs in association with Victoria University Press, pp. 1–6.

Smith, A. (2005b), 'From an alliance to a broad relationship: NZ and Thailand', in A. Smith (ed.), *Southeast Asia and New Zealand: A History of Regional and Bilateral Relations*. Wellington: NZ Institute of International Affairs in association with Victoria University Press, pp. 331–68.

Smith, R. (2002), 'Race, gender and authority in the workplace: theory and research', *Annual Review of Sociology*, **28**, 509–42.

Statistics NZ (2006), available at http://www.stats.govt.nz/Census/2006CensusHomePage. aspx (accessed 14 February 2008).

Statistics NZ (2008), 'Growing ethnic diversity', available at: http://www.stats.govt.nz/ analytical-reports/children-in-nz/growing-ethnic-diversity.ht (accessed 11 February 2008).

StatsNZ (2007), *Profile of New Zealander Responses, Ethnicity Question: 2006 Census*, Wellington: Statistics NZ.

Swarbrick, N. (2007), 'Indians', *Te Ara Encyclopedia of New Zealand*, available at: http://www.TeAra.govt.nz/NewZealanders/NewZealandPeoples/Indians/en (accessed 16 February 2008).

Talcott, G. (2000), 'The context and risk of organised illegal immigration to New Zealand: an exploration in policy and relevant research', Working Paper, Centre for Strategic Studies, Victoria University, Wellington.

Trlin, A., Henderson, A. and North, N. (2004), 'Skilled Chinese and Indian immigrant workers', in P. Spoonley, A. Dupuis and A. De Bruin (eds), *Work and Working in Twenty-first Century NZ*, Palmerston North: Dunmore, pp. 205–19.

United Nations (UN) (2007), 'Population Division – world population prospects', available at: http://esa.un.org/unpp/index.asp?panel=5#Asia (accessed 17 February 2008).

Vertovec, S. (1999), 'Conceiving and researching transnationalism', *Ethnic and Racial Studies*, **22** (2), 447–62.

Watts, N., Trlin, A., White, C. and North, N. (2007), 'Immigrant cultural capital in business: the New Zealand experience', in L. Dana (ed.), *Handbook of Research on Ethnic Minority Entrepreneurship*, Cheltenham, UK and Northampton, MA, USA: Edward Elgar, pp. 729–43.

Wong, G. (2003), 'Is saying sorry enough?', in Ip (ed.) (2003a), pp. 258–79.

World Economic Forum (WEF) (2007), *The Global Gender Gap Report 2007*, Geneva: WEF.

Yee, B. (2003), 'Coping with insecurity: everyday experiences of Chinese New Zealanders', in Ip (2003a), pp. 215–35.

Zanoni, P. and Janssens, M. (2003), 'Deconstructing difference: the rhetoric of human resource managers' diversity discourses', *Organisation Studies*, **25** (1), 55–74.

23 Israeli–Indian teams in Israeli high-tech organizations: a diversity perspective
Ayala Malach Pines and Nurit Zaidman

Background: foreign workers in Israel

A total of 190,000 foreign workers are employed in Israel today (the end of 2007 and start of 2008), about half of whom are employed with permits while the other half are illegal. In addition, another 50,000 Palestinians find odd jobs in Israel; only 10,000 of them arrive with work permits. Others make it through the breached border. Recently, another group of foreign workers joined the Israeli job market: 5,000 Sudanese refugees who infiltrated via Egypt. Their working conditions are particularly poor.

As high as these numbers seem, five years earlier, in 2003, approximately 300,000 foreign workers lived in Israel, 60 percent of them illegally. Half were from Asia (China, Thailand, the Philippines), 45 percent from Eastern Europe (mainly Romania and Moldovia), and the rest from African and Latin American countries.

Foreign workers have been widely employed in Israel since the 1980s. In the early 1990s, after Prime Minister Yitzhak Rabin barred most Palestinians from working inside Israel, foreign workers started arriving in large numbers. Due to closures and security concerns associated with the first and especially the second *intifada*, Israel began using foreign labor to replace Palestinian workers. In this way, contractors and industrialists gained an even cheaper workforce. While most foreign workers start out with legal permits, many become illegal simply by losing or changing jobs. Because of the high price they have usually paid to come to Israel, illegal workers are inclined to remain simply because they cannot afford to go home.

Nowadays, most of these foreign workers are employed in the construction business (55,000) and in the nursing sector (50,000) and about 30,000 are in the agricultural sector. There is no information about another 50,000. The employment terms of workers without permits are harsh and humiliating: they earn about US$2.5 per hour (US$2 in the agricultural sector, $3 in the construction industry) and lack any social benefits or professional protection, while being pursued by the police. In addition, they push out uneducated Israeli workers; and their presence results in minimized employment opportunities and declining salaries for Israelis with

504

similar skills. Foreign workers comprise about a quarter of all workers in the construction industry, 40 percent of the workers in the agricultural sector, and more than half in the nursing sector. If an employer is dishonest, refuses to pay, does not honor conditions of employment or subjects a worker to physical abuse, the foreign worker has no power to leave without becoming illegal and risking arrest and deportation. The current chapter focuses on a new type of foreign labours – workers in the high-tech industry.

Global workers in the high-tech industry

Contemporary globalization has intensified translational links through the revolution in communication and transport which has accelerated the movement of people, goods and information. Outsourcing of services such as call center staffing, payroll and administrative work, and information technology (IT) development has become a common way to create competitive advantage in the world of global business.

Specifically, offshore software development has seen tremendous growth in the last few years. This kind of outsourcing occurs when the contracting parties are in different countries and the software is developed in the developer's country, and then shipped to the buyer's organization. Countries such as Ireland, India and Israel have seen impressive growth in their software industries (Gopal et al., 2003). Since the workforce in India is relatively cheap, several major Israeli high-tech companies have turned to India to outsource their software development services.

However, offshore software development poses significant challenges. Failures in offshore software outsourcing suggest that it is becoming more complex to manage. The literature focuses on factors such as high coordination costs, distance, information security-related issues, lack of direct communication, cultural misunderstandings and infrastructure problems (Oza and Hall, 2005).

Research on distributed work teams is relevant to the understanding of the dynamics associated with the team, an important unit in the software development process. The literature discusses the effects of proximity, distance, face-to-face communication, conflicts and the effect of fuzzy boundaries of work teams (Kiesler and Cummings, 2002; Mannix et al., 2002; Mortensen and Hinds, 2002; Nardi and Whittaker, 2002).

Lakha (2005) studied the workplace experiences of Indian computer professionals working on temporary visas in Australia. Findings revealed that their presence in the translational workplace is marked by contested identity, concerns about security of employment and different understanding of what constitutes effective communication.

Oza and Hall (2005) studied the difficulties in managing offshore software outsourcing relationships from the perspective of Indian employees. They found that the main offshore software outsourcing difficulties discussed by the employees included cultural differences, expectation mismatch, language differences, loss of control, job loss and job transition.

Several studies show how different perceptions of hierarchy and transparency created problems in communication and knowledge transfer among members of Indian–Western teams in the high-tech sector (Lakha, 2005; Zaidman and Brock, 2009).

Regarding Israeli–Indian teams it was found that global norms, corporate governance, and IT culture created a competitive work environment as well as shared corpus of knowledge that is partially open to employees and outsourcing partners across the globe. Yet, not all aspects of this professional global culture are fully adopted by employees in global teams, especially if they are culturally diverse. The culture of the high-tech industry assumes open communication and knowledge transfer, yet socio-cultural structures produce different forms of knowledge transfer. For example, knowledge in hierarchical societies tends to transfer via hierarchical chains, moving in a top-down direction. Knowledge in egalitarian societies tends to fan out in all directions, flowing top down as well as bottom up.

Other aspects of these cultural structures, which have an impact on knowledge transfer, are the attribution of specific meaning (as well as power) to certain categories of people. For example, women are often segregated from men in Indian organizations, and there are norms of knowledge transfer related to women that are different from those related to the category of men. Furthermore, specific characteristics of the population involved might clash with the norms of the global high-tech culture as in the case of Israeli employees who tend to avoid systematic documentation of their work (Zaidman and Brock, 2009). These types of problems are especially problematic in global, or multicultural, teams.

Global teams

Today's global economy increasingly requires workers to collaborate in teams that cross cultural and geographic boundaries. These teams are becoming the norm in both business and non-governmental organizations (Bantel and Jackson, 1989; Adler, 2002; Distefano and Maznevski, 2000). Multicultural teams are task-oriented groups from different national cultures (Marquardt and Horvath, 2001). They are often semi-permanent groups, dynamic structural arrangements which are project-based and tend to have high member turnover (Townsend et al., 1998; Harvey and Novicevic, 2002).

Global teams outperform homogeneous teams at identifying problems and generating solutions using a variety of perspectives and skills (Watson et al., 1993; Maznevski, 1994). On the other hand, they do not often create the value expected of them. Instead, members clash and teams are either paralyzed into inaction or worse. As a result, most diverse teams perform worse than homogeneous ones (Distefano and Maznevski, 2000).

Managing cultural diversity and cross-cultural conflicts has become the most common challenge of multicultural teams (Marquardt and Horvath, 2001). Organizations that fail to keep and manage employees from different backgrounds can expect to suffer a significant competitive disadvantage compared to those that do (Cox and Blake, 1991). Management literature has started to address the way global teams need to be managed (for example, Distefano and Maznevski, 2000). It has been argued that the most productive teams are those in which differences are recognized, even nurtured. However, the most common teams suppress differences in ideas and perspectives (ibid.).

Studies on global teams tend to adopt a simplistic, linear and static approach. However, the environment in which global teams operate is dynamic and requires an understanding of complex influences and their relationship to organizational effectiveness. There is a need for a new approach that will capture the complex and contextual dynamic aspects of global teams in three levels: within the team, between the team and its organizational context, and between the team and its external environment (Maznevski and Athanassiou, 2006). There is also a need for a shift from a static approach to an approach that acknowledges the fact that teams are dynamic arrangements with high member turnover (Townsend et al., 1998; Harvey and Novicevic, 2002) and for a shift from the team to the employees who compose it (Bachmann, 2006).

In light of the inconsistent and even contradictory findings on the performance of global teams, conflicts between multicultural group members, social and cooperative behavior, idea generation and affective consequences in culturally diverse workgroups (ibid.), it is important to address the complexity involved in the functioning of a multicultural team as it is manifested in its natural setting.

Managerial implications are embedded in two major topic of research on multicultural teams: team *cohesion* and team *communication*.

Cohesion refers to the forces that bind members to each other and to their group (Guzzo and Shea, 1992) and typically result in positive outcomes (Stogdill, 1972; McGrath, 1984). Studies of team cohesion and team performance report a positive correlation between the two (Evans and Dion, 1991; Guzzo and Shea, 1992; Smith et al., 1994; Elron, 1997). It was found that multicultural teams were less cohesive than culturally homogeneous teams (Nahemow and Lawton, 1986; Wright and Drewery, 2002) due to, among other things, different perceptions of the environment, different motives, and communication norms (Shaw, 1981; Zaccaro, 1991; Bernthal and Insko, 1993; Wright and Drewery, 2002; Mason and Griffin, 2003; Knouse, 2006).

Communication in global teams has also been extensively discussed in the literature. Much of that research has focused on the geographical distribution of team members (Maznevski and Athanassiou, 2006) including, especially, research on 'virtual teams' and the technical aspect of communication in such teams such as the use of information systems. Other studies focused on the social aspects of communication including the need to understand communication processes in multicultural teams (Wheelan et al., 1998; Matveev and Nelson, 2004) and the importance of language (Chen et al., 2006).

The current chapter highlights the complexity and dynamics of global teams from a diversity perspective which shifts attention to the day-to-day reality of thousands of employees who work in the highly stressful, in addition to being highly successful and fast-growing, high-tech industry in Israel and India.

High-tech companies in Israel and in India

Israel has an unusually high number of high-technology (high-tech) companies and is among the world leaders in high-tech start-ups. About 4,000 high-tech companies make Israel the largest concentration of such companies in the world, outside of California. On the cutting edge of technological development in software, telecommunication, biotechnology and IT, Israeli high-tech and start-up companies are known for their creativity, innovation and ingenuity.

High-tech is the Israeli economy's primary engine of growth. Its influence on the Israeli GNP (gross national product) is enormous, bearing no proportion to its size in the general economy. Owing to the phenomenal success of the high-tech industry, high-tech entrepreneurs became Israel's new cultural heroes, figures to be respected and emulated (Lerner and Avrahami, 1999; Pines et al., 2005).

A similar growth characterizes the high-tech sector in India. According to India's National Association of Software and Service Companies (Nasscom), the country's IT sector grew from US$1.73 billion in 1994/95 to an estimated US$13.5 billion in 2001/02, reached US$17.2 billion during fiscal 2004/05, and is expected to approach US$31 billion in the year ending March 31, 2007 and US$60 billion by 2010.

Israeli and other foreign software companies have recognized the opportunities presented by the Indian professional and relatively inexpensive workforce. In response they not only trade actively with the Indian high-tech sector, but have also established subsidiaries and outsource operations.

The great success of the high-tech industry in India and Israel raised curiosity worldwide but little academic research attention. This chapter focuses attention on Israeli–Indian multicultural teams, those who actually carry much of the workload in Israeli high-tech companies and their Indian subsidiary centers.

Work in the high-tech industry

The contemporary culture of the high-tech industry is characterized by long work hours, the awareness that time is money, that the marketplace demands increasingly innovative tools, and that the competition for the production of the best and most cost-effective products is crucial for company survival (Kunda, 1992). Thus, high-tech organizations and employees work under huge pressures to perform well and within short timetables.

High-tech organizations emphasize both technical excellence and good employee relations (Mar et al., 1985; Hodson and Parker 1988). Knowledge, constant learning, and frank open communication are the primary prerequisite for the creation and making of new complex and sophisticated products (Hodson and Parker, 1988; Drucker, 1993).

Global teams must coordinate their work-related discussions across time zones and around travel schedules, using a wide variety of communication media tools, which tends to be more difficult and less productive than face-to-face communication (Lipnack and Stamps, 1997; Crampton and Hinds, 2004).

The contexts of multicultural teams

Contexts are sets of connections relevant to a particular phenomenon (Maznevski and Athanassiou, 2006). According to Geertz (1973), a context reveals hidden meanings and deeper understandings, or certain kinds of interpretation and explanation that can be cultural, social, political, religious economic or ecological (Dilley, 1999). The contexts that seem relevant to the understanding of employees' behavior in global teams include the team, the organization and the external local (cultural) as well as global (high-tech) contexts. While each of these contexts will be addressed independently, they are, of course, interconnected.

The team

As noted earlier, two of the most researched aspects of teams that are especially relevant for the behavior of individuals in multicultural teams are *team cohesion* (the forces that bind members to each other and to their group) and *team communication* (both face to face and virtual).

The organization
This consists of two dimensions – organizational culture and politics:

- *Organizational culture*, 'The way things are done' in an organization, influences the expectation and behavior of team members. Cultural values and assumptions (Schein, 2004) explain the behavior of team members and managers of global teams. Important in this context is the 'differentiation perspective' (Martin, 1992) that focuses on manifestations that have inconsistent interpretations such as ambiguities, and complexities.
- *Organizational politics* reflect organizational power. In response to changes in the global market, multinationals often go through organizational restructuring and downsizing which impact on employees' work satisfaction and psychological well-being (Burke and Greenglass, 2001). Organizational theory focuses on the way these manifestations of organizational politics, or 'upsetting organizations', impact on individuals.

Traditionally, organizational theory focused on social cohesion, commitment and success and paid little attention to organizations causing or facing disorganization, disorder and decay. But recently, a call was made for greater attention to the ways in which organizations disturb existing arrangements and create upsetting consequences (EGOS, 2008). An example is the requirement of *individuals* to work in multicultural teams.

The individual
Only sporadic research has focused on the responses of individuals in global teams, and those few studies presented conceptual analyses rather than data (for example, Hambrick et al., 1998; Bosch-Sijtsema, 2007). The lack of interest in the individual most likely reflects the dominance of the positivist approach in management research (Chapman, 1997; Piekkari and Welch, 2006) which implies that people are not active in shaping their physical and social reality (Orlikowski and Baroudi, 2002). Following recent developments in modern practice theory, this chapter focuses attention on the individual employee as an actor. Viewed from this perspective, actors' behavior can be viewed in terms of pragmatic choices, decision making, active calculating and strategizing (Ortner, 1984).

Culture
There is no single best definition of culture (Peng et al., 2000). Rather, researchers highlight various aspects of culture, adopting invariably imperfect but workable assumptions about what culture is. Culture

shapes, guides and even to some extent dictates behavior. It controls the definitions of the world for actors, limits their conceptual tools, and restricts their emotional repertoires (Ortner, 1984). Nevertheless, individuals can and do make pragmatic choices.

Indian culture is high in power distance (Carl et al., 2004) and low in assertiveness (Den Hartog, 2004). An essential element of Hindu social organizations, relationships and psychological make-up, is the concept of hierarchy (Sinha, 1990).

Israeli culture is very low in power distance (Gardiner, 1994; Meshulam, 1994; Hofstede, 2001) and high in assertiveness (Den Hartog, 2004). Israeli employees in high-tech organizations have been portrayed as less observant of departmental and hierarchical boundaries than Americans, and in general as less confined by the formal bureaucratic structure of the organization. Israeli employees are expected to 'think big' and take responsibility (Shamir and Melnik, 2002). The Israeli tendency toward work improvisations was noted in several studies (Meshulam, 1994; Hickson and Pugh, 1995; Shamir and Melnik, 2002).

An interesting and important question is: what effect do these two very different cultural contexts (Israeli and Indian) have on the stress and burnout of employees working in multicultural teams, in Israeli high-tech organizations?

Burnout and stress: the significant difference

Burnout is often conceptualized within the framework of stress (Farber, 1983; Hobfoll and Shirom, 2000; Cooper et al., 2001; Maslach et al., 2001). Hobfoll and Shirom (2000), for example, describe burnout as a consequence of exposure to chronic job stress. However, a recent study based on an application of existential theory, has demonstrated that while burnout may be a subcategory of stress, it has different antecedents, correlates and consequences (Pines and Keinan, 2005).

According to the existential perspective, the root cause of burnout lies in people's need to believe that their lives are meaningful, that the things they do are useful and important (for example, Pines, 1993). Victor Frankl (1976) wrote that 'the striving to find meaning in one's life is the primary motivational force in man' (p. 154). Today, for people who have rejected the religious answer to the existential quest, one of the most frequently chosen alternatives is work. People who choose this alternative try to derive from their work a sense of meaning for their life. They enter their career with high hopes, goals and expectations. When these hopes do not materialize, they feel they have failed, that their work is insignificant. They start feeling helpless and hopeless and eventually burn out.

Meaning plays a crucial role in coping with stress and burnout. It shapes the emotions the person experiences in a stressful encounter (Folkman and Moskowitz, 2000). The existential perspective, with its emphasis on meaning, can be applied to coping with the burnout of Israeli and Indian employees in multicultural teams, an interesting population from the perspective of burnout because they have not chosen to work with people (the traditional subjects of burnout research) yet find themselves in jobs in which they have to interact with foreigners whom they do not understand and at times do not respect, which highlights the similarity between the high-tech workers and the construction laborers.

Research has shown that Israelis, because of their daily confrontation with existential issues (brought about by the constant threat of terrorist attacks), because of their close-knit social networks, and because of their active and direct coping, tend to report low levels of burnout (Pines, 2004). Thus Israelis may experience similar levels of stress to their Indian counterparts, but report lower levels of burnout and a higher sense of meaning in their work. On the other hand, it is possible that the Indian low standard of living and their view of life as a transitory state may protect them from both stress and burnout.

The interest in workers who seem immune to burnout led to a recent investigation of Israeli 'serial' high-tech entrepreneurs, who go from one venture to the next, seemingly challenged by stress and immune to burnout (Pines and Kaplan, 2006). Findings of the study revealed an unusually low level of burnout despite high levels of stress.

Both the study of serial high-tech entrepreneurs and the search for multinational teams that may be immune to burnout are part of a shift in psychology away from negative aspects of humans toward 'positive psychology' (Seligman and Csikszentmihalyi, 2000).

Burnout, while experienced by the individual worker is always best analyzed and understood in the context of the team, the organization, the sector and the culture, based on the assumption that the kinds of relationships workers form are critical to the way they experience, express and cope with stress and burnout.

The focus on the individuals who shape the dynamic of global teams is based on the assumption that their behavior and level of stress and burnout are crucial determinants of these teams' success. To better understand this complex subject matter, an integrated approach is recommended which focuses on the employees (how they behave and strategize when they are forced to interact with people who are culturally different, spotlighting informal, often concealed reactions to challenging situations), in their multilayered context that includes the global team, the organization, the sector and the culture.

An important question that needs to be addressed is: what behaviors and strategies are used by Israeli versus Indian employees to cope with the stress and burnout inherent in their work, especially the stress caused by working with each other? These behaviors and strategies need to be analyzed from a relational perspective that includes: the team (cohesion and communication) the organization (organization culture, politics and upsetting aspects), the global (high-tech) context and the cultural (Indian/Israeli) context.

The relational perspective

Departing from the homologous, linear, simplistic and a-contextual traditions that tend to characterize organization and management studies, the relational perspectives are underpinned by a belief that social life is complex as it involves contextually situated phenomena that exist in irreducibly interconnected sets of relationships (Özbilgin, 2006). They do not treat individuals as functioning independently, but in terms of their interconnections and dynamic relationships with other individuals in an elaborate network of social systems.

As for the Indian–Israeli comparison, the best practice approach to cross-cultural comparisons in organizational research is a combination of 'emic' and 'etic' approaches (Schaffer and Riordan, 2003). The emic approach focuses on examining a construct as the people from within that culture understand it (Gudykunst, 1997). The etic approach focuses on comparing it across cultures (Schaffer and Riordan, 2003). An interpretative tradition (Prasad, 2005) describes 'the native's point of view' within specific contexts. Triangulation, a combination of qualitative methods, including especially an in-depth interview, has the advantage of producing a complete and contextual portrait (Ghauri, 2004).

Seven in-depth semi-structured interviews (Spradley, 1979; Saunders et al., 2003) were conducted with employees at different levels in the Israeli head quarters of C, a highly successful multinational company, as well as with two managers from another Israeli multinational software house that has a branch in India. The interviews were transcribed word for word (Spradley, 1979). In addition, observations were conducted during site visits to the organization's offices in Israel and India. The observations took place during work hours.

The interviews revealed that for many of the Israeli employees, working with Indian colleagues created major difficulties and caused both stress and burnout. A common response was disengagement or withdrawal as a form of informal resistance (Prasad and Prasad, 1998). The following are quotations obtained from Israeli employees working with Indians:

> *L*: frustration, frustration, simply frustration. On the one hand I feel that they simply don't understand me. Simply don't understand what I want. On the other

hand I am also angry, because after I have explained, when I ask something of them, they go and cause a blunder. I try to explain again and again and again and again. But how much can you? At some point I stop. My boss makes fun of me. He says: 'You've got what you've got'. One person here can do the work of four or five people there. I think that says a great deal about their quality. It is simply hard, very hard, to work with them, hard to get some value out of them fast. They don't get out of the box. That's the way they are. Narrow. Narrow in the way they look at things. God forbid an additional element will enter. No, nothing. From the beginning they have a problem understanding. Every work is monotonous, but I think that working with them you burn out faster, both because of their lack of understanding and because of the constant confrontation with difficulties. It burns you out. Look, I have been doing this work for four years, and the burnout started the minute we started working with the Indians. What burns me out is not the work here, what burns me out is the work with them. I don't want to do it any more. It is hard. I'm burned out. I've had it. They simply don't understand. They don't understand. They don't ask questions. They don't differentiate between what is of major importance and what is unimportant. We have high drop-out rates here. Many people are leaving. They are leaving because they are frustrated and burned out. Part of the frustration and burnout is India. India demands a lot of energy. After one telephone conversation with India I feel depleted. I have to take a break to get back to myself. It is very frustrating to see how they recycle mishaps, how they don't share information. When I come and I ask why they didn't share, they look at each other confused and 'sorry, sorry, sorry, sorry', but they don't give a reason, it didn't seem important . . .

E: There is some difficulty at work. They don't have the know-how. That's a fact. They don't have the experience. This means that the people who are under enormous stress here in Tel-Aviv have yet another task, to support India. We are trying to involve them, but it is difficult, very difficult, and it takes resources. They are incapable of working independently.

A: Technically they are not as good, and the people here don't like it. They are supposed to help us, and at the end we have to do the work, in the last minute and under pressure. It's very annoying. In other departments they stopped letting them develop. They let them do it several times, saw that they are not doing things right, so the easy solution is not to let them and then do it our-selves. Here we are trying to get them involved more and somehow overcome the problem, to teach them. People don't know how to make contact with them, they talk to them and they don't understand what is being said. There are many people who don't respect them, who don't respect their work, who think that they are doing a bad job. People avoid working with them. They approach me and others: 'Listen, this is urgent. I can't talk to them. You talk to them'. 'I don't understand them. I can't do it. Do me a favor. Ask me anything. I'll help you. But I don't want them to contact me'. That's what they say. Very few people will say 'It's fun'. I don't say it's fun either, but I am used to working with them, so it's not as hard for me and requires less effort . . . I have never heard them raise a voice. It may be related to the fact that they are our subordi-nates, but I have been there [India] and they never raise a voice there either. We are a more aggressive society . . .

Summary and conclusions

The diversity perspective adopted by the chapter, which starts out with the poorly paid and poorly treated foreign laborers, focuses attention on the new type of foreign workers – educated employees in the highly sophisticated and highly successful high-tech industry. Because today's global economy increasingly requires workers to collaborate in teams that cross cultural and geographic boundaries, the number of these new foreign workers has been growing steadily. India and Israel have seen impressive growth in their outsourcing of services, especially in the software industries. Since the workforce in India is relatively cheap, like other high-tech companies around the world, several major Israeli high-tech companies have turned to India to outsource their software development services. However, offshore outsourcing poses significant challenges including cultural misunderstandings.

The chapter argued that such challenges are best analyzed from a relational perspective which views them as existing in interconnected relationships involving (in the case of global teams in the high-tech sector) the individual workers (their stress, burnout and coping) the global team (its cohesion and communication), the organization (its culture, politics and upsetting aspects), the global sector (high-tech) and culture (Israeli versus Indian).

The behaviors and strategies used by Israeli versus Indian employees to cope with the stress and burnout inherent in their work, especially the stress caused by working with each other, can also be analyzed from a relational perspective that includes: the team (its cohesion and communication), the organization (its culture, politics and upsetting aspects), the global (high-tech) context and the cultural (Indian/Israeli) context.

Such an analysis is expected to make important theoretical contributions to diversity research by analyzing workers in global teams as foreign workers; to management research by shifting the focus of analysis to the individuals who shape the organizational field and by utilizing the relational perspective (which analyzes organizational entities in their contextual settings at micro (team), meso (organization) and macro (global sector and culture) levels of analysis; to critical organizational research by analyzing the challenges imposed by organizations when forcing employees to work in global teams; to burnout research by applying existential theory to understanding the difference between the causes and prevention of stress and burnout of workers in global teams; and to positive psychology by demonstrating the importance of meaning for workers' well-being.

In addition to its theoretical implication, this approach (especially when presented from a diversity perspective) has important practical implications for global companies (especially Israeli and Indian companies in the high-tech industry) by suggesting how to better manage and improve the functioning of multicultural teams. Another practical implication involves differential treatment of stress and burnout; in the case of burnout, the focus is on enhancing employees' sense of the work's importance.

Bibliography

Adler, N. (2002), *From Boston to Beijing: Managing with a World View*, Ohio: Southwestern.

Bachmann, A.S. (2006), 'Melting pot or tossed salad? Implications for designing effective multicultural workgroups', *Management International Review*, **46** (6), 721–47.

Bantel, K.A. and Jackson, S.E. (1989), 'Top management and innovations in banking: does the composition of the top team make a difference?', *Strategic Management Journal*, **10** (2), 107–24.

Bernthal, P.R. and Insko, C.A. (1993), 'Cohesiveness without groupthink: the interactive effects of social and task cohesion', *Group and Organization Management*, **18**, 66–87.

Bosch-Sijtsema, P. (2007), 'The impact of individual expectations and expectation conflicts on virtual teams', *Group and Organizational Management*, **32** (3), 358–88.

Burke, R.J. and Greenglass, E.R. (2001), 'Hospital restructuring and nursing staff well-being: the role of perceived hospital and union support', *Anxiety, Stress and Coping*, **14**, 93–115.

Carl, D., Gupta, V. and Javidan, M. (2004), 'Power distance', in House, R.J., Hanges, P.J., Javidan, M., Dorfman, P.W. and Gupta V. (eds), *Leadership, Culture, and Organizations: The GLOBE Study of 62 Societies*, Thousand Oaks, CA: Sage, pp. 513–63.

Chapman, M. (1997), 'Preface: social anthropology, business studies, and cultural issues', *International Studies of Management and Organization*, **26** (4), 3–29.

Chen, S., Geluykens, R. and Choi, C.J. (2006), 'The importance of language in global teams: a linguistic perspective', *Management International Review*, **46** (6), 679–96.

Cooper, C.L., Dewe, P.J. and O'Driscoll, M.P. (2001), *Organizational Stress*, Thousand Oaks, CA: Sage.

Cox, T.H. and Blake, S. (1991), 'Managing cultural diversity: implications for organizational competitiveness', *Academy of Management Executive*, **5** (3), 45–56.

Crampton, C.D. and Hinds, P.J. (2004), 'Subgroup dynamics in internationally distributed teams: ethnocentrism or cross-national learn', in Staw, B. and Kramer, R. (eds), *Research in Organizational Behavior*, **26**, Greenwich: JAI Press, pp. 231–63.

Den Hartog, D.N. (2004), 'Assertiveness', in House, R.J., Hanges, P.J., Javidan, M., Dorfman, P.W. and Gupta, V. (eds), *Leadership, Culture, and Organizations: The GLOBE Study of 62 Societies*, Thousand Oaks, CA: Sage, pp. 396–436.

Dilley, R. (1999), 'Introduction: the problem of context', in Dilley (ed.), *The Problem of Context*, New York: Berghan Books, pp. 1–15.

Distefano, J. and Maznevski, M. (2000), 'Creating value with diverse teams in global management', *Organizational Dynamics*, **29** (1), 45–63.

Drucker, P.F. (1993), *Post-Capitalist Society*, New York: Harper Collins.

EGOS (European Group of Organization Studies) (2008), 24th EGOS Colloquium 'Upsetting Organizations', July, Amsterdam.

Elron, E. (1997), 'Top management teams within multinational corporations: effects of cultural heterogeneity', *Leadership Quarterly*, **8** (4), 393–413.

Evans, C.E. and Dion, K.L. (1991), 'Group cohesion and performance', *Small Group Research*, **22**, 175–86.

Farber, B.A (ed.) (1983), *Stress and Burnout in the Human Service Professions*, New York: Pergamon.

Folkman, S. and Moskowitz, J.T. (2000), 'Positive affect and the other side of coping', *American Psychologist*, **55**, 647–54.

Frankl, V.E. (1976), *Man's Search for Meaning*, New York: Pocket Book.

Gardiner, M. (1994), 'Thoughts toward the formulation of an Israeli management model', in Shenhar, A. and Yarkoni, A. (eds), *Israeli Management Culture*, Tel Aviv: Gome (in Hebrew), pp. 99–108.

Geertz, C. (1973), *The Interpretation of Cultures: Selected Essays*, New York: Basic Books.

Ghauri, P. (2004), 'Designing and conducting case studies in international business research', in Marschan-Piekkari, R. and Welch, C. (eds), *Handbook of Qualitative Research Methods for International Business*, Cheltenham, UK and Northampton, MA, USA: Edward Elgar, pp. 109–24.

Gopal, A., Sivaramakrishnan, K., Krishnan, M.S. and Mukhopadhyay, T. (2003), 'Contracts in offshore software development: an empirical analysis', *Management Science*, **49**, 16–71.

Gudykunst, W.B. (1997), 'Cultural variability in communication', *Communication Research*, **24** (4), 327–48.

Guzzo, R.A. and Shea, G.P. (1992), 'Group performance and intergroup relations in organizations', in Dunnette, M.D. and Hough, L.M. (eds), *Handbook of Industrial and Organizational Psychology*, Palo Alto, CA: Consulting Psychologists Press, pp. 269–313.

Hambrick, D.C., Davison, S.C. and Snell, S.A. and Snow, C.C. (1998), 'When groups consist of multiple nationalities: toward a new understanding of the implications', *Organizational Studies*, **19** (2), 181–205.

Harvey, M. and Novicevic, M.M. (2002), 'The co-ordination of strategic initiatives within global organizations: the role of global teams', *International Journal of Human Resource Management*, **13** (4), 660–76.

Hickson, D.J. and Pugh, D.S. (1995), *Management Worldwide: The Impact of Societal Culture on Organizations around the Globe*, London: Penguin Books.

Hobfoll, S.E and Shirom, A. (2000), 'Conservation of resources theory: applications to stress and management in the workplace', in Golembiewski, R.T. (ed.), *Handbook of Organizational Behavior*, 2nd edn, New York: Dekker, pp. 57–81.

Hodson, R. and Parker, R.E. (1988), 'Work in high-technology settings: a review of the empirical literature', *Research in the Sociology of Work*, Greenwich, CT: JAI Press, pp. 1–29.

Hofstede, G. (2001), *Culture's Consequences: Comparing Values, Behaviors, Institutions and Organizations across Nations*, 2nd edn, Thousand Oaks, CA, and London: Sage.

Kiesler, S. and Cummings, J. (2002), 'What do we know about proximity and distance in work groups? A legacy of research', in Hinds, P. and Kisler, S. (eds), *Distributed Work*, Cambridge, MA: MIT Press, pp. 57–79.

Knouse, S. (2006), 'Task cohesion: a mechanism for bringing together diverse teams', *International Journal of Management*, **23** (3), 588–98.

Kunda, G. (1992), *Engineering Culture, Control and Commitment in a High-tech Corporation*, Philadelphia, PA: Temple University Press.

Lakha, S. (2005), 'Negotiating the transnational workplace: Indian computer professionals in Australia', *Journal of Intercultural Studies*, **26** (4), 337–59.

Lerner, M. and Avrahami, Y. (1999), 'Israel Executive Report. Research on entrepreneurship and economic growth', *Global Entrepreneurship Monitor*, Babson Park, MA: Babson College and London Business School.

Lipnack, J. and Stamps, J. (1997), *Virtual Teams: Reaching across Space, Time and Organizations with Technology*, New York: John Wiley.

Mannix, E., Griffith, T. and Neale, M. (2002), 'The phenomenology of conflict in distributed work teams', in Hinds, P. and Kisler, S. (eds), *Distributed Work*, Cambridge, MA: MIT Press, pp. 213–34.

Mar, B.W., Newell, W.T and Saxberg, B.O. (1985), 'The nature of high technology: editorial perspective', in Mar, Newell and Saxberg (eds), *Managing High Technology: An Interdisciplinary Perspective*, Amsterdam: Elsevier Science, pp. 3–16.

Marquardt, M.J. and Horvath, L. (2001), *Global Teams: How Top Multinationals Span Boundaries and Cultures with High-speed Teamwork*, Palo Alto, CA: Davies-Black.

Martin, J. (1992), *Cultures in Organizations: Three Perspectives*, New York: Oxford University Press.

Maslach, C., Schaufeli, W.B. and Leiter, P.M. (2001), 'Job Burnout', *Annual Review of Psychology*, **53**, 397–422.

Mason, C.M. and Griffin, M.A. (2003), 'Group absenteeism and positive affective tone: a longitudinal study', *Journal of Organizational Behavior*, **24** (6), September, 667–87.

Matveev, A.V. and Nelson, P.E (2004), 'Cross cultural communication competence and multicultural team performance: perceptions of American and Russian managers', *International Journal of Cross Cultural Management*, **4** (2), 253–71.

Maznevski, M.L. (1994), 'Understanding our differences: performance in decision-making groups with diverse members', *Human Relations*, **47**, 531–52.

Maznevski, M.L. and Athanassiou, N.A. (2006), 'Guest editors' introduction to the focused issue: a new direction for global teams research', *Management International Review*, **46** (6), 631–45.

McGrath, J. (1984), *Groups Interaction and Performance*, New Jersey: Prentice-Hall.

Meshulam, I. (1994), 'The impact of American management culture on Israeli firms', in Shenhar, A. and Yarkoni, A. (eds), *Israeli Management Culture*, Tel-Aviv: Gome (in Hebrew), pp. 213–24.

Mortensen, M. and Hinds, P. (2002), 'Fuzzy teams: boundary disagreement in distributed and collocated teams', in Hinds, P. and Kisler, S. (eds), *Distributed Work*, Cambridge, MA, MTI Press, pp. 283–308.

Nahemow, L. and Lawton, N.P. (1986), 'Similarity: and proprinquity: making friends with "different people"', in Street, R.M. and Porter, L.W. (eds), *Motivation and Work Behavior*, New York: McGraw-Hill.

Nardi, B. and Whittaker, S. (2002), 'The place of face-to-face communication in distributed work', in Hinds, P. and Kisler, S. (eds), *Distributed Work*, Cambridge, MA, MIT Press, pp. 83–110.

Nasscom, available at: http://www.nasscom.in.

Orlikowski, W.J. and Baroudi, J.B. (2002), 'Studying information technology in organizations: research approaches and assumptions', in Myers, M.D. and Avison, D. (eds), *Qualitative Research in Information Systems: A Reader*, London: Sage, pp. 51–77.

Ortner, S. (1984), 'Theory in anthropology since the sixties', *Comparative Studies in Society and History*, **26**, 126–66.

Oza, N. and Hall, T. (2005), 'Difficulties in managing offshore software outsourcing relationships: an empirical analysis of 18 high maturity Indian software companies', *Journal of Information Technology Case and Application Research*, **7** (3), 25–42.

Özbilgin, M. (2006), 'Relational methods in organization studies: a review of the field', in Kyriakidou, O. and Özbilgin, M. (eds), *Relational Perspectives in Organizational Studies: A Research Companion*, Vol. 13, Cheltenham, UK and Northampton, MA, USA: Edward Elgar, pp. 244–64.

Peng, K., Ames, D. and Knowles, E. (2000), 'Culture and human inference: perspectives from three traditions', in Matsumoto, D. (ed.), *Handbook of Cross-cultural Psychology*, Oxford: Oxford University Press, pp. 171–97.

Piekkari, R. and Welch C. (2006), Guest editors' introduction to the focused issue: 'Qualitative research methods in international business', *Management International Review*, **46** (4), 391–5.

Pines, A.M. (1993), 'Burnout – an existential perspective', in Schaufeli, W., Maslach, C. and Marek, T. (eds), *Professional Burnout: Developments in Theory and Research*, Washington, DC: Taylor & Francis, pp. 33–52.

Pines, A.M. (2004), 'Why Israelis are less burned out', *European Journal of Psychology*, **9** (2), 1–9.

Pines, A.M. and Kaplan, G. (2006), 'Why serial high-tech entrepreneurs don't burn out', paper presented at the *International Congress of Applied Psychology*, Athens, Greece, July.

Pines, A.M., and Keinan, G. (2005), 'Stress and burnout: the significant difference', *Personality and Individual Differences*, **39**, 625–35.

Pines, A.M., Levy, H., Utasi, A. and Hill, T.L. (2005), 'Entrepreneurs as cultural heroes:

a cross-cultural, interdisciplinary perspective', *Journal of Managerial Psychology*, **20**, 541–55.

Prasad, A. and Prasad, P. (1998), 'Everyday struggle at the workplace: the nature and implications of routine resistance in contemporary organizations', *Research in Sociology of Organizations*, **15**, 225–57.

Prasad, P. (2005), *Crafting Qualitative Research: Working in the Postpositivist Traditions*, New York: M.E. Sharpe.

Saunders, M., Lewis, P. and Thornhill, A. (2003), *Research Methods for Business Students*, London: Prentice-Hall.

Schaffer, B.S. and Riordan, C.M. (2003), 'A review of cross-cultural methodologies for organizational research: a best-practices approach', *Organizational Research Method*, **6** (2), 169–216.

Schein, E.H. (2004), *Organizational Culture and Leadership*, San Francisco, CA: John Wiley & Sons, Inc.

Seligman, M.E.P. and Csikszentmihalyi, M. (2000), 'Positive psychology: an introduction', *American Psychologist*, **55**, 5–14.

Shamir, B. and Melnik, Y. (2002), 'Boundary permeability as a cultural dimension, a study of cross cultural working relations between American and Israelis in high-tech organizations', *International Journal of Cross Cultural Management*, **2** (2), 219–38.

Shaw, M.E. (1981), *Group Dynamics: The Psychology of Small Group Behavior*, New York: McGraw-Hill.

Sinha, J.B.P. (1990), *Work Culture in the Indian Context*, New Delhi: Sage.

Smith, K.A., Smith, K.G., Olian, J.D., Sims, H.P., O'Bannon, D.P. and Scully, J. (1994), 'Top management teams' demography and process: the role of social integration and communication', *Administrative Science Quarterly*, **39**, 412–38.

Spradley, J.P. (1979), *The Ethnographic Interview*, New York: Holt, Rinehart and Winston.

Stogdill, R.M. (1972), 'Group productivity, drive and cohesiveness', *Organizational Behavior and Human Performances*, **8**, 26–43.

Townsend, A.M., DeMarie, S. and Hendrickson, A.R. (1998), 'Virtual teams: technology and the workplace of the future', *The Academy of Management Executive*, **12** (3), 17–29.

Watson, W.E., Kumar, K. and Michaelson, L.K. (1993), 'Cultural diversity's impact on interaction process and performance: comparing homogeneous and diverse task groups', *Academy of Management Journal*, **36**, 590–602.

Wheelan, S.A., Buzalo, G. and Tsumura, E. (1998), 'Development assessment tools for cross-cultural research', *Small Group Research*, **29**, 359–70.

Wright, N.S. and Drewery, G.P. (2002), 'Forming cohesion in culturally heterogeneous teams: differences in Japanese, Pacific Islander and Anglo experiences', *Cross Cultural Management*, **13**, 43–54.

Zaccaro, S.J. (1991), 'Nonequivalent associations between forms of cohesiveness and group-related outcomes', *Journal of Social Psychology*, **131**, 387–99.

Zaidman, N. and Brock, D. (2009), 'Knowledge transfer within and among multinationals and their subsidiaries: a culture-context approach', *Group and Organizational Management*, **3**, 1–32.

Index